AN EXPLORER'S GUIDE

Vermont

Vermont

Christina Tree & Sally W. Johnson

Principal Photography by Kim Grant

NINTH EDITION

The Countryman Press ✷ Woodstock Vermont

DEDICATION

Laura Howe
—C. T.

Stephen C. Terry and William West Terry
—S. W. J.

We welcome your comments and suggestions. Please contact Explorer's Guide Editor, The Countryman Press, P.O. Box 748, Woodstock, Vermont 05091, or e-mail countrymanpress@wwnorton.com.

Ninth Edition

ISSN 1523-9462
ISBN 0-88150-519-6

Maps by Moore Creative Designs, © 2002 The Countryman Press
Cover and interior design by Bodenweber Design
Text composition by PerfecType, Nashville, TN
Cover photograph by Dick Dietrich/Dietrich Photography

Published by The Countryman Press, P.O. Box 748, Woodstock, Vermont 05091

Distributed by W. W. Norton & Company, Inc., 500 Fifth Avenue, New York, NY 10110

Printed in the United States of America

10 9 8 7 6 5 4 3 2

EXPLORE WITH US!

We have been fine-tuning *Vermont: An Explorer's Guide* for the past 19 years, a period in which lodging, dining, and shopping opportunities have more than quadrupled in the state. As we have expanded our guide, we have also been increasingly selective, making recommendations based on years of conscientious research and personal experience. What makes us unique is that we describe the state by locally defined regions, giving you Vermont's communities, not simply its most popular destinations. With this guide you'll feel confident to venture beyond the tourist towns, along roads less traveled, to places of special hospitality and charm.

WHAT'S WHERE

In the beginning of the book you'll find an alphabetical listing of special highlights, with important information and advice on everything from antiques to weather reports.

LODGING

Prices: Please don't hold us or the respective innkeepers responsible for the rates listed as of press time in 2002. Some changes are inevitable. The 9 percent state rooms and meals tax and any built-in gratuities are included only where applicable. **Smoking:** State law bars smoking in all places of public accommodation in Vermont, including restaurants, and even in bars that don't qualify as "cabarets."

RESTAURANTS

Note the distinction between *Dining Out* and *Eating Out.* By their nature, restaurants listed in the Eating Out group are generally inexpensive.

KEY TO SYMBOLS

- The special value symbol appears next to lodging and restaurants that combine high quality and moderate prices.
- The kids-alert symbol appears next to lodging, restaurants, activities, and shops of special appeal to youngsters.
- ♿ The wheelchair symbol appears next to lodging, restaurants, and attractions that are partially or fully handicapped-accessible.
- 🐾 The dog paw symbol appears next to lodgings that accept pets (usually with a reservation and deposit) as of press time.
- ⚭ The wedding rings symbol appears beside inns that frequently serve as venues for weddings and civil unions.

We would appreciate your comments and corrections about places you visit or know well in the state. Please use the card enclosed in this book, or e-mail Chris: ctree@traveltree.net.

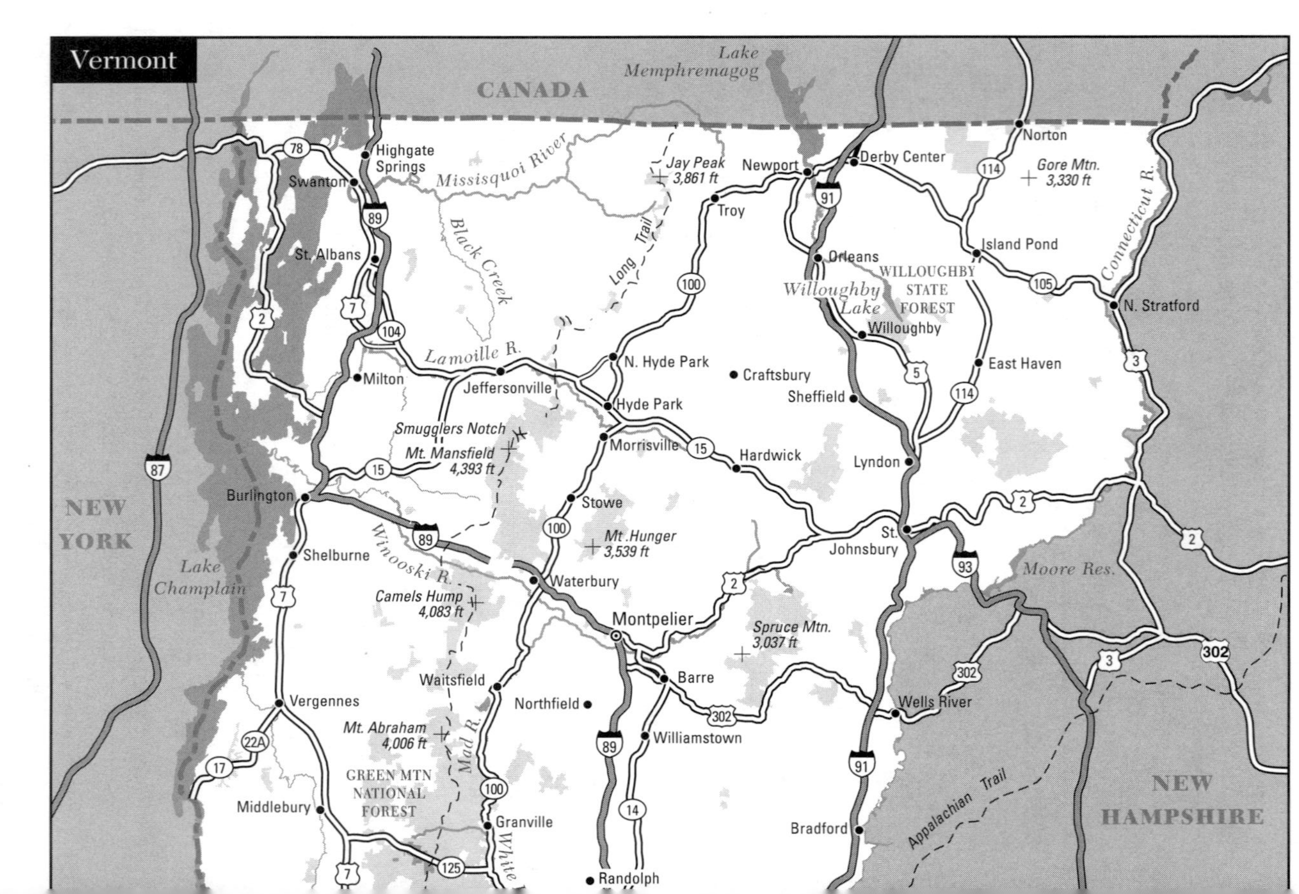
Vermont
CANADA
Lake Memphremagog
NEW YORK
NEW HAMPSHIRE
Lake Champlain
Highgate Springs
Swanton
St. Albans
Milton
Burlington
Shelburne
Vergennes
Middlebury
Jeffersonville
Smugglers Notch
Mt. Mansfield 4,393 ft
Camels Hump 4,083 ft
Mt. Abraham 4,006 ft
GREEN MTN NATIONAL FOREST
Waitsfield
Granville
Missisquoi River
Black Creek
Lamoille R.
Winooski R.
Mad R.
White
Long Trail
Jay Peak 3,861 ft
Newport
Troy
N. Hyde Park
Hyde Park
Morrisville
Stowe
Mt. Hunger 3,539 ft
Waterbury
Montpelier
Northfield
Barre
Williamstown
Randolph
Craftsbury
Hardwick
Sheffield
Lyndon
St. Johnsbury
Spruce Mtn. 3,037 ft
Wells River
Bradford
Derby Center
Orleans
Willoughby Lake
WILLOUGHBY STATE FOREST
Willoughby
Island Pond
East Haven
Norton
Gore Mtn. 3,330 ft
Connecticut R.
N. Stratford
Moore Res.
Appalachian Trail
78
89
7
2
104
15
87
22A
17
125
100
14
91
5
114
105
3
93
302

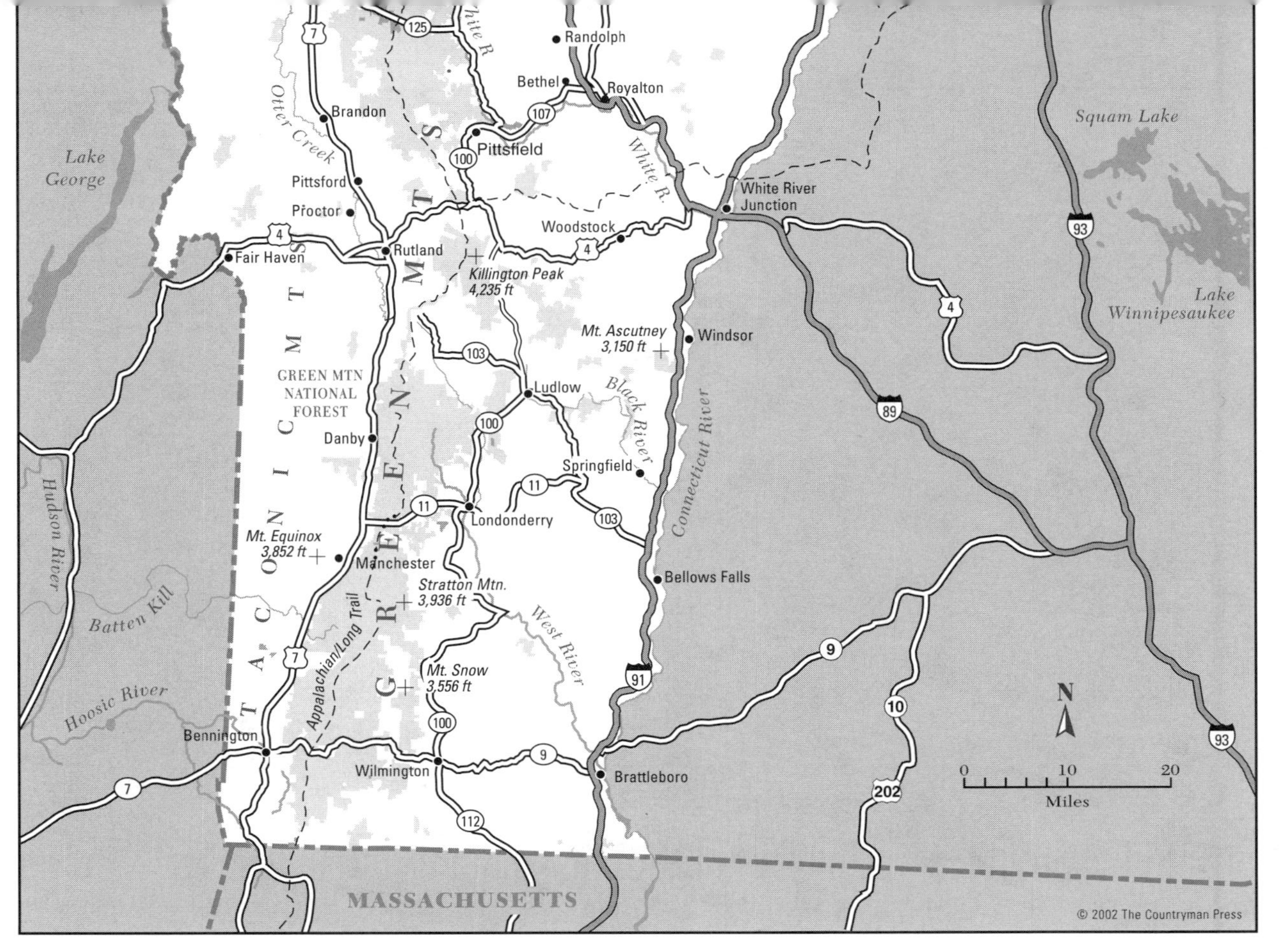
Randolph
Bethel
Royalton
Brandon
Otter Creek
Pittsfield
White R.
Lake George
Pittsford
Proctor
White River Junction
Squam Lake
Woodstock
Fair Haven
Rutland
Killington Peak 4,235 ft
Lake Winnipesaukee
Mt. Ascutney 3,150 ft
Windsor
GREEN MTN NATIONAL FOREST
Ludlow
Black River
Danby
Springfield
Connecticut River
Hudson River
Londonderry
Mt. Equinox 3,852 ft
Manchester
Bellows Falls
Stratton Mtn. 3,936 ft
Batten Kill
West River
Appalachian/Long Trail
Mt. Snow 3,556 ft
Hoosic River
Bennington
Wilmington
Brattleboro
TACONIC MTS
GREEN MTS
MASSACHUSETTS
N
0 10 20
Miles
© 2002 The Countryman Press

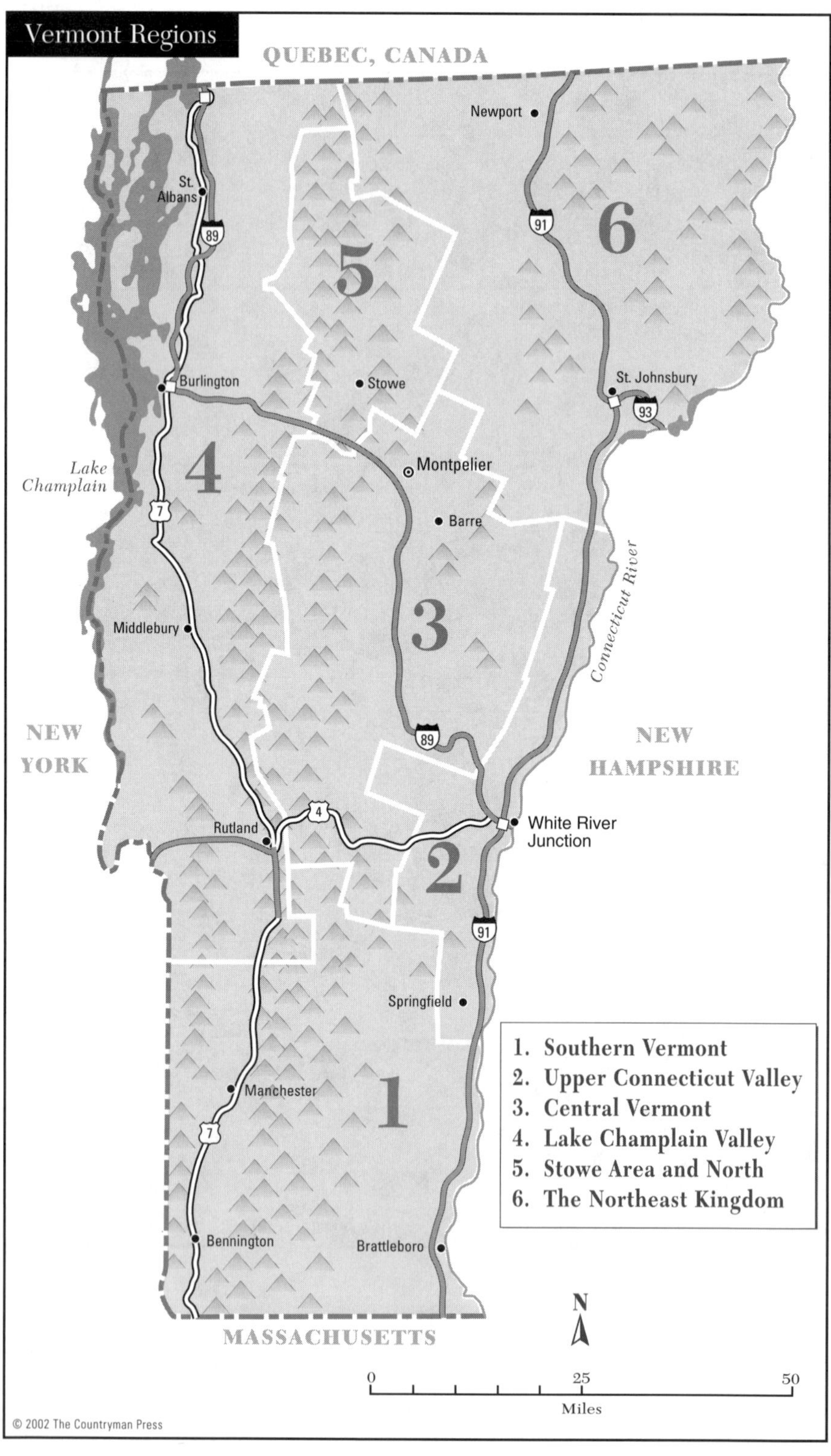
Vermont Regions
QUEBEC, CANADA
Newport
St. Albans
89
91
6
5
Stowe
Burlington
St. Johnsbury
93
Montpelier
Lake Champlain
4
7
Barre
Connecticut River
Middlebury
3
NEW YORK
NEW HAMPSHIRE
89
4
Rutland
White River Junction
2
91
Springfield
1. Southern Vermont
2. Upper Connecticut Valley
3. Central Vermont
4. Lake Champlain Valley
5. Stowe Area and North
6. The Northeast Kingdom
Manchester
1
7
Bennington
Brattleboro
N
MASSACHUSETTS
0
25
50
Miles

CONTENTS

10 INTRODUCTION

16 WHAT'S WHERE IN VERMONT

1 Southern Vermont

61 THE LOWER CONNECTICUT AND WEST RIVER VALLEYS

97 MOUNT SNOW/WILMINGTON AREA

115 BENNINGTON AREA

123 MANCHESTER AND THE MOUNTAINS

161 BELLOWS FALLS, SAXTONS RIVER, AND GRAFTON

173 OKEMO VALLEY REGION

2 Upper Connecticut Valley

195 UPPER VALLEY RIVER TOWNS

222 WOODSTOCK/QUECHEE AREA

3 Central Vermont

255 KILLINGTON/PLYMOUTH AREA

275 THE WHITE RIVER VALLEYS

295 SUGARBUSH/MAD RIVER VALLEY

316 BARRE/MONTPELIER AREA

4 Lake Champlain Valley

332 RUTLAND AND THE LOWER CHAMPLAIN VALLEY

344 ADDISON COUNTY AND ENVIRONS

375 BURLINGTON REGION

409 THE NORTHWEST CORNER

422 ST. ALBANS AND SWANTON

5 Stowe Area and North of the Notch

431 STOWE AND WATERBURY

457 NORTH OF THE NOTCH AND THE LAMOILLE VALLEY

6 The Northeast Kingdom

474 ST. JOHNSBURY, CRAFTSBURY, AND BURKE MOUNTAIN AREA

512 JAY PEAK AREA

523 NEWPORT AND THE NORTH COUNTRY

537 INDEX

INTRODUCTION

Welcome to the Green Mountain State and this ninth edition of the most comprehensive guide to its distinctive landscape, character, and places to see and stay. No other portrait of Vermont gathers so much practical information between two covers—so much, in fact, that even Vermonters find it useful.

We have divided the guide into areas whose boundaries usually coincide with those of the local chambers of commerce. Each section begins with a verbal snapshot of the area against a historical background, followed by advice on sources of information, getting around, things to see and do, and descriptions of just about every legal form of recreation, from skiing, horseback riding, sailing, hiking, swimming, canoeing, and golf to llama trekking and white-water rafting.

Then we give capsule descriptions of places to stay, representing roughly two-thirds of the resorts, inns, B&Bs, and farm stays—but omitting most motels. We try to be descriptive and reasonably candid about what we like and don't like. We visit regularly (many innkeepers tell us they see us more regularly than any other travel writers), and we describe many reasonably priced options, some of them real gems, that are found in no other book.

We critique upscale restaurants *(Dining Out)* and the everyday options *(Eating Out),* plus good delis, bakeries, and coffeehouses. Local entertainment, shops worth walking into, and special events round out coverage of virtually every city, town, and village.

Vermont is within a few hours' drive of 35 million people, and its popularity as a destination is growing. In summer, visitors seem to find their way to every corner. In winter they converge on those areas that offer the best alpine and cross-country skiing in the East. On fall foliage weekends, traffic congeals in places, and visitors without reservations find themselves sleeping in spare bedrooms. At that time of year it's best to come midweek—with reservations and this book. Vermont, after all, invented "foliage season" 50 years ago and has been promoting its autumn colors as a drive-through spectacle ever since. In the process it has developed a better system (see *Foliage* in "What's Where") for lodging "leaf-peepers" at peak periods than is found in other New England states.

Contrary to its image, Vermont's landscape varies substantially from north to south and even more from east to west. Rather than following the tried-and-true tourist routes (east–west Routes 9 and 4 and north–south Route 100), we suggest

A NOTE ON LODGING LISTINGS
We do not charge innkeepers to be included. It's worth noting that a large percentage of lodging guides charge lodging places a "processing fee," anywhere from $250 to $2,500—and that the web is also paid advertising. Within this edition we supply hundreds of web sites but we feel strongly that the Internet has increased rather than obviated the need for an honest, opinionated guidebook based on actual snoop-around rather than virtual research. Sure, this is the best search engine to visiting Vermont, but it's also much more: a combination of critical, current sleuthing and a sense of how to convey what's out there, based on decades of exploring and describing the Green Mountain State.

that (weather permitting) you drive the dramatic but well-surfaced "gap" roads (see *Gaps, Gulfs, and Gorges* in "What's Where") east or west across the state's relatively narrow width, bundling very different landscapes—mountain valleys and the broad sweep of farmland along Lake Champlain—into a few hours' drive.

While focusing on all the state's regions through the same lens (our format), we fervently hope that this book conveys the full spectrum of Vermont's beauty: the river roads of the Upper Valley, the high rolling farmland around Tunbridge and Chelsea, the glacially carved, haunting hills of the Northeast Kingdom, and the limestone farmsteads of Isle La Motte. Villages range from the self-consciously painted and pampering old resorts of Stowe, Woodstock, and Manchester to the equally proud but quiet villages of Craftsbury Common, Chelsea, and Newfane and the Victorian brick streetscapes of Brattleboro and Burlington.

Despite the inevitable inroads of today's shopping-center culture, Vermont has mostly preserved the character of the rural countryside that causes pangs of nostalgia in many urban visitors. Currently, for every acre of open land paved for a parking lot, at least 10 acres are added to the holdings of the Vermont Land Trust and are shielded from development. The administrators of Act 250, the pioneering land-use program, also still exercise sensible controls over new commercial development, deflecting sporadic efforts in the legislature to dilute the act's provisions. Vermonters, prudently and in a spirit of thrift, have not torn down the past. Abandoned farmhouses have been restored, and in a score of towns, adaptive preservation techniques have been thoughtfully applied to convert obsolete mills to other uses.

Vermont has never been a "rich" state. Except for machine tools, the Industrial Revolution skipped over it; as one political scientist noted, we leaped from "cow chips to microchips." Nevertheless, a few 19th-century family fortunes were made from lumber, wool, marble, and railroads. Tangible evidence of those entrepreneurs can be found in half a dozen stately homes that survive as inns, notably the Inn at Shelburne Farms, The Castle in Proctorsville, and the Hartness House in Springfield.

The 14 years of sovereignty as an independent country between 1777 and 1791 stamped Vermont with the indelible "contrary country" brand. Many examples of

TOURISM IN VERMONT

Contrary to common belief, tourism (for lack of a better word to describe the phenomenon of visitors "from away") is an integral part of Vermont's history, one that has affected its landscape—not just since the '50s but for 150 years.

Before the Civil War, southerners patronized mineral spas along the Connecticut River in Brattleboro and Newbury, and after the war Vermont's burgeoning railroads teamed up with the state's Board of Agriculture to promote farm vacations. Railroad guides also promoted Newport, with its elegant four-story Lake Memphremagog House ("one of the largest and finest hotels in New England"), and Lake Willoughby ("one of the most remarkable places in the continent"). Carriage roads were built to the top of Jay Peak, Mount Mansfield, and Mount Equinox, and of course there was a summit hotel atop Mount Mansfield (the highest peak in the state) as well as a large hotel beside the Green Mountain Inn in Stowe Village.

In the 1850s the Equinox House was recognized as one of New England's leading hotels. By 1862 the *Manchester Journal* could report that the previous summer, "Every house in the village was as full as a 'Third Avenue car,' almost entirely New Yorkers." Woodstock was equally well known in the right Manhattan circles by the 1890s.

All 19th- and early-20th-century visitors arrived by train (the exception being those who crossed Lake Champlain by ferry), and Vermont was slower than many other states to provide roads suitable to touring. The flood of 1927 washed out a number of major highways and bridges. In 1936 the proposal for building a federally funded, 260-mile Green Mountain Parkway the length of the state—passing just below the crests of Pico, Killington, and several other peaks—was roundly defeated in a public referendum.

After World War II, however, Vermont launched what may be the world's first and most successful campaign to turn off-season into peak season.

"If you can pick and choose, there is no better time for a motor trip through Vermont than in autumn," Abner W. Coleman wrote in the first issue of *Vermont Life,* a state publication. The autumn 1946 article continued: "To the color photographer, Vermont during the autumn months offers delights indescribable. Should film become more plentiful this year, hundreds of camera enthusiasts will be roaming around these hills, knocking themselves out in a happy frenzy

this spirit animated the state's subsequent history, from the years when Ethan Allen's Rabelaisian Green Mountain Boys wrested independence from the grip of Hampshiremen and 'Yorkers as well as from "The Cruel Minestereal Tools of George ye 3d," and blunted the British invasion of the Champlain Corridor. This spirit was later responsible for the abolitionist fervor that swept the state in the years before the Civil War and impelled Vermonters to flock to the colors in record

of artistic endeavor. For the autumn woods run the entire spectrum's course, from the blazing reds of the maple through the pale yellows of beech and birch to the violet of far-off mountain walls." The story was illustrated with the first of many vividly hued photos for which *Vermont Life* remains famous.

While Vermonters can't claim to have invented skiing, the state does boast America's oldest ski resorts. In the 1930s skiers began riding rope tows up slopes in Woodstock, at Pico, and on Mount Mansfield; after World War II Stowe became "Ski Capital of the East." Patrons at Mad River Glen built the country's first slope-side lodging, and in the early '60s nearby Sugarbush opened with the East's first bottom-of-the-lifts village. In ensuing decades more than a dozen Vermont ski areas have evolved into year-round resorts, several (Stowe, Sugarbush, and Killington) spawning full-fledged communities.

Vermont's ski communities mirror (in reverse) the story of its mill towns. Whereas mills were positioned on waterfalls—and no longer need the water to generate power—ski resorts have grown around mountains chosen for their good terrain and "dependable" snowfall. Only in recent years has it become apparent that access to enough water—to make snow—is crucial.

The question of whether skiing or any other manifestation of "tourism" (again that inadequate term) contributes to the preservation or destruction of the Vermont character and landscape can be argued interminably. But the fact is that it has been here for 150 years. Today, Vermont inns and B&Bs outnumber farms, and Vermont visitors outnumber cows.

Today's visitor is more likely than not to be welcomed by ex-visitors: More than 40 percent of the state's population of 608,827 has come "from away," a post–World War II phenomenon that has profoundly affected the cultural and political landscapes.

Much has been made of the proverbial "Vermont mystique," that indefinable quality of life and character. It is, we are happy to report, alive and well, especially along the back roads and in villages and hamlets where "neighboring" still reigns. While the portrait of the legendary Vermont Yankee—frugal, wary, taciturn, sardonic—has faded somewhat in today's homogenized culture, independent-minded Vermonters (many of them ex-"tourists") take care of each other, tolerate eccentricities, and regard the world with a healthy skepticism.

numbers when President Lincoln called for troops. They voted their consciences with much the same zeal when, in both world wars, the legislature declared war on Germany, in effect, before the United States did; and when Vermont and the United States observed their bicentennials in 1976–77, debates about secession drew crowds to the state's town halls!

The Authors

A flatland author, born in Hawaii, raised in New York City, and living near Boston, Chris Tree claims to be a professional Vermont visitor. Her infatuation with the state began in college.

"The college was in Massachusetts, but one of my classmates was a native Vermonter whose father ran a general store and whose mother [to whom Chris has dedicated this edition] knows the name of every flower, bird, and mushroom. I jumped at her invitations to come 'home' or to 'camp' and have since spent far more time in Vermont than has my friend. As a travel writer for the *Boston Globe,* I have spent more than 30 years writing newspaper stories about Vermont towns, inns, ski areas, and people. I interviewed John Kenneth Galbraith about Newfane, Pearl Buck about Danby. I rode the Vermont Bicentennial Train, froze a toe on one of the first inn-to-inn ski treks, camped on the Long Trail and in state parks, paddled a canoe down the Connecticut, slid over Lake Champlain on an iceboat as well as paddling it in a kayak, soared over the Mad River Valley in a glider, and hovered above the Upper Valley in a hot-air balloon. I have also tramped through the woods collecting sap, ridden many miles with Vermont Transit, led a foliage tour, collided with a tractor, and have broken down in a variety of places."

Sally West Johnson was born near Philadelphia and grew up in northern Maryland, but her family on the West side had long and deep ties to Vermont, in particular her mother, who spent much of her childhood as well as her college years in Middlebury. For years, the Johnson family—five children and two adults—would load into the family car for the annual 2-week ski vacation at Stowe. Those trips strongly influenced her decision to attend Middlebury College (class of 1972) and to move back to Vermont in 1979 after seven years in the wilds of Manhattan.

A journalist, Johnson spent years covering stories for the *Rutland Herald* that took her to every nook and cranny of Vermont. She has also written about Vermont for the *New York Times* and the *Boston Globe Magazine.* She is married to Stephen Terry, a native of Windsor, Vermont, and their son, Will, also can claim native status. They live in a restored 1800 Cape on the outskirts of Middlebury.

"Somehow, even as a kid, I knew I wanted to make my home here, without necessarily knowing what I would do to make a living. For me, the appeal of Vermont is in both its beauty and its human scale; we all tend to know each other up here, which keeps the politicians honest and the neighbors neighborly. To the extent we can capture that ethos and share it with visitors, I will feel that this book has achieved its goals."

Chris and Sally are deeply indebted to Peter Jennison, a sixth-generation Vermonter, who was born on a dairy farm in Swanton, attended one-room schoolhouses, and graduated from Middlebury College. After 25 years in the publishing business in New York City, he became a "born-again" Vermonter, returning to his native heath in 1972 and founding The Countryman Press. Peter coauthored this book during its first eight editions, and many of the best words in it remain his.

Chris wishes to thank Betsy Gentile, Patricia Long and William Hays in Brattleboro, Lynn Barrett of Dummerston, Lisa Shea of the Mount Snow Valley, Ed Egan of Okemo Valley, Richard Ewald, Pat Fowler, and Robert McBride of the Bellows Falls area, Thom and Joan Gorman and Susan Roy in the Mad River Valley, Beth

Kennett of Rochester, the Upper Valley's Catherine Carter, Quechee area's Gayle Ottmann and Susanne Schaefer, Dave Morrison for Woodstock, Killington's Kim Jackson, Jay and Karen Keller of Chelsea, Judy Hayward of Windsor, John Dumville of the Vermont Division of Historic Preservation, Diane Konrady of the Vermont Department of Tourism and Marketing, Jason Aldous of the Vermont Department of Agriculture, and agri-tourism director Jackie Folsom. Both authors are hugely grateful to Ann Kraybill, our ever-supportive editor at The Countryman Press.

Christina Tree
Sally W. Johnson

WHAT'S WHERE IN VERMONT

AREA CODE The area code for all of Vermont is **802.**

AGRICULTURAL FACTS AND FAIRS Some 1.34 million acres—of the state's total of 6 million acres—are devoted to agriculture. The farmhouse and barn are still a symbol of Vermont and every Vermont vacation should include a farm visit, whether to buy syrup, cheese, wool, or wine, maybe to pick apples or berries, tour the dairy operation, or to stay for a night or a week. Finding farms can be an excuse to explore unexpectedly beautiful backcountry.

Robert Eddy

Of course a "farm" isn't what it used to be. Just 1,525 of Vermont's 6,800 farms are now dairy, compared with 10,000 dairy farms 40 years ago. Even so, the average size of dairy herds has increased: With just 15 percent as many dairy farms, the state produces more than twice as much milk as it did 45 years ago. Vermont farms today are, however, more likely to raise goats or llamas, beef cattle or sheep, not to mention Christmas trees and flowers, vegetables, fruit, or trout. Bear in mind that before cows, there were sheep. In the 1830s and '40s, meadowland was far more extensive, and was populated by millions of sheep. When the Civil War ended, so did the push for wool blankets, and a significant number of sheep farms were wiped out. Luckily railroads were expanding to every corner of the state in the 1870s, and railroad companies teamed up with state agriculture departments to promote farms to "summer boarders."

Now farmers are once again looking to visitors as well as to new forms of agriculture to maintain their farms.

Within "What's Where" we suggest how to find a variety of agricultural products, from apples to wine. Request a packet of brochures from the Vermont Department of Agriculture (802-828-2416; 116 State Street, Drawer 20, Montpelier 05620-2901; www.state.vt.us/agric) or click onto the Vermont Farms! Association web site: www.vermontfarms.org; 1-802-877-VT-FARMS. The **Champlain Valley Exposition** in Essex (around Labor Day) is by far the state's largest agricultural fair; **Addison County Field Days** in early August, as well as the **Orleans County Fair** in Barton (5 days) and the **Bondville Fair** (2 days), both in late August, are the genuine thing, and the **Vermont State Fair** in Rutland (9 days, in early September) is big. The **Tunbridge World's Fair** (4 days in mid-September) is the oldest and most colorful of them all. See also in this chapter *Apples, Cheese, Christmas Trees, Farmers' Markets, Farms Open to the Public, Farm Stays, Gardens, Maple Sugaring, Pick Your Own, Sheep and Wool,* and *Wine.*

AIR SERVICE **Burlington International Airport** (802-863-1889) currently offers most of the scheduled (largely commuter) service in Vermont. Carriers include: **Delta Express** (1-800-221-1212), **Continental Express** (1-800-525-0280), **Northwest Airlink** (1-800-225-2525), **JetBlue** (1-800-538-2583) with reasonable fares to New York's JFK International Airport, **United Airlines** (1-800-241-6522), connecting with most U.S. points via Chicago, and **USAirways Express** (1-800-428-4322). From **Rutland State Airport** Continental Connection operated by **Colgan Air** (1-800-272-5488) flies to Boston and New York. **Lebanon Regional Airport** (603-298-8878), in New Hampshire just across the river from White River Junction, links the Upper Valley with New York and Boston and Philadelphia via **USAirways Express** (1-800-428-4322); the Hartford, Connecticut, airport, served by major carriers, is handy to much of central and southern Vermont on the eastern side of the Green Mountains, while busy **Albany Airport** (www.albanyairport.com) in New York is convenient for much of the western part of the state. Manchester (New Hampshire) Airport (www.flymanchester.com) is actually the largest airport in northern New England with a surprising number of daily domestic and international flights.

AIRPORTS Click on www.vermontairports.com for details about Vermont's 17 public-use airports, just two (see above) with scheduled flights but all accessible to private and some to charter planes. Request a copy of the *Vermont Airport Directory* from the Vermont Agency of Transportation (802-828-5754).

AMTRAK Amtrak service (1-800-USA-RAIL; www.Amtrak.com) has improved dramatically in recent years. Amtrak's *Vermonter* runs from Washington to Montreal with stops (at decent hours both north- and southbound) in Brattleboro, Bellows Falls, Claremont (New Hampshire), Windsor, White River Junction, Randolph, Montpelier, Waterbury, Burlington, and St. Albans. The *Adirondack* runs up the western shore of Lake Champlain en route from Manhattan to Montreal and stops at Port Kent, New York, across from the ferry to Burlington. The *Ethan Allen Express* connects Rutland with New York City (with special weekend ski-season runs and bus shuttles to Killington and Okemo) and Albany. All Vermont trains carry bicycles and skis in the baggage car.

ANTIQUARIAN BOOKSELLERS The **Vermont Antiquarian Booksellers Association** (VABA; www.valley.net/~vaba) publishes a pamphlet list of its more than 50 member stores, available in those stores.

ANTIQUING A pamphlet guide, *Antiquing in Vermont,* listing more than 120 members of the Vermont Antiques Dealers' Association (www.adntweb.com/vada), is available by sending a double-stamped, self-addressed, business-sized envelope to James Harley (88 Reading Farms Road, Reading 05062). The association sponsors an **annual antiques show** in September. Major concentrations of dealers can be found in Bennington, Burlington, Dorset, Manchester, Middlebury, Woodstock, and along Route 30 in the West River Valley. The **Weston Antiques Fair,** usually the first weekend in October, is the state's oldest and still one of its best. The state's largest group dealers are in Quechee and East Barre.

Kim Grant

APPLES During fall harvest season, the demand is not only for bushel baskets already filled with apples but also for an empty basket and the chance to climb a ladder and fill it with the many varieties of apples grown in Vermont—primarily in the Champlain islands, in the Champlain Valley around Shoreham, and in the lower Connecticut River Valley between Springfield and Brattleboro. Listings of orchards can be found under descriptions of these areas in this book and by requesting a map/guide to farms from the Vermont Apple Marketing Board (www.vermontapples.org) through the Department of Agriculture (802-828-2416; 116 State Street, Montpelier 05620-2901). From the earliest days of settlement through the mid-1800s more apples, it's said, were used for making hard cider and brandy than for eating and cooking. In 1810 some 125 distilleries were producing more than 173,000 gallons of apple brandy annually. Today wineries and cideries are once more making apple wines; the most visitor-friendly of these are: **Boyden Valley Winery** in Cambridge (802-644-8155; 802-226-7575), **Flag Hill Farm** in Vershire (802-685-7724), **Grand View Winery** near Montpelier (802-456-8810), **Putney Mountain Winery** (802-387-4610) in Dummerston, and **North River Winery** in Jacksonville (802-368-7557).

ART GALLERIES Vermont's principal collections of art (painting, sculpture, and decorative arts) are found in the **Bennington Museum** (works by Grandma Moses); the **Robert Hull Fleming Museum** at the University of Vermont, Burlington; the new **Arts Center at Middlebury College;** the **Athenaeum** in St. Johnsbury; the **Shelburne Museum** in Shelburne; the **Chaffee Art Center,** Rutland; the **Southern Vermont Arts Center,** Manchester; the **Thomas Waterman Wood Art Gallery,** Montpelier; the **Helen Day Art Center** in Stowe; the **Chester Art Guild** in Chester; and the **Chandler Gallery** in Randolph. Manchester and Woodstock offer an unusual number of private galleries, and Brattleboro is another art center. Both Burlington and Brattleboro sponsor open gallery tours the first Friday of every month.

ARTS COUNCILS Vermont's local arts councils organize films, festivals, and concerts throughout the year. Those listed here are the largest and sources of cultural happenings in their areas: **Arts Council of Windham County,** Brattleboro (802-257-1881); **Catamount Film and Arts Center,** St. Johnsbury (802-748-2600); **Crossroads Arts Council,** Rutland (802-775-5413); **Onion River Arts Council,** Montpelier (802-229-9408); **Pentangle Council on the Arts,** Woodstock (802-457-3981). The overall information source is the **Vermont Arts Council** (802-828-3291; 136 State Street, Montpelier 05633-6001; www.vermontartscouncil.org).

AUCTIONS Most major upcoming auctions are announced in the Thursday edition of Vermont newspapers, with a listing of items that will be up for bid. Auctions may be scheduled at any time, however, during summer months, advertised primarily on local bulletin boards and in shop windows. Among well-known auctioneers and auction houses: **William Dupras** of Randolph Center; **Butch Sutherland,** Woodstock; **C. W. Gray** of East Thetford, every Monday night, year-round (livestock); **Arthur Hicks,** Hicks' Commission Sales, Morrisville.

BALLOONING Year-round champagne flights are offered by Brian Boland at **Post Mills Airport** (802-333-4883). Also inquire at the **Stoweflake Resort** in Stowe (802-253-7355). Ascents are also offered by **Balloons Over New England** (1-800-788-5562) and **Killington Balloon Adventures** (802-291-4887). The **Annual Balloon Festival** in Quechee is held in June during Father's Day weekend.

BARNS Many barns along the highways and byways have distinctive touches, such as ornate Victorian cupolas, and still more are connected to farmhouses in the "extended" architectural style that served as shelter for the farmers' trips before dawn in deep snow. Just a dozen round barns survive in Vermont, all built between 1899 and World War I. The concept of the round barn is thought to have originated with the Shakers in Hancock, Massachusetts, where the original stone barn, built in 1824, is now the centerpiece of a museum. The Vermont survivors include: the **Moore barn** in East Barnet; the **Hastings barn** in Waterford; the **Metcalf barn** (Robillard Flats) in Irasburg; the **Parker barn** in Grand Isle, converted into a housing center for the elderly; two barns in Coventry; the **Powers barn** in Lowell; the **Parker barn** in North Troy; one in Enosburg Falls; and **Southwick's** in East Calais. In Waitsfield the **Joslin round barn** is now a cultural center with a swimming pool in its bowels, attached to the **Inn at Round Barn Farm;** in Strafford the **Round Barn Farm,** a 350-acre

Kim Grant

working dairy farm, takes guests. Round-barn addicts should check at local general stores for exact location and to secure permission to photograph the structures. Among other Vermont barns open to the public are the vast, five-story, 416-foot-long, Norman-style **Farm Barn** and the impressive stable and coach barn at Shelburne Farms in Shelburne. The round barn once in Passumpsic has been moved to the Shelburne Museum. Two lively, illustrated guides are *A Field Guide to New England Barns and Farm Buildings* by Thomas Visser and *Big House, Little House, Back House, Barn: The Connected Farm Buildings of New England* by Thomas Hubka (both from the University Press of New England).

BED & BREAKFASTS The hundreds of B&Bs we have personally inspected are listed under their respective locations in this book; they range from working farms to historic mansions, $55–350 per room.

BICYCLE TOURING In Vermont the distance via back roads from swimming hole to antiques shop to the next inn is never far. John Freidin, author of *25 Bicycle Tours in Vermont* (Backcountry Guides), introduced the whole notion of guided bike tours for adults back in 1972. Woodstock-based **Bike Vermont** (1-800-257-2226; www.bikevt.com; P.O. Box 207, Woodstock 05091) is now by far the state's largest, most respected inn-to-inn tour outfitter, offering a "sag wagon," renting 21-gear hybrid bikes, specializing in small (under 20) groups and a wide variety of Vermont destinations. **Bicycle Holidays** (1-800-292-5388) caters to those who prefer to travel without a guide but want a route mapped, inns reserved, and luggage transferred. Guided camping tours (with a sag wagon) are offered by **POMG** (Peace of Mind Guaranteed) **Bike Tours of Vermont** (802-434-2270; www.pomgbike.com). **Vermont Bicycle Touring** (1-800-245-3868) offers inn-to-inn biking tours to several destinations. **Cycle-Inn-Vermont** (802-228-8799; Box 243, Ludlow 05149) is an association of innkeepers whose establishments are a comfortable bike ride from each other. Participants are largely on their own, but rental equipment is available and baggage is transferred from inn to inn. Bicycle paths continue to grow and multiply in Vermont. **Stowe's "Rec" Path** and easy rentals make it an ideal place to sample the sport. The **Burlington Bike Path** follows the shore of Lake Champlain for 9 miles (rentals available); the 26-mile **Missisquoi Rail Trail** follows an old railbed from St. Albans to Richford; the **Bennington Historic Bike Route** leads bikers around local sights; and the 34-mile **D&H Recreation Trail** follows an abandoned railroad

VBT

bed almost 20 miles from Castleton to West Rupert, with the remainder in New York State. Within each chapter, we have described sources for local bike rentals. Note that many inns and outfitters offer shuttle service from Amtrak stops. See also *Mountain Biking.*

BIRDING While the hermit thrush, the state bird, is reclusive and not too easy to spot, Vermont offers ample opportunities for observing herons and ducks, as well as raptors like owls, hawks, falcons, ospreys, even bald eagles. Outstanding birding areas include the **Missisquoi National Wildlife Refuge** (802-868-4781) in Swanton, the **Dead Creek Wildlife Refuge** (802-759-2398) in Vergennes, and the 4,970-acre **Victory Basin** east of St. Johnsbury. The 255-acre **Green Mountain Audubon Nature Center** in Huntington (802-434-3068) is open year-round; inquire about guided walks and special programs (www.thecompass.com/audubon). The neighboring **Birds of Vermont Museum** (802-434-2167) in Huntington is well worth checking out, an exceptionally well-mounted display (in their natural habitats) of lifelike carvings of over 200 species, showing both male and female plumage, all the work of master carver Bob Spear of Colchester. The **Vermont Institute of Natural Science (VINS)** in Woodstock, but soon to move to Quechee (802-457-2779; www.vinsweb.org; open November to May except Sunday and daily the rest of the year), also has nature trails, a library, and a series of special programs. The institute's **Vermont Raptor Center** introduces visitors to the owls, hawks, and eagles of northern New England (26 species are in residence).

BOATING The official state map notes public boat-launch areas. A booklet, *Laws and Regulations Governing the Use and Registration of Motorboats,* is available from the Vermont Department of Public Safety, Marine Division, Montpelier 05602. Click onto boatsafe.com/vermont. (See also *Canoeing and Kayaking, Connecticut River,* and *White Water.*)

BOAT EXCURSIONS If you don't own a yacht, there are still plenty of ways to get onto Vermont rivers and lakes. Possible excursions include the ***Belle of Brattleboro*** (802-254-1263), which plies the Connecticut from Brattleboro, and Peacemaker Cruises (603-445-2371), which sails a scenic reach of the river above Bellows Falls; the ***Spirit of Ethan Allen II*** (802-862-8300), an excursion vessel based in Burlington; the **M/V *Carillon*** (802-897-5331), which offers narrated cruises from Larrabees Point in Shoreham up and down Lake Champlain near Fort Ticonderoga; ***Newport's Princess*** (802-334-6617) offers daily cruises of

Lake Memphremagog from the Newport City Dock; and the ***M/V Mountain Mills*** (802-464-2975), which sails on Lake Whitingham. For details, check under respective locations in this book. See also *Ferries.*

BOOKS For a complete bibliography, write for the *Books about Vermont* catalog from the Vermont Historical Society (109 State Street, Montpelier 05602; vhs@state.vt.us). In addition to the books we mention in specific fields or on particular subjects, here are some of the most useful current titles: *The Vermont Atlas and Gazetteer* (DeLorme); *Vermont Place Names: Footprints in History,* by Esther Swift (Vermont Historical Society); and *Lake Champlain: Key to Liberty,* by Ralph Nading Hill (The Countryman Press). *The Roadside History of Vermont,* by Peter Jennison (Mountain Press), is an informal narrative of what happened where and when along main travel routes. *Hands on the Land: A History of the Vermont Landscape,* by Jan Albers, published by the MIT Press for The Orton Family Foundation, is also essential reading for anyone truly interested in understanding why Vermont looks the way it does. Lovers of natural history should seek out *The Nature of Vermont* by Charles Johnson (University Press of New England). For children, *Vermont: The State with the Storybook Past,* by Cora Cheney (New England Press), is the best. A basic reference directory is *The Vermont Yearbook,* published by the National Survey, Chester. Civil War buffs will be rewarded by Howard Coffin's *Full Duty: Vermonters in the Civil War*; *Nine Months to Gettysburg: Stannard's Vermonters and the Repulse of Pickett's Charge;* and *The Battered Stars: One State's Civil War Ordeal During Grant's Overland Campaign* (all The Countryman Press). Our favorite current Vermont fiction writer is unquestionably Howard Frank Mosher of Irasburg, whose evocative novels include *Disappearances, Northern Borders, Where the Rivers Flow North,* and *A Stranger in the Kingdom;* the last two are now also films. Joseph Citro is the author of several books about occult occurrences and ghost stories in the state; his latest is *Green Mountains, Dark Tales* (University Press of New England). The Brattleboro-based mysteries of Archer Mayor, including *Open Season* and other titles in his Joe Gunther police-procedural series, are gaining momentum. And look for the charming little *Art of the State: Vermont* by Suzanne Mantell (Abrams). For a charming narrative guide to some off-the-beaten-path attractions, seek out *Off the Leash: Subversive Journeys around Vermont* by Helen Husher (The Countryman Press).

BREWERIES Civil War–era Vermont was New England's leading hops-producing state; in the United States only New York surpassed its production. In the late 19th century, however, temperance movements and other factors virtually eliminated its beer and wine industries. But Vermont brewing is back. Check out www.vermontbrewers.com. **Magic Hat Brewing Co.** (802-558-BREW) in South Burlington, **Harpoon Brewery** (1-888-HARPOON) in Windsor, and **Otter Creek Brewing** (1-800-473-0727) in Middlebury offer tours and tastings, while **Black River Brewing** (802-228-3100) in Ludlow, **Long Trail Brewing** (802-672-5011) in West Bridgewater, **McNeil's Brewery** (802-257-9102) in Brattleboro, **Jasper**

Kim Grant

Murdock's Alehouse at the Norwich Inn (802-649-1143), **Salt Ash Inn and Brew Pub** (1-800-SALT-ASH) in Plymouth, **The Shed** (802-253-9311) in Stowe, and **Trout River Brewing Co.** (802-626-3984) in Lyndonville all serve their own brews. **Rock Art Brewery** (802-635-9758) in Johnson welcomes visitors by appointment.

BUS SERVICE **Vermont Transit.** For a current timetable, contact Vermont Transit Co., Inc. (802-864-6811; 1-800-451-3292; 106 Main Street, Burlington 05401; www.vttransit.com). The major routes are (1) up the western side of the state from New York City and Albany via Bennington, Rutland, and Burlington to Montreal; (2) from Boston via White River Junction and Burlington to Montreal; you can connect to St. Johnsbury and Newport. Read the timetable carefully, and you will find that most corners of the state of Vermont—and a number elsewhere in northern New England—are served. Children under 12 travel at half price; one child under 5 can travel free. Inquire about overnight and multiday tours to Montreal, Boston, New York, and points south. Note that the new 345 Pine Street terminal in Burlington offers ample parking but is no longer downtown. At this writing the Montpelier terminal is a battered trailer that closes between buses and doesn't even post a schedule.

CAMPS, FOR CHILDREN For information about more than 50 Vermont summer camps for boys and girls contact the **Vermont Camping Association** (1-888-VTCAMPS; www.vermontcamps.org).

CAMPGROUNDS A *Vermont Campground Guide* advertising more than 70 private campgrounds and describing more than 30 state park campgrounds is published by the Vermont Campground Association (www.campvermont.com) and is available from the Vermont Department of Tourism (1-800-VERMONT). Also request a *Vermont State Parks Map Atlas* from the Vermont Department of Forests, Parks and Recreation (802-241-3655; 103 South Main Street, Waterbury 05671-0603; www.vtstateparks.com). State facilities include furnished cottages, unfurnished cabins, lean-tos, and tent and trailer sites. Fees vary with the class of the area; in 2002 the range was $12–20. Inquire about season passes. After January 1 through mid-May reservations can be made weekdays, 9–4 by phone: 802-479-4280 or 1-800-658-6934; after that phone the parks directly (each is listed as it appears geographically in the book). Vermont state park campsites are all screened by trees from neighboring sites and are well maintained; many parks have organized programs such as hikes, campfire sings, films, and lectures. Most parks are relatively uncrowded, especially midweek; the most popular parks are Branbury, Stillwater, Groton Forest, Quechee Gorge, and Lake St. Catherine. There are nine designated campsites within the 300,000-acre **Green Mountain National Forest** (sites available on a first-come, first-served basis for a maximum 14-day period at a modest charge). Camping is also permitted, without fee or prior permission, virtually anywhere on national forest land. Before you pitch your tent, however, we recommend that you visit one of the three district ranger offices; see *Green Mountain National Forest*. The **U.S. Army Corps of Engineers,** New England Division, has two camping areas in Vermont. **Winhall Brook**, at Ball Mountain Lake in Jamaica, it offers more than 100 campsites near flush toilets, showers, and swimming; for details phone 802-874-4881.

CANOEING AND KAYAKING Organized canoe and kayaking trips have increased in recent years. **Battenkill Canoe** (802-362-2800; 1-800-421-5268; Box 65, Route 313, West Arlington) offers day trips and inn-to-inn tours throughout the state; **Clearwater Sports** (802-496-2708; Route 100, Waitsfield 05673) offers guided tours, instruction, and special expeditions, as does **Umiak Outdoor Outfitters** (802-253-2317; 849 South Main Street, Stowe). **Vermont Canoe Touring Center** (802-257-5008; Route 5, Brattleboro) offers canoe rentals, shuttle service, and river camping on the Connecticut, just as **North Star Canoes** (603-542-5802), based in Cornish, New Hampshire, does for the scenic reach above the covered bridge, one particularly rich in camping spots (see "Upper Connecticut Valley"). **Wilderness Trails** (802-295-7620) offers similar trips on the neighboring stretch of the river, also on nearby ponds and on the White River. The stretch of the Lamoille River around Jeffersonville is served both by **Smugglers Notch Canoe Touring,** based at the Mannsview Inn (1-800-937-MANN), and by **Green River Canoe** (802-644-8851), based at Smugglers' Notch Resort. *The Vermont Guide to Fishing* map, free from the Vermont Fish and Wildlife Department (802-241-3700; 103 South Main Street, Waterbury 05676), notes falls, rapids, boulder fields, dams, and other potential dangers. A *Winooski River Canoe Guide* is $3 if you pick it up; $4 by mail from the Winooski Valley Park District, Ethan Allen Homestead, Burlington 05401. Recommended books: Roioli Schweiker's third edition of *Canoe Camping Vermont and New Hampshire Rivers* (Backcountry Guides) is a handy guide, and the *AMC River Guide: Vermont/New Hampshire* (AMC Books) is good for detailed information on canoeable rivers. (See also *Connecticut River* and *White Water*.)

VDT

CANOE AND KAYAK RENTALS Rentals are available from the canoe outfitters listed above and from the boat rental sources described in each chapter.

CATAMOUNT TRAIL See *Skiing, Cross-Country.*

CHEESE In recent years Vermont's production of cheese has increased to more than 100 million pounds annually and has become more varied, with sheep and goat as well as cow cheese winning top national and international honors. Of course a century ago most Vermont towns had a cheese maker to which farmers brought the day's surplus milk. **Crowley Cheese** (802-259-2340; 1-800-683-2602), established in 1882 and billed as "the oldest continuously operated cheese factory in the U.S.," is the only survivor of this era, and welcomes visitors to its wooden factory just west of Ludlow on Route 103 in Healdville (open weekdays 8–4; store open daily). This distinctive cheese is creamier than cheddar and still made the traditional way. **Cabot Creamery** (802-563-2231) in Cabot is the state's biggest, most famous producer, with a modern plant producing 12 million pounds of cheese a year. It includes a visitors center (closed only Sundays and January) and offers plant tours; Cabot also operates an annex in Waterbury Center, south of Stowe. Cabot continues to maintain quality as well as quantity. Award-winning **Vermont Shepherd Cheese** (802-387-4473), a rich, tangy sheep's milk cheese from Westminster, opens its "cave" to visitors from August through October, 10–2 (call for directions). **Grafton Village Cheese Company** (1-800-472-3866) in Grafton had its beginnings around 1890 and was resurrected by the Windham Foundation in 1966; visitors view the cheese making from outside, through a picture window. The **Plymouth Cheese Company** (802-672-3650) was founded in 1890 by Col. John Coolidge, father of President Coolidge, and at this writing plans to soon resume producing its old-fashioned Vermont granular curd cheese. At **Shelburne Farms** (802-985-8686; open daily, year-round), in Shelburne near Burlington, prizewinning cheddar is made from the milk of a single herd of Brown Swiss cows. In New Haven, **Orb Weaver Farm** (802-877-3755) produces a creamy, aged, Colby-type cheese made in small batches, entirely by hand (available in 2-pound wheels and 1-pound waxed wedges). In the northwest corner of the state goat cheese is made at **Willow Hill Farm** (802-893-2963) in Milton and at **Lakes End Cheeses** (802-796-3730) in Alburg. In nearby Highgate Center visitors are welcome at **Green Mountain Blue Cheese** (802-868-4193). The **Taylor Farm** (802-824-5690) in Londonderry (southern Vermont) is

Kim Grant

making a reputation with its Gouda, and in Randolph Center, minutes off I-89 exit 4 at **Neighborly Farms** (802-728-4700), you can walk down a hallway and view cows on one side and cheese making on the other (open daily Monday through Saturday, 10–5). **Vermont Butter & Cheese Company** in Websterville makes a wide variety of tantalizing goat cheeses, and **Blythedale Farm** (802-439-6575) in Corinth produces a variety of soft cheeses (a fine Vermont Brie, a Camembert, a Green Mountain Gruyère, and Jersey Blue), but neither is open to visitors. **Sugarbush Farm** (802-457-1757), set high on a hill in Woodstock, smokes and packages several varieties of cheddar cheese and welcomes visitors. Check out the Vermont Cheese Council's informative web site, www.vtcheese.com. Also see *The Cheeses of Vermont: A Gourmet Guide to Vermont's Artisanal Cheesemakers* by Henry Tewksbury (The Countryman Press), which includes a map of cheese makers that welcome visitors.

CHILDREN, ESPECIALLY FOR Look for the ✐ symbol in the margins throughout this book; it designates child-friendly attractions as well as lodging and dining. **Alpine slides** delight children of all ages at Bromley (where there is also a **DévalKart Ride**) as well as at Pico and Stowe. **Alpine lifts,** which operate in summer, are also a way of hoisting small legs and feet to the top of some of Vermont's most spectacular summits. Both **Mount Mansfield,** Vermont's highest peak, and **Killington Peak,** second highest in the state, are accessible via gondola on weekdays. **Jay Peak,** commanding as dramatic a view as the others, is also accessible on aerial tram. In southern Vermont, **Stratton's** gondola runs daily all summer and fall. **Santa's Land** in Putney is the only commercial attraction geared specifically to children. The **Shelburne Museum** has many exhibits that please youngsters, as does the **Fairbanks Museum and Planetarium,** St. Johnsbury, which is filled with stuffed animals, birds, and exhibits from near and far. The **Montshire Museum of Science** in Norwich is a real standout, with hands-on exhibits explaining many basic scientific mysteries; it's also good for waterside walks. The **Billings Farm & Museum** and **Vermont Institute of Natural Science,** both in Woodstock, are child pleasers. Over the past few years, as ski areas have come to compete for family business, most ski resorts have developed special programs for children; see the description for each ski area in the text. In summer, a number of ski areas, notably **Smugglers' Notch,** offer full day-camp programs for children. **The Tyler Place Family Resort** in Highgate Springs and the **Basin Harbor Club** in Vergennes are family-geared resorts with children's programs. (See also *Agricultural Fairs and Facts, Farms Open to the Public, Farm Stays, Boat Excursions,* and *Railroad Excursions.*)

CHRISTMAS TREES Christmas tree farms are plentiful throughout the state and most open after Thanksgiving, inviting customers to come tag the tree they want, leaving it to cut until the last moment. Check the Vermont Department of Agriculture web site, www.state.vt.us/agric, for a listing of growers and www.vermontfarms.org for a list of the more imaginative marketers. These include **Redrock Farm** (802-685-2282) in Chelsea, **Christ-**

mas Trees of Vermont (802-885-9597) in Springfield, and **Elysian Hills** (802-257-0233) in Dummerston, where you can pick out a tree in the summer or fall and have it shipped to you UPS at Christmas. In recent years, bed & breakfasts and inns have teamed up with farms to offer preholiday lodging packages that include a fresh Christmas tree (contact the Vermont Chamber of Commerce: 802-223-3443; www.vtchamber.com). For a do-it-yourself experience, contact the Green Mountain National Forest Service in Rochester (802-767-4261) and inquire about tagged trees you can cut for a nominal fee.

CIVIL UNIONS In the first year (2001) that Vermont sanctioned civil unions between couples of the same sex, 2,479 such ceremonies were performed with almost twice as many females as males taking vows. Only 479 couples were from Vermont. The post office in the central Vermont village of Gaysville has become a favorite venue for wedding pictures. Throughout this guide, we indicate venues that specialize in weddings and civil unions with the wedding ring symbol.

COLLEGES For information about all the state's colleges and universities, contact the **Vermont Higher Education Council** (802-878-7466; P.O. Box 47, Essex Junction 05453-0047; www.vtcolleges.org; vhec@aol.com).

CONNECTICUT RIVER New England's longest river rises near the Canadian/New Hampshire border and forms the border between that state and Vermont for some 255 miles. Not far below its source, it has been dammed into a series of lakes: five in New Hampshire's North Country above Pittsburg and two, Moore and Comerford Reservoirs, near St. Johnsbury. The 145 miles between Barnet and Brattleboro is punctuated by six dams, each creating deep pools that turn the river into a series of placid, narrow lakes. Check out Brattleboro, Bellows Falls, and the Upper Valley chapters for canoe and kayak rentals and boat excursions. *Boating on the Connecticut River* is a detailed guide available by sending a self-addressed envelope to the Connecticut River Joint Commissions (P.O. Box 1182, Charlestown, NH 03603). The commission also maintains an excellent web site, www.ctrivertravel.net. Another fine guide, *Canoeing on the Connecticut River,* is available by sending a SASE to PG&E National Energy Group, attn. Sarah White, 46 Central Parkway, Suite 100, Lebanon, NH 03766; 603-653-9200.

COVERED BRIDGES The state's 110 surviving covered bridges are marked on the official state map, on our maps, and are described in the appropriate chapters of this book under *To See.* Bridge buffs should secure a copy of *Covered Bridges of Vermont* by Ed Barna (The Countryman Press). Covered bridges are also found on www.historicvermont.org.

Kim Grant

CRAFTS More than 1,500 Vermonters make their living from crafts. There are also more than 100 retail crafts venues in the state, ranging from local shops to fine galleries. The dazzling **Vermont State Craft Center** at Frog Hollow in Middlebury and its branch stores in Manchester and Burlington each has its own educational program. Crafters also sell their wares at frequent events, ranging from farmers' markets and church bazaars to juried crafts shows and festivals. Within this book, we have described outstanding local crafts studios, galleries, and shops as they appear geographically and have also included major crafts festivals. Best of all is the **Open Studio Weekend,** held annually Memorial Day weekend, with more than 200 artisans in almost as many locations. Request a copy of the *Vermont Crafts Guide*, available at information centers and on request from the Vermont Crafts Council (802-223-3380; P.O. Box 938, 104 Main Street, Montpelier 05601-0938; www.vermontcrafts.com; vt1crafts@aol.com).

DINERS Vermont will not disappoint diner buffs. Hearty meals at reasonable prices can be found at the **Miss Newport** (good coffee), East Main Street, Newport; and at **Henry's Diner** (known for its Yankee pot roast, lobster roll, and generally good three squares) and the **Oasis,** both on Bank Street, Burlington. **Libby's Blue Line Diner,** Route 7 (just off I-89, exit 16), Colchester, is upscale and popular (you might dine on an eggplant burger). The **Parkway Diner** at 1696 Williston Road, South Burlington, is known for its Greek salad, lobster roll, and Parkway Special: roast beef on a pumpernickel roll. **Halfway House** on Route 22A, a few miles north of Shoreham Village, a local gathering spot, is open 5 AM–8 PM daily. The **Miss Lyndonville Diner** on Bond Street, Lyndonville, is admired for its pies (a breakfast special) and has been augmented by the nearby **Miss Vermont** (Route 5, St. Johnsbury Center), though lines are still long on Sunday morning. **Anthony's Restaurant** on Railroad Street in St. Johnsbury has expanded and is wheelchair-accessible but still offers great food at great prices. Just off 1-91 in Wells River the **P&H Truck Stop** is open 24 hours, 7 days a week, serving large, reasonably priced diner food quickly and cheaply. The **Wayside Restaurant and Bakery** (exit 7; follow signs for Route 302 and it's on your left) south of Montpelier, open 6:30 AM–9:30 PM daily, has expanded gradually over the years to become Vermont's ultimate family restaurant. **Blue Benn Diner,** 102 Hunt Street in Bennington, serves imaginative vegetarian as well as standard diner fare. Add to these the **Farina Family Diner**, Route 4 in Quechee Gorge Village; **Green Mountain Diner,** Main Street in Barre; **Cindy's Diner,** St. Albans; and **Don's Diner,** Bennington. **T. J. Buckley's** in Brattleboro may look like the battered vintage Worcester diner it is, but inside oak paneling gleams and the fare (dinner only, and only by reservation) is recognized as some of the best in the state. West Brattleboro also offers the **Chelsea Royal Diner,** west on Route 9, which, while a bit heavy on diner decor, is still a good family bet (wheelchair-accessible). In Chester, there is the **Country Girl Diner. Miss Bellows Falls Diner** is on the National Register of Historic Places, and the equally historic **Windsor Diner** has been nicely restored under new ownership and is famed for its clam chowder. The **Polka Dot** in White River Junction, and the **Fairlee Diner** in Fairlee, are also the real thing. See also *Highway Roadfood.*

EMERGENCIES Try **911** first. This simple SOS is finally reaching most corners of Vermont. Within this book, we have furnished the number of the medical facilities serving each area in each chapter. For state police phone 802-655-3435, for poison 802-658-3456, and for dental emergencies 1-800-640-5099.

EQUESTRIAN SPORTS Horses have become nearly as much a part of the Vermont landscape as the famous black-and-white Holsteins, and a dedicated equine aficionado can find plenty to see from late spring well into the fall. At the moment, Vermont has three polo clubs: **Sugarbush Polo Club** (802-496-8938), based in the Mad River Valley and Middlebury; **Green Mountain Polo Club** (Hildene: 802-362-1788), near Manchester; and **Quechee Polo Club** (802-295-7900). All hold games on Saturday and Sunday during the summer (usually at 1 PM); most games are free. The **Vermont Summer Horse Festival** (www.vermonthorse.org), the largest of several hunter-jumper shows around the state, takes place at the Harold Beebe Farm in East Dorset from early July through early August. The **Vermont Quarter Horse Association** (whinny.org/horseshow) hosts shows around the region in the summer. The VQHA season begins the first weekend of June at the Tunbridge Fairgrounds in Tunbridge. The **Green Mountain Horse Association** in South Woodstock holds **Dressage Days** in mid-July; see www.usdf.org/calendars for a complete list of dressage events. One of the newest equine activities to hit Vermont is **driving**. Pleasure-driving events are recommended for spectators: the website is www.americandrivingsociety.org.

Leight Johnson

EVENTS Almost every day of the year some special event is happening somewhere in Vermont. Usually it's something relatively small and friendly like a church supper, contra dance, community theatrical production, concert, or crafts fair. We have worked up our own "Special Events" for each region, and listings can also be found in various ways on the state's travel web site, www.1-800-VERMONT.com. Still, many of the best events are like fireflies, surfacing only on local bulletin boards and in the Thursday editions of local papers. In Burlington check out the free and fat *Seven Days*, a funky weekly listing of local arts and entertainment, available everywhere in town.

FACTORY OUTLETS Within the book, we have mentioned only a small fraction of the factory outlets of which we are aware. Our bias has been to favor distinctly made-in-Vermont products. Among our favorites: **Johnson Woolen Mills** (outstanding wool clothing for all ages) in Johnson; **Bennington Potters** (dinnerware, planters, etc.) in Bennington and Burlington; and **Vermont Marble** in Proctor. **Townshend Furniture** in Townshend is a long-established furniture factory worth checking, and **Shackleton Furniture** in Bridgewater, **Pompanoosuc Mills** in East Thetford, and **Copeland Furniture** in Bradford all sell seconds in their workshops. **Manchester** is known for its concentration of outlet stores specializing in quality clothing.

FARMERS' MARKETS From mid-June through early October you can count on finding fresh vegetables, fruit, honey, and much more at farm prices in commercial centers throughout the state. Click on www.state.vt.us/agric/farmmkt for a complete list. Major market venues include Burlington, Enosburg, Morrisville, Newport, St. Johnsbury, Norwich, Fair Haven, Middlebury, Montpelier, Rutland, Brattleboro, Manchester, Waterbury, Windsor, and Woodstock.

Kim Grant

FARMS OPEN TO THE PUBLIC For a list of farms open to the public for tours, to sell their products, or for farm stays, check out the Vermont Farms! Association web site, www.vermontfarms.org.

FARM STAYS A century ago, hundreds of Vermont farms took in visitors for weeks at a time. "There is no crop more profitable than the crop from the city," an 1890s Vermont Board of Agriculture pamphlet proclaimed, a publication noted by Dona Brown in *Inventing New England* (Smithsonian, 1995). Articles advised farmers on how to decorate, what to serve, and generally how to please and what to expect from city guests—much as B&B literature does today. Our own family found a farm stay so enrich ing that we returned year after year and are happy to see that the phenomenon is on the increase again. Within the book we have listed those farms that we have personally visited. For a list you can click on the Vermont Farms! Association's web site, www.vermontfarms.org. **Maple Crest Farm** (802-492-3367) in Shrewsbury deserves special mention because it remains in the same family who have been taking in guests on this working farm since the 1860s. In Rochester **Liberty Hill Farm** (802-767-3926) has pioneered the resurgence in farm stays by proving how successful they can be, and **Harvey's Mountain View** (802-767-4273), while no longer a working farm, still welcomes visitors precisely as it has for generations. **Berkson Farms** (802-933-2522) up in Enosburg Falls has been welcoming families for decades and encouraging them to share in farm chores. **Allenholm Farm** (802-372-5566) in South Hero offers B&B in the midst of a major apple orchard. **Round-Robin Farm** (802-763-7025), way off Sharon's beaten track, and **Emergo Farm Bed and Breakfast** (802-684-2215), on the edge of Danville Village, are also genuine working farms. We can also recommend **Echo Ledge Farm Inn** (802-748-4750) in East St. Johnsbury and **Rose Apple Acres** (802-525-6695) in North Troy. **Hollister Hill Farm** (802-454-7725) in Marshfield invites guests to participate in sugarmaking and take home the results of their labors, while **Rooster Ridge Farm** (802-472-8566) in Wolcott and **The Parent Farmhouse** (802-524-4201) in Milton, **Bittersweet Farm** (802-453-3828) in Bristol, and **Lilac Mountain Farm** (802-899-4180) in Jericho are all bed & breakfasts in bucolic farm settings. **Pie in the Sky** in Marshfield (802-426-3777) is a throwback to the 1960s back-to-the-land era; at the other extreme, there is lakeside Shelburne Farms, the state's most elegant farm, also the site of its most elegant inn: the **Inn at Shelburne Farms** (802-985-8686).

FERRIES On Lake Champlain, a number of car-carrying ferries ply back and forth between the Vermont and New York shores, offering splendid views of both the Green Mountains and the Adirondacks. The northernmost, the **Plattsburgh Ferry,** crosses from Grand Isle, Vermont, on Route 314 (year-round; 15-minute passage). From Burlington, the **Lake Champlain Ferries** cross to Port Kent, New York (1 hour). The **Essex Ferry** crosses from Route F-5 near Charlotte, Vermont, to Essex, New York (20 minutes). Check schedules (802-864-9804) for hours of operation and rates. All three of these are operated by the Lake Champlain Transportation Company, descendant of the line founded in 1828 claiming to be "the oldest steamboat company on earth." Near the southern end of the lake, the **Fort Ticonderoga Ferry** (802-897-7999) provides a scenic shortcut between Larrabees Point, Vermont, and Ticonderoga, New York. This small, car-carrying ferry makes the 6-minute crossing continuously between 8 AM and 9 PM during the summer season, less frequently in spring and fall. Service runs from late April through the last Sunday in October. Officially, the Fort Ti Ferry has held the franchise from the New York and Vermont legislatures since 1799.

FIDDLING Vermont is the fiddling capital of the East. Fiddlers include concert violinists, rural carpenters, farmers, and heavy-equipment operators who come from throughout the East to gather in beautiful natural settings. The **Northeast Fiddling Association** publishes newsletters the first Sunday of every month that list fiddling meets around the state (103 Vermont Route 14 North, East Randolph 05401; 802-728-5188). Annual fiddling events include the **Crackerbarrel Fiddle Festival,** Newbury, and the **National Championship Fiddle Contest** in Barre, usually the last Friday and Saturday in September. Fiddle festivals tend to start around noon and end around dusk.

FILM Three Vermont filmmakers have produced some notable low-budget films in recent years. Jay Craven's dramatizations of Howard Frank Mosher's novels—*Where the Rivers Flow North* and *A Stranger in the Kingdom*—are not only good films but evocative of life in the Northeast Kingdom not too long ago. Nora Jacobson's *My Mother's Early Lovers* rings true throughout. By the same token John O'Brien's films, *Vermont Is for Lovers* and *Man with a Plan,* go right to Vermont's still very real rural core. *Man with a Plan* actually launched its hero's real-life political campaign in 1998: To the amazement of the country, retired Tunbridge dairy farmer Fred Tuttle not only defeated a wealthy carpetbagger for the Republican nomination but won a respectable percentage of the vote for a U.S. senatorial seat.

FISHING Almost every Vermont river and pond, certainly any body of water serious enough to call itself a lake, is stocked with fish and has one or more access areas. Brook trout are the most widely distributed game fish. Visitors ages 15 and over must have a 5-day, a 14-day, or a nonresident license good for a year, available at any town clerk's office, from the local fish and game warden, or from assorted commercial outlets. Because these sources may be closed or time-consuming to track down on weekends, it's wise to obtain the license in advance from the **Vermont Fish and Wildlife Department** (802-241-3700; www.vtfishandwildlife.com). Request an application form and ask for a copy of *Vermont Guide to Fishing,* which details every species of fish and where to find it on a map of the state's rivers and streams, ponds, and lakes. Boat access, fish hatcheries, and canoe routes are also noted. The state's most famous trout stream is the **Battenkill River** in the southwest, focus of a fly-fishing school in Manchester Center offered by the **Orvis Company,** which has been in the business of making fishing rods and selling them to city people for more than a century (it also maintains an outstanding museum devoted to fly-fishing). Many inns, notably along Lake Champlain and in the Northeast Kingdom, offer tackle, boats, and advice on where to catch what. **Quimby Country** (802-822-5533; www.quimbycountry.com) is the state's only major fishing resort, a 19th-century lodge and cabins on Forest and Big Averill Lakes. Landlocked salmon can be found in some northern lakes; other common species include bass, walleye, northern pike, and perch. Federal fish hatcheries can be found in **Bethel** (802-234-5241) and **Pittsford** (802-483-6618), and state hatcheries are in **West Burke** (802-467-3660), **Bennington** (802-442-4556), **Grand Isle** (802-372-3171), **Roxbury** (802-485-7568), and **Salisbury** (802-352-4471). Ice anglers can

Kim Grant

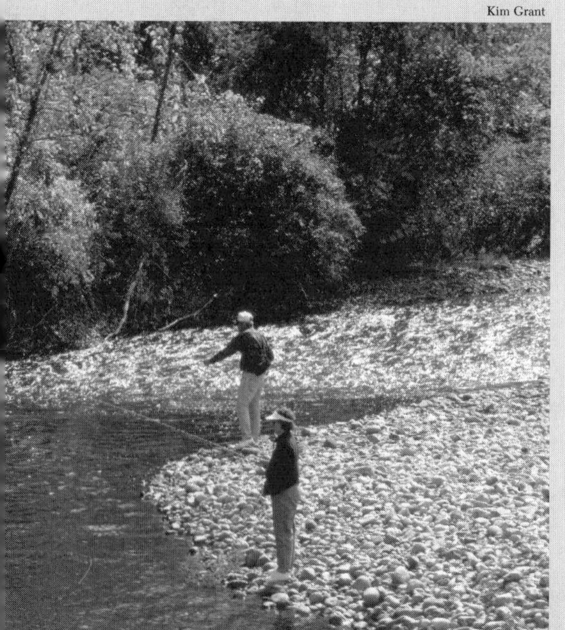

legally take every species of fish (trout only in a limited number of designated waters) and can actually hook smelt and some varieties of whitefish that are hard to come by during warmer months; the **Great Benson Fishing Derby** held annually in mid-February on Lake Champlain draws thousands of contestants from throughout New England. The **Lake Champlain International Fishing Derby,** based in Burlington (call 802-862-7777 for details), is a big summer draw. Books to buy include *The Vermont Atlas and Gazetteer* (DeLorme), with details about fishing species and access; the *Atlas of Vermont Trout Ponds* and *Vermont Trout Streams,* both from Northern Cartographics Inc. (Box 133, Burlington 05402); and *Fishing Vermont's Streams and Lakes* by Peter F. Cammann (Backcountry Guides). Within this book we have listed shops, outfitters, and guides as they appear within each region. **Vermont Outdoor Guide Association** (1-800-747-5905) represents qualified guides throughout the state; check out their informative web site, www.adventureguidesvt.com.

FOLIAGE Vermont is credited with inventing foliage season, first aggressively promoted just after World War II in the initial issues of *Vermont Life.* The Department of Tourism (see *Information*) maintains a foliage "hot line" and sends out weekly bulletins on color progress, which is always earlier than assumed by those of us who live south of Montpelier. Those in the know usually head for northern Vermont in late September and the first week in October, a period that coincides with peak color in that area as well as with the **Northeast Kingdom Fall Foliage Festival** (see "St. Johnsbury, Craftsbury, and Burke Mountain"). By the following weekend, central Vermont is usually ablaze, but visitors should be sure to have a bed reserved before coming, because organized bus tours converge on the state. By the Columbus Day weekend, when what seems like millions of families within driving distance make their annual leaf-peeping expedition, your odds of finding a bed are dim unless you take advantage of those chambers of commerce (notably Middlebury, Woodstock, Brattleboro, Manchester, Central Vermont, and St. Johnsbury) that pride themselves on finding refuge in private homes for all comers. During peak color, we recommend that you avoid Vermont's most heavily trafficked tourist routes; there is plenty of room on the back roads, especially those unsuited to buses. We strongly suggest exploring the high roads through Vermont's "gaps" (see *Gaps, Gulfs, and Gorges*) during this time of year.

GAPS, GULFS, AND GORGES Vermont's mountains were much higher before they were pummeled some 100,000 years ago by a mile-high sheet of ice. Glacial forces contoured the landscape we recognize today, notching the mountains with a number of handy "gaps" through which men eventually built roads to get from one side of the mountain to the other. Gaps frequently offer superb views and access to ridge trails. This is true of the **Appalachian, Lincoln, Middlebury,** and **Brandon Gaps,** all crossing the Long Trail and linking Route 100 with the Champlain Valley; and of the **Roxbury Gap** east of the Mad River Valley. Note, however, that the state's highest and most scenic gap of all is called a "notch" (**Smugglers Notch**

between Stowe and Jeffersonville), the New Hampshire name for mountain passes. Gaps at lower elevations are "gulfs," scenic passes that make ideal picnic sites: Note **Granville Gulf** on Route 100, **Brookfield Gulf** on Route 12, and **Williamstown Gulf** on Route 14. The state's outstanding gorges include: 163-foot-deep **Quechee Gorge,** which can be viewed from Route 4 east of Woodstock; **Brockway Mills Gorge** in Rockingham (off Route 103); **Cavendish Gorge,** Springfield; **Clarendon Gorge,** Shrewsbury (traversed by the Long Trail via footbridge); **Brewster River Gorge,** south of Jeffersonville off Route 108; **Jay Branch Gorge** off Route 105; and (probably the most photographed of all) the **Brown River** churning through the gorge below the Old Red Mill in Jericho.

GARDENS Vermont's growing season is short but all the more intense. Commercial herb and flower gardens are themselves the fastest-growing form of agriculture in the state, and many inns and B&Bs pride themselves on their gardens. Lodging places with especially noteworthy gardens include the **Basin Harbor Club** in Vergennes, the **Inn at Shelburne Farms** in Shelburne, **Judith's Garden B&B** and **Blueberry Hill,** both in Goshen, and the **Jackson House** in Woodstock. **Historic Hildene** in Manchester also features formal gardens. Request the *Vermont Perennial & Herb Display Gardens* brochure from the Vermont Department of Agriculture (802-828-2416; 116 State Street, Montpelier 05620; www.state.vt.us/agric/brochures). The Garden Conservancy publishes annual editions of the *Open Days Directory,* including a number of Vermont sites.

GENERAL STORES Still the hub of most small Vermont communities, general stores retain some shreds of their onetime status as the source of all staples and communication with the outside world. The most famous survivor is the **Vermont Country Store** in Weston and Rockingham, a genuine family business that has expanded into a Vermont version of L.L. Bean. Still, its thick catalog is a source of long underwear and garter belts, Healthy Feet Cream, shoe trees, and gadgets like a kit that turns a plastic soda bottle into a bird feeder. Within each chapter, we have described some of our personal favorites. "The General Store in Vermont," an oral history by Jane Beck, is available from the Vermont Folklife Center in Middlebury. Within this book we have described our favorite general stores as they appear geographically.

Christina Tree

GOLF More than 50 Vermont golf courses are open to the public and more than half of these have 18 holes, a half dozen justly famed throughout the country. A full program of lodging, meals, and lessons is available at **Mount Snow, Killington, Okemo, Stratton Mountain, Sugarbush,** and **Stowe**. The **Woodstock Inn, Lake**

Morey Inn, and others also offer golf packages. The Manchester area boasts the greatest concentration of courses. For a complete list see Vermont's official state map, and for descriptions see the glossy magazine, *Vermont Golf* (1-800-639-1941). *Vermont Golf Courses: A Player's Guide,* by Bob Labbance and David Cornwell (New England Press), is a useful book that describes all 50 of the courses open to the public, including detailed course maps, yardages, fees, opening/closing dates, and starting times.

THE GREEN MOUNTAINS Running 160 miles up the spine of this narrow state, the Green Mountains themselves range in width from 20 to 36 miles, with peaks rising to more than 4,000 feet. A part of the Appalachian Mountain chain, which extends from Alabama to Canada's Gaspé Peninsula, they were once far higher. The Long Trail runs the length of the range, and Route 100 shadows its eastern base. Also see *Hiking and Walking* and *Gaps, Gulfs, and Gorges.*

GREEN MOUNTAIN CLUB See *Hiking and Walking.*

GREEN MOUNTAIN NATIONAL FOREST The **Green Mountain National Forest** encompasses more than 300,000 Vermont acres managed by the U.S. Forest Service. It is traversed by 512 miles of trails, including the **Appalachian Trail** and the **Long Trail,** which follows the ridgeline of the main range of the Green Mountains (see *Hiking and Walking*). The forest harbors six wilderness areas. Use of off-road recreational vehicles is regulated. Information—printed as well as verbal—about hiking, camping, skiing, berry picking, and bird-watching is available from the ranger stations in Manchester Center (802-362-2307), Middlebury (802-388-4362), and Rochester (802-767-4261). Request a free "minimap" from the Green Mountain National Forest (802-747-6700; 231 North Main Street, Rutland 05701). All four offices maintain visitors centers, open weekdays 8–4:30; the magnificent visitors center in Rochester is also open 8–4 on weekends.

HANDICAPPED ACCESS With this edition we have included the wheelchair symbol ♿ to indicate lodging and dining places that are handicapped-accessible.

HERBS Herb farms are a growing phenomenon in rural Vermont—sources of live perennials and herbs; herbs dried into fanciful wreaths; sachets, potpourris, or seasonings distilled as scents. In our wanderings, we have happened on **Meadowsweet Herb Farm,** attached to a handsome farmhouse on a back road in Shrewsbury; and **Talbot's Herb and Perennial Farm** in Hartland, east of Woodstock off Route 4. A pamphlet guide, *Vermont Perennial & Herb Display Gardens,* is available from the Vermont Department of Agriculture (802-828-2416; 116 State Street, Montpelier 05620; www.state.vt.us/agric/brochures).

HIGH SEASON "High season," interestingly enough, varies in Vermont. While "foliage season" represents peak price as well as color everywhere, a ski condo can easily cost four times as much in February as it does in July. Meanwhile, a country inn may charge half its July price in February.

HIGHWAY ROADFOOD As we have cruised Vermont's interstates over the years, we have developed patterns of exiting for food at places where (1) food is less than a mile from the exit, and (2) food is good, and we strongly favor diners and local eateries over fast-food chains. Needless to say, wherever there's food, there's gas (no pun intended). All the following restaurants are described in their respective chapters.

Along **I-91,** south to north: *Exit 2* is handy to the many choices in downtown Brattleboro and to the **Chelsea Royal Diner,** west on Route 9. *Exit 4:* The **Putney Inn** is good for all three meals; around the corner is **Curtis' Barbecue** and just up Route 5 is the **Putney Diner.** *Exit 13:* Turn right over the bridge into Hanover, New Hampshire, or left into Norwich to **Alice's Patisserie & Cafe.** *Exit 15:* **The Fairlee Diner** is just north and **The Third Rail** is in the middle of the village on Route 5. *Exit 16:* The **Hungry Bear** is just off I-91; the **Bradford Village Store** in the middle of the village serves hot soups and deli sandwiches (try for the window seat) and the **Perfect Pear Café,** across the street, is several cuts above roadfood. *Exit 17:* **P&H Truck Stop** is worth a stop. *Exit 23:* Turn north onto Route 5 to find the **Miss Lyndonville Diner.** *Exit 25:* **Miss Newport Diner.**

Along I-89: *Exit 2:* **Brooksie's** is right there in the middle of Sharon. *Exit 3:* **Eaton's Sugar House** is right off the exit. *Exit 7:* Follow signs to Route 302 and the **Wayside Restaurant and Bakery,** a real find, is on your left. *Exit 10:* Turn left, then left again, and you are in the middle of Waterbury at **Arvad's.** *Exit 14W:* Burlington is just down the hill, worth a detour. *Exit 14E:* Turn right on Williston Ave. and head away from town to find Al's French Frys. *Exit 16:* **Libby's Blue Line Diner** is right there and great. Also see *Diners.*

HIGHWAY TRAVEL The **official state map,** updated annually (see *Maps*), comes free from local chamber of commerce information booths as well as from the state (see *Information*). **Interstate highway rest areas** with pay phones and bathroom facilities (usually open 7 AM–11 PM) are indicated on the state map. Along I-91 **Welcome Centers,** all open 7 AM–11 PM, are found northbound at **Guilford** (802-254-4593; with outside phones for making reservations 24 hours); northbound at **Bradford** (802-222-9369), southbound at **Lyndon** (802-626-9669), and at **Derby Line** (802-873-3311). Along I-89 there are rest areas at **Sharon,** north- and southbound; at **Randolph,** north- and southbound; and at **Williston,** north- and southbound, and there are more elaborate Welcome Centers at **Highgate** (802-868-3244, 7 AM–11 PM) and both north and southbound at **Georgia** (802-524-0018, open 7 AM–11 PM). The welcome center on I-93 is at **Waterford** (802-748-9368, 7 AM–11 PM). There are also visitors centers at the New York/Canadian border on Route 2 in **Alburg** (802-796-3980, open 10–6) and on the New York border on Route 4A in **Fair Haven** (802-265-4763, open 7 AM–9 PM). In Montpelier the **Capital Region Visitors Center,** 134 State Street (802-828-5981, open 8–8 daily), is the source of statewide information. **AAA Emergency Road Service:** 1-800-222-4357. For **road conditions** call 802-828-4894. See also *Weather, Highway Roadfood,* and *Diners.*

HIKING AND WALKING More than 700 miles of hiking trails web Vermont—which is 162 miles long as the crow flies but 255 miles long as the hiker trudges, following the **Long Trail** up and down the spine of the Green Mountains. But few hikers are out to set distance records on the Long Trail. The path from Massachusetts to the Canadian border, which was completed in 1931, has a way of slowing people down. It opens up eyes and lungs and drains compulsiveness. Even diehard backpackers tend to linger on rocky outcrops, looking down on farms and steeples. A total of 98 side trails (175 miles) meander off to wilderness ponds or abandoned villages; these trails are mostly maintained, along with the Long Trail, by the **Green Mountain Club** (802-244-7037; www.greenmountainclub.org), founded in 1910. The club also maintains 70 shelters, many of them staffed by caretakers during summer months. The club publishes the *Long Trail Guide* ($14.95), which gives details on trails and shelters throughout the system, as well as the *Day Hiker's Guide to Vermont* ($14.95; new again in 1999). These and other guides are sold in the

©Sports File/Dennis Curran

club's **Hiker's Center** (4711 Waterbury Road, Waterbury Center 05677; open 9–5 daily). The **Appalachian Trail Conference** (P.O. Box 807, Harpers Ferry, WV 25425) includes detailed descriptions of most Vermont trails in its *Appalachian Trail Guide to Vermont and New Hampshire* ($18.95), and a wide assortment of trails are nicely detailed in *50 Hikes in Vermont* (Backcountry Guides, $14.95). Backpackers who are hesitant to set out on their own can take a wide variety of guided hikes and walks. **Adventure Guides of Vermont** (1-800-747-5905; www.adventureguidesvt.com) and **Vermont Outdoor Guide Association** (1-800-425-8747; www.voga.org) can put you in touch with guides and adventure-geared packages throughout the state. Organized tours are offered by **Umiak Outdoor Outfitters** (1-800-479-3380), based in Stowe. **North Wind Inn Touring** (1-800-496-5771; www.northwindtouring.com) in Waitsfield offers 3- to 7-day hiking and walking tours around the world as well as Vermont, as does **Vermont Country Walkers** (802-244-1387; 1-800-464-9255), based in Waterbury. **Four Seasons Touring** (802-365-7937) in Townshend offers guided cross-country, snowshoeing, and hiking in the West River Valley of southeastern Vermont. Several inns also offer support services (route planning, baggage transfers) as well as meals and lodging. You might check outwww.Vermontinntoinnwalking.com. Within this book we suggest hiking trails as they appear geographically. Also note the recent proliferation of trail systems: In the Northeast Kingdom check out **Kingdom Trails** in East Burke, the **Vermont Leadership Center** near Island Pond, and the **Hazen's Notch Association**

Trails. We should also note that both Killington and Sugarbush offer ridge hiking from the top of their lifts. (See also *Birding, State Parks, Mountain Biking,* and *Nature Preserves.*)

HISTORY Vermont is a small state, but it had a dramatic life. In essence, the whole state is a living history museum, even though most towns were settled after the Revolution. Many, often overlapping, land grants issued by the royal governors of both New Hampshire and New York were not finally sorted out until 1791, when Congress admitted Vermont as the 14th state, after 14 years as an independent republic.

The Abenaki presence in Vermont is far more pervasive than was acknowledged until very recently. At today's **St. Anne's Shrine on Isle La Motte,** the spot presently memorialized as Champlain's first landfall on the lake that bears his name was certainly an Indian village and by 1666 a mission as well as a fort. It was abandoned in 1679 but remains an evocative place. A colossal granite stature of Champlain depicts an unnamed Indian guide at his feet. Nearby in present-day **Swanton,** the Indian village of Missisquoi became a mission village, a waystop for Abenaki headed for Montreal. Abenaki life is presented in an exhibit at the **Abenaki Museum** (100 Grand Avenue, Swanton; open Monday through Friday 8–4). Abenaki settlements are also recorded at Otter Creek, and the 18th-century tavern at **Chimney Point State Historic Site** in Addison has a well-mounted display that explains the territory's Native American and French colonial heritage. In Newport the new lakeside state office building displays the **Memphremagog Historical Society's** exhibit on northern Vermont Abenaki people, from Paleolithic through current times, and at **Fort at Number Four** in Charlestown, New Hampshire (see "The Upper Valley"), a community in which settlers and Indians lived side by side, the reconstructed fort exhibits Native American artifacts from Connecticut River Valley.

Bennington, chartered by the avaricious Gov. Benning Wentworth in 1749, the first chartered town west of the Connecticut River in the New Hampshire Grants, became the tinderbox for settlers' resistance to New York's rival claims, confirmed by King George in 1764. The desperate grantees found a champion in the protean Ethan Allen from Connecticut. This frontier rebel—land speculator, firebrand, and philosopher—recruited the boisterous Green Mountain Boys militiamen, who talked rum and rebellion at the Catamount Tavern in **Old Bennington,** roared defiance of the 'Yorkers, and then fought the British. Ethan's rambunctious life is reflected in the **Ethan Allen Homestead,** the farm north of Burlington where he died in 1789.

In Westminster, on the bank of the Connecticut River, the 1775 **"Massacre"** was thought, incorrectly, to have been the first armed engagement of the Revolution. But the death of William French, shot by a 'Yorker sheriff ("The Cruel Minestereal Tools of George ye 3d"), galvanized opposition to both New York and England, leading to a convention in Westminster in January 1777, where Vermonters declared their independence of everyone.

Formal independence was declared the following July, upriver in Windsor, where delegates gathered in Elijah West's tavern (now **The Old Constitution House**). They adopted a model constitution, the first to abolish slavery, before rushing off to attack the British, who had retaken Fort Ticonderoga. (While in Windsor, visit the **American Precision Museum,** a landmark reflecting early gun makers and the heyday of the machine tool industry.)

Ever since its discovery by Samuel de Champlain in 1609, Lake Champlain has been not only one of the nation's most historic waterways, but a strategic corridor in three wars. The French controlled the lake until 1759, when Lord Jeffery Amherst drove them out of Fort Carillon (now **Ticonderoga**) and then captured Montreal. In the American Revolution, the British used the lake as an invasion route to divide the colonies, but were thwarted when Ethan Allen's Green Mountain Boys captured Fort Ticonderoga in 1775.

Facing Ticonderoga across the lake's narrowest channel, the **Mount Independence State Historic Site** near Orwell dramatizes the struggle that ended with the decisive British defeat at Saratoga in 1777. As Burgoyne's British troops marched south, the only battle of the Revolution to have been fought on Vermont soil is commemorated at the **Hubbardton Battlefield** near Castleton, where a small force of Green Mountain Boys under Col. Seth Warner stopped a far larger British contingent. The invaders were soon repulsed again in the battle of Bennington—actually fought in New York—marked by the **Bennington Battle Monument** and by exhibits in the **Bennington Museum.**

The lake also figured in naval warfare when Benedict Arnold and a quickly assembled American flotilla engaged a heavier British squadron off Plattsburgh, New York, in the battle of Valcour Island in October 1776. One of Arnold's small gunboats, the *Philadelphia,* sunk by the British, was salvaged in 1935 and reposes in the Smithsonian. An exact replica is moored at the **Lake Champlain Maritime Museum** at Basin Harbor near Vergennes. A number of ships and other artifacts of that battle have been found buried in the mud on the lake bottom in recent years. In 1814 the British again tried to use Lake Champlain as an invasion route. Thomas McDonough moved his headquarters from Burlington to Vergennes and a shipyard at the mouth of Otter Creek. His small fleet barely managed to defeat British ships at Plattsburgh Bay, a bloody engagement that helped end the War of 1812.

With Vermont in the vanguard of the antislavery movement of the 1840s, the Underground Railroad flourished, notably at **Rokeby,** the home of the Robinson family in Ferrisburgh, now a museum. Evidence of the state's extraordinary record in the Civil War and its greater-than-average number of per-capita casualties may be seen in the memorials that dot most town and village greens. How Vermonters turned the tide of battle at Cedar Creek is portrayed in Julian Scott's huge and newly restored painting that hangs in the **State House** in Montpelier. The anniversary of the October 1864 **St. Albans Raid,** the northernmost engagement of the Civil War, is observed annually.

There are few 18th-century structures in the state, but the settlers who poured in after 1791 (the population nearly tripled, from 85,000 to 235,000 in 1820) built sophisticated dwellings and churches. **Dorset, Castleton, Chester** (Old Stone Village), **Middlebury, Brandon, Woodstock,** and **Norwich** are architectural showcases of Federal-style houses. Several historic, outstandingly splendid mansions built by 19th-century moguls are open to the public: the **Park-McCullough House,** North Bennington; the **Wilburton Inn** and **Hildene,** Manchester; **The Castle Inn,** Proctorsville; **Wilson Castle,** West Rutland; the **Marsh-Billings-Rockefeller National Historical Park,** Woodstock; and **The Inn at Shelburne Farms** (built by Lila Vanderbilt Webb), Shelburne.

Vermont's congressional delegations, especially in the 19th century, have always had more influence in Washington than the size of the state might indicate. For example, the **Justin Morrill Homestead** in Strafford, a spacious Gothic Revival house, reminds us of the distinguished career of the originator of the Land Grant Colleges Act, who served in Congress from 1855 to 1898.

State and local historical societies have faithfully preserved the cultural evidence. The **Vermont Historical Society Museum** (802-828-2291) in Montpelier houses permanent and thematic exhibits and maintains a research library in Barre. Arts, crafts, architecture, and transportation are featured in the **Shelburne Museum** in Shelburne. In Woodstock the **Billings Farm & Museum** re-creates a model 1890s stock farm and dairy and the **Marsh-Billings-Rockefeller National Historical Park** traces the state's environmental history. Outstanding collections of the ways people lived and worked can be found in town historical societies, notably the **Farrar Mansur House** in Weston, the **Sheldon Museum** in Middlebury, and the **Dana House** in Woodstock. For a lively, popular story of the state from its origins to the present, read Peter Jennison's *Roadside History of Vermont* (Mountain Press). A pamphlet guide to Vermont state historic sites, operated by the Division of Historic Preservation, is available at information centers throughout the state, and the sites are also profiled, along with events and historic roadside markers, at www.historicvermont.org. See also *Historical Societies.*

HISTORICAL SOCIETIES The attics of every town, historical societies are frequently worth seeking out, but because most are staffed by volunteers, they tend to be open just a few hours a week, in summer. Within each chapter we have tried to give accurate, current information. The Vermont Historical Society publishes a free booklet, *Passport to Vermont History,* listing hours and contact phones for more than 170. Information is also found at www.state.vt.us/vhs. Outstanding local historical societies are found in **Brattleboro, Brownington, Newfane,** and **Middlebury.** *Note:* On the last weekend of June the Vermont Historical Society sponsors the **Vermont History Expo,** currently held at the fairgrounds in Tunbridge, billed as "a celebration of Vermont's Story as Told by the Keepers of Its Treasures and Traditions." It includes a full schedule of folk songs, lectures, demonstrations, and much more, as well as displays.

HUNTING *Vermont Guide to Hunting,* a free pamphlet, lists and locates major wildlife management areas in the state and is available, along with a current *Digest of Fish & Wildlife Laws,* from the Vermont Fish and Wildlife Department (802-241-3700; 103 South Main Street, Waterbury 05671-0501). A nonresident small-game hunting license costs $35, a regular hunting license is $80, a combined hunting and fishing license is $100. A limited bow-and-arrow license is $50; a regular bow-and-arrow license is $15 on top of the regular hunting license. A nonresident trapping license is $300; an alien, nonresident trapping license is $500; both of these can be obtained only through the Fish and Wildlife Department. Of special interest may be the nonresident, 5-day small-game license for $20. A resident hunting license is $12, and trapping is $20. **Rifle season for deer** begins 12 days before Thanksgiving and lasts for 16 days, followed by **musket season. Bow-and-arrow season** also lasts 16 days, beginning the first Saturday in October; **hare and rabbit season** extends from the last Saturday in September to the second Sunday in March; **gray squirrel season** is from the last Saturday in September to the last Thursday before regular deer season. **Partridge and grouse** may be shot between the last Saturday in September and December 31, with a limit of four daily, eight in possession. **Black bear season** is determined annually, as is **moose season.** Licenses may be secured from local town clerks or wardens or ahead of time by mail from the Fish and Wildlife Department. In order to purchase a Vermont hunting or combination license, you must show or submit either a certificate proving you have satisfactorily completed a hunter safety course or a previous hunting or combination license.

ICE CREAM Vermont's quality milk is used to produce some outstanding ice cream as well as cheese. The big name is, of course, **Ben & Jerry's,** proud producers of what *Time* has billed "the best ice cream in the world." Their plant on Route 100 in Waterbury (featuring factory tours, free samples, real cows, and a gift shop full of reproductions in every conceivable shape) has quickly become one of the state's most popular tourist attractions. Other good Vermont ice creams include **Seward's** in Rutland, **Wilcox Brothers** in Manchester, and the **Mountain Creamery** in Woodstock.

INFORMATION **The Vermont Department of Tourism and Marketing** (802-828-3237; 1-800-VERMONT; fax: 802-828-3233; 6 Baldwin Street, 4th Floor, Drawer 33, Montpelier 05633-1301; www.1-800vermont.com; vttravel@dca.state.vt.us), offers excellent free aids: (1) **Vermont's official state map** includes symbols locating covered bridges, golf courses, picnic spots, ski areas, recreation sites, and boat-launch ramps. On the reverse side are descriptive listings of museums, galleries, and historic places, fishing and hunting rules and license fees, state and private campgrounds, state liquor stores, and hospital emergency rooms. (2) *Vermont Life Explorer* is a glossy magazine introducing the state. For information about specific parts of the state, the magazine refers visitors to 11 regional marketing associations, which we note as they apply to specific regions within each chapter of this book. On request you can also obtain the *Vermont Campground Guidebook.* The **Vermont Chamber of Commerce** (802-223-3443; fax: 802-828-4257; www.vtchamber.com; info@vtchamber.com) also publishes *Vermont Travelers Guidebook* and will send it on request, along with a *Vermont Attractions* map and pamphlet guides to shopping and country inns and B&Bs. We have noted local chambers of commerce town by town in

Christina Tree

each chapter of this book. In towns not served by a chamber, inquiries are welcomed by the town clerk. First-time visitors may be puzzled by Vermont's Travel Information System of directional signs that replace billboards (banned since 1967, another Vermont "first"). Stylized symbols for lodging, food, recreation, antiques and crafts, and other services are sited at intersections off major highways, at interstate rest areas, and at Welcome Centers, which are listed under *Highway Travel*.

INNS It's safe to say that we have visited more Vermont inns, more frequently, than anyone else living today. We do not charge for inclusion in this book, and we attempt to give as accurate and detailed a picture as space permits. We have described many inns in their respective towns, quoting 2001 rates. These prices are, of course, subject to change and should not be regarded as gospel. Summer rates are generally lower than winter rates (except, of course, at lake resorts); weekly or ski-week rates run 10–20 percent less than the per-diem price quoted. Many inns insist on MAP (Modified American Plan—breakfast and dinner) in winter but not in summer. Some resorts have AP (American Plan—three meals), and we have shown EP (European Plan—no meals) where applicable. We have attempted to note when 15 percent service is added, but you should always ask if it has been included in a quoted rate. Always add the 9 percent state tax on rooms and meals. It's prudent to check which, if any, credit cards are accepted. Within the text, special icons also highlight lodging places offering exceptional value, those that appeal to families, those that are handicapped-accessible, those that accept pets, and those that specialize in weddings and civil unions (wedding ring symbol).

LAKES The state famed for green mountains and white villages also harbors more than 400 relatively blue lakes: big lakes like **Champlain** (150 miles long) and **Memphremagog** (boasting 88 miles of coastline but most of it in Canada), smaller lakes like **Morey, Dunmore, Willoughby, Bomoseen,** and **Seymour.** Lakes are particularly plentiful and people sparse in Vermont's Northeast Kingdom. A century ago, there were many more lakeside hotels; today just a handful of these classic summer resorts survive: **Quimby Country** in Averill, **Highland Lodge** in Greensboro, the **Tyler Place** in Highgate Springs, the **Basin Harbor Club** near Vergennes, and the **Lake Morey Inn Resort** in Fairlee. There are a half dozen smaller, informal inns on scattered lakes, but that's about it. Still, you can bed down very reasonably within sound and sight of Vermont waters either by renting a cottage (more than half of those listed in *Four Season Vacation Rentals*, avail-

Kim Grant

able from the Vermont Department of Tourism and Marketing, are on lakes) or by taking advantage of state park campsites on **Groton Lake, Island Pond, Maidstone Lake, Lake Bomoseen, Lake Carmi, Lake Elmore, Lake St. Catherine,** and **Silver Lake** (in Barnard). On Lake Champlain, there are a number of state campgrounds, including those on **Grand Isle** (accessible by car) and **Burton Island** (accessible by public launch from St. Albans Bay). See *Campgrounds* for details about these and the free campsites on **Ball Mountain Lake,** maintained by the Army Corps of Engineers. There is public boat access to virtually every Vermont pond and lake of any size. Boat launches are listed on the state map.

LIBRARIES The small village of Brookfield boasts the state's oldest continuously operating public library, established in 1791. Most libraries that we mention here date, however, from that late-19th-century philanthropic era when wealthy native sons were moved to donate splendidly ornate libraries to their hometowns. Notable examples are to be found in **Barre, Chester, Ludlow, Wilmington, Rutland, Newport, Woodstock, St. Johnsbury,** and **Brattleboro.** Two of our favorite libraries lie within a short drive of each other: one on the common in **Craftsbury Common,** and the second—a converted general store—in **East Craftsbury,** where there is a special back room for youngsters, with a Ping-Pong table amid the books. Unfortunately, visitors may not check out books unless they happen to be staying within the community that the library serves. For research, the **Vermont Historical Society Library** in Barre is a treasure trove of Vermontiana and genealogical resources, as is the Wilbur Collection of the **Bailey-Howe Library** at the University of Vermont and the **Russell Collection** in Arlington. Three of the Vermont state colleges—Castleton, Johnson, and Lyndon—have collections of Vermontiana in the Vermont Rooms of their libraries.

LLAMA TREKKING **Northern Vermont Llama Treks** (802-644-2257) in Waterville and **Cold Hollow Llamas** (802-644-5846), Belvidere, are in northern Vermont. In the center of the state, try **Fernwood Llama Farm** (802-889-9611) in Tunbridge or **Woodstock Llama Trekking** (802-457-3722) in Woodstock/Quechee.

MAGAZINES *Vermont Life* (1-800-284-3243; www.vtlife.com), the popular and colorful quarterly published by the Agency of Development and Community Affairs and edited by Tom Slayton, is an outstanding chronicle of Vermont's people and places, featuring distinguished photographers. *Vermont Magazine,* the upbeat, statewide bimonthly launched in 1989, covers major issues, townscapes, products, and personalities, and reviews inns and restaurants (www.vermontmagazine.com). *Vermont History,* a quarterly scholarly journal, is published for members of the Vermont Historical Society. *Vermont Business People* (2 Church Street, Burlington 05401) is a tabloid-sized monthly that provides investigative reportage, analysis, and overviews of the state's economic doings from politically conservative and entrepreneurially aggressive points of view. *Seven Days* (802-864-5684; www.sevendaysvt.com), Burlington's free weekly tabloid of area arts and entertainment, is far more than a calendar of events.

MAPLE SUGARING Vermont produces an average of 400,000 gallons of maple syrup each year, more than any other state. No fewer than 2,400 maple growers tap an average of 1,000 trees each. About a quart of syrup is made per tap; it takes 30–40 gallons of sap to make each gallon of syrup. The process of tapping trees and boiling sap is stubbornly known as "sugaring," rather than syruping, because the end product for early settlers was sugar. Syrup was first made in the early 19th century, but production flagged when imported cane sugar was easy to come by. The Civil War revived the maple sugar industry: Union supporters were urged to consume sugar made by free men and to plant more and more maples. We urge visitors to buy syrup direct from the farm that has produced it any time of year (finding the farm is half the fun), but also to seriously consider making a special trip to a sugarhouse during sugaring season. It's then, not autumn, that sugar maples really perform, and it's a show that can't be viewed through a windshield. Sugaring season begins quietly in February as thousands of Vermonters wade, snowshoe, and snowmobile into their woods and begin "tapping," a ritual that may have changed technically as plastic tubing has replaced buckets, but the timing hasn't. Traditionally, sugaring itself begins on Town Meeting Day (the first Tuesday in March). The fact is, however, that sap runs only on those days when temperatures rise to 40 and 50 degrees during the day and drop into the 20s at night. And when the sap runs, it must be boiled down quickly. What you want to see is the boiling process: sap churning madly through the large, flat evaporating pan, darkening as you watch. You are enveloped in fragrant steam, listening to the rush of the sap, sampling the end result on snow or in tiny paper cups. Sugaring is Vermont's rite of spring. Don't miss a sugar-on-snow party: plates of snow dribbled with hot syrup, accompanied by doughnuts and dill pickles. The Vermont Department of Agriculture (802-828-2416) publishes the pamphlet guide *Maple Sugarhouses Open to Visitors* and also lists them by region on the web site www.vermontmaple.org. Be sure to call before going to check if there is sugaring that day. The one big **Vermont Maple Festival,** held the latter part of April in St. Albans, is a 3-day happening that includes tours through the local sugarbush (802-524-5800). At **Maple Grove Farm of Vermont,** "the world's largest maple candy factory" in St. Johnsbury, factory tours are offered Monday through Friday year-round, and the **Maple Museum** and gift shop is open May through late October. At **American Maple Products** (year-round) in Newport, you can see a movie about maple production; the story of sugaring is also dramatized

VDT

in the **New England Maple Museum** in Pittsford and in the maple museum at **Sugarmill Farm** in Barton. Within this book we list maple producers in the areas in which they are most heavily concentrated.

MAPS The **official state map** (see *Information*) is free and extremely helpful for general motoring in Vermont but will not suffice for finding your way around on the webs of dirt roads that connect some of the most beautiful corners of the state. Among our favorite areas wherein you are guaranteed to get lost using the state map: the high farming country between Albany, Craftsbury, and West Glover; similar country between Chelsea and Williamstown; south from Plainfield to Orange; and between Plymouth and Healdville. There are many more. We strongly suggest securing a copy of *The Vermont Atlas and Gazetteer* (DeLorme) if you want to do any serious back-road exploring, or *The Vermont Road Atlas and Guide* (Northern Cartographics); both are widely available at bookstores, gas stations, and general stores. The best regional maps for anyone planning to do much hiking or biking are published by **Map Adventures** (802-253-7489; 846 Cottage Club Road, Stowe 05672; www.mapadventures.com).

MONEY Don't leave home without MasterCard or Visa, the two credit cards that are far more readily accepted in Vermont than American Express or personal checks. Each inn has its own policy about credit cards and checks.

MOUNTAIN BIKING Several ski areas offer lift-assisted mountain biking: The **Mount Snow Resort Mountain Bike Center** (802-464-3333) was the first, offering 25 miles of trails spread over three of the ski resort's six peaks. **Stratton Mountain Resort** (802-297-4139), **Sugarbush Resort** (802-583-2381), **Killington** (802-422-6232), and **Jay Peak Resort** (802-988-2611; 1-800-451-4449) also now permit mountain biking on ski trails, accessible via lifts. In recent years, however, Vermont mountain-biking options have dramatically broadened beyond its ski mountains as the potential for its hundreds of miles of dirt and "Class 4" roads as well as cross-county trail systems has been recognized. **The Craftsbury Center** (1-800-729-7751) up in the Northeast Kingdom was the first place to rent mountain bikes and offer guided tours over dirt and abandoned logging roads. A former prep school now devoted to running and rowing as well as biking in summer and cross-country skiing in winter, it's set in high, rolling farm country with mountain views. In Randolph you can arrive with your bike via Amtrak and take advantage of the **Three Stallion Inn** network of trails. There's another magnificent trail system in the Burke Mountain area: **Kingdom Trails.** The hub of this system is **East Burke Sports** (802-626-3215), offering a 75-mile mix of alpine and cross-country-ski trails, several loops in East Burke Village, snowmobile trails maintained by VAST, cross-country trails up on Darling Hill, and several more miles of trails maintained by this nonprofit organization. For a map send $6 ($5 for the map, $1 for handling) to Kingdom Trails, P.O. Box 204, East Burke 05832. In southeastern Vermont, the **West Hill Shop** (802-387-5718) publishes its own map to an extensive network of singletrack trails and forgotten roads. We describe inns and bike shops that offer bike rentals in almost every chapter, but here we should mention **Blueberry Hill Inn** (1-800-448-0707), set high in Goshen with easy access to trails in the Moosalamoo region of the Green Mountain National Forest and to Silver Lake. In the Burlington area, the **Catamount Family Center** (802-879-6001) and **Bolton Valley** (802-434-2131) both offer extensive cross-country trail networks and rentals. Nominally priced **Map Adventures' Topographic Maps & Guides,** based in Stowe (802-253-7489), are useful map/guides outlining rides in various parts of Vermont: the Burlington and Stowe areas, the White River Valley, the Upper Valley, and southern Vermont, among others. **Adventure Guides of Vermont** (1-800-425-8727) is the way to find a guide, and maintains an excellent web site: www.voga.org. See also *Bicycle Touring.*

MOUNTAINTOPS While Vermont can boast only seven peaks above 4,000 feet, there are 80 mountains that rise more than 3,000 feet and any number of spectacular views, several of them accessible in summer and foliage season to those who prefer riding to walking up mountains. **Mount Mansfield,** which at 4,343 feet is the state's highest summit, can be reached via the Toll Road and a gondola. The mid-19th-century road brings you to the small Summit Station at 4,062 feet, from which the half-mile Tundra Trail brings you to the actual summit. The Mount Mansfield gondola, an eight-passenger, enclosed lift, hoists you from the main base area up to the Cliff House (serving light meals all day), from which a trail also heads up to the Chin. **Killington Peak,** Vermont's second highest peak at 4,241 feet, can be reached via a 1.2-mile ride on a gondola that takes you to a summit restaurant and a nature trail that even small children can negotiate. **Jay Peak,** a 3,861-foot summit towering like a lone sentinel near the Canadian border, is accessible via a 60-passenger tram (daily except Tuesday), and a "four-state view" from the top of **Stratton Mountain** is accessible via the ski resort's six-passenger gondola, "Starship XII" (daily in summer and fall). Other toll roads include the Auto Road to the 3,267-foot **Burke Mountain** in East Burke, the Toll Road to the 3,144-foot summit of **Mount Ascutney** in Ascutney State Park, and the road to the top of **Mount Equinox** in Sunderland. There are also chairlift rides to the tops of **Bromley** (you don't have to take the alpine slide down) and **Mount Snow** (weekends in summer, daily in foliage season).

MUD SEASON The period from snowmelt (around the middle of March) through early May (it varies each year) is known throughout the state as mud season for reasons that few visitors want to explore too deeply. It's worth mentioning that dirt roads can turn quickly into boggy quagmires, and travel off the main roads in this season can be challenging.

MUSEUMS Vermont museums vary from the immense **Shelburne Museum**—with its 36 buildings, many housing priceless collections of Americana, plus assorted exhibits such as a completely restored lake steamer and lighthouse—to the **American Precision Museum** in Windsor, an 1846 brick mill that once produced rifles. They include a number of outstanding historical museums (our favorites are the **Sheldon Museum** in Middlebury, the **Old Stone House Museum** in Brownington, and the **Dana House** in Woodstock) and some collections that go beyond the purely historical: **Bennington Museum** (famed for its collection of Grandma Moses paintings as well as early American glass and relics from the Revolution) and the **Fairbanks Museum and Planetarium** in St. Johnsbury. The **Billings Farm & Museum** in Woodstock shows off its blue-ribbon dairy and has a fascinating, beautifully mounted display of 19th-century farm life and tools. A detailed, 150-page catalog, *Vermont's Museums, Galleries & Historic Buildings*, is available from the **Vermont Museum & Gallery Alliance**, P.O. Box 489, Woodstock 05091 ($5.95, plus $1.50 postage and handling). Within this book, we have included all museums in their respective areas.

MUSIC The Green Mountains are filled with the sounds of music each summer, beginning with the **Discover Jazz Festival** (802-863-7992), more than 100 concerts held over a week around Burlington in early June. In Putney, a late-June through July series of three evening chamber music concerts each week are presented in the **Yellow Barn** (1-800-639-3819). In July and August options include the internationally famous **Marlboro Music Festival** (802-254-2394), at Marlboro College, presenting chamber music on weekends, and the **Vermont Mozart Festival** (802-862-7352; 1-800-639-9097), a series of 20 concerts performed at a variety of sites ranging from beautiful barns at the University of Vermont and Shelburne Farms to a Lake Champlain ferry and including some striking classic and modern churches and a ski area base lodge. **The Killington Music Festival** (802-773-4003) is a series of Sunday concerts at Ramshead Lodge in July and August, and the **Manchester Music Festival** (802-362-1956) brings leading performers to various venues around Manchester. Also well worth noting: the **Central Vermont Chamber Music Festival** (802-728-9133) at the Chandler Music Hall in Randolph in mid-August, **Summer**

Music School in Adamant (802-229-9297), concerts at the Town House in Hardwick by the **Craftsbury Chamber Players** (1-800-639-3443), and in Stowe, for a week in late July, at the **Performing Arts Festival** (802-253-7321). Other concert series are performed at the **Southern Vermont Arts Center** (Thursday and Sunday, 802-362-1405); at the **Fine Arts Center,** Castleton State College (802-468-4611, ext. 285); at the **Dibden Auditorium,** Johnson State College (802-635-2356); and at **Middlebury College Center for the Arts** (802-443-5007). The **North Country Concert Association** (43 Main Street, Derby Line 05830) schedules performances at sites throughout the Northeast Kingdom lake area. The **Vermont Symphony Orchestra,** oldest of the state symphonies, figures in a number of the series noted above and also performs at a variety of locations, ranging from Brattleboro's Living Memorial Park and the statehouse lawn to Wilson Castle, throughout the summer. In Weston, the **Kinhaven Music School** offers free concerts on summer weekends. The **Vermont Bach Festival** (802-257-4523), sponsored by the Brattleboro Music Center with performances in local churches and at Marlboro College, is a fitting climax to the season. See also *Fiddling.*

NATURE PRESERVES In recent years the **Vermont Land Trust** and many local land trusts have acquired numerous parcels of land throughout the state. Within each chapter in this book we note these where they appear under *Green Space.* Many of the most visitor-friendly preserves are owned by **The Nature Conservancy,** a national nonprofit conservation organization that has preserved close to 7 million acres throughout the United States since its founding in 1951. A *Vermont Project Directory,* available from The Nature Conservancy (802-229-4425; 27 State Street, Montpelier 05602), describes more than 100 properties.

OPERA HOUSES Northern New England opera houses are a turn-of-the-20th-century phenomenon: theaters built as cultural centers for the surrounding area, stages on which lecturers, musicians, and vaudeville acts, as well as opera singers, performed. Many of these buildings have long since disappeared, but those that survive are worth noting. The **Hyde Park Opera House,** built in 1910, has been restored by the Lamoille County Players, who stage four annual shows—one play, two musicals, and an annual foliage-season run of *The Sound of Music.* The **Barre Opera House,** built in 1899, is an elegant, acoustically outstanding, second-floor theater, home of the Barre Players; productions are staged here year-round. In Derby Line, in the second-floor **Opera House** (a neoclassical structure that also houses the Haskell Free Library), the audience sits in Vermont watching a stage that is in Canada. The **Chandler Music Hall** in Randolph and the Vergennes Opera House in Vergennes have been restored for varied uses.

PETS We note lodging places that accommodate pets with a symbol 🐾. We should note that while traveling with a dog or cat generally tends to rule out the possibility of staying in inns or B&Bs, some of Vermont's most elegant inns do permit them: the **Inn on the Common** in Craftsbury, **Topnotch** in Stowe, the **Basin Harbor Club** in

Sally Johnson

Vergennes, and the **Woodstock Inn and Resort** in Woodstock.

PICK YOUR OWN Strawberry season is mid- to late June. Cherries, plums, raspberries, and blueberries can be picked in July and August. Apples ripen by mid-September and can be picked through foliage season. For specifics on where, see *Apples* and *Farms Open to the Public.*

QUILTS A revival of interest in this craft is especially strong in Vermont, where quilting supply and made-to-order stores salt the state. The **Vermont Quilt Festival** (www.vqf.org) is held for three days in late June in Northfield, including exhibits of antique quilts, classes and lectures, vendors, and appraisals. **Shelburne Museum** has an outstanding quilt collection, and the **Billings Farm & Museum** holds an annual show.

RAILROAD EXCURSIONS The **Green Mountain Railroad** (802-463-3069; 1-800-707-3530; www.rails-vt.com) runs a number of excursion trains around the state. The *Green Mountain Flyer*, named for the fastest train on the old Rutland Railroad, runs between Bellows Falls on the Connecticut River and Chester (13 miles), with special foliage runs for another 14 miles to Ludlow and seasonal Santa Claus runs before Christmas. The *Vermont Valley Flyer* (802-463-4700) runs between Manchester, Arlington, and North Bennington in summer.

RENTAL COTTAGES AND CONDOMINIUMS *Four Season Vacation Rentals,* an annual booklet available from state information centers (see *Highway Travel*), lists upward of 200 properties, most of them either lakeside cottages or condominiums near ski areas but also including a variety of other housing, ranging from wooded summer camps by streams to aristocratic brick mansions with priceless views. *Vermont Rentals Magazine* (802-228-7158), 110 Main Street, Ludlow, is also available on request. Regional rentals are listed in each chapter.

Christina Tree

RESTAURANTS Culinary standards are rising every day: You can lunch simply and inexpensively nearly everywhere and dine superbly in a score of places where the quality would rate three stars in Boston or New York at three times the price. Fixed-price menus (prix fixe) have been so noted. We were tempted to try to list our favorites here, but the roster would be too long. Restaurants that appeal to us appear in the text in their respective areas. The range and variety are truly extraordinary. Note that we divide restaurants in each chapter into *Dining Out* (serious dining experiences) and *Eating Out* (everyday places). See also *Highway Roadfood.*

ROCKHOUNDING The most obvious sites are **Rock of Ages Quarry and Exhibit** in Barre and the **Vermont Marble Company Exhibit** in Proctor, which offers a new "Earth Alive" exhibit presenting local geological history interactively. Major exhibits of Vermont fossils, minerals, and rocks may be viewed at **Perkins Geology Hall,** University of Vermont, Burlington; and the **Fairbanks Museum** in St. Johnsbury. An annual **Rock Swap and Mineral Show** is held in early August, sponsored by the **Burlington Gem and Mineral Club.** Gold, incidentally, can be panned in a number of rivers, notably Broad Brook in Plymouth; the Rock River in Newfane and Dover; the Williams River in Ludlow; the Ottauquechee River in Bridgewater; the White River in Stockbridge and Rochester; the Mad River in Warren, Waitsfield, and Moretown; the Little River in Stowe and Waterbury; and the Missisquoi in Lowell and Troy.

SHEEP AND WOOL Specialty sheep and alpacas are multiplying quickly in Vermont. A number of farmers specialize in processing wool, among them **Mettowee Valley Farm** (802-325-3039) in Pawlet, **Country Casuals** (802-869-2360) in Cambridgeport, **Singing Spindle Spinnery** (802-244-8025) in South Duxbury, the **Lamb and Lamb Company** in Royalton (802-889-3417), **Maple Ridge Sheep Farm** in Randolph (802-728-3081), **Spring Hill Farm** (802-333-9023) in Fairlee, **Magnus Wools** (802-592-3320) in Barnet, **Round Barn Merinos** (802-877-6544) in Ferrisburgh, and **Wooly Hill Farm** (802-758-2284) in Bridport. Request a copy of the *Vermont FiberWorks Directory*, listing more than 80 producers, from the Vermont Department of Agriculture (802-828-2416), 116 State Street, Montpelier 05602. Inquire about the **Vermont Sheep and Wool Festival,** featuring sheep shearing, spinning, weaving, and plenty of sheep, held early autumn.

Kim Grant

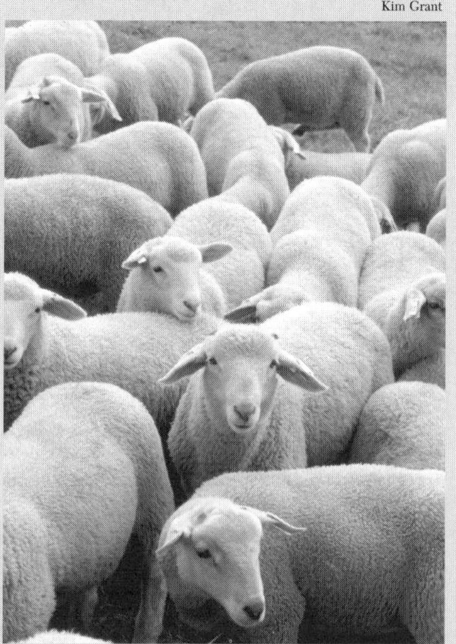

SHIPWRECKS Well-preserved 19th-century shipwrecks are open to the public (licensed divers) at three **Underwater Historical Preserves** in Lake Champlain near Burlington. The ***Phoenix,*** the second steamboat to ply Lake Champlain, burned to the waterline in 1819. The ***General Butler,*** an 88-foot schooner, fell victim to a winter gale in 1876. A coal barge, believed to be the ***A. R. Nowes,*** broke loose from a tug and sank in 1884. Contact the Division of Historic Preservation (802-828-3226) and the **Lake Champlain Maritime Museum** in Vergennes, which is charting underwater remains.

SKIING, CROSS-COUNTRY The **Vermont Ski Areas Association** now lists about 45 cross-country centers and tours in their *Vermont Winter Guide.* For desciptions and conditions click on www.xcountryski-vermont.com, www.voga.org, and www.pbpub.com. Within this book we have described each commercial touring center as it appears geographically. Given the dearth of natural snow in recent years, checking current conditions is now more important than ever. Vermont's most dependable snow can be found on high-elevation trails in **Stowe,** at **Craftsbury Center** in Craftsbury Common, **Hazen's Notch** in Montgomery Center, **Bolton Valley Resort** (between Burlington and Stowe), and **Blueberry Hill** in Goshen. **Mountain Top Inn** and **Mountain Meadows,** both in Chittenden (handy to Killington and Rutland) and **Grafton Ponds** in Grafton offer snowmaking on a short loop trail. All of the cross-country-ski centers mentioned above are located on the 300-mile **Catamount Trail,** a marked ski trail that runs (almost; it's now more than 90 percent complete) the length of the state. Contact the **Catamount Trail Association** (802-864-5794; 1 Main Street, Suite 308A, Burlington 05401; www.catamounttrail.org). Members ($25 per person, $40 per family) receive a regular newsletter and discounts at participating touring centers. You might want to request area maps; *The Catamount Trail Guidebook* is $17. *Adventure Skiing,* a map guide to cross-country trails in the Stowe/Bolton/Underhill area, is useful (802-253-7489). Inn-to-inn tours are possible between **Craftsbury Center Resort** and **Highland Lodge** in Greensboro; **Trapp Family Lodge** and **Edson Hill Manor** in Stowe; **Chipman House** in Ripton and **Churchill House Inn** in Goshen; and between **Village Inn** of Landgrove and **Nordic Inn** in Londonderry. **Mad River Glen** and **Bolton Valley** are two alpine resorts that specialize in telemarking. For details about marked cross-country trails in

Woodstock Inn and Resort

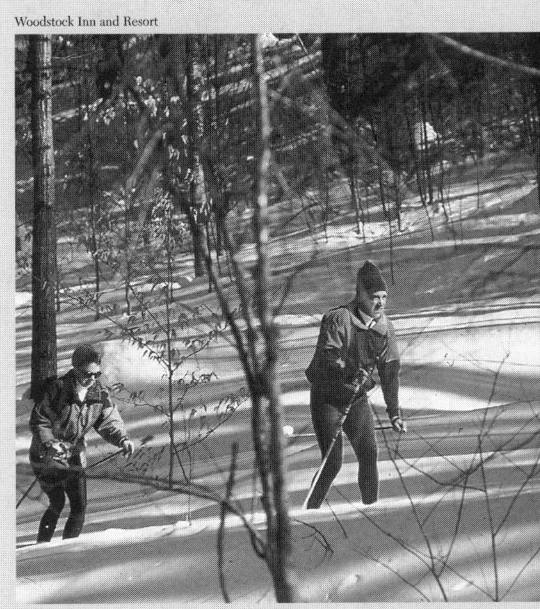

state preserves, contact the Department of Forests, Parks and Recreation (802-241-3655; Waterbury 05676), and for those within the Green Mountain National Forest request the ***Winter Recreation Map*** (see *State Parks*).

SKIING, DOWNHILL Since the 1930s, when America's commercial skiing began with a Model-T Ford engine pulling skiers up a hill in Woodstock, skiing has been a Vermont specialty. Fifteen ski areas are members of the Vermont Ski Areas Association and accessible with daily updated snow conditions and weather on the web site: www.skivermont.com. The Vermont Chamber of Commerce publishes a glossy *Vermont Winter Guide* (available free at www.vtchamber.com). Daily lift tickets are, of course, not the cheapest way to ski; all resorts deeply discount multiday lifts and lodging packages. **Killington/Pico,** the largest ski resort in the East, and **Mount Snow,** Vermont's second largest area, are all owned by the American Skiing Company; lift tickets and passes at one are honored at the others, and at ASC resorts in New Hampshire and Maine. **Sugarbush,** which was an ASC property, has been returned to local ownership. A number of long-established Vermont ski areas have become self-contained resorts. Both **Bolton Valley** and **Smugglers' Notch** cater to families; **Okemo, Stratton,** and **Sugarbush** offer varied skiing and facilities, appealing to a full range of patrons. Though no longer Vermont's biggest, Stowe remains Ski Capital of the East when it comes to the quantity and quality of inns, restaurants, and shops. We have described each ski area as it appears geographically. A 24-hour snow condition report for the state is available by calling the **Vermont Skiing Today SnowLine:** 802-229-0531 (November through June); or, again, you can check www.skivermont.com.

SLEIGH RIDES Sleigh rides are listed under *To Do* as they appear geographically in the book.

SNOWBOARDING An international sport first popularized by Burton Snowboards (born in Manchester, long since moved to Burlington, where we list details about its factory store), snowboarding lessons, rentals, and special terrain parks are offered at every major Vermont ski area except Mad River Glen (the only holdout in the East).

SNOWMOBILING Hundreds of miles of well-marked, groomed trails are laced together in a system maintained by the **Vermont Association of Snow Travelers (VAST).** VAST's corridor trails are up to 8 feet wide and are maintained by 145 local snowmobile clubs; for detailed maps and suggestions for routes, activities, and guided tours, contact the Vermont Association of Snow Travelers (802-229-0005; 41 Granger Road, Berlin 05641; www.snowmobilevt.com). Vermont has a reciprocal registration agreement with New York, Maine, New Hampshire, and Quebec; otherwise, registration is required to take advantage of trails within the state. Snowmobile rentals and tours are listed in the *Vermont Winter Guide* available through the Vermont Chamber (www.vtchamber.com.)

SNOWSHOEING Snowshoeing is experiencing a rebirth in Vermont, thanks to the new lightweight equipment available from sources like Tubbs

Robert Kozlow

Snowshoes in Stowe. Virtually all ski-touring centers now offer snowshoe rentals, and many inns stock a few pairs for guests.

SOARING **Sugarbush Soaring** (802-496-3730; Sugarbush Airport, Warren), in the Mad River Valley, is known as one of the prime spots in the East for riding thermal and ridge waves. The **Sugarbush Airport** is a well-established place to take glider lessons or rides or simply to watch the planes come and go. The **Fall Wave Soaring Encampment** held in early October draws glider pilots from throughout the country. Gliders and airplane rides are also available at the **Morrisville/Stowe State Airport** (802-888-5150) and **Post Mills Aviation** in Post Mills (802-333-9254), where soaring lessons are also a specialty, along with simply seeing the Connecticut Valley from the air.

SPAS Vermont is the setting for a select few of the country's finest spas. The oldest of these is **New Life Fitness Vacations,** directed by Jimmy LeSage at Killington. **Topnotch, Stoweflake Inn,** and the **Golden Eagle Resort** in Stowe and the **Equinox Hotel** in Manchester all offer full-service spa programs.

SPIRITUAL CENTERS/RETREATS The **Buddhist Meditation Center Karme Choling** (802-633-2384; www.klc.chambhala.org) is a long-established retreat in Barnet with many special programs. **Yoga Vermont** in Burlington (802-660-9718; www.yogavermont.com) draws Ashtanga Yoga pratitioners from throughout the country. The **Maple Forest Monastery and Green Mountain Dharma Center** in Hartland is the scene of a major retreat (families welcome) the first week in July (802-434-1103; www.plumvillage.org), and the **Weston Priory** (802-824-5409; www.westonpriory.org) in Weston is a long-established Benedictine monastery known for their music and offering retreats.

STATE PARKS Vermont's more than 50 exceptionally well-groomed state parks include camping and/or day-use facilities, and are so diverse an assortment of properties that no one image applies. Within this book we attempt to describe each as it appears geographically. Vermont state parks are also detailed in an exceptional web site **(www.vtstateparks.com)** and are part of the **Department of Forests, Parks and Recreation** (802-241-3665; 103 South Main Street, Waterbury 05671-0603), which manages more than 157,000 acres of state land, offering opportunities for hunting, fishing, cross-country skiing, mountain biking, snowmobiling, and primitive as well as supervised camping. Also see *Camping*.

SUMMER SELF-IMPROVEMENT PROGRAMS Whether it's improving your game of tennis or golf, learning to take pictures or to weave, cook, identify mushrooms, fish, or bike, or simply to lose weight, there is a summer program for you somewhere in Vermont. See *Tennis, Golf, Canoeing*, and *Fishing* for lodging and lesson packages. Prestigious academic programs include the **Russian School** at Norwich University (Russian only is spoken in all social as well as class activities; both undergraduate and graduate courses are offered; www.norwich.edu), intensive language programs at **Middlebury College** (among the offerings are Arabic and Japanese as well as more usual ones; www.middlebury.edu), and a writers' conference at the latter's Bread Loaf summer campus. Senior citizens can take advantage of some outstanding courses offered at bargain prices that include lodging as part of the **Elderhostel** program. For details, write to Elderhostel, 11 Avenue de Lafayette, Boston, MA 02111; www.elderhostel.org. The state's oldest, most respected crafts program is offered by **Fletcher Farm Craft School** (Ludlow 05149): off-loom weaving, creative needlework, quilting, pottery, raku, and stained glass, plus meals and lodging (minimum age 18). The **Vermont Studio Center** (802-635-7000) in Johnson has a national reputation. Working visual artists and writers come to renew their creative wellsprings or to explore completely new directions during intensive sessions that feature guidance and criticism by some of the country's premier artists. **Craftsbury Center** in Craftsbury has summer programs for all ages in running and sculling, and **Lyndon State** has a running camp.

Kim Grant

SWIMMING On the official state map, you can pick out the 36 day-use areas that offer swimming, most with changing facilities, maintained by the Vermont State Department of Forests, Parks and Recreation (weekdays: $1.50 per person 14 years and older, $2 for Sand Bar Park; weekends and holidays: $2.50 per person, $3 for Sand Bar Park). A similar facility is provided by the Green Mountain National Forest in Peru, and the U.S. Army Corps of Engineers has tidied corners of its dam projects for public use in Townshend and North Springfield. There are also public beaches on roughly one-third of Vermont's 400 lakes and ponds (but note that swimming is prohibited at designated "Fishing Access Areas") and plenty on Lake Champlain (see Burlington, Charlotte, Colchester, Georgia, and Swanton). Add to these all the town recreation areas and myriad pools available to visitors and you still haven't gone swimming Vermont-style until you have sampled a Vermont swimming hole. These range from deep spots in the state's ubiquitous streams to 100-foot-deep quarries (**Dorset Quarry** near Manchester and **Chapman Quarry** in West Rutland are famous) and freezing pools between waterfalls (see "Sugarbush/ Mad River Valley"). We have included some of our favorite swimming holes under *Swimming* in each section but could not bring ourselves to share them all. Look for cars along the road on a hot day and ask in local general stores. You won't be disappointed.

TENNIS Vermont claims as many tennis courts per capita as any other state in the union. These include town recreation facilities and sports centers as well as private facilities. Summer tennis programs, combining lessons, lodging, and meals, are offered at **Ascutney, Bolton Valley, Killington,** the **Village at Smugglers Notch, Stratton, Topnotch Resort** in Stowe, and at the **Bridges** in Sugarbush. Check *Tennis* under entries for each area.

THEATER Vermont's two long-established summer theaters are both in the Manchester area: the **Dorset Playhouse** and the **Weston Playhouse.** The **Green Mountain Guild** presents a series of summer musicals at the Killington Playhouse. Other summer theater can be found in Castleton, in Saxtons River, in Waitsfield (the **Valley Players**), in Warren **(Phantom Theater),** in Stowe (the **Stowe Playhouse** and the **Lamoille County Players** in Hyde Park), and **Northern Stage** at the Briggs Opera House in White River Junction. There's also the **Lost Nation Theater** in Montpelier. The **Flynn Theater** in Burlington and the **Paramount Theater** in Rutland are the scene of year-round live entertainment as well as film.

TRAINS See *Amtrak* and *Railroad Excursions.*

VERMONT PUBLIC RADIO Stations for those addicted to National Public Radio can be found throughout the state on the FM dial. In the Burlington area, tune into WVPS (107.9), in the White River Junction/Windsor area to WVPR (89.5), in the Rutland area to WRVT (88.7); WVPA (88.5) in St. Johnsbury; and WBTN (94.3) in Bennington.

WATCHABLE WILDLIFE Throughout Vermont, nonprofits and commercial enterprises offer frequent walks, workshops, hikes, bike tours, and other ways of heightening appreciation of the birds and animals, reptiles, fish, flowers, and other natural things to be seen. Request a copy of the free *Vermont Explorer's Guide Watchable Wildlife* pamphlet listing these events, published periodically throughout the year. It's available from the Vermont Department of Fish and Wildlife (802-241-3295) and on the web at www.nwf.org/northeast/index.html. See also *Birding* and *Hiking and Walking.*

WATERFALLS Those most accessible include: the falls at **Brewster River Gorge** in Jeffersonville; in **Bristol Memorial Forest Park,** Bristol; **Buttermilk Falls** (a popular swimming hole) in Ludlow; **Carver Falls** in West Haven (126 feet high); the falls in **Clarendon Gorge; Cow Meadows Ledges** in Newbury; **Duck Brook Cascades** in Bolton; the **East Putney Falls and Pot Holes; Glen Falls** in

VDT

Fairlee; **Great Falls of the Clyde River** in Charleston; **Hamilton Falls** in Jamaica; **Little Otter Creek Falls** in Ferrisburgh; **Middlebury Gorge** in East Middlebury; **Moss Glen Falls** in Granville Gulf; the **seven falls on the Huntington River** in Hanksville; **Shelburne Falls** in Shelburne; **Texas Falls** in Hancock; **Cadys Falls** in Morrisville; **Bingham Falls** in Stowe; and **Northfield Falls,** Northfield. This time around we finally found the magnificent but dangerous **Big Falls** in Troy. Most of these sites can be located on the invaluable *Vermont Atlas and Gazetteer* (DeLorme).

WEATHER REPORTS For serious weather travel information in Vermont, check with the Vermont highway department's weather line: 802-828-2648. Listen to ***An Eye on the Sky*** on Vermont Public Radio (see *Vermont Public Radio* for stations; www.fairbanksmuseum.com). In the show, produced by the Fairbanks Museum and Planetarium, Mark Breen and Steve Maleski make their reports on life's most constant variable both entertaining and informative. The Vermont Chamber of Commerce web site (see *Information*) also carries current weather information.

WEB PAGES In this edition we have hundreds of web sites within each region. Among the most helpful statewide sites are the following: **www.1-800-Vermont.com** is maintained by the Vermont Department of Travel and Tourism, with many informational leads and links; the Vermont Outdoor Guide Association maintains the best overall site for activies of every kind in the state: **www.voga.org; www.vtstateparks.com** includes locator maps and special programs related to state parks; **www.scenesofvermont.com** is an independently published mine of general information and links. The Vermont Chamber of Commerce is **www.vtchamber.com;** www.state.vt.usagric will get you to useful special listings.

WEDDINGS Destination weddings have become big business in Vermont, so big and so ubiquitous that in this edition we have added the wedding ring symbol for lodging places that specialize in them. Go to www.VermontWeddingGuide.com to request a free copy of the promotional *Vermont Wedding & Resource Guide* (remember it's all advertising): 1-800-860-5813 or info@weddingbook.net. One great wedding site that doesn't makes these listings is **Grand Isle Lake House** (802-865-2522) in the Champlain Islands, a turn-of-the-20th-century summer hotel currently maintained by the Preservation Trust of Vermont. Also see *Civil Unions*.

WHITEWATER During white-water season beginning in mid-April, experienced canoeists and kayakers take advantage of stretches on the **White,**

the **Lamoille,** and the **West Rivers,** among others. **White-water rafting** is also available on the **West River** during spring dam releases.

WINE Vermont has traditionally made apple and other fruit wines, but recently two wineries in the very northern reaches of Vermont have begun planting, harvesting, and fermenting grapes, with respectable results. These are **Boyden Valley Winery** (802-644-8151)—also good for premium apple wines—in Cambridge, and **Snow Farm Vineyard and Winery** (802-372-9463) in South Hero. **North River Winery** (802-368-7557), Vermont's long-established vintner, produces fruit wine; **Ottauquechee Valley Winery** (802-295-9463) in Quechee, **Flag Hill Farm** (802-685-7724) in Vershire, **Grand View Winery** (802-456-7012) in East Calais, and **Putney Mountain Winery** (802-387-4610) all make cider and apple wine. The newest addition is **Shelburne Vineyard** (802-734-1386) on the grounds of Shelburne Farms.

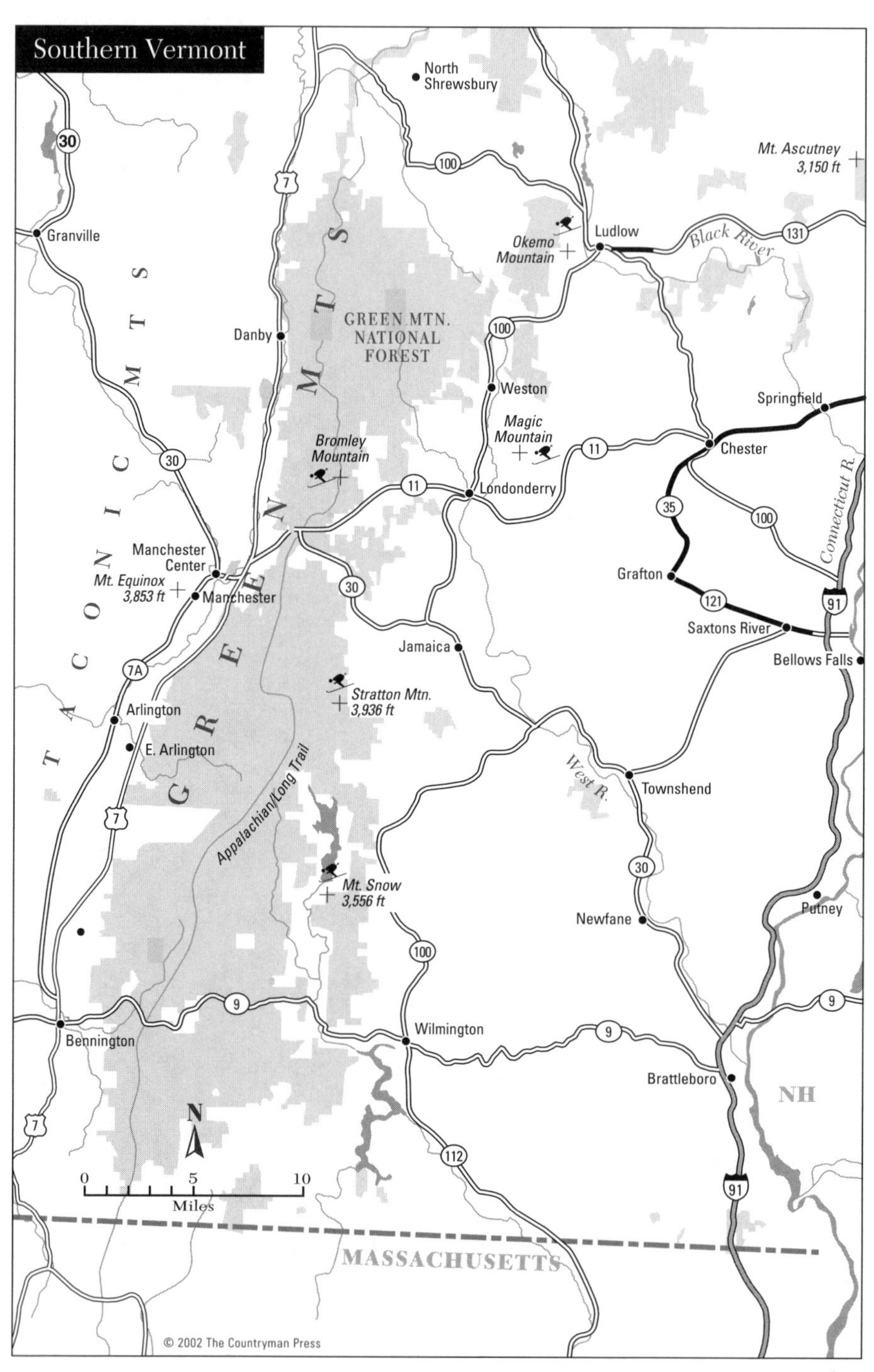
Southern Vermont
North Shrewsbury
Mt. Ascutney 3,150 ft
Granville
Ludlow
Okemo Mountain
Black River
TACONIC MTS
GREEN MTS
Danby
GREEN MTN. NATIONAL FOREST
Weston
Magic Mountain
Springfield
Chester
Bromley Mountain
Londonderry
Connecticut R.
Manchester Center
Mt. Equinox 3,853 ft
Manchester
Grafton
Saxtons River
Jamaica
Bellows Falls
Stratton Mtn. 3,936 ft
Arlington
E. Arlington
West R.
Townshend
Appalachian/Long Trail
Mt. Snow 3,556 ft
Putney
Newfane
Wilmington
Bennington
Brattleboro
NH
N
0 5 10
Miles
MASSACHUSETTS
© 2002 The Countryman Press

Southern Vermont

1

THE LOWER CONNECTICUT AND WEST RIVER VALLEYS

MOUNT SNOW/WILMINGTON AREA

BENNINGTON AREA

MANCHESTER AND THE MOUNTAINS

BELLOWS FALLS, SAXTONS RIVER, AND GRAFTON

OKEMO VALLEY REGION

Kim Grant

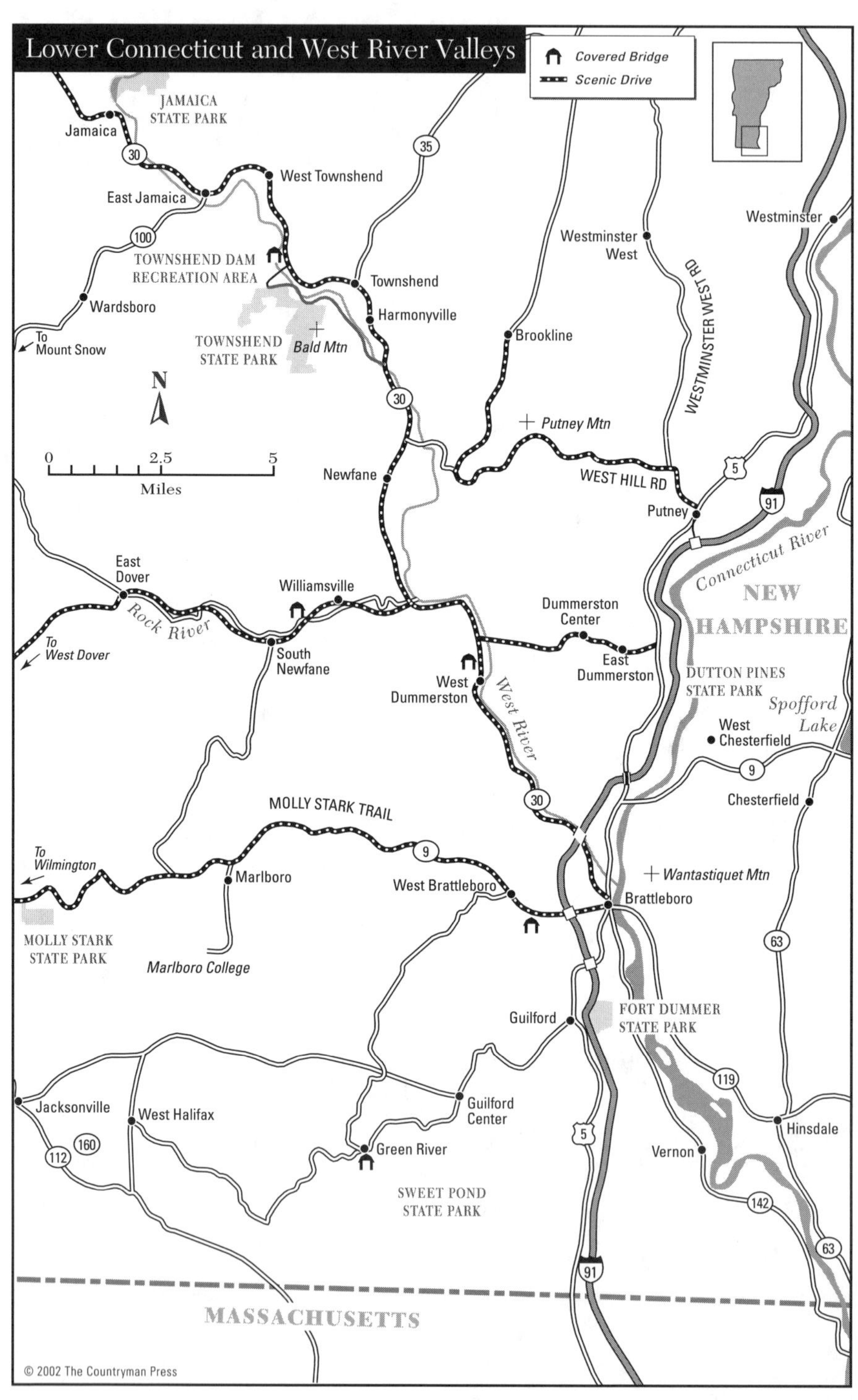
Lower Connecticut and West River Valleys
Covered Bridge
Scenic Drive
JAMAICA STATE PARK
Jamaica
30
West Townshend
East Jamaica
35
100
TOWNSHEND DAM RECREATION AREA
Townshend
Harmonyville
Wardsboro
To Mount Snow
TOWNSHEND STATE PARK
Bald Mtn
Brookline
Westminster West
WESTMINSTER WEST RD
Westminster
N
0
2.5
5
Miles
Putney Mtn
Newfane
WEST HILL RD
Putney
5
91
Connecticut River
NEW HAMPSHIRE
East Dover
Rock River
Williamsville
To West Dover
South Newfane
Dummerston Center
East Dummerston
West Dummerston
West River
DUTTON PINES STATE PARK
Spofford Lake
West Chesterfield
9
Chesterfield
MOLLY STARK TRAIL
To Wilmington
Marlboro
West Brattleboro
Wantastiquet Mtn
Brattleboro
MOLLY STARK STATE PARK
Marlboro College
63
Guilford
FORT DUMMER STATE PARK
119
Jacksonville
West Halifax
Guilford Center
Hinsdale
160
112
Green River
Vernon
SWEET POND STATE PARK
142
MASSACHUSETTS
© 2002 The Countryman Press

THE LOWER CONNECTICUT AND WEST RIVER VALLEYS

INCLUDING BRATTLEBORO, PUTNEY, NEWFANE, TOWNSHEND, AND JAMAICA

Wedged between the Green Mountains and the Connecticut River, Vermont's southeastern corner is a richly varied, poke-around kind of place. Brattleboro, in its southern corner, is the commercial and cultural hub, contrasting with the classic white-clapboarded, green-shuttered towns of Newfane, Townshend, and Jamaica, which are strung like pearls along the West River, and with equally rural Putney, up along the Connecticut.

"'Bratt' is a college town without a college," we were once told by a fellow patron at the Common Ground, a collective-run restaurant founded in 1971. Many of Brattleboro's movers and shakers are former members of the communes that once flourished in the nearby hills. It's an earnest, yeasty community in which the spirit of the '60s continues to build. The supermarket is a co-op showcasing Vermont cheeses; the movie house is a restored art deco theater. Downtown Victorian-era blocks house a mix of traditional and counterculture shops, and include an unusual number of bookstores, galleries, restaurants, and coffeehouses.

While it's one of the most accessible, this is far from the most touristed corner of Vermont. Beyond the widely scattered country inns, antiques dealers, and crafts shops lie swimming holes, and hiking trails that lead to unexpected vistas. The confluence of the Connecticut and West Rivers at Brattleboro is itself a beautiful, placid place to paddle.

GUIDANCE **Brattleboro Area Chamber of Commerce** (802-254-4565; www.brattleboro.com), 180 Main Street, Brattleboro 05301, is good for walk-in information (open year-round, Monday through Friday 8–5; Saturday 10–2). It maintains seasonal information booths manned by knowledgeable senior citizens on Route 9 in West Brattleboro and on Route 5 at the common, just north of the junction with Route 30. Public **rest rooms** are in the Robert S. Gibson Garden building on Main Street at the light, across from High Street (Route 9).

Putney has its own first-rate web site: www.putney.net, featuring its many artists and artisans, as well as lodging and dining. The **West River Valley** towns along Route 30 maintain www.westrivervalley.com.

BRICK MILL BUILDINGS AS SEEN FROM THE CONNECTICUT RIVER IN BRATTLEBORO

The **Southern Vermont Regional Market Organization** (1-877-887-2378; www.southernvermont.com) maintains a good web site for the entire region and sends out printed material.

Note: **The Southeast Vermont Welcome Center**, I-91 in Guilford (open daily 7 AM–1 AM) is the state's most elaborate visitors center (rest rooms).

Newspaper: The *Brattleboro Reformer* (802-254-2311) publishes a special Thursday calendar that's the best source of current arts and entertainment.

GETTING THERE *By bus*: **Greyhound/Vermont Transit** offers service from New York and Connecticut. **Peter Pan Bus Company** serves Boston via Springfield. The bus stop is on Route 5 at its junction with Route 9 west.
By train: **Amtrak** (1-800-USA-RAIL) trains from Washington, D.C., and New York City stop at the old downtown railroad station, now a museum.

GETTING AROUND **Brattleboro Taxi** (802-254-5411) will meet trains and buses. **Thomas Transportation** (1-800-526-8143) offers shuttle service to Boston's Logan Airport, Hartford's Bradley Airport, and Manchester Airport.

Parking: Main Street has metered parking: side streets are possible. A large parking area (Harmony Place) in the rear of the Brooks House is close to shops on High, Elliot, and Main Streets; access is from High Street (Route 9). Another large lot runs between High and Grove Streets.

WHEN TO GO In winter skiers tend to speed through, up Route 30 to Stratton or across Route 9 to Mount Snow, but in summer this is a favorite area both for day-tripping (from Boston, western Massachusetts, and Connecticut) and for longer stays in the many gracious inns and B&Bs. "Marlboro Season" (early July through early August) draws chamber music lovers, but other than that there is no single event or locale, just general beauty and many ways to enjoy it. Foliage brings more day-trippers, and it's wise to avoid the obvious roads (Route 9 and 30). Luckily, there are many options (see Scenic Drives).

MEDICAL EMERGENCY 911 serves this entire area. The medical facilities are at **Brattleboro Memorial Hospital** (802-257-0341), 17 Belmont Avenue, Brattleboro, and **Grace Cottage Hospital** (802-365-7357), Route 25, Townshend.

✷ Towns and Villages

Brattleboro. Vermont's largest town, "Bratt" is a largely 1870s brick and wrought-iron commercial hub for rural corners of three states. (Population swells from 12,000 at night to 30,000 by day.) It's a mix of native Vermonters, former commune members, and young people who keep arriving to study at one of several nearby educational institutions, including the burgeoning Brattleboro Music Center. Each year some 200 enroll in graduate programs at World Learning, begun in 1932 and best known for its Experiment in International Living program (now the School for International Training). Galleries, bookstores, boutiques, alternative shops, and restaurants now outnumber traditional stores. Sam's Outdoor Outfitters, Brown & Roberts Hardware, and Miller Brothers-Newton continue to thrive, but antiques and crafts stores have replaced former downtown anchors. On the first Friday of every month more than a dozen galleries and studios now host a Gallery Walk.

During its long history, this town has shed many skins. The site of Fort Dummer, built in 1724 just south of town, has been obliterated by the Vernon Dam. Gone, too, is the early-19th-century trading and resort town; no trace remains of the handsome, Federal-style commercial buildings or the two elaborate hotels that attracted trainloads of customers who came to take their water cures. The gingerbread wooden casino in Island Park and the fine brick town hall, with its gilded opera house, are also gone, as are the great slate-sided sheds in which hundreds of thousands of Estey organs were made.

Still, a motorist bogged down in the perpetual Main Street bottleneck notices Brooks House, built splendidly in 1869 as an 80-room hotel, once frequented by Rudyard Kipling, now converted to housing, offices, and shops. A couple of blocks down the 1930s art deco Latchis Hotel has been restored inside as well as out and, around the corner, Elliot Street is lined with specialty shops and restaurants.

Brattleboro is full of pleasant surprises. The former railroad station is now the Brattleboro Museum and Art Center. The Connecticut River is accessible by both excursion boat and rental canoe and can be viewed from a hidden downtown park and from the new Robert H. Gibson River Garden, a weatherproofed public space (with public rest rooms). The former Dunkin' Donuts is a Firefighter's Museum set in Doughnut Park. Live theater, music, and dance are presented without hoopla. The fanfare seems to be reserved for the annual winter carnival, begun aeons ago by Fred Harris, who also founded the Dartmouth Winter Carnival and the U.S. Eastern Amateur Ski Association.

Brooks Memorial Library (802-254-5290), 224 Main Street (open daily except Sunday), mounts changing exhibits of regional art and has a fine collection of 19th-century paintings and sculpture, including works by Larkin G. Mead, the Brattleboro boy who first achieved national renown by sculpting an 8-foot-high angel from snow one night and placing it at the junction of Routes 30 and 5. The

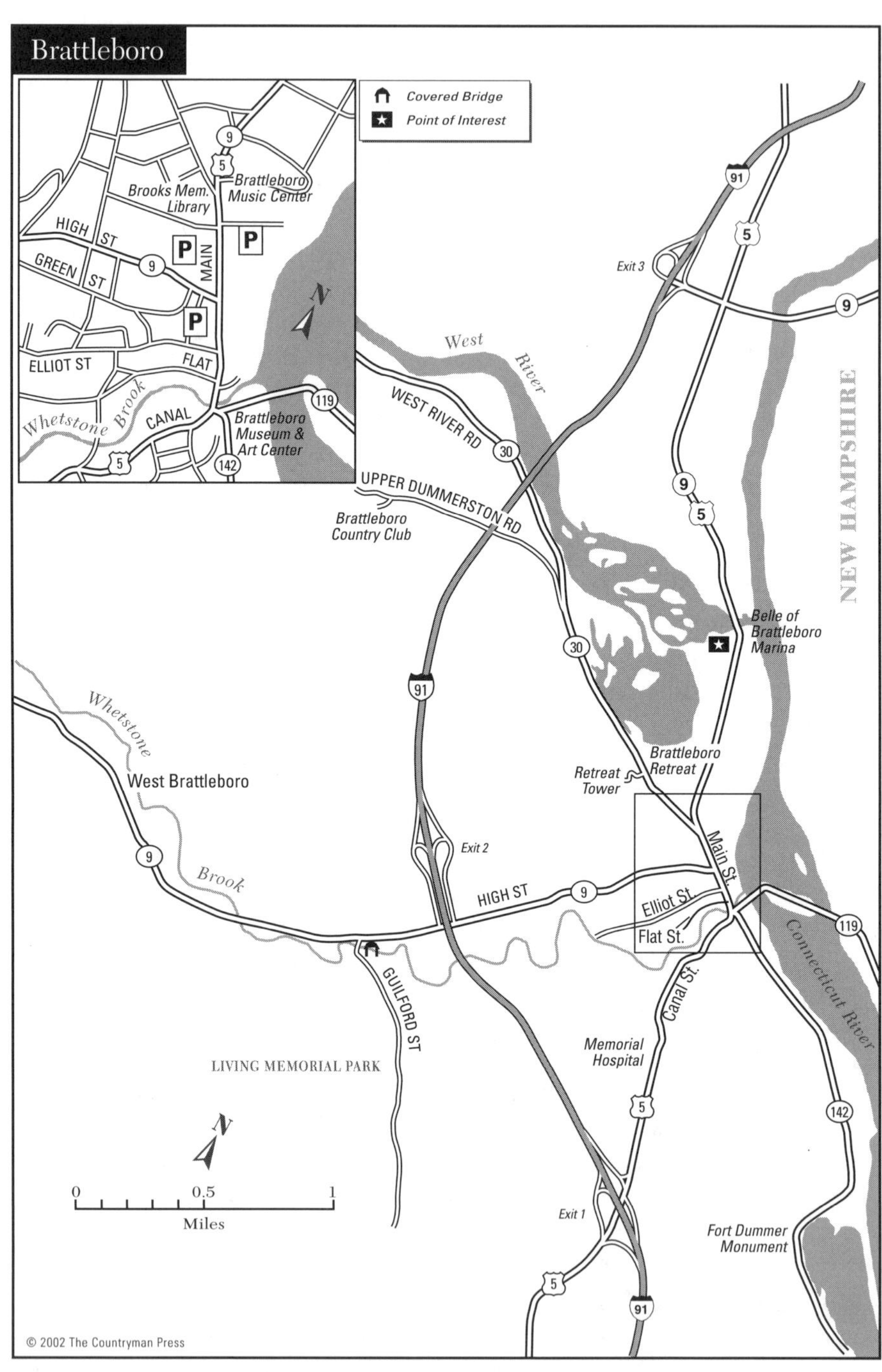
Brattleboro
Covered Bridge
Point of Interest
Brooks Mem. Library
Brattleboro Music Center
HIGH ST
GREEN ST
MAIN
ELLIOT ST
FLAT
Whetstone Brook
CANAL
Brattleboro Museum & Art Center
West River
WEST RIVER RD
UPPER DUMMERSTON RD
Brattleboro Country Club
Exit 3
NEW HAMPSHIRE
Belle of Brattleboro Marina
Whetstone
West Brattleboro
Brook
Retreat Tower
Brattleboro Retreat
Main St.
Exit 2
HIGH ST
Elliot St.
Flat St.
GUILFORD ST
Canal St.
Connecticut River
Memorial Hospital
LIVING MEMORIAL PARK
0 0.5 1
Miles
Exit 1
Fort Dummer Monument
© 2002 The Countryman Press

Brattleboro Historical Society (802-258-4957) maintains a "history room" (a restored 1800s classroom), a collection of Estey organs, and more than 7,000 photographs dating from the mid-1800s. It's on the third floor of the Municipal Building (230 Main Street; open Thursday 1–8 and Saturday 9–noon). Pick up the leaflet that describes the architectural walking tour of Main Street. The International Center on the 200-acre campus of **World Learning** (802-257-7751) on Kipling Road (off Route 5 just north of town), offers much the same view across the valley to Mount Monadnock that Rudyard Kipling enjoyed from Naulakha during the years that he lived there (1892–96).

Along Route 30 in the West River Valley

Newfane. A columned courthouse, matching Congregational church, and town hall—all grouped on a handsome green—are framed by dignified, white-clapboard houses, including two elegant inns. When Windham County's court sessions began meeting in Newfane in 1787, the village was about the same size it is now: 20 houses and two hotels. But in 1787, the village was 2 miles up on Newfane Hill. Beams were unpegged and homes moved to the more protected valley by ox-drawn sleighs in the winter of 1824.

Newfane inns have been famous for more than a century, at first because the whitewashed jail accommodated 25 paying guests, feeding them (as an 1848 poem says) "good pies and oyster soup" in the same rooms with inmates. By the time this facility closed (in the 1950s), the Old Newfane Inn—which incorporates much of its original hilltop structure—was beginning to acquire a reputation for gourmet fare. Economist John Kenneth Galbraith, a summer resident in the area since 1947, helped publicize the charms of both the village and the inn—whose onetime chef eventually opened the Four Columns Inn at the rear of the green.

Newfane Village is more than a place to dine, sleep, and stroll. It is the site of one of the state's oldest and biggest Sunday flea markets, and the immediate area

NEWFANE VILLAGE

Kim Grant

offers an unusual number of antiques shops. Beyond the stores and the remnants of the railway station (which served the narrow-gauge Brattleboro–Londonderry line from 1880 to 1936) is a fine old cemetery.

Newfane has bred as well as fed famous people. You'll learn about some of them in the exceptional **Historical Society of Windham County** (802-365-4148), Route 30, south of the common (open Memorial Day through October, Wednesday, Sunday, noon–5, and for special events). It looks like a brick post office. Displays change but the most interesting tale that's frequently told in the historical society displays is the story of John Wilson (see Brookline, below).

Brookline. Half as wide as it is long, Brookline is sequestered in a narrow valley bounded by steep hills and the West River. (Turn off Route 30 at the Newfane Flea Market.) Its population of 410 is four times what it was 50 years ago but a small fraction of what it was in the 1820s and '30s, when it supported three stores, three schools, two hotels, and a doctor. Those were the decades in which its two landmark brick buildings were constructed. One is a church, but the more famous is a round schoolhouse, said to be the only one in the country—and also probably the only school designed by a crook.

John Wilson never seems to have mentioned his past career as Thunderbolt, an infamous Scottish highwayman. In 1820, the obviously well-educated newcomer designed the circular schoolhouse. He gave it six large windows, the better (it was later noted) to allow him to see whoever approached from any side. Wilson taught only a term before moving to the neighboring (and more remote) town of Dummerston, just about the time that an Irish felon, "Lightfoot" Martin, was hanged in Cambridge, Massachusetts. In his confession (reprints are sold at the historical society), Martin fingered Wilson as his old accomplice, but with no obvious effect. Not long thereafter, Wilson added "Dr." to his name and practiced medicine in Newfane, then in Brattleboro, where he married, fathering a son before his wife divorced him "because of certain facts she learned." When he died in 1847, scars on Wilson's ankles and neck suggested chains and a rope. Today, several of Thunderbolt's pistols are preserved by the historical society and in Brattleboro's Brooks Library.

Unfortunately, the round schoolhouse is now virtually never open. In 1928, the town's first eight grades moved down the road to the current wooden schoolhouse. As the population dwindled through the '30s, '40s, and '50s, the building was used for town meeting, but that assemblage is now held in the vestry of the Baptist church, Brookline's second landmark. Built in 1836, the church has been beautifully restored, thanks to fund-raising efforts like the annual Musicale Sunday, usually held late in July, sponsored by the Ladies Benevolent Society.

Townshend. The next village green north on Route 30 is a full 2 acres, complete with Victorian-style gazebo. It's bordered on one side by a classic, white, 1790 Congregational church flanked by lovely clapboard houses, on others by a columned and tower-topped stucco town hall of the Leland and Gray Union High School (founded as a Baptist seminary in 1834), and by a clapboard commercial block. On the first Saturday in August the common fills with booths and games to benefit Grace Cottage Hospital, which has grown, unbelievably, out of the back side of a rambling old village home. (Known for the quality of its service, this is Vermont's first hospital to have installed a birthing bed.) West Townshend, farther along Route 30, is a three-corners with a photogenic church and general store.

TOWNSHEND GREEN

Kim Grant

The town also harbors stuffed-toy and furniture factories, a state park, a public swimming area, Vermont's largest single-span covered bridge, 15 cemeteries, and several good places to stay and to eat.

Jamaica. A small village clustered around its white Congregational church (1808) on Route 30, Jamaica is the kind of place you can drive through in 2 minutes, or stay a week. The village buildings are few but proud, and there is swimming and plenty of hiking as well as camping in **Jamaica State Park**. The village, which lies within the bailiwick of Stratton Mountain's resort community, also offers some surprisingly good shopping.

North along Route 5

Putney. This village's riverside fields have been heavily farmed since the mid–18th century, and its hillsides produce more than one-tenth of all the state's apples. Putney is an unusually fertile place for progressive thinking, too. Back in the 1840s, it spawned a group who practiced Bible Communism, the sharing of all property, work, and wives. John Humphrey Noyes, the group's leader, was charged with adultery in 1847 and fled with his flock to Oneida, New York, where they founded the famous silverplate company. Known today for experimental education rather than religion, Putney is the home of the Putney School, a coed, college preparatory school founded in 1935, with a regimen that entails helping with chores, including raising animals. Landmark College is the country's only fully accredited college specifically for dyslexic students and those with other learning disabilities. The Greenwood School, a prep school for dyslexic boys, and the Oak Meadow School, a pioneering support service for homeschooling, are also in town. In July the **Yellow Barn Music School and Festival** is housed in a barn behind the library; concerts are staged there and at other local venues throughout the month.

Putney Village is tiny but offers some interesting shopping, augmented on the first weekend after Thanksgiving by the annual **Putney Artisans Craft Tour** for which the studios of dozens of established craftspeople open their back-roads studios. Putney's scenic roads are also well known to serious bicyclists, and Putney Mountain (see *To Do—Hiking*) is beloved by both hikers and mountain bikers.

Putney's native sons include the late George Aiken, who served as governor before going on to Washington as a senator in 1941, a post he held until his retirement in

1975. Frank Wilson, a genuine Yankee trader who was one of the first merchants to enter Red China, built the first of his **Basketvilles,** "The World's Largest Basket Stores," in the village. The **Putney Historical Society** (802-387-5862), housed in town hall, is open by appointment.

South on Route 5

Guilford. Back-roaded by I-91 (which has no exit between Brattleboro and Massachusetts), this old agricultural town rewards with quiet rural scenery anyone who drives or pedals its roads. Check out **Sweet Pond State Park,** a former 125-acre estate with a large pond, good for swimming and boating, and circled by a nature path. Labor Day weekend is big here, the time for the old-fashioned **Guilford Fair** and for the annual 2-day, free concerts sponsored by Friends of Music at Guilford (802-257-1961) in and around the **Organ Barn.** The **Guilford Historical Society,** open Memorial Day through Columbus Day, Tuesday and Saturday, 10–2 and by appointment (call Addie Minott at 802-254-5910), maintains exhibits in the 1822 town hall, in the 1837 meetinghouse, and in the 1797 one-room brick schoolhouse.

✷ To See

MUSEUM ♿ **Brattleboro Museum and Art Center** (802-257-0124; web site: www.Brattleboromuseum.org), 10 Vermont Street (off Canal and Bridge Streets), Brattleboro. Open mid-May through early November, Tuesday through Sunday noon–6; $3 per adult, $2 for seniors and students, free under 12. The town's 1915 rail station makes a handsome home for changing exhibits that have varied wildly in recent years, from quilts to architecture to contemporary art. A historical room tells the story of Brattleboro's famed Estey Organ Co., which produced thousands of organs each year between the 1850s, and the company's demise in 1961. Inquire about frequent concerts, "twilight" guided walks, and for lectures related to the exhibits.

See also Historical Society of Windham County in Newfane under *Villages*.

GREEN RIVER BRIDGE AND GREEN RIVER FALLS IN GUILFORD

Alois Mayer

COVERED BRIDGES In Brattleboro, the reconstructed **Creamery Bridge** forms the entrance to Living Memorial Park on Route 9. North on Route 30 in West Dummerston, a Town lattice bridge across the West River is the longest still-used covered bridge in the state (for the best view, jump into the cool waters on either side; this is a popular swimming hole on a hot summer day). The **Scott Bridge,** Vermont's longest single-span bridge, stands by Route 30 in West Townshend just below the Townshend Dam, but it is closed to traffic. The region's oldest covered bridge spans the Rock River between Williamsville and South Newfane. The Green River in Guilford also boasts a covered bridge.

FOR FAMILIES **Brattleboro Retreat Petting Farm** (802-258-3714), 350 Linden Street, Route 30 just north of Brattleboro. Open Memorial Day through October, Wednesday through Sunday 10–4. Admission: $4.50 for 12 and over, $3.50 under 12. The Retreat's working dairy farm, which also includes llamas, pigs, emus, lambs, sheep, goats, oxen, donkeys, horses, chickens, kittens, shaggy Highland cattle, and a cow that visitors are invited to milk. A gift shop features Vermont products.

Butterfly Heaven and **D&K's Little Petting Farm** (802-874-4160), Route 30, Jamaica. Open daily year-round 9–5. $6 adult to either the Butterfly Heaven or Petting Farm, $8 for both, less for children and seniors. Dale and Karen Ameden began by creating a garden center featuring more than 1,000 varieties of perennials and acres of display gardens. They then added a petting farm with chicks, ducks, bunnies, Shetland sheep, pygmy goats, a Holstein calf, and more. Finally they built another big greenhouse and filled it with the plants butterflies love, along with paths, seats, and a jungle habitat for tropical birds at the far end. The result is enchanting. In all the complex covers 11 acres.

Santa's Land (802-387-5550; 1-800-726-8299), Route 5, Putney. Open daily 10–5 Memorial Day through Labor Day, weekends until Christmas. $12 for adults, $15 for children 3–12, $10 for seniors. Designed for children ages 2–8, this Christmas theme village includes an Igloo Pancake House, Christmas shops, Santa's home, reindeer, kiddie rides, barnyard and unusual animals, a Ferris wheel, Santa's Express Train, and, of course, Santa.

Connecticut River Fish Ladder, Vernon. The New England Power Company's 984-foot fish ladder helps American shad and Atlantic salmon return to their spawning grounds—51 pools in a 35-foot vertical rise. Best viewing is from late May through mid-July, 8–5 daily.

SCENIC DRIVES The hilly, heavily wooded country between the West and Connecticut River Valleys is webbed with roads, most of them dirt. Our favorites include:

Putney Mountain Road to Brookline. At the Putney General Store on Route 5, turn left onto Westminster West Road and left again about a mile up the hill onto West Hill Road. Not far above the Putney School, look for a dirt road on your right. It forks immediately; bear right to Putney Mountain. Trees thicken and sunlight dapples through in a way that it never seems to do on paved roads. Chipmunks scurry ahead on the hard-packed dirt. The few drivers you pass will wave. The road curves up and up—and up—cresting after 2.1 miles. Note the unmarked parking area on your right (see Putney Mountain under *To Do—Hiking*). The road then snakes down the other side into Brookline (see *Villages*).

The **Molly Stark Trail,** the 17 miles of Route 9 between Brattleboro and Bennington, is dedicated to the wife of Gen. John Stark, hero of the battle of Bennington. It passes by Marlboro (see *Scenic Drives* in "Mount Snow/Wilmington"), climbing high over Hogback Mountain before winding down into Wilmington. Very scenic but heavily trafficked during foliage season.

West Dummerston to West Dover. Beautiful in a car or on a bike, the 13 miles between Route 30 and Route 100 form a shortcut from Newfane to Mount Snow. Turn west off Route 30, 2 miles north of the covered bridge. Follow the Rock River (in summer, clumps of cars suggest swimming holes) west from West Dummerston and Williamsville, on through the picturesque village of South Newfane (the general store is a source of picnic fare); detour a half mile into the old hill village of Dover, very different from West Dover down on busy Route 100.

Route 30 from Brattleboro to Jamaica (you can loop back on Route 100 and either of the two routes sketched above) shadows the West River, passing two covered bridges and going through exceptionally picturesque villages of Newfane and Townshend, as well as by the Townshend Dam (good for swimming). Both villages offer first-rate crafts and antiques (see *Villages* and *Selective Shopping*).

East Dummerston to West Dummerston. A handy shortcut from Route 5 to Route 30 (or vice versa), just 2 miles up one side of a hill to picturesque Dummerston Center and 2 miles down the other. This was long known in our family as the Gnome Road because of the way it winds through the woods to Vermont's longest (recently refitted) traffic-bearing covered bridge (see *Covered Bridges*). It's generally known as the East/West Road.

Brattleboro to Guilford Center to Halifax and back. This can be a 46-mile loop to Wilmington and back; ask locally for shortcuts back up to Route 9. Take Route 5 south from Brattleboro to the Guilford Country Store (selling sandwiches), then right into Guilford Center (see *Villages*). Continue for a half mile and bear right on Stage Road to Green River with its covered bridge, church, and recently restored crib dam. Bear right at the church (before the bridge) and then left at the Y; follow Green River Road (along the river) and then Hatch School Road into Jacksonville. To complete the loop see *Scenic Tours, Jacksonville/Whitingham* in "Mount Snow/Wilmington."

✱ To Do

BICYCLING Some 200 miles of dirt and abandoned roads, along with miles of off-road trails, add up to a well-established mecca for bicyclists. The **Putney Bicycle Club,** the oldest in Vermont, organizes weekly (hard-core) mountain-bike tours. Check with the **West Hill Shop** (802-387-5718), open daily, I-91 exit 4, across from the Putney Inn. Since 1971 the hub of biking information throughout this area, the shop has published its own map, detailing four tours as well as Class 4 roads and off-road routes. It also provides mountain-bike rentals. **Brattleboro Bicycle Shop** (802-254-8644; 1-800-BRATBIKE), 178 Main Street, offers day rentals (hybrids) and plenty of advice about where to use them.

Mt. Riders (802-297-1745) in Rawsonville, 5 miles west of Jamaica, also rents mountain bikes.

BOATING **Vermont Canoe Touring Center** (802-257-5008), Brattleboro. Located at the cove at Veterans Memorial Bridge, Route 5, just north of the junc-

THE CONNECTICUT RIVER AROUND BRATTLEBORO IS WIDE AND SLOW FOR CANOEING

Kim Grant

tion with Route 30. Open daily Memorial Day weekend through Labor Day weekend 9–7, weekends in spring and fall. John Knickerbocker rents canoes and kayaks, and offers shuttle service, guided trips, and wilderness camping on the river. The 32 miles from Bellows Falls to the Vernon Dam is slow-moving water, as is the 6-mile stretch from below the dam to the Massachusetts border.

Connecticut River Tours (802-254-1263), Putney Road, Brattleboro. The 49-passenger, mahogany-trimmed *Belle of Brattleboro* offers several kinds of cruises Wednesday through Sunday and holidays, Memorial Day through Columbus Day.

Whitewater on the West River. Twice a year, once in spring and again in September, the Army Corps of Engineers releases water from the Ball Mountain Dam (802-874-4881) in Jamaica, creating whitewater fit for national kayak championships. The races are no longer run here, but commercial white-water rafters as well as white-water kayakers and canoeists take advantage of the flow, especially in fall, when many of the region's other white-water courses are dry.

Townshend Outdoors (802-365-7308), Route 30 south of Townshend Village. Open weekends year-round. Ann Griswold's consignment shop for sports equipment has canoes and kayaks, which can also be rented for use at the nearby Townshend Recreation Area (the dam) and other nearby lakes. You can rent tubes for use in the river, too. (The shop also sells and rents skis and snowshoes.)

FISHING In the **Connecticut River,** you can catch bass, trout, pike, pickerel, and yellow perch. There is an access on Old Ferry Road, 2 miles north of Brattleboro on Route 5; another is from River Road on the New Hampshire shore in Westmoreland (Route 9 east, then north on Route 63). For fishing boat rentals contact the **Marina Restaurant** (802-257-7563).

The **West River** is a source of trout and smallmouth bass; access is from any number of places along Route 30. In Vernon, there is a boat access on **Lily Pond;** in

Guilford, on **Weatherhead Hollow Pond** (see the DeLorme *Vermont Atlas and Gazetteer*).

GOLF **Brattleboro Country Club** (802-254-9864), Upper Dummerston Road, has recently expanded to 18 holes and includes a full driving range, practice areas, and instructional range. The **Windham Golf Club** (802-825-2517), Popple Dungeon Road in Windham, offers 18 holes. Also see Mount Snow and Stratton ski resorts; both offer golf schools and 27 holes.

HIKING **In Brattleboro,** a pleasant path up to the Retreat Tower, a 19th-century overlook, begins beside Linden Lodge on Route 30. Another trail follows the West River along the abandoned **West River railroad bed.** Access is off Route 5 north of town; take the second left turn after crossing the bridge. **Wantastiquet Mountain,** overlooking Brattleboro from across the Connecticut River in New Hampshire, is a good 1½-hour hike from downtown, great for picnics and views of southeast Vermont. See also Fort Dummer State Park under *Green Space* for a wooded trail south of town overlooking the Connecticut, and Townshend State Forest for a steep trek up Bald Mountain.

Putney Mountain between Putney and Brookline, off Putney Mountain Road (see *Scenic Drives*), is one of the most rewarding 1-mile round-trip hikes anywhere. A sign nailed to a tree in the unmarked parking area assures you that this is indeed Putney Mountain. Follow the trail that heads gently uphill through birches and maples, then continues through firs and vegetation that changes remarkably quickly to the stunted growth usually found only at higher elevations. Suddenly you emerge on the mountain's broad crown, circled by a deep-down satisfying panorama. The view to the east is of Mount Monadnock, rising in lonely magnificence above the roll of southern New Hampshire, but more spectacular is the spread of Green Mountain peaks to the west. You can pick out the ski trails on Haystack, Mount Snow, and Stratton.

Jamaica State Park offers a choice of three interesting trails. The most intriguing and theoretically the shortest is to Hamilton Falls, a 125-foot cascade through a series of wondrous potholes. It's an obvious mile (30-minute) hike up, but the return can be confusing. Beware straying onto Turkey Mountain Road.

Black Mountain Natural Area, maintained by The Nature Conservancy of Vermont (802-229-4425). Cross the covered bridge on Route 30 in West Dummerston and turn south on Quarry Road for 1.4 miles. The road changes to Rice Farm Road; go another 0.5 mile to a pull-off on the right. The marked trail begins across the road and rises abruptly 1,280 feet to a ridge, traversing it before dropping back down, passing a beaver dam on the way back to the river. The loop is best done clockwise. Beautiful in laurel season.

HORSEBACK RIDING **West River Stables at Meadowbrook Farm** (802-365-7668), Hill Road, Brookline. Roger Poitras has built a barn and ring across the way from the West River Lodge (see *Lodging—Bed & Breakfasts*) and offers English riding lessons featuring "centered riding" (using the Alexander technique), dressage, and jumping. **Winchester Stables** (802-365-9434), River Road in Newfane, also offers lessons. For trail rides see "Mount Snow/Wilmington" and "Manchester and the Mountains."

RAILROAD EXCURSION The ***Green Mountain Flyer*** (802-463-3069), based just north of this area in Bellows Falls, offers a 26-mile run in-season. (See "Bellows Falls, Saxtons River, and Grafton.")

SWIMMING 🖉 **Living Memorial Park,** west of downtown Brattleboro on Route 9, offers a public pool (mid-June through Labor Day). In the West River Valley at the **Townshend Lake Recreation Area** (802-874-4881) off Route 30 in West Townshend you drive across the top of the massive dam, completed in 1961 as a major flood-prevention measure for the southern Connecticut River Valley. Swimming is in the reservoir behind the dam, with a man-made beach and gradual drop-off, good for children. Changing facilities provided; small fee. The **West River** itself offers a few swimming holes, notably under the West Dummerston covered bridge on Route 30 and at Salmon Hole in Jamaica State Park. **Hamilton Falls,** accessible from the park, and **Pikes Falls,** also in Jamaica (ask directions locally), are favorite swimming holes, but not advised for children. Just off Route 30, a mile or so up (on South Newfane Road), the **Rock River** swirls through a series of shallow swimming spots; look for cars. In Guilford, there is swimming at **Sweet Pond State Park** (802-257-7406), a former 125-acre estate with a large pond circled by a nature path. Also handy to Brattleboro, **Wares Grove** is across the Connecticut River in Chesterfield, New Hampshire (9 miles east on Route 9, the next left after the junction with Route 63). This pleasant beach on Spofford Lake is good for children; there is a snack bar and makeshift changing facilities.

✷ Winter Sports

CROSS-COUNTRY SKIING **Brattleboro Outing Club Ski Hut** (802-254-4081), Upper Dummerston Road, Brattleboro. Trails through woods and a golf course, 16 km machine tracked, rentals, instruction. In **Living Memorial Park** (802-254-4081), Brattleboro, a 6 km trail through the woods is not only set but also lighted for night skiing. **West Hill Shop** (802-387-5718), I-91, exit 4 (across from the Putney Inn) is the source of cross-country information for the Putney area. **Townshend Outdoors** (802-365-7309), Route 30 south of Townshend Village, rents cross-country skis and snowshoes. **Jamaica State Park** in Jamaica (see *Green Space*) offers marked trails.

See also Grafton Ponds in "Bellows Falls, Saxtons River, and Grafton."

DOWNHILL SKIING The big ski areas are a short drive west into the Green Mountains, either to **Mount Snow** (Route 9 from Brattleboro and then up Route 100 to West Dover—see "Mount Snow/Wilmington Area") or up Route 30 to **Stratton** (see "Manchester and the Mountains").

SLEIGH RIDES **Fair Winds Farm** (802-254-9067), Upper Dummerston Road, and the **Robb Family Farm** (802-254-7664; 1-888-318-9087), 827 Ames Hill

Road, both offer sleigh rides within minutes of downtown Brattleboro. See also *Farms to Visit.*

SNOWMOBILES **River Bend Lodge** (802-365-7952), Route 30, Newfane, and **Stanley Bill Sales** (802-365-7375) in Townshend rent machines. Guided tours are offered by **High Country Snowmobile Tours** (802-464-2108; 1-800-627-SLED) in Wilmington.

✷ Green Space

Fort Dummer State Park (802-254-2610), Guilford. Located 2 miles south of Brattleboro on South Main Street. There are 61 campsites, including 10 lean-tos, and a dump station, a playfield, and a hiking trail through hardwoods with views of the river valley.

Jamaica State Park (802-874-4600), Jamaica. This 758-acre wooded area offers riverside camping, swimming in a great swimming hole, a picnic area, and an organized program of guided hikes. An old railroad bed along the river serves as a 3-mile trail to the Ball Mountain Dam, and an offshoot mile-long trail leads to Hamilton Falls. A weekend in spring and again in fall is set aside for white-water canoe races. There are 61 tent/trailer sites and 18 lean-tos. A large picnic shelter is handy to the swimming hole and a playground includes swings, a teeter-totter, and slides.

Ball Mountain Lake (802-874-4881), Jamaica. This 85-acre lake, created and maintained by the U.S. Army Corps of Engineers, is a dramatic sight among the wooded, steep mountains, conveniently viewed from the access road off Route 30. Over 100 campsites are available on Winhall Brook at the other end of the reservoir, open mid-May through Columbus Day; accessible off Route 100 in South Londonderry. For reservations phone 1-877-444-6777. A controlled release from this flood dam provides outstanding canoeing on the West River below Jamaica each spring and fall (see *To Do—Boating*).

Townshend State Park (802-365-7500), Townshend, marked from Route 30 south of town. Open early May through Columbus Day. Up a back road, an attractive, classic '30s Civilian Conservation Corps (CCC) stone and wood complex with a picnic pavilion. This is really an 826-acre state forest with 41 acres reserved for the park. The camping area (30 campsites, four lean-tos) is near the start of the 2.7-mile (steep) climb to the summit of Bald Mountain; trail maps are available at the park office.

Dutton Pines State Park (802-254-2277), Brattleboro. On Route 5, 5 miles north of town, this is a picnic area with a shelter.

Living Memorial Park, just west of Brattleboro on Route 9. This is an unusual facility for any community. It includes a swimming pool (mid-June through Labor Day), ice-skating rink (early December through mid-March), tennis courts, playground, camping sites, lawn games, a nine-hole golf course, and a ski hill serviced by a T-bar.

See also Sweet Pond State Park under *To Do—Swimming.*

✷ Farms to Visit

One of the state's concentrations of farms and orchards is here in the lower Connecticut River Valley, some offering "pick your own," others welcoming visitors to their farm stands, sugaring houses, or barns. Call before coming.

Note: **Brattleboro Farmer's Market** is held May through late October, Wednesday 10–2 at Merchants Bank Square across from the post office, and Saturday 9–2, Route 9 in West Brattleboro. This lively community coming-together showcases crafts and produce. Food vendors and, frequently, music and flowers are part of the scene.

Southern Vermont Working Farms, a map guide available from the Windham County Natural Resources Conservation District (802-254-5323), locates more than a dozen farms in this area.

APPLES AND MORE **Dwight Miller & Son** (802-254-9158), 581 Miller Road, East Dummerston. Open daily year-round. Syrup and seasonal pick-your-own apples, strawberries, and peaches, blueberries and raspberries, also selling pears, plums, and organic produce.

Green Mountain Orchards (802-387-5851), West Hill Road, Putney. Open daily in-season. Pick-your-own apples and blueberries; cider available in-season. Open in winter, selling apples.

CHEESE **Major Farm** (802-387-4473), Patch Road, Westminster West. Vermont Shepherd Cheese holds one the country's top awards for its distinctive, hand-pressed, sweet, creamy sheep's milk cheese. It is made April through October, then aged 4 to 8 months and available mid-August until the year's supply runs out in spring. The cave is open to visitors for tours and cheese tastings August through October, Thursday and Saturday 10–noon. Call for directions.

MAPLE SUGAR AND MORE **Robb Family Farm** (802-254-7664; 1-888-318-9087), 827 Ames Hill Road, Brattleboro. This 420-acre dairy farm has been in the same family since 1907, and visitors are welcomed here in a number of ways and in all seasons. In spring the sugarhouse is a fragrant, steamy place; year-round it's also the Country Shop (open Monday through Saturday 10–5, Sunday 1–5, closed Wednesday), stocked with maple products and floral items. Visitors are also welcome in the barn, moved here from Halifax in 1912 (50 of the 100-head herd are presently milked). Inquire about a Day on the Farm, beginning with breakfast, also about hayrides, sleigh rides, hiking, and the Apple Fritter Fest in October.

Lilac Ridge Farm (802-254-8113), Ames Hill Road, Brattleboro, is just before the Robb Family Farm (see above). Stuart and Beverly Thurber

THE CONNECTICUT RIVER VALLEY IS LINED WITH FARMS

Kim Grant

also milk 50 cows and produce maple syrup, and they grow Christmas trees. They invite visitors to come and walk around.

Franklin Farm (802-254-2228), Weatherhead Hollow Road, Guilford. A diversified family farm: dairy, maple sugaring, baked goods, fresh eggs, compost, and poultry.

Miller Farm (802-254-2657), Route 142, Vernon. One of Vermont's first registered Holstein farms (1887), in the Miller family since 1916. Farm tours offered.

Harlow's Sugar House (802-387-5852), Route 5 in Putney, is one of the most visitor-oriented operations, permitting you to pick your own apples, blueberries, and strawberries, and offering sleigh rides during sugaring season.

H & M Orchard (802-254-2711), Dummerston Center. One of the most accessible sugar shacks to observe "boiling" during sugaring season.

Sweet Tree Farm (802-254-4508), Route 5, Dummerston. The sugarhouse opens in March and continues through the summer months.

OTHER **Hickins Mountain Mowings** (802-254-2146), Black Mountain Road, Dummerston. Located off the high, wooded East/West Road (see *To See—Scenic Drives*), this is an outstanding family farm, noted for the quality and variety of its vegetables, flowers, maple syrup, pickles, jams, jellies, and fruitcakes. Open year-round, except Tuesday, until sunset.

Walker Farm (802-254-2051; www.walkerfarm.com), Route 5, Dummerston. A 200-year-old farm and garden center (open April 15 through fall, 10–6), specializing in hard-to-find annuals and perennials and garden books by local authors. A full line of produce June through Thanksgiving, featuring their own organic vegetables and local fruit. Display gardens, and calves for petting.

Dutton Berry Farm and Stand (802-365-4168), farm stand on Route 30, Newfane. This is a large, varied stand featuring produce from the family's Dummerston farm.

Fair Winds Farm (802-254-9067), Upper Dummerston Road. This small, diversified family farm offers horse-drawn sleigh and hayrides through the woods. Organic produce and fresh eggs are sold at their roadside stand on weekdays.

Elysian Hills (802-257-0233), Tucker Reed Road, Brattleboro. Bill and Mary Lou Schmidt maintain this tree farm (available for tagging in October) and also grow rhubarb for rhubarb wine, along with Gilfeather turnips for seed. Visitors welcome to walk the woodland trails.

✷ Lodging

COUNTRY INNS 🐾 ♿ **Four Columns Inn** (802-365-7713; 1-800-787-6633; www.fourcolumnsinn.com), Newfane 05345. This Greek Revival mansion, built in 1830 by Gen. Pardon Kimball to remind his southern wife of her girlhood home, fronts on Newfane's classic green. The 15 guest rooms vary from merely country elegant ($115–145) to deluxe (with gas fireplaces, $155–175) to extravagant suites (two-person whirlpool or soaking tub typically with a view of the gas fireplace, $190–340). The very best suite fills the space above the four columns, formerly a porch, with a Jacuzzi overlooking the green. Innkeepers Pam and Gorty Baldwin have brought comfort and color to the inn's common spaces as well, adding comfortable chairs, French doors, and a whimsical mural of Newfane in the tavern. While it's set in a splendid village (see Newfane under *Villages*), the inn backs onto 150 steep and wooded acres, good for walking or snowshoeing. Dining is a big attraction (see *Dining Out*), and facilities include a swimming pool. Rollaway $25. Rates increase in foliage season. Breakfast included.

ꝏ ♿ **Windham Hill Inn** (802-874-4080; 1-800-944-4080; www.windhamhill.com), West Townshend 05359. High above the West River Valley, this 1825 brick farmhouse is a luxurious retreat. Some of the 21 guest rooms have soaking tub, private deck, Jacuzzi, fireplace, or gas stove, and all have private bath and phone. All are carefully furnished with antiques and interesting art. Eight are in the White Barn Annex, some with a large deck looking down the valley. Common space in the inn itself include a music room with grand piano and an airy sun porch with wicker. Two sitting rooms are country elegant with wood-burning fireplaces, Oriental carpets, and wing chairs, and the dining room also has a fireplace, a formal dining table, and tables for two (see *Dining Out*). Innkeepers Grigs and Pat Markham have added a nicely landscaped pool overlooking the mountains and tennis court. The 160-acre property also includes an extensive network of hiking paths, groomed as cross-country trails in winter (when the frog pond freezes for skating). Inquire about weddings, both inside (there's a small conference center in the barn) and outside (for up to 150 guests). $210–345 B&B; $35 per extra person. Inquire about discounted packages. Add $45 per person, plus tax and gratuity, for dinner.

ꝏ 🐾 **Three Mountain Inn** (802-874-4140; 1-800-532-9399; www.threemountaininn.com), Route 30, Jamaica 05343. This 1790s inn in the middle of a classic Vermont village is currently undergoing a gradual but complete remake by energetic young innkeepers David and Stacy Hiler. At this writing the seven upstairs rooms and seven in neighboring Robinson House are a mix of the old-fashioned country-inn ambience created by the previous owners and newly decorated rooms with gas fireplaces. Sage Cottage in the garden now features a Jacuzzi tub, gas fireplace, two skylights and a stained-glass window, surround sound, and, of course, a TV/VCR. Common space includes the old tavern room with its large hearth and a cozy corner bar. There are two small dining rooms (see *Dining Out*). Jamaica State Park and its trails are a short walk (see *Green Space*) and Stratton Mountain (see *To Do—Downhill Skiing* in "Manchester and the Mountains") with its 27-hole golf course is a short drive. From $125 for small rooms in the inn to $325 for the cottage in high season; breakfast is included.

THE VIEW FROM THE LAWN OF THE WINDHAM HILL INN

Christina Tree

Old Newfane Inn (802-365-4427; 1-800-784-4427), Newfane 05345. Closed in November and April. Closed Monday. Under the same ownership for more than 30 years, this inn has changed little in the past two decades. The long, low-beamed dining room was a part of the original inn built up on Newfane Hill (see *Villages*), and there is a seemly sense of age and a formal atmosphere. The eight spotless guest rooms and two suites are furnished with antiques; $135–175 double (the high end is for a suite with living room, bath, and bedroom). No credit cards. The inn is best known for outstanding French-Swiss cuisine (see *Dining Out*).

ꝏ **The Inn at South Newfane** (802-348-7191; innatsouthnewfane@sover.net), South Newfane 05351. This elegant old country manor, with its sweeping lawn and pond, is sited in a tiny village, complete with church and covered bridge. Obviously a perfect setting for weddings, which, at this writing, dominate summer and fall business. Worth checking, however. There are six large guest rooms, all with high ceilings and private bath. $115–130 B&B. At this writing, the future of the public dining room is unclear.

Chesterfield Inn (603-256-3211; 1-800-365-5515; www.chesterfieldinn.com), P.O. Box 155, Chesterfield, NH 03443. On Route 9, 2 miles east of Brattleboro. The original house served as a tavern from 1798 to 1811 but the present facility is contemporary, with a large attractive dining room, spacious parlor, and 15 guest rooms scattered between the main house and the Guest House. All rooms have sitting area, phone, controlled heat and air-conditioning, optional TV, and wet bar, and some have a working fireplace or Jacuzzi. Innkeepers Phil and Judy Hueber have created a popular dining room and a comfortable, romantic getaway spot that's well positioned for exploring southern Vermont, as well as New Hampshire's Monadnock region. $150–250 includes a full breakfast.

BED & BREAKFASTS

In Brattleboro 05301

ꝏ 🐾 **40 Putney Road** (802-254-6268; 1-800-941-2413; frtyptny@sover.net), at that address. Just north of the town common and within walking distance of downtown shops and restaurants, this house with steeply pitched, gabled roof is said to be patterned on a French château. It was built in 1930 for the director of the neighboring Brattleboro Retreat. Rob and Mimi Hamlin, the new owners, love to cook, and light bistro fare is served with a selection of wine (Mimi is a former vineyard manager) and draft beer. Five tastefully furnished guest rooms, each with phone, TV, and private bath, include a two-room suite and a two-room cottage with a gas fireplace and full kitchen. We would request one of the rear two rooms overlooking the gardens, away from Route 5 (Putney Road), but front rooms are air-conditioned so noise is muted. Common space is plentiful and attractive, and landscaped grounds with working fountains border the West River. The $115–195 double rates include a full breakfast served, weather permitting, on the garden patio. The fireplace suite is $245 and the cottage, $175 double, $225 for four. Dogs possible.

ꝏ **Crosby House** (802-257-4914; 1-800-528-1868; www.crosbyhouse.com), 175 Western Avenue. A mansion built in 1868 and set in landscaped gardens, this is a special place with marble fireplace and baby grand piano in the parlor and superb detailing, augmented by cabinets and other examples of highly skilled woodworking by Lynn Kuralt's late husband, Tom. Each of the three guest rooms is well thought out and has a magnificent bed and bath; Winifred's Summer Retreat has both a paneled fireplace and a double whirlpool with separate shower. There are also two studio suites with cathedral ceilings and garden views and two cottages, one with a fireplace. $115–145 includes a full, heart-healthy breakfast served in the oak-paneled dining room or continental, served in your room.

The Artist's Loft B&B and Gallery (phone/fax: 802-257-5181; www.TheArtistsLoft.com), 103 Main Street. Artist William Hays and wife Patricia Long offer a middle-of-town spacious, colorful suite with a private entrance, queen-sized bed, and river view (private bath). This is a great spot if you want to plug into all that Brattleboro offers in the way of art, music, dining, and shopping; Patricia and William delight in sharing their knowledge about their adopted town. $118–145 includes continental breakfast.

MeadowLark Inn (802-257-4582; 1-800-616-6359; lark@together.net), Orchard Street, P.O. Box 2048. The town of Brattleboro includes some surprisingly rural corners, like this maple-walled ridge road. The large farmhouse, set in lawns, has been in Lark Eustace's family since 1958, and there is a hospitable, comfortable feel to the place. Common space includes a wraparound screen porch as well as a large living room. We prefer the old-fashioned, tastefully furnished rooms in the inn—which include three crisp, bright doubles ($95–105) and the Pine Room with a king bed, fireplace, and TV ($140)—to the two rooms in the 1870 coach house with Jacuzzi in the same room as the beds ($140). The coach house also has two more luxurious rooms with king bed, views, and refrigerator. The building has its own common space with a combination goldfish-tank/coffee-table centerpiece. Rates include a full country breakfast.

In Putney 05346

ꝏ ♿ **Hickory Ridge House** (802-387-5709; 1-800-380-9218; mail@hickoryridgehouse.com), RFD 3, Box 1410. An 1808 brick mansion, complete with Palladian window, set on 12 acres on a country road near the Connecticut River. There are six airy guest rooms in the inn and a two-bedroom cottage (two baths and full kitchen facilities, a wood-burning fireplace in the sitting room), painted in soft, authentic colors. They come with and without fireplace but all have private bath, phone, and (hidden) TV. The original Federal-era bedrooms are large, with Rumford fireplaces, and there's an upstairs sitting room. A first-floor room is handicapped-accessible. Longtime owners Jacki Walker and Steve Anderson don't mind telling you that they want to sell, but to the right people. A swimming hole lies within walking distance, and cross-country-touring trails are out the back door. $120–155 per couple; cottage is $310–350 per day.

ꝏ **Ranney-Crawford House** (802-387-4150; 1-800-731-5502), Westminster West Road. Arnie Glim, innkeeper of this 1810 brick Federal-style house on a quiet country road surrounded by fields, is an enthusiastic bicyclist who knows all the local possibilities for both touring and mountain biking. Four attractive guest rooms share two baths, and rates ($110–135) include a three-course breakfast.

Beckwood Pond (802-254-5900; 1-877-670-5900; www.beckwoodpond.com), 1107 Route 5. Alan and Helene Saxby are an Anglo-American couple who have lived on both sides of "the pond" and bring warmth and sophistication to this 1803 house. The five guest rooms are furnished with art and antiques, and the two-room suite features an intricately carved French bed from the early 1800s. All have European duvets and private bath. The 10-acre grounds include walking paths, good for cross-country skiing. $95–160 includes a three-course breakfast.

In the West River Valley

West River Lodge (802-365-7745; www.westriverlodge.com), 117 Hill Road, Newfane 05345, off Route 30. This may be the only Vermont farmhouse-turned-inn that's still dwarfed by its weathered red barn, one that hasn't been turned into "carriage house suites." Instead, since the 1930s, the inn has catered to horse lovers. Innkeepers Ellen Capito and Jim Wightman carry on the equestrian tradition (horses are boarded) but also welcome anyone who finds their way here, just a couple of miles but seemingly worlds away from Route 30. Instead of a pool, there is a swimming hole (10 feet deep with a totally private beach) on the West River. Riding lessons are still offered across the street (see *To Do—Horseback Riding*). There are eight guest rooms. $100 with private bath, $60–85, shared.

Boardman House (802-365-4086; 1-888-366-7182), village green, Townshend 05353. We like the friendly feel of this 1840s Greek Revival house tucked into a quiet (away from Route 30 traffic) corner of one of Vermont's standout commons. Sarah and Paul Messenger offer six attractive guest rooms, five with private bath. There's also a two-bedroom suite, a parlor, and an airy, old-fashioned kitchen. Breakfast usually includes fresh fruit compote and oven-warm muffins with a creative main dish. $70–75 for rooms, $110–120 for a suite.

Ranney Brook Farm (802-874-4589), Route 30, West Townshend. Set back in wooded grounds, this comfortable old house is just up the road from boating and swimming at Townshend Dam. It's an informal, relaxing place with a piano in the den, a "great room" in the rear (a 1790s barn), and a dining room in which a full breakfast is served family-style. Residents include a dog, two cats, and a parrot. The four rooms are upstairs; two have private bath. Diana Wichland is innkeeper and her husband John manages Miller Brothers-Newton, a long-established clothier in Brattleboro. $65–75 (no surcharge for foliage season).

Ascent of Nature (802-874-4424), 23 Turkey Mountain Road, Jamaica 04543. Becky and Tom Tolbert have turned this 1850s farmhouse into an informal B&B. Sited near the junction of Routes 100 and 30, it's not that far from either Stratton or Mount Snow. Turkey Mountain Road runs up alongside the property and leads up into the woods, a great place to walk. The three simply but nicely furnished rooms share one bath. The woodstove in the kitchen actually heats the kitchen and is used to prepare morning muffins. $65–75 includes full breakfast.

Rock River Bed & Breakfast (802-348-6301), 408 Dover Road, South Newfane 05301. Off the beaten path, between the West River and Mount Snow Valleys and on the edge of a small village, Chris and Nissa Petrak share their 1795 house with guests lucky enough to find them.

Two guest rooms are upstairs under the eaves and the prize room is down off the dining room, overlooking the gardens and Rock River. All rooms are furnished with family antiques and original art; the reasonable rates ($65–90) include a three-course breakfast.

In Guilford 05301

Green River Bridge House (802-257-5771), Green River. Joan Seymour has totally rehabbed a vintage-1791 house next to the covered bridge in this classic back-roads village. It's full of whimsical touches, like a former confessional as the reception window and specially designed ceilings to display her collection of crystal chandeliers. Amenities range from Jacuzzis to hair dryers. When we visited, renovations were still in progress but the three guest rooms were complete. Gardens and lawn stretch back along the river, a planned venue for weddings. $185–235 per couple includes a full breakfast.

OTHER LODGING **Latchis Hotel** (802-254-6300; fax: 802-254-6304), 50 Main Street, Brattleboro 05301. This downtown, art deco–style hotel first opened in 1939 and was resurrected after a thorough restoration. It has remained in the Latchis family throughout. Push open the door into the small but spiffy lobby, with its highly polished terrazzo marble floors. Surprises in the rooms include restored 1930s furniture, air-conditioning, and soundproof windows (a real blessing). Rooms are cheerful, brightly decorated, all with private bath, phone, fridge, and coffeemaker. The 27 rooms and three 2-room suites are accessible by elevator. The rooms to request are on the second and third floors, with views down Main Street and across to Wantastiquet Mountain. The hotel is so solidly built that you don't hear the traffic below. Some smoking rooms. For Windham Brewery and Lucca, both in the hotel, see *Where to Eat.* Rates from $75 for double rooms to $175 for suites, includes continental breakfast.

The Putney Inn (802-387-5517; 1-800-653-5517; www.putneyinn.com), Putney 05346. One of the oldest farmhouses in the area, this red-clapboard landmark was built by the first settlers. In the early 1960s, when the land was divided for construction of I-91, it was sold to local residents, who renovated the farmhouse without disturbing the posts and beams or the central open hearth. Plants and antiques add to the pleasant setting of the entry and large dining rooms. Twenty-five guest rooms occupy a motel-like wing, each with Queen Anne reproductions, bath, color TV, and phone. Pets are permitted but "must be smaller than a cow and not left alone in the rooms." The complex is set in 13 acres, with views of the river valley and mountains. Staff are helpful and friendly, and chef Ann Cooper has won many awards for her distinctly New England fare featuring local products (see *Dining Out*). At $88–158 per couple with a full breakfast, this is one of the best values around.

CAMPGROUNDS See *Green Space* for information on camping in Fort Dummer State Park, Jamaica State Park, Ball Mountain Lake, and Townshend State Park.

✷ Where to Eat

DINING OUT **T. J. Buckley's** (802-257-4922), 132 Elliot Street, Brattleboro. Open Wednesday through Sunday, 6–9. Reservations required.

RUDYARD KIPLING IN HIS STUDY AT NAULAKHA, C. 1895

RUDYARD KIPLING AND NAULAKHA

Rudyard Kipling first visited Brattleboro in the winter of 1892 and determined to build himself a house high on a hill in Dummerston (just north of the Brattleboro line), on property owned by his wife's family. The young couple then headed for Samoa to see Robert Louis Stevenson but got no farther than Yokohama, where their bank failed, taking virtually all their money. Returning to Vermont, they rented a cottage while building Naulakha; the name is a Hindi word meaning "great jewel." The shingled house is 90 feet long but only 22 feet wide, designed to resemble a ship riding the hillside like a wave. Its many windows face east, across the valley to the New Hampshire hills with a glimpse of the summit of Mount Monadnock. Just 26 years old, Kipling was already one of the world's best-known writers, and the two following years here were among the happiest in his life. Here he wrote the *Jungle Books.* Here the local doctor, James Conland, a former fisherman, inspired him to write *Captains Courageous* and also delivered his two daughters. Kipling's guests included Sir Arthur Conan Doyle, who brought with him a pair of Nordic skis, said to be the first in Vermont. Unfortunately, in 1896 a highly publicized falling-out with his dissolute brother-in-law drove the family back to England. They took relatively few belongings from Naulakha and neither did the property's two subsequent owners, who used it as a summerhouse. Happily, in 1992 it was acquired by Britain's Landmark Trust, which gutted, rewired, repaired, and replumbed it (a new septic system was required) but otherwise preserved every detail of the home as Rudyard and Carrie Kipling knew it. Though the house is not available for functions and rarely for tours, it can be rented for $1,200–2,600 per week and, depending on the season, for a few days at a time. There are four bedrooms (three baths). Some 60 percent of the present furnishings are original, including a third-floor pool table. A game of tennis, anyone, on the Kipling court? Or how about curling up with the *Jungle Books* on a sofa by the fire, only a few feet from where they were written? Or steeping in Kipling's own deep tub? For details about renting Naulakha contact The Landmark Trust USA (802-254-6868), c/o 707 Kipling Road, Dummerston 05301. *Rudyard Kipling in Vermont: "Birthplace of the* Jungle Books*"* by Stuart Murray (Images from the Past) offers an excellent descrption of Kipling's relation to and portrayal of the area.

FROM THE ORIGINAL ARCHITECTURAL DRAWING OF NAULAKHA, WHERE RUDYARD KIPLING LIVED 1893–96

From the outside this small but classic red-and-black 1920s Worcester diner looks unpromising, even battered. Inside, fresh flowers and mismatched settings (gathered from yard sales) brighten the tables, walls are oak paneled, and chef-owner Michael Fuller prepares the night's fish, chicken, and beef (vegetarian is also possible) in the open kitchen behind the counter. Fuller buys all produce locally and what's offered depends on what's available: On a July day the menu included bluefin tuna with roasted lobster stock, carrots, celery, fresh horseradish root, served with a risotto with a ginger/pheasant stock; and a chicken breast with white truffle and goat Fontina, served with flageolet beans (white) with fresh artichoke and julienned Romano beans. The $25 entrée includes salad; appetizer and dessert are extra. The wine list ranges from $20 to $60. No credit cards.

Peter Haven's (802-257-3333), 32 Elliot Street, Brattleboro. Open from 6 PM Tuesday through Saturday. Just 10 tables in this nifty restaurant decorated with splashy artwork, and with an inspired menu to match. The evening's entrées might include pasta del mar (a nest of linguine with a creamy pesto sauce topped with shrimp, scallops, and artichoke hearts), chicken in an Oriental sauce, and roasted boneless duck breast with a black currant and port sauce. Entrées $16.50–22.

The Four Columns Inn (802-365-7713), Route 30, Newfane. Serving 6–9 nightly except Thursday; Sunday brunch 11–2; reservations suggested. Chef Greg Parks has earned top ratings for his efforts, served in a converted barn with a large brick fireplace as its centerpiece. The emphasis is on herbs (homegrown), stocks made from scratch, and locally raised lamb and trout (the latter from the adjacent pond). While the menu changes frequently, it might include seared venison loin with a spiced Zinfadel glaze and sun-dried cherries, crispy free-range baby chicken with a porcini essence sauce, and grilled Black Angus with portobello mushrooms and a sweet-and-sour dipping sauce. Entrées $22–29.

Three Mountain Inn (802-874-4140), Route 30, Jamaica. Dinner by reservation only. While enjoying a candlelit dinner in front of the fireplaces in the two small dining rooms of this 18th-century village house, it's easy to imagine that you're in a colonial tavern. The frequently changing menus might include veal scaloppine with a champagne sauce and pan-roasted Maine scallops served with angelhair pasta and spicy peanut sauce. Entrées are $25–35. Save room for such desserts as Grand Marnier and white chocolate mousse.

✐ **The Putney Inn** (802-387-5517; 1-800-653-5517), just off I-91, exit 4, in Putney. Open for all three meals. An 18th-century house is now a popular restaurant, and executive chef Ann Cooper has won numerous awards and national acclaim for pastries and sauces. The dinner menu features classic New England dishes like roast breast of turkey with maple pecan stuffing, Vermont lamb with a rosemary Merlot sauce, and a native venison sampler with sweet potato pancakes and wild mushroom sauce. Traditional favorites include reasonably priced options like turkey and vegetable potpie in a bread bowl and Frank's Favorite Meat Loaf with three-onion sauce. Entrées $17.50–22.50.

Old Newfane Inn (802-365-4427), Route 30, Newfane Village. Open for dinner nightly except Monday. Reservations requested. The low-beamed old dining room is country formal. Chef-owner Eric Weindl is widely known for his Swiss-accented Continental menu with entrée choices like roast duckling au Cointreau à l'orange or rack of lamb for one ($14.95–26).

Windham Hill Inn (802-874-4080; 1-800-944-4080), West Townshend. This exceptionally attractive dining room overlooking a pond is open to the public by reservation. You could opt for the four-course prix fixe dinner for $45 or order à la carte: Dinner might begin with a crispy Asian noodle cake ($7) and include pan-seared American red snapper with black pepper tagliatelle and citrus-basil butter ($24).

Letamaya Restaurant (802-254-2352), 51 Main Street, Brattleboro. Open Tuesday through Saturday for lunch and dinner. Chef Hiroshi Hayashi, well known in southern New Hampshire for his Latacarta in Peterborough, has opened this small storefront restaurant featuring an "epicurean collage" of dishes, all prepared from scratch and using local ingredients. Appetizers include antipasto and nori rolls, and entrées ($16–22) range from Vermont country chicken simmered in wine, sour cream, and mustard sauce to pan-fried udon with herb ginger sauce. Organic wines and beers are served.

Lucca (802-254-4747), 6 Flat Street, Brattleboro. Open for dinner Wednesday through Sunday. Abel Anaya-Lucca hails from Ponce, Puerto Rico, but the large menu in this cheerful new bistro reflects many accents, most notably French. Dishes are so varied that everyone at a table tends to order something different and then sample. Servings are more than generous. Choices might range from eggplant layered with fire-roasted red peppers, red onions, portobello mushrooms, basil, fresh mozzarella, and sauce Provençal to filet mignon with a petit ragout of fresh chanterelles in a savory tart, smoked bacon whipped potatoes, and sauce bourguignon. Entrées $12–26. "Brasserie Fare" in the attractive bar includes escargots and burgers.

✷ Eating Out

In Brattleboro

Common Ground (802-257-0855), 25 Elliot Street. Open weekends for lunch, dinner, and Sunday brunch; other days and hours vary. Founded in 1971, this collective-run throwback has recently been revitalized. Dining rooms fill the high-ceilinged second floor of an old industrial building. Each month a new menu is printed showing the specialties, which run the gamut from Russian vegetable pie to lasagna and spanakopita. Beverages range from banana yogurt shakes through beer and wine. A bar/counter serves solo diners, but strangers routinely sit down at the same table and converse. Live entertainment Friday and Saturday night; anything goes.

Shin La Restaurant (802-257-5226), 57–61 Main Street. Open 11–9, closed Sunday. An attractive Korean restaurant known for homemade soups, dumplings, and other Korean fare. Recently expanded, it now includes a sushi bar in the adjacent storefront.

Riverview Cafe (802-254-9841), 36 Bridge Street. Open for all three meals, Tuesday through Sunday except winter when it's closed

Wednesday too. The best view in town, now under new ownership with chef Tristam Toleno, a graduate of Wesleyan and the New England Culinary Institute who worked in New York before returning to his native area. He has transformed this tired old place into an appealing space (with seasonal deck dining), and the moderately priced menu includes interesting soups and salads, and entrées like applewood-smoked spicy pork spareribs. Our one complaint about a Caesar's salad with free-range chicken was its size, not a lot for $8.25. We will, however, be back.

The Marina Restaurant (802-257-7563), Route 5, just north of the West River bridge. Open daily April through mid-October, less frequently off-season. Situated at the confluence of the West and Connecticut Rivers, the place has a great view and maximizes it, with a screen porch and patio as well as a recently expanded deck, and in winter there's fireside dining. The reasonably priced menu includes plenty of seafood and vegetarian choices, both at lunch and dinner, but also burgers. Full liquor license. A great place enjoy a margarita while watching the sunset.

Amy's Bakery Arts Café (802-251-1071), 113 Main Street. There are river views from tables in the back of this attractive storefront café, and the food is appealing too: spinach and cheese croissants, salads, and sandwiches, some with meat but plenty without.

Brattleboro Farmer's Market. If you happen into town around noon on a sunny Wednesday or Saturday, head for the farmers' market. On Wednesday it's downtown off Main Street by the Merchants Bank Building (look for the parking lot right there) with food vendors next to a small park overlooking the river. On Saturday it's just west of town by the Creamery Bridge. A live band and crafts, as well as produce vendors, are usually on hand.

Linda's Place (802-254-2713), 2 Main Street, across from the co-op. Open for breakfast and lunch. Located in the old brick Abbott Block, a small, pleasant café with good food and a surprisingly nice view down over the iron bridge.

Cafe Beyond (802-258-4900), 29 High Street. Open for breakfast and lunch. Back of the bookstore (see *Selective Shopping—Bookstores*), a café with delightful decor, a blackboard menu featuring panini, roll-ups, soups, and salads. Beverages range from espresso to microbrews. Works of local artists on display.

Walker's Restaurant (802-254-6046), 132 Main Street. Open for lunch and dinner until at least 10:30. Closed Sunday except during foliage and ski seasons. A reliable downtown waystop: a spacious dining room with brick walls, oak tables and full bar, soft lighting. For lunch a choice of burgers, soups, quiches, and sandwiches. The dinner menu includes the usual basics and and not-so-basics like mustard-herbed baked chicken. Inquire about live music. Children's menu.

Top of the Hill Grill (802-258-9178), 632 Putney Road. Open April to mid-November for lunch and dinner. You have to be looking for this unusual BBQ place. It comes up fast after the bridge, heading north on Route 5 out of town. You order, get a card, and then sit at a picnic table or in the weatherproofed outdoor dining space (with rest rooms) until your card is called (I was Queen of Hearts). The specialties are apple-smoked chicken and hickory-smoked pulled pork and ribs but you can also get a tempeh burger, roll-up, salad, or hot dog.

Gillies Seafood Restaurant and Raw Bar (802-257-9900), 209 Canal Street. Open Tuesday through Saturday 11–9, Sunday 3–9. Whoever the fish buyer is here, he's good. The specialty is Atlantic seafood. Try the crabcakes and chowder.

Back Side Cafe (802-257-5056), Green Street Extension. Open weekdays for breakfast, lunch, and dinner; Sunday brunch. A comfortable café featuring soups, salads, and Mexican specialties. Liquor license.

In Putney

Curtis' Barbeque (802-387-5474). Summer through fall, Wednesday through Sunday 10–dusk. Follow your nose to the blue school bus parked on Route 5 in Putney, just off I-91, exit 4. Curtis Tuff cooks up pork ribs and chicken, seasoned with his secret barbecue sauce, also foil-wrapped potatoes, grilled corn, and beans flavored with Vermont maple syrup. By far the best barbecue in the Northeast!

Putney Diner (802-387-5433), Main Street. Open 6 AM–9 PM daily. Another pleasant option in the middle of Putney Village, open for all three meals. Good for Belgian waffles, Philly cheese steak, and homemade vegetable lasagna. Pastries made daily.

Along Route 30

Townshend Country Inn (802-365-4141), Route 30, Townshend. Open daily year-round except Wednesday for dinner, also May through October for a Sunday buffet brunch. Said to have been a summer home for Grandma Moses, this pleasant restaurant specializes in roast Vermont turkey and offers a full menu at reasonable prices. Check out the Sunday buffet.

The Townshend Dam Diner (802-874-4107), Route 30, 2 miles north of the Townshend Dam. Open 5 AM–8 PM. Breakfast all day. Homemade French toast, homefries, muffins and biscuits, the "best dam chili," soups, and bison burgers (from the nearby East Hill Bison Farm), dinner staples like roast turkey, spaghetti, and garlic bread, daily specials.

Route 9 West

♿ **Jolly Butcher** (802-254-6043), West Brattleboro. Open daily for lunch and dinner. A popular steak house with an extensive salad and a good martini. Children's menu.

Ziter's Putney Inn Market & Deli (802-257-4994), 201½ Western Avenue (Route 9), West Brattleboro. Open Monday through Saturday 7–6, Sunday 8–6. A deli and café featuring the pastries and specialties from the Putney Inn kitchen.

Chelsea Royal Diner (802-254-8399), Route 9, West Brattleboro. Open 6 AM–9 PM. A genuine '30s diner that's been moved a few miles west of its original site (it's a mile west of I-91, exit 2). Plenty of parking and diner decor, serving breakfast all day as part of a big menu, also plenty of daily specials.

BREWS **Mocha Joe's** (802-257-7794), 82 Main Street, Brattleboro. Coffee is taken seriously here, roasted as well as brewed. Live music on weekends.

Coffee Country (802-257-0032), on the Harmony parking lot, Brattleboro. Good coffee, good food.

See also Cafe Beyond under *Eating Out*.

ICE CREAM ✐ **Page's Ice Cream** (802-254-3826), Route 9, West Brattleboro. Easy to miss in the strip (beside the Jolly Butcher), this yellow-clapboard ice cream stand has been a landmark for more than 50 years. Its ice cream is said to be lower in saturated fats and calories than commercial brands but that's not the point. It tastes good. We haven't tried all 14 flavors but can recommend the fresh peach, black raspberry, and sweet cream.

Windham Brewery (802-254-4747), in the Latchis Hotel. There's a pub menu to go with the ales, porters, and lagers on tap that are made on the spot.

McNeill's Brewery (802-254-2553), 90 Elliot Street, Brattleboro. Gold-medal-winning brew on tap. Games, food.

Twilight Tea Lounge (802-254-8887) Around the corner, under 51 Main Street, Brattleboro. Open Wednesday through Sunday, noon to varying hours. A barbershop for 75 years, this pleasant space is filled with mismatched tables and chairs and the aroma of rare teas. A cooperative, run by five young women, the venue for Thursday-night poetry and music.

Putney Mountain Winery (802-387-4610), at Scott Farm, Rudyard Kipling Road, Dummerston. Music professor and composer Charles Dodge has established a sensational reputation for the quality of his sparkling apple wines. Tastings are offered on weekends at Basketville (see *Selective Shopping*) in Putney and increasingly in the licensed tasting room at Scott Farm.

✷ Entertainment

ARTS CENTER **Hooker-Dunham Arts Center** (802-254-9276), 139 Main Street, Brattleboro. Call and check out what's going on at this middle-of-town venue. Offerings include theater, music, film, and lectures, and there's always a gallery show.

MUSIC **Yellow Barn Music Festival** (802-387-6637; 1-800-639-3819), Putney. Begun in 1969, this is a series of 25 chamber music concerts in July and early August. Performances are in a 150-seat barn located behind the public library in Putney Village. Artists include both well-known professionals and students from leading conservatories.

Brattleboro Music Center (802-257-4523), 15 Walnut Street, Brattleboro. Housed in a former convent, this burgeoning music school sponsors a wide variety of local musical events and festivals, including a Spring Festival of oratorios and pageants such as a

THE LATCHIS HOTEL, AN ART DECO LANDMARK, IS THE HOME OF THE LATCHIS THEATER

Kim Grant

winter/spring Chamber Music Series. Periodic concerts are presented by the Windham Orchestra and by the Community Chorus in area churches, and, most notably, the New England Bach Festival. The festival, a series of more than a dozen October concerts and lectures, has been held since 1969 in area churches and chapels, featuring choral performances conducted by the Swiss-born Blanche Moyse (founder of the Music Center in 1951). It's reviewed and celebrated as one of the Northeast's major annual events.

Friends of Music at Guilford (802-257-1961; 802-257-1028), Guilford. A series of concerts throughout the year at various locations. Note the free Labor Day weekend concerts under *Special Events.*

Vermont Jazz Center (802-254-9088), 72 Cotton Mill Hill, Studio 222, South Main Street, Brattleboro, stages frequent musical, vocal, and jazz happenings.

Also see the Marlboro Music Festival in "Mountain Snow/Wilmington Area."

THEATER **Whittemore Theater** at Marlboro College (802-257-4333) is the setting for frequent presentations.

Sandglass Theater (802-387-4051), Kimball Hill, Putney. October through Christmas and April and May, frequent summer performances in a variety of local venues. Based in a barn in Putney Village, the resident theater company performs original work combining live theater with puppetry. Also hosts guest performers.

MUSIC VENUES **Mole's Eye Café** (802-257-0771), corner of Main and High Streets, Brattleboro. A popular local hangout serving soups, chili, and sandwiches all day, with a full bar and frequent live and lively music until 1 AM.

Common Ground (802-257-0855), 25 Elliot Street. Live music Friday and Saturday night. See *Eating Out.*

Walker's Restaurant (802-254-6046) features jazz Thursday night. See *Eating Out.*

Gallery Walk. The first Friday of each month features music in Brattleboro's galleries.

Note: Check the *Brattleboro Reformer*'s Thursday listings of live music and entertainment at other area restaurants and cafés.

FILM The **Latchis Theater,** Main Street, Brattleboro, shows first-run films. For film buffs, this 900-seat movie house is itself a destination. Apollo still drives his chariot through the firmament on the ceiling; walls are graced with Doric columns, and the lobby floor bears the zodiac signs in multicolored terrazzo.

Kipling Cinemas (at Fairfield Plaza, Route 5 north of Brattleboro), a multiplex, also shows first-run films.

✷ Selective Shopping

ANTIQUES

In Brattleboro

Twice Upon a Time (802-254-2261), 63 Main Street. Open Monday through Saturday 10–6, Friday until 8, Sunday noon–5. "I always wanted a consignment shop that would be able to display anything that anyone wanted to give me," says Randi Crouse, proprietor of this truly amazing shop that now fills the entire three-level space created in 1906 for the E. J. Fenton Department Store. In the '50s it was chopped into smaller storefronts, but the two-story-high Corinthian columns, bubble glass, and wooden gallery are back, a setting for clothing, antique furniture, and furnishings. The markdown schedule is patterned on that of Filene's Basement. More than 100 dealers and a total of 4,000 consignors are represented. If there's something special you are looking for, chances are Crouse can find it.

Le Tagge Sale (802-254-9224), at the Marina Restaurant, Putney Road (Route 5 north). Open 10–5 Monday through Saturday. Down by the West River, a classic '50s roller-skating rink with a giant reflecting ball and music to match is filled with antiques, furniture, books, and art.

Along Route 30

More than two dozen dealers are found along this route. Pick up a copy of their pamphlet guide at the first place you stop. They include:

Newfane Flea Market (802-365-4000), just north of Newfane Village. Sunday, May through October. Billed as the largest open-air market in the state; usually 100 tables with assorted junk and treasure.

Jack Winner Antiques (802-365-7215; www.winnerantiques.com), Newfane. Specializing for over 30 years in 18th- and 19th-century formal and country furniture, equestrian antiques, and hunting prints.

Auntie M's Attic (802-365-9796), Route 30, south of Newfane Village. Open May through October, Thursday through Monday. A nice selection of antique china, furniture, glass, lamps, linens, and prints.

Nu-tique (802-365-7677), Newfane Village. Open May to October and by appointment. Books, including New England histories, poetry, military, children's; also old lamps, glass, sheet music, records.

Kim Grant

Riverdale Antiques (802-365-4616), Route 30, Harmonyville (between Newfane and Townshend). Open daily year-round, 10–5. More than 60 dealers selling quality antiques and collectibles.

Townshend Auction Gallery (802-365-4388), Route 30, Townshend. Over 30 years Kit Martin and Art Monette have established a solid reputation for their frequent auctions.

Old Corker's Antiques (802-874-4172; www.Oldcorkersantiques.com), Route 30, Jamaica. Open May through October, most days 10–5. Skip Woodruff specializes in antique fishing equipment and books, also snowshoes and the rustic furniture he makes himself. A great stop!

ART GALLERIES *Note:* The first Friday of each month is Gallery Walk in Brattleboro: open house with refreshments and music at downtown businesses that hang works by local artists and at studios as well as at formal galleries, usually 5–7.

Windham Art Gallery (802-257-1881), 69 Main Street, Brattleboro, showcases work by 50 members of an artists' cooperative. It's also the place to pick up a copy of the Arts Council of Windham County quarterly publication *Arts in the Season,* which lists current theater, poetry readings, and gallery shows throughout southeastern Vermont.

Artist's Loft Gallery (phone/fax: 802-257-5181), 103 Main Street, Brattleboro. Realistic landscapes of Brattleboro and Vermont are William Hays's forte.

The Art Building, 127 Main Street, Brattleboro, houses a dozen studios, open irregularly and for Gallery Walk. Visitors are welcome to stroll up any day and see whose door is open. The **River Gallery School** (802-257-1577) offers frequent classes and workshops here.

Tyler Gallery (802-257-4333), Rice Library, Marlboro College. Changing exhibits.

Elaine Beckwith Gallery (802-874-7234), Route 30/100, Jamaica Village. Open daily except Tuesday. Some 30 artists in a variety of styles and media are represented.

Sackett's Brook Gallery (802-387-8776), Putney Village. Open Thursday through Sunday, just up from the Putney General Store. Changing exhibits feature local artists.

See also Brattleboro Museum and Art Center (under *To See*), Hooker-Dunham Arts Center (under *Entertainment*), Vermont Artisan Designs (under *Crafts Shops*), Cafe Beyond (under *Bookstores*).

BOOKSTORES **The Book Cellar** (802-254-6026), 120 Main Street, Brattleboro. An outstanding, long-established, full-service bookstore, particularly strong on Vermont and New England titles.

Everyone's Books (802-254-8160), 23 Elliot Street, Brattleboro. This is an earnest and interesting alternative bookstore, specializing in women's books; also a great selection of children's and multicultural titles.

Collected Works Books & The Cafe Beyond (802-258-4900), 29 High Street, Brattleboro. An attractive, full-service bookstore with rooms that ramble on and back into the café (see *Eating Out*). Not a bad place to spend a rainy day.

Old & New England Books (802-

365-7074), West Street, Newfane. Open May to October. A delightful browsing place with an interesting stock of books old and new.

Brattleboro Books (802-257-0177), 34 Elliot Street. Open 9:30–6 daily except Sunday. An extensive selection of used and out-of-print books; has recently expanded into the adjoining storefront. Browsing encouraged.

Paperback Palace (802-258-4980), 48 Harmony Place (alias Basket's Bookstore), is a trove of used paperbacks.

Hearthstone Books (802-387-2100), at the junction of Route 5 and West Hill Road in Putney. Housed in the restored old tavern at the center of Putney Village, a full-service bookstore that invites browsing, with a frequently working hearth in the adjacent café.

CRAFTS SHOPS **Vermont Artisan Designs** (802-257-7044), 106 Main Street, Brattleboro. Open daily. Ever-expanding to fill three floors of a former department store, southern Vermont's outstanding contemporary crafts gallery displays the work of 300 artisans. Melange, a collection of interesting small shops, and Kitchen Sync, a culinary boutique, are part of this complex.

Green Mountain Spinnery (802-387-4528; www.spinnery.com), just off I-91, exit 4. Open Monday through Friday 9–5:30, Saturday 10–5:30. Labor Day through Thanksgiving, also Sunday noon–4. Founded as a cooperative more than 20 years ago, this is a real spinning mill in which undyed, unbleached wool from local flocks is sorted, scoured, picked, carded, spun, skeined, and labeled. You can buy the resulting yarn in various plies in natural and dyed colors. Knit-kits, patterns, buttons, and blankets are also sold and custom spinning is a specialty.

In Putney

Putney Clayschool (802-387-4395), Kimball Hill, open 10–5 daily except Thursday. A variety of functional stoneware and earthenware made, displayed, and sold.

Richard Bissell Fine Woodworking (802-387-4416), Signal Pine Road. Open Monday through Friday 8–5. Exceptional Shaker-inspired furniture, cabinetry, Windsor chairs.

Joshua Gold Pottery (802-387-2116), Westminster West Road, 3.7 miles north of Putney Village. Open July to January 1, Friday through Sunday 11–4 and by appointment. Fine, seemingly simple, functional, and sculptural pottery pieces noteworthy for the sophistication of their shapes and glazes. Worth a detour.

Brandywine Glassworks (802-387-4032), Fort Hill Road. Robert Burch hand-blows glass in his studio (call to see what he's doing); seconds of distinctive paperweights and other likely gifts are sold.

Note: On the weekend after Thanksgiving, Putney's two dozen artisans open their studios to visitors. Check out the **Putney Craft Tour and Sale** at www.putneycrafts.com.

Along Route 9

Lucy S. Gratwick Fine Handweaving (802-257-0181). Call for directions and hours: a colorful range of apparel and other items in cotton, silk, and wood.

Along Route 30
Taft Hill (802-865-4200), Harmonyville (Townshend). Open daily 11–5. Gifts and furnishings, featuring fine hand-painted glass and china created here at Crest Studio.

American Country Designs (802-874-4222), Jamaica Village. Open daily 9–5:30 except Tuesday. Local potter Susan Leader's bright, irresistible plates, vases, and pots with cheerful designs are the specialty here; also personalized wedding plates and a nice selection of crafts.

FACTORY OUTLETS **Townshend Furniture** (802-365-7720). Route 30, Townshend. Open weekdays 10–4, weekends until 5. Handcrafted, sturdy, attractive furniture made on the premises is sold at discount. Cherry Shaker and country pine are specialties.

Big Black Bear Shop at Mary Meyer (802-365-4160; 1-888-758-BEAR; www.bigblackbear.com), Route 30, Townshend, west of the village. Open daily. The original location of Vermont's oldest and largest stuffed-toy company. More than 500 designs, 20–70 percent off.

The Outlet Center (802-254-4594), Canal Street, Brattleboro; exit 1 off I-91. Open daily 9:30–8 except Sunday, 10–6. This former factory building that once produced handbags is an old-fashioned factory outlet center with 15 varied stores, worth checking.

SPECIAL SHOPS

In Brattleboro
Delectable Mountain (802-257-4456), 125 Main Street. Fine-fabric lovers make pilgrimages to Jan Norris's store, widely known for its selection of fine silks, all-natural imported laces, velvets, cottons, and upholstery jacquards. It's also offers a wide selection of unusual buttons.

Sam's Army and Navy Dept. Store (802-254-2933), 74 Main Street, Brattleboro. Open 8–6, until 9 on Friday, closed Sunday. The business that Sam Borofsky started in 1934 now fills two floors of two buildings with a full stock of hunting, camping, and sports equipment. Prices are reasonable, but people don't shop here for bargains. The big thing is the service—skilled help in selecting the right fishing rod, tennis racket, or gun. There are also name-brand sports clothes and standard army and navy gear. On the first day of deer hunting season (early November), the store opens at dawn and serves a hunter's breakfast (it also sells licenses). *Tip:* There's free popcorn every day, all day.

Brattleboro Food Co-op (802-257-0236), 2 Main Street. Open Monday through Saturday 9–9, Sunday 9–8; deli and fresh baked products. The cheese counter could just be the best showcase for Vermont cheese in the state; cheese from around the world also knowledgeably selected and presented (note the "cheese of the week"), also local produce, grains, wines, and a café.

Adavasi Imports (802-258-2231), 8 Flat Street. Shram and Elissa Bhanti keep prices low because they are also wholesalers, traveling to northwest India to buy their fabrics: linens and clothing hand-blocked with natural vegetable dyes; silk saris for $25;

cotton rugs; and wide variety of crafted items and jewelry. It's an exotic, fragrant emporium that keeps expanding.

Tom & Sally's Handmade Chocolates (802-254-4200), 55 Elliot Street. Locally made and worth a taste.

A Candle in the Night (802-257-0471), 181 Main Street. Donna and Larry Simons have built up a vast knowledge as well as inventory of Oriental and other handcrafted rugs over the decades.

Beadnicks (802-257-5114), 115 Main Street. Beads, baubles, whimsical wonders.

Borter's Jewelry Studio (802-254-3452). Gemstones; silver and gold jewelry handcrafted on the premises.

In Putney

Basketville (802-387-5509), Route 5. Open daily 8 AM–9 PM in busy seasons, 8–5 in slack seasons. The first of "The World's Largest Basket Stores" now scattered along the East Coast, it is also one of the oldest crafts producers in the state. Founded by Frank Wilson, an enterprising Yankee trader in the real sense, this is a family-run business. The vast store features woodenware, wicker furniture (filling the entire upstairs), wooden toys, and exquisite artificial flowers as well as traditional baskets and myriad other things, large and small. *Note*: Check out the Columbus Day weekend Basketville Seconds Sale.

Silver Forest of Vermont (802-387-4149), in the center of the village. A store worth checking out.

Offerings (802-387-2529), Kimball Hill. Open daily. A wide assortment of imported jewelry, much of it reasonably priced.

Along Route 30

Newfane Country Store (802-365-7916), Newfane. Quilts, Vermont cheese and maple syrup, plus toys and Christmas ornaments. The quilts and other quilted things are truly outstanding.

Lawrence's Smoke House (802-365-7751), Newfane. Corncob-smoked hams, bacon, poultry, fish, meats, and cheese are the specialties of the house. Catalog and mail order.

Jamaica Country Store (802-874-9151), Jamaica Village. Just a real country store, selling cheese, syrup, and souvenirs along with everything else.

✷ Special Events

February: **Brattleboro Winter Carnival.** Many events in Living Memorial Park (see *Green Space*); a full week of celebrations, climaxed by the Washington's Birthday cross-country-ski race.

Late June: Dummerston Center **Annual Strawberry Supper,** Grange Hall, Dummerston.

May through October: The **Brattleboro Area Farmer's Market,** Saturday on Route 9 at the Creamery Covered Bridge and Wednesday downtown. **Memorial Day Dawn Dance,** 8 PM–7 AM in Brattleboro.

July and August: **Yellow Barn Music Festival** in Putney (see *Entertainment—Music*).

July 4: A big **parade** winds through Brattleboro at 10 AM; games, exhibits, refreshments in Living Memorial Park (see *Green Space*); **fireworks** at 9 PM.

Late July (last Saturday): Annual **sale and supper** sponsored by the Ladies

Benevolent Society of Brookline; an old-fashioned affair with quality crafts. *Last weekend:* Events in Brattleboro both days climaxed by the **Riff Raff Regatta** Sunday, a raft competition off the Marina Restaurant at the confluence of the West and Connecticut Rivers.

First Saturday in August: **Grace Cottage Hospital Fair Day:** exhibits, booths, games, rides on the green in Townshend. Free concert series on Newfane common.

September: **Labor Day Dawn Dance,** 8 PM–7 AM, Brattleboro. Labor Day weekend in Guilford is observed both with the old-style **Guilford Fair** and with the annual 2-day music festival in **Guilford's Organ Barn** (802-257-1961). Concerts are free. **White Water on the West River,** Jamaica State Park; see *To Do—Boating.* **Heritage Festival Benefit** in Newfane, sponsored by the Newfane Congregational Church. **Putney Artisans Festival,** Putney Town Hall. *Last weekend:* **Apple Days** in downtown Brattleboro.

October: **Newfane Heritage Fair** on Columbus Day: crafts, dancing, raffle, sponsored by the Newfane Congregational Church.

Mid-October: The **Apple Pie Festival** in Dummerston features hundreds of Dummerston's famous apple pies, also crafts, at the Dummerston Center Congregational Church and Grange. **New England Bach Festival,** a series of major concerts in area churches sponsored by the Brattleboro Music Center (802-257-4523; see *Entertainment—Music*). The annual **Pumpkin Festival** on Townshend common features biggest-pumpkin and best-pumpkin-pie contests, plenty of vendors, food.

Weekend after Thanksgiving: **Putney Craft Tour**—some two dozen local studios open to the public, geared to Christmas shopping.

Early December: **Christmas Bazaar** on the common, Newfane.

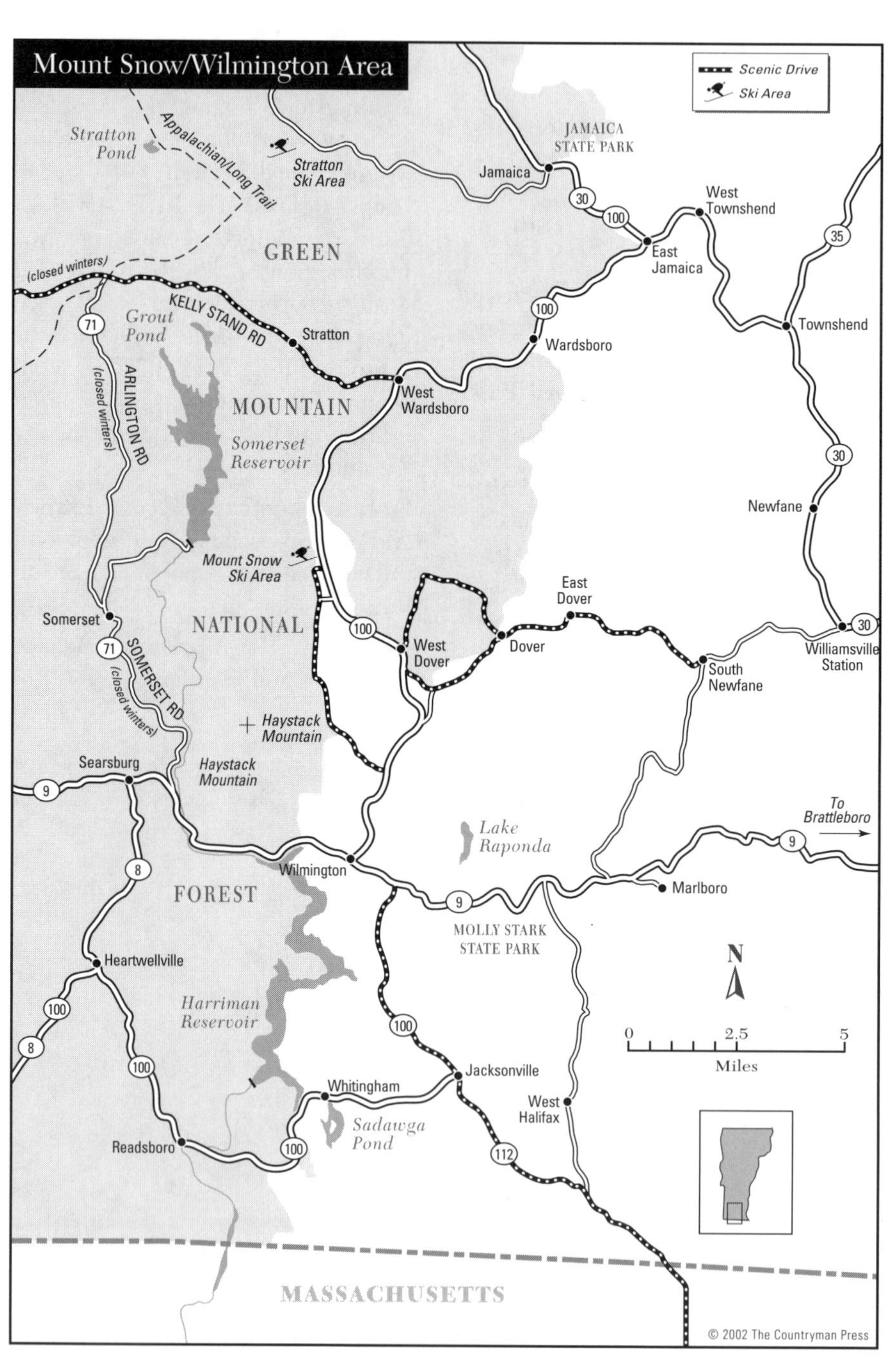
Mount Snow/Wilmington Area
Scenic Drive
Ski Area
Stratton Pond
Appalachian/Long Trail
Stratton Ski Area
JAMAICA STATE PARK
Jamaica
West Townshend
East Jamaica
GREEN
MOUNTAIN
NATIONAL
FOREST
(closed winters)
KELLY STAND RD
Grout Pond
Stratton
Wardsboro
Townshend
West Wardsboro
ARLINGTON RD
Somerset Reservoir
Newfane
Mount Snow Ski Area
East Dover
Somerset
Dover
West Dover
Williamsville Station
South Newfane
SOMERSET RD
Haystack Mountain
Searsburg
To Brattleboro
Lake Raponda
Wilmington
Marlboro
MOLLY STARK STATE PARK
Heartwellville
Harriman Reservoir
Miles
Jacksonville
Whitingham
West Halifax
Sadawga Pond
Readsboro
MASSACHUSETTS
© 2002 The Countryman Press

MOUNT SNOW/ WILMINGTON AREA

Mount Snow made its splashy debut as a ski destination in 1954. Reuben Snow's farm was transformed by ski lifts and trails, lodges, a skating rink, and an immense, floodlit geyser. Ski lodges mushroomed for miles around, varying in style from Tyrolean to '50s futuristic. By the early '70s, bust had followed boom, and the ski area was absorbed by one company after another. Acquired in 1994 by the American Ski Company, Mount Snow now incorporates Haystack, a long-established ski area in its own right, a few miles down the valley. Both have standout golf courses.

West Dover is a picturesque lineup of church, inn, and town offices, but much of the 9 miles of Route 100 between Wilmington and Mount Snow is a visual history of the ups and downs of the ski industry since the late '50s. Look closely, however, and you will find plenty to please. Perhaps because the valley's visitors come overwhelmingly from the New York City area, a number of inns and restaurants are several cuts above average. Beyond this narrow corridor, mountains rise on all sides. The village of Dover is a knot of white-clapboard buildings on the crest of a hill, a few miles east but palpably far farther away. Forest surrounds Route 100 north to the classic village of Wardsboro, south to the delightfully back-roaded towns of Jacksonville and Whitingham, and east to the college town of Marlboro, site of the world-class Marlboro Music Festival in July and August.

Although the surrounding hills were once lumbered extensively, they are now hauntingly empty. Two former logging villages actually lie at the bottom of sizable Harriman and Somerset Reservoirs, which have transformed the Deerfield Valley into one of the wateriest parts of Vermont, good for fishing, walking, boating, and swimming.

GUIDANCE **Southern Vermont Regional Marketing Organization** (1-877-887-2378; www.southernvermont.com) maintains a good web site and is a source of printed area information.

Mount Snow Valley Chamber of Commerce (802-464-8092; 1-877-887-6884; www.visitvermont.com) maintains a major Vermont Information Center on West Main Street in Wilmington (Route 9 west, seven doors from the junction of Routes 9 and 100). Pick up the useful *Mount Snow Valley Visitor's Guide.* The *Deerfield Valley News,* a local weekly, is a good source for current events.

GREEN MOUNTAIN HALL IN WHITINGHAM

Christina Tree

GETTING THERE The obvious route to Mount Snow from points south and east is I-91 to Brattleboro, then Route 9 to Wilmington. There are also two scenic shortcuts: (1) Route 30 north from Brattleboro 11.1 miles to the marked turnoff for Dover; follow the road through the covered bridge in South Newfane past Dover to West Dover; (2) turn off I-91 onto Route 2 in Greenfield, Massachusetts; follow Route 2 for 3.6 miles to Colrain Road (turn at Duck Pond Tavern) and proceed 17.3 miles to Jacksonville, where you pick up Route 100 into Wilmington. *From New York City:* **Edventures Bus Service** (802-464-2810; 212-921-9161).

GETTING AROUND **The MOO-ver** (802-464-8487) is a free community bus service operated by the Deerfield Valley Transit Association (DVTA). It connects points of interest in the valley, along Route 100 from the Deerfield Valley Health Center in Wilmington, picking up passengers at DVTA stops 7 AM–10 PM. Look for its Holstein cow logo.

WHEN TO GO High season is Christmas through February; in March snow is less dependable there than in other parts of the state. Golfers arrive in June, and in July and August both Art on the Mountain at Haystack and the Marlboro Music Festival draw a cultured crowd. Summer is, however, very low-key. Foliage usually fills every inn and restaurant during October's first three weekends.

MEDICAL EMERGENCY **911** now does it all.

✷ To See

SCENIC DRIVES **East along the Molly Stark Trail.** Wilmington is midway between Bennington (21 miles) and Brattleboro (20 miles) on Route 9, which is dedicated to the wife of Gen. John Stark, hero of the battle of Bennington. Five miles east of Wilmington you come to Hogback Mountain. Formerly a ski area, this is now a major overlook, said to offer a 100-mile view (weather dependent) facing south. This is also the site of the **Southern Vermont Natural History Museum** (802-464-0048; open Memorial Day through late October, 10–5). Larger than it looks from the outside, it displays mounted specimens of more than 500 New England birds and mammals in 80 dioramas, the collection of taxidermist Luman R. Nelson. When we visited live exhibits included two hawks and four hoot owls.

Marlboro. Continue along the Molly Stark Trail east some 5 miles to the turnoff to Marlboro Village, home of Marlboro College. From mid-July until mid-August its campus is the venue for the **Marlboro Music Festival** (see *Entertainment*). The **Marlboro Historical Society** (802-464-0329), with its collection of pictures, old farm tools, and antique furniture, is housed in the Newton House and the 1813 one-room schoolhouse on Main Street is open in July and August, Sunday 2–5. See *Selective Shopping* for the studios of notable Marlboro craftspeople. Continue into Brattleboro and return via the Dover Hill Road or follow the road past the college until the T, turn right, and you are soon in Jacksonville. See the following tours.

Jacksonville and Whitingham. From Wilmington follow Route 100, past Flames Stable (see *To Do—Horseback Riding*) and the turnoff for Ward's Cove (see *To Do—Swimming*), south 6 miles to the village of Jacksonville. At the junction of Route 100 and Route 112 stop by **Stone Soldier Pottery** (802-368-7077), open daily, known for it distinctive contemporary designs. Just down Route 112 is the **North River Winery** (802-368-7557) on Route 112 (open daily 10–5, except January through May, when hours are 11–5 Friday through Sunday), dedicated to producing fruit wines. We can speak for the full-bodied apple-blueberry, neither too dry nor too sweet. Green Mountain apple, cranberry-apple, and a number of other blends are offered (free samples come with the tour). Follow Route 100 south another 1.5 miles south and turn left on Town Hill Road (marked for the Brigham Young Monument) into Whitingham. At the top of Town Hill a monument commemorates the Mormon prophet who led his people into Utah and is hailed as the founder of Salt Lake City. He was born on a hill farm here, the son of a poor basket maker. The view takes in surrounding hills and there are picnic benches, grills, a playground, and parking area. Continue down the hill to Brown's General Store and turn right. Look on the right-hand side of the road near the top of this hill for a small marker that proclaims this to be the homestead site of Brigham Young: BORN ON THIS SPOT 1801 . . . A MAN OF MUCH COURAGE AND SUPERB EQUIPMENT. (BRIGHAM YOUNG FATHERED 57 CHILDREN BY 16 OF HIS 20 WIVES.) Before leaving the village, note the "floating island" in the middle of Sadawga Pond. Whitingham was once a busy resort, thanks to a mineral spring and its accessibility via the Hoosic Tunnel and Wilmington Railroad. The old railroad bed is now a 12-mile walking trail along this remote shore of Lake Whitingham. (Continue 1 mile south on Route 100 beyond the store, and take a right onto Dam Road; park and walk across the dam. Note the "Glory Hole," a large concrete overflow funnel that empties into the Deerfield River.)

Dover Hill Road, accessible from Route 100 via either Dorr Fitch Road in the village of West Dover or East Dover Road farther south (just below Sitzmark; see *To Do—Golf*). The road climbs steeply past the tiny village center of Dover. Here you could detour onto Cooper Hill Road for a few miles to take in the panorama of mountains. On an ordinary day, you can pick out Mount Monadnock in New Hampshire beyond Keene. You can either loop back down to Route 100 via Valley View Road or continue down the other side of the hill, through East Dover to the general store, covered bridge, and picturesque village center in South Newfane, following the Augerhole Road back to Route 9, or, if you are out for a real ride,

KELLY STAND ROAD

Kim Grant

continuing to Route 30, then south to Brattleboro and back to Wilmington on Route 9.

Handle Road runs south from Mount Snow, paralleling Route 100, turning into Cold Brook Road when it crosses the Wilmington line. The old farmhouses along this high, wooded road were bought up by city people to form a summer colony in the late 1880s. It's still a beautiful road, retaining some of the old houses and views.

Arlington/Kelly Stand Road heads west from West Wardsboro through the tiny village of Stratton. At 6.3 miles the Grout Pond turnoff is clearly marked and leads 1.3 miles to the pond. Hiking trails loop around the pond, through the woods, and continue to Somerset Reservoir (see *Green Space*). Beyond this turnoff is the monument to Daniel Webster, who spoke here to 1,600 people at an 1840 Whig rally. The hiking trail into Stratton Pond that begins just west of the monument is the most heavily hiked section of the Long Trail. It's possible (your vehicle and conditions permitting) to return to Route 9 through the Green Mountain Forest via the Arlington/Somerset Road (closed in winter). Roughly halfway down you pass the turnoff for Somerset Reservoir.

✷ To Do

AIRPLANE RIDES **North Air** (802-464-2196), Mount Snow Airport off Country Club Road, West Dover, offers scenic air rides.

BOATING **Green Mountain Flagship Co.** (802-464-2975), Route 9 west from Wilmington. Richard Joyce offers seasonal excursions on Lake Harriman aboard the M/V *Mt. Mills,* a twin-stacked pontoon vessel accommodating 65. Joyce caters to bus groups, but there are usually at least a half dozen seats left over. His narration of the logging history of the area is often accompanied by live music. Canoes and kayaks can be rented, too.

High Country Marine (802-464-2108; 1-800-627-7533), Route 9, on Lake Harriman. Rents jet boats or pontoon boat, wake boards, ski tubes.

Zoar Outdoor (1-800-532-7483; www.zoaroutdoor.com), Charlemont, Massachusetts. The Deerfield River flows south into Massachusetts, where regular dam releases power white-water rafting that's exciting enough to satisfy most jocks but do-able for children. This long-established outfitter also rents kayaks and sit-on-top canoes for lower stretches of the river. Charlemont is about 40 minutes south of Wilmington via Route 8A.

BOWLING **North Star Bowl and Mini Golf** (802-464-5148), Route 100, Wilmington, opens daily at noon for candlepin bowling; videos and pool tables, too.

CHAIRLIFT **Mount Snow** (1-800-245-SNOW). The lift operates on weekends in summer and daily throughout foliage season.

DAY CAMPS ✐ **Mount Snow Day Camps** (802-464-3333), Mount Snow. Mini Camp (ages 6 weeks to 12 months), Kids Camp (ages 5–8) and Sports Camp (ages 9–12) run during the summer, Monday through Friday 9–4. Activities include swimming, chairlift rides, arts and crafts, nature hikes, field trips, and more.

FISHING The **Deerfield** is known for rainbow and brook trout (the season is the second Saturday in April through October). The remote Harriman Bypass Reach, a 4.5-mile stretch of the river between the dam in Whitingham and Readsboro, is a good bet. Fly-fishermen can readily find guides. Note the **Taddingers/Orvis Fly Fishing School and Guiding Service** (802-464-6263), Route 100 north, Wilmington.

Harriman Reservoir is stocked with trout, bass, perch, and salmon; a boat launch is located off Fairview Avenue.

Somerset Reservoir, 5 miles west of Wilmington, then 10 miles north on the Somerset Road, offers bass, trout, and pike. There is a boat launch at the foot of the 9-mile-long lake. Smaller Sadawga Pond in Whitingham and Lake Raponda in Wilmington are also good for bass and trout; there is a boat launch on the former. Fishing licenses ($7) are available at Bill's Bait Shop, Whitingham; from the Wilmington town clerk; and at the Orvis dealership at Taddingers, Wilmington (see *Selective Shopping—Special Shops*).

GOLF **Mount Snow Country Club** (802-464-4254). Billing itself as "The Original Golf School," this program has been evolving since 1978. Weekend and 2- to 5-day midweek golf-school packages are offered May through September; the 18-hole, Cornish-designed championship golf course is also open on a daily basis.

Haystack (802-464-8301), Mann Road, off Cold Brook Road, Wilmington; clubhouse, 18 holes designed by Desmond Muirhead, full pro shop, newly upgraded with rave reviews.

Sitzmark Golf & Tennis Club (802-464-3384), Wilmington; 18 holes, club and cart rentals. No tee times.

HIKING Aside from the trails in Molly Stark State Park (see *Green Space*) and a short, self-guided trail atop Mount Snow, there are a number of overgrown roads leading to ghost towns. The Long Trail passes through the former logging town of Glastenbury (261 residents in 1880), and a former colonial highway in Woodford State Park (see *Green Space* in "Bennington Area") leads to a burying ground and 18th-century homesites. Somerset is another ghost town. The Hogback Mountain Overlook on Route 9 is the starting point for a hike up the old ski area access road to the Mount Olga fire tower. Inquire at the Mount Snow Valley Chamber of Commerce about accessing the 12-mile trail along the undeveloped shore of Lake Whitingham. Also see Grout Pond under *Green Space*.

Forest Care Nature Walks (802-254-4717). Lynn Levine leads popular group and individual treks in the summer and fall, discussing the ecology and wildlife in the area. Reservations needed a week ahead.

HORSEBACK RIDING **Flames Stables** (802-464-8329), Route 100 South, Wilmington. Western saddle trail rides, half-hour wagon rides, pony rides for young children.

Mountain View Stables (802-464-0615), Higley Hill Road, Wilmington. One-hour guided trail rides, English and Western saddles.

Whitingham Farm (802-368-2620) offers wagon rides using their Percheron/Morgan team, Blitz and Blaze.

HUNTING **Hermitage Sporting Clays and Hunting Preserve** (802-464-3511), Wilmington, consists of 200 acres and provides guided shoots with dogs, or you can try your hand at a round of 100 sporting clays. It is possible to use your own dog for a shoot. Reservations required. Pheasant hunts cost $295–395 per day.

LLAMA TREKKING **Green Mountain Expeditions** (802-368-7147), Whitingham, arranges picnic llama treks.

MOUNTAIN BIKING The **Mountain Bike School and Touring Center** at Mount Snow (1-800-245-SNOW) bills itself as "America's first and foremost mountain-bike school." It includes the Crisports Bike Shop with rentals and repairs and 45 miles of trails with lifts servicing a portion. Inquire about lodging/biking packages, clinics, and guided tours. **Alpine Traders** (802-464-8010), Route 100, West Dover. Open daily 8–6. Sales/rentals of Reflex mountain bikes.

SWIMMING There are several beaches on 11-mile-long Harriman Reservoir, also known as Whitingham Lake. **Mount Mills Beach** is 1 mile from Wilmington Village, posted from Castle Hill Road. **Ward's Cove Beach** is on Route 100 south of

Wilmington—turn right at Flames Stables (see *Horseback Riding*) and follow signs. Inquire locally about less publicized places.

Sitzmark Lodge (802-464-3384), north of Wilmington on Route 100, has a pool that is open to the public free of charge. Snacks and a bar are available poolside.

TENNIS The municipal courts at **Baker Field** in Wilmington are open to the public; also eight courts at Sitzmark (see above).

✷ Winter Sports

CROSS-COUNTRY SKIING **Hermitage Ski Touring Center** (802-464-3511), Wilmington. Outstanding 35 km, machine-tracked network (50 km total) includes a ridgetop trail with superb views, and elevations of 1,867–3,556 feet. Instruction, rental, repair, telemark guided tours (see also *Lodging—Inns* and *Dining Out*).

The **White House Winter Activity Center** (802-464-2135), Wilmington. A total of 25 km of tracked trails meander through the woods at elevations of 1,573–2,036 feet. Snowshoes are also available, and there's snow-tubing down the hill the inns stands on. Instruction, rentals, lodging (see *Lodging—Inns* and *Dining Out*), ski weeks.

Timber Creek Cross Country Touring Center (802-464-0999), West Dover. Just across Route 100 from the entrance to Mount Snow, a high-elevation, wooded system of trails that hold their snow cover; rentals, instruction available.

DOWNHILL SKIING/SNOWBOARDING ✐ **Mount Snow/Haystack** (information: 802-464-3333; snow report: 802-464-2151; reservations: 1-800-245-SNOW; www.mountsnow.com), West Dover. Owned by the American Skiing Company, the 767-acre area offers some 2,100 "on mountain" beds. There are five distinct areas here: the Main Mountain, the expert North Face, the Sunbrook Area, Carinthia Slopes, and Haystack (open weekends and holidays only). The vertical drop is 1,700 feet. The area also features two half-pipes and four terrain parks. Base area facilities include lodges, rental/repair shops, retail, and more. See the chapter introduction for the resort's history. *Lifts:* 23 chairlifts—3 high-speed and 1 fixed quad, 10 triples, 4 doubles. There are also two surface lifts and three Magic Carpets. *Ski/snowboard trails:* 132, including 33 "easier," 66 "more difficult," 26 "advanced," and 2 "double black diamonds." There are also 139 acres of hand-cleared "Tree Terrain."*Snowmaking:* 85 percent of the mountain. *Facilities:* Five base lodges, an upper lodge near the summit, the Snow Barn (nightclub with entertainment, dancing), and the Natural Life Center spa. *Ski school:* 85 instructors, Perfect Turn teaching methods—two clinics. *For children:* Perfect Kids; Mountain Camp (7–12); Mountain Riders (7–12); Snow Camp (4–6); Pre-Ski (3-year-olds); Child Care (6 weeks–5 years). *Rates:* Adults, weekdays Mount Snow and Haystack $49, Haystack only $27; weekends, holidays $55; young adult, $48; junior/senior, $34. *Special events:* Thankgiving and Christmas vacations; Fireworks and Torchlight Extravaganza; January, Snowmobile Snowcross; Feburary, Budweiser Aerial Assault and Boarderfest; March, Annual Reggae Festival. See www.mountsnow.com for full schedule.

DOGSLEDDING **Snowdoggin' Inc.** (802-380-2200) offers dogsled rides at Mount Snow and through the Green Mountains.

SLEIGH RIDES Sleigh rides are offered at **Adams Farm** (802-464-3762), Wilmington, with a refreshment stop at a cabin in the woods. They are also offered at **Flames Stables** (802-464-8329) on Route 100, south of Wilmington, and **Whitingham Farm** (802-368-2620) in Whitingham.

SNOWMOBILING **High Country Snowmobile Tours** (802-464-2108; 1-800-627-SLED) and Twin Brooks Snowmbile Tours (802-462-2054; 1-888-616-4054), both on Route 9 west in Wilmington, offer guided tours. **Sitzmark** (802-464-5498) on Route 100 north in Wilmington is now a snowmobile rather than a ski-touring center.

✷ Green Space

Molly Stark State Park (802-464-5460), Route 9 east of Wilmington Village. This is a 158-acre preserve features a hiking trail through the forest to 2,415-foot Mount Olga, from which there is a panoramic view. The 34 campsites include eight lean-tos. See *Campgrounds* in "What's Where" for state park fees and reservations.

Grout Pond Recreation Area (802-362-2307), west of West Wardsboro, off the Arlington (also known as the Kelly Stand) Road. A 1,600-acre piece of the Green Mountain National Forest designated for hiking, picnicking, fishing, boating, and camping. In summer a ranger resides at the Grout Pond Cabin, and campsites are available on a first come, first-served basis (6 vehicle sites, 11 walk-in campsites, and 4 sites accessible by canoe). Twelve miles of trails, which circle the pond and connect with Somerset Reservoir, are open in winter for skiing (they are not groomed). At the north end of the pond there are five picnic sites.

✷ Farms to Visit

Adams Farm (802-464-3762; www.adamsfamilyfarm.com), 15 Higley Hill Road, off Route 100, Wilmington. A sixth-generation, exceptionally visitor-friendly farm. Its Petting Farm (open daily except Tuesday July 1 through Labor Day, then weekends through Columbus Day) includes Rosie, the sow, in her swimming pool; Mr. McGregor's garden rabbits; a miniature horse; and goats, sheep, peacocks, turkeys, and geese. Visitors can gather fresh eggs, milk a goat, ride a tractor or pony, explore bear caves, or jump in the hay. Special events include a moonlight hayride and a sheep shearing festival. In winter there are horse-drawn sleigh rides. Inquire about afternoon tea. The Far Store and Quilt and Fiber Arts Loft features things locally crafted and otherwise produced.

Wheeler Farm (802-464-5225), Route 100 north of Wilmington Village. A third-generation working farm with Jersey and Dutch belted cows. Maple syrup is produced and sold, along with maple cream and sugar. Visitors welcome if you call before.

Boyd Family Farm (802-464-5618), East Dover Road, Wilmington. A working hillside farm, with pick-your-own flowers June through September, then pumpkins and Christmas wreaths.

North River Winery. See Jacksonville and Whitingham in *Scenic Driving Tours*.

✷ Lodging

This area can sleep more than 10,000 visitors on any one night, primarily in condominiums and ski lodges. The **Mount Snow Valley Chamber of Commerce** maintains a reservation line that includes inns as well as B&Bs (1-877-887-6884; www.visitvermont.com); the **Mount Snow Region Vacation Information Center** (1-800-451-MTSNOW, ext. 40; www.mountsnow-vt.com) operates a similar year-round service. Our listings focus on the inns and B&Bs.

RESORT ✐ **The Grand Summit Hotel and Crown Club** (802-464-6600; 1-800-261-9442; www.mountsnow.com), Mount Snow 05356. At the base of the ski lifts, this 198-room, condo hotel/conference center features one- to three-bedroom suites (many with kitchens) as well as the usual hotel rooms. Amenities include an outdoor pool and hot tubs, child care and arcade, and, of course, the adjacent ski lifts and, in summer, the golf and mountain-biking programs. **Harriman's Restaurant** is open for breakfast and dinner; **Harriman's Pub** has a bistro menu. Rates vary seasonally as well as for midweek and weekend stays: from $249 for a hotel room to $975 for the penthouse plus 8 percent service charge. Summer packages bring these prices down.

INNS

In Wilmington 05363

∞ ♿ **The White House of Wilmington** (802-464-2135; 1-800-541-2135; www.whitehouseinn.com). Built in 1915 on a knoll off Route 9 as a summer residence for Martin Brown, founder of Brown Paper Company, this is a Colonial Revival mansion with a longtime innkeeper, Bob Grinold. Public rooms are huge, airy, and light but also manage to be warm in winter—with the help of yawning hearths. In all seasons guests gather around the sunken bar. A total of 25 rooms, including 3 suites, are divided between the main house and the guest house. Two rooms have a balcony with fireplace, plus two-person whirlpool tub and two have a terrace with fireplace and whirlpool tub. There's a 60-foot outdoor pool, and a small indoor pool with whirlpool and sauna. In winter 43 km of cross-country trails are out the door. A full breakfast is included in the rates and dinner (see *Dining Out*) is served, along with a buffet Sunday brunch and a skiers' lunch in winter. Cash or checks preferred for accommodations. Rates range from $69 per person, B&B in the guest house, and from $74 per person double in the inn to $89 per person in the balcony rooms, plus 10 percent gratuity. Discounts on nonholiday midweek stays in both facilities.

✿ ✐ ♿ **Misty Mountain Lodge** (802-464-3961), Stowe Hill Road. Just 16 people can be accommodated in this informal old farmhouse set high on a hillside. There are six rooms (four with private bath, two with shared); one has a jetted whirlpool bath, and one is handicapped approved. Meals are served family-style and children feel welcome. Although ownership has recently changed, Vic and Donna Ruiz perpetuate the genial atmosphere for which this place is known. Guests can walk, cross-country ski, or relax by one of the gardens on the property, or settle down with a book by the fieldstone fireplace in the living room. $75–120 per couple; children 10 and under are free.

Nutmeg Inn (802-464-3351), P.O. Box 818. This delightful, 18th-century, roadside farmhouse on Route 9 west run by Dave and Pat Cerchio is a B&B that feels like an inn. It's on the edge of the village and offers 10 rooms, each nicely decorated with wallpaper, quilts, and braided rugs; four spacious one- and two-bedroom suites with fireplace and color TV/VCR and two-person whirlpool. All rooms and suites have central air-conditioning. There is a cozy living room, library, and BYOB bar, plus three intimate dining rooms for full, complimentary breakfasts. Food is important here. Summer rates: $89–199 double; fall, $109–299; winter, $99–289.

ꝏ **The Hermitage** (802-464-3511; www.hermitageinn.com), Coldbrook Road. Innkeeper Jim McGovern collects wines and art for this unusual and popular hostelry, which combines fine dining with cross-country skiing and pheasant hunting. There are some lovely rooms in the farmhouse annex; 14 of the 29 guest rooms are in the former Brook Bound, a mile down the road. Rates vary widely: from $60–125 double in Brook Bound, B&B, to $225–250 double, MAP, in the inn, plus 15 percent gratuity.

The Red Shutter Inn (802-464-3768; 1-800-845-7548; www.redshutterinn.com), Route 9. Renée and Tad Lyon preside over this big, gracious, 1890s house on the edge of the village with nine nicely furnished guest rooms including two suites with fireplace, one with a double whirlpool tub. The dining room, furnished with an assortment of old oak tables, has a good reputation and is open to the public (see *Dining Out*). From $110 double for cozy rooms in the carriage house to $180 for the spacious two-room Courtemanche Suite in the main house, B&B.

In West Dover 05356

The Inn at Sawmill Farm (802-464-8131; 1-800-493-1133; www.vermontdirect.com/sawmill), off Route 100. Closed early April to mid-May. Rod Williams is an architect, his wife, Ione, an interior decorator, and their son, Brill, an accomplished chef. Together the team has created one of Vermont's most elegant inns, a world-class hideaway in the Relais & Châteaux category, filled with antiques and splendid fabrics. The dining room is exceptional (see *Dining Out*). In summer, flowers are everywhere, inside and out; there is a swimming pool, tennis court, and two trout ponds. There are 20 beautifully appointed guest rooms, each different, 10 with working fireplace. $350–470 double occupancy, inn rooms, MAP; $450–850 double occupancy, fireplace rooms, MAP. The difference in rates depend on timing: cheapest midweek. Most expensive holiday and foliage seasons.

ꝏ ♿ **Deerhill Inn** (802-464-3100; 1-800-99-DEER9; www.deerhill.com), P.O. Box 136. After a hiatus of several years, Linda and Mike Anelli, former owners of Two Tannery Road, returned to West Dover and took over Deerhill, upgrading its flexible accommodations and dining rooms (see *Dining Out*). There are 15 luxurious rooms and suites, some in the old farmhouse, others in a newer wing. From the latter—especially on the galleried second floor—you enjoy a smashing view of Haystack and Mount Snow. One comfortable sitting room adjoins the tiny bar and two spacious dining rooms, walled with the work of local artists; upstairs is another big lounge for house guests, plus a library nook. In summer, flowers abound inside and out and around the patio of the new swimming pool. The Loft Room in the main house has its own terrace and private entrance, and the Oriental Room is a stunner. A lot happens here, too, especially during the valley's pre-Christmas festivities. Midweek, daily rates in the summer are $165–285 double B&B; $245–365 MAP, less off-season.

ꝏ **Doveberry Inn** (802-464-5652; 1-800-722-3204; www.doveberryinn.com), Route 100. A spacious, well-built inn on Route 100 near the Mount Snow access. There's a comfortable, large living room with fireplace and wine bar. Upstairs, each of the eight rooms is immaculate and bright, with private bath and full vanities (some of them copper), also with cable TV and video player, one with a fireplace and balcony. Request a back room overlooking the woods. Innkeepers Michael and Christine Fayette are culinary school graduates and prepare all of the northern Italian cuisine (see *Dining Out*). $90–110 daily per room with full breakfast in fall; $110–150 in winter. $90–110 spring and $80–105 in summer. MAP is available on request.

West Dover Inn (802-464-5207), Route 100. Built as the village inn in 1846 and now on the National Register of Historic Places, this handsome inn has been updated by Gregory Gramas and Monique Phelan to include modern amenities and antique appointments in each of its 12 guest rooms, 4 of which are fireplace suites with whirlpool tub. All rooms have private bath and cable TV. Guests enjoy a common room, with fireplace, as well as a publike cocktail lounge and casual fine-dining restaurant, Gregory's (see *Dining Out*). B&B rates: $100–145 per couple in summer; $120–200 in foliage season. Three-night minimum required during holiday periods.

ꝏ ✐ **Cooper Hill Inn** (802-348-6333; 1-800-783-3229), Cooper Hill Road, East Dover 05341. High on a hilltop on a quiet country road with one of the most spectacular mountain panoramas in New England, this sprawling inn changed owners as we went to press. When last seen it had 10 guest rooms, all with private bath, including two-room family suites, living room, dining room, game room, and roomy covered porch. Meals were served family-style; BYOB. Rates: $40 per person (double occupancy) April through September 21, $45 in fall foliage season; $44 winter, B&B; a 2-night winter weekend costs $110 per person with two breakfasts and a dinner; $110 in the fall, $90 in spring and summer. No credit cards.

BED & BREAKFASTS **Trail's End, A Country Inn** (802-464-2727; 1-800-859-2585; www.trailsendvt.com), 5 Trail's End Lane, Wilmington 05363, off East Dover Road. Unusual spaces in this ski lodge include a library and game room, a large living room with a two-story, fieldstone fireplace, and a dining space with large, round, hand-carved pine tables. The 13 rooms all have private bath and 4 have wood-burning fireplace; two fireplace suites also have canopy bed, refrigerator, microwave, and Jacuzzi. In summer check to see how your room is cooled. Facilities include a clay tennis court, a nicely landscaped heated pool, and paths leading out into the gardens and up the hill to the pond. Kevin Stephens serves dinner Saturday and on concert nights during the Marlboro Music Festival (see *Entertainment*). Guests have access to their own fridge, a plus in summer when no one wants to stray too far from the pool. $125–165 daily per room with breakfast in winter, $185–195 for suites, plus 15 percent gratuity; less in summer.

The Inn at Quail Run (1-800-34-ESCAPE), 106 Smith Road, Wilmington 05363. Nicely positioned above the valley, this ski lodge/inn is known for its breakfasts. Served in a flagstone-floored sun porch with mountain views, the morning menu might include a lobster-and-Boursin or crabmeat-and-avocado omelet or lemon-orange ricotta pancakes with Bob's special maple-glazed bacon (outsiders welcome). Common space is ample and includes a large living room with a piano and fireplace, and a small, inviting bar. Amenities include a heated pool and nine-person Jacuzzi. Children and pets are welcome but relegated to the lower level of the inn (the coolest in summer), off the game room.

Whetstone Inn (802-254-2500), 5550 South Road, Marlboro 05344. Handy to the Marlboro Music Festival (see *Entertainment*), this is a 1786 tavern with a Palladian window, part of the cluster of white-clapboard buildings—including the church and post office—that form the village core. Innkeepers Jean and Harry Boardman have been here more than 20 years, and there's a casually comfortable feel to the place. Most guests have been here before and have their own favorite rooms, of which there are 12, 7 with private bath and 3 with kitchen. $65–95. Breakfast is extra. There's swimming in a spring-fed pond.

Shearer Hill Farm (802-464-3253; 1-800-437-3104; www.shearerhillfarm.com), Shearer Hill Road off Route 9, 5 miles southeast of the village in Halifax. Keep going on this back road, bearing left at the fork, to Bill and Patti Pusey's simple, restored 200-year-old farmhouse a stone's throw from the Massachusetts border. Three rooms in the main house have private bath, and there is an annex with a ground-floor room and kitchenette, and two bedrooms and sitting room upstairs, all private baths. The pleasant large living room in the farmhouse has a VCR library. $90 double, $70 single with continental breakfast buffet. Cross-country skiing on the grounds.

The Candlelight Bed & Breakfast (802-368-2004; www.candlelightbandb.com), 3358 Route 100, Jacksonville 05342. An attractive B&B set above a rural stretch of Route 100; two guest rooms feature fireplaces; $90 per couple includes breakfast.

CONDO'S AND TOWN HOUSES

Mount Snow Condominums (802-464-7768; 1-800-451-4211). Four villages of various units from studios to three-bedroom town houses, with pools, saunas, hot tubs, and other facilities.

Snowresort Rentals (802-464-2177; 1-800-451-MTSNOW), Mountain Park Plaza, West Dover, has extensive listings of vacation homes and condos, ranging from small studios to five-bedroom condos for daily, weekend, monthly, or seasonal rentals.

CAMPING See Molly Stark State Park and Grout Pond Recreation Area in *Green Space*.

OTHER **The Amos Brown House,** the oldest house in the back-roads town of Whitingham, is currently under restoration by nonprofit Landmark Trust USA. The brick Cape-style farmhouse, built around 1800, with connected barn and sheds, is set in 30 acres of meadow and sugarbush on a quiet dirt road. For details about renting the house contact Landmark at 802-254-6868.

✷ Where to Eat

DINING OUT **Inn at Sawmill Farm** (802-464-8131), Route 100, West Dover. Open for dinner only, 6–9:30. The main dining room is the interior of a former barn, with fine chintz and old portraits. The linen-covered tables are set with sterling and fresh flowers; there is also a smaller, sun- and plant-filled dining room. The 34,000-bottle wine cellar was given the Grand Award from *Wine Spectator*. Specialties include roast duck in green peppercorn sauce, rack of lamb, and soft shell crab; generally there is also a wide choice of appetizers and irresistible desserts. One of the best in the state. Entrées $28–35.

Deerhill Inn (802-464-3100), off Route 100, West Dover. Michael Anelli presides over the kitchen of this luxurious establishment, with two attractive dining rooms lined with the work of local artists. You might begin dinner with crab-and-lobster-stuffed portobello mushrooms or steamed mussels with parsley garlic broth, and proceed to veal medallions with wild mushrooms and lemon cream sauce, or five-layer veal with roasted pepper sauce. Desserts are delectable. Entrées $20-30.

The Hermitage Inn (802-464-3511), Coldbrook Road, Wilmington. A popular, highly regarded restaurant with two dining rooms, fine art on the walls, and a mixture of arm- and wing chairs that all make for the elegance due the dishes. You might begin dinner with homemade venison sausage or game-bird pâté, proceed to chicken amandine, boneless trout, or the game-bird selection, with a wine chosen from among 2,000 labels. Sunday brunch. Entrées $15–30.

Le Petit Chef (802-464-8437), Route 100 north, Wilmington. Open for dinner daily except Tuesday. Elegant French dining in an old roadside house. This is a local favorite. Chef-

WILMINGTON

Kim Grant

owner Betty Hillman's French-accented menu might include poisson Mediterranean (shellfish poached in a zesty broth) and *côte de veau grillée* (grilled veal rib seasoned with herbs and a balsamic glaze, with straw potatoes and roasted stuffed tomato). Entrées $18–28.50. Reservations a must.

Doveberry Inn (802-464-5652), Route 100, West Dover. Closed Tuesday. This elegant inn is chef-owned and the accent is authentic northern Italian. The à la carte menu might include fennel and leek risotto followed by Gorgonzola and then wood-grilled veal chop. The Italian wine list is large. Entrées $19–31.

Gregory's (802-464-7264), Route 100, West Dover. The dining room at the West Dover Inn has a distinctive and seasonally changing menu. It might include curried crabcakes for starters, then applewood-smoked pork tenderloin. $17–28.

Two Tannery Road (802-464-2707), Route 100, West Dover. Open Tuesday through Sunday. The building itself is said to date in part from the late 1700s when it stood in Marlboro, Massachusetts, and it has moved several times within this valley, serving for a while as a summer home for Theodore Roosevelt's son. The bar began service in the original Waldorf Astoria (present site of the Empire State Building). The food is highly rated with a a large à la carte menu that might include Malay shrimp simmered in sweet and spicy lemon ginger sauce and chicken breast filled with Vermont ham and sharp cheddar. Entrées $21–30.

The Red Shutter Inn (802-464-3768), Route 9, Wilmington. Open Wednesday through Saturday in winter; daily except Tuesday in summer. The pleasant, oak-filled dining room provides a locally acclaimed "night-out" atmosphere. Appetizers usually include escargots with wild mushrooms, and entrées range from fresh Long Island duckling to linguine with chicken and shrimp. $19.50–25.50.

The White House of Wilmington (802-464-2135), Route 9 east, Wilmington. The wood-paneled dining room is warmed by a glowing hearth. The menu is extensive but usually includes several veal dishes, filet mignon, and boneless stuffed duck. $20.95–24.95.

EATING OUT **Poncho's Wreck** (802-464-9320), South Main Street, Wilmington. Open daily for dinner; lunch Friday through Sunday. Early-bird menu 4–6. A pubby, eclectic, casual atmosphere; specialties are Mexican dishes, fish, and smoked meats. Frozen drinks and a wide selection of beer. Try the artichoke hearts and chile rellenos, also a wide choice of seafood. Tends to fill up, so it's advisable to come very early or late. Inquire about live entertainment.

Dot's Restaurant (802-464-7284, 802-464-6476), Wilmington, is open 5:30 AM–8 PM, until 9 PM Friday and Saturday. This is a cheerful, pine-sided place in the middle of the village. There's a long Formica counter as well as tables, a fireplace in back, and wine by the glass. Stop by for a bowl of the hottest chili in New England. The soup and muffins are homemade, and the Reubens are first-rate. Its sibling is on Route 100 in Mountain Park Plaza.

Skyline Restaurant (802-464-3536), Route 9, Hogback Mountain, Marlboro. For more than 40 years, Joyce and Dick Hamilton have operated this restaurant with "the 100-mile view." The knottypine dining room has worn, shiny tables, fresh flowers, and a traditional New England menu. In winter, there's a fire. Specialties include homemade soups; homebaked brownies, pies, and turnovers; and a Vermonter sandwich.

Anchor (802-464-2112), South Main Street, Wilmington. Lunch and dinner, Sunday brunch. Same ownership as Poncho's, this is an informal fish place with a raw bar, fried clams, and daily specials like fried salmon slices in bacon and a sautéed mixed grill with lemon pepper sauce, plus ribs.

The Roadhouse Restaurant (802-464-5017), Route 100, Wilmington. Open for dinner daily except Wednesday. Considered one of the better deals in the valley because all dinners ($15.95–22.95) come with soup, bread, salad, and dessert, and the food is good. Entrées might include beef Stroganoff, Cornish game hen, baked salmon fillet, or back baby ribs.

Piero's Trattoria at the Orchard Inn (802-464-7147), Route 100, Wilmington. Just north of the village, this new chef-owned restaurant is a winner, featuring fare from the Marche region north of Rome. Appetizers feature bruschettas and polenta, and the specialty of the house is ravioli de Vitello: homemade pasta filled with veal, served with Gorgonzola, mushrooms, spinach, and a nutmeg cream sauce. Italian wines.

Alonzo's Pasta and Grille (802-464-2355), at the Crafts Inn, West Main Street, Wilmington. Open daily for lunch and dinner, breakfast on weekends. "Create-your-own-grill" specials (teriyaki steak, andouille sausage, for example); homemade pastas.

Mildred's Fine Foods Deli (802-464-1224), Route 9, Wilmington Village. Open 11–5. A source of standout deli sandwiches and wraps; eat in or take on a picnic.

BREWS **Bean Heads** (802-464-1208), Main and River Streets, Wilmington. Espresso, cappuccino, bagelry, soup, and sandwiches.

Maple Leaf Malt & Brewing (802-464-9900), 3 North Main Street, Wilmington. Open for lunch and dinner, full bar. The local micobrew in an attractive space, full bar, weekly entertainment.

✻ Entertainment

Memorial Hall Center for the Arts (802-464-8411), lodged in the McKim, Mead and White–designed theater next door to the historic Crafts Inn, Wilmington. The center sponsors a frequent theatrical, musical, and community events.

Mountain Park Cinema (802-464-6477), Route 100, West Dover, has two movie theaters for first-run films; matinees on rainy weekends.

APRÈS-SKI During ski season, the following places feature live entertainment or DJs on most nights. In summer, they come to life on weekends. On Route 100, between Wilmington and Mount Snow, look for **Andirons** (802-464-2114), **Deacon's Den** (802-464-9361), and **Snow Barn Entertainment Center** (the old Rubin's Barn at Mount Snow). The **Billiard Sanctuary** (802-464-9975), Route 100, music every Friday and Saturday.

✻ Selective Shopping

ANTIQUES **Wilmington Antique & Flea Market** (802-464-3345), junction of Routes 9 and 100. Open May through October Saturday and Sunday. Bills itself as southern Vermont's largest outdoor flea market.

Left Bank Antiques (802-464-3224), Routes 9 and 100, Wilmington. Country furniture, old paintings, and prints.

ARTISANS AND CRAFTS **Quaigh Design Centre** (802-464-2780), Main Street, Wilmington. This is a long-established showcase for top Vermont crafts; imported Scottish woolens are also a specialty. Lilias MacBean Hart, the owner, has produced a Vermont tartan.

John McLeod, Ltd. (802-464-8175), Route 9, Wilmington. Unusual wooden shapes to decorate your home (clocks, mirrors, cutting boards) are sold in the showroom of this woodworking shop on the western verge of the village; open daily.

Turnpike Road Pottery (802-254-2168), Marlboro. Open Saturday 1–4. Malcolm Wright makes distinctive wood-fired pottery.

Applewoods (802-254-2908), Marlboro. Open June to September 1, weekends 10–4 and by appointment. David and Michelle Holzapfel create amazing furnishings from burls and other wood forms.

Gallery in the Woods (802-464-5793), Marlboro. Dante Corsano makes widely respected tables, dressers, armoires—whatever you need. The lines are simple, and the craftsmanship is so exceptional that the pieces are striking. His wife, Suzanne, crafts equally striking pottery lamps in a range of soft hues. Many other artists are also featured.

Craft Haus (802-464-2164), Stowe Hill Road, Wilmington. Set high on a hillside, this is a gallery in Ursula Tancrel's home. The big attractions are works by folk artist Will Moses and Ursula's cloisonné and enamel-plated jewelry, which sells for far higher prices in urban stores. Open weekends 10–5 and at other times by appointment.

Kaos Fine Art Gallery (802-464-1414; www.kaosgallery.com), corner of Route 100 and Route 9, Wilmington. A slick new gallery featuring the works of its cofounders, Miki Boni, known for her portraits, and Karen Baker, a landscape artist.

SUMMER MUSIC FESTIVAL

Marlboro Music Festival, Persons Auditorium, Marlboro College. (For advance tickets write to Marlboro Music Festival, 135 South 18th Street, Philadelphia, PA 19103; 215-569-4690; after June 6, call the Marlboro box office, 802-254-2394; www.marlboromusic.org.) Concerts, primarily chamber music, are offered on Friday, Saturday, and Sunday, early July through mid-August. This unusual "festival" is a 7-week gathering of 70 or so world-class musicians who come to work together. It is held on this rural campus because Rudolf Serkin, one of its founders, owned a nearby farm. Pablo Casals came every year from 1960 to 1973. Some concerts are sold out in advance, but you can frequently find good seats before the performance (chairs are metal, and regulars bring cushions). There are (almost) always bargain-priced seats in the tent just outside the auditorium's sliding glass doors.

More Galleries: Pick up an *Art Galleries* map/guide to the burgeoning number of galleries.

BOOKSTORES **Bartleby's Books and Music** (802-464-5425), North Main Street, Wilmington, is a cheerful shop for new books (mostly paperbacks), greeting cards, cassettes, and compact disks.

Austin's Antiquarian Books (802-464-3727), Route 9 west, Wilmington.

SPECIAL SHOPS **Taddingers** (802-464-6263), Route 100, Wilmington. Seven specialty shops under one roof: antiques and fine prints, exclusive decorative accessories, Christmas Room, Nature Room, and an Orvis dealership, with gear for fly-fishing, fly-tying, and shooting, plus sponsorship of 1- and 2-day fishing schools.

Manyu's Boutique (802-464-8880), Main and River Streets, Wilmington, has casual, contemporary clothes and accessories for women.

Down in the Valley (802-464-2211), West Main Street, Wilmington. A long-established, genuinely off-price ski- and sportswear shop, featuring fleece outerwear.

Klara Simpla (802-464-5257), Route 9 west, Wilmington. A "holistic country store" with a following stretching the length of Route 9. Vitamins, homeopathic remedies, natural foods, a wide selection of books, and, of course, Birkenstock sandals are available. Upstairs are weekly sessions in massage therapy, yoga, chiropractic, acupuncture; also special workshops in such topics as nutrition and dowsing.

1836 Country Store Village (802-464-5102), West Main Street, Wilmington, has an eclectic stock of decorative brasses, pierced-tin lanterns, cotton calicoes, quilting supplies, cheese, and the usual souvenirs.

ART ON THE MOUNTAIN

A 9-day exhibit, late July through early August at Haystack (802-464-8671). One of the largest and best gatherings of craftspeople and their wares, displayed in Haystack's unusual glass-and-wood base lodge, daily 10–5.

Swe Den Nor Ltd. (802-464-2788), Route 100, West Dover. A long-established store with a wide selection of Scandinavian, contemporary, and country furniture; also lamps, paintings, and gifts.

✷ Special Events

Late January: **Harriman Ice Fishing Derby** on Lake Whitingham (802-368-2773).

April (Easter weekend): Nondenominational **sunrise service** on Mount Snow's summit with continental breakfast. Eggs hidden all over the mountain, good for prizes.

July through mid-August: **Marlboro Music Festival** (802-254-2394; see *Entertainment*).

August: **Deerfield Valley Farmers Day** (802-464-8092), Wilmington. Old-fashioned agricultural fair with midway, livestock exhibits.

November 25–December 25: **"Nights Before Christmas"** celebration—wreath sales, fashion shows, concerts, Festival of Lights, holiday tour of country inns, Living Nativity, and other events in the Mount Snow Valley.

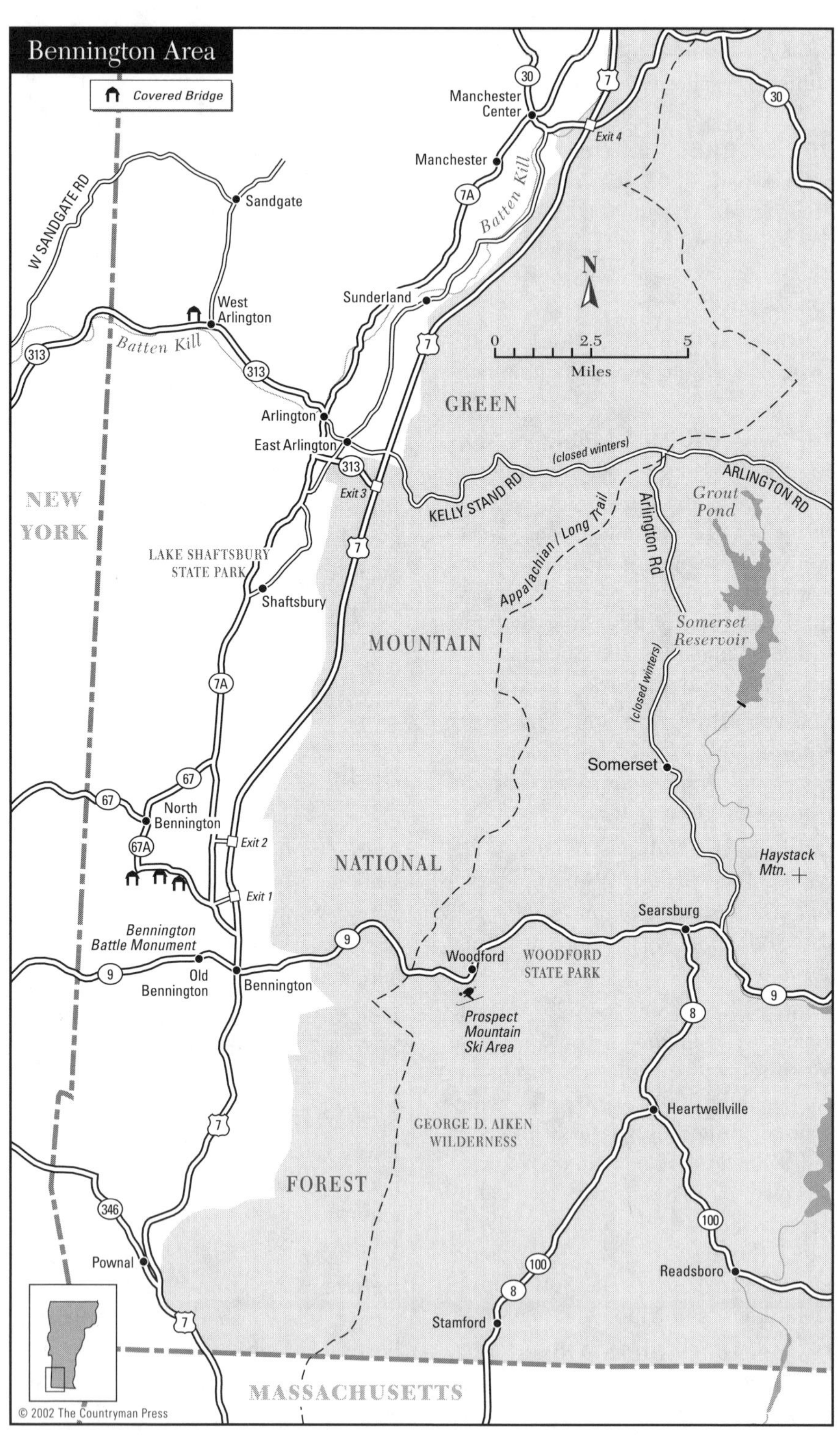

Bennington Area
Covered Bridge
Manchester Center
Manchester
Sandgate
W SANDGATE RD
Batten Kill
West Arlington
Sunderland
Exit 4
N
0 2.5 5
Miles
GREEN
MOUNTAIN
NATIONAL
FOREST
Arlington
East Arlington
Exit 3
KELLY STAND RD
(closed winters)
ARLINGTON RD
Grout Pond
Arlington Rd
Appalachian / Long Trail
NEW YORK
LAKE SHAFTSBURY STATE PARK
Shaftsbury
Somerset Reservoir
(closed winters)
Somerset
North Bennington
Exit 2
Exit 1
Haystack Mtn.
Searsburg
Bennington Battle Monument
Old Bennington
Bennington
Woodford
WOODFORD STATE PARK
Prospect Mountain Ski Area
GEORGE D. AIKEN WILDERNESS
Heartwellville
Pownal
Readsboro
Stamford
MASSACHUSETTS

BENNINGTON AREA

Vermont's southwest corner is dominated by Bennington, the state's fifth largest town, which is undergoing something of an industrial renaissance while retaining its historic luster. This growth has, in turn, led to a general improvement in places to stay and eat. The first town settled west of the Connecticut River in the New Hampshire Grants in 1749 and named for avaricious Gov. Benning Wentworth, Bennington became a hotbed of sedition when the "Bennington Mob," or Green Mountain Boys, formed in 1770 at Fay's Catamount Tavern under the leadership of Seth Warner and Ethan Allen to expel both the 'Yorkers (who claimed the territory) and, later, the British.

The battle of Bennington (more precisely, the battle for Bennington) on August 16, 1777, deflected General Burgoyne's occupation of the colonies when New Hampshire Gen. John Stark's hastily mobilized militiamen beat the tar out of Colonel Baum's overdressed Hessians on high ground near the Walloomsac River, across the New York border.

Today, Bennington is nationally known as the home of distinguished Bennington College, established in the early 1930s, as well as Southern Vermont College, headquartered in the Everett Mansion. It is also remembered fondly by collectors of Bennington pottery.

GUIDANCE A good visitors guide to Bennington County is provided by the **Bennington Area Chamber of Commerce** (802-447-3311; www.bennington.com), 100 Veterans Memorial Drive, Bennington 05201, which also has a well-supplied information center. The Regional Marketing Association (RMO) can be reached at 1-877-768-3766; www.sovermont.com.

GETTING THERE *By car:* Bennington lies at the convergence of Routes 7, 7A, 9, 67, and 67A. Going north can be confusing; watch the signs carefully to choose between the limited-access Route 7 to Manchester and the more interesting but slower historic Route 7A to Shaftsbury and Arlington.

By bus: **Vermont Transit** from Albany or hubs in Connecticut and Massachusetts.

MEDICAL EMERGENCY Bennington (911); Arlington (802-447-7911); **Southwestern Vermont Medical Center** (802-442-6361), 100 Hospital Drive, Bennington.

✱ To See

Historic Bennington Walking Tours, self-guided with a keyed map-brochure from the chamber of commerce (see *Guidance*)—also available at www.bennington.com—that describes Old Bennington, including the 306-foot, blue limestone shaft of the Bennington Battle Monument, dedicated in 1891; all the fine early houses along Monument Avenue; the Old Academy; Old First Church; the Burying Ground, where five Vermont governors and Robert Frost repose; and the venerable Walloomsac Inn, now a private home. A second walking tour of the downtown area includes the 1898 railroad depot (now a restaurant), constructed of blue marble cut to resemble granite; old mills; and Victorian homes.

Bennington Battle Monument (802-447-0550), Old Bennington. Open mid-April through October 31, daily 9–5, this Sandy Hill dolomite limestone shaft commemorates Gen. John Stark's defeat of General Burgoyne's invading British and Hessian forces at Walloomsac Heights, 5 miles to the northwest, on August 16, 1777.

MUSEUMS Bennington Museum (802-447-1571; www.benningtonmuseum.com), West Main Street, Route 9, Bennington. Open daily 9–6 June through October; 9–5 November through May. This really distinguished and growing collection features memorabilia from the battle of Bennington, including the oldest American Revolutionary flag in existence, plus early American glass, furniture, dolls and toys, historic Bennington pottery (notably an extraordinary 10-foot ceramic piece created for the 1853 Crystal Palace Exhibition), and a luxury 1925 Wasp touring car, the only surviving model of the rare automobiles made by Karl Martin in Bennington.

THE OLD FIRST CHURCH IN OLD BENNINGTON

Kim Grant

Particularly popular is a gallery of the largest collection of paintings by Grandma Moses (Anna Mary Robertson, 1860–1961), who lived in the vicinity. There's a gift shop and genealogical library. Admission.

The Park-McCullough House (802-442-5441), Route 67A in North Bennington. Open for tours late May through October and December, daily 10–3 except Tuesday and Wednesday. A splendid, 35-room Victorian mansion built in 1865 by Trenor W. Park, a forty-niner who struck it rich as a lawyer in California and later as a railroader. He built the house on part of the farm owned by his father-in-law, Hiland Hall, a representative to Congress and governor of Vermont. Park's son-in-law, John G. McCullough, became governor of Vermont in 1902 and raised his family in this capacious house. It has been open to the public since 1965 and is on the National Register of Historic Places, functioning as a community arts center. There's an appealing children's playhouse replica of the mansion and a stable full of carriages; also a gift shop, lunch counter, afternoon tea on the veranda. Admission.

Bennington Center for the Arts (802-442-7158; www.vermontartscenter.org), Route 9 at Gypsy Lane, houses four visual arts galleries and a theater for the Oldcastle Theatre Company, which performs May through December (see *Entertainment*).

The Shaftsbury Historical Society, Route 7A, is gradually developing a cluster of five historic buildings, including two schools. Open summer weekends 2–4 and serendipitously when the curator happens to be handy.

Hemmings Motor News (802-442-3101), 222 Main Street, is not really a museum, but it attracts large numbers of vintage-automobile buffs, Monday through Friday 9–5. Tours at 11 and 2; no charge. A few of its old-timer vehicles are parked at its Sunoco station branch on West Main Street near the Bennington Museum.

WINERY **Grand View Winery** (802-442-3636), Route 9W in Old Bennington. This outlet for the Grand View Winery in Calais is open daily for tastings, 11–5, with shorter hours in the winter.

COVERED BRIDGES Three stand just off Route 67A in North Bennington: **Silk Road, Paper Mill Village,** and the **Burt Henry.** There are two more in Arlington, and a driving tour of all five is available through the chamber.

✷ To Do

CANOEING **BattenKill Canoe Ltd.** (802-362-2800; 1-800-421-5268), River Road, off Route 7A, Arlington, is the center for day trips—with van service—canoe camping, instruction, rentals, and equipment. Customized inn-to-inn tours arranged.

GOLF AND TENNIS **Mount Anthony Country Club** (802-447-7079), 180 Country Club Drive (just below the Battle Monument): 18-hole golf course, tennis and paddle courts, pool, lunch and dinner (802-442-2617).

HORSEBACK RIDING **Kimberly Farms Riding Stables** (802-442-4354), 1524 Myers Road, Shaftsbury, offers trail rides, lessons, hayrides, inn-to-inn tours, and an overnight horse camp.

SKIING ✐ **Prospect Mountain** (802-442-2575; 802-442-5283), Route 9 east of Bennington. An intimate, friendly, family ski area, with cross-country (25 km), downhill, and telemark facilities, ski school, rentals and repairs, learn-to-ski packages, group rates, cafeteria, and bar. Moderate prices for all.

SNOWMOBILING **Twinbrooks Tours** (802-442-4054; 1-888-616-4054) in nearby Woodford offers snowmobile rentals, trail maps, and guided tours.

GREEN SPACE **Lake Shaftsbury State Park** (802-375-9979), 10.5 miles north on Route 7A, has swimming, picnicking, boating, and a nature trail on 26-acre Lake Shaftsbury.

Woodford State Park (802-447-7169), Route 9 east of Bennington. This 400-acre area includes 104 camping sites, 16 of them with lean-tos, swimming in Adams Reservoir, a children's playground, picnic spots, canoe and rowboat rentals.

✷ Lodging

INNS **The Four Chimneys Inn** (802-447-3500; 1-800-649-3503; www.fourchimneys.com), 21 West Road, Route 9, Old Bennington 05201. This stately, 1910 Colonial Revival home, once the estate of Phillip Jennings, offers 11 luxurious rooms, all with private bath, TV, and phone, some with fireplace and Jacuzzi. The owners, Harold and Christine Cullison, keep the grounds beautifully landscaped. Rates $105–205 double B&B, depending on the season. (See also *Dining Out*).

BED & BREAKFASTS **South Shire Inn** (802-447-3839), 124 Elm Street, Bennington 05201. This turn-of-the-20th-century Victorian mansion is a most attractive guest house, featuring 10-foot ceilings with plaster moldings, a library with a massive mahogany fireplace, an Italianate formal dining room, and comfortable bedrooms furnished with antiques. The five guest rooms in the main house, some with fireplace, have private bath; two can be joined as a suite. Four newer rooms, with Jacuzzi and TV, have been added in the old carriage house. $105–180 with breakfast; older children preferred.

Molly Stark Inn (802-442-9631; 1-800-356-3076; www.mollystarkinn.com), 1067 East Main Street, Bennington 05201. Six cozy bedrooms, all with private bath, some with Jacuzzi and/or woodstove, decorated with Americana, antiques, and quilts; wraparound porch. $70–95; $135–175 for the three guest cottages with Jacuzzi.

Alexandra B&B (802-442-5619; 1-888-207-9386; www.alexandrainn.com), Historic Route 7A at Orchard Road, Bennington 05201. Alex Koks and Andra Erickson, former proprietors of the Four Chimneys, have redecorated this attractive 1859 farmhouse. The 12 guest rooms with private bath have an English country house atmosphere. As Alex Koks is a master chef, breakfasts are very special. $85–145.

The Henry House (802-442-7045; 1-888-442-7045), 1338 Murphy Road, North Bennington 05257. Don and Judy Cole have five beautiful guest rooms in this restored historic place, built in 1769 on 25 acres, complemented by four common rooms. Among the guest rooms, the Ballroom, with its vaulted 14-foot ceiling, four-poster canopy bed, and a sitting area with working fireplace, is the most notable ($135). The other four are also distinctive: $85–100. Pets and children under 12 are not welcome.

Samuel Safford Inne (802-442-5934), 722 Main Street, Bennington 05201. Sandy Redding runs her B&B out of the oldest house in Bennington Village; it was restored during the Victorian period. She has five guest rooms, some with private bath, and serves a full breakfast. Rates range $59–125.

HoneyBee B&B (802-447-2941), P.O. Box 306, Church Street, Shaftsbury 05262. A beautiful 1840 Victorian home with a large front porch, five comfortable bedrooms and three working fireplaces. Full breakfast included. $70–125.

MOTELS **Vermonter Motor Lodge** (802-442-2529), Route 9, West Road, Bennington 05201. This motel, 2 miles west of Old Bennington, is an attractive miniresort with nicely decorated rooms and cabins, cable TV, room phone, swimming, boating, bass pond, Sugar Maple Inne Restaurant; $55–90 per room.

Paradise Motor Inn (802-442-8351), 141 West Main Street, Bennington 05201, close to the Bennington Museum (see *To See—Museums*), has 76 rooms and a nice restaurant on the premises; $59–94.

Knotty Pine Motel (802-442-5487; www.bennington.com/knottypine), 130 Northside Drive, Route 7A, Bennington 05201. The locals use this motel to put up their guests, which is always a good sign. There's a pool and a restaurant right next door. The clean, well-kept rooms range $50–82.

🐾 **Darling Kelly's Motel** (802-442-2322), 357 Route 7 south, Bennington 05201. This motel is set south of town on

THE PARK-MCCULLOUGH HOUSE

Christina Tree

5 acres with a pool. There are 24 rooms, and pets are allowed in some of them. A continental breakfast is included in the room rates: $43–87.

Harwood Hill Motel (802-442-6278; www.abnl.net/harwoodhill), 898 Harwood Hill Road, Bennington 05201. Planted right on top of a scenic hilltop in Bennington, its location right across the street from an apple orchard makes it a good choice for apple-blossom season (spring) and apple-picking time (fall). There are 16 rooms, some with refrigerator. Rates $40–75.

OTHER LODGING **Greenwood Lodge & Campsites** (802-442-2547), P.O. Box 246, Bennington 05201, 8 miles east of town on Route 9. Open May 20 through October 24. This rustic lodge/hostel and its campsites occupy 120 acres in Woodford, adjacent to the Prospect Mountain ski area (see *To Do—Skiing*). There are dorms for American Youth Hostel members and private family rooms; bring your own linen or sleeping bags. Three small ponds for swimming, boating, and fishing. There are hiking trails at Prospect Mountain. Inquire about the inexpensive rates.

✱ Where to Eat

DINING OUT **The Four Chimneys Inn** (802-447-3500), 21 West Road, Route 9, Old Bennington. Open daily for lunch and dinner in a gracious dining room and an enclosed porch. Lunch could start with a house specialty, mustard soup, and proceed with a smoked salmon croissant, chicken potpie, or omelets. Dinner (prix fixe $33.50) might include Burgundy-style snails followed by chicken breast with wild mushroom cream sauce, beef medallions and shrimp, or rack of lamb.

Bennington Station (802-447-1080), Depot Street, Bennington. Open for lunch and dinner daily. Train buffs love this place—a splendidly converted Romanesque railroad station built in 1897 of rough-hewn blue marble for the Bennington & Rutland Railroad. The exceptionally attractive restaurant features a collection of historic photos. For lunch, you could have Iron Horse Chili, Railroad Spikes (marinated and grilled beef strips), or a variety of salads and sandwiches. The dinner menu includes grilled duck salad, prime rib, New England chicken potpie, fish, various teriyakis, and BBQ ribs. Moderate.

Mount Anthony Country Club (802-442-2617), Bank Street just below the Bennington Battle Monument. Golf or no golf, you can enjoy at lunch or dinner in this scenic setting. For lunch, try the grilled portobello sandwich with artichokes and red peppers ($5.95) or the fancy chicken salad wrap ($6.95). For dinner, chef Grant Brown does a nice job with paella risotto with all manner of seafood ($19.95), fettuccine with homemade sausage and wild mushrooms ($12.95), or roasted rack of lamb with Beaujolais, honey, and lemon ($22.95). There's also room here for a banquet.

McMorland's Steak and Seafood (802-442-7500), 782 Harwood Hill, Bennington. Executive chef Brian McMorland's menu features a Yankee seafood bake with scallops, shrimp, and whitefish ($18.95), jumbo ravioli filled with smoked mozzarella and asparagus ($14.95), or a roasted half duck with sun-dried cherry and Grand Marnier sauce ($17.95). The bread pudding with Amaretto sauce ($3.95) is a house favorite.

EATING OUT ❀ **Blue Benn Diner** (802-442-5140), Route 7, near Deer Park, Bennington, open from 6 AM; breakfast all day, or lunch, which combines "road fare" with more esoteric items like eggs Benedict, tabbouleh, falafel, and herb teas.

Alldays & Onions (802-447-0043), 519 Main Street, Bennington. In this fish market and upscale deli-café, you can build your own sandwiches at lunch daily except Sunday, or splurge on rack of lamb with honey-thyme sauce for dinner (Thursday through Saturday).

Kevin's at Mikes Place III (802-442-0122), 27 Main Street, North Bennington. With soup, salads, burgers, steaks, and lots of hot snacks, this is everything a sports bar should be.

Fortune Cookie Chinese Restaurant (802-447-1111), 218 Northside Drive, Bennington. For those times when you need a change, this is decent Chinese food at decent prices. The special beef ($13.95) comes highly recommended by the locals.

Paradise Restaurant (802-442-5418), 141 West Main Street, Bennington. Open every day from lunch through dinner, the Paradise does all the traditionals—surf and turf, steaks, baked scrod, seafood Newburg—and much more. The Vermont roast turkey dinner ($10.95) is a good value and a favorite here. The early-bird menu is good until 6:30 PM, and there's a tavern serving wings, nachos, and burgers.

✷ Entertainment

Oldcastle Theatre Company (802-447-0564), Box 1555, Bennington. This accomplished theater company offers a full summer season of plays in the Bennington Center for the Arts. May through December.

✷ Selective Shopping

Camelot Village (802-447-0039), located just west of Old First Church on West Road in Bennington, can keep a shopper happy for a long time. The village has been growing over the years. It now includes the **Antique Center,** displaying the antiques and collectibles from more than 135 area dealers, and the **Craft Center** (802-447-0228), featuring the work of more than 250 regional artisans. **Fan-Tastic Gifts Country Store** offers homemade fudge, Vermont foods, maple products, and all sorts of gift items. **Yesterday, Today & Tomorrow** sells vintage clothing, hats, jewelry, and collectibles. Other stores include **Granite Lake Pottery, Occasional Flowers, Magic Sleigh, John McLeod Ltd.,** and **Vermont Soap & Candle.** There's even food, so you can spend a long time here.

BOOKSTORE **Bennington Bookshop** (802-442-5059), 467 Main Street. Vermont books, adult and children's titles, cards.

CRAFTS SHOPS **Hawkins House** (802-442-6463), 262 North Street, Route 7, Bennington, is a crafts market complex for the work of some 400 artisans in silver and gold, unusual textiles, handblown glass, pottery, quilts, cards, books, music, prints and woodcuts, stained glass, candles, and more. Open daily except Christmas and New Year's.

Oak Bluffs Cottage Pottery (802-823-5161), Route 7, 8 miles south of Bennington, has a full range of stoneware, baskets, and lamps.

Mahican Moccasin Factory (802-823-5294), Route 7, 5 miles south of Bennington, features a variety of deerskin, elk, and cowhide footwear, made in Pownal.

Bennington Potters Yard (802-447-7531), downtown on County Street, Bennington, is the high-tech place to get contemporary Bennington pottery, Catamount glass, and well-designed ovenproof cookware manufactured in North Bennington.

GALLERIES **Images from the Past** (802-442-3204), West Main Street, Bennington. Open daily April through December, winter weekends. Fascinating ephemera: postcards, prints, holograms, historic house boxes.

Bennington Center for the Arts (see *To See—Museums*)

SPECIAL SHOPS **The Chocolate Barn** (802-375-6928), Route 7A north of Shaftsbury, is an unusual combination: two floors of antiques, 56 varieties of hand-dipped chocolates, fudge, and special orders from antique candy molds. (There's another store at Routes 30 and 100 in Jamaica.)

Apple Barn & Country Bake Shop (802-447-7780). Near Bennington, there are cornfield mazes starting in September and haunted mazes for Halloween. Watch out for the pumpkin-eating dinosaur.

International Herbs (802-442-7870) in Bennington is one of the most complete herbal shops in the East, with herbs of every description packed into a relatively small space.

SPECIAL EVENTS *Late May:* **Bennington Mayfest** is a street festival, with crafts and entertainment.

June 1–2: **NAFA Flyball Tournament,** Southern Vermont College Athletic Center.

July: **Annual Bennington Museum Antique Show** (see *To See—Museums*).

Late July: **Pownal Valley Fair**—exhibits, antique tractor pull, bingo, music, fireworks, petting zoo, etc.

Late July: **Summer in the Park,** free concert series.

August 16–18: **Bennington Battle Day Weekend.**

Mid-September: **Antique and Classic Car Show,** Willow Park, Bennington.

December 31: **First Night Bennington.** Community wide celebrations.

MANCHESTER AND THE MOUNTAINS

INCLUDES ARLINGTON, DORSET, DANBY, LANDGROVE, LONDONDERRY, PAWLET, PERU

No Vermont community has changed more dramatically in recent years than Manchester. A summer resort since the Civil War, Manchester has also long been a place to stay while skiing at nearby Stratton and Bromley and on southern Vermont's most dependably snowy cross-country trails.

What's new is the breadth and depth of shopping in this proud old town: upward of 50 top-brand outlet stores and another 50 or so specialty stores and galleries. Manchester is also home to some of Vermont's best restaurants and places to stay, including one of its grandest resorts. Furthermore, the town is positioning itself as a cultural center for the state with the spectacular new Southern Vermont Arts Center, the Riley Rink at Hunter Park with its lengthy list of summer concerts, and two of the state's premier summer theaters, the Dorset Playhouse and the Weston Playhouse.

The white-columned, tower-topped, 180-room Equinox is as much a part of Manchester's current appeal as it was in the 1850s, the era in which the town's status as a resort was firmly established. Mrs. Abraham Lincoln and her two sons spent the summers of 1863 and '64 at the Equinox, booked again for the summer of '65, and reserved a space for the entire family the following season. The president, unfortunately, never made it.

Other presidents—Taft, Grant, Theodore Roosevelt, and Benjamin Harrison—came to stay at the Equinox, but it was Lincoln's family who adopted the village. Robert Todd Lincoln, who served as secretary of war under President Garfield, minister to Britain under Harrison, then president of the Pullman Palace Car Company, selected Manchester Village as his summer home, building Hildene, the lavish mansion that's now such an interesting place to visit. Other opulent "summer cottages" are sequestered off River Road and nearby country lanes.

Manchester Center and Village are both down in the wide Valley of Vermont, but Mount Equinox, a stray peak from New York's Taconic range, thrusts up a full 3,800 feet from the village, rising right from the back of its namesake hotel.

Luckily the 1930s Work Projects Administration plan to carve ski trails on Mount Equinox never panned out, and Manchester Village retains its serene,

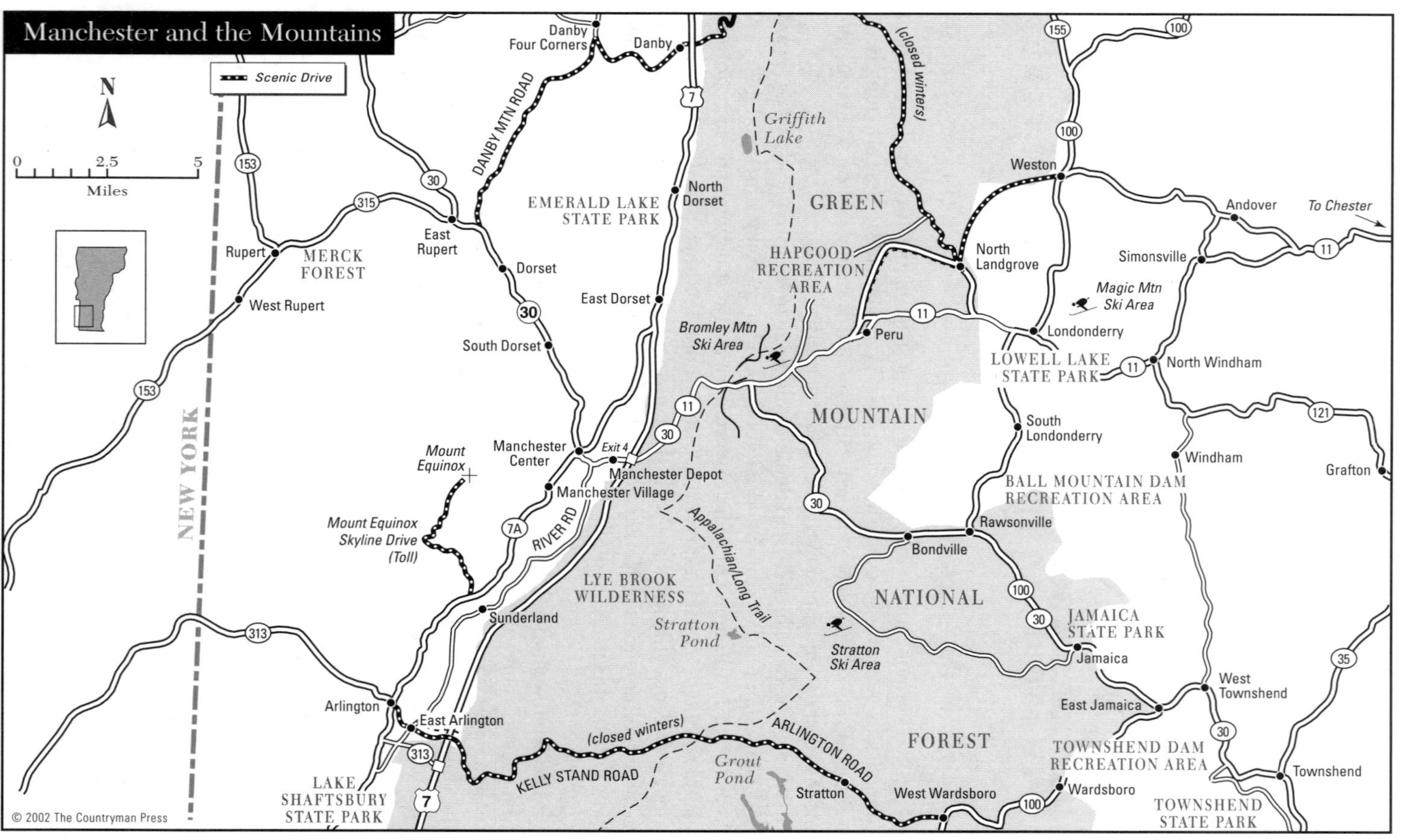

Manchester and the Mountains
Scenic Drive
N
0
2.5
5
Miles
NEW YORK
Danby Four Corners
Danby
DANBY MTN ROAD
EMERALD LAKE STATE PARK
North Dorset
East Dorset
Dorset
East Rupert
Rupert
MERCK FOREST
West Rupert
South Dorset
Griffith Lake
GREEN
MOUNTAIN
NATIONAL
FOREST
(closed winters)
HAPGOOD RECREATION AREA
Bromley Mtn Ski Area
Peru
Weston
North Landgrove
Londonderry
Magic Mtn Ski Area
Simonsville
Andover
To Chester
LOWELL LAKE STATE PARK
North Windham
South Londonderry
Windham
Grafton
BALL MOUNTAIN DAM RECREATION AREA
Rawsonville
Bondville
Manchester Center
Exit 4
Manchester Depot
Manchester Village
Mount Equinox
Mount Equinox Skyline Drive (Toll)
RIVER RD
Appalachian/Long Trail
LYE BROOK WILDERNESS
Stratton Pond
Stratton Ski Area
JAMAICA STATE PARK
Jamaica
East Jamaica
West Townshend
Townshend
TOWNSHEND DAM RECREATION AREA
TOWNSHEND STATE PARK
Wardsboro
West Wardsboro
Stratton
ARLINGTON ROAD
KELLY STAND ROAD
(closed winters)
Grout Pond
Sunderland
Arlington
East Arlington
LAKE SHAFTSBURY STATE PARK
© 2002 The Countryman Press

white-clapboard good looks. The hotel faces the Congregational church and gold-domed Bennington Courthouse, and the few tasteful stores include a branch of Frog Hollow, Vermont's premier crafts shop. Public buildings trail off into a line of mansions, spaced along marble sidewalks.

Discount shopping begins a quarter mile downhill in Manchester Center, a village with a different zip code and zoning. The center was "Factory Point" in the 19th century, when sawmills, marbleworks, and a tannery were powered by the Battenkill River's flow.

Fears that the former Factory Point might become Vermont's future factory outlet capital began in the mid-1980s, with the opening of a trendy wood-and-glass shopping complex at the traffic heart of town, the junction of Routes 7A and 11/30—known locally as "Malfunction Junction."

The strip malls, however, haven't materialized. Instead, outlets along Route 7A fill old homes and house-sized compounds, blending nicely with shopping landmarks like the Orvis Retail Store (supplying the needs of fishermen and other sportsmen since 1856).

The Green Mountains rise even within Manchester town limits to 3,100 feet on the east, then roll off into heavily forested uplands punctuated by picturesque villages like Peru, Landgrove, Weston, and Londonderry, all noteworthy for cross-country skiing and equally appealing in summer. Dorset and Danby are also well worth a visit.

GUIDANCE **Manchester and the Mountains Regional Chamber** (802-362-2100; www.manchestervermont.com), 5046 Main Street, Manchester Center. This clapboard chamber of commerce information booth is walled with pamphlets, good for general walk-in information. The chamber does not make reservations but does keep a running tally on space in member lodging places and on short-term condo and cottage rentals.

Stratton Mountain maintains a reservation and information service (802-297-4000 in-state; 1-800-THE-MTNS) and serves some 20 lodges, condo clusters, and inns on and around Stratton.

In winter, the **Bromley Village Lodging Service** (1-800-865-4786; www.bromley.com) also makes reservations for condominiums.

The Arlington Chamber of Commerce has merged with the Manchester Chamber but it maintains a volunteer-staffed information booth on Route 7A, which is open May through October.

Dorset Chamber of Commerce (802-867-2450; www.dorsetvt.com), P.O. Box 121, Dorset 05251.

Londonderry Chamber of Commerce (802-824-8178) maintains an information booth and office in the Mountain Marketplace (the Londonderry shopping center) at the junction of Routes 11 and 100.

GETTING THERE *By car:* From Bennington, Route 7 to Manchester is a limited-access highway that's speedy but dull, except for viewing Mount Equinox. You get a more interesting taste of the area, especially around Arlington, by clinging to historic Route 7A. From the southeast, the obvious access is I-91 to Brattleboro, then

Route 30 north. And from the Albany-Troy area, take NY 7 heading east into Vermont, where it becomes 9 east. In the center of Bennington, take VT 7 north to exit 4, or follow historic Route 7A.

By bus: **Vermont Transit** offers good service from New York and Montreal to Manchester; connections with Boston are via Williamstown, Massachusetts, or Rutland.

MEDICAL EMERGENCY **Manchester-Dorset Rescue Squad** (911).

Northshire Medical Associates (802-362-4440), Manchester Center.

Manchester Family Medical Clinic (802-362-1263), Route 7A, Manchester.

Mountain Valley Medical Clinic (802-824-6901), Route 11, opposite the Flood Brook School, 2 miles west of Londonderry, 3 miles east of Peru.

Carlos Otis Clinic (802-297-2300), at Stratton Mountain.

Tri Mountain Rescue Squad (802-824-3166). Bondville, Landgrove, Peru, and Stratton.

* Villages

In addition to Manchester, the area's picturesque places include: Arlington, 7 miles south along Route 7A; Weston, 15 miles to the northeast; Dorset, 8 miles to the northwest; Pawlet, another 7 miles to the north on Route 30; and Danby, 8 miles north of Dorset and 10 miles east of Pawlet.

Although never formally the capital of Vermont, **Arlington,** on Route 7A, was the de facto seat of government during most of the Revolutionary period. Fearing British attacks in the north, Vermont's first governor, Thomas Chittenden, moved south from Williston, liberated a Tory property in Arlington (the area known as Tory Hollow), and conducted affairs of state from there. Arlington recently was voted the most historic village in Vermont.

Many older visitors to Arlington fondly remember Dorothy Canfield Fisher, the author of 50 immensely popular, warmhearted novels and a judge of the Book-of-the-Month Club for 25 years. Another famous resident was illustrator Norman Rockwell, who lived in West Arlington from 1939 to 1953. Many of his illustrations of small-town Americans were done in and around Arlington.

Dorset. This pristine village is visible evidence that it takes money to "prevent the future." A fashionable summer refuge for years, few signs of commerce mar its state of carefully manicured nature. Today's tranquillity, making it a haven for artists and writers as well as the affluent, contrasts sharply with the hotheaded days of its youth. In 1776, the Green Mountain Boys gathered in Cephas Kent's tavern and issued their first declaration of independence from the New Hampshire Grants, signed by Thomas Chittenden, Ira Allen, Matthew Lyon, Seth Warner, and other Founding Fathers of Vermont. Today the Dorset Inn, said to be the state's oldest continuously operating hostelry, is the village focal point, along with the Dorset Playhouse, one of New England's most venerable summer theaters. The first marble to be quarried in North America came from Dorset, and one quarry is now a popular swimming hole. There is also a nine-hole golf course, the private Dorset Field Club (billed as the state's oldest), and a fine choice of places to stay.

Pawlet. Not far north of Dorset, this hamlet on Route 30 is an unexpected delight, with a mix of architectural styles in the buildings that cling to the rather steep slopes leading up from Flower Brook, over which Johnny Mach's General Store extends. Gib Mach has harnessed the rushing brook to a turbine that generates his electricity and has built a glass-topped counter at the end of a store aisle through which you can peer down at the water surging through the narrow gorge below. Next door, a former railroad station is now the Old Station Restaurant and Ice Cream Parlor, and a clutch of nearby shops are worth investigating.

Danby. A bypassed hamlet on Route 7 between Dorset and Wallingford, Danby is a vintage village known for fine marble quarries and as home base for Silas Griffith, an 1850s lumber baron who was Vermont's first millionaire. In the 1960s, novelist Pearl Buck bought seven buildings in the village and began to renovate them, and since her death inns, restaurants, and some intriguing shops have opened here.

Weston. A mountain crossroads that's a logical hub for exploring all of southern Vermont, this village of just 500 souls looms large on tourist maps. It's the home of one of the country's oldest and best summer theaters and the Vermont Country Store, New England's number one nostalgia outlet. The oval common is shaded with majestic maples, and a band plays regularly in the bandstand. Free summer concerts are also presented by the Kinhaven Music School high on a back road, and visitors are also welcome at Weston Priory, a small community of Benedictine monks, nationally known for the music sung and played at Sunday liturgies. Weston was actually one of the first villages in Vermont to be consciously preserved. The theater, the unusually fine historical collection in the Farrar Mansur House, and (indirectly) the Vermont Country Store all date from the "Weston Revival" of the 1930s. Today it offers exceptional lodging and dining as well as theater and shopping.

✷ To See

MUSEUMS ♿ **Southern Vermont Arts Center** (802-362-1405; www.svac.org), West Road, Manchester Center. Late May through October, daily 10–5 except Monday, and Sunday noon–5; December through mid-March, Monday through Saturday 10–5. Donation requested. The new Elizabeth deC. Wilson Museum, which opened in July 2000, is a work of art in itself with its soaring, light-filled galleries that house some first-class touring shows of paintings, sculpture, prints, and photography. Concerts and lectures are held in the adjacent, 430-seat Arkell Pavilion. Other special events throughout the year.

SOUTHERN VERMONT ARTS CENTER

Kim Grant

Light lunches are served in the Garden Café (see *Eating Out*), and there are extensive trails through the woods, among them a botany trail featuring rock formations, 67 varieties of wildflowers, and birches. Limited handicapped accessibility.

The American Museum of Fly Fishing (802-362-3300), Seminary Avenue and Route 7A, Manchester Village. Open May through October, 10–4 daily, the museum displays the beautiful flies of Mary Orvis Marbury as well as more than 1,000 rods and reels made by famous rod builders and owned by such luminaries as Daniel Webster, Bing Crosby, Ernest Hemingway, and presidents Hoover and Eisenhower. Don't miss it. $3 admission; students free.

Norman Rockwell Exhibition (802-375-6423), Route 7A, Arlington. Open daily 9–7. Housed in a Hudson River Gothic church are some 500 of the artist's *Saturday Evening Post* cover illustrations and prints. There's a 20-minute film, and a gift shop. Admission.

The **Dr. George A. Russell Collection of Vermontiana,** believed to be the third largest such collection, is housed in quarters behind the Martha Canfield Public Library, Arlington. Although not a museum (there are no displays), the collection is open to the public on Tuesday or by appointment with the curators, David and Mary Lou Thomas (802-375-6307). Dr. Russell, the country doctor immortalized in the Rockwell print that hangs in thousands of doctors' offices, collected Vermontiana for most of his long life and left his collection to the town. The collection includes Dorothy Canfield Fisher materials, a large selection of Norman Rockwell's work, many photographs from the period 1860–90, an extensive selection of town and country histories for Vermont and neighboring states, and a wealth of genealogical materials (deeds, letters, wills, account books, and diaries) for both the Arlington area and the state as a whole.

The Martha Canfield Public Library, Route 7A, Arlington (named for Dorothy Canfield Fisher's grandmother), holds a book sale under a tent on its lawn 10–5 Friday and Saturday and 1–5 Sunday from June 15 through foliage season. Books are sold at prices from 15¢ to 50¢, and records and jigsaw puzzles are also available at moderate prices. During peak holiday seasons, the sale is sometimes held weekdays as well.

HISTORIC HOMES ♿ **Historic Hildene** (802-362-1788; www.hildene.org), Route 7A, Manchester Village. Mid-May through October, 9:30–4; $8 adults; $4 youths 6–14. Limited handicapped accessibility. An impressive house among historic houses, this 24-room Georgian Revival manor is set on 412 acres, including formal gardens and paths that lead down into the Battenkill Valley. Bring a picnic lunch and plan to stay half the day. The tour begins with a wagon ride to the Carriage Barn, now a sophisticated visitors center with a slide show about Robert Todd Lincoln. You learn that he first came to the village as a boy with his mother for a stay at the Equinox House; his father was assassinated before the family could return, as they had intended, the following summer. It was Todd's law partner who later persuaded him to build this summer home adjacent to his own mansion. Todd died here in 1926, and members of the family lived here until 1975. Guides are familiar with at least one Lincoln and with the true character of the authenti-

Kim Grant

HISTORIC HILDENE, ROBERT TODD LINCOLN'S SUMMER HOME

cally furnished house. Tours include the restored formal gardens and a brief demonstration of the 1,000-pipe organ, which can be played both manually and with one of 240 player rolls on hand. Picnic tables outside command a view of the valley below, and there are numerous trails to stroll or—in winter, when the Carriage Barn becomes a warming hut—to explore on skis (see *Winter Sports—Cross-Country Skiing*). In summer, Sunday-afternoon polo matches are a popular spectator sport. Inquire about organ concerts and other special events.

♿ **Farrar Mansur House** (802-824-4399), village green, Weston. Open weekends Memorial Day through Columbus Day; in July and August, Wednesday through Sunday 1–4. Fee. Limited handicapped accessibility. Even if you have never set foot inside a historic house, make an exception for this one, built in 1797 as a tavern with a classic old taproom and seven fireplaces. Thanks to 1930s Work Projects Administration (WPA) artists, murals of Weston in its prime—in the 1840s it was twice the size it is today—cover the living room walls, and a number of primitive portraits hang in adjoining rooms, which are filled with furniture and furnishings donated by Weston families. Upstairs in the old ballroom, a rendition of townspeople dancing—each face is painted to resemble a specific resident—conjures the spirit of a town that knew how to have fun.

Weston Mill Museum, at the junction of Routes 100 and 155, Weston. Daily Memorial Day through Columbus Day, 10–5. Donations requested. This is a working restoration of a vintage mill. Note the work of David Claggett, a skilled tinmaker who uses 18th-century methods to make exceptional chandeliers, lanterns, sconces, and folk art.

SCENIC DRIVES **Mount Equinox** (802-362-1114). The summit of Mount Equinox is 3,825 feet high. Most of the mountain is owned by the Carthusian monks who occupy the monastery, which you can see from the top. A toll road (open May to November; $6 per car and driver; $2 per passenger) climbs more than 5 miles from Route 7 to the top. This can be a spectacular ride on a clear day, even more dramatic if the mountain is in the clouds and the road keeps disappearing in front of you. Be sure to drive back down in low gear and in total sobriety. There are also trails to the top.

Green Mountain National Forest Road Number 10, Danby to Landgrove. Closed in winter. The longest (14 miles) and most isolated of these byways, the road (beginning in Danby) climbs through the White Rocks Recreation Area, crossing a number of tempting hiking paths as well as the Long Trail. There are some fine views as you continue along, and you might want to picnic somewhere in the middle of the forest, as we did by a beaver pond. The road follows Tabor Brook down into Landgrove, itself a tiny, picturesque village.

Peru to Weston. From the village of Peru, an enticing, wooded road is paved as far as Hapgood Pond, then continues smoothly through Landgrove, a minuscule village with an outstanding inn (open to the public for dinner), set in rolling fields. The way to Weston is clearly marked.

East Rupert to Danby. Danby Mountain Road is the logical shortcut from Dorset to Danby, and it's quite beautiful, winding up and over a saddle between Woodlawn Mountain and Dorset Peak. Well-surfaced dirt, with long views in places. If you are coming from East Rupert, be sure to turn right at Danby Four Corners and follow Mill Brook into Danby.

✷ To Do

BICYCLING In Manchester, mountain-bike, hybrid-bike, and touring-bike rentals and touring information are available from **Battenkill Sports Cycle Shop** (802-362-2734; www.battenkillbicycle.com), open Monday through Saturday 9:30–5:30, in the Stone House, junction of Routes 7 and 11/30.

Stratton Sports (802-297-2200; 1-800-STRATTON), at Stratton Mountain, rents mountain bikes and offers terrain ranging from paved roads to cross-country-ski trails and (for expert bikers) a combination of service and ski trails down from the summit (the gondola hoists bikes as well as riders to the top); guided tours.

Mountain Riders (802-297-1745), junction of Routes 30 and 100 in Rawsonville, also on the Mount Snow Access Road in West Dover.

CAMPING **Green Mountain National Forest** (802-362-2307), District Ranger Office, Manchester. A public information office serving the southern third of the 275,000-acre Green Mountain National Forest is located on Routes 30 and 11 east of Manchester; open year-round, Monday through Friday 8–4:30. Maps and details are available about where to fish, hike, cross-country ski, and camp. All national forest campsites are available on a first-come, first-served basis.

NORCROSS WEST MARBLE QUARRY

Kim Grant

Emerald Lake State Park (802-362-1655), North Dorset. On Route 7, this area offers 105 campsites, including 36 lean-tos, also hiking and nature trails, among them a 3.4-mile, round-trip trek to a natural bridge.

Hapgood Pond Recreation Area, Peru. Acquired in 1931, this was the beginning of the Green Mountain National Forest. There is swimming, fishing, and limited boating on the 7-acre pond. Removed from the picnic ground and beach are 28 campsites (first-come, first-served basis). A pleasant, 8-mile forest trail threads through the woods.

Greendale Campground, 2 miles north of Weston on Route 100. There are 14 sites.

See also *Green Space* in "The Lower Connecticut and West River Valleys" for details about Jamaica State Park.

CANOEING The **Battenkill** makes for satisfying canoeing in the spring; the Manchester-to-Arlington section is relatively flat water but it gets difficult a mile above Arlington.

BattenKill Canoe Ltd. (802-362-2800), Route 7A in Arlington. An outfitter offering inn-to-inn canoe trips throughout the state and as far afield as Costa Rica and England, also rents canoes and offers shuttle service on the Battenkill.

DRIVING **Country Pursuits Centre** (802-362-7873), Manchester Village. Includes the Land Rover Driving School, Junior Off-Road, and the Fly Fishing School. An off-road instructional course and classroom area has been constructed for the driving school, and expert instructors are on hand to offer tips on driving both on- and off-road. Junior Off-Road is for children of all ages. Fly fishing lessons and guided trips.

FISHING Fly-fishing has been serious business in the Battenkill since the mid–19th century. The Orvis Company began manufacturing bamboo rods in Manchester Village near the spot where they are still produced.

The **Battenkill** is generally recognized as Vermont's best wild-trout stream; access is available at a number of places off Route 7A. Brown trout can also be found in Gale Meadows Pond, accessible via gravel road from Route 30 at Bondville. Emerald Lake in North Dorset is stocked with pike, bass, and perch; rental boats are available at the state park facility.

Orvis Fishing Schools (802-362-3622; 1-800-235-9763), the name in fly-fishing instruction as well as equipment; 3-day courses, offered twice weekly April through August.

Southern Vermont Fly Fisherman (1-800-682-0103). Chuck Kashner's guide service includes rods, reels, waders, flies, and a meal on full-day trips.

Battenkill Anglers (802-362-3184) is a Thomas & Thomas–sponsored fly-fishing school and outfitter.

Peter Basta (802-867-4103), P.O. Box 540, Dorset 05251, offers guide service and on-stream instruction.

GOLF The 18-hole **Gleneagles Golf Course** at the Equinox Country Club (802-362-3223), Manchester Center, which was established in the 1920s for guests of the Equinox House, in recent years has undergone a $3 million renovation and is open to the public. The **Dormy Grill** at the Gleneagles Clubhouse also offers pleasant noontime dining.

The Stratton Golf School (802-297-2200; 1-800-843-6867) offers weekend and midweek sessions, including professional instruction, use of the 27-hole course at the Stratton Mountain Country Club, and a special 22-acre "training site."

Windham Golf Club (802-875-2517), Popple Dungeon Road, Windham. An 18-hole course, built on the site of one of New England's largest and oldest potato farms. Facilities include a pro shop, carts, dressing rooms, and showers. The **Clubhouse** serves a Vermont country breakfast on weekends; salads, sandwiches, and burgers at lunch; and a tavern menu from 3:30 until closing.

The Practice Tee (802-362-3100), Route 7, Manchester Center. Open in-season, weather permitting, 9–7 weekdays, 8–7 weekends and holidays; lessons available.

HIKING From the Green Mountain National Forest District Office, request hiking maps for **Lye Brook Wilderness,** a 14,600-acre preserve south of Manchester with a 2.3-mile trail to the Lye Brook Waterfalls and the **Long Trail.** This Massachusetts-to-Quebec path doubles as the Appalachian Trail throughout the area; portions of the trail make good day hikes, either north over Bromley Mountain or south over Spruce Peak from Routes 11 and 30. The most heavily hiked stretch of the entire trail is the relatively level trek in from Kelly Stand Road to Stratton Pond; there are three shelters in the immediate area, and swimming is permitted. Griffith Lake, accessible from Peru and Danby, is a less crowded swimming and camping site on the trail. For details, consult the Green Mountain Club's *Long Trail Guide.*

Mount Equinox. Details about the rewarding, 6-mile Burr and Burton Trail from Manchester Village to the summit are available in *Day Hiker's Guide to Vermont* (Green Mountain Club). At 3,825 feet, this is the highest mountain in the state that is not traversed by the Long Trail. See also Equinox Preservation Trust under *Green Space.*

Tracks of Vermont (802-645-1938; www.explorevt.com), P.O. Box 252, Weston 05161. Organized day trips and longer outings.

HORSEBACK RIDING, ETC. **Horses for Hire** (802-297-1468), South Road, Rawsonville. Trail rides, sleigh rides, riding lessons, even in winter, weather permitting; $30 per person for a 1-hour ride. Half-day trips also available. English riding.

Karl Pfister (802-824-6320), Londonderry. Fall foliage carriage and wagon rides available by reservation.

Sunbowl Ranch (802-297-9210), at Stratton Mountain Resort, offers trail rides, donkey rides, lessons, and wagon rides.

Chipman Stables (802-293-5242), Danby Four Corners. Trail rides and lessons, both Western-style. Trail rides are $30 per person.

Petticoat Junction (802-362-3885) in Manchester offers carriage, wagon, sleigh, and small-group trail rides through the woods and meadows of Manchester.

HUNTING **Orvis Company** (802-362-3622; 1-800-548-9548) of Manchester (see *Fishing*) offers 2-day shooting courses ($775) in July and August; 3-day programs ($950) September through mid-October. Hunters move in groups of five through 10 stations in a simulated hunting course. Tuition includes guns and ammo, but not lodging.

The **British School of Falconry** (802-362-4780) at the Equinox Hotel, Manchester Village, offers introductory lessons, hawk walks, and pheasant hunting with hawks and falcons at the Tinmouth Hunting Preserve in Wallingford.

MOUNTAIN RIDES ✐ **Bromley Mountain** (802-824-5522; www.bromley.com), Route 11, Peru (6 miles east of Manchester). This 3,284-foot-high mountain offers excellent views of Stratton and Equinox Mountains. It is traversed by the Long Trail (see *Hiking*) and is also accessible by hiking the ski trails from the midpoint exit on the chairlift. This lift, serving the alpine slide, is open Memorial Day through mid-October, weather permitting, on weekends 10–5 and daily July through Labor Day 9:30–6 (fee). The **Bromley Alpine Slide,** the longest in this country, is a great ride with fabulous views whatever your age. The **DévalKarts** and the **Bromley Thrill Sleds** (similar to a winter luge) are big draws for the teen set. There are also miniature golf, a 24-foot climbing wall, a parabounce, a "trampoline thing," and an extreme zip line. Lunch, snacks, and drinks available at the base lodge.

Stratton Mountain (802-297-2200; 1-800-STRATTON; www.stratton.com) offers a four-state view from its summit, accessible by Starship XII gondolas from the ski resort (Route 30, Bondville). The gondolas run daily in summer and fall, 9:30–4:15. And there's lots of summer action in its Adventure Zone—skate park, climbing wall, boulders, and a cave.

NATURE WALKS AND WORKSHOPS ✐ **Vermont Institute of Natural Science** (VINS), in partnership with the Equinox Preservation Trust (802-362-4374; see *Green Space*), offers natural history walks and programs for adults, families, and children. The programs run year-round, geared to the season. $4–5 per adult, $1–2 for children.

SWIMMING **Dana L. Thompson Recreation Area** (802-362-1439), Route 30 north, Manchester, is open daily in summer, but hours for general swimming are limited; nominal fee.

Dorset Quarry, off Route 30 on Kelly Road between Manchester and Dorset (turn across from Mountain Weavers), is a deep, satisfying pool but not recommended for children. The upper quarry is the local skinny-dipping spot.

✐ **Hapgood Pond** in Peru, with its sand and calm, shallow drop-off, is favored by families with young children.

Emerald Lake State Park (802-362-1655), Route 7, North Dorset, offers clear lake swimming.

See also *Green Space.*

TENNIS ✐ **Stratton Mountain** (802-297-2200; 1-800-STRATTON: www.stratton.com) offers weekend and midweek clinics. There are 15 outdoor and 4 indoor courts. *Note:* Stratton Mountain offers full daycare and day camp in summer for children (6 weeks to 10 years old) of parents enrolled in the golf and tennis programs. A Junior Tennis Day Camp is also offered weekdays for children ages 7–15.

Dana L. Thompson Recreation Area, Manchester. Public courts are available with weekly memberships or on a per-hour basis.

Equinox Hotel Tennis (802-362-4700), Route 7A, Manchester Village. Three Har-Tru courts are open to the public for an hourly fee.

Dorset Tennis Club (802-362-2236), Route 7A, 4 miles north of Manchester. Indoor court; lessons.

TRAIN RIDES ✐ **The *Vermont Valley Flyer*** (802-463-3069; 1-800-707-3530), operated by the Green Mountain Railroad Corp., makes three round trips a day between Manchester and Arlington from the first of July to mid-October. $10 for adults, $6 children 3–12.

✱ Winter Sports

CROSS-COUNTRY SKIING **Viking Nordic Centre** (802-824-3933; www.vikingnordic.com), 615 Little Pond Road, Londonderry. The Viking trail system now includes 40 km of trails, 30 km groomed, 3 km lighted. There is a rental and retail shop and a café serving drinks, light breakfasts, and lunches. There are lessons, lunch tours to Weston, and bed & breakfast and inn-to-inn tours using a total of four local hostelries. The Viking Nordic Guest House also offers four bedrooms at the center; $400 per night including breakfast, snacks, and trail pass. Trail fee: $15 full day, $11 half day.

Wild Wings Ski Touring Center (802-824-6793), North Road, Peru. Tracy and Chuck Black run a family-oriented touring center located within the boundaries of the Green Mountain National Forest, 2.5 miles north of Peru. Trails are narrow, geared to the beginning and intermediate skier. This area tends to get a heavier snowfall than other local touring centers; the 25 km of trails are at elevations between 1,650 and 2,040 feet. Instruction and rentals. $9 trail fee.

Stratton Ski Touring Center (802-297-2200), Stratton Mountain. Based at the Sun Bowl (see *Horseback Riding*), a 20 km series of groomed loops plus adjoining backcountry trails. Guided backcountry tours as well as a variety of other tours are offered. $10 trail fee.

Hildene Ski Touring Center (802-362-1788), Manchester. The Lincoln Carriage Barn serves as a warming hut for this system of 12 km of groomed and mapped trails on the estate built by Robert Todd Lincoln (see Hildene under *To See—Historic Homes*). Trails meander through woods and fields on a promontory overlooking the Battenkill Valley between Mount Equinox and Lye Brook Wilderness. Lessons and equipment are available.

Equinox Ski Touring Center (802-362-3223) has 35 km of groomed trails and tracked terrain, snowshoeing, instruction, and rentals. This network includes trails on the golf course, up through the forests of the Equinox Preservation Trust (see *Green Space*), and around Equinox Pond.

DOWNHILL SKIING **Bromley** (802-824-5522), 3984 Route 11 in Peru, 8 miles east of Manchester. Founded in 1937 by Fred Pabst, of the Milwaukee brewing family, this is among the oldest ski areas in the country. It was also one of the first to have snowmaking, snow farming, a slope-side nursery, and condominiums. It retains its own following of those who like its friendly atmosphere and sunny trails. Boarders will enjoy Snowboard Heaven Terrain Park. *Lifts:* 10: 1 high-speed detachable quad, 1 fixed-grip quad, 4 doubles, 1 T-bar, 2 Mighty-Mites, and Magic Carpet. *Trails:* 43 trails—35 percent intermediate, 34 percent beginner, 31 percent expert. *Vertical drop:* 1,334 feet. *Snowmaking:* 80 percent of terrain from base to summit. *Facilities:* The base lodge offers two cafeterias as well as more formal areas. Skiers unload right at the base lodge; the driver then parks in an area across Route 11 and rides back on a shuttle bus. Valet parking is another option. *Ski school:* Ski and snowboard school. *For children:* The Bromley Learning Center includes a nursery for ages 6 weeks to 6 years. Mighty Moose for ages 3–5 and PigDog's Ski & Snowboard Mountain Club for 6-to 12-year-olds. *Rates:* $51 adults, $44 teens, $34 juniors, weekends; midweek, $46 adults, $38 teens, $32 juniors. Snowboard park $15.

Stratton (1-800-STRATTON; ski report: 802-297-4211; boarder line: 802-297-4545). Located atop a 5-mile access road from Route 30 in Bondville, Stratton is an unusually well-groomed mountain. This goes for its trails, facilities, lodges, and clientele. It ranks high among Vermont's major ski resorts, a big mountain with two separate areas: the original North Face and the distinctly sunnier Sun Bowl, the newer of the two. There are six terrain parks for snowboarders with two half-pipes and a super pipe. Thanks to the quantity of lifts, skiers are generally dispersed over the trail network. Stratton Village, a complex that includes a variety of shops, a dozen restaurants, a 91-room condo hotel, a 750-car garage, and 170 condominiums, dwarfs the base facility. A sports center includes a 25-yard-long pool, whirlpool, indoor tennis courts, racquetball courts, exercise equipment, and a lounge. (See also *Lodging*.)

A lot happens here in summer, too: There's a 70-foot climbing wall; a skate park with jumps, ramps, and rails; and an indoor family FunZone. *Lifts:* 14: a 12-passenger gondola, four 6-passenger high-speed detachable, four quads, one triple, one double chair, and two surface lifts. *Trails and slopes:* 90. *Vertical drop:* 2,003 feet. *Snowmaking:* 80 percent. *Facilities:* Restaurant and cafeteria in the base lodge, also cafeterias midmountain and in the new Sun Bowl Ranch. Chapel of the Snows at the parking lot, a little Bavarian-style church, has frequent nondenominational and Roman Catholic services. A shuttle bus brings skiers from inns on the mountain to the base lodge. Also a clinic, sports center, and shops and restaurants in the base area Village Square. *Ski school:* Ski and snowboard lessons. *For children:* Childcare Center for ages 6 weeks to 3 years. Mountain Riders 5–8 and 9–18. A separate base lodge for KidsKamp; combined ski and play programs are offered—Little Cubs (ages 4–6), Big Cubs (7–12), Junior Newcomers (7–12). *Rates:* $57 per adult midweek, $62 weekends and $64 holidays; $50–56 young adults and seniors; $42–46 juniors and super seniors. Many special packages.

Magic Mountain Ski Area (802-824-5645), Londonderry. Skiing and riding. A weekend lift ticket is $42, midweek $32.

ICE SKATING **Riley Rink at Hunter Park** (802-362-0150), a paradise for music lovers in the summer and sports enthusiasts in the spring, is transformed into an Olympic-sized ice-skating rink in the winter.

SLEIGH RIDES **Karl Pfister** (802-824-6320) in Landgrove offers the most remote, romantic sleigh ride around.

The **Equinox Hotel** and the stables listed under *Horseback Riding* also offer sleigh rides, as does **Merck Forest and Farmland Center** (see *Green Space*).

SNOWMOBILING A *Winter Recreation Map,* available free from the Green Mountain National Forest District Ranger Office (802-362-2307), Manchester, shows trails presently maintained in this area by the Vermont Association of Snow Travelers. **Classic Snow Tours** (802-824-6628), based at the Pinnacle Sun & Ski Lodge, junction of Routes 11 and 30, Manchester, offers tours and rentals.

✷ Green Space

Equinox Preservation Trust (802-362-4700), Manchester Village. A not-for-profit organization created in 1993 by Equinox Resort Associates and is administered through the Vermont Land Trust and The Nature Conservancy. Some 850 acres on Mount Equinox are now a user-friendly preserve. Secure a map/guide to the trail system (a portion is open to cross-country skiers) and inquire about the nature walks and seminars offered year-round, some geared to children, in conjunction with VINS (see *To Do—Nature Walks*). Horseback riding and mountain biking are also permitted on the ski trails in summer and fall. Be sure at least to walk the 1.2-mile loop through the hardwoods around Equinox Pond. *Note:* All parking for access to the trust property is at the parking lot of the Equinox Hotel (see *Lodging*).

Merck Forest and Farmland Center (802-394-7836), Route 315, Rupert. Some 2,800 acres of near wilderness, including Mount Antone, were set aside in the 1950s as a foundation by George Merck, of the Merck Drug Company. The area is now maintained through donations, and the forest offers year-round walks, talks, and facilities: foot and horse trails, picnic areas, a spring-fed swimming pond, 12 shelters, a farm museum, and a sugarhouse that produces 400 gallons of syrup. The **Merck Forest Summer Camp** has six 1-week sessions for children. Reservations are required for overnight use of the shelters. An extensive network of trails is marked for cross-country skiing.

Grout Pond, west of the village of Stratton, marked from Kelley Stand Road. Deep in the Green Mountain National Forest, this is a great spot for a picnic, complete with grills and a small beach.

See also *To Do—Camping.*

✷ Lodging

RESORT ⊘ **The Equinox** (802-362-4700; 802-362-1595; 1-800-362-4747; www.equinoxresort.com), Route 7A, Manchester Village 05254. The white-columned inn is composed of 17 distinct parts that have evolved over the past 229 years. It's still evolving. In the mid-1980s, it was revamped from its foundations up, an unavoidable process that left it sound but, many said, soulless. Thanks to a 1990s infusion of funds, the 136 rooms and 47 suites, most of them spacious and furnished in pine reproductions, have acquired modern plumbing and a brighter, more country-inn feel. The **Charles Orvis Inn** next door is composed of suites, each with a cherry-paneled kitchen, oak floors, gas fireplace, and separate living room and bedroom. Common rooms include a paneled bar, billiard room, and meeting space. The inn's public spaces are extensive and quite magnificent, the grandest in Vermont. Meals are memorable (see *Dining Out*). Facilities for which guests pay extra include the newly revamped, 18-hole golf course, a fitness center with outdoor and indoor pool, touring bikes, a 14-acre stocked trout pond, tennis courts, a cross-country-ski network, snowmobiling, hunting with falcons, and learning to drive Land Rovers ecologically off-road. You might want to make sure before booking that your stay does not coincide with one of the business groups that can preempt the public spaces. Rates: $189–589 at the Equinox, $569–899 at the Charles Orvis Inn. Inquire about midweek and MAP packages.

INNS AND BED & BREAKFASTS

In Manchester

♿ **The Inn at Ormsby Hill** (802-362-1163; 1-800-670-2841; www.ormsbyhill.com), 1842 Main Street, Manchester Center 05255. The inn is 2 miles southwest of Manchester Village on Route 7A, set in 2.5 acres of rolling lawns. The best views are from the back of the house. This gracious, elegant manor was the home of Edward Isham—Robert Todd Lincoln's law partner—and his family's home for 100 years. Its connection to Hildene (see *To See—Historic Homes*) is strong, spiritually and aesthetically.

THE EQUINOX

Kim Grant

Innkeepers Chris and Ted Sprague have doubled the number of guest rooms and obviously enjoyed distinctively decorating each in Waverly prints and exceptional antiques, all with fireplace and two-person Jacuzzi. The spacious Taft room, with its wood-burning fireplace and huge four-poster, is the unofficial honeymoon suite, but every one of the rooms is romantic enough to qualify. The downstairs Library suite is handicapped-accessible. Common space includes a formal parlor and an inviting library lined with bookshelves that hold many of Isham's personal volumes. The huge, many-windowed dining room with ornately carved hearth is the scene of bountiful breakfasts featuring, perhaps, strawberries with crème fraîche and wild mushroom risotto with sliced ham, capped with desserts like rhubarb crumble with vanilla ice cream. Chris Sprague is a chef of some renown, and dinner is also served to guests on Friday evenings. $150–350.

The Inn at Manchester (802-362-1793; 1-877-207-4440; www.innatmanchester.com), 3967 Main Street, Manchester 05254. A gracious old home, set back from Main Street, with an expansive front porch, big windows, gables, and a restored, vintage-1867 carriage house in back. The 18 rooms, all with private bath and air-conditioning, are named for flowers and herbs. There are also four suites, three with working fireplace. The dining room and parlors are imaginatively and comfortably furnished, and there is a TV and game room, warmed by an antique woodstove. Summer brings use of the pool in the back meadow and plenty of wicker on the flowery porch. Children over 8 are welcome. Ron and Mary Blake are the new owners of the inn. Rates are $129–249 per room, including breakfast and afternoon tea.

Manchester Highlands Inn (802-362-4565; 1-800-743-4565; www.highlandsinn.com), P.O. Box 1754, 216 Highland Avenue, Manchester Center 05255. Patricia and Robert Eichorn call their spacious Victorian inn "Manchester's best-kept secret." Recently repainted Victorian gray with rose and plum accents, it's on a quiet side street, a short walk from all the shops and restaurants but with an away-from-it-all feel, especially on the back porch and lawn (with its pool), both of which command an expansive view of Mount Equinox. The 15 guest rooms, all with private bath, are nicely decorated with family antiques and personal touches, many with canopy beds. Common space includes a comfortable living room, a wicker-filled sun room, and a TV room (with a library of movies to feed the VCR). In winter, the loss of the pool and porch is assuaged by the basement Remedy Room, with its bar and games—connected by "the tunnel" (decorated with guest graffiti) to the rooms in the carriage house, which, incidentally, are usually reserved for families. A very full breakfast featuring morning-glory muffins, maybe lemon soufflé pancakes and cheddar soufflés, is served, plus home-baked afternoon snacks and tea. $110–175 double; midweek and off-season specials.

1811 House (802-362-1811; 1-800-432-1811; www.1811house.com), P.O. Box 39, Manchester Village 05254. "A place to feel pampered" is the way the owners of this magnificent building describe what they offer. Parts of this mansion date back to the 1770s. It has been an inn since 1811, except for a few years during which it was owned by President Lincoln's granddaughter Mary Lincoln Isham. Public rooms are as elegant as any others to be found in New England, and the 14 guest rooms are in keeping, each with private bath, many with hearth. Innkeepers Bruce and Marnie Duff and Cathy and Jorge Veleta dispel any stuffiness in this rareified world. The cozy pub, replete with dartboards and a wide selection of single-malt Scotches, is open to the public from 5:30 to 8. An expansive lawn and newly redesigned English-style gardens overlook the Gleneagles Golf Course (see *To Do—Golf*). A wonderful full breakfast is included in the room rate, from $120 per person for a cozy double to $230 per person for a suite with a king-sized four-poster canopy bed, fireplace, and sitting room. Rates include gratuity. Children over 16 are welcome. Off-season rates available.

Reluctant Panther Inn & Restaurant (802-362-2568; 1-800-822-2331; www.reluctantpanther.com), 17–39 West Road, Manchester 05254. Renowned for its gourmet fare (see *Dining Out*), this mauve, yellow-shuttered village home also has 13 rooms, with five suites in the adjacent Porter House, each decorated with bright wallpaper and antiques. Seven rooms and all the suites have fireplace. Many suites feature two wood-burning fireplaces—one in front of the two-person whirlpool bath and a second in the bedroom. All have private bath, room phone, and cable TV. Breakfast is served to guests only, and, with the exception of dining hours, the living room and unique pubs make a peaceful and pleasant retreat. Innkeepers are Maye and Robert Bachofen. The inn is open year-round; the restaurant is open weekends only from November through April and closed Tuesday and Wednesday from May through October. Rates: $195–575 per room, including breakfast and dinner. No children under age 14.

The Village Country Inn (802-362-1792; 1-800-370-0300; fax: 802-362-7238; www.villagecountryinn.com), Box 408, Route 7A, Manchester 05254. This century-old, three-story Main Street inn has a long piazza lined with wicker and rockers. There are 33 rooms (18 suites and luxury rooms), 1 with Jacuzzi, some with gas fireplace, all with private bath, and many recently refurbished in lace, antiques, and chintz. Outside is a formal garden and gazebo, swimming pool, and patio; inside, an informal tavern and formal dining room. Rates, including breakfast, are $129–295 for a double, with a special dinner price for guests.

ꝏ **Wilburton Inn** (802-362-2500; 1-800-648-4944; www.wilburton.com), River Road, Manchester 05254. This is a brick, baronial, turn-of-the-20th-century mansion set up a hill and well off the main road on expansive grounds with long views of the Battenkill Valley. Common rooms are richly paneled and the living room is immense, complete with piano, comfortable window seats and couches, Oriental rugs, and an enormous hearth. Owners Georgette and Albert Levis have created unusual sculpture walks that reflect Albert's abiding interest in the human psyche. The house itself offers four suites and five bedrooms, and there are 25 rooms in outlying cottages, better suited to families as they offer more privacy and direct access to the seemingly limitless lawn—which harbors a pool and tennis courts. Breakfast is served at wrought-iron, glass-topped tables in the Terrace Room, and dinner, in the Billiard Room, is reminiscent of an exclusive men's club. Open year-round,

$110–300 per couple including a full breakfast and afternoon tea. Weddings are a specialty here.

The Inn at Willow Pond (802-362-4733; outside Vermont: 1-800-533-3533; www.innatwillowpond.com), Box 1429, Manchester Center 05255. Located 2.3 miles north on Route 7A, this inn offers 40 spacious guest rooms and suites in three separate, contemporary, Colonial-style buildings on a hillside overlooking the Manchester Country Club's golf course. The 18th-century Meeting House reception building contains the lofty main lounge, conference facilities, a fitness center with exercise equipment, two saunas, and a library. There's also an outdoor lap pool and a restaurant in a renovated 1770 house (see *Dining Out*). The larger guest rooms a feature fireplace and sitting area. Winter rates are $158 (for a small suite) to $348 for multiroom suites with a fireplace and full living room; all include continental breakfast. Full breakfast is served in the restaurant on weekends and holidays. Midweek and special off-season weekend rates available.

River Meadow Farm (802-362-1602), P.O. Box 822, Sugarhouse Lane, Manchester Center 05255. Off by itself down near the Battenkill south of Manchester Village, this is a beautiful old farmhouse with barns, built around 1797 and purchased in the 1820s by Manchester for use as a "poor farm." There are five bedrooms sharing two and a half baths, and guests have the run of the downstairs with its welcoming kitchen, pleasant living room, and dining room. Outside there is fishing on the Battenkill, ample space to hike, snowshoe, and cross-country ski—with a splendid view of Mount Equinox. Pat Dupree is a long-time Manchester resident who enjoys orienting her guests. Rates are $30 per person, full breakfast included.

Seth Warner Inn (802-362-3830), P.O. Box 281, Manchester Center 05255. This imposing vintage-1800 house is set back from Route 7A, southwest of Manchester Village, and it's a beauty—carefully restored by Stasia and Lee Tetreault. Rooms with open beams and stenciling are furnished in antiques and curtained in lace. Five bright guest rooms have country quilts and private bath. Common space includes a gracious living room, a hall library, and the dining room, in which guests gather for a full breakfast. $100–110 (fall) per room including breakfast.

The Battenkill Inn (802-362-4213; 1-800-441-1628; www.battenkillinn.com), P.O. Box 948, Manchester 05254. This 1840 Victorian farmhouse sits at the foot of the Mount Equinox Skyline Drive and backs onto meadows that stretch down to the Battenkill. The 11 guest rooms all have private bath and are furnished with antiques, and the common rooms include two sitting rooms and two small dining rooms—plenty of space to relax in. One room with a double bed and fireplace is fully handicapped-accessible. Your hosts are Cliff and Donna Ward. $130–180 per couple includes a full breakfast and complimentary hors d'oeuvres. Springtime midweek specials.

In Arlington 05250

The Arlington Inn (802-375-6532; 1-800-443-9442; www.arlingtoninn.com), 3904 Route 7A in the center of Arlington, occupies the 1848 Greek Revival mansion built by Martin Chester Deming, a Vermont railroad magnate, and has been used as an inn off and on since 1889. The 12 rooms and six suites in the main house and former carriage barn are spacious and furnished with Victorian antiques, and there's a formal parlor. Sylvester's Study on the ground floor is particularly impressive. Six new units, including two suites, have been installed in the adjacent 1830 parsonage; they have Drexel cherry four-posters and sleigh beds, TV, and air-conditioning. The inn is also known as a popular spot for dinner, and the gardens make a great spot for weddings or civil-union ceremonies. Rates range from $100 double occupancy to $265, including a full breakfast. Open all year.

ⓒⓓ **West Mountain Inn** (802-375-6516; www.westmountaininn.com), on Route 313 west of Arlington. Open year-round. A large, rambling former summer home with splendid views of the mountains and valley, converted and expanded into an inn. The 12 attractive rooms and six suites are named after famous people associated with Arlington, and a copy of Dorothy Canfield Fisher's *Vermont Tradition* is in every room. Breakfast and dinner are served daily; Sunday brunch on certain holidays. The inn's property includes more than 5 miles of walking and cross-country-ski trails, a bird sanctuary, seasonal gardens, and llamas in residence. A number of special events are featured, such as a St. Lucia Festival of Lights in early December, Leek and Fiddlehead Days in early May, and Ethan Allen Days (Father's Day weekend). Mary Ann Carlson gives complimentary African violets to guests who promise to take care of them. $169–223 for two, $275–300 for two MAP. (See also *Dining Out.*) There are also three town houses at the Historic Mill on the property.

Hill Farm Inn (802-375-2269; 1-800-882-2545; www.hillfarminn.com), 458 Hill Farm Road. Located off Route 7A north of the village, this historic farmstead, owned and managed by Kathleen and Craig Yanez, is set on 50 acres of land bordering the Battenkill River. The 1830 main building, 1790 guest house, and four seasonal cabins hold a total of 15 rooms, all with private bath. Licensed for beer and wine. Double rooms $75–160 includes full country breakfast. Children welcome at special rates.

The Inn on Covered Bridge Green (802-375-9489; 1-800-726-9480; fax: 802-375-9046; www.coveredbridge-green.com), 3587 River Road. Fans of Norman Rockwell can now actually stay in his former home, a pretty white 1792 Colonial next to a red covered bridge on the village green where Ethan Allen mustered his Green Mountain Boys. Clint and Julia Dickens offer nine bedrooms, all with private bath (four have two-person spa tubs), and two cottages. There's swimming, canoeing, and fly-fishing in the Battenkill, just a few hundred feet from the inn. The full country breakfasts are events, served on bone china with Waterford glass and silver. Rates range $150–250.

Country Willows B&B (802-375-0019; 1-800-796-2585; www.country-willows.com), 332 East Arlington Road. Anne and Ron Weber run this tidy, 1850s village historic landmark with four nifty guest rooms with private bath (two with claw-foot tubs), decorated in Victoriana. The West Mountain Room has a fine view, fireplace, and sitting area. There is a wraparound porch and a hammock for two. Rates range $110–145 per double including full country breakfast.

Ira Allen House (802-362-2284), Route 7A. A smartly renovated old roadside home with nine guest rooms, some set up for families. The inn's property across Route 7A fronts the Battenkill, good for trout fishing and, for the warm-blooded, a dip in a 10-foot-deep swimming hole. $65–80 per room with full breakfast.

ꝏ ✐ **Green River Inn** (802-375-2272; 1-888-648-2212; www.greenriverinn.com), 3402 Sandgate Road, Sandgate 05250 (off Route 313, 4 miles west from Route 7A, Arlington), has 14 renovated guest rooms, all with private bath, some with whirlpool and fireplace; sun room, deck, and special children's room. Jim and Betsy Gunn have a lot of ideas about what to do outdoors on their 450 acres. $90–185 B&B. They have an excellent dining room, so inquire about MAP.

In Danby 05739

✐ **Silas Griffith Inn** (802-293-5567; 1-800-545-1509), 178 Main Street, is the renovated 1891 mansion that once housed Vermont's first millionaire. George and Carol Gaines own this unusually comfortable, welcoming inn with its restored hardwood floors and carved bird's-eye, curly maple, and cherry woodwork. The 15 guest rooms, all with private bath, are divided between the main house and the converted carriage house, all furnished with antiques. You might want to request the room with the round porch (but no closet), or the room with the huge bed—one of several rooms that can be combined into a family suite sharing one bath. Common rooms include a large living room, well stocked with books, and a front parlor with TV, accessed by a wonderful "moon gate" door. The restaurant (in the carriage house) is locally popular (see *Dining Out*). Danby's intriguing shops are just down the street, there are some outstanding hiking trails just a few minutes' drive into the Green Mountain National Forest; Emerald Lake State Park is just 3 miles down Route 7. The inn's own 11 hilltop acres include a pool. Rates range $129–339, including full breakfast; discounts for weekdays and for a stay of several days.

ꝏ **The Quail's Nest** (802-293-5099; 1-800-599-6444; www.quailsnest-bandb.com), Box 221, 81 South Main Street, is a homey, pleasant B&B in an 1835 house. Greg and Nancy Diaz offer six guest rooms, all with private bath, furnished with antiques and handmade country quilts. There's a comfy living room and an interesting gift store out back. Rates $70–115. Nancy makes great maple-oat scones, part of a full breakfast.

In Dorset 05251

The Dorset Inn (802-867-5500), Church Street. A national historic site and the state's most venerable hostelry (in continuous operation since 1796) faces Dorset's historic green. It has been stylishly renovated by its owners, Sissy Hicks, former chef at the Barrows House, and Gretchen Schmidt. Known for its excellent cuisine (see *Dining Out*) and relaxing atmosphere, the inn has 31 guest rooms. It's within walking distance of antiques shops and the theater and offers a lineup of front-porch rockers from which you might not want to stir. Rates $180–230 double, including dinner and a full breakfast.

ꝏ ♿ **The Barrows House** (802-867-4455; 1-800-639-1620; www.barrows-house.com), Box 98. This exceptional miniresort on Route 30, now owned by Philadelphians Linda and Jim McGinnis, features attractive, flexibly arranged accommodations (18 rooms, 10 suites) in the main house and 7 rooms in adjacent buildings. The early-19th-century house is a short walk from the center of this historic village, but there is an out-in-the-country feel to the 12-acre grounds, which include a gazebo, heated outdoor swimming pool, sauna, and two tennis courts. In summer, bikes are available; golf and hiking are nearby. In winter, cross-country-ski equipment is available. There are comfortable sitting rooms in the main house and the bigger cottages, where large families or several friendly couples can be lodged. A convivial bar is wallpapered to resemble a private library. Dogs are welcome in two separate accommodations. The dining room and a guest room in one of the outer buildings are wheelchair-accessible. The dining room is outstanding (see *Dining Out*). $185–255 per couple including breakfast and dinner; less in the off-season.

🍴 ♿ **Inn at West View Farm** (802-867-5715; 1-800-769-4903; www.innatwestviewfarm.com), Route 30, just south of Dorset, is a small, well-groomed lodge with an appealing personality, once the focus of a 200-acre farm, now known especially for its exceptional cuisine. (The dining room—see *Dining Out*—remains the focal point of the inn. **Clancy's Tavern** offers lighter fare.) Christal Siewertsen is the innkeeper. The inn has a very pleasant living room with a fireplace in the old front parlor; common space also includes an inviting, wicker-filled sun porch. One downstairs room has been fitted for handicapped access, and the nine upstairs rooms are all furnished comfortably with cheerful paper and bright, crisp fabrics; all rooms are air-conditioned. Rates are $110–200, including full breakfast.

Marble West Inn (802-867-4155; 1-800-453-7629; www.marblewestinn.com), Dorset West Road. This Greek Revival house has seven marble columns on its marble front porches, and there are marble walkways and

THE DORSET INN

Kim Grant

three marble fireplaces. Now it offers eight well-decorated guest rooms (one a two-room suite with fireplace), an inviting living room, and a piano room that is the scene of impromptu concerts. The stencil work in the entrance hallway and on stairway walls is exceptional, and the high ceilings and bull's-eye moldings are pleasant reminders of an earlier era, as is the gracious hospitality of owner Paul Quinn. Guests mingle in the library for drinks (BYOB) and conversation. Rates are $90–175 per couple, including a candlelit, gourmet breakfast and afternoon tea. A 15 percent service charge is added. Please, no pets or children under 12.

Cornucopia of Dorset (802-867-5751; 1-800-566-5751; www.cornucopiaofdorset.com), 3228 Route 30, P.O. Box 307. This turn-of-the-20th-century home is one of Vermont's more elegant B&Bs. Donna Butman offers four meticulously decorated, air-conditioned bedrooms in the main house, each with canopy or four-poster bed, phone, and private bath; three with fireplace. There is also a cottage. The solarium, walled in glass, overlooks gardens and a manicured back lawn. Guests can also relax in the library or small living room, both with a fireplace, and on a back terrace under an awning. The cottage suite in the rear is a beauty, with a loft bedroom (with skylights), living room with fireplace, kitchen, and sun deck. The multicourse breakfast may feature puff pancakes, gingerbread waffles, or quiche Lorraine. A welcoming flute of champagne and a morning tray of coffee or tea are among the many amenities. Rooms are $150–275 for a double.

Dovetail Inn (802-867-5747; 1-800-4-DOVETAIL; www.dovetailinn.com), Route 30. An 1800s inn on the Dorset green with 11 bedrooms (all with private bath), run by Jean and Jim Kingston. Breakfast is served in the Keeping Room or in guest rooms. $65 for the smallest double room in low season; $195 for a two-room suite with a fireplace and TV, sleeping up to four. Ask about midweek rates.

In Weston 05161

Wilder Homestead Inn (802-824-8172), 25 Lawrence Hill Road. A classic, Federal-style brick house, beautifully transformed for B&B guests by warm hosts Patsy and Peter McKay. There are seven guest rooms, most with private bath, several with early-19th-century stenciling, each with a different decor. There's a huge hearth in the dining room; there's also an attractive library and living room and a full bar. All the sights of Weston are within an easy walk, and there's a waterfall across the street. $65–150 per couple B&B. No children under age 12. No smoking.

🏅 🐾 🖉 ♿ **Colonial House Inn & Motel** (802-824-6286; 1-800-639-5033; cohoinn@sover.net), Box 138, Route 100. A rare and delightful combination of nine motel units and six traditional inn rooms (shared baths), connected by a very pleasant dining room, a comfortable, sunken sitting room with dried flowers hanging from the rafters, and a solarium overlooking the lawn; there's also a fully equipped game room. Innkeepers John and Betty Nunnikhoven make all ages feel welcome, and most guests are repeats. Rates include memorable, multicourse breakfasts. Dinners are served family-style ($19.95). The inn is 2 miles south of the village, with lawn chairs facing a classic farmscape across the road; most guest rooms overlook a meadow. Rooms are $70–105 fall and winter, $54–86 spring and summer, B&B; $8 per child 4–12 years; $35–60 single. Ramp available for wheelchairs. Golf and theater packages. Pets are accepted in the motel units.

🐾 **The Darling Family Inn** (802-824-3223; innkeeper@thedarlingfamilyinn.com), Route 100. An 1830s house, exquisitely furnished with family antiques by Joan and Chapin Darling. The five guest rooms have private bath, canopy beds, fine quilts, and artistic touches. There are wide-plank floors throughout, and Joan has expertly painted the walls. Full country breakfasts, by candlelight, are included in the rates. In summer, the pool adds a nice touch. $85–145 per couple, including breakfast, except for guests in the two attractive cottages up on the hill (where pets are welcome).

In Peru 05152

🐾 **Johnny Seesaw's** (802-824-5533; 1-800-424-CSAW; www.jseesaw.com). Built as a dance hall in 1920 and converted into one of Vermont's first ski lodges, this is a wonderfully weathered, comfortable place. Within walking distance of the slopes in winter, it offers tennis and a pool in summer. There are 28 rooms—doubles, master bedrooms with fireplace in the main house, and family suites—

also four cottages with fireplaces, good for large families and small groups. There is a licensed pub (see *Dining Out*); "Yankee cuisine" dinners are à la carte and have a French accent. The living room boasts Vermont's first circular fireplace. $40–99 per adult B&B; add 15 percent service. Pets are okay.

✐ **The Wiley Inn** (802-824-6600; 1-888-843-6600; www.wileyinn.com), P.O. Box 7, Route 11, just 1 mile from Bromley. Its core is an 1835 house containing a delightful living room with fireplace, library, and dining room. A motel-like wing, now refurbished, includes two rooms with fireplaces within view of the whirlpool tubs in the bathrooms. Jerry and Judy Goldman extend a special welcome to families with the configuration of a number of rooms, as well as a game room with an on-line computer, TV, piano, and toys. Couples, on the other hand, may prefer the suitably quiet and romantic rooms in the original part of this rambling inn, with its total of eight rooms and four two-bedroom suites, all with private bath. Summer facilities include a backyard heated pool and play area; there's also a year-round outside hot tub. The inn's relatively small and attractive dining room is currently the Bromley Beach, an Italian bistro open weekends and holidays. Rooms, including a buffet breakfast, are $85–105 in summer and fall; suites, $145–185 for four people; in winter $95–125 for rooms, $180–200 for four people; the first child 12 or under is free in parent's room.

In Landgrove 05148

✐ **The Landgrove Inn** (802-824-6673; 1-800-669-8466; www.landgroveinn.com), 132 Landgrove Road. This red-clapboard building rambles back and around, beginning with the 1820 house, ending an acre or two away. The "Vermont continuous architecture" draws guests through a handsome lobby, past 16 crisp, bright rooms (all with private bath) that meander off in all directions, through the inviting Rafter Room Lounge (huge, filled with games and books), to the attractive dining room in the original house. Our favorite rooms are tucked up under the eaves in the oldest part of the inn, papered in floral prints and furnished with carefully chosen antiques but with new baths. Many rooms are well suited to families, who also will appreciate the heated pool, tennis court, a trout pond, lawn games, and paddle tennis court. In winter, you can take a sleigh ride or step out onto the 15-mile cross-country trail system that leads through the picturesque village of Landgrove (just a church, former school, and salting of homes cupped in a hollow), on into surrounding national forest. Bromley Ski Area is just 6 miles away, and Stratton is a 20-minute drive. Breakfast is an event here, served in the wood-beamed dining room with a many-windowed wall overlooking the garden. Dining is by candlelight, with a choice of six entrées prepared by a well-respected local chef (see *Dining Out*). $95–235 per couple B&B, $5–25 per child in the same room with parent; add 10 percent for service.

The Meadowbrook Inn (802-824-6444; 1-800-498-6445; www.meadowbinn.com), 24 Vermont Route 11. James and Elaine Nelson-Parker's forested retreat has eight guest rooms, all with private bath, five of them with fireplace, and four with two-person whirlpool tub, plus comfortable lounging areas. Their 26 km trail system is available to guests in all seasons for hiking, biking, nature walks, and cross-country skiing. Rates range $125–200 in high season, $100–200 in low season.

In and around Londonderry

Frog's Leap Inn (802-824-3019; 1-887-FROGSLEAP; www.frogsleap-inn.com), Route 100, Londonderry 05148. Formerly the Highland House and one of the oldest inns in the area, this is a classic Colonial, built in 1842 and set well back from the road above a sloping lawn. The estatelike place has 32 acres of pasture and forests with 1.5 miles of hiking and cross-country trails, an outdoor heated swimming pool, and a tennis court. There are eight rooms with private bath in the main house, and another eight (four of which are suites) with private bath in the annex, plus the Tad Pool House, which has a large two-bedroom suite with a kitchen and a deck overlooking the pool. B&B rates ($100–285 per room) include a continental breakfast delivered to your room as well as a full breakfast and afternoon tea; add $30 per person for MAP and a fine four-course dinner.

🏵 🖍 ♿ **The Londonderry Inn** (802-824-5226; www.londonderryinn.com), 8 Melendy Hill Road, South Londonderry 05155. On a knoll overlooking the West River, this 1826 dairy farm has been a country inn since 1940. The 24 guest rooms—some are suites—are decorated with folk-art-painted furniture and Chagall-inspired paintings on the walls, patchwork quilts and teddy bears on every bed. The large, bright public rooms include a huge stone fireplace, spring-fed pool, tropical birds, billiard room, movie room. Fresh-baked cookies are available every afternoon. Full hot buffet breakfast and afternoon tea are included in the room rates. Innkeepers Chrisman and Maya Kearn are glad to help guests plan daily itineraries. Children are welcome. Gift shop on premises. Room rates are the same year-round, holidays, and weekends and start at $136.

MOTELS **Palmer House Resort** (802-362-3600; 1-800-917-6245; www.palmerhouse.com), P.O. Box 657, Manchester Center 05255. A luxury motel with 50 rooms and suites with color TV, free coffee, a pool, whirlpool, and sauna, plus fishing in a private, stocked trout pond, tennis, and a nine-hole golf course; there's an adjacent restaurant. Continental breakfast is included in room rates of $75–175, $160–300 for suites, depending on the season.

♿ **The Manchester View** (802-362-2739; 1-800-548-4141; www.manchester-view.com), P.O. Box 1268, Route 7A, Manchester Center 05255. Pat Barnett owns this place just north of town with marvelous views. Thirty-five rooms with fridge, three 2-bedroom suites, and seven 1-bedroom suites (most with fireplace, living room, and two-person Jacuzzi); also handicapped-accessible units. A former barn now holds a breakfast room. Facilities include a heated outdoor pool in summer. Golf and tennis available at nearby Manchester Country Club. Rates are $90–225 based on double occupancy.

🏵 🖍 **Swiss Inn** (802-824-3442; 1-800-847-9477; www.swissinn.com), 249 Route 11, Londonderry 05148. From its exterior, this looks like a standard motel, but once inside, the differences are appealing. Joe and Pat Donahue feature Swiss dishes in their dining room (see *Dining Out*). Nineteen rooms, all with private bath, are large enough to accommodate families, and public space includes a library as well as a sitting room and bar. There's also an outdoor pool. $59–99 includes a full breakfast.

The Barnstead Inn (802-362-1619; 1-800-331-1619), Box 998, Manchester Center 05255. Just up Bonnet Street (Route 30), two blocks from the amenities of town, this is a genuine former hay barn converted into 14 motel units. It's all been done with consummate grace and charm, with many small touches like braided rugs and exposed old beams (but no room phones). There is also an outdoor pool and hot tub. $90–210 with breakfast on weekends.

The Weathervane (802-362-2444; 1-800-262-1317), Route 7A, Manchester 05254. Set back from the road with two picture windows in each of its 22 large units, each room has TV, free coffee, and hot chocolate. There is a "courtesy room" with books, games, and magazines; also a pool. $76–150 per couple, with breakfast in summer.

CONDOMINIUMS AND SKI LODGES **Stratton Mountain Inn** (1-800-STRATTON), at Stratton Mountain 05155, with 125 rooms, is the largest lodging facility on the mountain. Rooms have private bath, phone, and TV, and facilities include a large dining room, saunas, and whirlpools. On winter weekends $149–349 per room.

Stratton Village Lodge (1-800-STRATTON), adjacent to the Stratton base lodge, at Stratton Mountain 05155, has 91 studio-style units with kitchenette from $119 per person per day with lift ticket in winter. All resort guests have access to the sports center, with its indoor pool, exercise machines, and racquetball and tennis courts. Winter weekend rates: $229–439.

Stratton Condominiums (1-800-STRATTON), Stratton Mountain 05155. Roughly 250 of the resort's condominium units are in the rental pool at any given time, in a range of sizes and shapes; they run $69–109 per person per day with lift ticket midweek. All resort guests have access to the sports center and its indoor pool, exercise machines, and racquetball and tennis courts (a fee is charged).

Liftline Lodge (1-800-STRATTON), Stratton Mountain. Traditional 77-room European-style lodge is close to Stratton's lifts and village shops and restaurants. Two restaurants. Lift and lodging $59 per person. Weekends from $159 per room.

Long Trail House (1-800-STRATTON). The newest Stratton property has heated pool, hot tub, and sauna. Weekend and holiday rates start at $210.

Bromley Village (802-824-5458; 1-800-865-4786), P.O. Box 1130, Manchester Center 05255, is a complex of attractive one- to four-bedroom units adjacent to the ski area. Summer facilities include a pool and tennis courts. In winter, you can walk to the lifts; there is also a shuttle bus. Call for rates.

CAMPGROUNDS See *To Do—Camping* for a list of campgrounds in various state forests and parks.

✷ Where to Eat

DINING OUT **Chantecleer** (802-362-1616), Route 7A, East Dorset. Open 6–9:30, closed Monday and Tuesday in winter, closed Tuesday in summer. Long respected as one of Vermont's outstanding restaurants, Swiss chef Michael Baumann's establishment is known for such specialties as veal sweetbreads (prepared with sautéed shrimp and a fresh basil-tomato sauce with spaetzle; $28) and whole Dover sole ($35). Leave room for profiterole de maison or coupe Matterhorn. The setting is an elegantly remodeled old dairy barn with a massive fieldstone fireplace. There is an extensive wine list. Reservations essential. Expensive.

The Wilburton Inn (802-362-2500), River Road, Manchester Village. Dinner in the mansion's baronial billiard room is an event. You might start with lobster ravioli and proceed to cornmeal-encrusted trout with brown hazelnut butter sauce, poached salmon glazed with raspberry champagne, or roasted noisette of mountain lamb with garlic and rosemary. Moderate to expensive. Grill nights are Monday and Wednesday in the summer.

The Three Clock Inn (802-824-6327), Middletown Road, South Londonderry. Dinner daily except Monday. Reserve and request directions. After a couple of up-and-down years, this dining landmark is back on dependable ground with owner Serge Roche and his chef/partner, Michael Kloeti. The dining space is rustic, with low beams and glowing hearths. The à la carte menu changes frequently but might include grilled skate wings ($22) or veal Zurichoise ($23). Desserts might include a warm pear tart or crème caramel à l'orange ($7). There is an extensive wine cellar. Cooking classes are offered by Chef Michael.

Mistral's at Toll Gate (802-362-1779), off Routes 11/30 east of Manchester. Open for dinner daily except Wednesday. Reservations recommended. Chef Dana Markey and his wife, Cheryl, run this longtime dining landmark located in the old tollhouse once serving the Boston-to-Saratoga road. During warm-weather months a brook rushes along just under the windows. The menu might include tournedos of veal morel, salmon cannelloni, or sautéed veal pesto with fusilli. All are accompanied by a very long wine list. Entrées $22–30.

The Barrows House (802-867-4455), Route 30, Dorset. Open for dinner nightly, but weekends only in November. In a spacious, rather formal country dining room and its attached conservatory, both conscientiously appointed, diners can select from an à la carte menu that changes seasonally; nightly specials are also offered. Maine crabcakes or garlic-herb salmon roulade might be followed by pan-roasted veal tenderloin with pancetta, tomatoes, and shiitake mushrooms or grilled Vermont trout with cantaloupe-lime salsa. Entrées are $16–27, with "lighter-side entrées" as an option.

Inn at West View Farm (802-867-5715; 1-800-769-4903), Route 30, Dorset. Open for dinner Thursday through Monday. The Auberge Room is exceptionally attractive, and the food is dependably good. Entrées range $21–28 and might include braised short ribs, roasted wild king salmon, or coriander-crusted venison.

The Black Swan (802-362-3807), Route 7A, Manchester Village (next to the Jelly Mill; see *Selective Shopping—Special Shops*). Open for dinner daily except Wednesday. The food in this crisply decorated and managed old brick Colonial house is a treat for the senses. A representative dinner might begin with chilled strawberry soup or mussels steamed in white wine, garlic, and cream sauce, and proceed to scaloppine of venison ($19.95) or trout Piccata ($14.75). Lighter fare is served in the Mucky Duck Bistro.

Silas Griffith Inn (802-293-5567), 178 Main Street, Danby. This attractive, informal dining room, with a hearth and walls decorated with antique kitchen gadgets, is in the converted carriage house. The cuisine is French country, and dinner is served Thursday through Sunday 5:30–9 PM by reservation. You might dine on salmon, pork, ravioli, or trout. Entrées $15–29.

Reluctant Panther (802-362-2568), Route 7A, Manchester Village. Open for dinner nightly except Tuesday and Wednesday. The greenhouse dining room is particularly pleasant and can be the setting for a memorable evening, beginning with hors d'oeuvres in the sitting room. The menu changes daily but the appetizers might include steamed mussels with saffron-thyme sauce; the entrées, fillet of Arctic char; osso buco with creamy garlic-Parmesan polenta; or herbed pork tenderloin with rum-soaked fruit compote. The wine list is extensive. Expensive.

The Perfect Wife (802-362-2817), Routes 11/30, 1 mile east of the Route 7 overpass. Open Tuesday through Sunday 5–10 for dinner. Amy Chamberlain features locally raised chicken with chèvre and eggplant, sesame-crusted tuna, or the Howling Wolf vegetarian special. There's live music in the tavern every weekend. Entrées $5.95–22.

The Dorset Inn (802-867-5500), Church Street, Dorset. Open daily for breakfast, lunch, and dinner. Chef Sissy Hicks can be relied on for outstanding New England fare. Lunch might be Welsh rarebit ($10) or eggplant crêpes ($11). Dinner entrées include duck confit or turkey croquettes. Entrées $13–26.

The Equinox (802-362-4700), Manchester. Dinner is served in the formal, vaulted Colonnade dining room; Sunday brunch ($21 prix fixe) is a tradition for residents and visitors on holidays. The attractive Marsh Tavern is open for lunch and dinner daily, serving hearty soups, salads, pastas, and such specials as Devonshire shepherd's pie, lobster ravioli, Yankee pot roast, and various seafood selections at moderate prices. Entrées $10–24 in the Marsh Tavern.

Bistro Henry (802-362-4982) at the Chalet Motel, Routes 11/30, Manchester. Open for dinner daily except Monday. Dina and Henry Bronson run this Mediterranean-style dining room with a casual atmosphere, a full bar, and a *Wine Spectator* award for excellence. You might begin with a vegetable and Vermont goat cheese tart ($8) and dine on the pasta of the day or Merlot-braised lamb shank. Entrées are $16–22.

The Restaurant at Willow Pond (802-362-4733), Route 7 north of Manchester Center. A restaurant in a restored 1770s farmhouse. Dinner every night (but check in the off-seasons). The menu is "authentic" northern Italian. You might begin with a spinach salad, or grilled eggplant with a three-cheese-and-spinach stuffing and a fresh diced tomato and porcini mushroom sauce. Entrées include linguine alla pesto ($12.95) and veal Piccata ($19.95).

Swiss Inn (802-824-3442), Route 11, Londonderry. Open to the public for dinner daily except Wednesday, the Swiss Inn has a strong local following. While ownership is no longer Swiss, the current owner-chef seems to have the right touch with such dishes as Geschnetzeltes (veal à la Swiss), beef fondue, and chicken Lugano (chicken breast dipped in a Gruyère cheese batter); also Continental dishes like shrimp à la Marseilles and veal Marsala. Fondues are a specialty. Entrées run $13–23.

Johnny Seesaw's (802-824-5533; 1-800-424-CSAW), Route 11, Peru. A Prohibition-era dance hall, then one of New England's first ski lodges, this atmospheric inn is well worth a dinnertime visit even if you don't happen to be staying there. The extensive menu usually includes a choice of veal and seafood dishes and pork chops Vermont-style, but huge prime rib of beef is the house special (children can always get hamburgers or pasta as well as half-sized portions). Adult entrées: $12.95–19.95. Soft music played live on weekends.

The Landgrove Inn (802-824-6673), 132 Landgrove Road, Landgrove. Dinner by reservation Thursday through Sunday. This fine old inn is off by itself up dirt roads at the edge of a tiny village. Meals are by candlelight in a delightful old dining room with windows overlooking the garden. You might begin with a delectable butternut squash, apple, and onion soup, and dine on roast duck with blueberry sauce ($19) or rack of lamb ($25). Children's portions and delicious desserts.

Ye Olde Tavern (802-362-0611), 214 North Main Street, Manchester Center. Open daily from 5 PM for dinner. A 1790 tavern theoretically specializing in "authentic American" dinner dishes like roast tom turkey and pot roast, but seafood fettuccine is also on the menu, and the Tavern Seafood Stew is laced with vermouth, tomato, and fennel. The veal specialties all are priced at $19.50, and there's lots of prime rib. One of the better values in town.

Downstairs at the Playhouse (802-824-5288), Weston Playhouse, on the green in Weston. Open for dinner on theater nights beginning at 5:30; 5 on Sunday. A pleasant dining room by the falls, good, and then you're there. Reserve. (See also *Entertainment—Theater.*)

The Arlington Inn (802-375-6532), Route 7A, Arlington. There's a mauve-walled formal dining room and a more casual tavern. From a recent menu, you could select smoked warm duck salad ($10.95) as an appetizer and continue to lobster ravioli ($23.95), hazelnut-encrusted chicken ($21.95) or rosemary- and cedar-roasted salmon ($24.95). The prix fixe menu ($19.95), offered from Tuesday through Friday (not in foliage season), is a good value.

West Mountain Inn (802-375-6516), River Road, Arlington. Chef Larry Vellucci's dining room is open to the public by reservation 6:30–8:30 PM, Sunday through Friday, featuring a $35 prix fixe menu that might include pan-seared Chilean sea bass, spinach and roasted red pepper ravioli, or a Black Angus filet mignon.

See also the "The Lower Connecticut and West River Valleys" for Three Mountain Inn in Jamaica.

EATING OUT

In and around Manchester

The **Garden Café** at the Southern Vermont Arts Center (802-362-4220), West Road, Manchester Village. Open for lunch, May through mid-October, Tuesday through Saturday 11:30–3, Sunday noon–3. The food is fine and the setting is superb: a pleasant indoor room or the outside terrace, both with views over the sculpture garden and down the mountain to Manchester Village.

Little Rooster Cafe (802-362-3496), Route 7A south, Manchester Center. Breakfast and lunch from 7 AM; closed Wednesday. An offshoot of Chantecleer (see *Dining Out*), an "eclectic European café" serving exquisite waffles and omelets, café au lait and cappuccino, baguette sandwiches.

Expensive by breakfast and lunch standards, but special.

Laney's Restaurant (802-362-4456), Routes 11/30, Manchester Center. Open from 5 PM, this is a festive, kid-friendly spot, specializing in exotic pizza from a wood-fired brick oven, hickory-smoked ribs, grilled steaks, and salads; draft beer in frosted mugs.

Flat Road Diner (802-362-8126), Route 11/30, Manchester Depot. Closed Monday. An upscale diner with a pig motif, hubcaps on the walls, and a great breakfast/lunch menu served year-round. Dinner is served in the summer.

Best Diner (802-362-8171), Route 11/30, Manchester Depot. Very good food (the milk shakes are fabulous) at good prices in this upscale part of the world. Give it a try, especially with kids.

Gourmet Café and Deli, Route 7A, Manchester Center. Tucked back into one of Manchester Center's many shopping centers, this café offers great salads and sandwiches, plus a pleasant terrace to eat on in warm weather.

Sirloin Saloon (802-362-2600), Routes 11/30, Manchester Center. This is a large, many-cornered, Tiffany-lamp-lit, polished-brass place that's always packed; there's a huge salad bar and a children's menu.

Candeleros (802-362-0836), Main Street, Manchester Center, is a Mexican cantina open daily for lunch and dinner; there's a pleasant outdoor patio in summer.

The Buttery (802-362-3544), second floor at the Jelly Mill (see *Selective Shopping—Special Shops*), Route 7A, Manchester Center. An attractive, welcoming spot for lunch or brunch daily, starting at 10 AM: eggs Benedict or Blackstone, chicken salad with currants, soups, and sinful desserts.

Up for Breakfast (802-362-4204), 710 Main Street, Manchester. Breakfast Monday through Friday 6 AM–noon, weekends 7–1, dinner nightly 5:30–9. Bright, art-decked space with tables and a counter, an open kitchen, and blackboard menu specials—maybe a sausage, apple, and cheddar omelet, trout with eggs and hash browns, or wild turkey hash—and innovative specials later in the day as well. Worth climbing the stairs.

Mika's (802-362-8100), Avalanche Motor Lodge, Routes 11/30, Manchester. Open daily for lunch and dinner for fans of Chinese and Japanese cooking; sushi bar.

PELTIER'S GENERAL STORE IN DORSET

Kim Grant

Zoey's Deli & Bakery (802-362-0005), Routes 11/30, Manchester, serves breakfast and lunch daily 7–4. Nearly 20 varieties of specialty breads draw faithful customers.

For pizzas: **Christo's** (802-362-2408) on Main Street; **Marilyn Bruno's** (802-362-4469) on Center Hill; and **Manchester Pizza House** (802-362-3338) in the Manchester Shopping Center all offer high-quality pizza as well as salads, subs, grinders, and Italian lunches and dinners. All are in Manchester; all serve beer and wine and will deliver locally.

Elsewhere

Jonathon's Table (802-375-1021), Route 7A, Arlington. Keep your eyes peeled for the sign; the place is worth your trouble. Cheerful and done in lots of natural wood, Jonathon's Table is attracting both a local and a tourist crowd. Jonathon serves Veal Jonathon with a sherry and mushroom sauce ($15.95) and Vermont rainbow trout ($14.95) as well as steak, ribs, and pasta.

White Dog Tavern (802-293-5477), Route 7 north of Danby. Open for dinner Wednesday through Sunday. This is an 1812 farmhouse with a central chimney and three fireplaces, each serving as the focal point of a dining room. There's a cheery bar, and an outdoor deck in summer. The blackboard menu includes clams, shrimp, and the house special—chicken breasts à la Tom, served up with herbs, garlic, and melted cheese over spaghetti. Options might include blackened catfish and clams zuppa ($14–18).

The Barn Restaurant and Tavern (802-325-3088), Route 30, Pawlet. Open daily for dinner June through October. This is a genuine old barn with a huge fireplace and a view of the Mettawee River. A large menu offers something for everybody, but it's best known for seafood and steaks. There's also a salad bar and children's menu. Moderate.

Jake's Marketplace Café (802-824-6614), Mountain Marketplace at the junction of Routes 100 and 11, Londonderry. A local institution with a lively sports lounge, a lunch counter, and a pleasant pink dining room. Overstuffed sandwiches, salads, homemade soups, burgers. Pasta, steak, fish, personal pizzas ($11–21) are the dinner offerings. Lunch served only on weekends.

Gran'ma Frisby's (802-824-5931), Route 11 east of Londonderry. Open for lunch and dinner. When Magic Mountain Ski Area is open, you're lucky to get in the door of this wonderfully pubby place. Known for its fries and fresh-dough pizza, this is a friendly, reasonably priced find any time of year.

The Station Restaurant and Ice Cream Parlor (802-325-3041), School Street, Pawlet. Open 6 AM until 3 in winter, later in summer. If you think about it, railroad depots make perfect diners—with the counter and a row of stools down the length of the building and tables along the sides. This classic 1905 depot was moved here from another town and positioned above a babbling brook. It's a particularly pleasant place. Coffee cups bearing regulars' names hang by the door.

Mulligans (802-297-9293) at Stratton Mountain also has a Manchester Village locale (802-362-3663). This spacious, pleasant, family-priced restaurant is open for lunch and dinner; good for burgers, sandwiches, salads, and dinner options like Thai basil chicken and lobster and seafood manicotti. Children's specials include a Ninja Turtle Burger and Gorilla Cheese.

Outback Food & Spirits (802-297-FOOD), Route 30, Bondville, serves dinner daily from 7 PM, lunch on weekends, with live music on Saturday.

The Bryant House (802-824-6287), Route 100, Weston. Now owned by the neighboring Vermont Country Store (see *Selective Shopping—General Stores*), this fine old house belonged to one family—the Bryants—from the time it was built in 1827 until the family line petered out. Upstairs, a special room is set aside to look as it did in the 1890s. There are plenty of salads, sandwiches, and Vermont-style chicken pie. Lunch served 11:30–3. Try the homemade pie.

ICE CREAM AND SNACKS **Wilcox Brothers Dairy** (802-362-1223), Route 7A south, Manchester. Some of the creamiest, most delectable flavors in Vermont are made in this family-owned and -run dairy, available at the grocery store and in a variety of local restaurants. The dairy bar doesn't have a name, but it's 7 miles south of the blinking light in Manchester on the west side of the road.

Mother Myrick's Ice Cream Parlor & Fudge Factory (802-362-1560), Route 7A, Manchester Center. Open daily 11 AM–midnight in summer; fountain treats, cappuccino, sumptuous baked goods, and handmade chocolates and fudge concocted daily.

✷ Entertainment

MUSIC **Vermont Symphony Orchestra** (1-800-VSO-9293). Riley Rink at Hunter Park, on Route 7A, Manchester Center, serves as the distinguished orchestra's permanent summer home. When it's not on tour, especially around the Fourth of July weekend, the symphony's concerts in the arena are major events. The acoustics are fine, and one side of the arena swings up and open to permit part of the audience to picnic on a grassy bank.

Kinhaven Music School (802-824-3365), Lawrence Hill Road, Weston, a nationally recognized summer camp for young musicians, presents free concerts by students July through mid-August, Friday at 4 and Sunday at 2:30. Faculty perform Saturday at 8 PM. Performances are in the Concert Hall, high in the meadow of the school's 31-acre campus. It still looks more like a farm than a school. Picnics are encouraged.

Strattonfest (802-297-0100), Stratton Mountain, July and August. This series usually includes folk, jazz, classical, and country-western music on successive weeks.

Manchester Music Festival (802-362-1956; 1-800-639-5868), West Road, Manchester Center. A 7-week series of evening chamber music concerts in July and August, with performances at the Southern Vermont Art Center's Arkell Pavilion, Burr and Burton's Smith Center for the Arts, and the First Congregational Church in Manchester; also fall and winter performances in Manchester and Dorset.

THEATER **Dorset Playhouse** (802-867-5777). The Dorset Players, a community theater group formed in 1927, actually owns the beautiful playhouse in the center of Dorset and produces winter performances there. In summer, the Dorset Theatre Festival stages new plays as well as classics, performed by a resident professional group. Mid-June through October, 8:30 nightly; 5 and 9 PM Saturday.

Weston Playhouse (802-824-5288). Not long after the Civil War, townspeople built a second floor in their oldest church on the green and turned the lower level into a theater, producing ambitious plays such as Richard Sheridan's *The Rivals.* Theatrics remained a part of community life, and in the 1930s, a summer resident financed the remodeling of the defunct church into a real theater. Now billed as "the oldest professional theater in Vermont," the Weston Playhouse has had its ups and downs over the last half century or so, withstanding fire (in 1962 it burned to the ground) and two floods. Now nonprofit, with a company composed largely of professional Equity actors, it routinely draws rave reviews. Quality aside, Weston couldn't be more off-Broadway. The pillared theater (the facade is that of the old church) fronts on a classic village common and backs on the West River, complete with a waterfall and Holsteins grazing in the meadow beyond. Many patrons come early to dine "Downstairs at the Playhouse" and linger after the show to join cast members at the Cabaret (reservations for the Cabaret are frequently necessary). Performances are every night except Monday (plus Wednesday and Saturday matinees), late June through Labor Day weekend, plus a fall production. Tickets run $27–34.

FILM Manchester Twin Cinema (802-362-1229), Manchester Center.

WESTON PLAYHOUSE

Kim Grant

✷ Selective Shopping

ANTIQUES SHOPS See *Special Events* for the Weston Antiques Show and Stratton Antiques Festival.

Carriage Trade Antiques Center (802-362-1125), Route 7, north of Manchester Center. Open daily, displaying quality antiques representing more than 50 dealers.

Weston Antiques Barn (802-824-4097), open daily except Wednesday. One mile north of the village. A multiple-dealer shop.

Carlson's Antiques (802-867-4510), on the Dorset green. This two-story shop offers early American and Victorian furniture, paintings, glass, and china, plus textiles such as antique needlepoint pillows, hooked rugs, and fine linens. Closed Tuesday.

Danby Antiques Center (802-293-9984), Main Street, Danby. Open 10–5 daily April through December; Thursday through Monday from January through March. Displays American country and formal furniture and accessories from 24 dealers in 11 rooms and the barn.

Equinox Mountain Antiques Center (802-362-5459), Route 7A, Sunderland. Thirty-five dealers on two floors. Open 10–5 daily.

ART GALLERIES **West Wind Fine Art** (802-366-8126), 7352 Main Street, Route 7A north, Manchester Center, is an excellent new addition to the Manchester art scene. The gallery represents work by some fine American painters, including Richard Schmid and Nancy Guzik.

Southern Vermont Arts Center (see *To See—Museums*). In addition to its solo shows held throughout the year, the SVAC hosts a Members' Show in early summer and a National Fall Exhibition. There are also outdoor sculpture shows, May through October, and other special exhibits in winter.

Gallery North Star (802-362-4541), Route 7A, Manchester Village. Open daily 10:30–5:30. An offshoot of the Grafton gallery, showcasing Vermont-based artists.

Peel Gallery (802-293-5230), Route 7, 2 miles north of Danby Village. Represents 50 American artists whose works are dramatically displayed in a restored 18th-century barn. Margaret and Harris Peel launched this showcase 19 years ago. Shows and receptions are scheduled between Memorial Day and Columbus Day. Among those represented are Patrick Farrow, Sidney and Barbara Willis, and Larry Webster, along with several other nationally known artists. The gallery is open daily (except Tuesday) 10–5 year-round; open daily in July and August.

Tilting at Windmills Gallery (802-362-3022), Routes 11/30, Manchester Center. Open daily. An unusually large gallery with a wide selection of market-geared art.

Todd Gallery (802-864-5606), south edge of the village of Weston. Housed in an 1840s carriage barn, this attractive gallery displays owner Robert Todd's watercolors of Vermont and Ireland. Also whimsical photography and original sculpture, and unusual pieces crafted by Vermont artists. Closed Tuesday and Wednesday.

Beside Myself Gallery, Lathrop Lane, 4 miles north of Arlington off Route 7A. Open May 15 through October 15, 2–5 daily or by appointment, this gallery displays the work of contemporary regional artists: paintings, handmade paper, sculpture, and collages.

BOOKSTORES **The Northshire Bookstore** (802-362-2200), Main Street, Manchester Center, is highly regarded as one of the most complete in New England. The Morrows have filled the venerable Colburn House with a wide range of unusually well-displayed volumes, and in summer books overflow onto the porch. An amazingly wide range of adult titles, children's books, and records are featured, along with an extraordinarily comprehensive stock of current and classic paperbacks. The store and the Manchester Historical Society cosponsor frequent author lectures and book signings. The Morrows also run the **Next Chapter** (802-362-1006), a trove of used and antiquarian books, next door to the main store.

CRAFTS SHOPS **Frog Hollow at the Equinox** (802-362-3321), a few doors north in the same complex, is the third Vermont State Crafts Center, showcasing the work of state artisans, painters, sculptors, furniture makers, and jewelers.

The Porter House of Fine Crafts (802-362-4789), Green Mountain Village Shops, Manchester Center. Open daily 10–6. Unusual jewelry and handcrafts, clothing, toys, fabric art, kitchenware, alternative music.

Dorset Craft Center (802-362-8123), Route 30, Dorset. An old farmhouse has been converted into a studio showroom for baskets, pottery, candles, woodenware, stained glass, and quilts.

D. Lasser Ceramics (802-824-6183), 6405 Route 100, Londonderry. Open daily 9–6. A studio showroom with potters doing their thing, and shelves—inside and out—filled with bright pitchers and platters, bowls and vases, mugs and plates, all highly original and affordable. We're delighted with the multicolored "stix" we bought that hold either candles or flowers.

Vitriesse Glass Gallery (802-824-6634), Route 100, Weston Village. Open daily except Tuesday. Lucy Bergamini's intricate glass-bead jewelry is very special. The gallery also carries richly colored blown-glass vessels, goblets, and perfume bottles.

Danby Marble Company (802-293-5425), Route 7 north of Danby Village, open daily May through October and from November 20 through December 30. At first glance, this is just another array of marble bookends, lamps, chessboards, candleholders, trivets, and vases. Look more closely, though, and you'll find that this is a showcase for marble from throughout the East. (Danby itself is the site of what's billed as "the largest underground marble quarry in the world.") Tom Martin, owner of this store, cuts marble to whatever sizes and shapes you may desire.

Weston House Quilt Collection (802-824-3636), Route 100, Weston Village. Joanne and Richard Eggert have assembled one of the state's standout selections of both hand- and machine-made quilts and quilting fabrics, books, and notions.

Susan Sargent Designs (802-366-8017), Route 100, Weston Village. Open daily. The store features Sargent's striking designs woven into rugs, pillows, and throws. Other rugs, spreads, and curtains are also carried.

FACTORY OUTLETS Manchester merchants refuse to call these stores "outlets." Prices are slightly higher than at factory stores, but they're lower than retail. The list is lengthening quickly.

Manchester Commons and **Manchester Square,** the glass-and-wood anchor complex at and near the junction of Route 7A and Routes 11/30 in Manchester Center, presently house: Giorgio Armani, Emporio Armani, Baccarat, Boston Traders, Brooks Brothers, Coach, Cole Haan, Crabtree & Evelyn, Garnet Hill, Dansk, Joan & David, Ellen Tracy, Jones New York, Donna Karan, Tommy Hilfiger, Movado, Polo/Ralph Lauren, Seiko, and Timberland, among others.

Equinox Square, a smaller complex tucked behind Friendly's, houses Burberry's and Christian Dior, among others.

Manchester Marketplace Outlet Shops (next to Dexter Shoe) harbors more shops.

Designer Outlets Center, also on Route 7A south near its junction with Routes 11/30, houses six more shops, including Anne Klein and Van Heusen.

J. K. Adams Co., Factory and Factory Store, Route 30, has a complete line of its fine wood products: sugar maple butcher blocks, knife racks, spice racks, cheese and carving boards, with complementary accessories. Discounted "seconds" on the second floor.

GENERAL STORES **The Vermont Country Store** (802-824-3184), Route 100, Weston Village. Open year-round, Monday through Saturday 9–5. Established by Vrest Orton in 1946 and billed as America's first restored country store, this pioneer nostalgia venture also includes one of the country's first mail-order catalogs. The orig-

OUTLET SHOPS IN MANCHESTER

Kim Grant

inal store (actually an old Masons Hall) has since quintupled in size and spilled into four adjacent buildings. The specialty of both the catalog (which accounts for 75 percent of the company's business) and the store is the functional item that makes life easy, especially anything that's difficult to find nowadays—jumbo metal hairpins, hardwood coat hangers, slippery-elm throat lozenges, garter belts. Lyman, the present Orton-in-charge, has a penchant for newfangled gadgets, such as a plastic frame to hold baseball caps in dishwashers. He's a zealot when it comes to basics that seem to have disappeared, and he frequently finds someone to replicate them, as in the case of the perfect potato masher. The store's own line of edibles features the Vermont Common Cracker, unchanged since 1812, still stamped out in a patented 19th-century machine.

J. J. Hapgood Store (802-824-5911), off Route 11, Peru. Daily 8:30–6. Nancy and Frank Kirkpatrick's genuine general store has a potbellied stove, old-fashioned counters filled with food, and some clothing staples; geared to locals as well as tourists.

Peltier's General Merchandise (802-867-4400), Route 30, Dorset Village. A village landmark since 1816: staples and then some, including

A SIGN OUTSIDE THE VERMONT COUNTRY STORE IN WESTON Kim Grant

almost any kind of fish on request, baking to order, Vermont products, wines, and gourmet items like hearts of palm and Tiptree jams. Because there are no lunch or snack shops in Dorset, this also serves the purpose; good for picnic fare.

Mach's General Store (802-325-3405), Route 30, Pawlet Village. The focal point of this genuine old emporium is described under Pawlet (see *Villages*), but the charm of this family-run place goes beyond its water view. Built as a hotel, it's filled with a wide variety of locally useful merchandise.

The Weston Village Store (802-824-5477), Route 100, Weston. Open daily. A standard country emporium catering to visitors.

SPECIAL SHOPS **Orvis Retail Store** (802-362-3750), Route 7A, Manchester Center, supplying the needs of anglers and other sportsmen since 1856. Known widely for its mail-order catalog, the second oldest in the country, Orvis specializes in the fishing rods made in the factory out back; also other fishing tackle and gear, country clothes, and other small luxury items—from silk underwear to welcome mats—that make the difference in country, or would-be country, living. Don't miss the "bargain basement."

Herdsmen Leathers (802-362-2751) Manchester Center. Open daily, year-round, calling itself "New England's finest leather shop": coats, boots, shoes, and accessories; watch for sales.

The Jelly Mill, Route 7A, Manchester Center. Open daily 10–6. A three-story barn filled with folk art, crystal, cards, crafts, toys, and other assorted gifts.

Equinox Village Shops. This cluster of historic buildings across from the Equinox hotel in Manchester Village includes the Claire Murray Shop and Irish Too, a collection of Irish gifts and clothing.

Equinox Nursery, Route 7A, south of Manchester. An outstanding farm stand and nursery managed by three generations of the Preuss family; good for picking vegetables, berries in-season. Especially famous in the fall for the 100,000 pounds of pumpkins it produces, also for its display of scarecrows and pumpkin faces. Sells pumpkin bread, pie, ice cream, and marmalade, along with other farm stand staples, annuals, perennials, and shrubs. During January and February, the family usually makes 1,000 jars of jams and jellies.

Candle Mill Village (802-375-6068) in East Arlington is a charming hamlet of specialty shops next to two waterfalls. It is located in the Candle Mill, operated locally, stocking 50,000 candles from all over the world, including one that weighs 248 pounds. There's also the **Happy Cook,** the **Rosebud Toy Company,** and the **Bearatorium.** Nearby are an **Antiques Center,** the **Village Peddler,** and the **Scandinavian Country Shop.** One of the ubiquitous Green Mountain Boys, Remember Baker—the builder and first owner of the mill—is commemorated by a monument.

Vermont Country Bird Houses (802-293-5991), Main Street, Danby. Imaginatively hand-carved birdhouses in various architectural styles, with steeples, cupolas, bell towers, and the like, by Jim Kardas. Open daily.

✷ Special Events

March: Spring skiing, sugaring.

April: Trout season opens; Easter parades and egg hunts at ski areas. White-water canoeing on the West River (see "Lower Connecticut and West River Valleys").

May: **Vermont Symphony Orchestra** performs at Hunter Park; Hildene opens (see *To See—Historic Homes*).

June: **Strawberry festivals** in Dorset; the annual **Antique and Classic Car Show** at Hildene (see *To See—Historic Homes*) and **vintage sports car climb** to Equinox Summit; **Hildene Peony Festival** (see *To See—Historic Homes*).

July: Manchester and Dorset host an **old-fashioned Fourth,** a daylong celebration that culminates in fireworks. The **Vermont Summer Festival Horse Show** comes to Manchester for three weeks.

July through mid-August: **Kinhaven Music School** concert series (see *Entertainment—Music*); **Dorset Playhouse** and **Weston Playhouse** open (see *Entertainment—Theater*); a **major antiques show** is held at Hildene Meadows in even years, at Dorset in odd ones. **Manchester Music Festival** (see *Entertainment—Music*). The **Vermont Symphony Orchestra** takes up residence at Hunter Park. **Strattonfest** at Stratton Mountain Resort (see *Entertainment*).

August: **Southern Vermont Crafts Fair**—juried exhibitors, entertainment, food, and music at Hildene; **Wine & Food Festival** at Stratton Mountain Resort (second week). **Norman's Attic** in Arlington is a townwide tag sale. **Storytelling Festival** at Stratton Mountain (late August).

September: The month is chock-full of antiques shows around the area; the biggest is the annual **Vermont Antiques Dealers Association Show** at Riley Rink in Hunter Park. **Peru Fair:** Just 1 day (the fourth Saturday), considered one of Vermont's most colorful (and crowded), it includes a pig roast, crafts, food, and entertainment. **Stratton Quilt Festival.**

October: **Weston Antiques Show,** first weekend, one of the state's oldest and most respected, staged in the

Weston Playhouse (see *Entertainment—Theater*). **Hildene Farm, Food & Folk Art Fair** at the Meadowlands.

November: Harvest dinners and wild-game suppers abound; check local papers and bulletin boards.

December: **Christmas Prelude** (weekend events in Manchester including Vermont's largest potluck dinner, first three weekends) and **Candlelight Tours** of Hildene (between Christmas and New Year's; see *To See—Historic Homes*), including sleigh rides, refreshments in the barn, music on the organ. A **tour of the historic inns** of Manchester Village takes place the first two Saturdays of December. There's a **Winter Solstice Walk** at Merck Forest in Rupert.

BELLOWS FALLS, SAXTONS RIVER, AND GRAFTON

Forty years ago Grafton, a derelict backroads village, was restored to picturesque perfection. Now it's nearby Bellows Falls that's reviving. The two are, however, very different places. In contrast to Grafton's steepled church and stagecoach inn, the icons in Bellows Falls are a brick, Florentine-style tower and a 1920s diner.

A village of 3,500 residents within the town of Rockingham (total population: 6,800), Bellows Falls is a late-19th-century brick mill and railroad center sited at one of the largest drops in the entire length of the Connecticut River. Its buildings cascade too, down glacial terraces so steep that steps connect the brick downtown with Victorian homes above and with surviving mill buildings down by the river. Geologists tell us that 400 to 600 million years ago two continents collided and separated at this site. Local historians say that it's no accident that this was a sacred place for Native Americans, as evidenced by carvings still visible at the foot of the Great Falls.

One of America's first canals, built in 1802 to ease river traffic around the great falls, still flows behind downtown shops, and passenger trains still rumble through the tunnel built in 1851 beneath the village square. Bellows Falls remains an Amtrak stop; rail buffs can switch here to the *Green Mountain Flyer* for an excursion up along the Connecticut and then the Williams River to Chester. But without a car, or at least two wheels, you will miss Grafton, the Old Rockingham Meeting House, and Saxtons River, a delightfully unrestored village that's also in the town of Rockingham, one with a first-rate summer theater.

GUIDANCE **Great Falls Regional Chamber of Commerce** (802-463-4280), corner of Bridge Street in the square, maintains a web site (www.gfrcc.org) and a walk-in information center, serving towns on both sides of the Connecticut River. It's open weekdays 10–2, with rest rooms. Pick up the *Guided Walking Tour* and *Building on the Past* pamphlets. The best web site for Bellows Falls tourist info is www.bellowsfalls.org.

A new **Connecticut River By-Way Interpretive Center** (www.ctrivertravel.net) on Depot Street, across from the train depot, offers displays and information for the surrounding area on both sides of the river, as well as rest rooms. Open daily in summer, weekdays off-season.

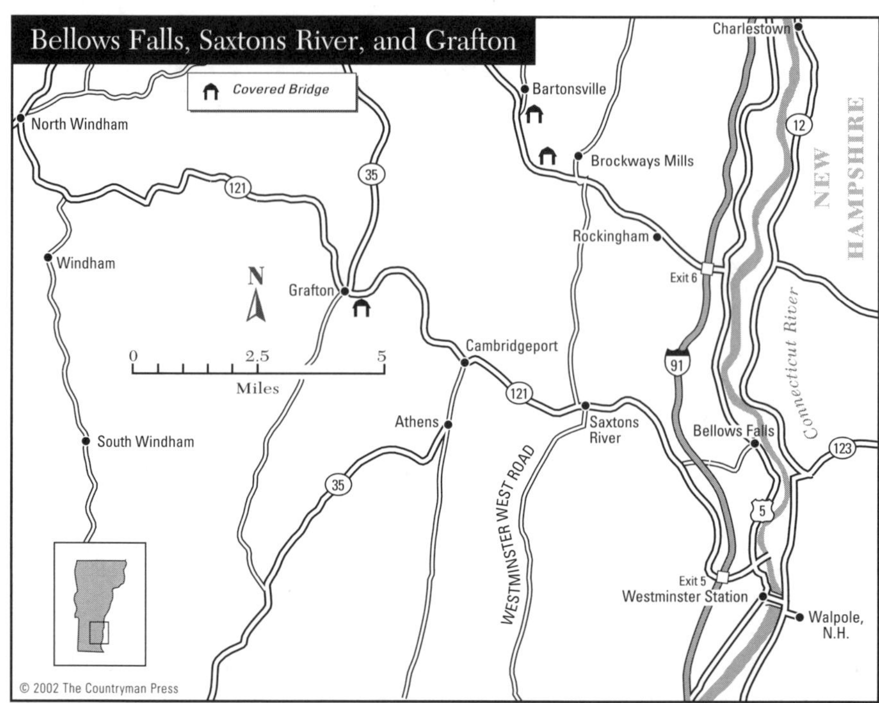

In **Grafton** the Daniels House Gift Shop/Café (802-843-2255), behind the Old Tavern, is open daily, year-round except March and April, and has rest rooms. Pick up a walking tour brochure. Web site: www.windham-foundation.org.

Southern Vermont Regional Market Association (1-877-887-2378; www.southernvermont.com). Maintains a web site and sends out printed material for this entire region.

GETTING THERE *By bus:* **Vermont Transit** from points in Connecticut and Massachusetts stops at Bellows Falls (at Fletcher's drugstore in the square).

By train: **Amtrak** trains stop at Bellows Falls en route to New York City and Washington. Call 1-800-USA-RAIL.

WHEN TO GO Grafton's Christmas-card look draws winter guests, but serious cross-country skiers should know that snow here can be iffy. In spring water surges over the dam in Bellows Falls, but summer brings theater to Saxtons River and it's the preferred season on both sides of the Connecticut River. But it is still pretty quiet, with the exception of July 4. Foliage season is busy.

MEDICAL EMERGENCY 911.

Bellows Falls Health Center (802-463-1360).

VILLAGES Bellows Falls. Viewed from above the dam at Bellows Falls, the Connecticut River resembles a glassy, narrow lake. The view from below the village, however, is very different. Instead of thundering falls, what you usually see is a power station between two narrow water channels and several bridges. The Bellows Falls Canal Co. was the first in the country to obtain a charter and it was an amazing feat, easing flatboats through a series of locks, substantially expanding navigation up the Connecticut. The creation of the canal also formed the island separating the village from the Connecticut River, which for much of the year is now reduced to a modest cascade, dropping through the half-mile gorge beneath the dam. It's on the island that the 1920s railroad station stands, serving Amtrak and the *Green Mountain Flyer* (see *To Do—Railroad Excursion*).

In 1869 William Russell developed the novel idea of making paper from wood pulp, using logs floated down from both sides of the river. He went on to found International Paper. The canal was put to work powering mills, and it still powers turbines generating electricity.

Despite major fires, much of the village architecture dates from the 1890s, the period depicted in a building-sized mural just south of the square. Rockingham Town Hall, with its Florentine-style tower, includes the town-owned New Falls Cinema (see *Entertainment*) and Fletcher's Drug, the bus stop. The surrounding square is lined with a lively mix of shops and restaurants.

Bellows Falls is also known as the home of Hetty Green (1835–1916), who parlayed a substantial inheritance into a $100 million fortune; she was called the Witch of Wall Street, to which she traveled by day coach, looking like a bag lady in threadbare bombazine. The **Bellows Falls Historical Society** maintains displays in the **Rockingham Free Library and Museum** (open summer Fridays, 2–4; 802-463-4270), Westminster Street, and in the **Adams Grist Mill** (Saturday and Sunday 1–4 in July through October). The mill ground grain from 1831 until 1961; the old machinery is all in place.

Grafton. Prior to the Civil War, Grafton boasted more than 1,480 residents and 10,000 sheep. Wool was turned into 75,000 yards of Grafton cloth annually; soapstone from 13 local quarries left town in the shape of sinks, stoves, inkwells, and foot warmers. But then one in three of Grafton's men marched off to the Civil War, and few returned. Sheep farming, too, "went west." An 1869 flood destroyed the town's six dams and its road. The new highway bypassed Grafton. The town's tavern, however, built in 1801, entered a golden era. Innkeeper Marlan Phelps invested his entire California Gold Rush fortune in adding a third floor and double porches, and his brother Francis organized a still-extant cornet band. Guests included Emerson, Thoreau, and Kipling; later both Woodrow Wilson and Teddy Roosevelt visited.

By 1940, however, the Tavern was sagging, and nearly all the 80-some houses in town were selling—with plenty of acreage—for just $3,000–5,000. It

A MURAL IN DOWNTOWN BELLOWS FALLS

Christina Tree

GRAFTON TOWN HALL

Kim Grant

wasn't until 1963 that Matthew Hall, a summer resident descended from the town's first pastor, hit on a suitable use for the fortune his aunt Pauline Fiske had left for a worthy cause. Incorporated in 1963, the resulting Windham Foundation first focused on the town's rotting core, restoring the store, a **blacksmith shop,** and the **Old Tavern** (see *Lodging*). It went on revive the cheese factory, to bury the village wiring, and eventually to acquire many buildings and 2,000 acres with marked footpaths on which visitors can walk or cross-country ski down past the pond, into the woods, and home again. In the the Daniels House behind the Tavern pick up a pamphlet ***Walking Tour of Grafton.*** The **Grafton Historical Society Museum** (802-843-2584; www.graftonhistory.org), 147 Main Street, is open weekends and holidays Memorial Day through Columbus Day 10–2 ($3 admission).

✐ **The Grafton Museum of Natural History** (802-843-2111; www.nature-museum.org) is on the Townshend Road just south of the village. Open Saturday year-round 10–4, Sunday too in summer, it focuses on local flora and fauna, with hands-on exhibits for children. Children should also find their way around to the back of the Windham Foundation Center to the **Sheep Shed,** a visitor-friendly barn that usually houses some lambs. The **Grafton Village Cheese Company** (802-843-2221) in the village is open Monday through Friday 8:30–4; Saturday and Sunday 10–4. To produce its Covered Bridge Cheddar, vats of fresh milk are heated and the curd is cut by hand, tested, drained, milled, salted, molded, and pressed before aging.

Saxtons River, like Bellows Falls, is a village in the town of Rockingham. Said to be named for a surveyor who fell into the river and drowned, it's best known as the home of the Vermont Academy (founded in 1876, a private prep school since 1932). This village of 541 souls is also not a bad place to stay, eat, and shop. The **Saxtons River Historical Museum** (802-869-2566; open summer Sundays, 1–4:30) is housed in a former Congregational church built in 1836 at the western end of the village. Its collection includes art, tinware, toys, Civil War memorabilia, and a furnished Victorian parlor and kitchen.

Walpole, New Hampshire. Few villages are as historically and phsically linked (by two bridges) as Bellows Falls and Walpole, New Hamphire. Bellows Falls is named for Walpole's founder, Col. Benjamin Bellows, who owned land on both side of the river. Walpole's village is a white wooden classic, graced by fine old churches and dozens of clapboard mansions, set high on a plateau above the river. Some buildings date from the early and mid–19th century, when this was a popular summer resort with several large inns. Louisa May Alcott wrote here, and Emily Dickinson visited. James Michener came to research the chapter of *Hawaii* about a departing missionary family. Current creative residents include filmmaker Ken Burns. The **Walpole Historical Society** (603-756-3308; open May through October, Wednesday and Saturday 2–4) is exceptional. Also see *Lodging* and *Where to Eat*.

✷ To See

COVERED BRIDGES There are four covered bridges in the area: two in Bartonsville (1.5 miles north of Route 103 and the other east off Route 103); one in Grafton; and one in Saxtons River off Route 121, noteworthy for its "flying buttresses" (replaced in 1982).

ROCKINGHAM MEETING HOUSE
Vermont's oldest unchanged public building is off Route 103 between Chester and Bellows Falls, and open Memorial Day through Columbus Day, 10–4 (50¢ admission). Built as a combination church and town hall in 1787, this Federal-style structure stands quietly above its graveyard. It's striking inside and out. Inside, "pigpen"-style pews each accommodate 10 to 15 people, some with their backs to the minister. The old burying ground is filled with thin old markers bearing readable epitaphs.

ALONG THE CONNECTICUT RIVER IN BELLOWS FALLS ✐ The **Fish Ladder and Visitors Center** (802-463-3226) of the New England Power Company on Bridge Street in Bellows Falls is one of a series of ladders constructed on the Connecticut River to return Atlantic salmon and American shad to their native spawning grounds.

✐ **Native American petroglyphs.** On the Vermont side of the river, visible from the Villas Bridge. Etched into two separate rock surfaces you see a series of round heads. Note the prominent figure with a neck and shoulders and rays or feathers, assumed to denote power. Said to date in age anywhere from 300 to 2,000 years, the carvings are said to have been created by the Abenaki tribe who fished at the foot of the falls. Unfortunately the carvings have been eroded by logging and railroad blasting and years ago were painted bright yellow to make them easier to see.

✷ To Do

BICYCLING **Grafton Ponds** (802-843-2400) in Grafton rents mountain bikes for use on dirt roads radiating from the village and on its cross-country trails.

BOATING ***Peacemaker*** **Cruises** (603-445-2371), 22 West Street, North Walpole, New Hampshire. Just across the bridge from Bellows Falls Bill Gallagher offers

ROCKINGHAM MEETING HOUSE

Kim Grant

regularly scheduled (late May through mid-October, weekends at 2) 2-hour cruises on *Peacemaker,* his canopied pontoon boat. The cruise takes you upriver between cornfields, past Herrick's Cove, a particularly beautiful spot at the confluence with the Williams River. Chances are you will spot a blue heron in the cove and swallows soaring and swooping by the dozens around their nests in the riverbank. The boat accommodates 16, and is available for charters.

GOLF **Bellows Falls Country Club** (802-463-9809), Route 103, Rockingham. Scenic nine-hole course; clubhouse with bar and lunchroom.

Windham Country Club (802-875-2517; www.windhamgolf.com), 6802 Popple Dungeon Road. Formerly Tater Hill, 18 holes with a pro shop.

RAILROAD EXCURSION ***Green Mountain Flyer*** (802-463-3069; 1-800-707-3530; www.rails-vt.com), 54 Depot Street, Bellows Falls. Round trips available Tuesday through Saturday, July 3 through September 1; twice-daily round trips during foliage season (September 15–October 14). Inquire about special runs in February and March. Based in the same handsome 1920s railroad station that serves Amtrak, this excursion is operated by the Green Mountain Railroad; its rolling stock includes some turn-of-the-20th-century cars. The 13-mile (one-way) route is along the Connecticut River, past covered bridges, then up the Williams River and through wooded rock cuts, which include the spectacular Brockway Mills gorge. $12 round trip for adults, $8 per child 3–12.

CROSS-COUNTRY SKIING **Grafton Ponds** (802-843-2400), Townshend Road, Grafton. You'll find 30 km of groomed trails meandering off from a log cabin warming hut, over meadows, and into the woods on Bear Hill. Snowmaking, rentals, and instruction, plus ice skating and snowshoeing.

SWIMMING **Grafton Swimming Pond,** Route 121, 1 mile west of the village, is an oasis for children.

✷ Lodging

INNS ∞ ♿ **The Old Tavern** (802-843-2231; 1-800-843-1801; www.old-tavern.com), Main Street, Grafton 05146, where Routes 35 and 121 intersect. The brick core of this splendid building dates back to 1788, but the double-porched facade is mid–19th century. The stylish interior (vintage 1965) tastefully re-creates a formal early American setting. More than 40 rooms are divided among the inn and nearby houses, a few of which can be rented in their entirety. Guest rooms have private bath, but no TV or air-conditioning. Common rooms are formal and elegant. The Phelps Barn has a fireplaced lounge. In summer there are nearby tennis courts and a sand-bottomed swimming pond; in winter, cross-country skiing. Youngsters are welcome in some cottages. Pets are not permitted, but you can bring your horse (there's a stable). $135–$395 per room depending on the room and season. Houses sleeping eight or nine people are $550–950; 10 percent senior discount.

Inn at Saxtons River (802-869-2110), Main Street, Saxtons River 05154. This vintage-1903 inn with a distinctive square, five-story tower has an attractive streetside pub and a large, popular dining room (see *Dining Out*). The 16 rooms (all with private bath) are $120–130, $20 per extra person, including a buffet breakfast.

The Walpole Inn (603-756-3320; www.walpoleinn.com), Main Street, Walpole, NH 03608. Totally rehabbed in 1999, this 1760s tavern, best known for its dining, offers eight comfortable upstairs guest rooms, some with gas fireplace. $130–160.

BED & BREAKFASTS **The Inn at Woodchuck Farm** (802-843-2398), Middletown Road, Grafton 05146. Open year-round. This 1780s farmhouse sits high on a hill, on a back road above Grafton. The porch, well stocked with comfortable wicker, has a peaceful, top-of-the-world feel, and there are views from the elegant living room and dining room, too. Operated as an inn by the Gabriel family for more than 30 years, it offers six rooms, four of them corner rooms with private bath (one with a fireplace) in the main house. In the west wing, an upstairs studio has its own kitchen and glass doors that open onto a private deck with views of the woods. Downstairs is a spacious suite with a king-sized canopy bed and a fridge, microwave, and coffeemaker sequestered in a hand-carved armoire. By the pond, the old barn has been rejigged to offer some great spaces. You can have either a double room with fireplace, two rooms with fireplace, or the whole barn with a two-story living room, woodstove, kitchen, and view of the pond. Spruce Cottage offers privacy and seclusion. Furnished in antiques, it is fully equipped and sleeps up to seven people ($375 per day). There's a sauna in the woods next to the pond, which is good for swimming, fishing, and canoeing, and the 200 rolling acres are laced with walking trails. No smoking. $89–260 B&B.

PORCH ROCKERS AT THE GRAFTON INN

Kim Grant

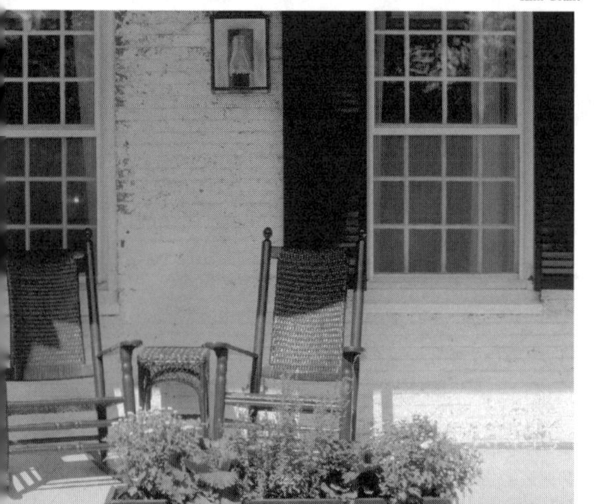

River Mist B&B (802-463-9023; 1-888-463-9023; www.river-mist.com), 7 Burt Street, Bellows Falls 05101. This Queen Anne Victorian town house with wraparound porches reflects the way the town's onetime mill owners lived. Michael Verone offers lacy guest rooms with private bath at $120. Includes a very full breakfast. Less off-season.

The Inn at Valley Farms (1-877-327-2855; www.innatvalleyfarms.com), Wentworth Road, Walpole, NH 03608. A farmhuse dating from 1774, set on a 105-acre farm. Common rooms are elegant, and there's an inviting sun porch and gardens. In addition to attractive guest rooms and suites in the house there are two 3-bedroom cottages. $95–125 for rooms, $125–155 for the two-room garden suite, $120–160 per night for the cottages.

Readmore Bed & Breakfast & Books (802-463-9415; www.readmoreinn.com), 1 Hapgood Street, Bellows Falls 05101. New in 2002: Dorothy and Stewart Read's Victorian house offers ample common space and six guest rooms, all with private bath, three with Jacuzzi and fireplace. One is a two-bedroom suite. The Reads are antiquarian book dealers; rooms are themed with appropriate books (gardening, history, etc.). $150–270 includes breakfast.

✷ Where to Eat

DINING OUT **Oona's** (802-463-9830), 15 Rockingham Street, Bellows Falls. Open for lunch and dinner nightly, live music on Thursday, and jazz the first Saturday of each month. Oona Madden's storefront restaurant is the heart of the new Bellows Falls. It's colorful and comfortable, with an eclectic menu that changes daily, moderate at lunch and upscale at dinner. $20 for golden sea bass with a sweetened grapefruit-tarragon butter sauce. Wednesday is Tapas Night.

The Old Tavern (802-843-2231), Grafton, serves dinner and Sunday brunch in the formal dining rooms or in the more casual Pine and Garden rooms. Recently rave reviews have been celebrating the food and wine to be sampled in this formal old dining room amid fine portraits and Chippendale chairs. A spring menu might include roasted lamb chop with morels, fiddleheads, and a white wine demiglaze with herbed popover and sautéed green beans. The wine list is both extensive and reasonably priced. Entrées $21–30.

Inn at Saxtons River (802-869-2110), Main Street, Saxtons River. Open for lunch and dinner daily except Monday; known for Sunday brunch. This attractive inn's dining room gets mostly good reviews. The à la carte menu is unusually large. You might begin with marinated and grilled shrimp cocktail and dine on pan-seared duck breast with gingered fig sauce ($18). This is the obvious spot to dine before productions at the Saxtons River Playhouse (see *Entertainment*) around the corner.

✐ **Leslie's** (802-463-4929), Rockingham. Route 5 just south of I-91 exit 6, a 1790s tavern with seven fireplaces, serving dinner. Closed Tuesday. Chef-owned for two decades, known for homemade pasta and home-grown produce. Veal and organically raised chicken are served a variety of ways and there's always a vegetarian plate. Entrées $15–20.

Averill's Restaurant & Bob's Tavern (802-369-2327), Route 121, Saxtons River. Open Monday through Saturday 5:30–10 for dinner; 4–closing in the tavern. Attractive and owner operated with a large choice of entrées that might include spanakopita or steak *au poivre* ($10–17). In the tavern you can always get a hamburger and fries ($5). Nightly specials.

The Walpole Inn (603-756-3320), Main Street, Walpole. Open for dinner. A traditional dining setting and menu with a good rep. The summer menu might range from a crispy duck and ginger salad to rack of lamb ($16–27). The specialty, served Friday and Saturday, is herb-crusted prime rib.

EATING OUT *Note:* Also see Oona's for lunch.

Miss Bellows Falls Diner (802-463-9800), 90 Rockingham Street, Bellows Falls. Open daily except Monday from 6 AM through dinner. Inside and out this Worcester Diner #771 is still pure, unhokey 1920s.

THE MISS BELLOWS FALLS DINER

Alan Fowler

Pizza Paul and Mary (802-869-2222), Main Street, Saxtons River. Open daily 11–9 except Monday. Besides a catchy name, this village eatery offers unusual pizza toppings—like pesto, artichoke, and avocado—also burgers, subs, and antipasti.

Joy Wah (802-463-9761), Rockingham Road (Route 5), Bellows Falls. Full-service Chinese fare in a Victorian farmhouse perched on a knoll overlooking the Connecticut River; includes all the familiar dishes on its lengthy menu. Open daily for lunch and dinner.

Anatolia (802-463-2384), 111 Rockingham Street, Bellows Falls. Open daily 11–11. Spaghetti and meatballs, rib eye, pizzas, and Greek salad are on the menu, but the real specialties here are from Somet and Michrican Eroglu's homeland. Try the Turkish gyro or Anatolia sampler. Half portions available for children.

China Wok (802-463-9885), 92 Rockingham Street, Bellows Falls. Open daily for lunch and dinner. No MSG and a pleasant atmosphere combine with a wide, reasonably priced selection.

The Cafe (802-463-1336) Rockingham Street, Bellows Falls, next to Oona's Restaurant. Good for cappuccino at breakfast and for soup and sandwiches at lunch.

L. A. Burdick Café (603-756-2882), 47 Main Street, Walpole, New Hampshire. Open 7 AM–8 PM daily. This is home base for the nationally known chocolatier with cafés in Cambridge and Edgartown, Massachusetts. This new café serves not only chocolates and pastries but also a menu to complement them, including wine.

Frank's Franks (802-463-9800), Rockingham Street, Bellows Falls. A small eatery with two surprises: a river view and superb fried fish. The franks are fine too.

Entertainment

THEATER AND FILM **Saxtons River Playhouse** (802-869-2030), Westminster West Road, Saxtons River Village. Late June through August, musicals and popular plays, Monday through Saturday at 8 PM; Sunday at 7. Also some matinees and children's theater on Thursday, Friday at 2, as well as after-show cabarets.

New Falls Cinema (802-463-4766), on the square in Bellows Falls, operated by the Rockingham recreation department, Friday through Tuesday shows first-run flicks at $3 ($1.50 on bargain days). This fine old vaudeville house is also the venue for live performances.

Front Porch Theater Company (802-463-9791; www.frontporchtheater.org). A communtiy theater group performs in town hall during the school year, not to be confused with **The Front Porch Theater Summer Series,** which features varied musical and performance groups on various Bellows Falls porches. For details contact Village Square Booksellers (see *Selective Shopping*).

MUSIC The **Flying under Radar Series** folk music Thursday evening at Oona's Restaurant is now a stop on the national folk music circuit.

The **Grafton Cornet Band** performs in either Grafton or Chester (sometimes in Townshend) on summer weekends.

ARTS **Main Street Arts** (802-869-2960), Main Street, Saxtons River. This local arts council sponsors dance and musical performances, parades, cabarets, recitals, and a midwinter solstice celebration (The Revels) as well as art classes and the Jelly Bean crafts shop.

Great River Arts Institute (603-756-3638; www.greatriverarts.org), P.O. Box 639, Walpole, NH 03608. Workshops in writing and a variety of visual arts are offered.

✷ Selective Shopping

ANTIQUES SHOPS **Grafton Gathering Places Antiques** (802-875-2309), 748 Eastman Road, open daily year-round except Tuesday. A two-story country barn filled with early country and period furniture and accessories.

Sign of the Raven (802-869-2500), Route 121 east, Saxtons River. Open 10–5 (by chance or appointment—call ahead). Antiques and fine American paintings.

GALLERIES **Three Rivers Gallery** (802-463-1991), Canal Street in the Exner Block, Bellows Falls. A showcase for the best of local art, custom furniture, and decorative accessories. Check out William Accorsi's whimsical sculptures in his gallery/studio next door.

A SIGN AT THE GRAFTON VILLAGE CHEESE COMPANY

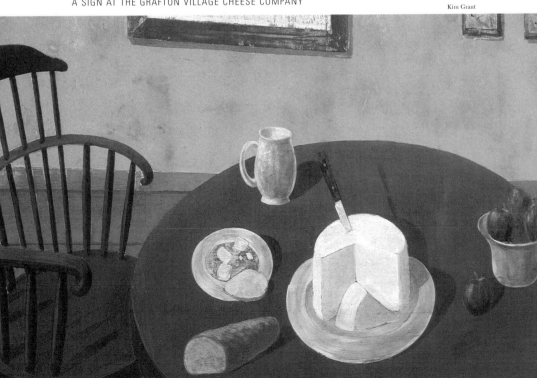

Kim Grant

Gallery North Star (802-843-2465), Townshend Road, Grafton Village. Six rooms in this Grafton Village house are hung with landscapes and graphic prints, oils, watercolors, and sculpture.

The Framery of Vermont (802-463-3295), 115 Rockingham Street, Bellows Falls. The particular focus here is the Connecticut River Valley, its landscape, flora, and fauna.

SPECIAL SHOPS **Vermont Country Store,** Rockingham Village (www.vermontcountrystore.com), Route 103. An offshoot of the famous Vermont Country Store in Weston, this is also owned by Lyman Orton and houses a Common Cracker machine, which visitors can watch as it stamps out the hard round biscuits. The store also sells whole-grain breads and cookies baked here, along with a line of calico material, soapstone griddles, woodenware gadgets, natural-fiber clothing, and much more. There is also an upstairs bargain room.

Village Square Booksellers (802-463-9404), 28 The Square, Bellows Falls. Open Monday through Saturday 9–6, Friday until 7, and Sunday noon–4. Patricia Fowler's independent, full-service bookstore offers poetry readings and other special programs, also features local photography by Alan Fowler.

Jelly Bean Tree (802-869-2326), Main Street, Saxtons River. Open daily April through December, noon–5. A crafts cooperative run by local artisans and carrying the work of many more on consignment: pottery, macramé, leather, weaving, batik, and hand-sewn, -knit, and -crocheted items.

Sam's Outdoor Outfitters (802-463-3500; www.samsoutdoor.com), 78 The Square, Bellows Falls, bills itself as "the biggest little store in the world." A branch of the Brattleboro store but still big.

Caboose Corner (802-463-4575), 676 Missing Link Road, Route 5, Bellows Falls. Open Wednesday through Sunday, noon–8 PM. Model trains and accessories in an old Rutland Railroad caboose.

FARMS TO VISIT **Hidden Orchard Farms** (802-843-2499), Grafton. Pick-your-own apples, blueberries, and raspberries. Apple cider and pumpkins. Maple syrup and natural fruit and berry preserves, fruit butters. The store is in the old fire station in Grafton Village.

Allen Brothers Farms & Orchards (802-722-3395), Route 5, 2 miles south of Bellows Falls. Open year-round, daily. Offers pick-your-own apples and potatoes, also sells vegetables, plants and seeds, honey, syrup, and Vermont gifts.

✷ Special Events

July 4 weekend: A big **parade** in Saxtons River.

Early August: (early), **Old Home Days & Transpo,** Bellows Falls. A full weekend of events—railroad excursions, live entertainment, art show, Rockingham Meeting House Pilgrimage, spectacular fireworks supplied by the Lisai family.

OKEMO VALLEY REGION

INCLUDING LUDLOW AND CHESTER

Okemo is the name of a mountain, not a valley, but it's a popular ski mountain and in this is this era of "branding" the label applies to a large and varied region. Okemo towers 3,300 feet above Ludlow, a lively village on the eastern edge of the Green Mountains. North of town Route 100 threads a chain of lakes, through a steep-sided valley, and Route 103 angles off to climb west through Mount Holly to Belmont or Hortonville and Shrewsbury, beautiful high country. To the east Route 131 follows the Black River through the small mill villages of Proctorsville and Cavendish and Route 103 shadows the Williams River, south to Chester, the region's other handsome old crossroads community.

GUIDANCE **Okemo Valley Regional Chamber of Commerce** (802-228-5830; www.VacationinVermont.com), P.O. Box 333, Ludlow 05149. A walk-in information office in the Marketplace, across from Okemo Mountain access road on Route 103 (look for the clock tower), has menus, events listings, and lodging brochures. The chamber also maintains a seasonal information booth on the green in Chester (802-875-2939). Rest rooms both places. Request the current issue of the *Okemo Valley Regional Guide*. For lodging in the Chester area also check out www.chesterlodging.com, and for other area lodging www.okemo.com.

MEDICAL EMERGENCY **911** covers the area. **Ludlow Health Center** (802-228-4362), 8 Main Street, is open daily with emergency care. **Springfield Hospital** (802-885-2151), 25 Ridgewood Road, Springfield, offers 24-hour emergency care. Also see "Rutland."

GETTING THERE *By bus:* **Vermont Transit** (802-862-9671) stops two times per day in Ludlow at the Okemo Marketplace en route from Rutland to Boston.

By air: See "Rutland" for service from Boston.

GETTING AROUND **George's Shuttle Service** (1-800-208-3933), based in Weathersfield, provides transport by reservation to and from the railroad stations in Bellows Falls and Rutland and airports throughout New England.

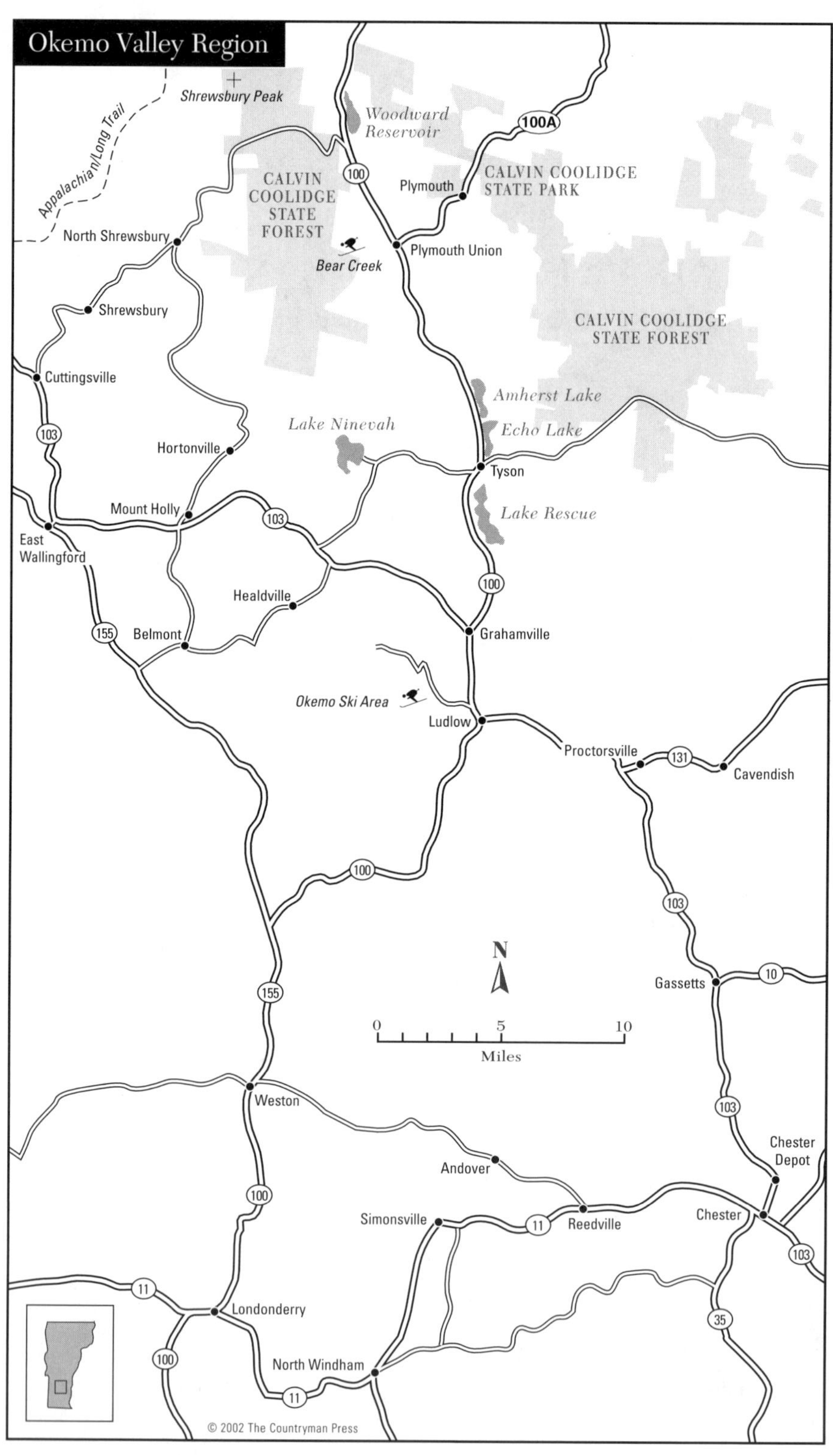
Okemo Valley Region
Shrewsbury Peak
Appalachian/Long Trail
Woodward Reservoir
100A
CALVIN COOLIDGE STATE PARK
CALVIN COOLIDGE STATE FOREST
Plymouth
100
North Shrewsbury
Plymouth Union
Bear Creek
Shrewsbury
CALVIN COOLIDGE STATE FOREST
Cuttingsville
Amherst Lake
103
Lake Ninevah
Echo Lake
Hortonville
Tyson
Mount Holly
Lake Rescue
East Wallingford
103
100
Healdville
155
Belmont
Grahamville
Okemo Ski Area
Ludlow
Proctorsville
131
Cavendish
100
103
N
Gassetts
10
0
5
10
Miles
155
Weston
103
Chester Depot
Andover
100
Simonsville
11
Reedville
Chester
103
11
Londonderry
35
100
North Windham
11
© 2002 The Countryman Press

Okemo Mountain Resort (802-228-4041) offers a free shuttle to the village during peak times in ski season.

WHEN TO GO Nearby lakes make Ludlow as much of a summer place to be as Chester and the hill towns. In winter Okemo is the big draw; cross-country skiers also head for Andover and Shrewsbury.

TOWN AND VILLAGE **Ludlow** (population: 2,700) boomed with the production of "shoddy" (fabric made from reworked wool) after the Civil War, a period frozen in the red brick of its commercial block, Victorian mansions, magnificent library, and academy (now the Black River Museum). In the wake of the wool boom, the General Electric Company moved into the steepled mill at the heart of town and kept people employed making small-aircraft engine parts until 1977. Okemo opened in 1956, but for years it was a sleeper—a big mountain with antiquated lifts on the edge of a former mill town. Ski clubs nested in the Victorian homes, and just a few inns catered to serious skiers. Tim and Diane Mueller bought the ski area in 1982, and it has been evolving ever since as one of New England's most popular ski resorts, known for the quality of its snowmaking, grooming, and on-mountain lodging and other facilities. A major golf course has recently been added that doubles as a full-service cross-country-ski center.

The effect on Ludlow has been dramatic. The old General Electric plant has been turned into condominiums. Other lodging options as well as restaurants have multiplied. For a sense of Ludlow B.O. (Before Okemo) visit the **Fletcher Library** (802-228-8921), Main Street, Ludlow. Open Monday through Friday 10–5:30, Saturday 10–1 and 6:30–8:30, it offers reading rooms with fireplaces; old-style, green-shaded lights; and century-old paintings of local landscapes. The **Black River Academy Historical Museum** (802-228-5050), at the corner of Smith and High Streets, is open June through Labor Day Tuesday through Sunday noon–4, then through mid-October just Friday and Saturday, same hours. A steepled, brick school building, built in 1889, the academy's reputation drew students from throughout New England. One large room is dedicated to Pres. Calvin Coolidge, class of 1890. Other rooms in the four-story building are filled with exhibits about mining, lumbering, railroading, farming, and other segments in the history of the Black River Valley. $2 adults, free under age 12.

Lake Pauline and Lake Rescue harbor rental cottages, as do Lake Ninevah and Echo and Amherst Lakes, which are just north of the town line. In warm-weather months, however, Ludlow's big attraction is its location and abundant rental housing stock, making it an ideal base from which to explore much of southern and central Vermont.

Chester (population: 2,700) encompasses three distinct villages within a few miles, each of them worth noting. The village of Chester itself is a beauty, sited at the confluence of three branches of the Williams River and of five major roads. Its stringbean-shaped village green is lined with shops and restaurants, including the double-porched old Fullerton Inn. Across the street (Route 11) is a fine old brick schoolhouse, its ground floor now occupied by the **Chester Art Guild** (802-875-

3767; manned daily by volunteers by June through October), with changing exhibits and frequent special events. Upstairs the **Chester Historical Society** (802-875-6211; open June through October, Saturday and Sunday 2–5) presents the town's colorful history, including the story of Clarence Adams, a prominent citizen who broke into more than 50 businesses and homes between 1886 and 1902 before being apprehended.

Don't miss Chester's **Stone Village** up on North Street (Route 103): a double line of 30 buildings faced in gneiss, a rough-hewn, gleaming mica schist quarried from nearby Flamstead Mountain. Cool in summer, warm in winter, stone houses are a rarity in New England. All of these are said to have been built by two brothers in the pre–Civil War decade, with hiding spaces enough to make them a significant stop on the Underground Railroad.

Midway between Main and North Streets is **Chester Depot,** a pleasant old traffic center that resembles neither of these places. The well-kept Victorian depot serves as the northern terminus for the *Green Mountain Flyer* (see *To Do*), spilling more than 100 passengers at a time to browse and stroll.

SCENIC DRIVE From Ludlow head north 2 miles on Route 100, then west on 103, 5 miles to Healdville and the sign for the Crowley Cheese Factory. In the 1880s every Vermont town had its cheese factory to process surplus milk, but Crowley Cheese, which the family had begun making in the 1820s, was distributed up and down the East Coast. The three-story wooden building, built in 1882 by Winfield Crowley, is now billed as America's oldest cheese factory. It's a 2-mile detour down a side road but well worth the effort. Visitors are welcome weekdays, 8–4, to watch the shower-capped employees "cutting," "raking," and otherwise turning 5,000 pounds of fresh milk into 500 pounds of cheese (see *Selective Shopping*).

CROWLEY CHEESE FACTORY

Christina Tree

Route 103 climbs on to **Mount Holly** and on continues anther 5 miles to Cuttingsville (see Vermont Industries in *Selective Shopping*). U.S. Sen. Jim Jeffords lives nearby and can frequently be found at the Over Easy Restaurant. Turn up the road ("Town Hill") posted for Shrewsbury, a gem of a town with dense forest and long vistas, seemingly on the roof of this area that straddles central and southern Vermont. **Shrewsbury Center** is marked by a white wooden church set back on a knoll beside two face-to-face taverns, now both B&Bs. One of these, **Maple Crest Farm,** remains in the same family that built it in 1808 and has been taking in guests since the 1860s. Although the dairy herd is gone, this is still a working farm with more than 30 head of beef cattle and some 300 acres in hay. Stop and take in the view and the quiet. In **North Shrewsbury,** 2 more miles up the hill, is the **W. E. Pierce General Store** (presently closed), with a '50s gas pump out front. A signs across the road points to **Meadowsweet Herb Farm** just down Eastham Road. Here Polly Haynes sells the herbal blends and vinegars, potpourri, party dips, and more and maintains display gardens (see *Selective Shopping*). The farm's brochure directs visitors back down dirt roads to Mount Holly, but adventurous and careful drivers (with good brakes) should head back up to North Shrewbury and take the right just past the store. This is **CCC Road,** one of Vermont's steepest and most scenic routes, open in summer only. It's 6 miles seemingly straight down—with superlative mountain and valley views—to Route 100 in Plymouth.

Turn south (right) on Route 100 for 2 miles and left on Route 100A to **Plymouth Notch,** perhaps the first rural Vermont village to appear in publications throughout the world—on August 2, 1923, the day Calvin Coolidge was sworn into office here as the 30th U.S. president. It's now the **Calvin Coolidge Historic Site** (for a full description, see "Killington/Plymouth Area"). Make your way back to Route 100; from Plymouth it's a scenic 9-mile ride south past a chain of lakes to Ludlow.

✷ To Do

BIKING **Mountain Cycology** (802-228-2722), Ludlow, across from the Grand Union. No rentals but equipment, repair, guidebooks, and local advice as well as sales.

Bike Vermont (1-800-257-2226; www.BikeVermont.com) offers a choice of inn-to-inn tours in this area.

BOATING **Northern Excursions** (802-228-4957), Ludlow, offers canoes, kayaks, and tubes for fishing, wildlife viewing, photography, and camping.

Echo Lake Inn (802-228-8602), Route 100, Tyson, rents canoes and other boats. (See *Lodging*.) Rentals are also available at **Camp Plymouth State Park** (802-672-3612) off Route 100 in Tyson. Nearby Lake Ninevah is quieter, with some beautiful marshes and woods.

FISHING Public access has been provided to Lake Rescue, Echo Lake, Lake Ninevah, Woodward Reservoir, and Amherst Lake. Fishing licenses are required except under age 16. The catch includes rainbow trout, bass, and pickerel. There is also fly-fishing in the Black River along Route 131 in Cavendish, and the 6-mile stretch from the green metal bridge in Downers to the covered bridge is stocked and maintained as a trophy trout section, stocked each spring with 1.5-pound brown trout and 18-inch rainbows.

GOLF The **Okemo Valley Golf Club** (802-228-1396), Fox Lane, Ludlow. A new, 18-hole championship "heathland-style" course featuring wide fairways with dips, ripples, rolls, and hollows said to suggest Scottish links. The Golf Academy also utilizes an 18-acre outdoor Golf Learning Center with a 370-yard-long driving range and four practice greens. Also new: a Golf Operations & Academy Center with a 6,000-square-foot indoor practice area, a computerized virtual golf program, classrooms, and changing rooms with showers. The Club House includes a fully stocked Pro Shop and Willie Dunn's Grill (see *Eating Out*).

Windham Golf Club (802-875-2517; www.windhamgolf.com), 6802 Popple Dungeon Road, Windham (off Route 11, not far from Chester). Formerly Tater Hill, this is an 18-hole course with a pro shop and practice range.

HORSEBACK RIDING AND HORSE-DRAWN RIDES **Cavendish Trail Horse Rides** (802-226-7821), Twenty Mile Stream Road, Proctorsville, offers guided tours and pony rides. Trail rides are offered at **Hawk Inn and Mountain Resort** on Route 100 in Plymouth (see "Killington/Plymouth Area").

RAILROAD EXCURSION ✐ ***Green Mountain Flyer*** (802-463-3069; 1-800-707-3530; www.rails-vt.com), 54 Depot Street, Bellows Falls. From late June through Labor Day one daily round trip, twice daily during foliage season. Rolling stock includes some turn-of-the-20th-century cars. The 13-mile (one way) route to Chester Depot is along the Connecticut River, past covered bridges, then up the Williams River and through wooded rock cuts, which include the spectacular Brockway Mills gorge. $12 round trip for adults, $8 per child 3–12.

SELF-IMPROVEMENT VACATIONS **Fletcher Farm Craft School** (802-228-8770), Route 103 east, Ludlow. Operated since 1948 by the Society of Vermont Craftsmen, this old farmstead on the eastern edge of town offers dorm-style lodging and pleasant studio space for the 86 classes held during July and August. Subjects include early American decoration, stained glass, basketry, weaving, woodcarving, quilting, oil and watercolor painting, spinning, and rug hooking and braiding. Meals are family-style.

SWIMMING ✐ **West Hill Recreation Area** (802-228-2849), West Hill off Route 103 in Ludlow, includes a beach (with lifeguard) on a small, spring-fed reservoir; also a snack bar and playground/picnic area.

Buttermilk Falls, near the junction of Routes 100 and 103. This is a swimming hole and a series of small but beautiful falls (turn at the VFW post just west of the intersection).

✐ **Camp Plymouth State Park** (802-672-3612), off Route 100 at Tyson. Beach on Echo Lake, picnic area, food concession, volleyball, horseshoes, playground, and beach but no lifeguard.

Star Lake in the village of Belmont in Mount Holly is also a great place for a swim.

✷ Winter Sports

SNOWMOBILE RIDES ✐ **C&B Guided Rides** (802-259-2666) caters especially to families with children and groups, night and day.

CROSS-COUNTRY SKIING **Okemo Valley Nordic Center** (802-228-8871), junction of Routes 100 and 103, Ludlow. A café and a rental shop are surrounded by the open roll of the golf course; there are also wooded and mountain trails adding up to 28 km (including 20 km of skating lanes), also 10 km of dedicated snowshoe trails. The clubhouse offers a fireplace, restaurant and lounge, changing rooms and showers. Rentals. $17 adult, $14, $12.

Also see Grafton Ponds in Grafton (in "Bellows Falls, Saxtons River, and Grafton") and Viking Nordic Centre in Londonderry (in "Manchester and the Mountains").

DOWNHILL SKIING **Okemo** (information: 802-228-4041; snow reports: 802-228-5222; reservations: 1-800-78-OKEMO; www.okemo.com). A big mountain (boasting Vermont's fourth highest vertical drop), Okemo is a destination ski and snowboard resort with a small-resort feel. It's one of the few resorts with a real town right at its base, one with lodging, restaurants, grocery and specialty stores. It's also far larger than it looks from its base. Surprises begin at the top of the initial chairlifts, where you meet a wall of three-story condominiums and find your way down to the spacious Sugar House base lodge—from which the true size of the mountain becomes apparent. This is a ski area of many parts. Beginners and lower-intermediate skiers can enjoy both the lower southwest and upper northeast sides of the mountain—entirely different places in view and feel. From the summit, beginners can actually run a full 4.5 miles to the base. Expert skiers, on the other hand, have the entire northwestern face of the mountain, served by its own chair. There are also a number of wide, central fall line runs down the face of Okemo. World Cup is a long and steep but forgiving run with sweeping views down the Black River Valley to the Connecticut River. Solitude Peak, with snowmaking on eight trails served by a quad chair, is another haven with long cruisers, bump runs, beginner terrain, and the Solitude Village. The most recent enhancements include a 420-foot-long super pipe and a newly renovated Snow Stars

A VIEW OF OKEMO MOUNTAIN AND ITS TRAILS

Center for kids. Site work has begun at Jackson Gore, a 546-acre expansion area with its own access off Route 103. At this writing construction of the Jackson Gore Inn, along with new trails and lifts, is set to begin. *Lifts:* 14: 7 quad chairs (including 3 high-speed), 3 triple chairs, and 3 surface lifts. *Trails and slopes:* 98 trails and glades covering 520 acres—25 percent novice, 50 percent intermediate, 25 percent advanced expert. *Vertical drop:* 2,150 feet (highest in southern Vermont). *Snowmaking:* Covers 95 percent of trails (495 acres). *Facilities:* Base lodge with cafeteria; midmountain Sugar House base lodge with cafeteria; summit lodge and cafeteria; Solitude Day Lodge. *Note:* Gables, in the Solitude Day Lodge, run by the New England Culinary Institute, is not your usual cafeteria (open 11–3). *Ski school:* Okemo's Cutting Edge Learning Center is staffed by 250 instructors. Children's programs include Snow Star Skiers (ages 4–7), Young Mountain Explorers (ages 7–12), and Get Altitude (ages 3–16). Children's snowboard programs are Snow Star Riders (ages 5–7) and Young Riders (ages 7–12). Ski and snowboard programs include Women's Ski Spree and Adult Snowboard Camps. Senior discounts available on group lessons; an Adaptive Program includes discounted ski and snowboard lessons (reservations required) and tickets. The state-approved Penguin Day Care Center serves children 6 weeks to 8 years and offers supervised indoor and outdoor activities. A Mini Stars ski program is also available for ages 3 and 4. Inquire about Kids' Night Out evening programs, available 6–10 PM in-season. *Lift tickets:* $54–59 adult, $47–50 for young adults (13–18) and seniors ages 65–69; $35–38, ages 7–12 and 70-plus. Rates include tax, and the range reflects midweek and holiday pricing; savings on multiday tickets are substantial.

✱ Lodging

RESORTS **Okemo Mountain Resort** (802-228-4041; 1-800-78-OKEMO); www.okemo.com) is a ski resort that's open year-round, with nearly 700 on-mountain condominiums and a new 18-hole golf course as well as a variety of weatherproofed sports facilities. See *Condominiums* in this section, and *Golf* and *Winter Sports* under *To Do*.

Also see Hawk Mountain Resort in Plymouth, described in "Killington /Plymouth Area."

INNS ⚭ **The Andrie Rose Inn and Luxury Suites** (802-228-4846; 1-800-223-4846; www.andrieroseinn.com), 13 Pleasant Street, Ludlow 05149. Michael and Irene Maston preside over this complex on a quiet back street with unexpectedly luxurious rooms and suites and a reputation for fine dining. The inn itself is a turn-of-the-20th-century house in which the old detailing has been carefully preserved, but the feel—thanks to skillful decor and skylights—is light filled and cheerful. Five of the nine upstairs guest rooms ($80–130 in summer, $120–205 in fall and winter) have whirlpool tub and all are furnished with antiques and designer linens. Summit View features a skylight framing the summit of the mountain. Next door the Federal-style Guesthouse contains townhouse suites geared to families (each with kitchen facility and washer/dryer) as well as suites for two; also next door is Solitude, an 1840s Greek Revival building with seven luxury suites featuring bedside whirlpool tub for two facing a gas fireplace. See *Dining Out* for details about the $38 per-person prix fix emenu. Guests in the main house breakfast in the dining room while those without kitchen facilities in the neighboring buildings receive breakfast in a basket. Amenities include shuttle service to and from Okemo. Suites are $200–250 in spring and summer; $120–525 in fall and winter.

The Governor's Inn (802-228-8830; 1-800-GOVERNOR; www.thegovernorsinn.com), 86 Main Street, open year-round except December 23–26. William Wallace Stickney, governor of Vermont 1900–1902, built this Victorian house with its ornate slate, hand-painted fireplaces. Now it is a gourmet getaway (see *Dining Out*), owned by Jim and Cathy Kubec. The eight upstairs guest rooms are furnished with antiques, and a suite features a whirlpool bath and sitting area. The living room is small but elegant; full bar service is offered guests in the den. Dinner is served Thursday through Sunday, open to the public (with 48-hour prior reservation). Breakfast and tea are served in a cheery back room, warmed by the sun and a woodstove. $165–315 B&B double in fall and winter, $105–230 in low season; add $90 per couple MAP; add 18 percent for service.

Echo Lake Inn (802-228-8602; 1-800-356-6844; www.echolakeinn.com), Route 100 in Tyson, but the mailing address is P.O. Box 154, Ludlow 05149. One of the few survivors of the many Victorian-style summer hotels (although parts of the building predate the Victorian era) that once graced Vermont lakes, the inn is four stories tall with a long white porch, lined in summer with pink geraniums and red rockers. Now winterized, it offers 23 rooms, all with private bath. There are six condo units in the adjacent Carriage House. The living room is homey and informal, with hooked rugs and wooden chairs grouped around the fireplace and TV. There's also the inviting Stone Tavern and a low-beamed dining room (see *Dining Out*), both open to the public. Summer facilities include tennis courts and a pool. At the dock on Echo Lake across the road, rowboats and canoes are available to guests. $79–430 B&B. Inquire about MAP rates and special packages. Add 18 percent to MAP.

ꝏ **The Fullerton Inn** (802-875-2444), 40 Common, P.O. Box 188, Chester 05143. Formerly the Inn at Long Last. Jerry and Robin Szawerda now own this big, old-fashioned, 1920s-style hotel, and they have renovated guest rooms, adding sitting rooms and ceiling fans. Common space includes the immense old lobby and a pub as well as the formal dining room (see *Dining Out*), and a sunny breakfast room. $109–149 double.

ꝏ **The Castle** (802-226-7222; 1-800-697-7222; www.thecastle-vt.com), P.O. Box 207, Routes 131 and 103, Proctorsville 05153. Quarry and timber baron Allen Fletcher, elected governor of Vermont in 1913, built this imposing neo-Jacobean stone manor on a knoll, importing European artisans in 1901 for the oak and mahogany woodwork and detailed cast-plaster ceilings. It's now owned by the neighboring Cavendish Point Hotel. Weddings are the specialty. The 10 rooms are ponderously regal, 6 with gas or wood-burning fireplace and 2 with whirlpool bath. Also see *Dining Out*. $149–289 MAP in winter; somewhat lower in summer.

BED & BREAKFASTS

In the Ludlow area

The Okemo Inn (802-228-8834; out of state: 1-800-328-8834), junction of

Routes 100 north and 103, Ludlow 05149. Open year-round except for 2 weeks in April and November. Ron Parry has been here longer than any other local innkeeper, and this 1810 home is well kept and effortlessly welcoming. There are 11 nicely furnished guest rooms, most with two double beds, all with private bath. In the living room a table in front of the hearth is made from old bellows, and the dining room has low, notched beams; there's also a TV room, a sauna, and in summertime a pool. Ten-speed bikes are available but no one has requested one in years. $75–160 per day B&B for two people. Add 10 percent for service.

♿ **The Golden Stage Inn** (802-226-7744; 1-800-253-8226; www.goldenstageinn.com), 399 Depot Street, P.O. Box 218, Proctorsville 05153. Sandy and Peter Gregg are at the helm of this handsome, historic house. An inn in the 18th century, it belonged to the Skinner family for 100 years, beginning in 1830. There is a suite and eight guest rooms, one named for the writer and performer Cornelia Otis Skinner. Dining areas include the solarium, the inn's greenhouse. The inn is centrally air-conditioned, and a swimming pool is set in gardens. $89–199 B&B, MAP available.

Okemo Lantern Lodge (802-226-7770; 1-800-732-7077), P.O. Box 247, 329 Main Street, Proctorsville 05153, a former mill owner's mansion, is rich in ornately carved butternut and stained glass. The dining room takes center stage downstairs. Jennifer Keegan and Alex Bordas offer 10 guest rooms, ranging from small to large enough for a king-sized bed; all have private bath. Our favorites are on the third floor. In warm-weather months the inn is popular with bicyclists and families; it's a casual, comfortable inn with a swimming pool out back. $80–125.

In Chester 05143

Henry Farm Inn (802-875-2674; 1-800-723-8213; www.henryfarminn.com), Green Mountain Turnpike. There's a nice out-in-the-country feel to this old place, set in 50 rolling acres. Larger than other farmhouses of the period, it was built in 1760 as a stagecoach stop and retains its pine floors, beehive oven, and sense of pleasant, uncluttered simplicity. The nine rooms are large, all with small bathroom. Two of the rooms are suites with kitchen. What you notice are the quilts and the views. A path leads to the spring-fed pond up the hill, and a swimming hole in the Williams River is just across the road. Inquire about frequent quilting workshop weekends. Your hosts are Patricia and Paul Dexter and their enterprising son Joseph. Children welcome. $80–155 includes a country breakfast.

Stone Cottage Collectables (802-875-6211), 196 North Street, Chester 05143. Chris and Ann Curran are your hosts at this 1840 stone house in Chester's Stone Village historic district. Three sitting rooms are furnished with antiques and collectibles and there is also a pleasant patio, deck, and garden. There are two guest rooms with private bath but the find here is a glorious queen-bed room, with fireplace, created by the former owner, best-selling author Olivia Goldsmith (*The First Wives Club*). Room rates, including full breakfast, are $95 for the queen-bed room and $80 for the full-bed room. The Currans also operate a shop here, featuring radios and tubes, cameras, and stamps as well as antiques.

♿ **Inn Victoria** (802-875-4288; 1-800-732-4288), on the green, Chester. Yellow brick with purple shutters, a mansard roof, and columned porch, this showy

Victorian has seven antiques-furnished guest rooms and a suite (sleeping six to eight). All rooms have queen-sized beds, three have Jacuzzis, and the first-floor garden room is handicapped-accessible. Jack and Janet Burns have added an outdoor hot tub and a deck and serve tea. No children under 15 please. From $110 for a small room to $165 for a suite, breakfast included.

The Chester House (802-875-2205; 1-888-875-2205), 266 Main Street, on the green. Common space includes a keeping room with fireplace (beer and wine are served). Room 1 has a queen bed and a whirlpool bath; Room 2, queen bed plus steam bath and sitting area; Room 4, queen bed, sitting area, and whirlpool. All have telephone and air-conditioning. Paul Anderson and Randy Guy are your hosts. $89–169 B&B.

Hugging Bear Inn & Shoppe (802-875-2412; 1-800-325-0519), 244 Main Street. A teddy bear lover's haven with bears on the beds of six guest rooms (private bath). The place teems with them: teddy bear wallpaper, teddy bear sheets and shower curtains, and more than 6,000 stuffed bears in the shop behind the kitchen. Georgette Thomas believes that people don't hug enough. Everyone is invited to hug any bear in the house, and the atmosphere here is contagiously friendly. Rates are $65–95 single, $90–145 double. For extra people: $50 for children under age 15, $25 adult. Full breakfast is included.

Night with a Native Bed & Breakfast (802-875-2616), 266 Depot Street. Doris Hastings is a sixth-generation Vermonter who obviously enjoys accommodating guests in a house that conveys a lively interest in many things. The two small, antiques-decorated bedrooms have private bath. Breakfast is included. $75–95 per couple.

UP IN THE HILLS

The Inn at High View (802-875-2724; www.innathighview.com), 753 East Hill Road, Andover 05143. An attractive inn set high on 72 acres of East Hill, with some of the best views of any inn in Vermont. A portion of the house dates back to the 18th century, but it's been a ski lodge for decades, one of the first to cater to cross-country skiers; there is 15 km trail network out the back door. In summer a pool is set in the rock gardens. There are six rooms and two suites (each two rooms), all very attractively furnished. Request a room with access to the hot tub. There's also a sauna. A game room in the basement is fitted with videos and games for kids; there's a gazebo out on the lawn for weddings. Hosts Greg Bohan and Sal Massaro enjoy an enthusiastic repeat business. Saturday night Sal cooks elegant Italian fare ($30; BYOB). $125–155 for rooms, $165–175 for suites, includes breakfast. Pets possible.

Crisanver House (802-492-3589; 1-800-492-8089; www.crisanver.com), 1434 Crown Point Road, Shrewsbury 05738. Set high on 115 acres of woods and meadows, with panoramic views, this is a find—but it's booked many weekends for weddings. The 1802 portion of this house has recently been restored and offers eight attractive guest rooms, all with down comforters and pillows, exposed beams, original art, robes, and individual heat control. The casually elegant living room has a fireplace and grand piano, and a downstairs game room has table tennis and a pool table. Innkeeper Carol Davenport Calotta has recently added two minisuites in the neighboring cottage,

Maple Crest Farm (802-492-3367), RR Box 120, Cuttingsville 05738. This handsome, white-brick farmhouse sits high on a ridge in the old hilltop center of Shrewsbury. It was built in 1808 as Gleason's Tavern and is still in the same family. In the 1860s, they began taking in guests and have done so off and on ever since. The Smiths offer three antiques-filled rooms (the front ground-floor room with a half bath is our favorite) sharing two baths and two charming apartments that can accommodate small families. "Every piece of furniture has a story," says Donna Smith—and she knows each one. Ask about a rocking chair or spool bed, and you'll begin to sense who has lived in this unusual house down through the years. Books and magazines are everywhere, and if you look closely, you'll see that they're carefully selected, focusing on local and Vermont tales and history. The Smiths raise beef cattle, hay, and are noted for the quality of their maple syrup, produced in the sugarhouse at the peak of the hill; the same sweeping view can be enjoyed in winter on cross-country skis. You can walk off in any number of directions. $35–80. Breakfast extra. No credit cards.

MAPLE CREST FARM

Christina Tree

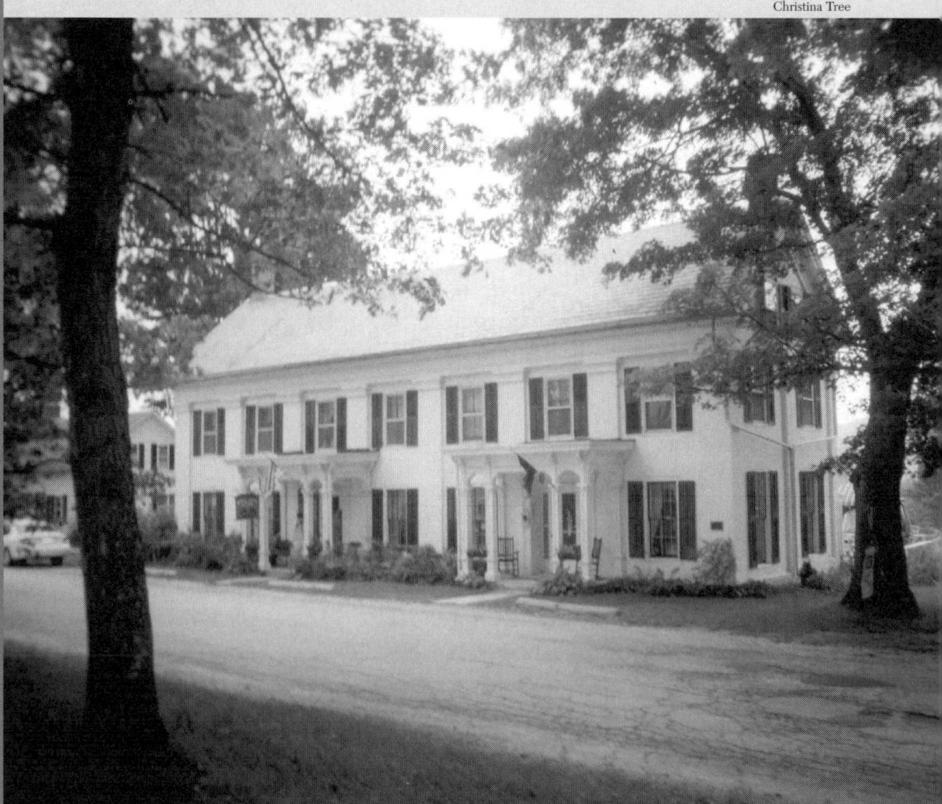

and a barn has been designed to accommodate 120 people for weddings and parties. In summer there's a heated pool and in winter, cross-country skiing. $100–120 for rooms with shared bath, $110–160 with private bath, $150–200 for minisuites, including afternoon tea, full breakfast, and shuttle service from Rutland airport, bus stop, and train station. Inquire about dinner.

High Pastures (802-773-2087; 1-800-584-4738), Cold River Road, Shrewsbury 05738. Taffy Maynard's 200-year-old restored farmhouse is a beauty, set on 126 acres traversed by the Appalachian/Long Trail. This is very much the family's home, but there are five antiques-furnished guest rooms, two with private bath, one with a crazy window and two skylights. Unexpected extras include a pool, tennis court, and cross-country trails as well as well-patronized bird feeders. $70–85 double.

The Buckmaster Inn (802-492-3720; www.buckmasterinn.com), 20 Lottery Road, Shrewsbury 05738. Built as the Buckmaster Tavern beside the Shrewsbury church in 1801, the house is owned by Richard and Elizabeth Davis, who have lightened and brightened its decor. Eight to 10 guests can be accommodated in four rooms (private baths). There is a spacious living room, a library with fireplace and TV, and a long, screened-in porch that's especially inviting in the summer and fall. The Davises are enthusiastic hosts who can tell you what to see and do. $89 double includes a continental-plus breakfast featuring home-baked goodies.

OUT IN THE COUNTRY

The Inn at Cranberry Farm (802-463-1331; www.cranberryfarminn.com), 61 Williams River Road, Chester 05143. Set in 60 acres off by itself near Brockway Mills, a contemporary lodge with an open-beamed, two-story living room and library obviously designed for numbers—ideal for weddings, but couples are very welcome. There are 11 guest rooms, all with private bath, some handicapped-accessible, some with fireplace. $150–225 includes a full breakfast and tea.

Old Town Farm Inn (802-875-2346; 1-888-232-1089), 665 Vermont Route 10, Chester 05143. This former "Town Farm" is in Gassetts, a village midway between Chester and Ludlow. Long known to families as a reasonably priced ski lodge, the old place with its wide-board floors has been nicely rehabbed by Michiko and Alex Hunter. There are now eight comfortable guest rooms, all with private bath. It's set in 11 acres with a pond. $79–129 with breakfast. This is also now a popular place to dine on sushi (see *Eating Out*).

Rowell's Inn (802-875-3658), Route 11, Simonsville, Andover 05142. Open year-round. This distinctive, double-porched, brick stage stop has been serving the public off and on since 1820. Skip and Louise Haley offer six comfortable guest rooms with private bath, one with a working fireplace. Two spacious spaces on the third floor have been carved from the old ballroom, furnished grandly with antiques and Oriental rugs. Located midway between Londonderry, Weston, and Chester, the inn is off by itself with some fine walks and cross-country skiing out the back door. $120–205 B&B; MAP plan offered.

The Combes Family Inn (802-228-8799; 1-800-822-8799), East Lake Road, Ludlow 05149. Ruth and Bill Combes have celebrated their 23rd anniversary as innkeepers, welcoming families to their peaceful 1891 former dairy farm home. There are 11 guest rooms, all with private bath—6 in the farmhouse and 5 in an attached unit (where pets are allowed). B&B double rates: $65 spring, $90 summer, $154 winter. Ruth's hearty Vermont-style dinners are available nightly by reservation at $16 per adult and $8 for kids. Add 15 percent service charge in winter, 10 percent other times.

Stone Hearth Inn (802-875-2525; www.thestonehearthinn.com), Route 11 (1 mile west of the village), Chester 05143. Under ownership by Chris Clay and Brent Anderson, this rambling 1810 farmhouse is a comfortable, informal place. The 10 guest rooms all have private bath; common space includes a library, sitting room, and recreation room wih games, TV, and a hot tub. The tavern at one end of the inn is fully licensed with a pool table and casual menu. $69–149 double, B&B.

Whitney Brook (802-226-7460), 2433 Twenty Mile Stream Road, Proctorsville 05153. Jim and Ellen Parrish welcome guests to their pretty 1870 farmhouse on a quiet road. There are four guest rooms, three with queen beds and one with a double and a single. Two rooms have private bath, two share. Guests enjoy a private living room downstairs and a sitting room upstairs. $55–95.

Popple Fields (802-875-4219; www.popplefields.com), 1300 Popple Dungeon Road, P.O. Box 636, Chester 05143. It took Conrad Delia 10 years (1989–1999) to build this amazing reproduction 18th-century house, and it's a beauty, remarkable for its beauty and detailing, right down to a colonial-style bar. It's way out on a back road, set in 18 rolling acres. There are four guest rooms, two with private bath, and Conrad has made much of the furniture, too (he operates a Windsor chair and cabinet shop on the premises). Marylin Delia serves a full buffet breakfast in the large country kitchen. No children under 15 please. $90–150.

MOTELS **Best Western** (802-228-8188; www.bestwesternludlow.com), 93 Main Street, Ludlow 05149. Years ago Fire Chief Rick Harrison built a 14-unit motel onto the back of his 1825 home. It's now a 48-unit motel decorated with a range of rooms and suites, from antiques-decorated to contemporary. All units have phone, cable TV, full bath, and in-room coffee, and there's a pool. $65–300.

Cavendish Pointe Hotel (802-226-7688; 1-800-438-7908; www.okemo-cavendishpointe.com), Route 103, Cavendish 05142. A contemporary motor inn with 72 fairly large rooms. Facilities include an indoor pool, hot tub/spa room, game room; also a restaurant-bar that opens only during ski season. $69–189.

All Seasons Inn Motel (802-228-8100; 1-888-228-8100), 112 Main Street, Ludlow 05149. A mansard-roofed house in the middle of the village has been turned into 17 units, all with cable TV, phone (with voice mail), and refrigerator; 6 have kitchenette. Free shuttle-bus service. $65–175.

CONDOMINIUMS **Okemo Mountain Resort** offers nearly 700 condominium units, all booked through the Okemo Mountain Lodging Service (802-228-5571; 1-800-78-OKEMO; RFD 1, Ludlow 05149). Obviously they are far cheaper in summer than winter. They include: **Okemo Moun-**

tain Lodge, a three-story hotel at the entrance to the resort, really a cluster of 55 one-bedroom condos, each with a sleeping couch in the living room. There's a compact kitchen with eating counter and a fireplace; enough space for a couple and two children ($95–240). **Kettle Brook** has one-, two-, and three-bedroom nicely built units salted along trails ($135–436). **Winterplace,** set high on a mountain shelf, consists of 17 buildings with a total of 250 units ranging in size from two bedrooms to three bedrooms plus a loft. Residents have access to a fitness center with indoor pool ($135–436). **Solitude Village** is a ski-in/ski-out complex of one- to five-unit condos and town houses plus a lodge with indoor/outdoor heated pool and a service area with a restaurant, ski shop, and children's learning center ($135–436). **Ledgewood Condominiums** are three- and four-bedroom units with garages accessed by their own trail ($175–562).

✷ Where to Eat

DINING OUT *Note:* Also see The River Tavern at Hawk Inn and Mountain Resort in Plymouth, in the Killington chapter.

Nikki's (802-228-7797), Route 100/103, Sunshine Market Place, Ludlow. Dinner nightly from 5 PM. Not the fanciest place in the area but one of the most pleasant. Operated by Bob Gilmore since 1976, the dining area and menu continue to evolve. The exposed wood and brick walls are garnished with stained and beveled glass, and there are booths, an inviting bar area, and gleaming coffee machines. One table is downstairs in the wine cellar. New England bouillabaisse (fresh salmon, littleneck clams, and scallops in a simmering tomato seafood broth) is a specialty, and we are told that the osso buco con orecchiette is excellent. The wine selection is exceptional. Entrées $5–28.

The Governor's Inn (802-228-8830; 1-800-468-3766; www.thegovernorsinn.com), 86 Main Street, Ludlow. Now owned by Jim and Kathy Kubec, this remains Ludlow's most famous restaurant, open to nonguests on Friday and Saturday nights with 48 hours' advance reservations. The single seating begins at 7 PM with hors d'oeuvres and cocktails served in the parlor. Guests then move on to the Victorian dining rooms, where they are served by waitresses in period dress. Each evening's menu is fixed. On a summer night you might begin with crabcakes followed by a salad of marinated vegetables, pineapple, and tortellini, then a sorbet and roasted stuffed game hens topped off by apricot Victorian. Prix fixe $50 per person.

Echo Lake Inn (802-228-8602; www.echolakeinn.com), Route 100 north in Tyson. Open to the public for dinner. The dining room, with print wallpaper and shades of mauve, is attractive. Chef Kevin Barnes has

ECHO LAKE

Kim Grant

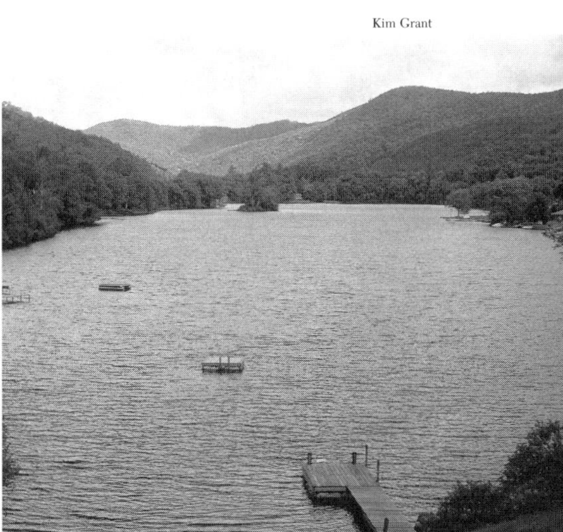

established an enviable reputation over the past decade. His menu ranges from spinach cannelloni to sautéed ostrich medallions in lingonberry sauce. Entrées $17–25.

The Castle (802-226-7222), intersection of Routes 131 and 103, Proctorsville. Open for dinner Thursday through Saturday. The interior of this stone mansion is a rich blend of American oak, Mexican mahogany, and French marble. Feast on beef Wellington or lobster Armagnac. Entrées $37–49.

The Andrie Rose Inn (802-228-4846; www.andrieroseinn.com). Open to the public by reservation Friday and Saturday with a set, four-course dinner at $38 per person. Chef-owner Irene Maston's menu on a summer Friday included a choice of Cavendish Farm quails with nectarine and plum stuffing in an Asian-spiced sauce or seed-crusted halibut fillet in roast garlic and red pepper broth.

Fullerton Inn (802-875-2444), 40 The Common, Chester. Open nightly Tuesday through Saturday. This pleasant dining room is surprisingly casual with a varied menu ranging from focaccia bread pizza to steak Oscar. Live entertainment on Saturday night.

EATING OUT

In Chester

Raspberries and Tyme (802-875-4486), on the green. Open daily, serving delectable breakfasts 8–11; lunches 11 AM–closing; dinner 5–9. The only problem with this place is getting in. In summer, even with the porch tables, it's frequently a crunch so come early or late. Great salads, simmering soups, and a wide choice of sandwiches are named for a variety of village establishments. The Misty Valley Books veggie bagel (spinach, tomato, grated carrots, broccoli, and sprouts with hummus on their own garlic-herb spread under melted Vermont cheddar) is a best-seller. Lisai's Market Reuben burger is memorable.

Baba-A-Louis Bakery (802-875-4666), Route 11 west, Chester. Closed April and November, as well as Sunday and Monday, but otherwise open 7 AM–6 PM. This is the other great lunch option in town, a long-established bakery in relatively new expanded quarters with an open kitchen and self-serve lunch fare that includes soups and a salad bar as well as quiche and panini. Breakfast options include sticky buns and cinnamon twists, and no one leaves without a loaf of this top-drawer bakery's specialty breads. Friday only, pizzas are available from 3 to 6.

Country Girl Diner, junction of Routes 11 and 103, Chester. An authentic, Silk City Diner made in Patterson, New Jersey, in the early '40s. It's a homey, popular spot open Monday through Saturday 5:30 AM–8 PM, Sunday 7 AM–8 PM. Classic diner and diner fare.

Rose Arbour Tea Room (802-875-4767), just off the green, Chester. Tea served daily 10–5 except Monday. A combination gift store and tearoom. Coffee and lemonade are also served to accompany the chicken salad with fruit garnish and diablo chocolate cake.

In and around Ludlow

Harry's Cafe (802-259-2996), Route 103, Mount Holly. Open 5–10, Tuesday through Sunday. Trip Pierce took the funky old Backside Restaurant and turned it into a light, airy space with good art and a woodstove. "It's open season on whatever you want to eat" is the way Pierce describes the wildly eclectic menu: Thai-style teriyaki and red curry, shrimp and tortellini, fish-and-chips, and New York sirloin. Specialties include grilled steak or chicken sliced thin, wrapped with lots of jack cheese and onion in a flour tortilla, topped with more cheese, baked until golden, and served with salsa and sour cream. Try the burrito if you want the best (and most food) for the least money.

Japanese Cusine by Michiko at the Old Town Farm Inn (802-875-2345; 1-888-232-1059). Open Wednesday through Sunday by reservation. Gassetts, really Nowheresville halfway between Chester and Ludlow, isn't exactly where you expect to find a first-rate Japanese restaurant, but that's where Michiko Hunter presides over the kitchen of this old family-geared lodge, turning out tantalizing and reasonably priced sushi. It's BYOB, and desserts include green tea and ample walnut ice cream made at the inn.

Sam's Steak House (802-228-5622), 91 Route 103, just east of downtown Ludlow. Formerly Michael's, open for dinner nightly with midweek specials. Known for filet mignon you can cut with a butter knife as well as sinful desserts and a great salad bar.

Dunne's Grille (802-228-1387), at the Okemo Valley Golf & Nordic Center, Route 100. Open year-round for lunch and dinner, serving surprisingly affordable and good food. Try the shrimp with capers and olives in a red sauce.

Ludlow Cooking Co. (802-226-7251), 29 Main Street, Ludlow. Open 11–10. Good for sandwiches, deli items, and rich desserts, mostly Italian-style dinner menu (also meals-to-go), but homestyle suffed cabbage is a specialty.

DJ's Restaurant (802-228-5374), 146 Main Street, Ludlow. Open from 4:30 for dinner. A downtown eatery that's been upscaled, best known for its broiled scallops and shrimp, extensive salad bar, and nightly specials.

Cappuccino's Cafe (802-228-7566), 41 Depot Street, Ludlow, serves dinner Tuesday through Sunday; reservations suggested. Chef-owner Steve Degnan and his wife Dawn have created a pleasant ambience and a varied menu with nightly specials; full bar.

Pot Belly Restaruant and Pub (802-228-8989), 130 Main Street, Ludlow. Open for dinner nightly and lunch most days. First opened in a storefront in 1974, this zany place has expanded into a great space; good for live entertainment (swing and blues bands, jug band music, and rock 'n' roll on weekends), and victuals ranging from popcorn shrimp, Pot Belly chicken, or ribs to chocolate peanut butter pie. A Belly burger or the Cajun chicken sandwich is a good bet at lunch, and you can always get a Belly burger at dinner, too.

BREWS **Black River Brewing Company** (802-228-3100), Route 103, Proctorsville, makes several ales, porters, and stouts (among them Big Buck, Fish Tale, Long Term Disability, Stump Jumper), which can be sampled and downed in its English pub. Wings and sweet-potato-chip nachos are among the specialties.

A State of Bean (802-228-4131), at the base of the Okemo Access Road, features overstuffed chairs and couches, serves fresh-baked muffins and pastries, homemade soups, sandwiches, salads, desserts, and a variety of coffee drinks.

✷ Selective Shopping

ANTIQUES SHOPS

In Chester

Stone House Antiques (802-875-4477), Route 103 south, is an antiques mall with 125 dealers and a touristy collection of country crafts. See also Stone Cottage Collectables under *Lodging—Bed & Breakfasts.*

ART GALLERIES **Chester Art Guild** (802-875-3767), on the green, Chester (see description under *Villages*).

Crow Hill Gallery (802-875-3763), Flamstead Road, Chester. This is a great excuse to ride up Crow Hill; the contemporary gallery shows the work of Jeanne Carbonetti and other local artists. Open Wednesday through Sunday, 10–5.

Grist Mill Gallery of Fine Art (802-875-3415), just off Route 103, Chester Depot. This distinctive, old red gristmill lends itself nicely to exhibit space for Allison Kibbe's original landscapes.

John James Audubon Art Gallery, 98 Winery Road, off Route 103, Proctorsville. Open Tuesday through Sunday, noon–5. Joseph Cerniglia sold his winery and bought a big collection of Audubon prints.

Red Barn Gallery (802-875-2784), Main Street, Chester. Half a mile west of the village green, featuring paintings by Ruth Harrison.

BOOKS AND MAPS **Misty Valley Books** (802-875-3400), on the green, Chester, open daily. An unusually friendly, well-stocked bookshop; browsing is encouraged and book and author readings are frequent, making it a lively cultural center.

The National Survey (802-875-2121), Chester Village, off the green. Open Monday through Friday 9–5, Saturday 10–4. Founded in 1912 by two sons of Chester's Baptist minister, the National Survey publishes maps for many states, foreign governments, industries, and other groups throughout the world. The store carries a large selection of maps, also old brochures.

Over Andover (802-876-4348; call for directions), open July through October, Thursday through Monday 11–5 and weekends year-round. A barn full of rare and unusual used books (specialties include King Arthur, Thomas Merton, and C. S. Lewis).

CRAFTS **Bonnie's Bundles** (802-875-2114; www.bonniesboundlesdolls.com), Stone Village, Route 103, Chester. Open weekends and by appointment. Housed in an 1814 stone house, a doll lover's find. Bonnie Waters handcrafts wonderfully original dolls.

Craft Shop at Fletcher Farm (802-228-4348), 611 Route 103, east of Ludlow. Open late June to mid-September, 9:30–5, and weekends from Memorial Day. Work by members of the Society of Vermont Craftsmen.

FOOD AND FLOWERS **Crowley Cheese Factory and Shop** (1-800-683-2606; www.crowleycheese-vermont.com), Route 103, 5 miles northwest of Ludlow. See *Scenic Drive* for the history of this exceptional cheese, which is sharper and creamier than cheddar. The factory (802-259-2340) is open 8–4, Monday through Friday, and the shop (802-259-2210) on Route 103, which carries other Vermont products as well, is open daily 10–5:30.

Meadowsweet Herb Farm (802-492-3565; www.meadowsweetherbfarm.com), 1130 Eatham Road, North Shrewsbury. See *Scenic Drive*. The shop in this 1860 farmhouse features herb wreaths, potpourri, and culinary blends as well as herbal soaps, gift baskets, and more. Perennial herbs and geraniums are grown year-round in the solar greenhouse and sold as seedlings. A picnic bench overlooks the gardens, open daily 9–5, May through October and holidays.

Green Mountain Sugar House (802-228-7151), Route 100, 4 miles north of Ludlow. You can watch syrup being produced in March and April; maple candy is made throughout the year on a weekly basis. This is also a place to find freshly pressed cider in September. The gift and produce shop is open daily 9–6 "most of the time."

Black River Produce (802-226-7484), Route 103 in Proctorsville.The purveyor of fruits and vegetables to the area's best restaurants, an exceptional source of fruit, vegetables, fresh breads, cheese, seafood, and flowers, excellent prepared foods, lobsters steamed to go, chowder and fish-and-chips on Friday.

Singleton's Store (802-226-7666), downtown Proctorsville. A long-established family-run grocery store just east of Route 103 on Route 131 in the middle of Proctorsville has kept abreast of the demands of the area's condo owners while continuing to cover the basics: a Vermont liquor store, fishing and hunting licenses, rods and reels, guns and ammo, sporting goods, outdoor wear and boots, plus fine wines, choice meats, a standout deli, and a gun shop; the specialty of the house is smoked and marinated meat (an average of 350 pounds of meat sold per day).

Crow's Bakery, Route 131, Proctorsville. A full array of delicious homemade breads, pastries, desserts, and heart-warming soups.

Belmont General Store, across the street from Star Lake in Belmont Village. Former Nikki's Restaurant chef Chris Kelly and his wife Louisa have turned this general store into a source of homemade bread and pastries, lunch and dinner menus to go, as well as local eggs and other produce.

SPECIAL SHOPS **Vermont Industries Factory Store** (802-492-3451; 1-800-826-4766), Route 103 in Cuttingsville, open daily 10–5:30. A big barn full of hand-forged, wrought-iron products—freestanding sundials, sconces, candleholders, corn driers, hanging planters, chandeliers, and a wide range of fireplace accessories. The distinctive floor lamps sell for substantially more in stores throughout New England.

Clear Lake Furniture (802-228-8395; www.clearlakevt.com), 322 Route 100 north, Ludlow. The workshop and showroom for elegantly simple custom-made pieces in cherry, curly maple, oak, and walnut by Brent Karner and Frank Procopio. Open Monday through Saturday 9–6, Sunday noon–5.

Inn Victoria Teapot Shop (802-875-4288), 321 Main Street, Chester. Teapots in all shapes and sizes and tea accessories.

Forlie-Ballou (802-875-2090), off Main Street, Chester Village. Worth checking. Suzy Forlie and Mary Ballou carry a fine selection of women's clothing and accessories.

SPECIAL EVENTS *February–March:* **Okemo WinterFest** includes "the Ludlow Olympics," tobogganing, snow sculpture contest, fireworks, ski races, and torchlight parade. Call 802-228-4041 or 802-228-6110 for details.

July 1: **Fletcher Farm Arts and Crafts Fair,** Route 103, Ludlow; **St. Joseph's Carnival; horse show and community picnic,** Chester.

August: **Chester Outdoor Art Show. Vermont State Zucchini Festival,** Ludlow. Four days of "zucchini madness" include a costume parade, Z-buck auction, and other events. **Thursday-evening concerts** on the Chester green all month.

September (last weekend): **Fall Crafts Fair,** Chester.

Early December: Victorian Christmas Walk and Parade, Ludlow.

December: **Overture to Christmas,** Chester, usually the second Saturday. Tree-lighting and candlelight caroling procession from church to church.

Upper Connecticut Valley

2

UPPER VALLEY RIVER TOWNS

WOODSTOCK/QUECHEE AREA

Kim Grant

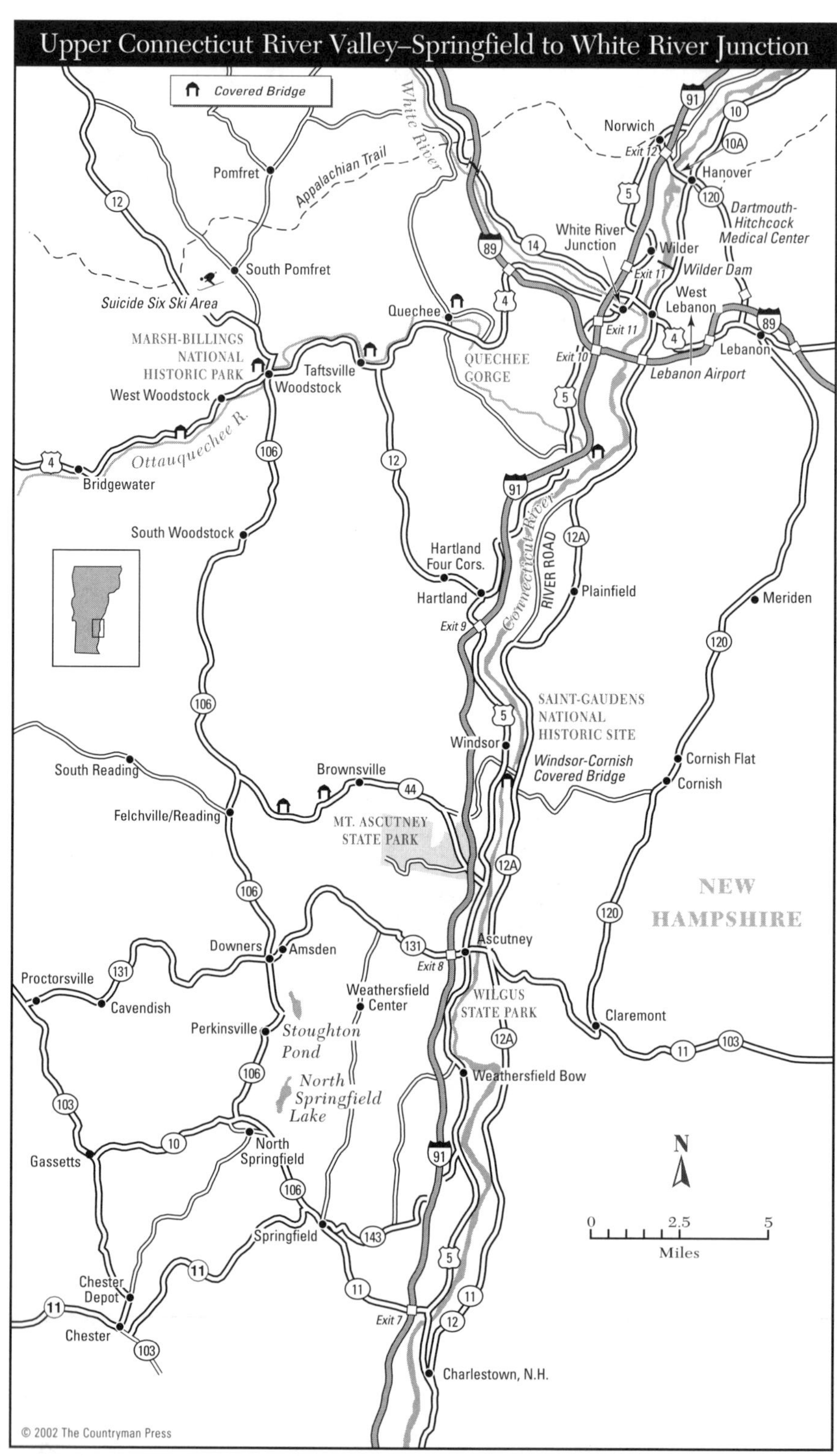
Upper Connecticut River Valley–Springfield to White River Junction
Covered Bridge
Pomfret
Appalachian Trail
White River
Norwich
Exit 12
Hanover
Dartmouth-Hitchcock Medical Center
White River Junction
Wilder
Exit 11
Wilder Dam
West Lebanon
Lebanon
Lebanon Airport
Exit 10
South Pomfret
Suicide Six Ski Area
Quechee
MARSH-BILLINGS NATIONAL HISTORIC PARK
Taftsville
Woodstock
West Woodstock
QUECHEE GORGE
Ottauquechee R.
Bridgewater
South Woodstock
Hartland Four Cors.
Hartland
Exit 9
Connecticut River
RIVER ROAD
Plainfield
Meriden
SAINT-GAUDENS NATIONAL HISTORIC SITE
Windsor
Windsor-Cornish Covered Bridge
Cornish Flat
Cornish
South Reading
Brownsville
Felchville/Reading
MT. ASCUTNEY STATE PARK
NEW HAMPSHIRE
Downers
Amsden
Ascutney
Exit 8
Proctorsville
Cavendish
Weathersfield Center
WILGUS STATE PARK
Claremont
Perkinsville
Stoughton Pond
North Springfield Lake
Weathersfield Bow
Gassetts
North Springfield
Springfield
Chester Depot
Chester
Exit 7
Charlestown, N.H.
N
0 2.5 5
Miles
© 2002 The Countryman Press

UPPER VALLEY RIVER TOWNS

The Upper Valley ignores state lines to form one of New England's most beautiful and distinctive regions. Its two dozen towns are scattered along the Vermont and New Hampshire banks of the Connecticut River for some 20 miles north and south of Dartmouth College.

Upper Valley is a name coined in the 1950s by a local daily, the *Valley News,* to define its two-state circulation area. The label has stuck, interestingly, to the same group of towns that, back in the 1770s, attempted to unite politically. But the Dartmouth College–based supporters of their "New Connecticut" were thwarted by larger powers, namely New York and New Hampshire, along with the strident Vermont independence faction, the Green Mountain Boys. On July 2, 1777, delegates met at Elijah West's tavern in Windsor to declare Vermont a "free and independent state," bounded on the east by the Connecticut River.

The Upper Valley itself prospered, a fact that's obvious from the exquisite Federal-era meetinghouses and mansions still salted through this area. The river belongs to New Hampshire, thanks to a decree by King George III that still holds, which means that state is responsible for maintaining the bridges. Of the dozens of bridges that once connected the two states, only 10 survive, but they include the longest, historic covered bridge in the United States (connecting Windsor with Cornish). The Upper Valley area phone book includes towns on both sides of the river (it's a local call back and forth, although the area code is now needed), and Norwich and Hanover's Dresden School District reaches well into Vermont. Several Independence Day parades start in one state and finish across the bridge in the other. And the Montshire Museum, founded on the New Hampshire side of the river and now splendidly rooted on the Vermont bank, combines both states in its name.

The cultural center of the Upper Valley remains the Dartmouth campus in Hanover, graced with a major theater and museum. With the nearby medical complex and the West Lebanon shopping center strip (a popular escape route from Vermont's sales tax), it forms a genuine hub, handy to the highways radiating, the way rail lines once did, from White River Junction. Since the 1820s, the area's industrial core has been in at its southern end, in Springfield and Windsor, both of which have produced far more than their share of inventors. At the northern end of the valley summer camps have lined the shores of Lakes Morey and Fairlee for more than a century.

Beyond these redbrick towns and old resort enclaves, farms still spread comfortably along the river, all the way from Weathersfield Bow to a similar oxbow in Newbury. They are backed in places by steep hills, including Mount Ascutney, a monadnock thrusting 3,144 feet straight up from the banks of the river (site of both a state park with a summit road and a self-contained ski resort). The stretch of both road (Route 5) and river north from Wilder Dam to Newbury offers unexpected vistas of the White Mountains, and its inns cater to bicyclists, canoeists, and kayakers.

Thanks to decades of acquisitions, greenups, and cleanups by numerous conservation groups, the Connecticut River itself has enjoyed a genuine renewal, with campsites and inns spaced along the shore; visitors and residents alike are discovering its beauty.

GUIDANCE An excellent, noncommercial web site, www.ctrivertravel.net, covering the entire stretch of the Connnecticut shared by Vermont and New Hampshire is maintained by the **Connecticut River Joint Commissions.** In 2002 this bistate commission is opening "waypoint" information centers in Windsor and Fairlee. **The Upper Valley Welcome Center** (802-281-5050) in the railroad station in downtown White River Junction (open daily, 8–7, with rest rooms), is also the site of an evolving transportation museum. Also see www.uppervalleychamber.com.

The **Springfield Area Chamber Commerce** (802-885-2779; www.springfieldvt.com) answers phone queries year-round (weekdays, 8–5) and maintains the 18th-century **Eureka Schoolhouse** (Route 11, near I-91) as a seasonal information booth. **The Windsor–Mount. Ascutney Area Chamber of Commerce** (802-674-5910) also answers phone queries; also see www.vacationinvermont.com. **The Quechee Chamber of Commerce** (802-295-7900; 1-800-295-5451; www.quechee.com) also covers the heart of the Upper Valley.

GETTING THERE *By car:* Interstates 91 and 89 converge in the White River Junction–Lebanon area, where they also meet Route 5 north and south on the Vermont side; Route 4, the main east–west highway through central Vermont; and Route 10, the river road on the New Hampshire side.

By bus: White River Junction is a hub for **Greyhound/Vermont Transit** (802-295-3011).

By air: The Lebanon (New Hampshire) Regional Airport is served by **USAirways Express** (1-800-428-4322) from Boston and New York.

By train: **Amtrak** (802-295-7160; 1-800-875-7245) stops in White River Junction and Windsor en route to and from New York's Penn Station and Washington, D.C. Baggage cars carry bikes. At this writing, there is one daily train southbound (10:20 AM) and one northbound (6:20 PM). Inquire about connections between St. Albans and Montreal.

GETTING AROUND Several local cab companies connect with planes, buses, and trains. Try **Big Yellow Taxi** (802-281-8294).

WHEN TO GO The Upper Valley, with the exception of Mount Ascutney Ski Resort, is best explored in summer and fall.

MEDICAL EMERGENCY 911 now serves this area.

Dartmouth-Hitchcock Medical Center (603-650-5000), 1 Medical Center Drive, off Route 120, between Hanover and Lebanon, is recognized as one of the best teaching hospitals in New England.

Local medical facilities include **Springfield Hospital** (802-885-2151), 25 Ridgewood Road, Springfield, and **Mount Ascutney Hospital** (802-674-6711), County Road, Windsor.

✷ Villages

Springfield. Situated at the confluence of the Connecticut and Black Rivers, Springfield boomed with Vermont's tool industry in the 19th and first half of the 20th century and has suffered as that industry has atrophied. Beyond the defunct factories and the powerful falls, the town's compact downtown shows interesting signs of life. Among the gracious 19th-century mansions in residential neighborhoods terraced above it are the Hartness House (see *Lodging*) and at 9 Elm Street the **Springfield Art & Historical Society** (802-885-2415; open May through mid-October, Tuesday through Friday noon–5; Saturday 2–5), with collections of pewter, Bennington pottery, toys and dolls, primitive paintings, and costumes, and puts on periodic art shows. See *Green Space* for the new Toonerville Trail along the Black River.

Weathersfield Center. On a scenic old north–south road between Springfield and Route 131 stands this nearly secret gem of a hamlet with its brick 1821 Meeting House and Civil War memorial, a particularly sobering reminder of how many young Vermonters served and died (12 boys from just this small village) in that war. The **Weathersfield Historical Society,** housed in the Reverend Dan Foster House (open late June to early October, Thursday through Monday 2–5), displays Civil War memorabilia, archival photos, an old forge, and the last wildcat killed in Weathersfield (1867). It was Weathersfield native William Jarvis who transformed the economy of Vermont—and the rest of northern New England—by smuggling 4,000 sheep out of Spain during his term as U.S. consul in Lisbon. That was in 1810. By 1840 there were upward of 2 million sheep in Vermont.

THE HISTORIC MEETING HOUSE IN WEATHERSFIELD

Kim Grant

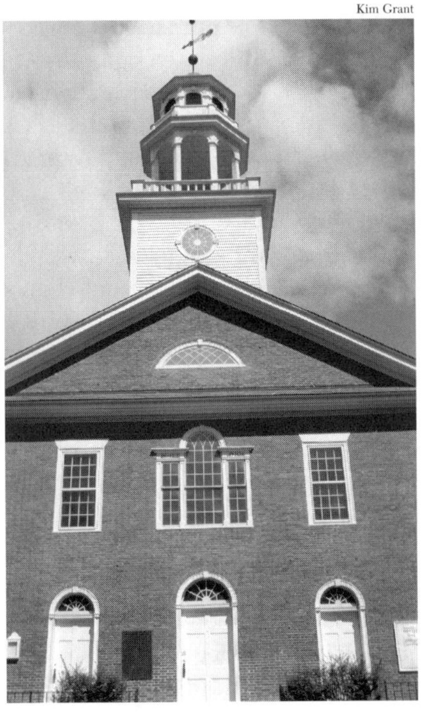

Windsor. In *Roadside History of Vermont*, Peter Jennison notes that while it is known as the "Birthplace of Vermont" (see Old Constitution House under *To See*), Windsor can also claim to be the midwife of the state's machine tool industry. Windsor resident Lemuel Hedge devised a machine for ruling paper in 1815 and dividing scales in 1827. Asahel Hubbard produced a revolving pump in 1828, and Niconar Kendall designed an "under hammer" rifle, the first use of interchangeable parts, in the 1830s in the picturesque old mill that's now the American Precision Museum (see *To See—Museums*). Windsor's mid-19th-century prosperity is reflected in the handsome lines of the columned **Windsor House,** once considered the best public house between Boston and Montreal. It now houses a Vermont State Craft Gallery and the Preservation Institute (www.preservationworks.org), which offers training programs in preservation skills. The Italianate building across the street was designed in 1850 by Ammi Young as a post office (the oldest federal post office in continuous use in the United States) with upstairs courthouse (which served as Woodrow Wilson's summer White House from 1913 to 1915; the president spent his summers in Cornish, just across the Windsor-Cornish Covered Bridge (*To See—Covered Bridges*). Cornish was at the time an artists and writers colony that had evolved around sculptor Augustus Saint-Gaudens (see *To See—Historic Sites*). The colony nurtured artist Maxfield Parrish; his painting *Templed Hills* hangs in the Vermont National Bank branch that is next to Windsor House (Parrish left it in perpetua to the bank's tellers for "keeping my account balanced"). It depicts a mountain that resembles Mount Ascutney, towering above water that resembles Lake Runnemede. The lake is now a town-owned conservation area, good for walking and bird-watching, that's sequestered behind the town's mansion row, just north of the bank. South on Main Street, across from the red and chrome Windsor Diner (Worcester Diner #835) stands the vintage 1798 **Old South Congregational Church.** Designed by Asher Benjamin, the church fortunately retains its classic beauty despite several renovations. Also worth noting: the contemporary St. Francis of Assisi Roman Catholic Church and its panels depicting the the Seven Sacraments donated by noted American painter George Tooker. On the common (off Main Street), St. Paul's, built in 1832, is Vermont's oldest Episcopal church. Townsend Cottage, across the square, is a striking example of 1840s Carpenter Gothic style. North of town a riverside, visitor-geared industrial park features the Simon Pearce glass factory and Harpoon Brewery. South of town 3,144-foot-high Mount Ascutney rises from the river's edge, a state park offering seasonal camping, hiking, a road to the top, and a self-contained ski resort in winter. A nominally priced *Architectural & Historical Walking Tour of Windsor* booklet prepared by Historic Windsor is sold at the Windsor State Craft Gallery.

White River Junction, located at the confluence of the Connecticut and White Rivers and the junction of Interstates 91 and 89, was once a bustling, often raucous railroad hub. While its periphery serves the interstates with brand-name motels and fast-food stops, the redbrick downtown, with its venerable Hotel Coolidge and the Polka Dot Diner, still caters to train passengers. Horace Wells of White River Junction was, incidentally, the first person to use laughing gas as an anesthetic for pulling teeth. White River Junction is actually a village in Hartford, a town that also includes Quechee, Hartford Village, Wilder, and West Hartford.

Chris McKinley

AMTRAK'S *VERMONTER* PULLS INTO WHITE RIVER JUNCTION

Hanover, New Hampshire—Dartmouth College. Chartered in 1769, Dartmouth is the ninth oldest and one of the most prestigious colleges in the country, and its handsome buildings frame three sides of an elm-shaded green. The fourth side is lined with visitor-friendly buildings: the large, college-owned Hanover Inn, Hopkins Center entertainment complex, and the Hood Museum of Art (see *To See—Museums*). Note the white information kiosk on the green, staffed during the summer months. Most visitors find their way into **Baker Memorial Library** to see the set of murals by famous Mexican painter José Clemente Orozco (which some alumni once demanded be removed or covered because of the artist's left-wing politics). When the kiosk is closed, guided tours are offered by the admission office (603-646-2875) in McNutt Hall by student members of Green Key.

Norwich, one of the prettiest towns in Vermont, was settled in 1761 by a group from Marshfield, Connecticut. It has always had close ties to Hanover (just across the bridge) and was itself the original home of Norwich University (founded 1819), which moved to Northfield after the Civil War. The village is an architectural showcase for fine brick and frame Federal homes. Note the Seven Nations House, built in 1832 as a commercial "tenement." Across the way is the Norwich Inn, dating back to 1797 and with a popular brewpub as well as dining room, the hospitable heart of town. Sequestered down by the river (east of I-91), the recently expanded Montshire Museum (see *To See—Museums*) offers insights into ways the world and universe go round as well as into how the river shapes the immediate environment; it also offers trails through its 110 acres. King Arthur Flour's flagship Baker's Store and Baking Education Center on Route 5, south of town, draws devotees from throughout the county.

Thetford has an unusual number of post offices per capita: There are six villages in all. Thetford Center has a friendly general store and handsome brick Methodist

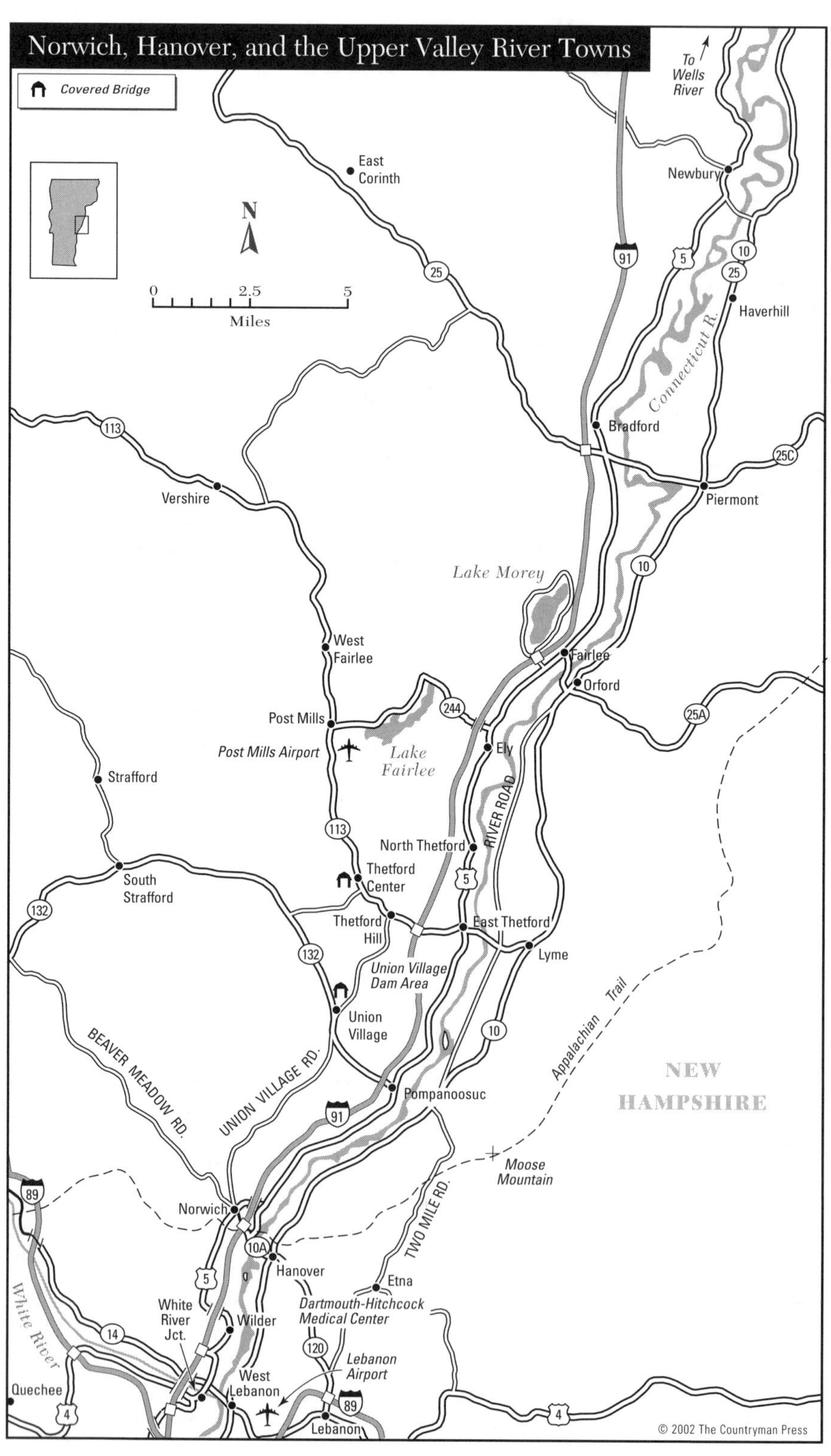
Norwich, Hanover, and the Upper Valley River Towns
Covered Bridge
N
0
2.5
5
Miles
To Wells River
East Corinth
Newbury
Haverhill
Connecticut R.
Bradford
Piermont
Vershire
Lake Morey
Fairlee
Orford
West Fairlee
Post Mills
Post Mills Airport
Lake Fairlee
Ely
Strafford
RIVER ROAD
North Thetford
Thetford Center
South Strafford
Thetford Hill
East Thetford
Lyme
Union Village Dam Area
Union Village
BEAVER MEADOW RD.
UNION VILLAGE RD.
Appalachian Trail
NEW HAMPSHIRE
Pompanoosuc
Moose Mountain
TWO MILE RD.
Norwich
Hanover
Etna
Dartmouth-Hitchcock Medical Center
White River Jct.
Wilder
White River
Lebanon Airport
West Lebanon
Quechee
Lebanon
© 2002 The Countryman Press

church. Thetford Hill is a beauty, the site of Thetford Academy, the Parish Players (see *Entertainment*), and the **Thetford Historical Society** (open August Sundays 2–5) and its Historic Library (open year-round, Monday and Thursday 2–4 and Tuesday 10–noon).

THETFORD CENTER METHODIST CHURCH

Christina Tree

Fairlee Village, shelved between the Palisades and a bend in the Connecticut River, is a plain cousin to aristocratic Orford, New Hampshire (well known for its lineup of elegant Federal-era houses), just across the river. But we like it better. Check out Chapman's, a 19th-century pharmacy that has expanded in unusual directions. Summer camps and inns line nearby Lake Morey. Samuel Morey, a resident of Orford and a lumberman in Fairlee, was the inventor of the first steamboat: In 1793, 14 years before Fulton launched his *Clermont,* Morey was puffing up and down the river in a primitive craft barely big enough to hold him and his firewood. The remains of the little steamer are believed to lie at the bottom of Lake Morey, scuttled by its builder when the $100,000 in stock offered him by Robert Fulton turned out to be worthless. Morey also patented an internal combustion engine in 1825. Lake Fairlee, also lined with children's camps and with a public swim beach, straddles the town line and is best accessed from Route 244 west of Ely.

Bradford, at the confluence of the Waits River and the Connecticut, is built on terraces of land above the floodplain. Buildings along the Connecticut side of its main street (Route 5) have another level below, and a golf course is sequestered down there behind the downtown. Favorite sons include James Wilson, an ingenious farmer, who made America's first geographical globes in the early 1800s. Today the town is a good waystop for lunch and dinner and offers unexpectedly good shopping.

Newbury and Haverhill. The northern reaches of the Upper Valley are defined by these two unusually beautiful towns, both with handsome villages. Haverhill (New Hampshire) actually includes several very different villages. Newbury, Vermont, was known in the 19th century as a mineral spa, but the big old resort hotel has long since vanished.

✷ To See

MUSEUMS ✐ **Montshire Museum of Science** (802-649-2200; www.montshire.org), 1 Montshire Road, Norwich. Open daily 10–5 except Thankgiving, Christmas, and New Year's Day; $6.50 per adult, $5.50 per child ages 3–17. Use of the trails is free. Few cities have a science museum of this quality, and the superb exhibits plus extensive trails along the Connecticut River add up to one of New

John Gilbert Fox

THE MONTSHIRE MUSEUM OF SCIENCE IN NORWICH HAS DOZENS OF FASCINATING EXHIBITS FOR CHILDREN

England's outstanding sights. Don't be put off by the entrance fee. Do you know which common fruits and vegetables float in water? Do you know the difference between a nebula and a nova? The museum's avowed goal is to demystify natural phenomena, and it does so in a way that's fun. Exhibits change but usually include an aquarium of northern New England fish, a display on the physics of the bubble, and another on weather. All exhibits (even the boa constrictor) are "hands-on." New outdoor Science Park exhibits focus on water and how moving water shapes landscapes. A new wing features the natural environment of the Upper Connecticut River Valley. There's also a playground and a gift shop; inquire about workshops, guided hikes, special events, and exhibits. (See also *Green Space*.)

Hood Museum of Art (603-646-2808), Dartmouth green, Hanover, New Hampshire. Open Tuesday through Saturday 10–5 and Sunday noon–5; until 9 PM Wednesday. Free. An outstanding collection of art, ranging from Assyrian bas-reliefs donated by missionary graduates in the 1850s to works by Italian masters and American 18th- and 19th-century artists, is displayed in the downstairs galleries. A narrow flight of stairs rises dramatically to the high, skylit Lathrop Gallery, hung with such modern masterpieces as Picasso's *Guitar on a Table,* a gift of Nelson Rockefeller, class of 1930. Rothko, Picasso, and at least one outsized canvas by Dartmouth graduate Frank Stella are usually on display. There are frequently changing special exhibits.

American Precision Museum (802-674-5781), South Main Street, Windsor. Open May 30 through November 1, Monday through Friday 9–5; Saturday, Sunday, and holidays 10–4; $5 per adult, $3.50 seniors, $2 ages 6–12; family $14. An important, expanding collection of hand and machine tools, assembled in the 1846 Robbins, Kendall & Lawrence Armory, itself a national historic landmark. The firm became world famous in 1851 because of its displays of "the American system" of manufacturing interchangeable parts, especially for what became the renowned Enfield rifle. Special exhibits vary from year to year.

HISTORIC SITES

Fort at Number Four (603-826-5700; www.fortat4.com), Route 11, Charlestown, New Hampshire. Open Memorial Day through late October, 10–4; $8 adult, $7 seniors, $4.50 children, under 6 free. Conjuring a little-remembered chapter in New England history, this riverside stockade replicates the fort that stood nearby during the French and Indian Wars in the 1740s. The original fell once but withstood repeated attacks.

The complex includes a Great Hall, barns, and furnished living quarters. Costumed interpreters prepare meals, perform chores and crafts. Inquire about special events and reenactments.

THE AMERICAN PRECISION MUSEUM IN WINDSOR

Kim Grant

The Old Constitution House (802-828-3501; www.historicvermont.org), North Main Street, Windsor. Open late May through early October, Wednesday through Sunday, 11–5. Nominal admission. This is Elijah West's tavern (but not in its original location), where delegates gathered on July 2, 1777, to adopt Vermont's constitution, America's first to prohibit slavery, establish universal voting rights for all males, and authorize a public school system. Excellent first-floor displays trace the history of the Republic of Vermont; upstairs is the town's collection of antiques, prints, documents, tools, and toys. Special exhibits vary each year, and a path out the back door leads to Lake Runnemede.

The Saint-Gaudens National Historic Site (603-675-2175), Cornish, New Hampshire. Grounds open daily, dawn to dusk. Buildings open 9–4:30 daily late May through October. $4 adults; free under age 17. Includes the sculptor's summer home, barn-studio, sculpture court, and formal gardens, which he developed and occupied between 1885 and his death in 1907. The property was accepted by the National Park Service in 1964. Augustus Saint-Gaudens loved the Ravine Trail, a quarter-mile cart path to Blow-Me-Up Brook, now marked for visitors, and other walks laid out through the woodlands and wetlands of the Blow-Me-Down Natural Area. Saint-Gaudens was one of several artists who formed a summer colony in Cornish, a group that included poets Percy MacKaye, Witter Bynner, and William Vaughn Moody; Winston Churchill, the American novelist whose summer estate was used as the vacation White House by President Woodrow Wilson in 1914 and 1915; Ethel Barrymore, Charles Dana Gibson, Finley Peter Dunne, and Maxfield Parrish. Summer visitors can enjoy examples of the artist's work.

Note: Bring a picnic lunch for Sunday-afternoon chamber music concerts, at 2 PM in July and August.

COVERED BRIDGES

The **Windsor-Cornish Covered Bridge** is the longest such span not only in (or partly in) Vermont but also in the United States. Never mind those rumors of a new covered bridge somewhere; this is the real thing, originally constructed in 1866 (admittedly it has been rebuilt). There are also three covered bridges across the Mill Brook (just north and south of Route 44) in Brownsville, and three in

Robert Kozlow

MOUNT ASCUTNEY RISES BEHIND THE WINDSOR-CORNISH COVERED BRIDGE

Weathersfield: The **Titcomb Bridge** is on Route 106 across from the elementary school; the **Upper Falls Bridge** is on Upper Falls Road (turn south off Route 131 about 0.3 mile west of its junction with Route 106); and the **Salmond Bridge** is on Henry Gould Road (turn north off Route 131, 2.4 miles east of its junction with Route 106). The vintage-1870 **Baltimore Covered Bridge,** originally in North Springfield, has been moved to sit beside the Eureka Schoolhouse (see *Guidance*) on Route 11 in Springfield, just off I-91.

✷ To Do

BALLOONING **Post Mills Airport** (802-333-9254), West Fairlee. Veteran balloonist Brian Boland offers early-morning and sunset rides year-round. On the summer evening we tried it, the balloon hovered above hidden pockets in the hills, and we saw a herd of what looked like brown-and-white goats that, on closer inspection, proved to be deer. After an hour or so, we settled down gently in an East Bradford farmyard and broke out the champagne. $200 per flight includes champagne.

Also see "Woodstock/Quechee" for two balloonists and New England's largest balloon festival.

BICYCLING Route I-91 drains a large percentage of traffic from Route 5, but this old highway along the river is still fairly busy. On the New Hampshire side of the river, search out the River Road that runs 8 miles north from Route 12A just north of the Saint-Gaudens site (see *To See—Historic Sites*) on through Plainfield. Also find the River Road from Route 10 north of Hanover (just north of the Chieftain Motel) through Lyme, rejoining Route 10 in Orford. Route 10 from Orford to Haverhill is also particularly beautiful, as is Route 5 in Vermont, between Fairlee and Norwich.

For inn-to-inn guided tours in this area, contact **Bike Vermont** (802-457-3553; 1-800-257-2226), and for self-guided tours, **Bicycle Holidays** (802-388-2453). **Juniper Hill Inn** in Windsor and **Silver Maple Lodge** in Fairlee (see *Lodging*)

cater to bicyclists, offering packages that combine biking and canoeing. **POMG** (1-888-635-BIKE) offers vehicle-supported camping tours.

Note: Amtrak's *Vermonter*, serving this corridor (see *Getting There*), carries bicycles. It's possible to detrain in Bellows Falls (26 miles south of Windsor; see "Southern Vermont"), Windsor, or White River Junction and explore this area on two wheels. We suggest, however, consulting some of the above bike-geared resources before you come.

BIKE RENTALS **Ascutney Mountain Resort** (802-484-3511) in Brownsville rents mountain bikes and offers 32 km of trails. **Wilderness Trails** (802-295-7620), Quechee, offers mountain-bike rentals and mapped trails.

BOATING With its placid water and lovely scenery, the Connecticut River through much of the Upper Valley is ideal for easygoing canoeists. Information on primitive campsites along this stretch of the Connecticut River can be found on the **Upper Valley Land Trust's** web site, www.UVLT.org. The **Connecticut River Joint Commissions** (603-826-4800; www.ctrivertravel.net) has published a useful *Boating on the Connecticut River* guide. Canoeing the Connecticut can, admittedly, be a bit of a slog. The headwind is as infamous as the lack of current. So what? Why does canoeing have to be about going great distances? For study programs and guided educational canoe trips on the river, contact the **Montshire Museum of Science** (802-649-2200; see *To See—Museums*).

North Star Canoes (603-542-5802), Route 12A at Balloch's Crossing in Cornish, New Hampshire, just across the river from Windsor. John Hammond will shuttle patrons to put-ins either 3 or 12 miles above the Cornish-Windsor Covered Bridge so that they can paddle downstream toward the river's most famous landmark. Roughly half of North Star's patrons camp, either at **Wilgus State Park** (802-674-5422; see *Green Space*) or at another site in Windsor. This is probably New England's most picturesque livery: The check-in desk in the barn is redolent of bales of hay, and John Hammond may well be out front shoeing horses; the canoes are stacked behind the farmhouse.

Wilderness Trails (802-295-7620), Quechee, offers rentals and guided canoe and kayak trips, as well as shuttle service, for a stretch of the Connecticut north of that serviced by North Star Canoe.

The **Ledyard Canoe Club** (603-643-6709), Hanover, New Hampshire, is billed as the oldest canoe club in America. It's named for a 1773 Dartmouth dropout who felled a pine tree, hollowed it out, and took off downriver (with a book of Ovid's poems), ending up at Hartford, 100 miles and several major waterfalls downstream. Hidden beyond Dartmouth's slick new rowing center, Ledyard is a mellow, friendly, student-run place. The canoeing and kayaking center for the 40 miles above Wilder Dam, it offers kayaking clinics as well as canoe and kayak rentals. No shuttle service.

Fairlee Marine (802-333-9745), Route 5 in Fairlee, offers pontoon, canoe, kayak, and rowboat rentals on the 40-mile stretch of the Connecticut above the Wilder Dam; the river is calm and relatively quiet.

FISHING You can eat the brown and rainbow trout you can catch in the Connecticut River. There's a boat launch at Wilder Dam, another just north of Hanover, and another on the Vermont bank in North Thetford. Guides and classes in fly-tying and fly-fishing are offered by **Lyme Angler** (603-643-1263), a source of fishing gear and tips, 8 South Main Street, Hanover.

River Excitement (802-457-4021), P.O. Box 65, Hartland Four Corners 05049. Guided trips on the upper Connecticut River and trout streams, good for beginners through experts. Fly-fishing and spinning equipment, cameras and superb food provided.

Also see Wilderness Trails in *Boating*.

GOLF **Crown Point Country Club** (802-885-2703), Weathersfield Station Road, Springfield. 18 holes, rolling terrain.

Windsor Country Club (802-674-6491); nine holes on Route 5, north of Windsor.

Hanover Country Club (603-646-2000), Rope Ferry Road, off Route 10, Hanover, New Hampshire. A classy, 18-hole course with pro shop and lounge, open May through October.

Lake Morey Inn Resort (802-333-4311; 1-800-423-1211) in Fairlee features an 18-hole golf course on which the Vermont Open has been played for more than 40 years.

Bradford Country Club (802-222-5207); nine holes down by the river.

HANG GLIDING **Mount Ascutney** is one of the prime spots in the country for hang gliding. For lessons, equipment, or a shuttle or flight, check with **Morningside Flight Park** (603-542-4416) in Claremont, New Hampshire.

HORSEBACK RIDING See Kedron Valley Stables in "Woodstock/Quechee."

SWIMMING **Union Village Dam Area,** Thetford (west on Route 132 from Norwich), offers swimming, picnicking, and fishing.

✐ **Storrs Pond Recreation Area** (603-643-2134), Reservoir Road, Hanover, New Hampshire, has a pool, pond, and camping; admission.

✐ **Treasure Island** (802-333-9625), Thetford, on Lake Fairlee, is a pleasant public beach with lifeguards and a tennis court; admission.

The beach at **Mill Pond** in Windsor is town owned, open to the public for a fee. **Stoughton Pond** between Downers and Amsden, south of Route 131 or north from Route 106, near Springfield Dam Lake. **North Springfield Lake** also offers picnicking and swimming.

✷ Winter Sports

CROSS-COUNTRY SKIING **Lake Morey Inn Resort** (802-333-4800), Fairlee, maintains 12 miles of groomed trails. $8 trail fee.

See also *Cross-Country Skiing* in "Woodstock/Quechee."

DOWNHILL SKIING 🖉 **Ascutney Mountain Resort** (802-484-7711; snow report and lodging reservations: 1-800-243-0011; www.ascutney.com), Brownsville (I-91 exit 8 or 9). A family-geared, self-contained resort. Current owners Steve and Susan Plausteiner have added major improvements, increasing snowmaking to 95 percent and adding the North Peak area to the mountain, substantially increasing its vertical drop and its expert trails; it is served by a new mile-long fast quad chair. Facilities include a 215-room condo hotel, a sports center—with indoor pool and weight and racquetball rooms—a full restaurants, and a base lodge. *Lifts:* One quad, three triple, one double chairlift, one Wonder Carpet. *Slopes and trails:* 56. *Vertical drop:* 1,800 feet. *Snowmaking:* 95 percent. *Nursery/child care:* From 6 weeks. *Rates:* Adults $44 midweek, $49 weekend and holiday, juniors (7–16) and seniors (65–69) $21 midweek, $39 weekend and holiday; adult Sunday morning: $39 day, junior $27. Half day $36, 26.

ASCUTNEY MOUNTAIN RESORT David Brownell

See also *Downhill Skiing* in "Woodstock/Quechee" and the "Okemo Valley."

✳ Green Space

🖉 **Wilgus State Park** (802-674-5422; 802-773-2657), 1.5 miles south of exit 8, I-91, off Route 5, Windsor. This small, quiet campground on the Connecticut River is ideal for canoeists, as many lean-tos and tent sites are on the riverbank. Car shuttle service available; playground, picnic tables, hiking trails, canoe rentals.

In Springfield the **Toonerville Trail,** a new 10-foot-wide, paved recreation path good for bicycling and walking, follows the Black River along an old trolley line from the trailhead on Route 11 (behind the Robert Jones Industrial Center) 3 miles to another parking area on Route 5, just north of the Cheshire Bridge across the Connecticut. Just south of this bridge a service road leads to Hoyt's Landing, a recently upgraded put-in on the river, also a scenic picnic spot. At the Eureka Schoolhouse information center (see *Guidance*) on Route 11 ask directions to the Springfield Nature Trail on the northern fringe of town. It winds through 50 acres of fields and woods.

Ascutney State Park (802-674-2060). Rising out of the valley to an elevation of 3,144 feet, Mount Ascutney is set in more than 2,000 acres of woodland. The 3.8-mile paved road to the summit begins on Route 44A, off Route 5, between Ascutney and Windsor. Of the four hiking trails to the summit, we recommend the 2.9-mile ascent from Weathersfield with an 84-foot waterfall about halfway (the trailhead is on Cascade Falls Road, 3.5 miles north off Route 131). The 3.2-mile Brownsville Trail begins on Route 44 between Windsor and Brownsville; the 2.7-mile Windsor Trail starts on Route 44A in Windsor. Granite was quarried here as early as 1808, and there was a popular summit house. Tent sites, trailer sites, and lean-tos can be reserved. The ski slopes and self-contained Ascutney Mountain Resort (see *Lodging*) are accessible from Route 44 in Brownsville.

♿ **Montshire Museum of Science Trails,** Norwich. The museum's 110 acres include a 12-acre promontory between the Connecticut River and the marshy bay at the mouth of Bloody Brook. The quarter-mile trail leading down through tall white pines to the bay is quite magical. The 1.5 mile Hazen Trail runs all the way to Wilder Village. These trails are hard-packed, accessible to strollers and wheelchairs.

Thetford Hill State Park (802-785-2266 and January through May: 1-800-299-3071). Open mid-May through Labor Day. Just off I-91, exit 14, 1 mile south of Thetford Hill on the Union Village Road. Developed by the Civilian Conservation Corps in the 1930s, 177 acres with a campground (14 tent/trailer sites, two lean-tos, hot showers), hiking and cross-country trails (maintained by Thetford Academy) and swimming in the Union Village Reservoir.

See also Quechee Gorge Recreation Area in "Woodstock/Quechee."

✷ Lodging

Note: Listings are in geographical order, south to north.

RESORTS **Ascutney Mountain Resort** (802-484-7711; 1-800-243-0011), Brownsville 05037, includes a 215-room condo hotel with flanking condominiums at the base of the ski area. Accommodations range from standard hotel rooms to three-bedroom suites with kitchen and fireplace and outdoor deck, furnished in reproduction antiques. Facilities include the full-service Harvest Inn Restaurant and a sports center, also tennis courts and indoor and outdoor pools, and extensive alpine trails (see *Downhill Skiing*) in winter. Summer features tennis programs and children's adventure camps (ages 4–10). Summer and fall from $75 for a room to $269 for a three-bedroom condo; winter: $75–90 per room to $330–470 three-bedroom condo. Inquire about packages. Five-day midweek packages are $99–139 per person, skiing and lodging included, cheaper for kids.

♿ **Lake Morey Resort** (802-333-4311; 1-800-423-1211), Fairlee 05045. On the shore of Lake Morey, this sprawling, lakeside landmark has been reclaimed by the Avery family, who initially transformed it into a resort in the 1920s but sold it in the early 1990s. Over the past year they have virtually gutted and rebuilt it, reducing the number of rooms (there are now 137), redoing bathrooms, phone lines, the works. The formerly '50s-style public spaces have also been totally revamped but the splendid lake view remains key, along with a player-friendly 18-hole golf course. Facilities include indoor and outdoor swimming pools, tennis and racquetball courts, a fitness center, cross-country-ski and snowmobile trails in winter, and access to the Dartmouth Skiway. Grounds have also been newly landscaped. Winter: $80–126 per room, $94–141 MAP; summer: $125–195 EP per room, $95–130 MAP per person, including use of sports facilities. Ask about packages.

INNS ∞ ♿ **Hartness House** (802-885-2115; 1-800-732-4789; www.hartnesshouse.com), Orchard Street,

Springfield 05156. In 1903 James Hartness built himself a stone and shingle mansion set in 32 acres on a parklike bluff. The inventor (Hartness patented 120 machines), aviator (he held one of the first 100 pilot's licenses in the United States and built Vermont's first airport), astronomer, and governor (1920–22) installed one of the first tracking telescopes in the country at the end of a 240-foot underground corridor connected to the mansion in 1910. It's still in use (inquire about tours), and since 1939 the mansion has been an inn with 40 old-fashioned guest rooms, 10 in the main house, the remainder in a connecting motel-like annex, each with private bath, phone, and color TV. There's a formal feel to the large lobby, with its traditional check-in desk, and to the pub and dining room (see *Dining Out*). The innkeepers span two generations and six members of the Blair family. Facilities include a swimming pool and nature trails. $99–150 double includes breakfast. Weddings are a specialty.

Juniper Hill Inn (802-674-5273; 1-800-359-2541), 153 Pembroke Road, off Route 5 on Juniper Hill Road. Set high on a hill above its impressive drive, with a magnificent view of Mount Ascutney and the Connecticut River Valley, this splendid 28-room mansion, built by Maxwell Evarts in 1901, combines Edwardian grandeur with the informal hospitality of innkeepers Rob and Susanne Pearl and their corgis Cuddles and Tucker. Adult guests (and children over 12) can relax by the hearth in the huge main hall, in a second living room (with TV), or in the library, with its leather armchairs and unusual hearth. One of Vermont's most romantic getaways, the inn offers no fewer than 11 guest rooms with fireplace (all but the two on the third floor are wood-burning). All 16 guest rooms have private bath and are furnished with flair and genuinely interesting antiques. We never can decide which we like best, but Room 7 is a beauty, with rose floral paper, cream trim, a fireplace, and a garden view. We like to sit at the desk overlooking Mount Ascutney, and both Rooms 2 and 3 have balconies with this view. Guests gather for meals in the dining room, a deep burgundy (it works) with floor-to-ceiling fireplace. Reserve for candelight dinners (see *Dining Out*). Inquire about the Yankee Rambler Package, using rental canoes and 18-speed mountain bicycles. On the other hand, we could easily spend a day walking around Lake Runnemede, a hidden conservation area that's great for birding, and by the pool. Rates $90–180 per room, full breakfast included; add $25 for an additional person; add 17.5 percent gratuity on meals and beverages.

Norwich Inn (802-649-1143), Box 908, 225 Main Street, Norwich 05055. Originally built as a stage stop by Jasper Murdock in 1797, this cheerful inn now has a total of 27 rooms divided among the main building, the Vestry, and a backyard motel, all with private bath, telephone, and cable TV. Innkeepers Sally and Tim Wilson have redecorated the guest rooms, and the public rooms are attractive and welcoming. Less formal and expensive than the Hanover Inn across the river, this is very much a gathering place for Dartmouth parents, faculty, and students. A brew pub, Jasper Murdock's Alehouse, features 15 varieties of inn-made brew (see *Eating Out*). The dining rooms are open for breakfast, lunch, and dinner (see *Dining Out*). Rates run from $65 in the off-season in the motel to $149 for a two-bedroom suite in the Vestry. All three meals are served. Dogs are permitted in one twin-bedded room in the motel.

🐾 **The Pond House at Shattuck Hill Farm** (802-484-0011; www.pondhouseinn.com), P.O. Box 234, Brownsville 05037. Vermont native David Raymond and Gretel Schuck have created a real gem of a place, an 1830s Cape by the side of a steeply rising back road, with views across fields to mountains. We love the square dining room with its pumpkin pine floors and original six-over-six windows, and we love the spare, tasteful way the three guest rooms are furnished, each with private bath. Breakfast might feature orange French toast, and the dinner menu might include tuna with artichoke hearts or wild mushroom risotto. The 10-acre grounds include a croquet court and gardens as well as the pond. Horses and polite dogs can be accommodated. In winter there's skating, sledding, and cross-country skiing. Dinner and full breakfast are included in $160–175 per couple.

BED & BREAKFASTS **The Inn at Windsor** (802-674-5670; 802-236-5561), 106 Apothecary Lane, Windsor 05089. Working away steadily since 1983, Larry Bowser and his wife Holly Taylor have been restoring the vintage 1786 Green Mansion, set above Main Street in downtown Windsor and handy to paths around Lake Runnemede and to Mill Pond. Guests enter through a landscaped garden, are asked to remove their shoes, and are then given freshly laundered slippers. Both guest rooms have antique woodstoves built into the hearth, and there is a working fireplace in the suite. All three rooms are interestingly, eclectically furnished, as is the gathering space around the original kitchen hearth and a contemporary breakfast room. The old buttery is now a guest party complete with fridge. $105–165 includes a full breakfast.

🐾 🖍 **Mill Brook Bed & Breakfast** (802-484-7283), Box 410, Route 44, Brownsville 05037. Kay Carriere creates extravagant breakfasts for guests at her 1880s farmhouse near Mount Ascutney. She also goes the extra mile to make guests comfortable in her two frilly rooms and three suites, all with private bath and names like Columbine and Raspberry. Fresh baked goods and hot drinks are always available, and there are no fewer than four common rooms, as well as a hot tub on the back deck. Inquire about the swimming hole. Children and some pets welcome. $70–140 double.

🖍 **Burton Farm Lodge** (802-484-3300), 27 Cross Road, West Windsor 05089-9713. An old farmstead by a large trout pond on a back road near Mount Ascutney. The feel here is that of a homey farm, not your usual B&B. There are two rooms (shared bath). Families are welcome, and children will feel at home immediately. German spoken. $70–80 per couple includes breakfast; $10 per extra person.

⚭ **The Sumner Mansion** (802-436-3386; 1-888-529-8796; www.sumnermansion.com), junction of Routes 5 and 12, Hartland 05048. Mary Louise and Ron Thorburn, who entertained so well when they owned the Inn at Weathersfield, now preside over this beautifully restored and furnished brick landmark on the National Register, really in a class of its own and specializing primarily in weddings (performed under Vermont's third oldest sugar maple) and reunions (January through March). The brick mansion, designed in 1803 by Asher Benjamin, has a formal parlor and five air-conditioned guest rooms with private bath, but the big attractions here are the huge, glass-enclosed dining room and lofty library/music room, surrounded by extensive lawns and gardens. $120–150 per couple B&B includes breakfast and high tea. Inquire about rental of the the entire property.

See also **Bailey's Mills B&B** in Reading, described in "Woodstock/Quechee."

Stonecrest Farm (802-296-2425; 1-800-730-225; www.stonecrestfarm.com), 1187 Christian Street, P.O. Box 409, Wilder 05088. Gail Sanderson's vintage-1810 home, sited on 2 acres just a few miles from Dartmouth College, offers six antiques-furnished rooms with private bath. Common space includes a large formal living room well stocked with books, along with a woodstove and French doors opening onto a stone terrace. Note the curved oak staircase. $139–154 per couple with full breakfast in high season. A good place for solo travelers.

Beaver Meadow (802-649-1053; www.beavermeadowbb.com), 319 Beaver Meadow Road, Norwich 05055. Margo and Rob Titus offer three antiques-furnished rooms with private bath in their 1850s farmhouse. It's on a country road just a mile from the center of town and less than 3 miles from Dartmouth College. $90–110 includes a full breakfast. In summer Lilac Cottage is $115 per night.

Silver Maple Lodge & Cottages (802-333-4326; 1-800-666-1946; www.silvermaplelodge.com), 520 U.S. Route 5 South, Fairlee 05045. Situated just south of the village on Route 5, Silver Maple was built as a farmhouse in 1855 and has been welcoming travelers for more than 80 years. Now run by Scott and Sharon Wright, it has eight nicely appointed guest rooms in the lodge and seven separate, pine-paneled, shaded cottages. The farmhouse has cheerful sitting rooms with exposed 200-year-old hand-hewn beams in the living room and dining room, where fresh breads appear with other continental breakfast goodies. The newest cottages with kitchenette and working fireplace are real beauties. Play horseshoes, croquet, badminton, or shuffleboard on the lawn, or rent a bike or canoe. Scott will also arrange a ride in a hot-air balloon for you at neighboring Post Mills Airport. Scott grew up on a Tunbridge farm and takes pride in introducing visitors to Vermont. $59–89 per couple. Pets accepted in the cottages.

Peach Brook Inn (802-866-3389), Doe Hill, off Route 5, South Newbury 05051. Ray and Joyce Emery have opened their spacious 1837 home with its splendid view of the Connecticut River. What a special place! Common space includes two nicely furnished parlors with exposed beams and a fireplace, an open kitchen, and a screen porch with a view of Mount Moosilauke across the river. The house is on a country lane in the almost vanished village of South Newbury, once connected to Haverhill, New Hampshire, across the river by a long-gone covered bridge. Plenty of farm animals are within walking distance. There are three comfortable guest rooms; $60–65 with shared bath, $70–75 with private, including full breakfast. No smoking. No children under 10, please; under 18 are $10.

Glenwood (802-866-3396; glenwood@together.net), 4354 Route 5, Newbury, 05051. In an early-19th-century house on the fringe of this handsome village John and Carolyn Keats and their two young daughters offer three comfortable-looking, antiques-furnished guest rooms, two with shared and one with a private bath. $50–75 includes taxes as well as breakfast. Floors are wide planked, there's a working fireplace in the living room, and breakfast is served at the dining room table. An efficiency rental unit (attached but with a separate entrance) with two bedrooms, a living room, and full kitchen is $550–700 per week.

♿ **The Whipple Tree Bed & Breakfast** (802-429-2076; 1-800-466-4097; www.whipple-tree.com), 487 Stevens Place, Wells River 05081. This is a real find, a contemporary house, designed to be a B&B, perched higher than any other on the Vermont side of the valley, set in no less than 500 acres with spectacular views east to the White Mountains. Bill and Carol Bailey are about as deeply rooted in the area. Bill is descended from Gen. Jacob Bailey, charged during the American Revolution by George Washington to build the famous Bayley-Hazen Road across the Northeast Kingdom. The six spacious guest rooms all have private bath (General Jacob features a gas fireplace and soaking tub), also phone and TV, and the many-windowed common space is immense. Extras include a hot tub, exercise and game room, and meeting space. $140–190. $15 per extra person.

HOTEL **The Hotel Coolidge** (802-295-3118; 1-800-622-1124; Hotel.Coolidge@valley.net), White River Junction 05001, is as one of the last of the old railroad hotels. All 50 elevator-served guest rooms have private bath, phone, and TV. Some are depressingly small, but others are quite roomy and attractive, and the family suites (two rooms connected by a bath) are a real bargain. The hotel sits across from the Amtrak station and next to the Briggs Opera House (see *Entertainment*). Local buses to Hanover and Lebanon stop at the door, and rental cars can be arranged. Search out the splendid Peter Michael Gish murals in the Vermont Room, painted in 1950 in exchange for room and board while the artist was studying with Paul Sample at Dartmouth. Owner-manager David Briggs, a seventh-generation Vermonter, takes his role as innkeeper seriously and will arrange for special needs. $59–79 per room double. Children free.

HOSTEL **The Hotel Coolidge** (802-295-3118). A wing of the Coolidge, described above, is a Hostelling International facility with dorm-style beds and access to a self-service kitchen and laundry. Private family rooms are also available by reservation. $20.71 (tax included) with special double and children's rates.

LODGING WORTH CROSSING THE RIVER FOR **Moose Mountain Lodge** (603-643-3529; moosemountainlodge.com), Etna, New Hampshire 03750. Open June through October, December 26 through mid-March, Wednesday through Sunday. This is the most alpine inn in all of New England, perched high on a steep hill behind Hanover, just off the Appalachian Trail with spectacular views to the west across the Connecticut River to the Green Mountains. Kay and Peter Shumway have been here since 1975 and obviously enjoy what they do, greeting guests like old friends and preparing memorable meals from the freshest ingredients. The 11 guest rooms are small but attractive, with handmade log beds and five shared baths. Inside and out, the lodge has plenty of pine. It was built of stones and logs cleared from this hill. The 350 acres include a deep pond just outside the door, ample woods, and meadows with long views. In winter it offers 50 miles of cross-country-ski trails. $200 per couple MAP in winter includes lunch, $90 MAP in summer and fall; $55 for children 12 and under MAP.

Loch Lyme Lodge and Cottages (603-795-2141; 1-800-423-2141), Route 10, RFD 278, Lyme, New Hampshire 03768. The main lodge is open through foliage season; the cabins, Memorial Day to mid-September. There are four rooms in the inn and 22 brown-shingle cabins (11 with cooking facilities) spread along a wooded hillside overlooking a lake called Post Pond. The big attraction here is a private beach with a float and a fleet of rowboats and canoes; also a Windsurfer. Two tennis courts, a baseball field, basketball court, volleyball net, and recreation cabin are there for the using, and baby-sitting is available for parents who want time off. Lunch and dinner are served, and a take-out lunch bar is open for sandwiches and cones. Loch Lyme was founded in 1917 and has been owned and managed by Paul and Judy Barker's family since the 1940s. No credit cards. Pets permitted in cabins. From $53 single and $68 double off-season to $96 double in summer (including breakfast). Housekeeping cabins are $550–800 per week; children's rates.

Piermont Inn (603-272-4820), 1 Old Church Street, Piermont, New Hampshire 03779 (across the bridge from Bradford, Vermont). A 1790s stagecoach stop with six rooms, four in the adjacent carriage house (only the two in the inn are open year-round), all with private bath. The two in the main house are outstanding, both carved from the tavern's original ballroom, high-ceilinged and spacious, with writing desks and appropriate antiques. The carriage house rooms are simple but cheery; one is handicapped-accessible. Common space includes a living room with fireplace, TV, wing chairs, and a nifty grandfather clock. Charlie and Karen Brown are longtime Piermont residents who enjoy tuning in guests to the many ways of exploring this upper (less touristed) part of the Upper Valley, especially to canoeing the river (they offer a canoe and informal shuttle service). Breakfast is full, and dinner can be arranged. Rooms in the main house are $95–110; in the carriage house (summer only), $60–70. Breakfast is included in winter.

The Gibson House (603-989-3125; www.gibsonhouse.com), RR 1, Box 193, Haverhill, New Hampshire 03765. Artist Keita Colton has restored Haverhill's classic 1850 Greek Revival stagecoach stop and offers five fantasy rooms, lavishly and imaginatively decorated, and breakfasts to match. The house fronts on Route 10 but the sun porch and terraces overlook gardens and the Connecticut River.

Where to Eat

Note: Listings are in geographical order, south to north.

DINING OUT **Penelope's on the Square** (802-885-9186), Springfield. Open daily for lunch and dinner except Sunday. Polished woods, stained glass, and greenery, an attractive setting for dining from a large menu. Choices range from beef filet flambéed in brandy ($21.95) to Rosie's

Scrod ($14.95) and baked lasagna ($9.95). Children's menu.

Hartness House (802-885-2115), 30 Orchard Street, Springfield. Closed Monday. Open for lunch and dinner weekdays, dinner only on weekends. The dining room in this venerable landmark is now Victorian red, greens, and golds. The chef is Michael Hofford and the menu might include beer-battered fish-and-chips, roast pork loin with onion confit and sautéed apples, or pan-seared halibut with an orange, ginger, carrot sauce. Entrées $12.95–19.95.

Seed House Café at the 1815 House (802-484-1815), junction of Routes 44 and 106, Reading. Open Friday through Sunday evenings, but check. A handsome brick tavern actually built in 1806, serving as a public house until the 1870s and then (until the 1950s) as headquarters for Budd Hawkins' Seeds. Peter Bennett turned it into a restaurant again, specializing in his own "comfort food," dishes like Wiener schnitzel, beef stew (with red wine and garlic), and ham steak. Quail and thin-sliced duck breast are also apt to be on the menu. Entrées $16–22. See also the Seed House Café under *Eating Out*.

Windsor Station Restaurant (802-674-2052), Depot Avenue, Windsor. Built as a passenger train station (it remains an Amtrak stop), now decorated in natural wood plus velvet and brass. It serves reasonably priced dinner with entrées from chicken Kiev or amandine and veal Madeira to the Station Master filet mignon topped with shrimp, asparagus, and hollandaise sauce. A children's menu is available. Inexpensive to moderate.

Juniper Hill Inn (802-674-5273), Route 5 north of Windsor. Dinner by reservation, Tuesday through Saturday. Reserve. Patrons are asked to come at 6:15 for a drink before. Innkeeper Susanne Pearl is the chef, offering a four-course prix fixe menu that might include herb-crusted rack of lamb and maple-glazed salmon fillets. $35 per person. The wine list is respectable.

Skunk Hollow Tavern (802-436-2139), Hartland Four Corners, off Route 12 north of I-91, exit 9. Dinner Wednesday through Sunday. Reservations suggested. Carlos Ocasio's split-personality restaurant is simply one of the best places around, hidden away in a small village that's easily accessible both from the Connecticut and the Ottauquechee River Valleys. Patrons gather downstairs in the pub to play darts and backgammon and to munch on fish-and-chips, mussels, or pizza; the generally excellent, more formal dining is upstairs in the inn's original parlor. The menu changes every few months but staples include Chicken Carlos and fish-and-chips. Variables might be red pepper shrimp with Oriental pasta or shiitake chicken; always salad of the day and homemade soups. $6.95–19.95. Live entertainment Wednesday and Friday nights.

Karibu Tulé's A Taste of Africa (802-295-4243), 2 North Main Street, White River Junction. Open for dinner. *Ka-ree-bu Yu-lay* means "welcome, let's dine" in Swahili. The menu features authentic African and world cuisine, from Moroccan couscous and Kenyan pillau (jasmine rice cooked with a blend of spices, peas, and carrots) and peanut chicken stew from Mali. Chapati bread is always served, and there are daily specials. Moderate to expensive.

Tip-Top Café (802-295-4411), Tip-Top Bakery Building, 85 North Main Street, White River Junction. Open Monday through Friday 8–5; lunch

11:30–2. Dinner served Thursday through Saturday, 5:30-9:30, late-night light menu Friday and Saturday. This bright and polished new café in a rehabbed industrial building offers a simple but sophisticated dinner menu. Appetizers include house-made duck confit on a bed of mesclun; entrées include salmon, chicken, duck, beef, and pasta dishes. Excellent desserts include tarte Tatin, chocolate mocha cake. Limited but intelligently chosen wine list. Appetizers $6; entrées $12–16; sides $4; dessert $4–6.

La Poule à Dents (802-649-2922; www.lapoule.com), Main Street, Norwich. Open for dinner nightly from 6; reservations required. The name means "as scarce as hen's teeth," a way of noting that the best things in life are rare; this is one of the more formal, upscale places in the Upper Valley. The touch is French and the ingredients local. An à la carte menu in the beamed dining room of this 1820s house might feature smoked seafood sausage with crispy sweet potatoes and lobster vinaigrette to start, followed by grilled garlic-rubbed tenderloin of pork served with Stilton gnocchi and port wine reduction sauce. Entrées: $21–26. The wine list is a point of pride.

Norwich Inn (802-649-1143), Main Street, Norwich, popular locally for breakfast, lunch, and dinner, also Sunday brunch. Although the dining rooms are traditional, they are bright and inviting, far from stuffy. The menu changes every few months, but a dinner menu might include scallion shrimp tempura and sesame-crusted tofu as appetizers and sautéed veal medallions as well as vegetarian stuffed sweet bell pepper among the entrées, priced $15.95–19.95.

Colatina Exit (802-222-9008), Main Street, Bradford. Open daily, 5–10 PM; weekends until 11. This is a real Vermont trattoria that's been here more than 26 years: candles in Chianti bottles, Italian scenes on the walls, checked (green, mind you) tablecloths, and a variety of pastas and specials like grilled shrimp primavera ($12.95) and seafood cioppino ($13.95). Note family-style specials.

Peyton Place (603-532-4886; www.peytonplacerestaurant.com), Route 10, Orford, New Hampshire. Open Wednesday through Saturday 5:30–10:30; closed Wednesday in winter. Reservations recommended. A fixture for years in Bradford, this legendary restaurant (named for owners Jim, Heidi, Sophie and Shamus Peyton) recently moved down the river a way and across into Orford, New Hampshire (it's a half mile down Route 10 from the Fairlee-Orford bridge). Its new home is the vintage 1773 Mann Tavern, which includes a genuine old pub room (with a new pub menu) as well as more formal dining rooms. Dinner entrées might range from rack of lamb with wild mushrooms ($24, $46 for two) to vegetarian ravioli, handmade to order ($15). Ice creams and sorbets are handmade. Wine and spirits are served.

The Perfect Pear Café (802-222-5912; www.theperfectpearcafe.com), the Bradford Mill, Main Street, Bradford. Dinner reservations recommended. Open Tuesday through Saturday for lunch and in summer (same days) for dinner. Winter days may vary. Chef-owners Eric and Nancy Harting have created a charming, 50-seat bistro serving fresh, sophisticated food. You might begin with pumpkin and walnut ravioli in Gorgonzola cream sauce and dine on horseradish-crusted sea bass over mashed potatoes garnished with sweet chive oil. Dinner entrées: $11.95–19.95.

See also "Woodstock/Quechee" for the Simon Pearce Restaurant, the Parker House Inn, and the Meadows at Marshland Farm, all in Quechee.

EATING OUT **Morning Star Café** (802-885-6987), 56 Main Street, Springfield. Open Monday through Saturday from 7 AM, until 5 Monday and Tuesday, until 9 Wednesday and Thursday, and until 9:30 Friday and Saturday. A very welcome addition, an airy storefront with high ceilings, widely spaced tables, and good espresso, chai, and latte, pastries, a light deli. The dinner menu changes constantly; perhaps grilled boneless pork chops with cider-glazed mushrooms ($14.95) and mussels steamed in garlic with white sauce and farfalle pasta ($12.95). There's a wine list.

McKinley's (802-885-9186), on the square, Springfield. Same fern-bar atmosphere as Penelope's (see *Dining Out*) but a different menu. A good lunch stop: burgers, taco salad, sandwiches, pastas, and soups.

Country Creemee Restaurant, Downers Corner (junction of Routes 131 and 106), Amsden. Seasonal. Locals will tell you that everything tastes good here; we always get the super-long hot dog to consume at a picnic table under the trees.

Seed House Café at the 1815 House (802-484-1815), open Friday through Sunday evenings, junction of Routes 44 and 106, Reading. Burgers, sandwiches, salads, reasonably priced fare like fettuccine Alfredo and grilled chicken sandwiches. All grilling done over charcoal.

Brownsville General Store (802-484-7480), Route 44 just west of the entrance to Ascutney Mountain Resort. A regular general store with busy gas pumps but also with a big red Aga cookstove behind the lunch counter, a clue to the quality of soups and daily specials like chicken and biscuits. Bread is fresh baked, and there's a full deli.

Dan's Windsor Diner (802-674-5555), 135 Main Street, Windsor. Open Friday and Saturday 6 AM–8 PM. Sunday through Thursday 6 AM–2:30 PM; Friday and Saturday until 8 PM. Dan Kirby has spiffed up this 1952 classic Worcester diner, now famous up and down the river for its clam chowder. Specialties include meat loaf, liver and onions, and macaroni and cheese, along with omelets, burger baskets, and pies.

Shepherd's Pie Restaurant and Deli (802-674-9390), 131 Main Street, Windsor. Open from 7 AM (Sunday from 8) for breakfast through lunch and dinner until 8 PM; closing Sunday, at 3 PM. Every town should have a comfortable gathering spot like Sharon Shepherd's tangerine-walled storefront. The food is fine, judging from a generous chicken quesadilla one summer day and a rather unorthodox but tasty shepherd's pie on a chilly autumn evening. Specialties include soups, vegetarian dishes, and "Ralphies" (baked, breaded chicken breast, sliced and rolled into a tortilla with a choice of toppings). The deli is a sandwich source for picnicking on the river, the Mill Pond, or Lake Runnemede.

See also Skunk Hollow Tavern under *Dining Out*.

Gandy Dancer Café (802-280-2233), 39 Front Main Street, White River Junction. Open 8–4 weekdays, for Sunday brunch (9:30–1:30), and for pretheater dinners. *Gandy dancer* is a name for the men who laid railroad track, and this bright new café faces the Amtrak station across the tracks. Sara Deestender bakes muffins and pastries, breakfast wraps, and panini to go with morning espresso. The lunch specialties are roll-ups, freshly made quiche, and soups. Brunch specialties include Belgian waffles, quiche, and warm croissants with cheese. On Friday and Saturday evenings dinner is served before Northern Stage productions at the neighboring Briggs Opera House (reserve).

The Polka Dot (802-295-9722), North Main Street, White River Junction. Open 5 AM–7 PM. A little too real for some folks but a classic diner with chrome, photos of old trains, stools, and booths, known for soups and honey-coated fried chicken, specials like tuna-noodle casserole, good pies.

River City Cafe (802-296-7113), 15 Main Street, White River Junction. Open weekdays 8–4, Saturday 9–3. Good for breakfast pastries, lunch soups and salads, coffee all day.

Jasper Murdock's Alehouse in the Norwich Inn (802-649-1143), Main Street, Norwich. Open 5:30–9. The house brew comes in many varieties (see *Brews*). The Alehouse is a green-walled, comfortable pub; the bill of fare changes frequently but usually includes crabcakes, a pub cheeseburger, shepherd's pie, and a roasted pepper and eggplant sandwich.

Alice's Patisserie and Cafe (802-649-2846), Main and Elm Streets, Norwich. Open Tuesday through Friday 9:30–5:30; to 3 Saturday. Under new ownership with a greater emphasis on pastries and take-home dinners; also a café, good for leek and potato soup or marinated artichoke hearts with roasted red peppers and black olive spread on a freshly baked baguette, or a fruit tart and cappuccino.

The Third Rail (802-333-9797), Route 5, Fairlee. Open except Sunday for lunch and dinner; reservations advisable for dinner in summer. This roadside house with friendly pub and several small, cheerful, and informal dining rooms is under new ownership. Appetizers include "rail rolls" (blackened chicken, mushrooms, onions, and Brie wrapped in a flour tortilla and deep-fried); entrées ($8.75–14.95) range from vegetable strudel and roasted vegetable lasagna to pork spareribs and hand-cut grilled rib eye.

Fairlee Diner (802-333-3569), Route 5, Fairlee. Closed Tuesday, otherwise 5:30–2, until 7 Thursday and 8 Friday. Turn left (north) on Route 5 if you are coming off I-91. This is a classic wooden diner built in the '30s (across the road from where it stands), with wooden booths, worn-shiny wooden stool tops, and good food. The mashed potato doughnuts are special, and both the soup and the pie are dependably good. Daily specials.

Bradford Village Store (802-222-4617), Main Street, Bradford. Housed in a former 19th-century hotel, this is a classic general store but with Crock-Pots full of good soup, chili, or stew; a deli and daily specials for $3.99; tables are in the back—including a booth with the best river view in town.

The Hungry Bear (802-222-5288), Bradford, Route 5 (just off I-91), open daily 7 AM–7 PM, until 8 on Saturday, evolved from a hamburger stand into a dependable roadfood stop, good for generous servings of whatever you order, from oversized pancakes through soups and sandwiches to nightly specials.

✎ **Warner Gallery Restaurant** (802-429-2120, just off I-91, exit 17, on Route 302, Wells River. Open Tuesday through Saturday 5 AM–9 PM, Sunday 11–8. A dependable (90 percent of the time) family restaurant with some atmosphere. Entrées usually include the mixed grill ($14.95) and roast turkey ($12.95). There's a children's menu, and Sunday brunch is billed as "best in the Northeast."

✎ **P&H Truck Stop** (802-429-2141), just off I-91, exit 17, on Route 302, Wells River. Open 24 hours. Dozens of rigs are usually parked outside on one side, and the license plates on cars in the other lot is usually quite amazing. This is a classic truck stop with speedy service, friendly waitresses, and heaping portions at amazing prices.

BREWS **Jasper Murdock's Alehouse** in the Norwich Inn (802-649-1143), Main Street, Norwich. Open 5:30–9. Brewmaster Timothy Wilson prides himself on reviving the New England tradition of inns brewing their own beer (his brews are sold nowhere else). Jasper Murdock's Ales, crafted from English malts, come in four varieties (our favorite is Whistling Pig Red) and have a strong local following.

Harpoon Brewery (1-888-HARPOON; www.harpoonbrewery.com), south of exit 9, north of Windsor on Route 5. Open Tuesday through Saturday, 10–6 except major holidays (check); tour (and tastings) are usually at 11, 1, and 3. Founded in Boston in 1986 and still Boston based, Harpoon purchased this, the former Catamount Brewery, in 2000. The "visitors center" here consists of a shop, which doubles as a "beer garden," selling deli sandwiches and, well, beer.

✷ Entertainment

MUSIC AND THEATER **Hopkins Center for the Arts** (603-646-2422), Dartmouth green, Hanover, New Hampshire. Three theaters, a recital hall, and art galleries feature year-round programs of plays, concerts, and films.

✎ **Northern Stage** (802-291-9009), at the Briggs Opera House, White River Junction. This excellent community theater group offers semiprofessional productions year-round. Special children's theater classes and summer arts education classes.

The Parish Players (802-785-4344), based in the Eclipse Grange Hall on Thetford Hill, is the oldest community theater company in the Upper Valley; its September-through-May repertoire includes classic pieces and original works; summer presentations vary.

In the past few seasons, venues have burgeoned for folk, blues, and hard-to-label, idiosyncratic performers. The **Lebanon Opera House** (603-448-2498), on the green in Lebanon, New Hampshire, is one of the most active. **Opera North** (603-643-1946) stages semiprofessional performances of a very high standard including one major opera, usually at the Lebanon Opera House, every August. Smaller performances are offered at other times of the year in various locations in the Upper Valley.

FILM **Dartmouth Film Society** at the Hopkins Center (603-646-2576), Dartmouth green, Hanover, New Hampshire. Frequent showings of classic, contemporary, and experimental films in two theaters.

The Nugget (603-643-2769), South Main Street, Hanover, New Hampshire. Four first-run films nightly.

Fairlee Drive-In (802-333-9192), Route 5, Fairlee. Summer only; check local papers for listings.

MUSIC **The Club Car** (802-674-5551; www.windsorstation.com), next to Windsor Station (see *Dining Out*) opens at 7 PM Friday and Saturday for live jazz and blues.

✷ Selective Shopping

BOOKSTORES **The Norwich Bookstore** (802-649-1114), Main Street, Norwich. This nifty, bright, very personalized shop in a classic house next to the post office has a knowledgeable staff, a great children's section, and frequent readings and signings by authors and illustrators.

The Dartmouth Bookstore, (603-643-3616), 33 South Main Street, Hanover, New Hampshire. A full-service independent bookstore on the campus of Dartmouth College.

I Wonda Book Shoppe (802-674-5503), Main Street, Windsor, under the Tuxbury Shops. An eclectic stock of gifts, books.

The Hundredth Monkey Bookstore (802-295-9397), 3 North Main Street, White River Junction. Used, antiquarian, and new books.

ARTS AND CRAFTS **Vermont Craft Gallery** at Windsor House (802-674-6729). Open daily 10–5; Sunday 11–4. An attractive retail showcase-gallery for Vermont craftspeople: two floors of glass, ceramics, furniture, jewelry, prints, toys, a book corner, plus a series of instructional programs.

Cider Hill Farm (802-674-5293), Hunt Road, 2.5 miles west of State Street, Windsor. Sarah Milek's commercial display garden (see *Farms*) is the setting for Gary Milek's studio, displaying his striking Vermont landscapes done in egg tempera, the botanically correct floral prints, and stunning cards made from them.

South Road Pottery (802-222-5798), 3458 South Road, Bradford. Open May through October daily, 10–5; otherwise by appointment. Worth searching out both for back-road locale and for Bruce Murray's distinctive, functional pottery: butter and condiment dishes, teapots, bowls, mugs, lamps, trays, and more.

FACTORY TOURS AND SHOPS **Simon Pearce Glass** (802-674-6280), Route 5, north of Windsor. Open daily 9–5. Pearce operated his own glassworks in Ireland for a decade and moved here in 1981, acquiring the venerable Downer's Mill in Quechee and harnessing the dam's hydropower for the glass furnace (see *Selective Shopping* in "Woodstock/Quechee"). He subsequently built this additional, 32,000-square-foot facility down by the Connecticut River. Designed to be visitor friendly, it includes a catwalk above the factory floor—a fascinating place from which you can watch glass being blown and shaped. Of course, there's a big showroom-shop featuring seconds as well as first-quality glass and pottery.

King Arthur Flour Baker's Store (802-649-3361; 1-800-827-6836; www.kingarthurflour.com), Route 5, Norwich. Open Monday through Saturday 9–6; Sunday 10–4. This home as well as prime outlet for the country's oldest family-owned flour company (since 1790) draws serious bakers, and would-be bakers, from several time zones. The vast post-and-beam store itself is a marvel, its shelves stocked with every conceivable kind of flour

Kim Grant

GLASSBLOWING AT SIMON PEARCE IN WINDSOR

and baking ingredient along with a selection of equipment and cookbooks. Bread and pastries are made in the adjacent bakery (with a glass connector allowing visitors to watch the hands and skills of the bakers). Next door is the new Baking Education Center, offering baking classes ranging from beginner to expert, from piecrusts to braided breads and elegant pastries.

Stave Puzzles (802-295-5200), off Route 5, 1 mile south of Norwich and I-89, exit 13. Turn at the sign for Olcott Commerce Park, and take the drive after UPS. The handcrafted wooden jigsaw puzzles made here are the Rolls-Royces of the pastime. Some are cut and put together in multiple-choice fashion; all are mounted on mahogany. Their prices are impressive, too: A 150-piece lobster trap is $695, the 400-piece three-dimensional baseball game is $1,895. Made-to-order puzzles incorporating family photos are a specialty, but pictures of the final product never come with the puzzle pieces. Visitors are welcome to inspect display drawers filled with puzzles and to peer into the puzzle works itself.

Pompanoosuc Mills (802-785-4851), Route 5, East Thetford. Open weekdays 9–1, Saturday 9–5, Sunday noon–5. Dwight Sargeant began building furniture in his riverside house, a cottage industry that has evolved into a riverside factory, with showrooms throughout New England. Furniture is made to order. Check out the big tent sale Memorial Day weekend.

Copeland Furniture (802-222-5300; www.copelandfurniture.com), 64 Main Street, Bradford. Open Monday through Friday 10–6, Saturday 9–5. Contemporary, cleanly lined, locally made furniture in native hardwoods displayed in the handsome showroom in the converted 19th-century brick mill across from Bradford Falls. Seconds.

SPECIAL SHOPS **Vermont Salvage Exchange** (802-295-7616), Railroad Row, White River Junction, for doors, chandeliers, moldings, mantels, old bricks, and other architectural relics.

Briggs Ltd. (802-295-7100), 12 North Main Street, White River Junction. Hunting supplies and Orvis tackle, as well as Woolrich and Pendleton clothing for men and women.

Dan and Whit's General Store, Main Street, Norwich. Next to the Norwich Inn, a general store among general stores: great bulletin board, groceries, buttons, hardware, clothing, advice.

Chapman's (802-333-9709), Fairlee. Open daily 8–6, until 5 on Sunday. Since 1924, members of the Chapman family have expanded the stock of this old pharmacy to include 10,000 hand-tied flies, wines, Mexican silver and Indonesian jewelry, used books, and an unusual selection of toys—as well as nightcrawlers and manila envelopes. Check out the antiques in the barn. This time we bought a wooden puzzle and a stove mitt.

Farm-Way, Inc. (1-800-222-9316), Route 25, Bradford. One mile east of

I-91, exit 16. Open Monday through Saturday until 8 PM. Billed as "complete outfitters for man and beast," this is a phenomenon: a family-run source of work boots and rugged clothing that now includes a stock of more than 2 million products spread over 5 acres: tack, furniture, pet supplies, syrup, whatever. Shoes and boots remain a specialty, from size 4E to 16; 10,000 shoes, boots, clogs, sandals, and sneakers in stock.

FARMS **Cider Hill Farm** (802-674-5293), Hunt Road, 2.5 miles west of State Street, Windsor. Growers of herbs and perennials, creators of herb wreaths, dried-flower arrangements, herbal blends, and apple cider.

Killdeer Farm (802-649-2852) has a farm stand on Route 5 just south of Norwich. Open every day from May through October, with a wide variety of Vermont products, baked goods, and fruit, as well as bedding plants and organic vegetables.

Norwich Farmers' Market, south of Norwich on Route 5. Open Saturday 9–1 from May through October. A real happening, this is the place to see and be seen on summer Saturdays. Local farmers bring produce, wool, baked goods, flowers, and handmade crafts; live music under the gazebo.

Cedar Circle Farm (802-785-4101), East Thetford. Famous for its four varieties of cantaloupes; also good for local peas and strawberries.

Crossroad Farm (802-333-4455), on the crossroad between Routes 113 and 244, Post Mills. Fresh local produce sold at a seasonal stand near the shores of Lake Fairlee.

4 Corners Farm (802-866-3342), just off Route 5, South Newbury. Bob and Kim Gray sell their own produce and flowers. An exceptionally pretty farm, just off but up above the highway.

Special Events

July and August: Sunday-afternoon (2 PM) **lawn concerts** at the Saint-Gaudens National Historic Site (603-675-2175) in Cornish, New Hampshire; free with admission to the grounds; bring a picnic.

July: On Saturday night at the Old Grange Hall (historical society: 802-824-5294) in Brownsville (West Windsor) **baked bean and salad suppers** have been held since 1935. **Windsor Heritage Days** celebrate Vermont's birthplace as a republic, the weekend following July 4. **Connecticut Valley Fair,** Bradford (midmonth). **Cracker Barrel Bazaar,** Newbury (802-866-5521), third or final weekend, includes plenty of fiddling.

August: **North Haverhill (New Hampshire) Fair:** old-style fair with ox and tractor pulls, pig races, etc. **The Quechee Scottish Festival** is big, Quechee (see "Woodstock/Quechee").

September: **Apple Festival** at King Arthur Flour, Norwich. **Octoberfest** at the Harpoon Brewery, Windsor.

October: The annual **Vermont Apple Festival** (802-885-2779), Springfield, is held Columbus Day weekend and includes a crafts show. **Festival Windsor** is an annual autumn celebration.

November: **Annual Wild Game Supper** in Bradford (802-222-4721), the Saturday before Thanksgiving, when hungry visitors pour into the Congregational church for this feast.

WOODSTOCK/QUECHEE AREA

Cradled between Mount Peg and Mount Tom and moated by the Ottauquechee River, Woodstock is repeatedly named among the prettiest towns in America. The story behind Woodstock's good looks, which include the surrounding landscape as well as historic buildings, is told at the Marsh-Billings-Rockefeller National Historical Park, the country's only national park to focus on the concept of conservation.

The Ottauqechee River flows east through Woodstock along Route 4 toward the Connecticut River, generating electricity as it tumbles over falls beneath the covered bridge at Taftsville and powering Simon Pearce's glass factory a few miles downstream in Quechee Village. Below Quechee it has carved Vermont's "Grand Canyon," 163-foot-deep Quechee Gorge, spanned by a Route 4 and by a high, spidery railroad bridge.

The Woodstock Railroad carried passengers and freight the 20 miles east from Woodstock to White River Junction between 1875 and 1933. How to ease current traffic congestion, which includes 18-wheelers headed for Rutland as well as tour buses and tourists in summer and fall and skiers in winter, remains a very real challenge. Route 4 is the shortest way across "Vermont's waist," and an ever-growing stream of vehicles continues to wind up the valley, filing through the middle of Woodstock, around its exquisite green, and on through the village of West Woodstock, following the river west into Bridgewater (past another born-again mill).

Our advice: Get off Route 4. Turn off at Quechee Gorge and walk the canyon rim. Turn off into Quechee Village and follow River Road to Billings Farm. Continue on Route 12 beyond the national park , north to Barnard. Follow Route 106 south from the Woodstock green into horse country. Like most of the world's famously beautiful and heavily touristed areas, especially those that are also home to sophisticated people who could live anywhere, the Ottauquechee River Valley offers visitors plenty to see and do superficially and still more, the more you explore.

GUIDANCE **The Woodstock Area Chamber of Commerce** (802-457-3555; 1-888-496-6378; www.woodstockvt.com), 18 Central Street, Woodstock 05901, keeps an information booth open on the green, June through October (802-457-1042) and publishes *Window on Woodstock,* a useful free pamphlet guide. The chamber

STATELY BUILDINGS ON THE GREEN IN WOODSTOCK

also finds beds for stranded fall foliage leaf-peepers. Rest rooms are available in the town hall, west of the green.

The Quechee Chamber of Commerce (802-295-7900; 1-800-295-5451; www.quechee.com), P.O. Box 160, Quechee 05059, maintains an information booth on Route 4 at Quechee Gorge, open mid-May through mid-October.
Also check out www.easternvermont.com, the web site for the state's regional marketing organization for this area.

GETTING THERE *By car:* Route 4 west from I-91 and I-89.

By train: Amtrak to White River Junction.

By bus: Vermont Transit to White River Junction, with connections to and from Rutland via Woodstock; tickets at the Whipple Tree, Central Street, Woodstock (see *Selective Shopping*).

MEDICAL EMERGENCY **911** now covers the area.

PARKING In Woodstock itself parking can be a problem during crunch times. There's a free lot by the river on Pleasant Street.

WHEN TO COME This area is as genuinely year-round as Vermont gets. Marsh-Billings-Rockefeller National Historical Park and the Billings Farm Museum are open May through mid-October but Woodstock's early-December Wassail Weekend is its most colorful event, and January through March bring cross-country and alpine skiing.

✷ Villages

Woodstock. In the 1790s, when it became the shire town of Windsor County, Woodstock began attracting influential and prosperous professionals, who, with

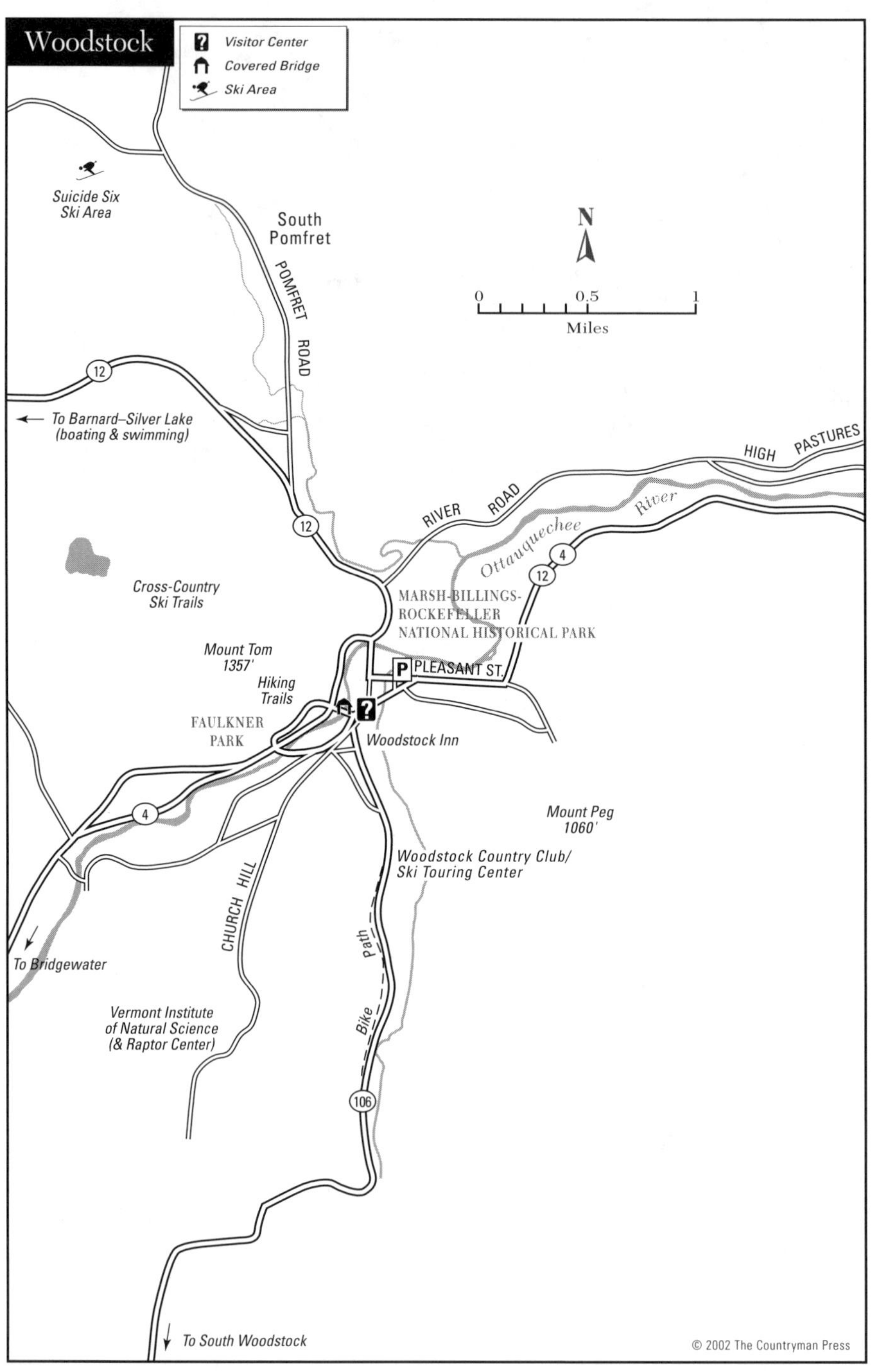
Woodstock
Visitor Center
Covered Bridge
Ski Area
Suicide Six
Ski Area
South
Pomfret
POMFRET ROAD
N
0
0.5
1
Miles
12
To Barnard–Silver Lake
(boating & swimming)
HIGH PASTURES
RIVER ROAD
River
Ottauquechee
12
4
12
Cross-Country
Ski Trails
MARSH-BILLINGS-
ROCKEFELLER
NATIONAL HISTORICAL PARK
Mount Tom
1357'
P
PLEASANT ST.
Hiking
Trails
FAULKNER
PARK
Woodstock Inn
4
Mount Peg
1060'
Woodstock Country Club/
Ski Touring Center
CHURCH HILL
Bike Path
To Bridgewater
Vermont Institute
of Natural Science
(& Raptor Center)
106
To South Woodstock
© 2002 The Countryman Press

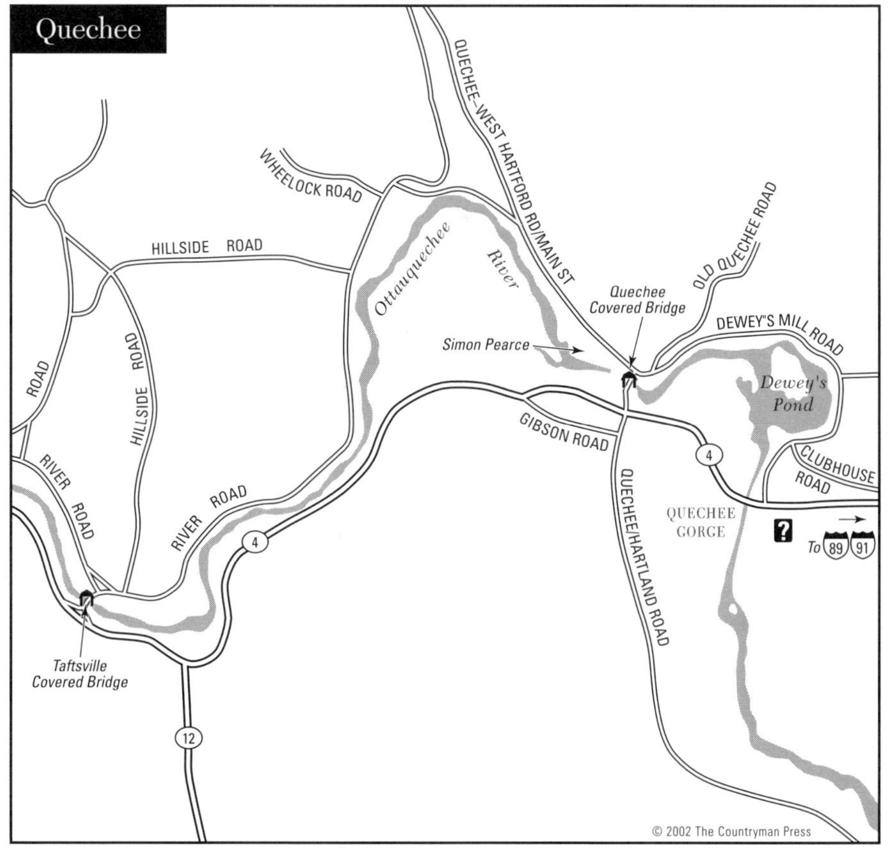

local merchants and bankers, built the concentration of distinguished Federal houses that surround the elliptical green, forming an architectural showcase that has been meticulously preserved. In the 19th century it produced more than its share of celebrities, including Hiram Powers, the sculptor whose nude *Greek Slave* scandalized the nation in 1847, and Sen. Jacob Collamer (1791–1865), President Lincoln's confidant, who declared, "The good people of Woodstock have less incentive than others to yearn for heaven."

Three eminent residents in particular—all of whom lived in the same house but in different eras—helped shape the current Woodstock (see accompanying box).

"Innkeeping has always been the backbone of Woodstock's economy, most importantly since 1892 when the town's business leaders and bankers decided to build a new hotel grand enough to rival the White Mountain resorts," Peter Jennison writes in *Woodstock's Heritage.* By the turn of the 20th century, in addition to several inns, Woodstock had an elaborate mineral water spa and golf links, and it had become Vermont's first winter resort, drawing guests from Boston and New York for snowshoeing and skating. In 1934 America's first rope tow was installed here, marking the real advent of downhill skiing

Courtesy Billings Family Archives

FREDERICK BILLINGS BY KURTZ, C. 1873

GEORGE PERKINS MARSH (1801–1882), FREDERICK BILLINGS (1823–1890), AND LAURANCE ROCKEFELLER (BORN 1910)
Three men in particular have helped shape Woodstock's landscape. The first, George Perkins Marsh, born and raised here, had damaged his eyesight by age 7 by devouring encyclopedias and books on Greek and Latin. Sent outdoors, he studied the woods, fields, birds, and animals with equal intensity. As a man he noted the effects of logging on the landscape (60 percent of Vermont's virgin forest was harvested in the first half of the 19th century) and the resulting floods and destruction of fisheries. Later, traveling in the Middle East as the U.S. ambassador to Turkey, Marsh noted how once-fertile land had become desert. He wrote: "I fear man has brought the face of the earth to a devastation almost as complete as that of the moon."

Marsh wrote *Man and Nature* at age 63, while U.S. ambassador to Italy. Published in 1864, it is widely recognized as the first book to acknowledge civilization's effect on the environment, and the first to suggest solutions. In contrast to Henry David Thoreau (*Walden* appeared in 1854), Marsh doesn't idealize wilderness. Instead, he attempts to address the interdependence of the environment and society as a whole.

Man and Nature isn't an easy read but it greatly influenced this country's nascent sciences of forestry and agriculture as well as many of the era's movers and shakers, among them Frederick Billings. Raised in Woodstock, Billings departed at age 25 for San Francisco. That city's first lawyer, he made a fortune registering land claims and speculating in land during the Gold Rush. As a returning son who had "made good," Billings spoke at the 1864 Woodstock Fair, remarking on the rawness of the local landscape, the hills denuded by logging and sheep grazing. In 1869 he bought the old Marsh farm and transformed the vintage-1801 house into a mansion. On Mount Tom he planted more than 100,000 trees, turned a bog into Pogue Pond, and created the carriage roads. Billings's primary home was in New York and as president of the Pacific Northwest Railroad (the reason Billings, Montana, is named for him), he toured the country extensively. He continued, however, to retreat to Woodstock, creating a model dairy farm on his property, a project sustained after his death, through thick and thin, by his wife and two successive generations of Billings women.

In 1934 Frederick Billings's granddaughter Mary French (1910–1997) married Laurance Rockefeller in Woodstock. John D. Rockefeller Jr. had been largely responsible for creating more than 20 state and national parks and historic sites, and Laurance inherited his father's commitment to conservation and quickly became an effective advocate of ecotourism. In the 1950s, Mary Rockefeller inherited the Billings estate in Woodstock and Laurance bought and replaced the old inn, incorporating the golf course and Suicide Six ski area into one resort. He also created the Woodstock Foundation, a nonprofit umbrella for numerous village projects (see Woodstock under *Villages*) and for collecting local antique farm tools and oral histories, opening the Billings Farm and Museum in 1983. In 1992 the Marsh-Billings-Rockefeller National Historical Park was created. It opened in 1998.

Courtesy Billings Family Archives

GEORGE PERKINS MARSH BY G. P. A. HEALY, C. 1820

Kim Grant

THE ROCKEFELLER MANSION AT MARSH-BILLINGS-ROCKEFELLER NATIONAL HISTORIC PARK

By the early 1960s, however, the beloved Woodstock Inn was creaky, the town's ski areas had been upstaged, and the hills were sprouting condos. Laurance Rockefeller acquired the two aki areas (upgrading Suicide Six and closing Mount Tom) and had the 18-hole golf course redesigned by Robert Trent Jones Sr. In 1969 he replaced the old inn. Rockefeller also created the Woodstock Foundation, a nonprofit umbrella for such village projects as acquiring and restoring dozens of historic homes, burying power lines, and building a new covered bridge by the green. In 1992 it opened the Billings Farm and Museum. The Marsh-Billings-Rockefeller National Historical Park, which includesg the neighboring Rockefeller mansion and surrounding 550 forested acres on Mount Tom, opened in 1998.

Woodstock itself remains a real town with a lot going on. Events chalked on the "Town Crier" blackboard at the corner of Elm and Central Streets are likely to include a supper at one of the town's several churches (four boast Paul Revere bells), the current film at the theater in town hall, as well as events at the Historical Society and guided walks or talks at the Vermont Institute of Natural Science (VINS).

THE JERSEYS ARE FRIENDLY AT THE BILLINGS FARM & MUSEUM

Note: The Woodstock Historical Society has published detailed pamphlets and guides available at Dana House (see *Also See*). For a brief history of the town, see Peter Jennison's informative and nominally priced *Woodstock's Heritage.* There is also a **Woodstock Walking Tour,** kdann@zoo.uvm.edu, summer through foliage season, Friday through Monday, 10 AM and 2 PM and by appointment; $6 for adults, $3 for children. Kevin Dann is a fount of local history and lore.

Quechee, on Route 4, some 6 miles east of Woodstock, is one of five villages in the township of Hartford. In the mid– and late 19th century life revolved around the J. C. Parker and Co. mill, which produced a soft baby flannel made from "shoddy" (reworked rags). A neighboring mill village surrounded the Dewey Mill, which made baseball uniforms for the Boston Red Sox and the New York Yankees. In the 1950s, however, both mills shut down. In the '60s the Dewey Mill virtually disappeared beneath a flood-control project (see North Hartland Lake under *Green Space*) and 6,000 acres straddling both villages was acquired by the Quechee Lakes Corporation, the largest second-home and condominium development in the state. Thanks in good part to Act 250, Vermont's land-use statute, the end result is unobtrusive. Most homes are sequestered in woods; open space includes two (private) 18-hole golf courses. In Quechee Village the mill is now Simon Pearce's famous glass factory and restaurant, and the former mill owner's mansion is the Parker House Inn (see *Lodging—Inns*). Dramatic Quechee Gorge (see *Green Space*) is visible from Route 4 but is best appreciated if you follow the trail to the bottom. Tourist-geared shops and eateries continue to proliferate along Route 4, but, along back roads, so does village conservation land.

✷ Must See

Note: Listings are organized geographically, east to west.

Quechee Gorge, Route 4, is one of Vermont's natural wonders, a 3,000-foot-long, 163-foot-deep chasm sculpted 13,000 years ago. Visible from the highway, it is now encompassed by a state park that includes hiking trails along the rim and down into the gorge. See *Green Space.*

Visitors Center for Billings Farm & Museum and the Marsh-Billings-Rockefeller National Historical Park, Route 12 north of Woodstock Village. Open late May through October daily 10–5. The parking lot and visitors center at Billings Farm serves both the farm and national park with displays on Marsh, Billings, and Rockefeller and a theater showing *A Place in the Land,* Charles Guggenheim's award-winning documentary dramatizing the story of all three men. Rest rooms and a gift shop.

🖋 **Billings Farm & Museum** (802-457-2355; www.billingsfarm.org). Admission: $8 adult, $7 over 65, $6 ages 13–17, $4 ages 5–12, $1 ages 3–4. Open daily May through October and for special events throughout the year. Exhibits demonstrate life on Frederick Billings's model "gentleman's" farm in the 1890s: plowing, seeding, cultivating, harvesting, and storing crops; making cheese and butter; woodcutting and sugaring. The 1890 farm manager's house has been restored. Visitors can also observe what happens on a modern dairy farm with a prize winning Jersey herd. There are also sheep and two friendly 2,000-pound workhorses, Ruth and Kate. The cows are milked daily at 3 PM. Inquire about special events, like apple days and wool days in fall; Thanksgiving weekend and Christmas weekend celebrations; sleigh rally in mid-February; and periodic demonstrations and crafts exhibits, including quilts in mid-August.

Marsh-Billings-Rockefeller National Historical Park (802-457-3368;

www.nps.gov/mabi), Route 12 north of Woodstock Village. Mount Tom carriage roads and forest trails (see *Green Space*) are open year-round. Mansion tours are offered late May through October and are limited to a dozen visitors at a time (advance reservations are advised: $4 adult, $2 seniors). The **Carriage Barn** (late May through October, 10–5; free), an elegant space with dark beadboard walls and the feel of a library, features an exhibit: *Celebrating Stewardship—People Taking Care of Places.* It positions Marsh, Billings, and Rockefeller within the timeline of America's conservation history. Multimedia displays profile individuals practicing conservation around the world. Visitors are invited to record their own conservation stories on computers. More unusual still for a national park is the reading area with its conference-sized table (crafted from wood harvested on Mount Tom) with relevant books, including children's stories. The Queen Anne mansion is well worth visiting. Notable 19th-century furniture, Tiffany glass porcelains, and American art aside, it offers a sense of the amazing individuals who lived there. The guided, interpretive tour—about an hour—begins in the former carriage house.

✷ Also See

The Dana House (home of the Woodstock Historical Society, 802-457-1822), Elm Street, Woodstock. Open 10–5, May through October and certain winter weekends. Nominal admission; 40-minute tours on the hour. John Cotton Dana was an eminent, early-20th-century librarian and museum director whose innovations made books and art more accessible to the public. Completed in 1807 and occupied for the next 140 years by the Dana family, this historic house has an interesting permanent exhibit portraying the town's economic heritage and an admirable collection of antiques, locally wrought coin silver, portraits, porcelains, fabrics, costumes, and toys. The John Cotton Dana Library is a research and reference center.

The Vermont Institute of Natural Science/Vermont Raptor Center (802-457-2779; www.vinsweb.org), 1.5 miles southwest of the village of Woodstock at 27023 Church Hill Road. Open year-round, Monday through Saturday 10–4; $7 per adult, $4 students 12–18, $3 children 5–11, $1 children 3–4. A beloved institution, VINS styles itself a living museum and clinic devoted to birds of prey. Resident raptors include bald eagles, peregrine falcons, snowy owls, and more than 20 other species. The 78-acre property offers extensive hiking trails. Exhibits of flora and fanua include a rare herbarium collection. VINS also houses the distinguished Pettingill Ornithological Library and a gift shop. Inquire about frequent lectures, bird-fern-and-wildflower walks, and about the daily (June through October) raptor-in-flight demonstration.

✐ **The Norman Williams Public Library** (802-457-2295), on the Woodstock green. Open daily except Sunday and holidays. A recently renovated Romanesque gem, donated and endowed in 1883 by Dr. Edward H. Williams, general manager of the Pennsylvania Railroad and later head of Baldwin Locomotives. It offers children's story hours, poetry readings, and brown-bag summer concerts on the lawn.

COVERED BRIDGES There are three in the town of Woodstock—the **Lincoln Bridge** (1865), Route 4, West Woodstock, Vermont's only Pratt-type truss; the

Middle Bridge, in the center of the village, built in 1969 by Milton Graton, "last of the covered-bridge builders," in the Town lattice style (partially destroyed by vandalism and rebuilt); and the notable red **Taftsville Bridge** (1836), Route 4 east, utilizing multiple king- and queenposts and an unusual mongrel truss. The Taftsville Bridge overlooks a hydroelectric dam, still in use.

SCENIC DRIVES The whole area offers delightful vistas; one of the most scenic shortcuts is the North Road, which leaves Route 12 next to Silver Lake in Barnard and leads to Bethel. Another is Cloudland Road from River Road, and River Road itself, from Quechee to Woodstock.

✷ To Do

BALLOONING **Balloons Over New England** (800-788-5562; www.balloonsovernewengland.com) and **Killington Balloon Adventures** (802-291-4887), both based in Quechee, offer flights above the valley. The **Quechee Balloon Festival** on Father's Day weekend in June is New England's premier balloon festival, featuring rides as well as live entertainment and crafts (see *Special Events*).

BICYCLING **Bike Vermont** (802-457-3553; 1-800-257-2226; www.BikeVt.com), Box 207, Woodstock. Vermont's most experienced, most personalized, and altogether best inn-to-inn tours, offers weekend, 5-, and 7-day trips through much of Vermont. Twenty-one-speed Trek and Cannondale hybrids are available for rent. Tours are also offered to Ireland.

Cyclery Plus (802-457-3377), Route 4 in West Woodstock. Randy Koetsier has rentals and local bike maps (a marked bike path leads east from the village into Woodstock; (River Road to Quechee Village is a designated bike trail).

Wilderness Trails (802-295-7620), Clubhouse Road at the Quechee Inn. Complete outdoor equipment rental for the whole family and maps

Woodstock Sports (802-457-1568), 30 Central Street, Woodstock, has bike rentals.

BOATING **Wilderness Trails** (802-295-7620), Clubhouse Road at the Quechee Inn, offers guided canoe and kayak trips, also rentals and shuttle sevice on the Connecticut, White, and Ottauquechee Rivers, also in the Dewey Mills Waterfowl Sanctuary. Inquire about island camping.

Silver Lake State Park (802-234-9451) in Barnard rents rowboats (see *Green Space*).

FISHING **Vermont Fly Fishing School** (802-295-7620), the Quechee Inn at Marshland Farm. Marty Banik offers lessons as well as providing tackle and guided fishing on Dewey's Pond, and the Connecticut, White, and Ottauquechee Rivers.

GOLF AND TENNIS **Woodstock Country Club** (802-457-2114), part of the Woodstock Inn and Resort (see *Resorts*), offers one of Vermont's oldest and most

Woodstock Inn and Resort

CROSS-COUNTRY SKIERS AT THE WOODSTOCK SKI TOURING CENTER

prestigious 18-hole golf courses, designed by Robert Trent Jones. There are also 10 tennis and two paddle tennis courts. Facilites include a pro shop, putting green and practice range, lessons, electric carts, a restaurant and lounge.

Vail Field, Woodstock. Two public tennis courts and a children's playground.

Quechee Gorge Mini Golf (802-296-6669), Route 4, next to Quechee Gorge, 18 holes.

HEALTH SPA **Woodstock Health & Fitness Center** (802-457-6656), part of the Woodstock Inn and Resort, Route 106, recently renovated with indoor tennis and racquetball, lap pool, whirlpool, aerobic and state-of-the-art fitness equipment; flexible memberships and day-use options; pro shop.

HORSEBACK RIDING Woodstock has been an equestrian center for generations, especially for the hardy Morgans, which are making a local comeback in South Woodstock.

Kedron Valley Stables (802-457-1480), Route 106, South Woodstock. Generally recognized as one of the best places to ride horseback—if you know how but don't happen to own a horse—in New England. Learn to ride or spiff up your skills in the ring, take a guided trail ride ($35), a weekend vacation, a 6-day riding clinic (with accommodations at Kendall Homestead; see *Lodging—Other Lodging*) or a 4-day inn-to-inn tour that averages 20 miles a day, 5 hours in the saddle. Over the years, Paul and Barbara Kendall have pieced together a network of paths to link appealing inns. They lead riders over hiking and recreation trails, dirt roads, and meadows. Inquire about carriage, wagon, and sleigh rides.

The Green Mountain Horse Association (802-457-1509), Route 106, South Woodstock. Sponsor of the original 100-mile ride, an annual event around Labor Day that draws entrants from all over; shows, trials, and other popular events.

LLAMA TREKKING **Woodstock Llama Trekking** (802-457-3722; 802-457-5117; www.woodsstockllamatrek.com), The Red Cupboard, Route 4, West Woodstock. The nine male llamas are penned on Route 4, but Brian Powell leads patrons on trails up through the woods to a scenic picnic spot.

ROCK CLIMBING ✐ **The Wall** (802-457-2221; www.vermontrocks.com), just east of the intersection of Routes 4 and 12, Quechee. Call for hours and rates. This new indoor rock climbing gym and bouldering cave draws serious local climbers year-round. Equipment rentals and instruction for adults and children; birthday parties a specialty. Also includes an outdoor driving range.

POLO **Quechee Polo Club.** Matches most Saturday afternoons in July and August on the field near the center of the village.

SWIMMING **Silver Lake State Park** (802-234-9451; 802-773-2657), 10 miles north on Route 12 in Barnard, has a nice beach, and there's another smaller one right next to the general store.

✐ **The Woodstock Recreation Center** (802-457-1502), 54 River Street, has two public pools, mostly for youngsters.

✷ Winter Sports

CROSS-COUNTRY SKIING The trail system on **Mount Tom** ranks with some of the best groomed in New England. It's composed largely of 1880s carriage roads climbing gently from the valley floor (700 feet) to the summit (1,250 feet), skirting a small lake, and finally commanding a view of the village below and down the Ottauquechee Valley. The system offers vistas in many directions and a log cabin heated with a woodstove. Buy tickets and pick up a map at the **Ski Touring Center** (802-457-6674). Located at the Woodstock Country Club, Route 106 south of the village, part of the Woodstock Inn and Resort, the center has mapped, marked, and groomed 60 km of varied trails, from gentle terrain to forest- and uplands, including Mount Tom and Mount Peg. Group and individual lessons; guided, 4-hour picnic tours; rentals; salesroom; lockers; bar-restaurant; $12.50 per adult, $8.25 junior.

Wilderness Trails (802-295-7620), Clubhouse Road at the Quechee Inn, has 18 km of track-set trails, including easy loops through the woods and meadows around Quechee Gorge, offering fine views of its waterfalls, also harder trails down into the gorge. Snowshoe rentals are also offered.

DOWNHILL SKIING ✐ **Suicide Six Downhill Ski Area** (802-457-6661), South Pomfret, 5 miles north of Woodstock on Pomfret Road. Heir—on the other side of the hill—to the first ski tow in the United States, which was cranked up in 1934. Once operated by Bunny Bertram, now in the Ski Hall of Fame, Suicide Six is now part of the Woodstock Inn and Resort complex and has a base lodge finished with native woodwork. Its beginners area has a J-bar ($6 for all day); two double chairlifts climb 655 vertical feet to reach 22 trails ranging from easy to The Show Off and Pomfret Plunge, plus a half-pipe for snowboarders. Lessons, rentals, restaurant. Weekend/holiday lift rates are $44 for adults and $28 for seniors and children; weekdays (with just the big chair running) it's $25 adult, $20 seniors and children.

✐ **Quechee Club Ski Area** (802-295-9356), Quechee, is open weekends and during school vacations. It "feels like a neighborhood playground devoted to introducing kids to the delights of winter," a *New York Times* writer declared. "Kids ages 4 and up can enroll in group lessons and older children roam the hill's eight trails on their own." Lift tickets: $24 adult, $20 junior for a full day, $18 and $14 for a half day (Sunday morning is $17); free for ages 6 and under. Less for 2- and 3-day passes. Inquire about 2 hours of afternoon skiing.

ICE SKATING **Silver Lake,** by the general store in Barnard. **Vail Field,** Woodstock, is maintained by the local

THE WOODSTOCK INN ON A WINTER'S NIGHT

Woodstock Inn and Resort

hockey and skating committee and is lighted for night skating. Free. **Woodstock Sports** (802-457-1568), 30 Central Street, Woodstock, offers skate and ski rentals. **Wilderness Trails** (see *Cross-Country Skiing*) in Quechee also rents skates and clears the pond on its property and across the road.

✷ Green Space

Mount Tom's 1,250-foot summit towers above the village of Woodstock. It's one of Vermont's most walked and walkable mountains. From Mountain Avenue in the village itself **Faulkner Park** (donated by Mrs. Edward Faulkner, one of Woodstock's most thoughtful philanthropists) features a trail patterned on Baden-Baden's "cardiac" walks. A marked, 1.6-mile path zigzags up to the summit (bring a picnic; a bench overlooks the village). The **Marsh-Billings-Rockefeller National Historical Park** encompasses more than 500 acres on the back side of Mount Tom, with 30 miles of footpaths that were originally carriage roads, including a trail and picnic tables at Pogue Pond. Enter on Route 12 at the park (follow signs) or at the trailhead on Prosper Road, just off Route 12. Inquire about frequent seasonal programs offered by the national park (802-457-3368). Also see *Cross-Country Skiing* for winter use.

Mount Peg Trails begin behind the Woodstock Health & Fitness Center on Route 106 (ask directions at the desk). Open May through October. One is roughly 5 miles round trip, a peaceful walk up along easy switchbacks beneath pines with picnic bench at the summit, with views west down the valley to Killington.

Eshqua Bog, off Hartland Hill Road, Woodstock. A 40-acre sanctuary managed by the New England Wild Flower Society and The Nature Conservancy with a white-blazed loop trail circling through 8 acres of wetlands, with orchids blooming in summer. Ask directions locally.

Quechee Gorge State Park (802-295-2990; January through May: 1-800-299-3071), off Route 4, Quechee. This 611-acre preserve encompasses the gorge (see *Green Space*), and trails along its rim lead down (south of Route 4) into the gorge, which should be approached carefully. At the north end of the gorge, under a spillway, is a fine, rockbound swimming hole, accessible by easy stages through the pine woods at the west end of the bridge. Look for picnic tables under the pines on Dewey Mills Road. The campground (open mid-May through October 15) offers 47 tent/trailer sites, seven lean-tos, and a dump station.

North Hartland Lake Recreation Area (802-295-2855) is a 1,711-acre acre preserve created by U.S. Army Corps of Engineers to control the confluence of the Ottaquechee and Connecticut Rivers. It offers a sandy beach, wooded picnic area with grills, and a nature trail. Access is poorly marked, so ask directions at the Quechee information booth (see *Guidance*).

Silver Lake State Park (802-234-9451; January through May, 1-800-299-3071), Route 12, Barnard. Open mid-May through October 15. On Silver Lake, good for fishing, swimming, and boating (rentals available). The park offers a snack bar and wooded campground with 40 tent/trailer sites and seven lean-tos. Hot showers.

Dewey Pond Wildlife Sanctuary, Dewey Mills Road, Quechee. Originally a millpond, this is a beautiful spot with nature trails and a boat launch, good for bird-watching and fishing.

Hurricane Forest, Route 5, White River Junction. This 500-acre town forest harbors a pond and many miles of trails. Ask directions at the Quechee information booth (see *Guidance*).

Also see Vermont Institute of Natural Science under *To See*.

✷ Lodging

RESORTS ✐ **The Woodstock Inn and Resort** (802-457-1100; 1-800-448-7900; www.woodstockinn.com), on the green, 05091, is the lineal descendant of the 18th-century Eagle Tavern and the famous "old" Woodstock Inn that flourished between 1893 and 1969, putting the town on the year-round resort map. Today's grand, 146-room, air-conditioned, Colonial-style edition, owned by Laurance S. Rockefeller, reflects the owner's meticulous standards. It was extensively remodeled in 1989–91 with the addition of a townhouse wing, the luxurious Richardson's Tavern, and expansion of the dining and meeting rooms. The comfortably furnished main lobby is dominated by a huge stone fireplace where 5-foot birch logs blaze in winter. There's a spiffy main dining room, plus coffee shop, library, gift shop, conference facilities, putting green, and swimming pool. Guests have access to the scenic 18-hole Woodstock Country Club for golf and tennis (it's a fine cross-country-ski center in winter) and to a splendid indoor Sports Center, plus downhill skiing at the historic Suicide Six area and wagon and sleigh rides. (See *To Do—Golf, Health Spa,* also *Winter Sports.*)

The creature comforts of these pearly precincts, beautifully appointed and run in most respects, make this Vermont's premier place to stay and play. Current regular-season rates are $179–339 ($119–234 in spring and November "Value Seasons"); spacious porch and/or fireplace suites in the new Tavern Wing are $365–539; and there is a separate cottage, the Justin Morgan House, which has a full kitchen. Children under 14 free when staying in the same room with an adult. MAP available at $63 per person per day. Check out ski and golf packages.

Twin Farms (802-234-9999; 1-800-894-6327; fax: 802-234-9990; www.twinfarms.com), Barnard 05031. Ironically, the shades of Sinclair Lewis, whose novels satirized the materialism of American life in the '20s, and Dorothy Thompson, the acerbic foreign correspondent, hover over this 300-acre, luxurious Shangri-la that used to be their country home. Here and now, an exclusive group of corporate CEOs, heads of government, royalty, and celebrities are welcome to unwind, frolic, and be rich together in sybaritic privacy. Of the four stylish rooms in the main house, Red's is only $900 a day; Dorothy's, $1,050. New cottages have been added since the place opened in 1993 and range from $900 to $2,500, all including Lucullan meals at any hour, open bars, and the use of all recreational amenities, including the former Sonnenberg ski lift, a fully equipped fitness center, Japanese Furo, croquet court, pond, and mountain bikes. The common rooms and guest quarters display an extraordinary collection of modern art, by David Hockney, Frank Stella, and Roy Lichtenstein, among others. Accommodations at Twin Farms are by reservation only. There's a 2-night minimum on weekends, 3 nights over holidays, and full payment is due 30 days before arrival. The entire enclave can be yours for $20,000 a day.

INNS ∞ 🐾 ✐ **The Kedron Valley Inn** (802-457-1473; 1-800-836-1193; www.kedronvalleyinn.com), Route 106, South Woodstock 05071. Since acquiring this venerable miniresort in 1985, Max and Merrily Comins have worked tirelessly, gingering up decor, appointments, and cuisine, without depleting its 19th-century charm. The mellow brick inn has been welcoming visitors since 1828 and served as a stop on the Underground Railroad. The complex now includes the neighboring Tavern Building (built in 1822 as the village store) and a Vermont log motel unit, which sits beside an acre-plus swimming pond with sandy beach. The Kedron Valley Stables (see *To Do—Horseback Riding*) are just up the road. The 28 nicely decorated guest rooms, all with private bath, include 5 suites and several rooms with Jacuzzi and private deck. While rooms vary, all have canopy or antique oak beds and 16 have a fireplace or Franklin stove. Quilts from the family's 60-piece museum-caliber collection decorate guest rooms and the large, low-beamed dining room (see *Dining Out*). Merrily has prepared her own detailed guides to the area (including one for dogs) but guests should allow time just to sit on the expansive columned porch with its rockers and flowers. Room rates are $130–248 double, B&B. Discounts available for May and June and midweek, off-peak periods year-round. The inn can host a reception for up to 200 and organizes weddings, using the village church and a horse-drawn carriage or sleigh.

∞ **The Jackson House Inn** (802-457-2065; 1-800-448-1890; www.jacksonhouse.com), 37 Old Route 4, West Woodstock 05091. This luxuriously appointed and equipped 1890 farmhouse has been expanded to include 15 exceptionally beautiful rooms and an outstanding restaurant (see *Dining Out*). Four acres of manicured grounds, gardens, and a spring-fed swim pond add to its appeal. Rates range from $195 for the Josephine Bonaparte room on the ground floor, furnished in the French Empire style, to $340 for one of the four new minisuites, three of which have a thermal massage tub for two. One minisuite, the Christine Jackson on the first floor, has a Brazilian mahogany four-poster queen bed, a gas fireplace, and French doors to the brick patio and garden. Rates include a memorable breakfast and a predinner glass of wine and hors d'oeuvres. Your hosts are Carl and Linda Delnegro.

∞ ✐ **The Quechee Inn at Marshland Farm** (802-295-3133; 1-800-235-3133; www.quecheeinn.com), Quechee Main Street, Quechee 05059, is an attractive, rather formal, restored and enlarged 18th-century farmhouse, once the home of Vermont's first lieutenant governor. It's near the Ottauquechee River and its dramatic gorge. The sitting room and 24 guest rooms (including 2 suites) have been newly redecorated, and the dining room is above average. Guests have access to the nearby Quechee Club for golf, downhill skiing, and swimming. The inn maintains its own 18 km of groomed cross-country-ski trails, bike and canoe rentals, and a fishing school (see also Wilderness Trails under *To Do—Bicycling, Fishing,* and *Winter Sports—Cross-Country Skiing*). Rates range from $170 to $240 in high seasons, $90–130 in low.

Parker House Inn (802-295-6077; www.theparkerhouseinn.com), 1792 Main Street, Quechee 05059. An imposing redbrick mansion built in 1857 by Vermont Sen. Joseph Parker beside his flannel mill on the Ottauquchee River, this inn is best known for food (see *Dining Out*) but it's also a comfortable and surprisingly informal place to stay. Chefs Walt and Barbara Forrester are warm hosts. The downstairs parlors are now dining rooms, but there is a small second-floor sitting room with a TV, a sunny downstairs reading nook, a breakfast room, and a riverside porch. The seven guest rooms all have private bath. Four on the second floor are high-ceilinged and antiques furnished, while three on the third are less formal. Ours had a pull-out couch and was plenty large enough for a family. $115–150 includes a full breakfast.

The Lincoln Inn (802-457-3312), Route 4, West Woodstock 05091. This 200-year-old, pleasantly renovated farmhouse on the river—next to the covered bridge—has six cheery guest rooms with bath, hand-hewn beams in the library, and a fine dining room in the hands of its Swiss chef-owner. Breakfast and tax are included in the $125 rate, which is higher in foliage season.

THE TAFTSVILLE GENERAL STORE

Kim Grant

BED & BREAKFASTS

In Woodstock 05091

The Charleston House (802-457-3843; www.charlestonhouse.com), 21 Pleasant Street. This luxurious, recently expanded Federal brick town house (vintage 1835) in the middle of the village is especially appealing, with period furniture in eight bedrooms, all with private bath and air-conditioning, several with fireplaces and Jacuzzi. Rates are $110–225 and include full breakfast in the dining room or continental breakfast bedside. Your genial hosts are Willa and Dixi Nohl (Dixi for many years managed Burke Mount ski area in the Northeast Kingdom).

Three Church Street (802-457-1925). In one of the grander Federal houses near the green, Eleanor Paine holds hospitable court, serving bountiful breakfasts. There are spacious sitting rooms and 11 guest rooms, 6 with private bath ($85–125 B&B), plus swimming pool and tennis court. Solo travelers feel comfortable here, and pets are permitted. This is also a great house to rent in its entirely for a wedding.

Canterbury House (802-457-3077; 1-800-390-3077), 43 Pleasant Street. Bob and Sue Frost's village Victorian has eight rooms with private bath (our favorites are the original second-floor bedrooms in the front) and air-conditioning. Guests meet around the hearth in the large, gracious living room. From $100 for a back room overlooking the parking lot to $165 for the Monk's Tale, which has a fireplace and cable TV. Full breakfast.

Ardmore Inn (802-457-3887; 1-800-497-9652), 23 Pleasant Street. A meticulously restored Victorian town house with classy Irish overtones and five spacious rooms, each with private marble bath. The Sheridan Room on the ground floor includes an extra-large bathroom with a walk-in shower and Jacuzzi. Guests use the elegant parlor, dining room, and screened veranda. $85–150 includes breakfast and afternoon tea.

The 1830 Shire Town Inn (802-457-1830; www.1830shiretowninn.com), 31 South Street. Directly across from the Woodstock Inn, one block south of the green, Arlene Gibson's 1830 home has three comfortable rooms with private bath. Our favorite is the downstairs, very private Woodstock Room, set into the rocks with a leafy view. The common rooms feature wide-pine floors, hand-hewn beams, a fireplace, and good art. $85–125 includes a hearty country breakfast.

Barr House (802-457-3334), 55 South Street. Kay Paul, a sixth-generation Vermonter and the retired Woodstock Inn bartender, and Jim, the former fire chief, offer two charming rooms (request the one with a skylight) with shared bath in a trim saltbox across from the Woodstock Inn's golf course/cross-country-ski center. Solo travelers feel welcome. $60 single, $70–80 double including a full breakfast.

Woodstock House (802-457-1758), Route 106, 3 miles south of the village. Mary Fraser offers her guests five rooms (three with private bath, two shared) in her comfortable, early-19th-century farmhouse with exposed beams and wide-board floors. Children welcome. $85–95 with a full breakfast.

The Woodstocker (802-457-3896; 1-800-457-3896), 61 River Street (corner of Route 4). The arrangement of rooms in this rambling wooden addition to a classic 1830s Cape is explained by its former life as an apartment house. Tom and Nancy Blackford offer two suites with living room, kitchen, and deck (great for families) and seven more spacious rooms with private bath, most with air-conditioning. $85–175 double with big buffet breakfast.

The Village Inn of Woodstock (802-457-1255; 1-800-722-4571), 41 Pleasant Street, is an informal, purple-painted Victorian manse with fireplaces, oak wainscoting, and pressed-tin ceilings. David and Evelyn Brey offer seven comfortable rooms with private bath. $95–160 with full breakfast.

Winslow House (802-457-1820), 429 Woodstock Road (Route 4), West Woodstock 05091. A mile west of the village, Jeff and Kathy Bedis have fitted their five bright, spacious guest rooms with every possible comfort: bedside lights, cable TV, air-conditioning, individually controlled heat, phone, and refrigerator as well as private bath. Three are suites with sitting rooms. This is a Federal farmhouse with common rooms tastefully furnished in comfortable antiques. It backs on the town playing fields and a path along the Ottauquechee. $95–125 double, more during foliage. Pets are accepted but children only over age 8.

Deer Brook Inn (802-672-3713), 535 Woodstock Road (Route 4), Woodstock 05091. Five miles west of Woodstock and 10 miles east of Killington's Skyeship Gondola, Brian and Rosemary McGinty's restored 1820 farmhouse is set back in fields across the road from the

Ottauquechee River. It has a nice feel and antique charm, light-filled and unfussily but appropriately furnished with antiques. The floors are wide pine; a graceful couch faces the living room hearth, and beds are covered with Rosemary's homemade quilts. Each room has a full bath and climate-controlled heat and air-conditioning. A ground-floor two-room suite with a sitting room is good for families. Our favorite of the four second-floor rooms is number 1, with its skylight above the bed and in the bathroom. $85–140 includes a full breakfast.

Carriage House of Woodstock (802-457-4322; 1-800-791-8045; www.carriagehousewoodstock.com), Route 4, West Woodstock 05091. Debbie Stanglin welcomes guests to this refurbished Victorian farmhouse with a wraparound porch and parlor with fireplace. The nine attractive guest rooms have queen bed and private bath, some with cable TV and whirlpool tub. A full breakfast and afternoon snack are included in $95–185.

In Taftsville 05073

Applebutter Inn (802-457-4158), Happy Valley Road. This is gem of a B&B, a rare melding of an exceptionally beautiful house with taste and warmth. A former Jersey farm, off the main drag, the house is a graceful 1850s Federal, with pillars and gables, which Bev and Andy Cook have deftly extended in back to create a bright, spacious dining area/library. There is also an elegantly comfortable yellow living room with a fireplace and the house is furnished throughout with 18th-century antiques; wide-pine floors show between Oriental rugs. The six guest rooms, named for varieties of apples, all have private bath and vary in size from the Granny Smith Room with skylights, a cannonball double and twin bed, and a sitting area (good for a family) down to the Baldwin Room with a double bed and hall bath. Bev is known for her inimitable, natural-foods breakfasts (just about the best muffins in the area), included in $70–135 rate.

Eben House (802-457-3769), Happy Valley Road. Bob and Betsy McKaig's hearty hospitality animates this comfortable 1845 brick cottage with two guest rooms and baths and thoughtful amenities like a guest fridge; request the Calvin Coolidge Room in the back, near the brook. $105–125 with full breakfast; no children or credit cards, however.

In Quechee 05059

The Pippin Inn (802-296-3646; 1-800-9-PIPPIN; www.pippininn.com), 696 Dewey Mills Road. Just upriver from Quechee Gorge, Mark and Patricia Pippin have renovated the mid-1800s Dewey family mansion. Sited on a tree-lined avenue, featuring picture windows and a pillared double porch, it's an unusual hideaway. At this writing there are three antiques-furnished two-room suites, an exercise room, lounge, and billiard parlor ($155–195). Twelve more rooms are planned for this year.

Herrin House Inn (802-296-7512; 1-800-616-4415; www.herrinhouseinn.com), P.O. Box 312, Quechee-Hartland Road. No one was home when we stopped by to see this new, totally renovated farmhouse but obviously no expense had been, spared to tidy it inside and out, creating four luxurious guest rooms, handsome common space, and an "enchanted cottage." $140–275 depending on room and time. It's sited on 20 acres with a pond for fishing and ice skating.

In Barnard 05031

♿ **Maple Leaf Inn** (802-234-5342; www.mapleleaf.com), P.O. Box 273,

Route 12. Gary and Janet Robison opened up this sparkling new place in a faithfully reproduced turn-of-the-20th-century Victorian farmhouse, designed specifically as a B&B. Stenciling, stitchery, and handmade quilts decorate the seven guest rooms, each with a capacious private bath, king-sized bed, sitting area, telephone, and TV/VCR. Most guest rooms have wood-burning fireplace and whirlpool bath. The parlor, library, and dining room are bright and inviting. Rates are $120–230 with full breakfast. The Country Garden Room on the main floor has easy access for anyone who needs special assistance, and a whirlpool bath.

Inn at Chelsea Farm (802-234-9888; www.innatchelseafarm.com), Route 12. Some places just click the moment you walk in, and for us this classic white Cape, set back from Route 12 and surrounded by its fields, was one of those places. Inside spaces flow from the living room with its fireplace and are filled with quiet light and nicely decorated; the art is original and good. The three guest rooms, each named for a season (there's no "winter"), are also bright and comfortable without being fussy, and fitted with fine linens and down comforters. Host Wendy Fox spent much of her life managing a prestigious small guest house in Bermuda and hospitality comes naturally. Children are welcome; there are pet sheep in the field. Silver Lake State Park and its beach are just up the road. $115–130 per couple includes a full breakfast.

South of South Woodstock

Bailey's Mills Bed & Breakfast (802-484-7809; 1-800-639-3437), RR 1, Box 117, Reading 05062. As happens so often in Vermont, surprises lurk at the end of a back road, especially in the case of this venerable guest house, a few miles west of Route 106. With a two-story porch and fluted columns, Bailey's Mills resembles a southern antebellum mansion. The 17-room brick home includes 11 fireplaces, two beehive ovens, a dance hall, and an 1829 general store, all part of an ambitious manufacturing complex established by Levi Bailey (1766–1850) and operated by his family for a century. Today, Barbara Thaeder offers several comfortable rooms, two with working fireplace, each with a cozy sitting area and private bath, tastefully furnished with antiques. A spacious solarium makes Mom's Room an especially appealing suite. The library with its Rumford fireplace has a large collection of fascinating books and is furnished, as is the dining room, with family antiques and "old stuff." Paths lead off across the meadows into the woods and to the millpond (swimmable). Barbara is an avid conservationist, a member of Green Hotels of Vermont. $90–155 with breakfast; slightly higher in foliage season and over some holidays; and special rates for "Rent the Inn" extended stays and packages. (Ask about the adjacent Spite Cemetery.)

Greystone Bed & Breakfast (802-484-7200), Box 85, Reading 05062, 11 miles south of Woodstock on Route 106. This is an 1830s house, faced with stone quarried from a ledge across the road. Connie Miller offers two bedrooms with private bath (one can can be a family suite) on the second floor and and a suite with a king or twin beds, sitting room, and private bath on the third; $85 for the bedrooms, $100 for two in the suite; lower midweek. Rates include a full breakfast. An enthusiastic rider, Connie is active in the nearby Green Mountain Horse Association.

Kim Grant

THE DINING ROOM AT SIMON PEARCE OVERLOOKS THE OTTAUQUECHEE RIVER

MOTEL 🏵 ✐ **Pond Ridge** (802-457-1667), Route 4, West Woodstock 05091. Set way back from Route 4, 1.5 mile west of Woodstock, and in 6.5 landscaped acres with a picnic/barbecue area bordering the Ottauquechee River (swimming, fishing), this is a real find. Christine and David Coates offer 14 units fitted with two double beds or one queen as well as air-conditioning, cable TV, and coffee machines, also six apartments with full kitchens, great for families. Rooms are $49–99 (more in foliage), and a two-bedroom apartment is $125–135. Children 6 and under are free; a cot is $10.

Also see Farmbrook Motel in "Killington/Plymouth Area."

OTHER LODGING ✐ **Quechee Lakes Resort** offers several hundred rental units, ranging from small condos to six-bedroom houses, all with access to resort facilities, which include the golf courses and clubhouse with its indoor pool and squash courts. Several local Realtors specialize in these rentals, including **Quechee Vacation Rentals** (802-295-3186; 1-800-262-3186), **Quechee Lakes Rentals** (802-295-1970; 1-800-745-0042), **Carefree Quechee** (802-295-9500), and **Quechee Associates** (802-295-9500).

✐ **Kendall Homestead** (802-457-2734), Route 106, South Woodstock 05071. This fine old family house on a knoll close to the Kedron Valley Stables (see *To Do—Horseback Riding*) has three bedrooms and baths, plus sitting rooms and kitchen and laundry facilities. Good spot for families or groups of horse riders; available by the day, weekend, week, or month; inquire for flexible rates.

Note: For camping at the area's two state parks see *Green Space.*

✱ Where to Eat

DINING OUT **The Prince and the Pauper** (802-457-1818; www.princeandpauper.com), 24 Elm Street, Woodstock. Open daily for dinner (reservations advised) except for late-fall and early-spring vacations. Nouvelle and Continental cuisine in a candlelit, elegantly rustic setting. Owner-chef Chris Balcer has, over more than 20 years, created and upheld consistently superior standards. A recent sampling of the $38 prix fixe dinner included, among a choice of seven starters, smoked pheasant ravioli and pan-seared Maine scallops with Madras curry beurre blanc, followed by a salad, then a choice of a half dozen entrées, including Cantonese roast duckling and tournedos of veal with Hudson Valley foie gras and cider reduction. Patrons tend to linger in the premium wine bar, where you can also dine on the bistro menu, featuring the likes of Mom's Meatloaf (a blend of beef, pork, and veal served with garlic mashed potatoes and crispy onion rings), Maine crabcakes, and a choice of hearth-baked pizzas (bistro entrées: $12.95–19.95). One of the state's best; "worth every calorie and dollar," we said in the first edition of this book, and 20 years later we have no reason to change our minds.

The Barnard Inn (802-234-9961), 10 miles north of Woodstock on Route 12, Barnard. Open Tuesday through Sunday from 5, dinner 6–9. Reservations advised. Chef-owners Ruth Schimmelpfenning and Will Dodson operated restaurants in San Francisco before bringing their considerable energy and talent to bear on this elegant 1796 brick house with its nicely appointed formal rooms. Starters ($7–17) might include fried green tomatoes with a herb polenta cake or mussels with a garlic, sun-dried tomato cream sauce; and a half dozen entrée choices ($24–29) might include porcini-dusted Ahi tuna with sweet corn whipped potatoes and a port wine reduction sauce or rack of lamb served with couscous, sun-dried tomatoes, and local vegetables. Desserts ($6.50) include Ruth's Tahitian vanilla bean crème brûlée. In far less formal Max's Tavern patrons can dine on smoked turkey with pesto bangers and mash ($10) or a half of an herb-roasted chicken ($12). A large selection of wines and beers are available by the glass.

Simon Pearce Restaurant (802-295-1470; www.simonpearce.com), The Mill, Quechee. Open for lunch (11:30–2:45) and dinner (reservations advised) 6–9 daily. This is a cheerful, upbeat, contemporary place for consis-

SOUTH WOODSTOCK MEETING HOUSE

tently superior food, served with its own pottery and glass, overlooking the waterfall. The patio is open in summer, and its Irish soda bread and Ballymaloe brown bread alone are worth a visit. Lunch entrées could be spinach and cheddar cheese in puff pastry or beef and Guinness stew; at dinner, main courses might be crisp roast duckling with shiitake ginger sauce or slow-roasted Maine salmon with native corn salad and lobster vinaigrette or wild mushroom fricassee. Dinner entrées $18.50–34.50.

Parker House Inn (802-295-6077; www.theparkerhouseinn.com), 1792 Quechee Main Street, Quechee. Open for dinner daily 5:30–9; reservations please. Innkeepers Barbara (the pastry chef) and Walt Forrester (a Culinary Institute of America graduate) offer simply good American food in the elegant front rooms of their classic brick Victorian mill owner's mansion. In summer tables are set on the outdoor terrace overlooking the Ottauquechee River. Dinner might commence with pan-fried shrimp and catfish cakes with sweet red pepper lemon relish and roasted garlic aioli ($8.95); and entrées might include grilled marinated pork chops with grapes and raisins ($19).

The Woodstock Inn and Resort (802-457-1100; www.woodstockinn.com), on the green, Woodstock. Open for dinner and Sunday brunch. The cheerfully contemporary main dining room, with its alcoves and semicircular bay, is an especially attractive setting for the sumptuous Sunday brunch buffet ($24.95) and executive chef Daniel Jackson's truly superior dinners. You might start with New England lobster and crabcakes with smoked corn and spicy remoulade, or a duet of house-smoked Atlantic salmon, and continue with miso-glazed Chilean sea bass napped with a fresh orange-ginger reduction, or roasted rack of lamb with a fava bean cassoulet and cracked peppercorn lamb jus. Entrées $24–30. Lighter fare and breakfast and lunch are served in the less expensive Eagle Café.

The Jackson House Restaurant (802-457-2065), Route 4 west, Woodstock. Open Wednesday through Monday. This latest entrant in the area's world of fine dining offers sophisticated cuisine in surroundings of understated (but sometimes noisy) simplicity. Chef Andrew Turner offers a $55 prix fixe menu that could begin with ravioli or sweetbreads with leek puree, free-range chicken with truffle essence, followed by sesame-crusted monkfish and lobster with lemongrass soy broth, or grilled venison medallions with chestnut spaetzle and red cabbage, topped off with a chocolate velvet mousse torte with raspberry ice cream. Vegetarian and vegan menus are are also offered.

The Kedron Valley Inn (802-457-1473; www.kedronvalleyinn), Route 106, 5 miles south of Woodstock. Chef Jim Allen has won applause for stylish "nouvelle Vermont" cuisine. Open for dinner (reservations suggested). This is one of Vermont's oldest inns, and the large, low-beamed dining room is country elegant. Appetizers might include prosciutto-wrapped grilled portobello mushrooms, marinated, grilled, and sliced ($7.50). A wide choice of entrées range from raviolis stuffed with an array of vegetables and cheeses to oven-roasted rack of lamb seared with sesame oil, ginger, and garlic. All entrées ($18–26) come with salad and breads. A lighter menu is available in the tavern, and children's drinks and "cocktails" are served. The award-winning wine list is a point of pride.

Wild Grass (802-457-1917), Gallery Place, Route 4, Woodstock. Open daily for dinner, featuring an appealing "intercontinental" menu that includes crispy sage leaves with dipping sauces or grilled marinated shrimp with avocado, tomato, and red onion as starters and a wide choice of entrées, from stir-fried tempeh to grilled Jamaican jerk pork loin. Entrées $14.25–17.50.

The Meadows at the Quechee Inn at Marshland Farm (802-295-3133; www.quecheeinn.com), Clubhouse Road, Quechee. Open nightly, this romantically rustic dining room's dinner menu might include entrées ($18.50–22.50) such as horseradish-crusted Atlantic salmon and pancetta-wrapped Angus tenderloin, as well as a "supper menu" with lighter entrées ranging from French onion soup with salad to grilled flatiron steak ($10–16).

The Lincoln Inn (802-457-3312), Route 4, West Woodstock. Open Friday through Monday. Chef-owner Kirt Hildgrand is Swiss trained and worked in top hotels in London, Bermuda, and New York before orchestrating this attractive fireside dining room. Popular selections include shrimp amoureuse, with a Pernod-scented dill sauce served in a heart-shaped pastry shell; pan-seared red snapper; and sautéed veal medallions with melted Brie. Entrées $15–25.

See also Skunk Hollow Tavern under *Dining Out* in "Upper Valley River Towns" and The Corners Inn in "Killington/Plymouth Area."

EATING OUT **Bentley's Restaurant** (802-457-3232), Elm Street, Woodstock, an oasis of Victoriana and plants, is open daily for lunch and dinner, featuring everything from brawny hamburgers and croissant sandwiches to veal Marsala and Jack Daniels steak. Frequent live entertainment, disco dancing weekends.

Pane e Salute Italian Bakery (802-457-4882), 61 Central Street, Woodstock. Open for lunch 12–2:30, for Sunday brunch 10–2, and Friday and Saturday for dinner (reservations recommended). This small café/bakery has acquired a passionate following in a short time. Classic peasant soups (mostly vegetarian), panini (premade bar sandwiches), and a wide choice of pastas, salads, and daily specials are offered at lunch. Sunday brunch plates include baked omelet with zucchini, tomato, and Parmigiano, and rosemary-roasted chicken. The dinner menu includes a pasta course ($12) as well as entrées ($16). Beer and wine, and of course espresso, cappuccino, and café latte, are served. Breads are also sold.

Spooner's (802-457-4022), Route 4 east (in the Sunset Farm Barn), Woodstock. Open daily for dinner from 5:30. A natty, informal, relatively inexpensive family restaurant specializing in beef and seafood, also a salad bar. Families are welcome; children's menu.

Mountain Creamery (802-457-1715), Central Street, Woodstock, serves breakfast daily 7–11:30, lunch until 3, pastry and espresso until 6. This is the local meeting place: a bright, friendly, comfortable eatery good for freshly made soups, sandwiches, salads, daily specials, and their own handmade ice cream as well as apple pie. Pies and cakes are also for sale.

FireStones (802-295-1600), Route 4, Waterman Place, Quechee. Open daily for lunch and dinner and Sunday brunch.

Bill Decklebaum and David Creech, proprietors of Bentley's (see above), also operate this rustic, lodgelike restaurant, with a big wood-fired oven as centerpiece, featuring made-to-order flatbreads, fire-roasted shrimp marinated in Long Trail Ale, fire-roasted chicken, and steaks. Children's menu; outdoor deck.

Umpleby's, "makers of fine baked goods" (802-672-1300), The Mill, Route 4, Bridgewater. Open 7:30–5:30; closed Monday. Charles Umpleby specializes in breads (try the crazy wheat) but also bakes genuine European-style croissants and raspberry brioche for breakfast, delectable leek and onion tarts, sausage rolls, and individual quiches to go with homemade soups, served up by wife Carolyn.

Farina Family Diner and Restaurant (802-295-8955), Quechee Gorge Village. Open year-round from 7 AM for all three meals; closed Tuesday. A genuine 1946 Worcester Diner #787 that stood in Holyoke, (Massachusetts), was moved here in 1991 and expanded to include a rear dining room. Booths up front, tables in the back, fresh-brewed coffee and an all-American menu. Children's menu.

Ott Dog Snack Bar (802-295-1088), Route 4, Quechee Gorge. Open mid-May to mid-October. Family owned with the motto "Not fast food. Good food fast." Fresh soups and five different kinds of hot dogs are the specialties.

The Wasp Diner, Pleasant Street, Woodstock. Join Woodstock's hardworking fraternity for breakfast or lunch at the counter.

PICNICS On a beautiful summer or fall day the best place to lunch is outside. In Woodstock itself there's Teagle's Landing, right on Central Street by the river, and Faulkner Park on Monument Avenue. See *Green Space* for other ideas.

The Village Butcher (802-457-2756), 18 Elm Street, Woodstock, provides tasty deli specials to go, along with its top-flight meats, wines, and baked goods, plus homemade fudge.

Woodstock Farmers' Market (802-457-3658) has a thoughtful deli case, plus soups and sandwiches, fresh fish, free-range chicken, meals to go, Baba à Louis bread, and cookies.

✷ Entertainment

Pentangle Council on the Arts (802-457-3981; www.PentangleArts.org), Town Hall Theater, 31 The Green, Woodstock. First-run films are shown Friday through Monday evenings at 7:30 in the Town Hall Theater. Live presentations at town hall and at the Woodstock Union High School include a variety of musical and other live entertainment. Check the Town Crier blackboard at the corner of Elm and Central Streets for current happenings.

✷ Selective Shopping

ANTIQUES SHOPS The Woodstock area is mecca for antiques buffs. There are two big group galleries: **Quechee Gorge Village Antique Mall** (802-295-1550), Route 4, east of Quechee Gorge, open daily, is one of new England's largest antiques collectives with some 450 dealers represented. The **Antiques Collaborative** (802-296-5858), Waterman Place, Route 4 at the blinking light in Quechee, is also open daily and shows representative stock from some 150 upscale dealers: period furniture usually in good condition, silver, Oriental rugs, and more.

Among more the more than dozen individual dealers: **Wigren & Barlow** (802-457-2453), 29 Pleasant Street, is Woodstock's most elegant antiques shop, with a large selection of fine country and formal furniture, decorative accessories, and garden appointments (open daily April through November; by chance in winter); **Church Street Antiques** (802-457-2628), west of the green in Woodstock, has a wide variety: furniture (usually includes antique high chairs), mirrors, Quimper and Majolica ware (open Wednesday through Saturday 10–5, Sunday 1–5); at **American Classics** (802-457-4337), 71 Central Street, Woodstock, carefully selected, upscale folk art and antiques fill several second-floor rooms (open daily 10–5:30); **Pleasant Street Books** (802-457-4050), 48 Pleasant Street, Woodstock, carries 10,000 selected titles in all fields (open daily 11–5 in summer and fall; by appointment off-season); **Fraser's Antiques** (802-457-3437), Happy Valley Road, just off Route 4 in Taftsville, has a good stock of early American furniture and accessories; **Who Is Sylvia?** (802-457-1110), 26 Central Street, in the old village firehouse, houses two floors of great vintage clothing and accessories for men as well as women; **Mill Brook Antiques** (802-484-5942), Route 106, Reading (11 miles south of Woodstock), has a shop and barn full of early American furniture, primitives, stoneware, china, quilts, and more (open year-round but call ahead).

ART GALLERIES Galleries come and go in Woodstock. At present they include: **Woodstock Folk Art** (802-457-2012), 8 Elm Street, Woodstock, specializes in contemporary carvings, prints, and antiquities. **Stephen Huneck Studio** (802-457-3206), 49 Central Street, Woodstock, offers the celebrated St. Johnsbury woodcarver's fanciful animals of all kinds adorning furniture, wall reliefs, jewelry, and other witty, uncommon pieces. **Gallery on the Green** (802-457-4956), corner of Elm Street, Woodstock, features original art, limited-edition prints, photography, and occasionally sculpture, from New England artists. **Polonaise Art Gallery** (802-457-5180), 15 Central Street, Woodstock, features contemporary and traditional styles in paintings and sculpture. **Robert O. Caulfield Art Gallery** (802-457-1472), 71 Central Street, Woodstock, is the artist's studio; realistic oil and watercolor landscapes and street scenes.

ARTISANS **Charles Shackleton Furniture** and **Miranda Thomas Pottery** (802-672-5175; 1-800-245-9901; www.shackletonthomas.com), The Mill, Route 4, Bridgewater, and at 23 Elm Street, Woodstock. Open daily, 10–5:30 at both places; inquire about mill tours. This couple met at art school in England and again at Simon Pearce Glass. Charles was an apprentice glassblower before he switched to furniture making; Miranda founded the pottery studio there, and the showroom carried both their work. But no longer. They have since acquired the western third of the Bridgewater Mill, and Charles works with more than two dozen fellow crafters to produce exquisite furniture. It's made to order, but models are displayed (along with seconds at the mill), complemented by

Charles Shackelton Furniture/Miranda Thomas Pottery

CHARLES SHACKLETON FURNITURE AND MIRANDA THOMAS POTTERY ARE BASED AT THE MILL AT BRIDGEWATER CORNERS

MILLS

The Bridgewater Mill, also known as "The Old Inn Marketplace" and "The Mill," Route 4, Bridgewater. The core of this vast, yellow wooden mill dates back to the 1820s, when it worked cotton, switching to wool in the 1840s, supplying woolen uniforms and blankets for the troops in several wars. In the 1970s when it closed the building was saved by a local bootstrap effort and became a hive of small shops. It has had its ups and downs since, but current occupants are a rich mix. By far the most famous are **Charles Shackleton Furniture** and **Miranda Thomas Pottery** (see *Artisans*), whose shop and workspace are accessible from the west entrance. **The Bridgewater Country Store** (802-672-3332) showcases some 20 vendors, ranging from local maple producers and Vermont Flannel to a large selection of country furniture that's new but been"distressed" by an Amish group in Jamesport, Missouri. The store also includes many antiques, mostly large pieces, upstairs (there's actually an elevator). The Mill's upper floors are partially filled with offices and artists' studios, launching pads for enterprises like **David Crandall's** (802-672-5475), custom-styled 18-karat gold jewelry. Crandall began on the second floor but has since moved to prime first-floor space beside Shackleton/Thomas at the west entrance. The central, oldest part of The Mill is a wonderfully mixed bag. Down in the basement, occupying space that was used not so long ago to incubate the Long Trail Brewery (now housed in a spiffy brewery just up Route 4; see "Killington/Plymouth Area"), is the **Hillbilly Flea Market** (802-672-1094; open Thursday through Sunday, 10–5). Obviously based on the "one man's junk is another man's treasure" theory, its contents ("10 loads of stuff arrive and disappear each week") range from old bottles and car parts to used furniture. On the first floor, beyond the village post office, is the **Sun of the Heart Bookstore** (802-672-5151, open daily 10–6). The mill's oldest tenant, it's a genuinely bright spot at its heart, an independent shop reflecting owner Akanakha Perkins's interest in many New Age subjects. Also well worth checking is **Vermont Ski & Sports** (802-672-3636), an outlet for retail shops by that name in Ludlow and Killington. The aromas of baking, suffusing much of the first floor, emanate from **Umpleby's** (802-672-1300), a small café tucked in a back corner, overlooking the Ottauquechee River (see *Eating Out*).

Simon Pearce Glass (802-295-2711; www.simonpearce.com), The Mill, 1760 Main Street, Quechee. The brick mill by the falls in the Ottauquechee was the 19th-century home of J. C. Parker and Co., producing "shoddy": wool reworked from soft rags. Parker was known for fine baby flannel. It closed for a spell, then served as offices for Quechee Lakes Resort. In 1985 Simon Pearce opened it as a glass factory, harnessing the dam's hydropower for his glass furnace. Pearce had already been making his original glass for a decade in Ireland, and here he quickly established a reputation for his distinctive production pieces: tableware, vases, lamps, candlesticks, etc. Visitors can watch glass being blown and can shop for individual pieces from the retail shop, along with Simon Pearce pottery. The shop (802-295-2711) is open 9–9 daily; pottery throwing can be viewed daily 9–4 and glassblowing 9–5. The Simon Pearce Restaurant (see *Dining Out*), overlooking the falls, is justifiably one of Vermont's most popular. Simon Pearce now also operates a large, visitor-friendly glass and pottery factory in nearby Windsor (see *Selective Shopping* in "Upper Valley River Towns") as well as in Maryland and Pennsylvania. His glass and pottery are sold in over 270 stores throughout the country.

Miranda's distinctive pottery, hand-thrown and carved with traditional designs, such as rabbits, fish, and trees. Her pottery is housed in a former worker's cottage in the mill's parking lot.

Woodstock Clayworks (802-672-5005), Route 4 west (5 miles west of Woodstock, 2 miles east of Bridgewater), open May through October. Barbara Thompson Knutson's work is both whimsical and functional and includes birdbaths, planters and vases, teapots and mugs. The gallery itself is set in a garden, well worth visiting. We treasure her simple clay centerpiece that holds both flowers and candles.

FossilGlass (802-457-4102), 25 South Street, Woodstock. Christina Salusti's distinctive glassware is sold in top shops around the country, but Woodstock is home. This new store showcases the full spectrum of her work and serves as an outlet. Hand-spun plates, bowls, and platters are unusually shaped and frequently partially colored; the surfaces suggest fossil imprints.

Peter Bramhall (802-672-5141), Bridgewater Center. The back-road studio of this unique glassblower may be visited by appointment.

Woodstock Potters (802-457-1298), Mechanic Street, Woodstock, has a studio-workshop for stoneware and hand-painted porcelains, plus gold and silver jewelry.

Also see Simon Pearce under *Mills*.

BOOKSTORES **The Yankee Bookshop** (802-457-2411), Central Street, Woodstock, carries an unusually large stock of hardbound and paperback books for adults and children, plus cards; features the work of local authors and publishers. **Shiretown Books** (802-457-2996), 9 Central Street, Woodstock, is an intimate, very personalized shop that has a carefully selected stock of books for adults and children. Also see Sun of the Heart Bookstore under *Mills*.

SPECIAL SHOPS

In Woodstock Village

F. H. Gillingham & Sons (802-457-2100; 1-800-344-6668), Elm Street, Woodstock, owned and run by the same family since 1886, is something of an institution, retaining a lot of its old-fashioned general-store flavor. You'll find plain and fancy groceries, wine, housewares, and hardware for home, garden, and farm. Mail-order catalog.

✐ **Woodstock Pharmacy** (802-457-1306), Central Street. Open daily 8–6 and Sunday morning until 1. Another Woodstock institution that has branched out well beyond the basics, especially good for stationery and (downstairs) for children's toys and books.

Unicorn (802-457-2480), 15 Central Street, Woodstock, is a treasure trove of unusual gifts, cards, games, toys, and unclassifiable finds.

The Vermont Workshop (802-457-1400), 73 Central Street, Woodstock, features a wide selection of gifts and crafts, furniture, rugs, and lamps.

Arjuna (802-457-3350), 20 Central Street, Woodstock, is a small cornucopia of unusual collectibles and items from around the world, plus funky jewelry.

The Whipple Tree (802-457-1325), 7 Central Street, has yarns, knitting, sewing, and art supplies (and Vermont Transit bus tickets).

Also see FossilGlass under *Artisans*, and check out *Antiques*.

East of Woodstock Village

Fat Hat Factory (802-296-6646), at the corner of Route 4 and Clubhouse Road, Quechee, offers "spirited hats and carefree clothing," most of it made right here: skirts, pants, and sweaters as well as hats.

New England Specialties Shoppe (802-295-6163), Route 4, Quechee. The Laros's store, east of the gorge, has an especially large and carefully selected stock of Vermont products, from cheese, syrup, and preserves to sweatshirts and toys. In the same complex look for **Ottauquechee Valley Winery** (802-295-9463), sequestered behind the Mesa Home Factory Store. It's a relatively new offshoot of North River Winery in Jacksonville, producing a half dozen fruit wines from pears and apples, rhubarb, and a blend of blueberries and apples.

✐ **Quechee Gorge Village** (802-295-1550; 1-800-438-5565; www.quecheegorge.com), Route 4 at Quechee Gorge. The most elaborate of several Route 4 shopping complexes, it includes the Antiques Center (see *Antiques*) and Farina Family Diner (see *Eating Out*), also an arts and crafts center, general store, and Christmas Loft. A seasonal miniature train for small tourists circles the property.

Talbot's Herb & Perennial Farm (802-436-2085), Hartland-Quechee Road, 3 miles south of the blinker on Route 4. Field-grown herbs, dried flowers and wreaths, greenhouse. Open daily 9–5, from early April through October.

Taftsville Country Store (802-457-1135), Route 4 east, Taftsville. Refurbished and restocked, this 1840 landmark carries carefully chosen Vermont gifts as well as a good selection of cheeses, maple products, jams, jellies, smoked ham, and bacon, plus staples, wine, and books.

Sugarbush Farm (802-457-1757; 1-800-281-1757), RR 1, Box 568, Woodstock, but located in Pomfret: Take Route 4 to Taftsville, cross the covered bridge, go up the hill, turn left onto Hillside Road, then follow signs. *Warning:* It's steep. Beware in mud season, but it's well worth the effort: Sample seven Vermont cheeses, all packaged here along with gift boxes, geared to sending products to far corners of the world. In-season, you can watch maple sugaring, walk the maple and nature trail, meditate in the Luce family's small woodland chapel, or visit with their farm animals.

Scotland by the Yard (802-295-5351), Route 4, 3 miles east of Woodstock, imports tartans and tweeds, kilts, capes, coats, sweaters, skirts, canes, books, records, oatcakes, and shortbreads.

Elsewhere

Red Cupboard Gift Shop (802-457-3722), Route 4, West Woodstock, has a broad selection of Vermont-made gifts, jams, jellies, and a variety of maple products.

High Brook Horse and Harness (802-457-4677), Route 106, South Woodstock, is a "country store" for horses and horse people—saddlery, harnesses, equestrian clothes, supplies, and gifts.

✷ Special Events

Note: Check the **Town Crier blackboard** at the corner of Elm and Central Streets in Woodstock for the week's happenings.

February (Washington's Birthday): A week of **Winter Carnival** events sponsored by the Woodstock Recreation Center (802-457-1502)—concerts, Fisk Trophy Race, sleigh rides, square dance, torchlight ski parade.

May: Woodstock **Memorial Day Parade.**

Late June: **Quechee Hot Air Balloon Festival** (802-295-7900), Father's Day weekend—a gathering of more than two dozen balloons with ascensions, flights, races, crafts show, entertainment.

July 4: **Crafts Fair,** Woodstock—music and fireworks display in the evening at the high school. **Woodstock Road Race,** 7.4 miles (802-457-1502).

August: **Quechee Scottish Festival,** third Saturday: pipe bands, sheepdog trials, Highland dancing, more than 50 clans. **Billings Farm Quilt Show.**

Mid-October: Quechee **antiques and crafts festivals. Apple & Crafts Fair,** Woodstock.

Early December: **Christmas Wassail Weekend,** which includes a grand parade of carriages around the Woodstock green, Yule log lighting, concerts.

Central Vermont

3

KILLINGTON/PLYMOUTH AREA

THE WHITE RIVER VALLEYS

SUGARBUSH/MAD RIVER VALLEY

BARRE/MONTPELIER AREA

Kim Grant

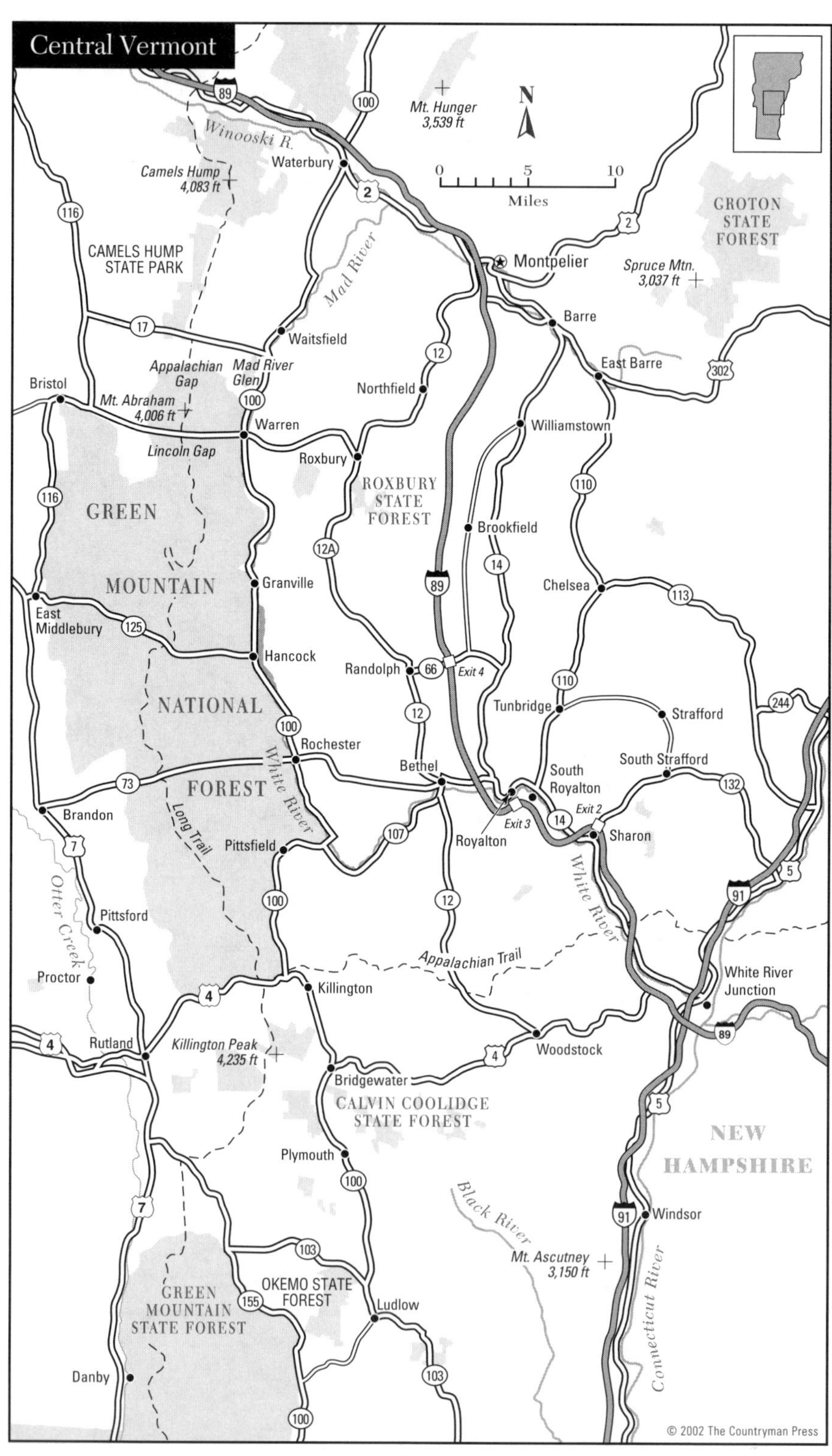

Central Vermont
89
100
Mt. Hunger
3,539 ft
N
Winooski R.
Waterbury
Camels Hump
4,083 ft
2
0
5
10
Miles
116
CAMELS HUMP
STATE PARK
Mad River
Montpelier
2
GROTON
STATE
FOREST
Spruce Mtn.
3,037 ft
Barre
17
Waitsfield
12
Appalachian
Gap
Mad River
Glen
East Barre
302
Bristol
Northfield
Mt. Abraham
4,006 ft
100
Warren
Williamstown
Lincoln Gap
Roxbury
ROXBURY
STATE
FOREST
110
116
GREEN
Brookfield
12A
14
MOUNTAIN
Granville
89
Chelsea
113
East
Middlebury
125
Hancock
Randolph
66
Exit 4
110
NATIONAL
Tunbridge
Strafford
244
12
100
Rochester
South Strafford
White River
Bethel
South
Royalton
73
FOREST
132
Brandon
Long Trail
Exit 3
14
Exit 2
Royalton
Sharon
7
Pittsfield
107
Otter Creek
100
12
White River
5
91
Pittsford
Appalachian Trail
Proctor
White River
Junction
4
Killington
89
4
Rutland
Killington Peak
4,235 ft
4
Woodstock
Bridgewater
CALVIN COOLIDGE
STATE FOREST
5
NEW
HAMPSHIRE
Plymouth
100
Black River
7
91
Windsor
103
Mt. Ascutney
3,150 ft
GREEN
MOUNTAIN
STATE FOREST
OKEMO STATE
FOREST
155
Ludlow
Connecticut River
Danby
103
100

KILLINGTON/PLYMOUTH AREA

Killington is the largest ski resort with the longest ski season in the East. It boasts seven mountains and the most extensive snowmaking system in the world. It's said that some 18,000 visitors can bed down within 20 miles.

Killington Peak, the second highest summit in the state, is flanked by other mountains and faces another majestic range across Sherburne Pass. Although the road through this upland village has been heavily traveled since the settling of Rutland (11 miles to the west) and Woodstock (20 miles to the east), there was never much of anything here. In 1924, an elaborate, rustic-style inn was built at the junction of Route 4, the Appalachian Trail, and the new Long Trail. A winter annex across the road was added in 1938, when Pico (now part of Killington) installed one of the country's first T-bars. But the logging village of Sherburne Center was practically a ghost town in 1957 when Killington began.

Condominiums cluster at higher elevations while lodges, inns, and motels are strung along the 5-mile length of Killington Road and west along Route 4 as it slopes ever downward through Mendon to Rutland. Ski lodges are also salted along Route 100 north to the pleasant old town of Pittsfield, and in the village of Chittenden, sequestered up a back road from Route 4, near a mountain-backed reservoir. In summer, this is exceptional hiking and mountain-biking country. The K1 Express Gondola, to the summit of Killington Peak, carries bikes. What Killington terms "Endless Adventures" include major golf and tennis programs and plenty of family-geared activities. Summer also brings theater and ballet, a series of musical, horsey, and other events, and—because this is still primarily a winter resort area—substantial savings on summer accommodations. Southeast of Killington, down Route 100 and a few miles up Route 100A, stands the village of Plymouth Notch, looking much the way it did on August 3, 1923, when Calvin Coolidge was sworn in by his father as the 30th president of the United States in his kerosene-lighted home. Now the President Calvin Coolidge State Historic Site, it's arguably the only Vermont village in which the story of its remarkable residents as well as its buildings have been preserved.

GUIDANCE **Killington Lodging and Travel Service** (1-800-621-6867), Route 4, located in the Shops at the Shack. Open daily 8 AM–9 PM mid-November through May, the bureau keeps a tally on vacancies and makes reservations. A wide variety

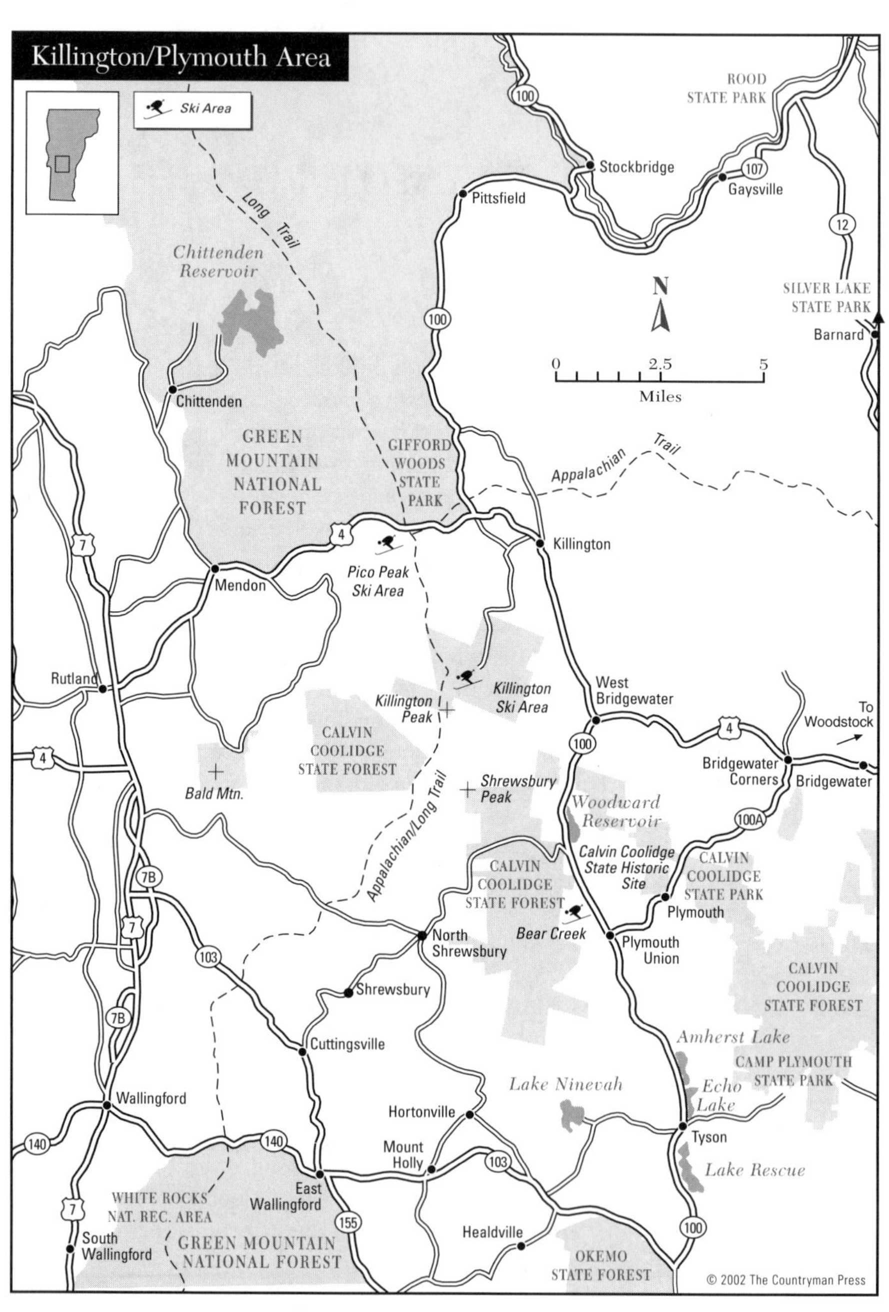

Killington/Plymouth Area
Ski Area
Long Trail
Chittenden Reservoir
Chittenden
GREEN MOUNTAIN NATIONAL FOREST
GIFFORD WOODS STATE PARK
Pittsfield
Stockbridge
ROOD STATE PARK
Gaysville
SILVER LAKE STATE PARK
Barnard
N
0 2.5 5
Miles
Appalachian Trail
Killington
Mendon
Pico Peak Ski Area
Killington Ski Area
Killington Peak
Rutland
West Bridgewater
To Woodstock
Bridgewater Corners
Bridgewater
CALVIN COOLIDGE STATE FOREST
Bald Mtn.
Shrewsbury Peak
Appalachian/Long Trail
Woodward Reservoir
Calvin Coolidge State Historic Site
CALVIN COOLIDGE STATE PARK
Plymouth
Bear Creek
Plymouth Union
North Shrewsbury
Shrewsbury
Cuttingsville
Amherst Lake
CAMP PLYMOUTH STATE PARK
Echo Lake
Lake Ninevah
Wallingford
Hortonville
Tyson
Mount Holly
Lake Rescue
East Wallingford
WHITE ROCKS NAT. REC. AREA
Healdville
South Wallingford
OKEMO STATE FOREST
© 2002 The Countryman Press

of 2- to 5-day ski packages are available Summer packages are available by phoning 1-877-4KTIMES. The web site for all information related to the area is www.killington.com.

GETTING THERE *By rail:* **Amtrak's *Ethan Allen Express*** (1-800-USA-RAIL) from New York City stops in Rutland. Departures from NYC are 2:45 and from Rutland, 1:10, with a special Sunday train at 5:05.

By bus: Vermont Transit stops en route from Rutland to White River Junction at Killington Depot, Route 4 near the access road. Most inns will pick up guests. *By plane:* Rutland Airport is served by **USAirways Express** operated by Colgan Air (1-800-786-2579) from Boston. For direct service from New York see "Burlington Region."

WHEN TO GO In theory Killington's ski season begins mid-November and runs through May but the full trail system rarely opens before Christmas, and by Easter it's pretty much all over. Given its size and high profile, Killington attracts more ski-weekers than other New England areas, enough for a lively midweek atmosphere but still leaving ample room on the slopes (not always true during February weekends and school vacations). July through foliage season is pleasant: plenty to do and a wide choice of places to stay at off-season prices.

MEDICAL EMERGENCY Dial **911.**

Rutland Regional Medical Center (802-775-7111), 160 Allen Street, Rutland.

✷ To Do

AERIAL RIDES The **Killington K1 Express** runs from Killington Base Lodge to the top of Killington Peak (see the box). During foliage season (mid-September to Columbus Day), the **Killington Skyeship Express,** a speedy, eight-passenger gondola, operates runs from Route 4 to an elevation of 3,800 feet. Both cost the same, and for both the phone is 802-422-6200.

BICYCLING **Killington Mountain Bike Center** (802-422-6232; 1-877-4KTIMES). The Killington K1 Express Gondola operates Memorial Day through Columbus Day hoisting bicyclists and their bikes to Killington Peak,

KILLINGTON PEAK

On a clear day the view from the summit of the state's second highest mountain (4,241 feet) encompasses five states. It sweeps northwest to the Adirondacks, east to the White Mountains, and north along the spine of the Green Mountains. It's the spot on which the Rev. Samuel Peters in 1763 is said to have christened all that he could see "Verd monts." The K1 Express Gondola (daily, Memorial Day through Labor Day, then daily mid-September through Columbus Day; 802-422-6200) hoists visitors up from the Killington Base Lodge to the Peak Restaurant (open for special dinners in foliage season) just below the summit, and a nature trail leads to the peak. Round trip gondola: $13 per adult, $8 juniors and seniors, $31 per family; one-way: $9 and $5.

accessing 45 miles of marked trails; $8 for a trail pass, $20 for a ride on the gondola. During foliage season, the Skyeship is also available. Guided tours, instruction, bike rentals and packages.

True Wheels (802-422-3234; www.truewheels.com), top of the Killington Road, also rents mountain bikes. The only place on the mountain for bike repair, and a great source of info for local trail and road riding.

CAMPING See *Green Space.*

CANOEING AND KAYAKING **Chittenden Reservoir** is a sublime place to canoe or kayak, an expansive 674 acres and backed by mountains. Boat access is at the end of Chittenden Dam Road.

Blue Ridge Outfitters (802-747-4878; www.blueridgeoutfitter.com) rents and delivers both kayaks and canoes.

Kayak King (802-422-3070; www.kayakking.8m.com) in Killington offers kayak rentals on Kent Pond.

FISHING Licenses are available from the Killington town clerk, River Road, and also from sporting goods stores and state park rangers. Landlocked salmon and trout can be had in Chittenden Reservoir; trout are the catch in Mendon Brook. There also is fishing in Kent and Colton Ponds, and the White, Tweed, and Ottauquechee Rivers. Woodward Reservoir on Route 100 south and Echo Lake in Tyson (accessible from Plymouth Camp State Park) are also good fishing.

Stream & Brook Fly-fishing at the Cortina Inn (802-773-3333; www.streambrook.com) features a 2-day beginner's program. The inn has a practice pond; day two is spent on local rivers and streams. Inquire about guided trips.

FOR FAMILIES ✐ **Killington/Pico Adventure Center** (802-422-6200) is physically divided between the base areas of Pico, down on Route 4, and of Killington itself. Open Memorial Day to late June on weekends, then daily through Labor Day, 10–5. An Adventure Center Pass covers everything; $30–40 per day adult, $25–35 age 12 and under and 65-plus. Passes are also available for single activities.

At Pico: The Alpine Slide. Patrons ride a triple chairlift up and then slide down a total of 3,410 feet; the slide begins halfway up the mountain with a sweeping view of the valley to the west. Lunch and snacks are served at a snack bar. "Endless Activities" here also include the "bungee thing," miniature golf (19 holes), and chairlift rides.

At Killington: Water slides, outdoor climbing wall, skateboard and in-line skate park, and mountain boarding, as well as mountain biking and a hiking center.

✐ **Mountain Meadows Munchkins** (802-775-1010), 285 Thundering Brook Road, Killington 05751. Based at Mountain Meadows Lodge (see *Lodging—Resorts*), this unusual program geared to children from 6 months and up is open to drop-ins as well as lodge guests. Farm animal care, hikes on the Appalachian Trail, fishing, boating, and swimming are part of the program for older children. Children's theme meals, story and movie nights are also offered.

CHITTENDEN RESERVOIR Christina Tree

GOLF **Killington Resort** (802-422-6700), Killington Road, Killington, has its own 18-hole, 6,326-yard, par-72 course designed by Geoffrey Cornish. Weekend clinics and golf packages. PGA professional instruction, rental clubs. The **Mountain Golf School** (1-800-343-0762), at the Killington Resort, features 2-day weekend and 3-day midweek instructional programs.

Green Mountain National Golf Course (802-422-GOLF; www.GMNGC.com), Barrows-Towne Road and Route 100, Killington. This highly rated 18-hole course opened in 1996 and includes a clubhouse, three practice teeing areas, four target greens, and an 8,000-square-foot putting green.

HEALTH SPAS/FITNESS **Cortina Health Club** (802-773-3333), Cortina Inn, Route 4, Killington. Heated indoor pool, whirlpool, exercise room, saunas, massage, facials, exercise classes.

Pico Sports Center (802-747-0564), Route 4, Killington. A 75-foot Olympic lap pool, aerobics area, fitness and cardiovascular room, Jacuzzi, saunas, tanning, massage, fitness evaluations.

The Spa at the Woods (802-422-3139), Killington Road. Built as the heart of a deluxe condo complex but open to drop-ins, an unusually attractive, full-service spa with pool, Jacuzzi, and a full massage and body treatment menu.

Mountain Green Health Club (802-422-3113), center of Killington Village. Located in the Mountain Green complex, a club with a 54-foot indoor lap pool, Jacuzzi, aerobics classes, steam rooms, sauna, massage.

New Life Hiking Spa (1-800-228-4676; www.newlifehikingspa.com), based at the Inn of the Six Mountains (see *Lodging—Lodges*). Early May through October. Since 1978 Jimmy LeSage has been refining and fine-tuning fitness programs (2 to 10 days and longer) that combine sensible eating and moderate exercise. The daily regimen begins with a prebreakfast walk and includes body conditioning, yoga, and hiking. Meals are varied, and the focus is on increasing energy and stamina (a good solo vacation).

HIKING **Deer Leap Trail,** off Route 4 behind The Inn at Long Trail (see *Lodging—Lodges*), is the most popular short hike: a 45-minute one-way trek up a winding, moderately steep path that yields a panoramic view from the top of a 2,490-foot cliff. You can continue along the Long Trail to Chittenden Reservoir

Vermont Division for Historic Preservation

THE CALVIN COOLIDGE STATE HISTORIC SITE

CALVIN COOLIDGE AND PLYMOUTH NOTCH

Calvin Coolidge (1872–1933) is best remembered for his dry wit and thrift, his integrity and common sense, all famously Vermont virtues. The village of Plymouth Notch—in which Coolidge was born, assumed the presidency, briefly governed the country (in the summer of 1924), and is buried—is said to be the best-preserved presidential birthplace in the nation. It may also be the best-preserved Vermont village, offering an in-depth sense of the people who lived there.

In the spirit of Coolidge himself, the village remains low-key: no 1920s costumed interpreters, no multimedia displays. The cheese factory built by the president's father, John Coolidge, showcases the history of Vermont cheese making and produces its own granular curd cheese. The square-steepled Union Christian Church, with its acoustically superb interior, is the setting for frequent concerts and lectures. The general store sells pickles, afghans, and some Vermont specialty foods like dilled carrots and Moxie—reportedly Coolidge's favorite drink (it was, after all, Prohibition).

"Colonel" John Coolidge became storekeeper here in 1868, and his son Calvin was born on the Fourth of July, 1872, in the modest attached house. The family moved across the street to the larger "Coolidge Homestead" when he was 4 years old, and it was there, because he happened to be home helping with the haying, that Vice Pres. Calvin Coolidge learned of Pres. Warren Harding's unexpected death and, at 2:47 AM on August 3, 1923, was sworn in, by his father, as 30th president of the United States.

"I didn't know I couldn't" was the reply Coolidge Sr. gave when reporters asked how he knew he could administer the presidential oath of office. "Colonel John" was a former state senator, a notary public, and the village sheriff as well as shopkeeper. His terse response typifies the dry wit for which his son would later became known.

It should come as no surprise that in this classic Vermont village you encounter a classic Vermont family. The Coolidges were hardworking (up before dawn for chores), self-sufficient (you see an intricate quilt that was stitched by Cal at age 10 and a graceful carriage built his father), and closely linked to the land. Coolidge is buried with seven generations of his family in the small graveyard across the road from the village. Village residents numbered 29 during Coolidge's presidency, and a high percentage of these formed the Old-Time Dance Orchestra, which played in the dance hall above the general store. This same room served as the office of the summer White House for a dozen days in 1924. At the time Calvin and his wife Grace were grieving the death of their son Calvin Jr., a promising 16-year-old who had died due to a complication from an infected blister he acquired while playing tennis at the White House.

Plymouth resident Ruth ("Midge") Aldrich opened several tourist cabins (prefab jobs brought up from Boston) to accommodate the Secret Service and a Top of the Notch Tea Room to serve a steady stream of the Coolidge-curious. Plymouth Notch, however, never hit the big time as a tourist attraction, perhaps because, while he continued to visit "The Notch," President Coolidge himself retired to private life not here but in his adopted home, Northampton, Massachusetts. After graduating from nearby Amherst College, Coolidge had opened a law practice in Northampton, and it was there that he met his wife (fellow Vermonter Grace Anna Goodhue, who was teaching there at the Clarke School for the Deaf), and served as mayor. He represented Northampton in the Massachusetts legislature before becoming governor of the Bay State, and he died in Northampton.

It was Aurora Pierce, the family housekeeper, who fiercely preserved the Coolidge Homestead, adamantly opposing even minor changes, like plumbing and electricity. Not until Aurora's death in 1956 did the Vermont's Historic Sites Commission assume management of the house and its contents (which Grace Coolidge had deeded to them). The state had already purchased the 1840s village tavern that had also been Calvin's mother's home, turning it into a lunchroom and information center.

The President Calvin Coolidge State Historic Site presently encompasses 25 buildings, the majority of the village. Eleven buildings, including the cheese factory, the 1840s church, the general store, and its upstairs hall (restored to look just as it did as the office of the summer White House) and the hand-hewn Wilder Barn (housing farm implements and horse-drawn vehicles), are open to the public. A stone-faced visitors center (with changing exhibits) has been added, power lines have been buried (electricity actually didn't reach Plymouth until after Calvin's death), and roads have been paved. Otherwise the village looks about as it did in the 1920s, sitting quietly at the foot of East Mountain. It's set in 560 acres presently owned by the Vermont Division for Historic Preservation, surrounded by the 500-acre Coolidge State Park, in turn abutting the 18,000-acre Calvin Coolidge State Forest. The President Coolidge State Historic Site (802-672-3773; www.historicvermont.org/Coolidge) is open daily late May through mid-October, 9:30–5. Admission: $6.50 per adult, children 14 and under free.

PRESIDENT CALVIN COOLIDGE

Vermont Division for Historic Preservation

(spot a car) or branch east at the Maine Junction on the Appalachian Trail. Consult hiking guides for details. This trail also connects with Gifford Woods State Park (see *Green Space*).

Bald Mountain. This 3-mile, 3-hour round-trip hike is in Aiken State Forest, off Stratton Road from Route 4 in Mendon. The blue-blazed circle trail begins opposite the entrance to **Tamarack Notch Camp.**

Fox Creek Inn (see *Lodging—Inns*) shuttles hikers to the Long Trail as part of the Country Inns Along the Trail program (www.inntoinn.com).

Killington Hiking Center (802-422-6200) at Killington base lodge. Pick up a hiking map to the mountain and its lifts. Inquire about "Hike and Stay" packages.

HORSEBACK RIDING **Mountain Top Stables** (802-483-2311), Chittenden. Pony and trail rides, geared to various abilities, are offered Memorial Day through Columbus Day, also group and private instruction, sleigh rides.

Hawk Center (802-672-3811), at Salt Ash, Route 100, in Plymouth, offers lessons, trail rides, and hayrides.

Riverside Farm Stables (802-746-8544; www.riversidefarm.com), 7 miles north of Killington on Route 100 in Pittsfield. Guided mountain trail rides, dinner rides, lessons, hayrides. The antiques shop here caters to nonriders in the family.

TENNIS **Killington School for Tennis at the Cortina Inn** (802-773-3331), Route 4, Killington. Weekend and 5-day, midweek packages are available Memorial Day to early September, using nine outdoor courts and the Village at Killington. It also features a Junior Tennis Academy.

Summit Lodge (802-422-3535), Killington Road. Six outdoor courts are available to the public (see *Lodging—Lodges*).

Public courts are also maintained by the towns of Chittenden and Killington.

✷ Winter Sports

CROSS-COUNTRY SKIING **Mountain Meadows Ski Touring Center** (802-775-7077; 1-800-221-0598), Thundering Brook Road off Route 4, Killington. One of Vermont's oldest and most serious touring centers, set high (1,500–1,800 feet) on the rolling acreage of the Mountain Meadows Lodge (see *Lodging—Resorts*); 60 km total, 40 km set; 1.5 miles lit; snowmaking; instruction, rentals, also telemark lessons and rentals. Tours of the backcountry available.

Mountain Top Ski Touring Center (802-483-6089), Chittenden. A total of 110 km of trails (70 km set) begin at Mountain Top Inn (see *Lodging—Resorts*), an ideal location at 1,495–2,165 feet, with sweeping views of Chittenden Mountain and Reservoir; rentals and lessons, limited snowmaking, and a log cabin warming hut in the woods at the intersection of trails.

DOWNHILL SKIING ✐ **Killington Resort** (switchboard: 802-422-3333; information: 802-422-6200; www.killington.com), Killington. With seven parking lots, seven

Rob Bossi

KILLINGTON RESORT

base lodges, six interconnected mountains—plus Pico—and an entirely separate novice area, Killington is unquestionably big. When it was purchased by the American Skiing Company in 1996, it was dubbed the Beast of the East. Thanks to its four entry points and far-flung network of lifts and trails, the crowds are neatly dispersed throughout the area. The virtually self-contained Ramshead Family Mountain features a family center for rentals, skier development program registration, child care, food court emporium, and Snow Play Park. *Lifts:* 32, including 12 quads (5 high-speed) plus the Skyeship and K1 Express Gondolas, 4 doubles, 6 triples, 8 surface lifts (52,973 rides per hour). *Trails and slopes:* 200. *Vertical drop:* 3,050 feet. *Snowmaking:* 62 miles of trails, with 1,850 snowguns. *Snowboarding:* Super pipe with 12-foot walls, three terrain parks. *Facilities:* Six cafeterias, five ski rental shops, one mountaintop restaurant, four lounges. *For children:* Comprehensive Perfect Kids ski and snowboard coaching program based at the Family Center. Children 12 and under ski and ride free when accompanied by an adult with a 5-day pass; kids 5 and under ski free with an adult. *Special programs:* School for Ski Professionals, for Snowboard Professionals, Women's Snowboard Clinics, early-December Ski Raceweek and Snowboard Freeriding and Carving Camp, Women's Turn, Mogul Clinic Weekends. *Rates:* 1-day—adult $62 weekend/$59 midweek, young adult $57/52, junior $39/36. Multiday rates and interchangeable tickets (with other ASC resorts) can bring adult tickets down to $42 per day.

Bear Creek Mountain Club (802-672-4242; www.bearcreekclub.com). The chairlift operates Thursday through Sunday in-season at the former Round Top ski area. Plans call for this to be the centerpiece of a second-home development, but ski tickets are available to the public (in 2002: $50 adult for a full day, $30 junior), space permitting. Skiers are limited to 250 per day on the 16 trails. Inquire about lifetime memberships.

SLEIGH RIDES **Cortina Inn** (802-773-3333), Route 4 East, Mendon. Wednesday, Saturday, and some holidays.

SNOWMOBILING **Killington Snowmobile Tours** (802-422-2121), based at Killington, offers snowmobile tours plus tours to Killington Peak for Wednesday-night dinner.

SNOWSHOEING **Killington Snowshoe Tours,** based at Beattie's Trailside Lodge (802-773-9791) on Route 100 north, offers scheduled morning and afternoon tours on winter Saturdays and Sundays, rentals anytime.

✷ Green Space

Calvin Coolidge State Forest. This 18,000-acre preserve, which actually includes Killington Peak, is scattered through seven local towns and divided by Route 100 into two districts. The recreational center is Coolidge State Park (summer: 802-672-3612; winter: 802-885-8891; 1-800-299-3071), Route 100A east of Plymouth Notch. Open mid-May to mid-October, these 500 acres include a campground (60 campsites including 35 lean-tos, a dump station, picnic area, and rest rooms with hot showers), picnic shelter, and hiking and snowmobile trails. In another part of the forest Camp Plymouth State Park, off Route 100 in Tyson, served as a Civilian Conservation Corps (CCC) camp in 1933 and offers a the beach on Echo Lake (picnic area, food concession). Inquire about gold panning and trails into the abandoned village of Plymouth Five Corners. North of the turnoff for Route 100A the steep CCC Road (marked for Meadowsweet Farm) climbs away from Route 100 into the western swatch of the forest, with beautiful views back down the valley. It's unfortunate (but sensible) that this road is closed in winter because it harbors some of the area's snowiest cross-country trails, accessible only by going the long way around through Shrewsbury (see *Scenic Drives* in "Okemo Valley").

Gifford Woods State Park (summer: 802-775-5354; winter: 802-885-8891; 1-800-299-3071), a half mile north of Route 4 on Route 100, Killington. The campground (27 tent/trailer and 21 lean-to sites, hot showers) is patronized by hikers on the Appalachian Trail, which runs through the park. Across the road is the Gifford Woods Natural Area, a 7-acre stand of virgin hardwoods (sugar maple, yellow birch, basswood, white ash, and hemlock). Trails lead up to Deer Leap Mountain (see *Hiking*) and to the lovely waterfalls where Kent Brook enters Kent Pond. In winter cross-country trails connect with Mountain Meadows (see *To Do—Cross-Country Skiing*).

✷ Lodging

Note: Killington's Skyeship Gondola on Route 4 also put the inns of Plymouth to the southeast is within easy reach, and lodging in both Woodstock (see "Woodstock/Quechee") and Ludlow (see "Okemo Valley") within 14 miles. See *Guidance* for central reservations numbers.

RESORTS ✐ **The Killington Grand Resort Hotel & Conference Center** (1-888-64-GRAND), 228 East Mountain Road, Killington 05751. At the base of the lifts, this 200-room, vintage-1997 facility offers standard hotel rooms, also studios and one-, two-, and three-bedroom suites (with kitchen). It's immense, with endless corridors and Vermont's biggest meeting space (the Grand Ballroom), ergo conventions. The rooms are, however, irreproachably comfortable. Amenities include an outdoor heated pool, health club, on-site daycare, Ovations Restaurant (see *Dining Out*), and a café. It's close not only to the base lodge, but in summer to the golf course. Summer rates range from $150 for a hotel room, in winter $266; a one-bedroom suite (four people) goes for $227 in summer, $400 in winter. Better values year-round if combined with a sports package.

Hawk Inn and Mountain Resort (802-672-3811; 1-800-685-4295; www.hawkresort.com), Route 100, Plymouth 05056. Set on 1,200 acres and owned by longtime residents Brenda and Jack Geishecker, this ranks among Vermont's most luxurious resorts. Lodging options include freestanding "mountain villas" salted away on hillsides with splendid views, also the townhouse-style Ledges Villas along the Black River and the 50-room Hawk Inn and River Tavern. Situated halfway between Killington and Okemo (theoretically 10 minutes from each) and 3 miles from the trails at Bear Creek Mountain Club, the resort is well positioned for alpine skiers and offers its own extensive cross-country system as well as a heated outdoor pool, a spa, and ice skating and sleigh rides. In summer, there is tennis, horseback riding, swimming, mountain biking, fly-fishing, as well as canoeing, kayaking, sailing, and rowing on Lake Amherst. The heart of the inn itself is a 19th-century farmhouse, and rooms are in modern wings. Each is decorated differently. Some have whirlpool bath; all are equipped with down comforters, featherbeds, and large-screen TV. The spa boasts New England's largest indoor/outdoor pool and its largest hot tub. In winter, rates are $310–440 per couple in the inn, $375–750 in the Ledges Villas, and $450–900 in the freestanding mountain villas; in summer: $280–390; off-season: $230–320. Inn rates include breakfast. See *Dining Out* for the River Tavern, which also offers a pub menu, fireside. Lunch is served poolside during the summer.

Cortina Inn and Resort (802-773-3333; 1-800-451-6108; www.cortinainn.com), Killington 05751. This modern luxury lodge on Route 4 is designed for the average American family out to pamper themselves. Innkeepers Bob and Brenda Harnish are enterprising hosts who offer a full summer program: tennis with pros using eight courts; a fitness center with whirlpools, saunas, exercise machines, and indoor pool; a game room; and special hiking, fishing, and picnicking expeditions. The grounds include an extensive nature- and a touring-trail systems connecting with both the Mountain Meadows and Mountain Top trail networks in winter. Afternoon tea is served in the two-story lobby, which has a round hearth in the center and exhibit space for local sculpture and art in the gallery. There are 96 rooms and suites, a variety of individually decorated spaces, some suites with fireplace and whirlpool bath (Room 215 is immense), some suites with lofts, and five rooms that are wheelchair-accessible. Summer rates $124–159 per couple B&B; in winter $159–194 B&B. Children $5 in the same room with parent. Pets cost $5 too. The Cortina dining rooms are Zola's Grille and casual Theodore's Tavern (see *Dining Out* and *Eating Out*). Inquire about tennis, golf, and ski packages.

Mountain Meadows Lodge (802-775-1010; 1-800-370-4567; www.mtmeadowslodge.com), Thundering

Brook Road, Killington 05751. The main building is an 1856 barn, nicely converted to include an informal dining room, spacious living room with a lake view, and game room. Now run by Michele and Mark Werle, the inn is geared to families year-round, catering to people who like the outdoors in warm-weather months and as well as in winter. This is a hospitable, thoroughly relaxing kind of lodge. There are 20 guest rooms, many of them great for families, all with private bath. A sauna and outdoor Jacuzzi are among the amenities. In summer, there is a swimming pool and 100-acre Kent Pond, which abuts the property and is good for fishing and canoeing as well as swimming; the town tennis courts are just down the road. In winter, this is a major ski-touring center (see *Cross-Country Skiing*). Mountain Meadows Munchkins Children's Center is open to the public for daycare as well as to guests, and introduces kids to farm animals and nature. Weekdays: $85–140 per couple B&B; $150–200 for a family room plus $10 per child 4–10, $20 age 11 and up. Weekends: $116–140 per night per couple B&B, $152–176 MAP; $186–270 in the suites with $15 per child 10 and under, $38 age 11 and up.

Mountain Top Inn (802-483-2311; 1-800-445-2100; www.mountaintopinn.com), Mountain Top Road, Chittenden 05737. Closed April through Memorial Day and after Columbus Day until mid-December. Set on 337 rolling acres overlooking Chittenden Reservoir, this self-contained resort is known for horseback riding and cross-country skiing. On our most recent visit it was looking a shade tired, but what we saw of the 35 rooms (two double beds, private bath) seemed comfortable. There are also six cottages and four chalets. In addition to stables and the cross-country center, facilities include a heated pool, tennis, lawn games, sauna, canoeing, horseback riding, a five-hole golf course and driving range, claybird shooting, and fly-fishing. $168–268 for a cottage unit includes breakfast. Children 6 and under are free; $26 under and $42 over age 12. Add $42 per couple for dinner plus a 15 percent service charge. Inquire about weekend packages.

INNS **The October Country Inn** (802-672-3412; 1-800-648-8421), junction of Routes 4 and 100A, Bridgewater Corners 05035. Handy to Killington and Woodstock (8 miles) as well as most of the things to do and see in this chapter, yet sequestered up a back road with hiking trails that lead past the swimming pool to the top of a hill for a sweeping, peaceful view. This old farmhouse has a large, comfortable living room with inviting places to sit around the hearth and at the big round table in the dining room—not to be confused with the other cheery dining room in which guests gather around long tables for memorable meals, which can be Greek, Mexican, Asian, French, or, occasionally, American. Innkeepers Edie and Chuck Janisse offer candlelit dinners featuring homemade bread, cakes, homegrown vegetables and herbs, and wine. Breakfasts are equally ambitious, geared to fuel bikers in summer and skiers in winter. The 10 guest rooms (8 with private bath) vary in size; many have queen-sized beds, and all are carefully decorated. $145–165 includes dinner and breakfast for two year-round.

♿ **Fox Creek Inn** (802-483-6213; 1-800-707-0017; www.foxcreekinn.com), 49 Dam Road, Chittenden 05737. This is backwoods luxury in a superb house built by the inventor William Barstow, who retired here after selling his various holdings for $40 million right before the 1929 stock market crash. Ann and Alex Volz offer eight carefully furnished guest rooms, all with private bath, most with Jacuzzi, and a couple with gas fireplace. The Honeymoon Suite, also good for a family of four, has two fireplaces and a two-person Jacuzzi. Guests gather around the big stone fireplace in the paneled den, in the comfortable living room, and at the cozy bar. Candlelight dinners are a point of pride (see *Dining Out*). There is swimming, canoeing, and fishing in the Chittenden Reservoir just down the road, and in winter you can cross-country ski. Rates are $149–199 B&B, $179–289 MAP. Add 15 percent gratuity.

ꝏ 🏵 ♿ **The Vermont Inn** (802-775-0708; 1-800-541-7795; www.vermontinn.com), Killington 05751. Set above Route 4 with a view of Killington and Pico, this is a 19th-century farmhouse with a homey feel to its public rooms—the living room with woodstove, the pub/lounge with fireplace, a game room, and an upstairs reading room, a welcome nook in the evening when the dining room is open to the public (see *Dining Out*). Summer facilities include a pool, tennis court, and lawn games. The sauna and hot tub are available year-round. Innkeepers Megan and Greg Smith offer 18 guest rooms, ranging from smallish to spacious, all bright with brass and antique or canopy bedstead and private bath. Five have a fireplace, one with a Jacuzzi and one, wheelchair-accessible. $50–110 per couple B&B in summer, $80–180 B&B in fall and winter. Add $45 per couple for dinner and 15 percent gratuity.

🐾 **Red Clover Inn** (802-775-2290; 1-800-752-0571; www.redcloverinn.com), Box 7450, Woodward Road, Mendon 05701. Texans Mary and Dave Strekecki and Melinda Davis preside at this handsome 1840s landmark, set in its 13 acres. Several of the 14 rooms have all the bells and whistles: cathedral ceiling, a whirlpool from which you can operate (via remote control) the gas fireplace, TV, VCR, etc. All rooms are attractive, each different, with plenty of light. Our favorite is Tuscany, with a queen bed, skylights, and a double soaking tub. Common space is ample, and the dining rooms are public (see *Dining Out*). Facilities include a landscaped pool and small pond. $170–495 per couple MAP. Pets permitted in the carriage house.

The Pittsfield Inn (802-746-8943; 1-877-746-8943; www.pittsfieldinn.com), P.O. Box 685, Pittsfield 05762. Located 8 miles north of Killington in the center of the village on a handsome green, this double-porched old tavern has been welcoming guests since 1835. The inn had just changed hands as we go to press; call for updated information.

Salt Ash Inn (802-672-3748; 1-800-SALT-ASH), Route 100, Plymouth 05056. Built as an inn in the 1830s, presently owned by Paul Reitz and David Rosen, this is a special place. A pub in the former general store retains the original grocery counter and wooden post office boxes (where Calvin Coolidge picked up his mail), and a circular hearth serves the purpose of the old potbellied stove. The 17 rooms all have private bath; facilities include a heated outdoor pool and hot tub. Daily $99–159 per room B&B; weekends $330–415 per couple, including Saturday-night dinner and two full breakfasts.

LODGES **Summit Lodge** (802-422-3535; 1-800-635-6343), Killington

Road, Killington 05751. A meandering 45-room ski lodge in which guests are greeted by two majestic St. Bernards. Facilities include Maxwell's Restaurant and the inviting Saints Pub plus whirlpools, saunas, five tennis courts, outdoor heated swimming pool (geared for winter use, too), lawn games, and a courtesy bus to the Killington lifts. $49–140 per person B&B; many packages.

✎ **The Inn of the Six Mountains** (802-422-4302; 1-800-228-4676; www.six-mountains.com), Killington Road, Killington 05751. A 103-room, four-story, Adirondack-style hotel with gabled ceilings, skylights, balconies, and a two-story lobby with a fieldstone fireplace. Common spaces include a second-floor sitting room and a third-floor library. There is also a spa with lap pool, Jacuzzis, sauna, and exercise room, plus a dining room. The building is, unfortunately, right on Killington Road and in summer bus groups may predominate. In winter, $281 per person for 2 days includes skiing, lodging, and breakfast; children free in same room with parent. In summer, $99–299 per couple.

The Inn at Long Trail (802-775-7181; 1-800-325-2540; www.innatlong-trail.com), Route 4, Killington 05751. Closed in shoulder seasons. This is the first building in New England specifically built to serve as a ski lodge. It began in 1938 as an annex to a splendid summer inn that has since burned. Designed to resemble the inside of the forest as much as possible, the interior incorporates parts of trees and boulders and is a casual place. The inn caters to through-hikers on the Appalachian and Long Trails and outdoorsmen of all sorts. The 22-foot-long bar is made from a single log, and a protruding toe of the backyard cliff can be seen in both the pub and the dining room. The 14 rooms are small but cheery (2 are family suites), and there are 5 two-room suites with fireplace. The hot tub is used only in winter. Dinner is served varying nights in the restaurant, but you can usually count on McGrath's Irish Pub (see *Eating Out*). Summer rates are $68–98 per room B&B; in winter, $320–428 per couple per weekend MAP; ask about ski weeks. Gratuity is 10 percent.

✎ **Cascades Lodge** (802-422-3731; 1-800-345-0113; www.cascadeslodge.com), 58 Old Mill Road, Killington 05751. The MacKenzie family's neat, contemporary, 46-room hostelry is practically next to the Killington base lodge. Some rooms have balconies, and there's an indoor pool, sun deck, whirlpool, sauna, lounge, and a highly rated restaurant (see *Eating Out*). Rates: $99–109 in summer, $119–199 in fall and winter. Children stay and eat free in summer and fall.

Beattie's Trailside Lodge (802-422-3532; 1-800-447-2209), 115 Coffee House Road, Killington 05751, off Route 100 north. This is a homey, old-fashioned, downhill-ski-oriented place catering to groups. Meals and the 33 rooms are family-style, with bunk rooms (sleeping up to nine) or double

CILLY GENERAL STORE IN PLYMOUTH

Christina Tree

beds, 22 with private bath. There's a hot tub, a big, comfortable living room, and an outdoor heated pool. It's a great place for a family reunion. (Ask what groups are booked for the time you plan to be there.) $35–78 per person MAP in winter, $79 double B&B in summer. In winter there's snowshoeing and cross-country skiing on the adjacent Green Mountain National Golf Course.

Butternut on the Mountain (802-422-2000; 1-800-524-7654), Box 306, Killington Road, Killington 05751. Open year-round except May and June. A family-owned motor lodge with 18 large standard rooms with color TV and phone. Facilities include an indoor heated pool, whirlpool, fireside library and lounge, game room, laundry facilities, and Mrs. Brady's Restaurant (see *Eating Out*). $56–200 per room with continental breakfast; ski packages available. Pets accepted in summer.

BED & BREAKFAST **Fox and Pheasant Inn** (802-422-8770), Box 305, Killington 05751. The former Sunrise Village reception center at the foot of Bear Mountain has been converted into a six-bedroom guest house by Charlie Brunell and Nina Tasi. Four of the oversized rooms have a fireplace; all have a sitting area and private bath (one with whirlpool). Guest rooms, the fireplaced living room, TV den, and dining room are furnished with contemporary Vermont pieces. $100–140 double in low season, $140–195 in high, with continental breakfast.

MOTEL **Farmbrook Motel** (802-672-3621), Route 100A, Plymouth 05056. An unusually attractive 12-unit motel 3 miles from Coolidge's birthplace (see the Calvin Coolidge box; the brookside grounds have outdoor fireplaces, picnic tables. Some rooms sleep five; two kitchenettes. Rates: $50–75, slightly higher during foliage and holidays.

CONDOMINIUMS The Killington Travel Service/Lodging Bureau (1-800-621-6867 in ski season; otherwise 1-877-458-4637) serves hundreds of mountain properties, including: **Killington Resort Villages,** 600 condo units in a half dozen clusters including **Sunrise Mountain Village,** high on the mountain. In summer this becomes a miniresort in its own right, nicely landscaped and filled, primarily, with Florida retirees who have discovered the value of long-term rentals. Amenities include pools and whirlpools for each condo cluster. In winter you can walk to the lifts, and while the village is not "slope-side" (it's a schlep or shuttle to the base lodge), you are right at the nerve center of Killington's vast lift and trail network. Winter rates range upward from $232 per person for 5-day, 5-night packages. In summer packages start at $41 and in fall at $51 per person per day. **Pico Resort Hotel** on Route 4 in Killington abuts the Pico base lodge. The 152 units are well done: one-bedroom suites in the Village Square; two-, three-, and four-bedroom units in the village, with phone and marble-faced fireplace. The sports center here has a 75-foot indoor pool, Nautilus equipment, aerobics room, Jacuzzi, saunas, and lounge. Same prices as Killington Resort Village.

CAMPGROUNDS See *Green Space* for information on camping in Calvin Coolidge and Gifford Woods State Parks.

✱ Where to Eat

DINING OUT **Hemingway's** (802-422-3886), Route 4, Sherburne Flats, east of Killington. Closed Monday and Tuesday. Between Linda's eye for detail in the decor and service and Ted's concern for freshness, preparation, and presentation, the Fondulas have created one of the most highly rated dining experiences in New England. Chandeliers, fresh flowers, and floor-length table linens grace the peach-colored, vaulted main room, while a less formal atmosphere prevails in the garden room and stone-walled wine cellar. Specializes in "regional, classic cuisine" like grilled pheasant with Beaujolais, filet of beef with potato galette and roasted shallots, almond-crusted swordfish, Napoleon of sea bass with tarragon pastries, and rich desserts. Four-course prix fixe menu $48–65 but inquire about midweek specials; wine-tasting menu $72–90.

The Corners Inn Restaurant (802-672-9986), Route 4, Bridgewater Corners. Open for dinner Wednesday through Sunday. Reservations suggested. Known for the unusual ways he uses fresh, local ingredients, chef-owner Brad Pirkey has created an informal, standout small restaurant in an 1890 farmhouse. In winter request a table near the fireplace, and in summer, on the terrace. There's also a friendly bar. Specials on a summer night included beef Wellington and lobster spring rolls, and the menu ranged from homemade pastas with sweet Italian sausage, prosciutto, mushrooms, garlic, and roasted red peppers to veal with wild mushrooms and artichoke hearts. Entrées $12.95–18.95.

♿ **The River Tavern** (802-672-3811) at Hawk Inn and Resort, Route 100, Plymouth. Open for breakfast daily, lunch in-season, dinner year-round. Dinner reservations recommended. Chef Frank Van Overbeeke opened two well-known restaurants in Boston before settling his family into the Green Mountains. The restaurant itself is country elegant, with windowed walls framing the landscape. A summer dinner menu might feature rack of lamb with slow-roasted vegetables and a drizzle of goat cheese, or grilled, aioli-crusted tuna with littleneck clams in a garlic broth, served with a Greek salad. Entrées $19–24. Pub menu also available.

The Countryman's Pleasure (802-773-7141), just off Route 4, Mendon. Open 5:30–9 daily. Known for its top-drawer Austrian/German specialties: veal schnitzel cordon bleu, sauerbraten, goulash, and so on. The attractive dining rooms occupy the first floor of a charming house. A long wine list and 28 beers as well as international coffees and non-alcoholic wines and beers are served. The atmosphere is cozy, informal. Entrées $9.95–18.95. Senior and children's menu.

♿ **The Vermont Inn** (802-775-0708; 1-800-541-7795), Route 4, Killington. Open for dinner nightly. Chef Stephen Hatch has captured first place three times in the Killington-Champagne Dine Around Contest. It's a pleasant inn dining room with a fireplace and a varied menu that changes nightly. Entrées could include rack of lamb, Delmonico steak *au poivre,* tenderloin of pork with mushrooms, or vegetarian pasta. Children's menu available. Entrées $12.95–20.95.

Zola's Grille at the Cortina Inn (802-773-3333), Route 4, Killington. Open daily. Dinner in this spacious, nicely decorated dining room could start with a lump crab and bell pepper salad, followed by roasted venison or orange- and maple-glazed pork loin. Entrées $15.50–21.50. The Sunday buffet brunch is a winner at $14.95.

Red Clover Inn (802-775-2290), Route 4, Mendon. Reservations please. Open from 6 PM except Sunday. There are three country-inn-style dining rooms, two with fireplace, all air-conditioned. The menu changes daily but on a summer night might include baked Brie wrapped in almond phyllo with fresh fruit among the starters and crab-stuffed baked shrimp on top of homemade tagliatelle. Entrées $20–30.

Choices Restaurant (802-422-4030), Glazebrook Center, Killington Road, Killington. Open Wednesday through Sunday for dinner; Sunday brunch 11–2. This combination bistro-brasserie-pub has a huge menu of savory appetizers, salads, soups, raw bar, sandwiches, pastas, and such entrées as Shaker-style smoked pork loin with knockwurst and Cornish Hen Calvin Coolidge. Chef Claude has also added dishes from his former high-end restaurant (Claude's), such entrées as veal mignon and breast of duck cassis. Entrées $12.50–22.

Fox Creek Inn (802-483-6213), 49 Dam Road, Chittenden. Open for dinner Tuesday through Sunday with one seating at 7:30 PM. In this intimate (five tables), golden-colored dining room the menu changes nightly. Appetizers might include Maryland crabcakes with a spicy hollandaise sauce, followed by a salad and choice of veal Marsala or sun-dried tomato and cheese ravioli and a dessert for a prix fixe of $25. The wine selection is a point of pride.

♿ **The Moondance Grille** (802-422-2600), the Woods Resort & Spa, Killington Road. Open for dinner and Sunday brunch. Chef-owned by Marc Andrew and Lori Scott, this new restaurant at in the attractive spa building has an eclectic, mouthwatering menu ranging from vegetable and goat cheese empanada with roasted tomatillo sauce ($12.95) to certified Angus tenderloin marinated in grilled rosemary and olive oil ($23.95).

🖍 ♿ **Ovations Restaurant** (802-422-6111), Killington Grand Resort, is open daily 11–9:30. This is a family-geared hotel dining room with soups and salads served all day and dinner selections ranging from pasta to a wild grill: charbroiled elk medallions, orange marinated duck breast, and boar sausage ($29.95).

EATING OUT 🖍 **Grist Mill** (802-422-3970), Killington Road on the Summit Lodge grounds. Open for lunch and dinner, Sunday brunch. This is a new building, nicely designed to look like a gristmill that has always stood on Summit Pond (there's a 90-year-old waterwheel). The inside is airy and pleasing, dominated by a huge stone hearth. The menu ranges from steaks and veal dishes through grilled swordfish to vegetable stir fry. There's a children's menu and blackboard specials.

McGrath's Irish Pub and the **Inn at Long Trail** (802-775-7181), Route 4, Killington. The pub is open nightly, the restaurant, during the high season. The 22-foot-long bar is made from a single log, and a protruding toe of the backyard cliff can be seen in both the pub and the dining room. The first place to serve Guinness on tap in Vermont, the pub boasts Vermont's largest selection of Irish whiskey and features Irish country and folk music in the pub on weekends. The house specialties are Guinness stew and shepherd's pie.

🖍 **Casey's Caboose** (802-422-3795), Killington Road, Killington. Open daily from 3 PM. The building incorporates a circa-1900 snowplow car and a great caboose to house the coveted tables in the place, but you really can't lose: The atmosphere throughout rates high on our short list of family dining spots. Free buffalo wings during happy hour. Burgers and salads all day and a great children's menu. Entrées: $18.95 for penne pasta with shrimp and garlic, $17.95 for ribs, $20.95–26 for filet mignon.

Cascades Lodge Restaurant (802-422-3731), top of Killington Road at Killington Village. Open daily, featuring big breakfasts. Locally known as a good dinner bet with a menu ranging from fettuccine Alfredo ($12.95) to paella ($26.95). Pub fare also available.

Charity's Tavern (802-422-3800), Killington Road, Killington. Open daily for lunch and dinner; brunch (11:30–3) Saturday and Sunday. Tiffany shades, 1880s saloon decor, and wooden booths—this is the place for French onion soup, a Reuben, or vegetarian casserole at lunch; steak is a good dinner choice. Informal, satisfying.

Mother Shapiro's (802-422-9933), Killington Road, Killington. The most popular place on the mountain for breakfast (open at 7:30 AM), good for lunch and dinner, too. A pubby, friendly place with big burgers and monster deli sandwiches, homemade soups, specials.

Peppino's Ristorante Italiano (802-422-3293), near the foot of Killington Road. A traditional, reasonably priced Italian restaurant with predictable menu and decor, reliable.

Mountain Meadows Lodge (802-775-1010). This pleasant, family-geared lodge (see *Lodging—Resorts*) offers casual dining with a choice of vegetarian dishes ($8.95–11.95) as well as entrées like veal Napoleon (veal medallions sautéed with fresh apples and mushrooms in a brandy cream sauce) for $15.95. Children are welcome; inquire about children's themed dining.

Back Behind Saloon (802-422-9907), junction of Routes 4 and 100 south, West Bridgewater. Open for dinner nightly. A zany atmosphere (look for the red caboose and antique Mobil gas pump), barnboard, stained glass, a big hearth. Specialties like venison and saloon roast duck augment basic American fare: steaks and chicken, generous portions. Entrées on the high side ($13.95–22.50). Children's menu.

Theodore's Tavern (802-773-3331), Cortina Inn, Route 4. A good bet for casual dining and après-ski.

Crazy Mountain (802-422-2113) in front of the Comfort Inn, Killington Road. Open from breakfast through dinner. An inviting gathering place with sofas, tables, pottery, periodicals, coffee, beer, soups, salads, wrap sandwiches, and blackboard specials.

Sugar & Spice (802-773-7832), Route 4, Mendon. Open 7–2 daily. A pancake restaurant housed in a large replica of a classic sugarhouse and surrounded by a 50-acre sugarbush. Besides dining on a variety of pancake, egg, and omelet dishes, along with soups and sandwiches, you can watch both maple candy and cheese being made several days a week. Gift shop.

♿ **Mrs. Brady's** (802-422-2020), Killington Road at Butternut on the Mountain. The atmosphere is casual and colorful, and the menu features a salad bar, steak, and seafood; includes a great American burger platter and gobbler (turkey on a grinder with stuffing and gravy), as well as baked stuffed lobster. There are also pasta, veal, and steak dishes; stir fries; plus pizza and a children's menu.

Ppeppers Bar & Grill (802-422-3177), in the Killington Mall, open daily 7 AM–11 PM, is a popular spot for breakfast, lunch, dinner, and take-out food.

PIZZA **Outback Pizza** (802-422-9885), Killington Road. Open from 3 in spring and winter, from 5 in summer and fall. Features wood-fired stone-baked pizza with prime ingredients.

Pizza Jerks (802-422-2304). A local favorite, part of a virtual café with Internet access.

See also "Rutland and the Lower Champlain Valley." Rutland is an exceptionally good "eating-out" town.

✷ Entertainment

MUSIC The **Killington Music Festival** (802-773-4003), a series of mostly chamber music concerts in Snowshed Lodge and at a scattering of other local sites; weekends in July and August.

APRÈS-SKI **The Wobbly Barn** (802-422-3392), Killington Road, Killington. A steakhouse (dinner 5–11) with plenty of music, dancing, blues, rock 'n' roll. Ski season only.

The Nightspot (802-422-9885), Killington Road, Killington. Dancing nightly to a DJ. Free ski tuning and happy-hour hors d'oeuvres nightly.

McGrath's Irish Pub at the Inn at Long Trail (802-775-7181), Route 4, Killington. Live Irish music on weekends to go with the Gaelic atmosphere and Guinness on tap. It's a great pub with a 22-foot-long bar made from a single log and a boulder protruding from the back wall.

Pickle Barrel (802-422-3035), Killington Road, Killington. "Some of the finest rock 'n' roll bands in the East."

✷ Selective Shopping

Bill's Country Store (802-773-9313), at the junction of Routes 4 and 100, Killington, stocks a broad spectrum of Vermont products, including cheese, maple goodies, deerskin gloves, and woodwork.

The Shops at the Shack and **The Ski Shack** (802-773-3600), Route 4 at Killington Road, Killington. Open daily 9–5:30. This place has just about everything in the way of sports clothes and equipment for adults and kids, much at discount prices; boutique name-brand shops include Nordica, North Face, Children's Shop, and Nike.

See also the Marketplace at Bridgewater Mill in "Woodstock/Quechee."

Long Trail Brewing Company (802-672-5011; www.longtrail.com), Route 4 west at Bridgewater Corners, produces Long Trail Ale as well as Pollenator, India Pale Ale, Stout, Black-berry, Wheat, and Harvest. Tastings and pub fare, daily noon–5.

✷ Special Events

January through March: Frequent **alpine ski races** for all ages at Killington and Pico.

Memorial Day weekend: **Rage Weekend** with **Killington Triathlon:** ski, mountain bike, cross-country run.

June–July: **Futures Golf Tour,** Green Mountain National Golf Course, Killington.

July 4: **Calvin Coolidge Birthday Memorial,** Plymouth.

July and August: **Killington Music Festival** (802-773-4003).

August: **Killington Renaissance Festival**

Columbus Day weekend: **Sheep and Wool Festival. Brewer's Fest,** Killington.

THE WHITE RIVER VALLEYS

"Vanishing Vermont" could be the subtitle for this chapter. As I-89 sweeps up through central Vermont in a grand 52-mile arc—from White River Junction to Montpelier—it yields a series of panoramas. Motorists see the high wall of the Green Mountains beyond the Braintree Range on the west and catch glimpses of an occasional valley village. What they don't see is one of Vermont's best-kept secrets: the classic old villages, abrupt valleys, and hill farms along the White River and its three branches.

The White River rises high in the Green Mountains above Granville Gulf and rushes down through Hancock, widening and slowing among farms in Rochester, keeping company with Route 100 until Stockbridge, where its course dictates a dogleg in the highway. Turning sharply east and carving a narrow valley for Route 107 (the Gaysville reach is an especially challenging one for kayakers during spring freshets), the river reaches Bethel, and begins to parallel Route 14 and I-89. As it courses through the Royaltons and Sharon on its way to the Connecticut River, tubing and fishing possibilities increase with the input of the three northern branches.

Each of these streams, rising some 20 miles north of of the main stem of the river, has carved its own valley. The First Branch, shadowed by Route 110, threads six covered bridges, lush farmland, and the unselfconsciously beautiful villages of Chelsea and Tunbridge. The Second Branch begins above the picturesque village of Brookfield, known for its floating bridge, and flows south along Route 14. The Third Branch rises in Roxbury, conveniently near a fish hatchery, and flows south through a lonely valley (along Route 12A) to Randolph, one of the few I-89 exits and an Amtrak stop as well as the only commercial center of any size in this entire area.

Beautiful as these valleys are, the high east–west roads that connect them, climbing up over the hills and down into the next valley, are more rewarding still. To begin exploring this back-roaded and unresortified heart of Vermont, you might exit in Sharon and climb through the Straffords to Tunbridge and north to Chelsea, west to Brookfield, then south to Randolph, on down Route 12, and west over Rochester Mountain. See *Scenic Drives* for tours that can pleasantly fill many days.

GUIDANCE **Randolph Area Chamber of Commerce** (802-728-9027; fax: 802-728-4705; www.randolphvt.com), 31 Route 66, Randolph 05060. Phone answered year-round, information center maintained Memorial Day through mid-October at

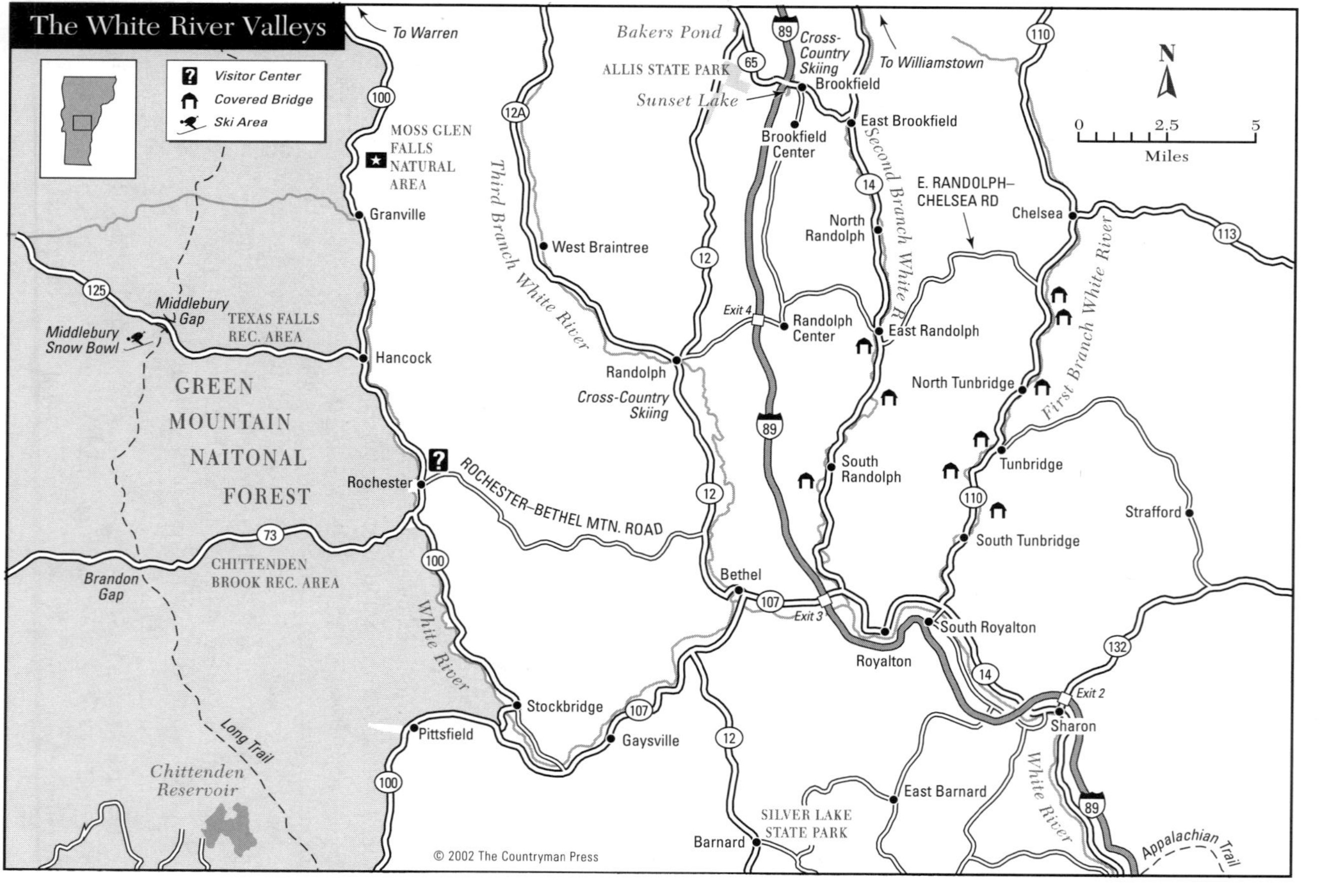
The White River Valleys
Visitor Center
Covered Bridge
Ski Area
To Warren
Bakers Pond
ALLIS STATE PARK
Sunset Lake
Cross-Country Skiing
To Williamstown
Brookfield
East Brookfield
Brookfield Center
MOSS GLEN FALLS NATURAL AREA
Granville
West Braintree
Third Branch White River
Second Branch White River
E. RANDOLPH–CHELSEA RD
Chelsea
North Randolph
First Branch White River
Middlebury Gap
TEXAS FALLS REC. AREA
Middlebury Snow Bowl
Hancock
Exit 4
Randolph Center
East Randolph
Randolph
Cross-Country Skiing
North Tunbridge
GREEN MOUNTAIN NAITONAL FOREST
Rochester
ROCHESTER–BETHEL MTN. ROAD
South Randolph
Tunbridge
Strafford
South Tunbridge
CHITTENDEN BROOK REC. AREA
Brandon Gap
Bethel
Exit 3
South Royalton
Royalton
White River
Exit 2
Sharon
Stockbridge
Pittsfield
Gaysville
Long Trail
Chittenden Reservoir
East Barnard
SILVER LAKE STATE PARK
Barnard
Appalachian Trail
0
2.5
5
Miles
N
100
12A
65
89
14
110
113
125
12
73
107
132

State Plaza just off I-89, exit 4 (next to the Mobil station); the chamber offices are just west on Route 66 across from the Montague Golf Club. Request a map brochure.

Green Mountain National Forest Ranger Office and Visitors Center (802-767-4261), Route 100 in Rochester. Open 8–4 daily. A magnificent new center (rest rooms) with detailed information on hiking, biking, picnicking, bird-watching, camping, and other recreation in this part of the GMNF.

Eastern Vermont Rivers & Byways (1-888-848-4199), the state's marketing organization for this region, publishes a magazine and maintains a web site, www.easternriververmont.com.

The Herald of Randolph (802-728-3232), Box 309, Randolph, carries local news and events for Orange and northern Windsor Counties.

GETTING THERE *By bus:* **Vermont Transit** buses stop just off I-89 at White River Junction and Randolph.

By train: **Amtrak's *Vermonter*** (1-800-USA-RAIL). Randolph and White River Junction (see "Upper Valley River Towns") are stops for trains from Washington, D.C., New York City, and Springfield and Amherst, Massachusetts, with connecting bus service to Montreal; the baggage car has bike racks.

By car: This area covers a wide, hilly swath of Vermont. I-89 runs diagonally across it but with only three exits (Sharon, Bethel, and Randolph). Towns are connected by beautiful old east–west ridge roads as well as north–south valley roads. See *Scenic Drives* for suggested routes.

GETTING AROUND *Taxi:* **JT's Taxi & Courier** (802-728-6209) is based in Randolph.

Car rental: **Especially Imports** (802-728-4455), Route 66, Randolph, can arrange to meet you at the train.

WHEN TO GO Brookfield and Rochester offer winter cross-country skiing, and Tunbridge draws Vermonters for the Vermont History Expo in June and the World's Fair in September. March brings sugaring; in May there's kayaking and in summer, tubing along the lower reaches of the White River. Given its scattering of appealing places to stay and its farms and back-roads scenery, this is a rewarding getaway area anytime except mud season (April and early May).

MEDICAL EMERGENCY **911** now serves the area.

Gifford Medical Center (802-728-4441), 44 South Main Street, Randolph.

✱ Villages

Sharon Village. An old commercial center at the junction of the river road (Route 14) and the high road (to Strafford), this remains a cluster of services just off I-89. Brooksie's offers roadfood; the columned Sharon Trading Post is a classic general store with a serious meat department, also selling local maple products.

The **Sharon Historical Society,** also at this crossroads, is open summer Sundays (1–3) and in early August on Old Home Day, a lively event at which guests over 70 can eat free at the chicken pie supper.

South Royalton Village. On a bend in the river and off Route 14, this classic railroad village frames an outsized green with an elevated bandstand and a Civil War cannon. A granite arch recalls the 1780 raid on Royalton by more than 300 Native Americans commanded by an English lieutenant. The railroad hotel, an 1887 brick Queen Anne–style commercial block, the train depot, and many of the clapboard buildings within eyeshot have all received a new lease on life thanks to the presence of Vermont's first and only law school. Founded in 1972 and headquartered in a tower-topped old school building, Vermont Law School now draws students from around the country. In the village of Royalton, north on Route 14, most buildings predate the Civil War.

Tunbridge. Some 20,000 people jam into this village of 400 for four days each September. They come for the **Tunbridge World's Fair,** said to have originated in 1761 when the town received its charter from George III to hold two fairs each year. In fact, the fair dates back to 1867. Sited in a grassy, natural bowl by a bend in the river, it has everything an agricultural fair should have: a midway, livestock displays and contests, a Floral Hall, collections of old-time relics, dancing, sulky racing, a fiddlers contest, horse pulls, a grandstand, and more. Known as the "Drunkards Reunion" during a prolonged era when it is claimed that anyone found sober after 3 PM was expelled as a nuisance, it is now billed as a family event. The fairgrounds are also the site of the annual June Vermont History Expo, showcasing Vermont historical societies from around the state. Tunbridge boasts four covered bridges (see our map), a fishing hole, and a photogenic brick Methodist church (in South Tunbridge).

THE GREEN IN SOUTH ROYALTON

Kim Grant

Christina Tree

TWIN GENERAL STORES DISTINGUISH CHELSEA VILLAGE

Strafford. If it were any nearer a highway this quietly spectacular village would be mobbed with tourists but, happily, it's 15 miles northwest of I-91, 9 miles north of I-89, and not on the way to anywhere except Tunbridge. Coming *from* Tunbridge, the road climbs steeply through woods and fields, finally cresting and beginning its downhill run through beautifully restored farms with ponds out back (pools would be too garish), stables, and other signs of wealth not evident on the western side of the mountain. Aristocratic homes—which include the Gothic Revival Justin Morrill Homestead (see *To See*)—cluster near the common, at the head of which stands the churchlike white-clapboard Town House, built in 1799, so classic it's a staple of New England photo books.

Chelsea. Chelsea has been hailed as one of the few remaining bastions of "Vermont character." It is a town with not one but two picturesque commons and an unusual survival rate of dairy farms and maple producers. Noteworthy buildings include a steepled church, the Orange County Courthouse, a brick library, its own bank (since 1822), and many Federal-era homes, one now the outstanding Shire Inn (see *Lodging—Inns*). An amazing number of services—post office, restaurants, barber, and fish and wildlife office—are compressed into a small space. The commercial heart of town revolves around twin 1818 brick buildings that both house general stores, one of which (Will's) is known for its ice cream.

Brookfield. "Pond Village," as it's known, easily ranks among the most picturesque four corners in all New England. It boasts the state's oldest continuously operating library (established in 1791) and Sunset Lake, traversed by a recently rebuilt floating bridge, buoyed by barrels (the lake is too deep to support a pillared span). During the summer, much of its traffic stops midway to fish, and on the last Saturday in January it is a coveted viewing point for one of New England's last ice-harvest festivals. At the center of the village is Green Trails Inn, with extensive cross-country trails (see *Lodging—Inns*). Ariel's Restaurant, overlooking the pond, draws diners from a 50-mile radius (see *Dining Out*). Allis State Park, a few miles west, offers camping, picnicking, and a sweeping view (see *Green Space*). The

Marvin Newton House, Ridge Road in Brookfield Center, is an eight-room home built in 1835, now housing local historical exhibits (open Sundays in July and August, 2–5; $2; 802-276-3959).

Bethel. At the confluence of the White River and its Third Branch as well as of Routes 107 and 12, this was once a major source of white granite used to face such buildings as Washington, D.C.'s, Union Station. An eight-sided former school, now a community center, stands on Route 14 in West Bethel.

Randolph. Randolph Center (east on Route 66 from I-89 exit 4) is clearly the oldest of the five Randolphs. It's a lineup of brick and clapboard Federal-era mansions along a main street that was cut unusually wide with the idea that this might be the state capital. Instead, it is now a quiet village in which life centers on Floyd's General Store and the nearby complex of Vermont Technical College, grown from the grammar school built here in 1806. According to a historical marker, musician and schoolmaster Justin Morgan brought a young stallion from Massachusetts to his home here in 1789 (Justin Morgan the man lies buried in the nearby cemetery; the grave of Justin Morgan the horse is marked by a simple stone off Route 110 in Chelsea). Randolph remains a horsey community, but with the arrival of the railroad in the mid–19th century, population shifted from the center down to the valley, 3 miles west (now the other side of I-89). It's here that Amtrak now stops, at the station on Main Street, steps from the Chandler Music Hall, a lively town-owned performance center (see *Entertainment*). The **Randolph Historical Society Museum** (802-728-5398), upstairs in the police station, exhibits memorabilia, with the emphasis on railroading; three rooms are furnished in circa-1900 style. (Open May through October, Sunday 2–4, and by appointment. $1 per adult.)

Rochester straddles Route 100 in a quiet valley between the Green Mountains and the Braintree Range. It has a large village green, a reclusive summer population, and a suprising spread of lodging options, from luxurious hideaways to a working farm. The approach over Rochester Mountain (see *Scenic Drives*) provides panoramic views and a delightful alternation of field and forest. North of the village on Route 100 the magnificent new **Green Mountain National Forest Visitors Center** (see *Guidance*) orients sportsmen, picnickers, and hikers to the largely uninhabited western portion of the town that lies within the GMNF. The Bingo area, in particular, offers swimming holes, abandoned town roads, cellar holes, and Civil War–era cemeteries. Rochester is also a center for mountain biking and for cross-country skiing (see *To Do*). The **Rochester Historical Society,** housed over the library, is open Tuesday and Thursday 1–4 and Saturday 9–noon. Summer brings **Chamber Music Society** programs at the Federated Church and Sunday-evening concerts on the green.

* To See

Floating Bridge at Sunset Lake, Brookfield Village. First built in 1820 and replaced six times since, this is the only heavily used bridge of its kind in the country. It's quite picturesque.

Joseph Smith Memorial and Birthplace (802-763-7742), Darby Hill Road, South Royalton. Open year-round during daylight hours, seasonal guided tours, late May through mid-October, Wednesday through Sunday. A marker on Route 14 (1 mile southeast of the village) points you up a steep, 2-mile hill to a complex maintained by the Mormon Church. It includes paintings, sculpture, exhibits, and a film housed in two buildings. A 38½-foot-high shaft, cut from Barre granite in 1908, marks the site of the farm on which the founder of the Church of Jesus Christ of Latter-day Saints was born in 1805 and lived until he was 10. Each foot on the shaft marks a year in the life of the prophet, who was murdered by a mob in Carthage, Illinois, in 1844. The 360 well-maintained acres include picnic tables.

COVERED BRIDGES There are four covered bridges in Tunbridge: the **Cilley Bridge,** south of the junction of Route 110 with Strafford Road and built in 1883; the **Howe Bridge** (1879), east off Route 110 in South Tunbridge; and in North Tunbridge, the 1845 **Flint Bridge** and 1902 **Larkin Bridge,** both east of Route 110. The **Mill Bridge** (1883), crushed by ice in the winter of 1999, has been rebuilt. In Randolph, two multiple kingpost bridges, both built in 1904, are just off Route 14 between East Randolph and South Randolph. In Chelsea, there is the **Moxley** or **Guy Bridge,** an 1886 queenpost, east off Route 110.

SCENIC DRIVES **The Quickie Tour:** Sharon to South Royalton via Strafford and Tunbridge (22 miles). Take I-89 to exit 2, Sharon, good for gas and food (see *Villages*), and climb Route 132 to Strafford, site of the Justin Morrill Homestead and the Town House. Continue up and over the hills and down into Tunbridge (see *Villages*). If time permits turn north on Route 110 for 5 miles and past three covered bridges (see above) to Chelsea, a good place to stay (see *Villages*). Otherwise turn south on Route 110 for the 5 scenic miles back (past one covered bridge) to Route 14 at South Royalton (see *Villages*) and pick up I-89 again at exit 3 in Royalton, or turn back down Route 14 to Sharon. En route you pass the turnoff for the Joseph Smith Memorial.

Royalton to Randolph via Granville Gulch (117 miles). Take I-89 to exit 3, just west of Eaton's Sugar House. The low road west (Route 107) follows the White River to Route 100, but the high road over **Rochester Mountain** saves 11 miles and is beautiful besides. At the junction in Bethel take Route 12 north a little more than 2 miles and turn left onto Camp Brook Road. At the height-of-land the view is a panorama of the Green Mountains ahead. Keep to the main road (the one with the line down the middle) until a T, and turn left (it's marked) for the descent into Rochester (see *Villages*). Turn north on Route 100 and, 4 miles up, note the Hancock Hotel and the turnoff for Middlebury Gap, Route 125 (see below). Continuing north on Route 100, the mountain walls close in as you near **Granville Gulf** and **Moss Glen Falls.** Turn off Route 100 into **Warren Village** (see "Sugarbush/Mad River Valley") and follow signs 2 miles to East Warren, where you turn onto the **Roxbury Mountain Road.** Be sure to pull out near the top for a look back down the valley. It's a popular soaring center, and you may see a glider or hawks riding the thermal waves. Continue downhill to Route 12A and turn south, following the railroad tracks and the Third Branch of the White River past the turnoff for Braintree Hill (see *Picnicking*) to Randolph and back to I-89, exit 4.

Randolph Center, Brookfield, Chelsea (27 miles). Take I-89 to exit 4 and turn

JUSTIN MORRILL AND HIS HOMESTEAD

Justin Morrill Homestead (802-828-3015), Route 132, Strafford Village. Open Memorial Day through Columbus Day, Wednesday through Sunday 11–5; $2; tours on the hour. Justin Morrill never went to college but is remembered as the congressman who sponsored the Land Grant Colleges Acts (one in 1862 and another in 1890) that created more than 76 present institutions, currently enrolling some 2.9 million students. Many have evolved into state universities. The son of a Strafford blacksmith, Morrill made enough money as a country storekeeper (which he parleyed into a chain of stores) to retire at age 38 and enter politics on an antislavery and temperance platform. He served in Congress for 44 years (1855–98), never finding much time to spend in his striking, 17-room Gothic Revival mansion because he kept getting reelected. A man who was instrumental in the design and construction of the Washington Monument and the Library of Congress, Justin Morrill helped design his own house and (now restored) gardens and orchard. The icehouse and carriage barn are fitted with interpretive panels about Morrill and with the many national events in which he played a role. Inside and out, this is a fascinating house, well maintained by the Vermont Division of Historic Preservation. Inquire about frequent events: the annual garden party, croquet tournament, faux painting, landscape gardening, village walks, and more.

JUSTIN MORRILL HOMESTEAD IN STRAFFORD

east into Randolph Center (see *Villages*), then north along a glorious ridge road (marked TO BROOKFIELD) to Brookfield (see *Villages*) with its famous floating bridge across Sunset Lake, leading to Allis State Park. Even addicted as we are to shotcuts, we recommend passing up the gravel road from East Brookfield to Chelsea; go around through East Randolph (6 miles south on Route 14, then turn onto the road marked for Chelsea. It's 6 more miles). Chelsea (see *Villages*) is a good place to stay and from which to explore the Barre/Montpelier area. Otherwise return on Route 110 and Route 14 to I-89, passing six covered bridges.

Middlebury Gap. Robert Frost Memorial Drive is too glorious a stretch of road to pass by. From Route 100 in Hancock turn onto Route 125 west and take the short detour into **Texas Falls** (see the box). Route 125 continues to climb through Middlebury Gap (the Long Trail crosses at an altitude of 2,149 feet). Then it's on through the Green Mountain National Forest until the rambling yellow, wooden Bread Loaf Inn and its annexes unexpectedly appear, banked in hydrangeas. Owned by Middlebury College, this 1860s hotel is nationally known for its summer literary programs. Note the turnoff just west for the **Robert Frost Cabin.** A dirt road leads to the Homer Noble farm; a short way past the farm is the cabin in which Robert Frost spent 23 summers. Continue to the Robert Frost Wayside (see *Green Space* in "Addison County"). Return the way you came or continue to Middlebury and return to Route 100 via Brandon Gap (Route 73), Appalachian Gap (Route 117) or Lincoln Gap (see "Sugarbush/Mad River Valley").

✷ To Do

BIKING In Randolph the **Three Stallion Inn** (see *Lodging—Inns*) offers its own network of trails and rents bikes. They sell a map published by the local White River Valley Trails Association that details 240 miles of riding including miles of Class 4 roads (public but not maintained for vehicles) and singletrack grass and dirt trails. Theoretically you can take Amtrak to Randolph (baggage cars carry bikes). Frequent bicycle races are staged at the Green Mountain Stock Farm (surrounding the inn).

Green Mountain Bikes (802-767-4464; 1-800-767-7882; www.greenmountainbikes.com), Route 100 in the village of Rochester. Doon Hinderyckx is a fount of information about local trails in and beyond the national forest. He offers guided tours and rents and sells mountain and cross bikes.

Also check with the Green Mountain National Forest Visitors Center (see *Guidance*) and this chapter's *Scenic Drives*.

BOATING While most of the White River is navigable in high water (May through July), the 20-mile stretch from Rochester to Bethel is especially popular with canoeists, tubers, and kayakers. A good place to put in is at the cement bridge just south of Rochester. For boat rentals see "Sugarbush/Mad River Valley."

FISHING Trout abound at the junction of the Tweed and White Rivers, downstream of Bethel, above Randolph, and below Royalton. Fly-fishing enthusiasts find the Bethel area good for large rainbow and brown trout, while below Royal-

TEXAS FALLS

Texas Falls, Hancock. On Route 125 west of Route 100 a sign points to the road to the falls. It's a quarter mile. The falls are an exceptional series of shoots and pools, rimmed by interesting rock formations and spanned by footbridges. Swimming is not permitted, but a short, steep (be careful) trail leads down to the falls. A quarter mile farther up the road is a picnic area with grills and outhouses.

ton there are bass, spring walleye, and trout.

Fishing licenses are available at **Tracy's Midway,** a convenience store and gas station on North Main Street in Sharon.

Baker's Pond on Route 12 in Brookfield has a parking area and boat launch, good for trout fishing. There is a boat access on **Rood Pond** in Williamstown and a canoe access on **Sunset Lake** in Brookfield, also stocked with trout. The floating bridge is a popular fishing spot.

White River National Fish Hatchery, Gaysville (Bethel), Route 12/107 west of Bethel Village, raises imprint salmon for the Connecticut River restoration program.

Roxbury State Fish Hatchery, Route 12A in Roxbury, raises brookies and Atlantic salmon, over 350,000 fish per year. It abuts the Third Branch of the White River, and the fishing downstream can be amazing.

GOLF **Montague Golf Club** (802-728-3806), Randolph. One of the oldest courses in Vermont, 18 holes. The Second Branch of the White River winds through it. Light fare is served in the clubhouse; lessons offered. *Note:* A driving range maintained by the Three Stallion Inn (see *Lodging—Inns*) is just west on Route 66.

The White River Golf Club (802-767-GOLF), Route 100, Rochester. Nine holes, clubhouse with a restaurant serving lunch (dinner by arrangement). Open May 1 through October 31. Next to it is a driving range (802-767-3211).

HIKING The **Green Mountain National Forest** (see *Guidance*) harbors numerous trails. On Route 100 itself in Granville Gulf there are two short nature trails. At Moss Glen Falls, the half-mile loop on the west side of the road is more rugged than the 1-mile loop on the east side.

In **Allis State Park,** Brookfield (off Route 12; see *Green Space*), a 2.5-mile trail circles down through meadows and back up through woods. A trail leads from the picnic area to a fire tower with one of the best views in central Vermont (on a clear day, from Killington/Pico to Mount Mansfield to Ascutney). The Bear Hill Nature Trail is another reason for finding this special place.

HORSEBACK RIDING **Riverside Farm Stables** (802-746-8544; www.riverside-farm.com), Route 100, Pittsfield offers trail and pony rides for its stretch of the Route 100 corridor.

LLAMA HIKING **Heart of Vermont Llama Hikes** (802-889-9611), Fernwood Llama Farm, Spring Road, Tunbridge. Memorial Day through Columbus Day: Picnic hikes, moonrise hikes, half- and full-day hikes offered through the rural countryside. Fiber and fiber products also sold.

FARMS TO VISIT **Vermont Technical College** maintains a demonstration farm in Randolph Center (802-728-3395). Visitors can tour the sugarhouse, apple orchard (pick your own), and dairy barn.

Neighborly Farms of Vermont (802-728-4700; 1-888-212-6898), North Randolph Road, Randolph Center. Rob and Linda Dimmick and their three young children run an organic dairy and make organic cheeses that they sell at the farm and through area stores. Visitors are welcome to see the cows and watch cheese making (call ahead).

Maple Ridge Sheep Farm (802-728-3081) in Braintree, said to be the oldest and largest Shetland sheep farm in the country, produces fleece, machine-washable sheepskin, yarn, knit and woven items, meat. Call first.

PICNICKING **Brookfield Gulf,** Route 12 west of Brookfield. Picnic facility, nature trail.

Braintree Hill, Braintree Hill Road (off Route 12A just west of downtown Randolph). A great picnic spot with an early cemetery and sweeping views to the White Mountains. The handsome Braintree Meeting House here is open by appointment and on Old Home Day (first Sunday in August).

Bingo Brook in Rochester off Route 73 in the national forest. Picnic sites with grills by a mountain stream, good for fishing and swimming.

Also see Allis State Park in *Green Space*, Texas Falls in *To See,* and the Robert Frost Wayside in *Scenic Drives.*

SWIMMING Ask locally about various swimming holes in the First, Second, and Third Branches and the main stem of the White River. In Randolph Center, there is a man-made beach, bathhouse, and picnic area. At **Lake Champagne,** there is swimming at a private campground that charges admission. There is also a pool at the recreational park in Randolph.

TUBING Tubing on the White River is so popular that you can rent tubes a number of places along the stretch from Gaysville to South Royalton. Sources at this writing include **White River Valley Camping** (802-234-9115) and **Gaysville Trading Company** (802-234-9118), both in Gaysville, and the **Stockbridge General Store** (802-234-9118).

✷ Winter Sports

CROSS-COUNTRY SKIING **Green Mountain Ski Touring Club** (802-728-9122; 1-800-424-5575), Three Stallion Inn, off Route 66, Randolph. Fifty km of groomed and tracked trails weave through woods and meadows; instruction and rentals available; marked from Route 66.

Green Trails Ski Touring Center (802-276-3412), Brookfield. Some 33 km of trails meander around frozen ponds, through woods, and over meadows at elevations of 1,132 to 1,572 feet. A ski shop offers rentals and instruction.

Nordic Adventures (802-767-3272), Route 100, Rochester Village. Dean Mendell offers a full line of cross-country equipment and snowshoes, lessons, and guided tours. **Green Mountain National Forest** (see *Guidance*) maintains trails in Rochester on Liberty Hill and at Chittenden Brook.

✷ Green Space

Allis State Park (802-276-3175), Brookfield. Open May 30 through September 15. A camping area with 22 sites, 4 with lean-tos (no hook-ups), each on a wooded loop road separate from the picnic area, in which you can choose tables on a windy hilltop or under a pavilion. A hiking trail (see *To Do—Hiking*) commands a fine view of the valley northward.

Green Mountain National Forest (GMNF). Among the highlights of the Rochester district of the GMNF are the Long Trail and the Texas Falls Recreation Area (see *To See*). A good short hike is from Brandon Gap north two-thirds of a mile to the cliffs of Mount Horrid, where there are views to the east. Because of the abundance of other things to do in this area, be sure to drop into the new GMNF Visitors Center (see *Guidance*) 2 miles north of the Rochester green on Route 100 (802-767-4261).

✷ Lodging

INNS ⚭ **The Shire Inn** (802-685-3031; 1-800-441-6908; www.shireinn.com), Chelsea 05038. This is precisely the kind of Vermont country inn that everyone fantasizes about: a classic 1832 Federal-era brick mansion furnished with antiques, rooms with canopy beds and working fireplaces (all private bath), set right on the green of a handsome-yet-workaday village. It's the kind of place that could easily be too stiff and self-conscious, but thanks to Jay and Karen Keller, you'll feel right at home from the moment you enter the sunny parlor with its elegant hearth. Be sure to arrive in good time for dinner, a five-course candlelight event that might begin with a three-layer vegetable terrine followed by a pear sorbet, then chicken Wellington, veal Sicilian, or a vegetable ravioli with basil sauce, followed by a salad and irresistible dessert (wine is served). Upstairs Jay has laid a fire that's waiting when you fall into that canopy bed. The breakfast selection might include apple pancakes, herb-cheese omelets, and spinach quiche. The Kellers are delighted to tune in guests to the possibilities of things to see and do; bicycles and cross-country skis (snowmobile trails web the area) are provided. You might, however, want to just find yourself a corner of the flower garden. The six rooms are $110–155 B&B, $185–225 including dinner plus 15 percent service. No smoking. Children under 7 inappropriate except in the nearby two-bedroom cottage, in which pets are also accepted ($145 per day).

⚭ **Green Trails Inn** (802-276-3412; 1-800-243-3412; www.greentrailsinn.com), Brookfield 05036. It all began with Jessie Fiske, a Brookfield native who became one of the first women professors at Rutgers University, in New Jersey. She rented rooms to her students and associates, who spent summers horseback riding and "botanizing" with Miss Fiske. The present inn consists of 12 rooms (9 with private bath) and one suite, some in the 1790s Guest House (one room retains its 18th-century stenciling), more in the inn, which offers a large hearth and a sunny dining room. The horses are gone, but the trails are still good for walking and cross-country skiing (33 km are marked and groomed). The inn sits just across from the floating bridge and a small beach on Sunset Pond, which invites canoeing and fishing. Nina Gaby and Craig Smith are your friendly hosts. Jessie Fiske's old riding ring up on the hillside is now a frequent site for weddings for up to 250 people. Rates are $90 per couple (shared bath) to $160 for the two-room suite with a fireplace, breakfast included; MAP available in winter. *Note:* Ariel's Restaurant (see *Dining Out*) is across the street.

ꝏ **Three Stallion Inn** (802-728-5575; 1-800-424-5575; www.3stallion-inn.com), off Route 66, Randolph 05060. Geared to sports-minded guests, especially cross-country skiers and mountain bikers, in addition to fishermen and golfers. This stone farmhouse is set on 1,300 acres of pasture and woodland, with some 33 miles of singletrack trails, part of an old estate—the Green Mountain Stock Farm. The lively Morgan Pub and Lippitt's Restaurant (see *Eating Out* and *Dining Out*) are off away from the rest of the inn. Facilities include a fitness room, a whirlpool and sauna, two tennis courts, and an outdoor lap pool. The adjoining Montague Golf Club is 18 holes (see *To Do—Golf*), and the inn also maintains a driving range. There's swimming and brown trout in the Third Branch of the White River, which runs through the property, and a trout pond invites catch-and-release. The 15 guest rooms include 3 family suites and range from $120 (shared bath) to $155 double for a room with private bath. Continental breakfast included; MAP and group packages available. Inquire about weddings and special packages.

Tupper Farm Lodge (802-767-4243; www.tupperfarmlodge.com), RR 1, Box 149, Rochester 05767. An 1820s farmhouse on Route 100, known for its friendly atmosphere and good cooking. Roger and Anne Verme have been welcoming guests since 1971. They accommodate 30 in 10 rooms, most with private bath. They cater to skiers and bicyclists with bountiful breakfasts and candlelit dinners. The swimming hole is across the road in the White River. $40–54 per person MAP, $60 per couple. B&B rate available in summer only; ski-week and children's rates.

BED & BREAKFASTS **Cooper-Webber House** (802-767-4742), Route 100 (Box 436), Rochester 05767. Ron and Sandy Brown have skillfully restored this magnificent vintage-1830s Federal house in the center of Rochester Village. Enter through the screened patio furnished with rocking chairs into a big country kitchen. Beyond: comfortable, uncluttered common spaces with fireplaces. Three guest rooms are unfussily furnished with early-19th-century-style (but comfortable) four-poster beds and handmade quilts. One room with a private bath, two with shared. An upstairs library with a woodstove is stocked with irresistible books. $70–75 includes a full breakfast.

🐾 **Greenhurst Inn** (802-234-9474; 1-800-510-2553), Bethel 05032, a Victorian mansion on the western fringe of Bethel, across Route 107 from the river. There are 13 guest rooms, 7 with private bath (the most cheerful on the third floor); these include a spacious tower room ($90) and the Victorian Suite, tucked under the eaves with a skylight. Longtime innkeeper Lyle Wolfe has a library of 4,000 books. $50–95 double per room; $100 for Victoria's Suite, with a sitting room and private bath; breakfast included. Dogs accepted.

The New Homestead (802-767-4751), Rochester 05767. Don't be put off by the funky exterior of this old house in the village. Inside it's clean and comfortable, with an eclectic mix of art and attractive quilts: five rooms, three with private bath, two with shared. $55 per room year-round includes a sumptuous breakfast of homegrown eggs, jams, spuds, and homemade bread. Your hosts are Sandy Haas and David Marmor.

Brookfield Guest House (802-276-3146), Pond Village near the floating bridge 05036. Former Bostonians George and Connie Karal offer a sophisticated B&B with a large verandah in the middle of this special village, steps from Sunset Pond and its floating bridge. The two new suites are beauties, especially the ground-floor green room with private bath, sleeping three. Upstairs two rooms share a bath. $95–125 per couple includes a full breakfast. No children under 10 please.

Inn at Johnnycake Flats (802-485-8961; www.johnnycakeflats.com), RR 1, Carrie Howe Road, Roxbury (off Route 12A) 05669. Off the beaten track, but handy to Sugarbush, geared to guests with an interest in nature. Hosts Debra and Jim Rogler have traveled in New Zealand, Australia, and throughout the States and enjoy tuning guests into their surroundings, beginning with the 16 surrounding acres with sheep and two frog ponds. The house was an early-1800s stage stop, and the living room fireplace is made from handmade bricks. There are three guest rooms furnished with antiques and Debra's quilts. Choose from double or twin beds; a two-bunk room can work for children. From $65–85 (for the room with private bath and a little library), a country breakfast included. Guests are welcome to use the innkeepers' snowshoes, cross-country skis, and bicycles.

FARMS 🍼 **Liberty Hill Farm** (802-767-3926; www.libertyhillfarm.com), 511 Liberty Hill Road, Rochester 05767. This is a working, 150-head dairy farm set in a broad meadow off Route 100—a great place for families. Bob and Beth Kennett's own sons are grown but they remain family geared, with cribs, high chairs, plenty of toys, some chicks, and kittens. The 150-year-old farmhouse has seven guest rooms (five with double beds, one with two single beds, and a room with five single beds) and four shared baths; families can spread into two rooms sharing a sitting room and bath. Meals are served family-style, and Beth makes everything from scratch. In summer you can hear the gurgle of the White River (good for trout fishing as well as its swimming hole) from the porch, and in winter you can ski off into the village across the meadows. $70 per adult, $30 per child under 12, MAP.

∞ 🐾 🍼 **Harvey's Mountain View Inn** (802-767-4273), Rochester 05767.High above the valley in the North Hollow area, this spot offers spectacular mountain views. While it's no longer the working farm it was for six generations of Harveys (it's been in the family since 1809), Don and Maggie continue to welcome guests as they have since 1960. The 10 rooms (2 with private bath) are clean and comfortable, suited for family reunions, small groups, and weddings. There's also a two-bedroom housekeeping cottage (pets permitted) and a heated pool. Open year-round. $35–75 per person includes a hearty breakfast *and* dinner.

✐ **Round Robin Farm** (802-763-7025), Fay Brook Road, Strafford 05072. This is a 350-acre working dairy farm with one of Vermont's famous 10-sided round barns (built in 1917). It's been in the family for six generations. What's offered is the big old house or rooms therein (two rooms with double bed and two with twins) and a fridge with the fixings for making your own breakfast. Cross-country ski or walk woods and meadows. No smoking and no pets, please. A double room is $30 per person per night. Inquire about the price for the whole house.

Placidia Farm Bed & Breakfast (802-728-9883), Randolph 05060. This is an apartment in a hand-hewn log home (deck, kitchen, bedroom, and living room) on a large farm with its own pond. A full breakfast in Viola Frost-Latinen's plant-filled sun porch is included. $100 per couple; $45 each additional person.

MOTEL **The Columns Motor Lodge** (802-763-7040), Sharon 05065. A small, neat motor lodge attached to an old house. Located in Sharon Village, just off I-89, it has a nice gift shop and is across from both the general store and Brooksies Family Restaurant (see *Eating Out*), a good waystop. Cal and Joanne Keyler charge $42–48 double.

SECOND HOMES AND COTTAGES **Hawk North, Vermont's Mountain Hideaway** (1-800-832-8007; www.vthideaway.com), P.O. Box 529, Route 107, Pittsfield 05762. Hawk homes are nicely designed vacation houses, hidden away in the woods on sites scattered among Rochester and Stockbridge. No longer related to Hawk Mountain Resort, Hawk North maintains a check-in office at the junction of Routes 100 and 107. Each of the 10 homes is individually owned, and decor varies, but all offer spacious living/dining room and deck, full kitchen, and two to four bedrooms. Some have sauna and/or hot tub. Rates fluctuate wildly with the season: $240–475 per night for two to four bedrooms.

Birch Meadow Farm (802-276-3156), RD 1, Box 294A, Brookfield 05036, East Street off Route 65 south. This is Mary and Matt Commerford's woodsy hideaway, with three modern log cabins equipped for housekeeping. There are TVs and woodstoves, plus a B&B suite in the main house, which sits high on a hill with splendid views. $99–110 per couple, $15 each additional adult, $5 per child.

CAMPGROUNDS **Lake Champagne Campground** (802-728-5298), P.O. Box C, Randolph 05061. Open Memorial Day weekend through mid-October. A 150-acre property with fields, a 3-acre swim lake, hot showers, mountain views, and facilities for tents through full-sized RVs.

Chittenden Brook Campground in the Green Mountain National Forest (802-767-4261), 5.3 miles west of Rochester on Route 73. The 17 campsites are fitted with picnic tables and grills; there are hand-operated water pumps and vault toilets. The surrounding forest provides good fishing, hiking, and birding. No trailers over 18 feet. No hook-ups or showers.

Note: Primitive camping is permitted almost everywhere in the Green Mountain National Forest.

Allis State Park (summer: 802-276-3175; winter: 802-885-8891; reservations: 1-800-299-3071). Named for Wallace Allis, who deeded his Bear Mountain Farm to the state as a campground and recreational area. Sited on the summit of Bear Mountain, it includes a picnic area and trail to the fire tower, also 18 tent and 8 lean-to sites, each with a picnic table and fireplace. Hot showers but no hook-ups.

✷ Where to Eat

DINING OUT **Ariel's Restaurant & Pond Village Pub** (802-276-3939), Brookfield. Reservations requested. Open Thursday through Saturday with a full menu; Tuesday, Wednesday, and Sunday with a pub menu. Overlooking Sunset Lake in the middle of "Pond Village," this restaurant is known as one of the best places to eat in Vermont. Lee and Richard are chef-owners who specialize in Mediterranean and Pacific Rim dishes, unusual combinations of ingredients and spices. On an August day you might begin with a crabcake in pastry with mango slices and avocado puree ($9.25), and dine on seared sea scallops with a fresh corn and chive risotto and pesto butter sauce ($19.50) topped off with plum crisp with buttermilk sorbet. Pub entrées are in the $8.75–11.75 range and are child friendly.

The Inn at Idlewood (802-763-5236), Route 132, Sharon. Open Friday and Saturday by reservation year-round. Chef-owners Alex Bird and Marcy Marceau have both studied in France and are known as caterers but have established a huge reputation for their small dining rooms. "We don't turn tables," Alex stresses. "You are here for the evening." The ever-changing menu is a five-course dinner with a choice of entrées. One May night it included pan-seared Cavendish quail in mahogany glaze and roasted sea bass on a bed of fennel and roasted pepper. The choice of three desserts included choclate walnut brandy torte. The prix fixe is $40–48 (depending on your choices) and there's a long wine list, a mix of Californian and French. Inquire about weddings.

Stone Soup Restaurant (802-765-4301), on the green, Strafford. Open for dinner Thursday through Sunday 6–9. Reservations strongly suggested. There is no sign for this elegantly rustic restaurant that has acquired a strong following over the past two decades. You step from Strafford's handsome green into a cheery tavern room with a large hearth. The candlelit, low-beamed dining rooms are beyond. On our last visit, the blackboard menu included eggplant soup, osso buco, and garlic and lime chicken. Note the attractive herb garden. Personal checks, but no credit cards. Entrées $18.95–25.95.

♿ **Lippitts at the Three Stallion Inn** (802-728-5575), off Route 66 (just off I-89), Randolph. Open for dinner. At this writing the executive chef is from the Caribbean island of Anguilla and the sous chef specializes in Pacific Rim cuisine, a combination that can result in surprisingly successful dishes. The menu might include grilled salmon Niçoise with mesclun salad, roasted potatoes and onions, and olives ($14.95) and pasta purses filled with four cheeses, served with braised rainbow Swiss chard and finished Alfredo sauce ($15.95). Also see the Morgan's Pub under *Eating Out*. On summer Sundays there's a concert on the deck with live music by local bands.

Fox Stand Inn (802-763-8437), Route 14, Royalton. Dinner, Tuesday through Saturday; Sunday noon buffet. Homegrown beef and farm produce served in a landmark 1818 stagecoach inn. Never open when we stop by but local residents vouch for it; patio dining in summer. Moderate.

EATING OUT Roadfood, listed geographically south to north, off I-89.

I-89, exit 2

Brooksies Family Restaurant (802-763-8407), Sharon. A genuine family restaurant with counter service on one side and a slightly classier addition on the other. The diner opens early for breakfast and has a full lunch and dinner menu. Meals on the restaurant side can begin with baked stuffed mushroom caps and include roast duckling flambé, filet mignon, or spaghetti with meatballs. This is a traditional stop for many ski-bound families. Good pies.

Dixie's Country Kitchen (802-763-8721) Route 14 in Sharon on the way to South Royalton. Open for lunch and dinner. Good roadfood, seafood, steak, and $6.95 specials.

South Royalton House (802-763-8315) on the green, South Royalton. A historic railroad hotel, now owed by the Vermont Law School, serving lunch and dinner. Terrace dining in summer, with specials under $10.

Chelsea Station (802-763-8685) on the green, South Royalton. Booths, a counter, breakfast from 6 AM, a friendly atmosphere, and a basic menu.

I-89, exit 3

Eaton's Sugar House, Inc. (802-763-8809; 1-888-VT-MAPLE). Located at the junction of Routes 14 and 107 in Royalton, just off I-89. Open daily 7–7. A good old-fashioned family-owned restaurant featuring pancakes and local syrup, sandwiches, burgers, and reasonably priced daily specials. Try the turkey club made with fresh-carved turkey on homemade bread. Vermont maple syrup, cheese, and other products are also sold (see *Selective Shopping*).

Route 110 in Chelsea

Dixie's II, Chelsea. In the middle of the village, housed in a classic old brick bank building. This cheerful spot with a blackboard menu opens at 6:30 AM for breakfast; open for lunch and dinner except on Sunday and Monday, when it closes at 2 PM.

The Pines, Chelsea Village. Open from 3 PM. A friendly rural pub with a pool table, the local gathering spot and the food is fine.

Route 12 north of Bethel

Onion Flats (802-234-5169) north of Bethel. Roadfood, good cones, and onion rings.

I-89, exit 4 in Randolph

Debbie's Corner Café (802-728-6062), 2 Merchant's Row. Open for breakfst and lunch, known for omelets and specialty sandwiches.

Morgan's Pub at the Three Stallion Inn (800-424-5575), off Route 66 (just off I-89), Randolph. This is a popular local gathering place with a tavern menu that usually includes a char-grilled black Angus burgers and grilled chicken sandwichs.

Along Route 100

Rochester Café & Country Store

(802-767-4302), Route 100, Rochester Village. Open early for breakfast until 11:30, lunch until 4. Terrible coffee, great fries, good burgers and ice cream.

Kristina's Café, Merriam House, Route 100, Rochester. Just north of the general store and gas pumps, this recently rehabbed complex includes a 12-table café. Scheduled to open in June 2002, it will offer espresso, wholesome breakfast breads and muffins, soups, sandwiches, and salads.

Little Village Coffee Shop (802-767-9999), Rochester. Open Tuesday through Friday 8–3 and Saturday 10–3, then for live music 7–10. Gregg and Anne Ryan's comfortable space featuring organic coffees, herbal teas, baked goods. Also conversations and products for "sustainable living."

Old Hancock Hotel (802-767-4976), Hancock, at Route 125. Open weekdays 6–8, Friday and Saturday until 9. A 19th-century village hotel known for its breads, muffins, and pies, good roadfood. Pick up a sandwich to take to nearby Texas Falls (see *To See*).

✷ Entertainment

The Playhouse Movie Theatre, Main Street, Randolph, the oldest movie house in the state. Shows first-run flicks.

Randall Drive-In Movie Theatre, Route 12 in Bethel, operates in summer only.

✷ Selective Shopping

CHRISTMAS TREES **Redrock Farm** (802-685-2282), 53A Strafford Turnpike, Chelsea. Drop by any day of the year and pick out a balsam fir or white spruce (up to 6 feet) and it will be shipped to you via UPS at Christmas. A full-sized tree is $36 plus shipping; wreaths, too. Walt Rockwood and Jean Peterson usually take coffee breaks at 10 AM and 3 PM, good times to visit. Fishermen are welcome to test their skills on the pond.

The Green Mountain National Forest permits cutting your own Christmas tree (under 20 feet tall and in specific areas) providing that you obtain a tree tag ($5) from the town of Rochester.

SUGARHOUSES These maple producers sell syrup year-round and welcome visitors into their sugar shacks during March production periods.

Silloway Farms (802-728-5253, 802-728-5503), Boudro Road, Randolph Center, welcomes up to 20 visitors at a time.

Vermont Technical College Farm (802-728-3395, 802-728-3391), Randolph, Route 66 east off I-89, invites visitors to tour sugaring operations.

North Hollow Farm (802-767-4255), Route 100, Rochester. Maple syrup, gift baskets.

Eaton's Sugar House (802-763-8809), junction of Routes 14 and 107, just off I-89, exit 3. An old-fashioned, family-run, maple-focused complex in which you can watch maple candies being made and find a wide selection of maple treats, in addition to Vermont cheese and other products. A good place to get Christmas greens. See also *Eating Out*.

SPECIAL STORES **Michael Egan Blown Glass** (802-767-4547), Route 100, Granville beside the Only Village Store (see below). Open 10–5; closed Tuesdays. Don't pass up this new roadside studio. Mad River Valley native Michael Egan shapes Venetian-style, freehand blown-glass into spectacular vases, pitchers, and a variety of housewares as well as art glass.

Only Village Store (802-767-4711; outside Vermont: 1-800-828-1005), Route 100, Granville. This complex includes the **Hemenway Bowl Mill,** making decorative wooden bowls since 1857 with present machinery dating from the 1880s. Good for woodenware, toys, crafts, cards, books, clothing, baskets, smoked meats, cheeses, maple products, specialty foods, antiques. Antiques are also sold.

The Raptor Store (802-767-3552). Noted bird carver Floyd Scloz **[[Au: "Scloz" correct?]]** operates a small store exhibiting his work and selling carving supplies. Inquire about the Vermont Raptor Academy, series of workshops that regularly draw students from around the country.

Judy Jensen Clay Studio (802-767-3271), Route 100 down behind the Rochester Café. Open daily. Jensen's work ranges from tiny vases to large urns, tile to chess sets, sculpture, hand made cards, and plenty of highly decorative functional ware. She also displays work in fiber, wood, glass, iron, and paper.

Cover to Cover Books (802-728-5509), 27 North Main Street, Randolph. A full-service store selling new and old books, also cards, gifts; inquire about poetry readings.

Old Schoolhouse Books (763-2434), 106 Chelsea Street, on the green, South Royalton. An interesting selection of old and new books.

Irene Collins (802-765-4335) Route 132, South Strafford Village. Open April through mid February, Thursday through Saturday 11–5, Sunday 1–5. This mix of top quality designer and vintage clothing store is well worth a stop. Check out the new branch (same hours) in Rochester Village.

Merriam House, Route 100, Rochester. This handsome, newly rehabbed building includes a branch of the Irene Collins store described above, and Kristina's Café (see *Eating Out*).

✷ Special Events

January (last Saturday): **Brookfield Ice Harvest Festival:** ice cutting, ice sculpting, hot food, sledding, skating, skiing.

February: Strafford Winter Carnival.

March: Open sugarhouses.

Mid-June: **Vermont History Expo,** a two-day gathering of Vermont historical societies, varied events at the Tunbridge Fairgrounds.

July: **July 4 parade** in Strafford, a bigger one in Randolph. **Chandler Players** perform at Chandler Music Hall, Randolph. **Chelsea Flea Market:** 150 dealers cover both greens.

July, August: **Summer music school,** workshops at the Mountain School, Vershire. **Huntington Farm Show,** Strafford. **Brookfield Blues Festival**

CHANDLER MUSIC HALL

Chandler Music Hall (802-728-9133), Main Street, Randolph. A fine, acoustically outstanding music hall built in 1907 and restored to mint condition. It is now open year-round for musical and theatrical performances: chamber music, blues, jazz, opera, folksingers, the Vermont symphony, and Mud Season Talent Show.

VDT

HARVESTING ICE AT THE FLOATING BRIDGE IN BROOKFIELD

(off Route 65 in Brookfield, August). The **South Royalton Town Band,** in business for more than a century, gives free concerts on the green Thursday evening. **Sharon Old Home Day** (see *Villages*).

September: **New World Festival** (Sunday before Labor Day) at the Chandler Music Hall in Randolph features Celtic music, in addition to food and crafts. **World's Fair,** Tunbridge. **New England Mountain Bike Festival** (last weekend), Green Mountain Stock Farm, Randolph: a three-day noncompetitive event with guided rides for all ability levels.

October (Columbus Day weekend): **Lord's Acre Supper,** sale and auction, Barrett Hall, Strafford.

November: **Annual Hunters' Supper,** Barrett Hall, Strafford.

SUGARBUSH/MAD RIVER VALLEY

There were farms and lumber mills in this magnificent valley before Mad River Glen began attracting skiers in 1948, but the unique look and lifestyle of this community has been shaped by three ski areas, just as truly as the earlier villages grew around mills and commons. Its present character has been evolving since the '60s, when Sugarbush and then Glen Ellen (the two have since merged) triggered an influx of ski-struck urbanites who formed polo and fox hunt groups, built an airport, and opened and patronized a gliding school, specialty shops, and fine restaurants. Young architects eager to test new theories of solar heating and cluster housing designed New England's first trailside homes, first bottom-of-the-lift village and condominiums. Most of these settling skiers have remained, their numbers now augmented by their grown children and second-home owners who have come to retire. It's a well-heeled, active, ecological- and community-minded group.

Physically just 4 miles apart, philosophically Sugarbush and Mad River Glen seemed at opposite poles of the ski world in the '90s. By then it was painfully clear that northern New England's natural snow is too fickle a base for the big business that skiing had become, and that to make snow you need water. The two ski areas faced this challenge in their own ways.

Lacking a reliable source of water, Mad River Glen simply ignored it. This "ski it if you can" mountain continues to operate the nation's oldest lift, and it became the country's first cooperatively owned ski area (some 2,000 shares are currently divided among 1,600 shareholders). It also remains the only area in the East that bars snowboarders, featuring telemarking and animal tracking instead.

Water for making snow was, however, essential for the survival of Sugarbush, a major ski resort and the Valley's workhorse. Luckily, in 1995 it was bought by the Maine-based American Ski Company and acquired a 63-million-gallon snowmaking pond (to store water siphoned from the Mad River during peak flows) and other needed infrastructure improvements. In 2001, it again lucked out. The six-mountain, 115-trail skiing/riding resort is now owned by Summit Ventures, a limited partnership composed of long-time Valley skiers who have been involved with both of its resorts and have an understanding of how the two complement each other.

A few years ago the very question of what to call this magnificent valley (Mad River? Sugarbush?) would have sparked a debate, but residents now agree: It's the Mad River Valley, named for the river down its center. Seven miles wide, it is

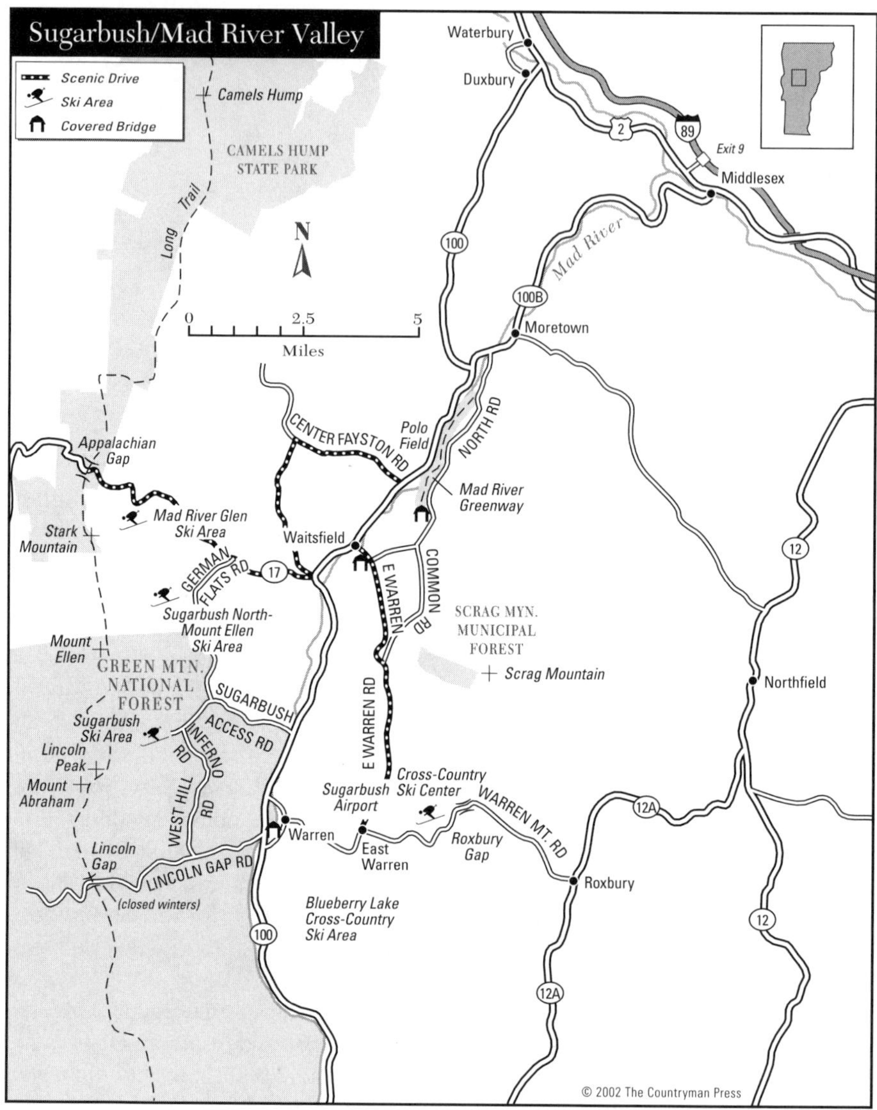

magnificent, with meadows stretching to the Roxbury Range on the east. In summer and fall, there is hiking on the Long Trail over some of the highest peaks in the Green Mountains, soaring in gliders above the valley, mountain biking on ski trails and high woods roads, a choice of horseback-riding options, fishing and swimming in the Mad River itself, not to mention outstanding golf, tennis, polo, and cricket.

With direct links to the Champlain Valley via the scenic roads through Appalachian and Lincoln Gaps on the west, this is a logical lodging and dining hub from which to explore some of Vermont's most magnificent and varied landscapes, especially during foliage season. Dining and shopping is as good as any resort area in the East. Several thousand visitors can bed down here on any given night, but it's far from obvious where. Visitors tend to drive right through on Route 100 (the

Valley spine), seeing nothing more than the clump of roadside shops in Waitsfield, missing Warren Village (6 miles south, just off Route 100) entirely. "The Valley" (as it's known locally) lacks the high-profile image enjoyed by rival Green Mountain resorts to north and south—which is fine by residents and regulars.

GUIDANCE **Sugarbush Chamber of Commerce** (802-496-3409; lodging: 1-800-82-VISIT; www.madrivervalley.com), Box 173, Waitsfield 05673. A walk-in visitors center in the General Wait House, Route 100, Waitsfield, is open year-round 9–5 weekdays, Saturday 9–1. During crunch times, vacancies are posted after 5 PM, in the lobby, near the courtesy phone. Request the free guide.

Green Mountain National Forest Ranger District Office and Visitors Center (802-767-4261), Route 100 in Rochester. Open 8–4. While this magnificent new information center is 25 miles south of Warren, it's worth knowing it's there (see "The White River Valleys") as a resource for exploring much of the area immediately west and south of the Valley.

GETTING THERE *By bus and train:* Waterbury, 12 miles north of Waitsfield, is the nearest **Vermont Transit** and **Amtrak** stop.

By air: Burlington Airport is 45 miles away; see *Getting There* in "Burlington Region" for carriers.

By car: Valley residents will tell you that the quickest route from points south is I-89 to Randolph and 15 miles up Route 12A to Roxbury, then 8 miles over the Roxbury Gap to Warren. This is also the most scenic way (the valley view from the top of the gap is spectacular), but be forewarned that this high road can be treacherous in winter. In snow, play it safe and take I-89 to Middlesex, exit 9, then 100B the 13 miles south to Waitsfield.

GETTING AROUND During ski season, shuttles circle between condos at the top of the access road and restaurants and nightspots. Many inns have their own transport to the lifts.

Valley Transit's "Mad Bus" runs year-round, with increased frequency in winter. This is free public transportation that ties the Valley floor to all three mountain base areas. Much more than a shuttle—clean, modern 26-passenger buses. Nine buses run in winter 7 days a week and until 1:30 AM on Saturday night.

C&L Taxi (802-496-4056) and **Morf Transit** (802-864-5588; 1-800-696-7433) offer local and long-distance service.

Note: Waitsfield–Champlain Valley Telecom offers free local calls on some pay phones (but not all, so check) scattered around the Valley.

WHEN TO GO Christmas week through February is high season, high volume, especially in a snowy season when Mad River Glen is wide open. Midweek during this same period is cheaper and far quieter. Ditto for March when the man-made snow base at Sugarbush is deep and weekend crowds have eased. By mid-April it's all over, and forget May and June, but come for the Warren Fourth of July parade and the many events that follow. As noted above, thanks to the gap roads (see *Scenic Drives*), this is an ideal hub for foliage. After the leaves fall it's dead until mid-December.

MEDICAL EMERGENCY 911 or ambulance (802-496-3600). **Mad River Valley Health Center** (802-496-3838), Route 100, Waitsfield.

✷ Villages

Note: The Mad River Valley includes Moretown (population: 653) to the north and Fayston (population: 1,040), an elusive town without a center that produced potatoes in the 1860s and was an important lumbering presence into the early 20th century. It's home to Mount Ellen and Mad River Glen ski areas and to inns along Route 17 and the German Flats Road.

Warren Village. The village center of the long-established farm town of Warren (population: 1,681) is a compact clapboard cluster of town hall, steepled church, and bandstand, with a double-porched general store by a waterfall across from an inn. At first glance the village doesn't look much different from how it did in the 1950s when Route 100 passed through its center, but the effect of Sugarbush, the ski resort that's way up an access road at the other end of town, has been total. The Pitcher Inn's self-consciously plain face masks an elegant restaurant and some of the most elaborate (and expensive) themed rooms in Vermont (see *Dining Out* and *Lodging*); the Warren Store (once a stagecoach inn itself) stocks a mix of gourmet food and upscale clothing and gifts (see *Selective Shopping—Special Shops*). Arts, antiques, and crafts are within an easy walk, and a covered bridge spans the Mad River. The village is the setting for one of Vermont's most colorful July 4 parades.

Waitsfield. The most populous (around 1,600) of the Valley's towns and its commercial center, home to Mad River Canoe, among several companies, and to two small, tasteful shopping malls that flank Route 100 on land that was farmed until the 1960s. The old village center is a half mile up Route 100, a gathering of 19th-century buildings, including a library and church, on and around Bridge Street (it's a covered bridge). Much larger and denser than it first looks, the village offers a sophisticated mix of boutiques and services, a movie house with a wine bar, and several first-rate restaurants. Changing historical exhibits are displayed in the General Wait House. Benjamin Wait, you learn, had been a member of Vermont's famed Rogers' Rangers and weathered dozens of French and Indian Wars battles, as well as serving in the Revolution before founding the town at age 53 in 1789. He later was pitted against his fellow settlers on the question of where to put the common. He wanted it just about where the commercial center is today (the original common has been left high and dry out on Joslin Hill Road). Largely denuded of its woods during its era as a logging and sheep-farming community, the town is now mostly wooded and home to more people than ever.

THE SLOPES OF MOUNT ELLEN RISE BEHIND THE WAITSFIELD FEDERATED CHURCH

Sugarbush Resorts/David Brownell

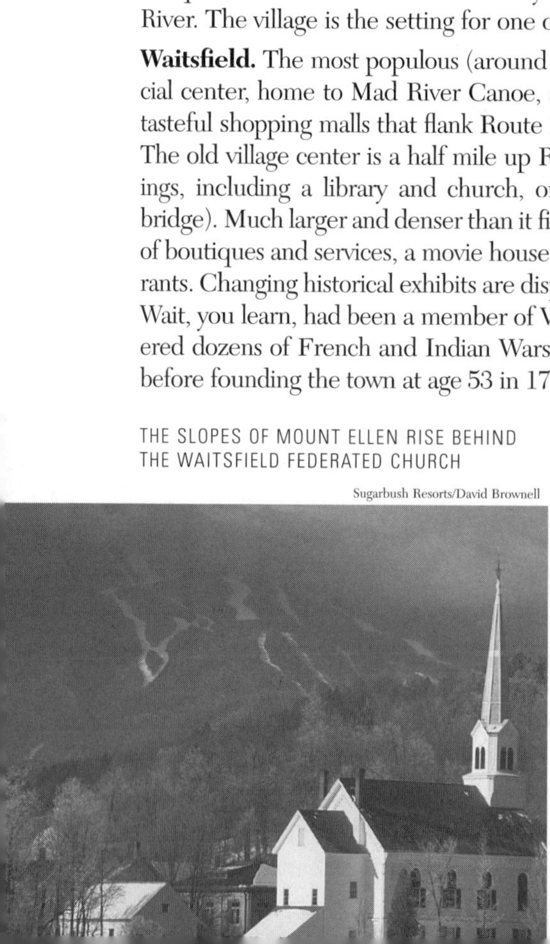

✷ To Do

In winter, the Valley's magnets are its alpine and cross-country-ski areas, but in summer there are no chairlifts, no slides, no factory outlets, just an unusual number of activities to pursue. Check the following list!

BICYCLING The Valley's wide variety of terrain, from smooth dirt roads to technical singletrack, lends itself to mountain biking. For rentals and service, check **Clearwater Sports** (802-496-2708), **Inverness Ski Shop** (802-496-3343), and **Stark Mountain Bike Works** (802-496-4800), all on Route 100 in Waitsfield. The routes listed here under *Scenic Drives* are also popular bike routes. Rentals and tours available. **Bike Vermont** (1-800-257-2226) offers weekend tours based at the 1824 House Inn (see *Lodging—Bed & Breakfasts*).

Mad River Greenway. A 3-mile trail follows the Mad River from a parking area on Trembly Road (turn off Route 100 north of Waitsfield at the sign for the Mad River Inn).

CANOEING ✐ **Clearwater Sports** (802-496-2708), Route 100, Waitsfield. Barry Bender offers learn-to-canoe and -kayak programs, full-moon canoe cruises on Waterbury Reservoir, camping excursions, also a children's day program (ages 9–13) and a 5-day wilderness camp program for 9- to 13-year-olds.

Vermont Pack & Paddle Outfitters (802-496-9006), based in Waitsfield, offers kayaking and canoeing tours.

FARMS ✐ **Mountain Valley Farm** (802-496-9255). Reservations required, but visitors are welcome to visit the barnyard animals—chickens, ducks, sheep, and horses. Wagon rides and sleigh rides are also offered.

Rootswork (802-496-2474; rootswork@madriver.com), East Warren Schoolhouse. This nonprofit organization is devoted to promoting and nurturing local agriculture. A retail store sells farmstead cheeses, vegetables, and appropriate books.

VERMONT ICELANDIC HORSE FARM IN WAITSFIELD

Kim Grant

FISHING Numerous streams offer good fly-fishing. The chamber of commerce (see *Guidance*) keeps a list of a half dozen guide services. Vermont fishing licenses are required and can be bought at **Kenyon's Variety Store,** Route 100, Waitsfield.

Vermont Pack & Paddle (802-496-9009) in Waitsfield offers guided fly-fish and ultralight fishing tours.

FITNESS CENTERS **Sugarbush Health & Racquet Club** (802-583-6700), Sugarbush Village, Warren. An outstanding complex with indoor and outdoor pools, indoor and outdoor Jacuzzis, whirlpool, sauna, steam room, exercise room, indoor squash, tennis and racquetball courts, massage room, aerobics studio, 11-station Nautilus, and a full range of cardiovascular equipment. The **Valley Rock Gym** (802-583-6754), part of this complex, features an indoor climbing wall, open 3–9 PM.

The Bridges Family Resort and Tennis Club (802-583-2922; 1-800-453-2922), Sugarbush Access Road, Warren. A year-round health and tennis club with indoor and outdoor tennis, heated pools, fitness center, hot tub, and sauna.

GOLF **Sugarbush Golf Course** (802-583-6725), Warren, at the Sugarbush Inn (see *Lodging—Resorts*). An 18-hole, Robert Trent Jones Sr. course, PGA rate 42, par 72; car and club rental, lessons, practice range, café. Inquire about golf/lodging packages.

HIKING *Walks & Rambles in Vermont's Mad River Valley* ($2.95), available at the chamber of commerce (see *Guidance*), unlocks the area's many superb hiking secrets.

The **Long Trail** runs along the ridge of the Green Mountains here and is easily accessible from three places: the two gap roads and the Sugarbush Bravo chairlift (weekends only). From the Lincoln Gap Road (the gap itself is 4.7 miles west of Route 100) you can hike a short way south to Sunset Ledge for a view of the Champlain Valley and Adirondacks. The more popular hike, however, is north from the gap (be advised to start early; parking is limited) to the Battell Shelter and on to Mount Abraham (5 miles round-trip), a 4,052-foot summit with spectacular views west, south as far as Killington Peak, and north as far as Belvidere Mountain. From Mount Abraham north to Lincoln Peak (accessible by the Sugarbush Resort chairlift) and on to Mount Ellen (4,135 feet) is largely above tree line; 3,600-foot General Stark Mountain to the north is best accessed (still a steep 2.6-mile hike) from Route 17 at Appalachian Gap. For details about the two shelters, contact the **Green Mountain Club** (802-244-7037). Mill Brook Inn's Joan Gorman also recommends beginning 2.1 miles up Tucker Hill Road at the small parking area (on the left) at the CAMEL'S HUMP STATE FOREST sign. Follow the blue blazes through the stand of pines known as "the Enchanted Forest" to the top of Dana Hill Road (approximately 1 hour round-trip, good for skiing and snowshoeing).

Mad River Glen (802-496-3551) offers a full schedule of guided backcountry trips and bird-watching tours.

HORSEBACK RIDING **Vermont Icelandic Horse Farm** (802-496-7141), Fayston Road, Waitsfield. Year-round. These strong, pony-sized mounts were brought to Iceland by the Vikings, but are still relatively rare. Karen Winhold uses them for half- and full-day trail rides and (seasonal) inn-to-inn treks from her stable in Waitsfield Common. The horses have an unusually smooth gait (faster than a walk, gentler than a trot). Skijoring is offered in winter.

Dana Hill Stable (802-496-6251), Route 17, Fayston. Clinics, extensive coaching weeks.

MINIGOLF ✐ **Lots-O-Balls** (802-244-5874), Route 100, in Duxbury, between Waitsfield and Waterbury. Open in-season from 11 AM, a great 19-hole miniature golf course.

POLO **Sugarbush Polo Club.** The oldest and most active polo club in Vermont holds matches every Wednesday during summer months and a USPA-sanctioned tournament on July 4. Lessons available. Contact the Sugarbush Chamber of Commerce (802-496-3409) for current dates and contacts.

SCENIC DRIVES **East Warren Road.** If you miss this road, you miss the heart of the Valley. From Bridge Street in Waitsfield Village, cross the covered bridge, bear right onto East Warren Road, and continue the 6 miles to East Warren. The views are of the Green Mountains set back across open farmland. For an overview of the Valley, take the Roxbury Gap Road up to the pullout (be careful, because there are not many places to turn around). From East Warren, loop back the 2 miles through Warren Village to Route 100.

Bragg Hill Road. The views from this peerless old farm road are magnificent: down across pastures and the narrow valley cut by the Mill Brook to Mount Ellen. Begin at Bragg Hill Road (off Route 100 just north of the Route 17 junction) and drive uphill, continue as it turns to dirt, and follow it around (bearing left); it turns into Number 9 Road and rejoins Route 17.

Granville Gulf. Drive Route 100 south from Warren and the Valley quickly disappears, replaced by a dark, narrow, and twisty pass, part of the Granville Gulf State Reservation. At the height-of-land, the Mad River begins its north-flowing course toward the Gulf of St. Lawrence and the White River rises, flowing south to eventually empty into Long Island Sound. A few miles south **Moss Glen Falls** spills down a steep cliff by the road. Granville itself is a wood-milling town and the vintage 1857 **Hemenway Bowl Mill** (see *Selective Shopping*) here forms the centerpiece for crafts and antiques shops. To turn this 20-mile drive into a day trip, continue to Hancock and across the Middlebury Gap to Middlebury, back across Appalachian or Lincoln Gap (see below) to the Mad River Valley

SOARING **Sugarbush-Warren Airport** (802-496-2290; 1-800-881-SOAR), Warren. Respected as one of the East's prime spots for riding thermal and ridge waves. Glider lessons, rides, food; open daily May through October. Solo and private lessons, rides, vacations available for all ages. From $97 for one person, $108 per couple for 20 minutes. Come just to see who's gliding in and out; lunch at the Diner Soar Deli and sandwiches.

SUMMER DAY CAMPS ✐ **Sugarbush Resort** (802-583-2381), the **Bridges Family Resort and Tennis Club** (802-583-2922; 1-800-453-2922) in Warren, **Clearwater Sports** (802-496-2708) in Waitsfield, and the **Sunrise Montessori School** (802-496-5435) in Waitsfield all offer summer day camps. For ages 13 and up there's even a weeklong **Junior Soaring Camp** (802-492-2708) at the Sugarbush Airport (see *Soaring*). **Mad River Glen** also offers nature-geared day camps in summer.

SWIMMING South of Warren Village, the Mad River becomes a series of dramatic falls and whirlpools cascading through a gorge. The most secluded swimming hole is by the **Bobbin Mill** (the first right off Route 100 after Lincoln Gap Road, heading south); park by the gravel pit and follow the path through the pines to a series of pools, all icy cold. Ask locally about **Warren Falls** and the best spot for skinny-dipping. The **Lareau Farm swimming hole** (now a town park) in the Mad River, south of Waitsfield on Route 100, is best for kids**. Blueberry Lake** in Warren is now owned by the Green Mountain National Forest; the **Ward Fishing Access area** on Route 100B in Moretown is another good bet. **Bristol Falls** is just about 10 miles from Warren via the Lincoln Gap Road (see *Scenic Drives*). The **Sugarbush Sports Center** (see *Fitness Centers*) features a large, L-shaped outdoor pool with adjacent changing facilities, café, bar, and Jacuzzi; the **Bridges Family Resort and Tennis Club** (see *Fitness Centers*) offers indoor and outdoor pools and swimming lessons. Many inns also have outdoor pools. At the **Inn at Round Barn Farm** (802-496-2276), East Warren Road, Waitsfield, the lap pool is in the barn.

TENNIS The Bridges Family Resort and Tennis Club (802-583-2922; 1-800-453-2922), Sugarbush Access Road, Warren, offers indoor and outdoor courts and year-round tennis clinics for both adults and juniors.

WALKING AND RUNNING The Mad River Path Association (802-583-8181) maintains several ever-evolving recreation paths in the Valley, namely: the **Warren Path,** beginning near Brooks Field at Warren Elementary School (Brook Road, Warren); the **Millbrook Path** in Fayston, running along the hill through the woods (blue blazes) between Millbrook Inn and Tucker Hill Lodge, on up across German Flats Road to the Inn at Mad River Barn; the **Mad River Greenway** (see *Bicycling*); and the **Village Path,** which begins at Fiddlers' Green and heads south to the Irasville Cemetery and beyond. See also *Hiking* and *Scenic Drives.*

✷ Winter Sports

CROSS-COUNTRY, TELEMARK SKIING, AND SNOWSHOEING Ole's Cross-Country Center (802-496-3430), at the airport, Warren. Forty km of machine-tracked trails radiate out across the meadows and into the woods with elevations ranging from 1,120 to 1,640 feet. This is a hidden treasure at the heart of the valley—with views of the mountains on both sides. Rentals and instruction. Breakfast and lunch served weekends 10–3, otherwise soups and sandwiches 9–5 here at the DinerSoar Deli.

Blueberry Lake Cross-Country Ski Center (802-496-6687), Plunkton Road, Warren. On the scenic, east side of the Valley, a total of 60 km of secluded trails.

Local trail: Puddledock in Granville Gulf State Reservation on Route 100, south of Warren: 3.5 miles of ungroomed trails marked with red metal triangles; map available at the registration box.

Check out the ***Mad River Valley Snowshoe Trails*** map/guide ($2.95) published by Map Adventures (802-253-7489) in Stowe, detailing 15 tours and identifying local animal tracks. **Clearwater Sports** (802-253-2317), Route 100, Waitsfield, offers rentals, along with custom and group tours.

Telemarking is a longtime specialty at **Mad River Glen** (802-496-3551). Inquire about midweek rentals, lesson and lift packages, and special events; also about guided tracking on snowshoes. Inquire about the frequent schedule of snowshoe treks and rambles.

DOWNHILL SKIING **Sugarbush** (information: 802-583-2381; ski report: 802-583-SNOW; www.sugarbush.com; lodging reservations: 1-800-53-SUGAR). Two separate trail systems on two major peaks—3,975-foot Lincoln Peak at Sugarbush South and 4,135-foot Mount Ellen at Sugarbush North—originally two different ski areas—were linked in 1995 by a 2-mile (9½-minute) quad chair traversing the undeveloped Slide Brook Basin that separates them. Snowmaking coverage, long adequate at Mount Ellen, was also tripled to cover substantially more terrain at Lincoln Peak. Sugarbush skiers will tell you how fortunate their resort was to be sidelined during the era in

GAP DRIVES

Appalachian Gap. Even if you are not continuing down the other side, be sure to drive up Route 17 past the Mad River Glen base area to its high point (there's parking at the trailhead for the Long Trail) and look down across the Champlain Valley, across the lake, to the Adirondacks in the distance. This is a great sunset ride.

Lincoln Gap is the steepest of Vermont's east–west gap roads (nothing allowed in tow, good brakes required, closed in winter), and the most spectacular. It begins on Route 100 just below Warren Village and climbs for 3 miles, seemingly straight up to the top of the 2,424-foot-high Lincoln Gap, where there's a pullout, a trailhead for the Long Trail (see *Hiking*). Next come magnificent vistas south, across farm fields (this stretch of road is unpaved in wide places and paved when it narrows). The village of Lincoln, clustered around a good general store, is about as quiet as Vermont gets. Continue through West Lincoln and down to Bartlett Falls in Rocky Dale (see Bristol in *Villages* in "Addison County and Environs").

For the **ultimate foliage loop** drive west over the **Appalachian Gap** (Route 17) 16 miles from Waitsfield to Route 116, then 2 miles south on Route 116 to the Lincoln Gap Road and head back east 14 miles to Warren.

which a large percentage of New England's best ski trails were smoothed, widened, and generally homogenized. In particular they are thankful that the Castle Rock trails, recognized throughout the country as some of the meanest, most natural, and most interesting expert terrain at any major American ski resort, survive. *Lifts:* 18—7 quads, 3 triples, 4 doubles, and 4 surface. Lifts operate 9–4, 8:30–4 weekends and holidays. *Trails:* 115; 20 acres of patrolled tree skiing; 468 skiable acres. *Vertical drop:* 2,650 feet. *Snowmaking:* 285.5 acres overall. *Facilities:* Cafeterias, lounges, ski shops, rentals, restaurants, sports center, condominiums. *Ski school:* Sugarbush Ski and Snowboarding School clinics, special teen program; women's clinics, guided backcountry skiing. *Snowboarding:* Rentals, lessons, terrain parks. *For children:* Nursery from infancy; special morning and afternoon programs for older kids. *Rates:* In 2001–2, $48–55 adults, $29–35 juniors and seniors; cheaper with lodging packages.

Mad River Glen (802-496-3551; in-state snow reports: 1-800-696-2001; outstanding web site: www.madriverglen.com). In 1995 one of New England's oldest major ski areas (the first to offer slope-side lodging) becamethe first to be owned cooperatively by its skiers, retaining its enviable reputation as one of the most challenging yet friendliest places to ski. Its vertical drop puts it in the big league, but the number of lifts and trails remains consciously limited. The Sunnyside Double Chair was replaced in 1998, the first capital improvement since 1982, and access to the summit of Stark Mountain (3,836 feet) is via the vintage-1948 single chair (the only one left in the country). All trails funnel into the central base lodge area, the better for families—many of whom are now third-generation Mad River skiers—to meet. Many trails are off the ski map. A favored place for telemarking, it's the only place in New England in which snowboarding is outlawed. Although completely lacking in snowmaking, on a good snow day it's the region's best ski buy. *Lifts:* Four chairs, including the single plus the Callie's Corner Handle Tow. *Trails and slopes:* 20 expert, 10 intermediate, 14 novice, a total of 800 skiable acres. *Vertical drop:* 2,000 feet. *Snowmaking:* 15 percent, which includes top to bottom on the Practice Slope, also other high-volume, low-elevation areas. *Facilities:* Base lodge, cafeteria, and pub; also the Birdcage, halfway up the mountain, serving sandwiches, drinks;

CROSS-COUNTRY SKIING AT SUGARBUSH

Schriebl

ski shop, rentals, ski school. *For children:* Cricket Club Nursery for 6 weeks to 6 years; programs for ages 3 to 17 include Junior Racing and Junior Mogul programs. *Rates:* $32 adults on weekdays and weekends, $42 on holidays, $22–26 juniors (14 and under), $30 on holidays; half-day, multiday rates. Under 6 and over 70 ski free.

SKIJORING Inquire about this sport (also about winter horseback riding) at **Vermont Icelandic Horse Farm** (802-496-7141) in Waitsfield (see *Horseback Riding*).

SNOWMOBILING Eighty miles of local trails are maintained by the Mad River Ridge Runners; snowmobile registration can be purchased at **Kenyon's Store,** Route 100, Waitsfield.

ICE SKATING **Sugarbush Inn** (802-583-6100; 1-800-537-8427) in Warren offers skating on flooded tennis courts. **The Skatium** at Mad River Green Shopping Center in Waitsfield (lighted) offers rentals, also available from neighboring **Inverness Ski Shop** (802-496-3343); free day and night skating on the groomed hockey rink at Brooks Recreation Field off Brook Road in Warren.

SLEIGH RIDES **Mountain Valley Farm** (802-496-9255) in Waitsfield offers sleigh rides, as does **Mad River Carriage Co.** (802-496-2104) off East Warren Road in Waitsfield.

✷ Lodging

Note: The Sugarbush-based (1-800-53-SUGAR) reservation service is open 9–5 daily, 8–8 during high ski season, serving roughly half the Valley's condos and 21 inns and B&Bs.

RESORTS **Sugarbush Inn** (802-583-6100; 1-800-537-8427), Warren 05674. The centerpiece of this complex is the fairly formal, 46-room Sugarbush Inn, with a 24-hour front desk, room phones, a library and sitting room, and an outdoor pool. $80–115 per couple, breakfast included, service extra.

The Bridges Family Resort and Tennis Club (802-583-2922; 1-800-453-2922), Sugarbush Access Road, Warren 05674. A self-contained resort just down the access road from the Sugarbush main lifts and base lodge. Facilities include indoor tennis, squash, an indoor pool, saunas, Jacuzzi and exercise room, and 100 condo-style units ranging from one to three bedrooms, each with fireplace, sun deck, TV, and phone, some with washer and dryer. $165–285 for a one-bedroom, $215–285 for a two-bedroom, and $330–585 for a three-bedroom unit; cheaper the longer you stay; inquire about ski and tennis packages.

INNS The inns listed below serve dinner as a matter of course; B&Bs may serve dinner on occasion.

Pitcher Inn (802-496-6350; 1-888-TO-PITCH; www.pitcherinn.com), Warren 05674. Designed by architect David Sellers to look like it's been sitting here in the middle of Warren Village for a century, the white-clapboard inn just opened in the 1997–98 winter season, replacing a building that had burned. Inside, however, the inn offers some extraordinary spaces, notably a cozy small library with books and a hearth, far from the large, elegant dining room that's open to the public (see *Dining Out*). Each guest room was designed by a different architect to convey a different aspect of local history. The Lodge, for instance, suggests a Masonic lodge (once a major social force in the Valley), with a ceiling painted midnight blue and delicately studded with stars, and obelisk-shaped posts on the king-sized bed. From a bedside switch in the Mountain Room, you can make the sun rise and set over the mountains painted on the facing wall. Bathrooms are splendid. Two of the 11 rooms are suites. $350–550 includes breakfast in the inn, $600 in the suites.

Millbrook Inn & Restaurant (802-496-2405; 1-800-477-2809; www.millbrookinn.com), Route 17, Waitsfield 05673. Open year-round except April, May, and late October to Thanksgiving. This 19th-century farmhouse is a gem. You enter through the warming room, actually heated by a woodstove in winter. The living rooms invite you to sit down. The heart of the ground floor, however, is the dining room, well known locally as one of the best places to dine in the Valley (see *Dining Out*). Each of the seven guest rooms is different enough to deserve its own name, but all have stenciled walls, bureaus, antique beds with firm, queen- or king-sized mattresses, and private bath. Our favorite is the Shell Room with a wedding-ring-patterned quilt on the antique bed with its shell-shaped inlaid headboard and a picture of Thom's grandparents on the wall. A ski lodge since 1948, Millbrook has become a true country inn since Joan and Thom Gorman took over in 1979. They are constantly redecorating and landscaping the garden (breakfast is served on the patio, weather permitting) and have acquired the small ski house on the wooded hillside across the brook. In winter $130–150 per couple MAP; in summer, $120 MAP, $80 B&B. Inquire about the ski house. Children ages 6 and older are welcome. Pets by prior approval.

Inn at Mad River Barn (802-496-3310; www.madriverbarn.com), 2849 Mill Brook Road, Waitsfield 05673. Betsy Pratt, former owner of Mad River Glen Ski Area, preserves the special atmosphere of this classic 1940s ski lodge, with its massive stone fireplace and deep leather chairs, and a dining room filled with mismatched oak tables and original 1930s art. The food (breakfast only in summer, dinner too in winter) is fine, as are the pine-walled guest rooms, all with private bath (those in the annex come with small kitchenette). In summer, the appeal of the place is enhanced by the pool, secluded in a grove of birches, and by the deck overlooking landscaped gardens, a setting for weddings and receptions. In winter, a trail connects with Mad River Glen. $80–135 per room includes breakfast. Dinner is $15 extra; special children's rates. Add 8 percent service charge in winter.

Tucker Hill Lodge (phone/fax: 802-496-3983; 1-800-543-7841; www.tuckerhill.com), Marble Hill Road, Waitsfield 05673. A classic 1940s ski lodge with a fieldstone hearth in the living room and 18 newly renovated rooms under new ownership by David Jackson. All rooms have private bath, phone, TV, and data port. $59–169 per double room, $169–399 for a suite sleeping four to six. Including continental breakfast. Also see The Steak Place in *Dining Out*.

Sweet Onion Inn (802-767-3734), Route 100/125, P.O. Box 66, Hancock 05748. The former Hancock Inn is now a pleasant B&B catering to vegetarians, serving family-style breakfast and dinner using whole and unprocessed fresh and organic ingredients, animal-, dairy-, and egg-free whenever possible, sweetened naturally. $135 double with private bath, $120 with shared, MAP. Single $105 and $90; B&B rates also available.

BED & BREAKFASTS ⚭ **The Inn at Round Barn Farm** (802-496-2276; www.innattheroundbarn.com), East Warren Road, Waitsfield 05673. Named for its remarkable round (12-sided) barn built in 1910, now a cultural and reception center with a lap pool and greenhouse on its ground floor, this old farmhouse is one of New England's most elegant bed & breakfasts. Innkeeper Anne Marie DeFreest offers 12 antiques-furnished rooms, 7 with gas fireplace, several with steam shower and/or Jacuzzi, all overlooking the meadows and mountains. Guests who come in winter are asked to leave their shoes at the door and don slippers to protect the hardwood floors. Common space includes a sun-filled breakfast room, a stone terrace, a book-lined library, and a lower-level game room with pool table, organ, TV, VCR, and a fridge stocked with complimentary soda and juices. From $99 midweek for double room with a regular shower, to $275 on weekends in high season for a room with marble fireplace, canopy king bed, and Jacuzzi. Prices include gourmet breakfast and afternoon edibles. A series of workshops ranging from cooking classes to watercolor and photography are offered mid-April through mid-August. Weddings are a specialty of the barn, which also serves as a venue for summer concerts (see *Entertainment*). In winter, the inn maintains an extensive cross-country network. Children 15 and older accepted.

⚭ ✐ **The Lareau Farm Country Inn** (802-496-4949; 1-800-833-0766; www.lareaufarminn.com), Route 100, Waitsfield 05673. Guests feel right at home, checking in via the kitchen and settling into the two sitting rooms (one with a fireplace) or onto the broad, columned back porch that overlooks an expansive spread of lawn that stretches down to a great (10-foot-deep) swimming hole and backs into a steep wooded hill. This is a 150-year-old farmhouse set in a wide meadow and the Mad River, a total of 67 acres with trails to walk or ski. Susan Easley, a warm host, offers 12 guest rooms and a suite with Jacuzzi, all nicely furnished with antique beds, quilts, and rockers. $70–110 for a double room with private bath, $60–80 with shared bath, includes a full breakfast (2-night minimum on weekends). $100–135 for the suite. Children are welcome "with well-behaved parents," and families occupy rooms along an ell off the main house. Weddings are a specialty; dinner on weekends is served in the American Flatbread Kitchen (see *Eating Out*) in the adjoining barn.

⚭ **West Hill House** (802-496-7162; 1-800-898-1427; www.westhillhouse.com), 1496 West Hill Road, Warren 05674. A gabled farmhouse off in a far corner of the golf course but convenient both to Sugarbush lifts and to the village of Warren. Dotty Kyle, an irrepressible chef, and Eric Brattstrom, a former contractor who can't stop himself from improving and expanding the place, offer seven guest rooms, including two suites, all with private bath with either a Jacuzzi tub and shower or steam bath/tub/shower combo and all with gas fireplace. The four-poster suite, up its own spiral staircase, has all the bells and whistles: fireplace, four-poster canopy queen-sized bed, study with daybed, and a bath with Jacuzzi and fireplace. Guests gather around the dining room table for multicourse breakfasts (with, perhaps, a vegetable soufflé), also for candelight dinners (on request). The house offers an unusual amount of common space: a living room, library with fireplace, and sun room with views to the mountains. Step out the front door to cross-country ski or play golf, out the back into 9 wooded acres. $125–190 year-round. Inquire about family reunions and weddings.

Mountain View Inn (802-496-2426), 1912 Mill Brook Road, Waitsfield 05673. This typical Vermont house is bigger than it looks, accommodating 14 in seven nicely decorated rooms. Guests gather around the wood-burning stove in the living room and at the long harvest table for breakfast. Fred and Susan Spencer are genial hosts. Handy to Mount Ellen, Mad River Glen, and the Mill Brook Path. $110–150 per couple B&B.

1824 House Inn (802-496-7555; 1-800-426-3986; www.1824house.com), 2150 Main Street (Route 100), Waitsfield 05673. North of the village, the gabled house is a beauty, decorated with an eye to room colors, Oriental rugs, and well-chosen antiques, in addition to comfort. Innkeepers Jack Rodie and Carol Davis have both led bike tours in their varied careers and they cater to outdoor-minded guests, hikers as well as bikers, recommending routes and offering shuttle service at the end of trails. The eight guest rooms vary, but all have private bath and feather bed. There are gracious drawing and dining rooms with fireplaces and an outside hot tub. The 22-acre property invites walking and cross-country skiing. There's also a good swimming hole in the Mad River, just across the road. $115–145 per room includes a full breakfast and afternoon tea.

The Featherbed Inn (802-496-7151; www.featherbedinn.com), Route 100, Waitsfield 05673. Clive and Tracey Coutts devoted three years to restoring this early-19th-century farmhouse before hanging out their shingle. The two-room Beatrice Suite has a pencil-post canopy bed and wet bar; the Ilse Suite offers a cathedral ceiling and a queen-sized sleigh bed; all the rooms have feather bed. There are also eight more traditional rooms. Common spaces are tasteful and inviting, from the living room with its woodstove and grand piano to the den with TV. Set back from Route 100, the house overlooks lawn and fields. Rates include a full breakfast. $95–145.

Deer Meadow Inn (802-496-2850; 1-888-459-9183; www.deermeadowinn.com), P.O. Box 242, Warren 05674. Off by itself in the middle of the valley near the airport (the hub for cross-country trails in winter). A traditional Vermont house set in 35 acres with three attractive, antiques-furnished guest rooms, all private bath and phone. Two spring-fed ponds on the property are good for swimming and fishing (trout and bass). $125 includes a breakfast.

The Mad River Inn (802-496-7900; 1-800-832-8278; madriverinn@madriver.com), P.O. Box 75, off Route 100, Waitsfield 05673. A house with turn-of-the-20th-century detailing, like fine woodwork and large picture windows with lace etchings in the living room. The nine guest rooms are furnished with an eye to Victorian fabric, color, and antiques. The house overlooks a gazebo, meadow, and the Mad River, and it's handy to a good swimming hole. Facilities include an outdoor Jacuzzi and a downstairs game room and BYOB bar. Rates from $89 for the smallest room with a private but hall bath to $135 for the largest with private bath on a weekend; a three-course breakfast and afternoon tea are included. Children welcome. Weddings a specialty.

The Sugartree Inn (802-583-3211; 1-800-666-8907; sugartree@madriver.com), Sugarbush Access Road, Warren 05674. This is a modern ski lodge, but Frank and Kathy Partsch have done their utmost to create a country-inn atmosphere. The nine rooms have quilts, canopy and brass beds, and private bath; a large oak-furnished suite has a gas fireplace. Guests gather by the fireplace in the living room, and breakfast is served in the adjoining dining room. Breakfast specials include chocolate chip pancakes. $99–175 per couple B&B.

Weathertop Lodge (802-496-4909; 1-800-800-3625), 755 Mill Brook Road, Waitsfield 05673. The atmosphere is that of a ski lodge rather than a country inn, but it's appealing any time of year. The common room has a fieldstone fireplace, stereo, piano, cable TV, video games, and VCR. There's also a fitness center with an array of exercise machines and the hot tub and sauna. The nine rooms are large, with two queen beds and a full bath—but Bill and Gail Mulconnery have redecorated with country-inn-style fabrics and furnishings. $98–175 per room.

MOTEL **Wait Farm Motor Inn** (802-496-2033; 1-800-887-2828), Waitsfield 05673. Paul Lavoie's eight motel units, four with kitchenette, as well as two double rooms in the main house, constitute this friendly family business. $50–70 per couple.

CONDOMINIUMS The Valley harbors more than 400 rental condominium units, many clustered around Sugarbush (Lincoln Peak), more scattered along the access road, and some squirreled away in the woods. No one reservation service represents them all.

Sugarbush Village Condominiums (802-583-3333; 1-800-537-8427). The resort manages a total of 250 condominium units in the rental pool, ranging from suites to four-bedroom mountain homes. Winter rates: $300 for a slope-side two-bedroom condominium, from $200 if not slope-side; from $70 per night, $420 per week for a one-bedroom condo in summer.

Sugarbush Resort Condos (802-583-6100; 1-800-537-8427; fax: 802-583-3209). A total of 200 units, most walk-to-the-slopes, with health club access. From $150 for a one-bedroom, $285-400 for two-bedroom, up to $700 for a four-bedroom unit. Less off-season.

The Battleground (802-496-2288; 1-800-248-2102), Route 17, Fayston 05673. An unusually attractive cluster of 26 town houses, each designed to face the brook or a piece of greenery, backing into each other and thus preserving most of the 60 acres for walking or ski touring (the area's 60 km network of trails is accessible). In summer there is a pool, tennis and paddle tennis courts, and a play area for children. Mad River Glen is just up Route 17. Rates (2-night minimum) for two-, three-, and four-bedroom units are $160–225 per night in summer, $200–500 in winter.

Powderhound Lodge (802-496-5100; 1-800-548-4022; fax: 802-496-

5163), Route 100, Warren 05674. The old roadside farmstead now serves as reception, living, and dining rooms—with a downstairs pub—for the 44 condo-style apartments clustered in back. Each of these consists of two rooms, one with two beds and another lounging/dining space with two more daybeds and a TV; token cooking facilities. There are also four motel units with phone and TV. It's all nicely designed and maintained, nothing fancy but a good deal for families and couples who like the privacy of their own space with an option to mix with fellow guests. Summer facilities include a swimming pool, a clay tennis court, and lawn games, and there's a hot tub for year-round use, plus a winter shuttle to the mountain. $79–125 in winter, with many 2- and 3-day (also midweek) ski packages; $70–100 in summer plus 3 percent service. Pets are $5 per night plus 12 percent added to the room rate.

✷ Where to Eat

DINING OUT *Note:* The Valley restaurants are unusual in both quality and longevity. Most have been around for quite some time and, like most culinary landmarks, have their good and bad days.

Pitcher Inn (802-496-6350), Warren Village. Open for dinner and Sunday brunch. The elegant inn dining room features an à la carte menu to match, orchestrated by chef Sue Schickler. You might begin with sorrel soup with smoked salmon crouton and dine on grilled black bass with Thai green curry, coconut basmati rice, and green Romano beans or a grilled vegetable Napoleon with mozzarella, pesto, and brown butter vinaigrette. Entrées $24–34. The choice of wines by the glass is large, and the wine list itself is long and widely priced.

Chez Henri (802-583-2600), Sugarbush Village. Open for lunch, brunch, and dinner. (Check in the off-season.) A genuine bistro. In 1963 Henri Borel relinquished his position as food controller for Air France to open this snug, inviting café with a fireplace, marble bar (imported from a Barre soda fountain), and terrace for dining out front in summer. After dinner, the back room becomes a disco, open until 2 AM (nightly in winter, Friday through Sunday in summer). Dinner entrées usually include roast duck with a fruit and pepper sauce and bouillabaisse, but most items change frequently so that longtime patrons can always find something new. Lunch on pasta Provençal or French onion soup. Entrées $15–26.

Millbrook Inn & Restaurant (802-496-2405), Route 17, Waitsfield. Open for dinner except April, May, and late October to mid-December. For more than 20 years Thom Gorman has been the chef and Joan Gorman the pastry chef, hostess, and waitress in their attractive dining room, a double parlor with hearth and French doors opening on a garden. (The couple reenergize during the months they close by hiking, backpacking, kayaking, and camping in the world's far corners.) They offer an eclectic, changing menu that might range from eggplant Parmesan to scampi and always includes a fish of the day and an "innkeeper's choice," along with a few Indian dishes, a legacy of Thom's Peace Corps days. We recommend the badami rogan josh, a wonderfully spiced (local) lamb dish. All dinners include Joan's anadama bread, as well as salad and starch—but save room for one of her freshly made pies, cakes, or ice creams. Wine and beer are served. Entrées $10.50–17.95.

The Spotted Cow (802-496-5151),

Bridge Street Marketplace, Waitsfield. Open for lunch and dinner daily except Monday. Reserve for dinner. This is Jay Young's latest project (Bermuda born and bred, Young owned the Sugarbush Inn for many years, then Jay's in the Mad River Green). Small and stylish, this is an in spot. The Bermuda fish chowder we sampled for lunch was superb. Dinner might be grilled breast of duckling with forest mushrooms, dried cherries and port, applejack maple and pork sausage stuffing, saffron, basmati rice, and haricots verts. Entrées $18.95–24.95.

The Common Man Restaurant (802-583-2800), German Flats Road, Warren. Dinner only, closed Monday off-season. Reservations suggested. A mid-19th-century barn hung with chandeliers and warmed by an open hearth, this is a Vermont dining landmark, still owned by Michael Ware who opened it in 1972, that continues to earn good reviews. The menu changes weekly but many signature dishes don't. Appetizers might include a crab and scallop mousse with a mushroom and white wine sauce; entrées range from ricotta ravioli to a ragout of Vermont venison in ale. Desserts are tempting and the wine list, extensive. Entrées $14–25.

Bass Restaurant (802-583-3100), Sugarbush Access Road, Warren. Open nightly for dinner. This culinary landmark has lost its long-standing chef but Stratis Bass remains continues to oversee the dining room, a stepped space that's pleasantly lit with a long, inviting bar and dining areas. Entrées might include slow-roasted lamb shank served with bean cakes and finished with mint (delicious!) and baked eggplant and Swiss chard timbale finished with artichokes and lemon. The dessert tray is fairly irresistible. Entrées $10.25–18.50.

Michael's Restaurant at the Powderhound (802-496-3832), Route 100, Warren. Open for dinner Thursday through Sunday. Michael Flanagan, one of the Valley's favorite chefs, has a loyal following and gets rave reviews, featuring "Vermont ingredients, global flavors." It's an eclectic menu, perhaps including spice-grilled tuna loin served with udon noodle salad and wasabi aioli; a Malay-style seafood hot pot; a serious, not-for-wimps vegetable platter; and a Mexican sampler. Entrées $11.96 (southern-barbecued tofu) to $17.95 ("real Vermont steak").

The Steak Place (802-496-3025), Tucker Hill Lodge, Route 17, Waitsfield. Theoretically open for dinner nightly, but check. USDA prime beef is what this place is about, and it's too new for a fair review. Steaks from $17.95 for a Kansas City strip to $32.95 for porterhouse.

The Warren House Restaurant & Rupert's Bar (802-583-2421), Sugarbush Access Road, Warren. Open for dinner daily from 5:30. Formerly Sam Rupert's, this attractive place still offers inviting, low-key bar and fine dining: entrées like roasted Atlantic salmon wih chèvre glaze and garden sprouts or balsamic-braised New Zealand lamb shank. Entrées $12.95–18.95.

EATING OUT **The Den** (802-496-8880), just north of the junction of Routes 100 and 17 in Waitsfield. Open daily for lunch and dinner until 10:30, sandwiches until 11. The cheerful, pubby heart of the Valley; booths, stained glass, a summer patio. The menu is large and always includes a homemade soup, a wide choice of burgers, and a salad bar; dinner entrées might include a grilled half duckling and jerk pork as well as house steak. A wide selection of beers.

Egan's Big World Pub and Grill (802-496-5557), Madbush Falls Motel, Route 100, Waitsfield (near the Sugarbush Access Road). Named for local extreme skier John Egan (who skis the world). The atmosphere is casual, friendly, and lively—a brewpub with booths and a more formal (but not really) dining area: terrific burgers, pastas, salads, a great marinated eggplant (served with spinach, red peppers, and Vermont goat cheese), and (winter only) a dynamite Hungarian goulash. Egan's Extreme Ale is the house brew.

American Flatbread Kitchen (802-496-8856), at the Lareau Farm Country Inn, Route 100, Waitsfield. Open Friday and Saturday 5:30–9:30, year-round (more or less). George Schenk's distinctive pizza is baked in a primitive, wood-fired oven heated to 800 degrees; the results are distributed to stores from Florida to Chicago. On weekends the kitchen becomes an informal dining space featuring flatbread (toppings include cheese and herb, sun-dried tomato, homemade sausage with mushroom) and exceptional salads whose dressing boasts homemade fruit vinegar. Also specials such as grilled vegetables with garlic-herb sauce and oven-roasted chicken. Dine in or take out. Beer served. Each night Schenk writes a dedication, always food for thought.

THE WARREN STORE IN WARREN VILLAGE

Kim Grant

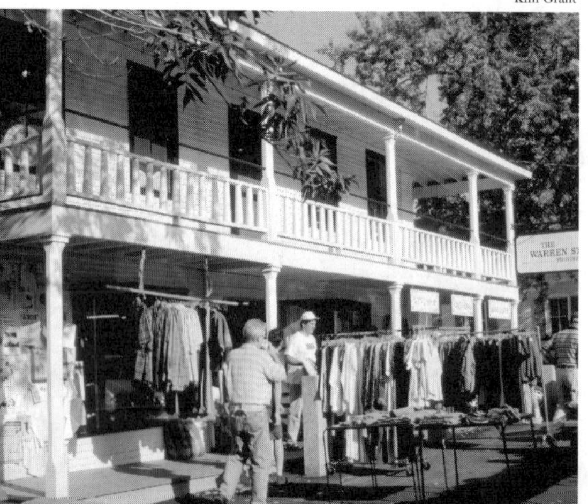

Jay's (802-496-8282), Mad River Green Shopping Center, Route 100, Waitsfield. Open for breakfast, lunch, dinner, and Sunday brunch. A family restaurant, bright and spacious, with an immense menu. Dinner might be chicken pesto, pasta pillows filled with broccoli and Vermont cheddar in a curry cream sauce, or Jay's Giant Burger. Children's menu, pizzas; full liquor license.

Miguel's Stowe-Away (802-583-3858), Sugarbush Access Road, Warren. Serving meals 5:30–10. An offshoot of Stowe's successful Mexican Stowe-Away. Pollo and pescado augment a choice of fajitas, chiles, enchiladas, and burritos; also good for sopas, ensaladas, and cerveza.

Valley Pizzeria (802-496-9200), 4752 Main Street (Route 100), Waitsfield. Open 11–9:30, Sundays 4–9:30. Closed Wednesday. New York–style pizza (not too thick or too thin) with a wide variety of toppings, hand tossed and baked in a stone oven. Eat in or take out; burgers and salads also served. Try the Greek pizza. No beer or wine.

Hyde-Away Inn (802-496-2322), Route 17, Waitsfield. Pub open from 4:30, dining room 5:30–9:30. An informal, affordable restaurant with plenty of appetizers and soups, sandwiches, and burgers. The dinner menu might include crabcakes, Mexican lasagna, and broiled salmon, served with homemade bread and salad.

Warren Store (802-496-3864), Warren Village. Open daily 8–7, Sunday until 6. Year-round the bakery produces French and health breads, plus croissants and great deli food and sandwiches; in summer a deck overlooks the small waterfall.

Three Mountain Cafe, Mad River Green Shopping Center, Waitsfield. The café and espresso bar features croissants, pastries, and chocolate truffles to go with the coffee.

Hancock Hotel (802-767-4976), junction of Routes 100 and 125 (Middlebury Gap Road). Open 6 AM–9 PM weekdays, until 9 Sunday. A genuine 19th-century village hotel that now bills itself as "Vermont's Home Bakery," good for the basics with nightly specials, featuring homemade bread, muffins and pies. Beer and wine served. Pick up a sandwich and take it to nearby Texas Falls (see *To See* in "The White River Valleys").

✷ Entertainment

Green Mountain Cultural Center (802-496-7722) at the Joslyn Round Barn, Waitsfield. This concert and exhibit space in a classic round barn is the setting for a series of summer concerts, along with workshops and a major foliage-season art exhibit. The **Valley Players** (802-583-1674), a community theater company, produces three or four plays a year in its own theater just north of Waitsfield Village, Route 100. The **Phantom Theater** (802-496-5997 in summer), a local group with New York City theater community members, presents original plays and improvisational performances for children and adults at Edgecomb Barn in Warren. Also note **Mad River Chorale** performances in June and December (check with the chamber of commerce: 802-496-7907). The **Mad River Flick** (802-496-4200), Route 100 north, Waitsfield: first-run films; wine, snacks served; video games.

APRÈS-SKI **The Blue Tooth** (802-583-2656), Sugarbush Access Road, Warren. A ski-season "mountain saloon"; open from 3 PM in ski season for après-ski snacks and drinks, moderately priced dinners, live entertainment, dancing. **The Hyde-Away** (802-496-2322) is the hot spot near Mad River Glen (Route 17).

✷ Selective Shopping

ANTIQUES **Warren Antiques** (802-496-4025), Warren Village. Open daily 10–5 May through October, then by appointment. Victoriana, furniture, ephemera.

Barn-It All Antiques and Collectibles (802-496-7007), Warren Village. Two stories of nostalgia: furniture, glassware, pottery, and so on.

ART GALLERIES ꝏ **The Bundy Fine Arts Center** (802-496-5055), Bundy Road (off Route 100), Waitsfield. Open Thursday through Friday 10–4, Saturday 11–6, Sunday 12–6. An interesting building that offers a mix of good art, in addition to a sculpture garden around and beyond a reflecting pond. A popular site for weddings.

Kristal Gallery (802-496-6767), East Warren Road. Open year-round, daily 10:30–6. Hanni Saltzman mounts a genuinely interesting mix of oils and watercolors; in summer there's also a sculpture garden.

Parade Gallery (802-496-5445) in Warren Village offers an affordable selection of prints and original art.

Black Newt Ironworks Sculpture Studio (802-496-5843), Route 100,

Waitsfield Village. A converted town barn and former blacksmith shop is studio space for John Matusz, who sculpts in steel and stone.

Bridge Street Bakery (802-496-0077), Bridge Street, Waitsfield. Artist owned, a café most notable for its local paintings, prints, and photography (all for sale).

Bridge Street Studio & Gallery (802-496-4917), Bridge Street, Waitsfield. Artist-owned gallery upstairs in an old hotel.

CRAFTS SHOPS AND GALLERIES **Tulip Tree Crafts** (802-496-2259), Village Square, Waitsfield. Judy Dodds runs this exceptional store featuring folk art, pottery, antiques, cards, and quilts. Judy herself is a fiber artist, specializing in quilted wall hangings. Her husband silk-screens T-shirts, and the shop offers an unusual variety.

Artisans Gallery (802-496-6256), Route 100, Waitsfield. Open daily 10–6. A highly selective collection of furniture, baskets, canes, rugs, glass, decoys, ornaments, photography, and much more.

Michael Egan Blown Glass (802-767-4547), Route 100, Granville. Open 10–5; closed Tuesday. Don't pass up this new roadside studio near the Hemenway Bowl Mill. Valley native Michael Egan shapes Venetian-style freehand blown glass into spectacular vases, pitchers, and a variety of housewares as well as art glass.

Cabin Fever Quilts (802-496-2287), the Old Church, Waitsfield. Closed Tuesday, otherwise open 10–5. Machine-sewn, hand-tied quilts come in a range of sizes and patterns, priced $175–400; also pillows, gifts, and quilt fabrics.

Waitsfield Pottery (802-496-7155), Route 100 across from Bridge Street. Ulrike Tesmer makes functional, hand-thrown stoneware pieces, well worth a stop.

Luminosity Stained Glass Studio (802-496-2231), the Old Church, Route 100, Waitsfield. This is a very special shop. Since 1975, Barry Friedman has been fashioning Tiffany lampshades and a variety of designs in leaded and stained glass; the shop also carries some interesting jewelry. Items are priced from $15 for great necklaces to $15,000 for an exquisite lamp.

Bradley House in Warren Village showcases work by an amazing variety of local craftspeople. It's a trove of hand-loomed rugs, woven baskets, quilts and pillows, wooden bowls, metalwork, furniture, fabric art, pottery, handblown glass, and more. Open daily.

FARM STAND **Hartshorn's Farm Stand** (802-496-5816) sells maple products, Christmas trees, pumpkins, and locally respected produce, and stages a Halloween haunted happening.

SPECIAL SHOPS **Warren Store and More,** Warren Village. Staples, wines, and the deli and bakery are downstairs (see *Eating Out*); upstairs is one of Vermont's best-kept secrets, an eclectic selection of clothing, jewelry, and gifts. We treasure everything we have bought here, from earrings to a winter coat.

All Things Bright and Beautiful (802-496-3397), Bridge Street, Waitsfield. There are an incredible number of stuffed animals and unusual toys on two floors of this old village house.

The Store (802-496-4465), Route 100, Waitsfield. Since its 1965 opening, this exceptional shop has grown tenfold, now filling two floors of an 1834 meetinghouse with superb early American, French, and English antiques, cookware, tabletop gifts, collectibles, lifestyle books, Vermont gourmet products, and children's toys and books from around the world.

The Hemenway Bowl Mill Store (802-828-1005), Route 100, Granville. Open daily, 9–5. Look for the VERMONT ONLY sign on Route 100. The bowl mill has been making wooden salad and decorative bowls since 1857. A selection of cutting boards, bird feeders, toys, and Vermont products also carried, along with country antiques.

Tempest Book Shop (802-496-2022), Village Square, Waitsfield. This family-run bookstore is a trove of titles in most categories, including children's books. We like their motto: "A house without books is like a room without windows" (Horace Mann).

SUGARHOUSES **Eastman Long & Sons** (802-496-3448), Tucker Hill Road, Waitsfield. "Sonny" Long sets 6,000 taps high on 100 wooded acres that have been in his family for generations. He maintains that the higher the elevation, the better the syrup, and he welcomes visitors to his roadside sugarhouse (featuring a new Vermont-made, totally lead-free evaporator and two reverse osmosis machines used to reduce the sap volume by 70 percent) during sugaring season. "A sugarmaker has to be a plumber and electrician these days," Long jokes, relating hair-raising stories of what one small animal can to to an intricate web of tubing, at night, in the middle of a sap flow. "On summer weekends, I sit in my van and sell syrup down at the junction of Route 100 and 17 for far less than anyone can buy it at local stores," he says, "and still people tell me I'm charging too much."

Palmer's Maple Products (802-496-3675), East Warren Road, Waitsfield. Delbert and Sharlia Palmer sell syrup from their farm on this scenic road.

✷ Special Events

Note: Check with the chamber of commerce (see *Guidance*) and its web site (www.sugarbushchamber.org) for weekly listings of special events.

February: **Winter Carnival,** Sugarbush.

March: Annual **New England Telemark Festival,** Mad River Glen.

April: **Sugarbush Triathlon**—canoe, kayak, bicycle, cross-country-ski races (more than 400 competitors), Sugarbush.

July 4: Outstanding **parade,** Warren Village.

July and August: Summer productions by the **Valley Players** and by the **Phantom Theater** (see *Entertainment*). **Green Mountain Polo Tournament,** Warren.

August: **Vermont Festival of the Arts** runs 10 days throughout the Valley.

Labor Day weekend: 2-day **crafts exhibits.**

Early October: **Soaring Encampment** throughout the Valley. **Sugarbush Antique Car Show.**

December: **Christmas celebrations** throughout the Valley.

BARRE/MONTPELIER AREA

Any attempt to understand the character of Vermont entails a visit to Montpelier: a stroll through the Vermont Historical Society Museum and into the ornate but informal statehouse built of Vermont granite and marble. Good food and pleasant shopping are nearby on State and Main Streets.

An exit on I-89, Montpelier is also at the hub of old roads radiating off into the hills, including Route 2, which runs all the way to Bangor, Maine, and Route 302 to Portland, which begins here as central Vermont's big commercial strip, "the Barre-Montpelier Road."

Billed as "the granite capital of the world," Barre continues to quarry, cut, and sculpt its high-quality gray granite, now used primarily for tombstones. The big attraction is the Rock of Ages Quarry in Graniteville, southeast of town, but Barre's Main Street has plenty to offer and its two cemeteries showcase the work—ranging from quirky to spectacular—of generations of Barre sculptors. The newly opened Vermont History Center (headquarters for the Vermont Historical Society), the recently restored old Labor Hall, and the Barre Opera House, one of Vermon's most beautiful and liveliest theaters, are all right downtown.

Southwest of Montpelier is the proud old town of Northfield, home of Norwich University and of no less than five covered bridges. East Barre and East Montpelier are both rural villages. Head either northeast on Route 2 or southeast or Route 302 to quickly find yourself in little-touristed farm country and forest.

GUIDANCE In Montpelier the **Vermont Department of Tourism** maintains a classy and friendly information center (802-828-3981) with rest rooms in a clapboard house across the street from the capitol at 134 State Street. It's open 7 AM–8 PM weekdays.

In **Barre** the Old Pinsly Depot just off in downtown Barre is now a combinatin welcome center and showcase for the evolving Granite Museum (802-476-4605). Open Monday through Friday 8:30–12:30, Saturday 10:30–4:30. It offer rest rooms, area information, and exhibits.

Central Vermont Chamber of Commerce (802-877-887-3678; www.central-vt.com). Publishes a helpful booklet guide to the area, keeps track of member vacancies during foliage season, and maintains a walk-in center open weekdays 8:30–5 at 33 Stewart Street at Berlin Corners (just off I-89 exit 7; take your first left).

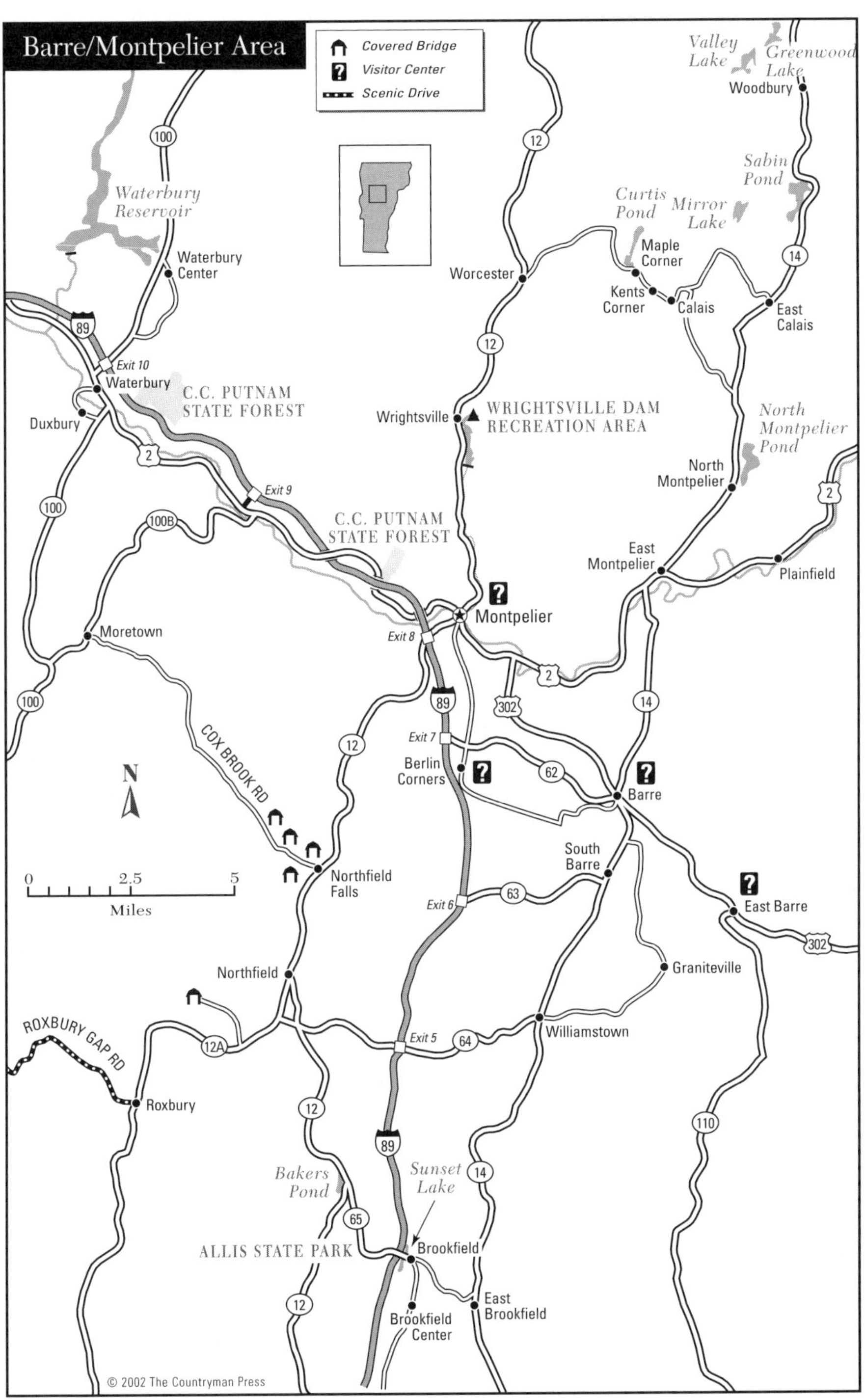
Barre/Montpelier Area
Covered Bridge
Visitor Center
Scenic Drive
Waterbury Reservoir
Waterbury Center
Waterbury
Exit 10
Duxbury
C.C. PUTNAM STATE FOREST
Exit 9
C.C. PUTNAM STATE FOREST
Moretown
COX BROOK RD
Northfield Falls
Northfield
ROXBURY GAP RD
Roxbury
Bakers Pond
ALLIS STATE PARK
Sunset Lake
Brookfield
Brookfield Center
East Brookfield
Williamstown
Exit 5
Exit 6
Exit 7
Exit 8
Berlin Corners
Montpelier
Worcester
Wrightsville
WRIGHTSVILLE DAM RECREATION AREA
Valley Lake
Greenwood Lake
Woodbury
Sabin Pond
Curtis Pond
Mirror Lake
Maple Corner
Kents Corner
Calais
East Calais
North Montpelier Pond
North Montpelier
East Montpelier
Plainfield
Barre
South Barre
East Barre
Graniteville
Miles
0
2.5
5
N
© 2002 The Countryman Press

GETTING THERE *By bus:* **Vermont Transit** (1-800-451-3292) from Boston to Montreal, connecting with New York and Connecticut service, stops in Montpelier at a disgraceful trailer off State Street that is otherwise closed and doesn't even post the schedule.

By train: **Amtrak** (1-800-USA-RAIL; www.Amtrak.com) stops in Montpelier Junction, a mile west of town on the other side of I-89.
Ground transfers: **Wheels Transportation** (802-223-2882; 1-877-227-0771).

By car: For **Montpelier** take I-89, exit 8. At the second traffic light, make a left, crossing the river on Bailey Avenue. At the light, turn right on State Street. The red-clapboard house that houses the information center (see *Guidance*) is on your right, a good place to park. The capitol and Vermont Historical Society are a short way up across the street.

To reach **Barre** take I-89 to exit 7 and follow signs for Route 62, a divided highway to Main Street.

WHEN TO GO This is a rare corner of Vermont that varies little from season to season. Come January through April to see the Vermont Legislature in action.

MEDICAL EMERGENCY **911** now works for this entire area. **Central Vermont Medical Center** (802-229-9121) is in Berlin off Route 62; exit 7 off I-89.

✱ Towns

Montpelier. The smallest and possibly the most livable of the nation's state capitals, Montpelier is a town of fewer than 9,000 people, with band concerts on summer Wednesdays, high school playing fields just a few blocks from the capitol. The gold dome of the statehouse itself is appropriately crowned by a green hill rising steeply behind it. A new path leads right up that hill into **Hubbard Park,** more than 110 leafy acres with windy roads, good for biking and jogging. The new **Stone Cutters Way** down along the Winooski River is also a pleasant bike or jog. The **State House,** the **Vermont Historical Society Museum,** and the **T. W. Wood Art Gallery** are all must-see sights. Montpelier, moreover, is home base for the **New England Culinany Institute (NECI),** currently enrolling some 650 students and staffing three of the town's oustanding restaurants.

Precisely why this narrow floodplain of the Winooski was selected as Vermont's statehouse site in 1805 is uncertain, as is why it was named for a small city in the Languedoc region of France. The fact is, however, that Vermont's first legislators picked a town noted for its unusual number of whiskey distilleries and named it for a town best known for its wine and brandy. It's also true that Montpelier is unusually accessible, by roads both old and new, from every corner of central and northern Vermont.

Barre. This is a city of 9,900 people, surrounded by a town of 7,000. Motorists caught in Main Street's perpetual traffic may ponder the conspicuous absence of granite in the facades of the commercial buildings. Most date from 1880–1910, during which the community's population jumped from 2,000 to 12,000, swollen by stonecutters and craftsmen from Scotland, Eastern Europe, Italy, and French

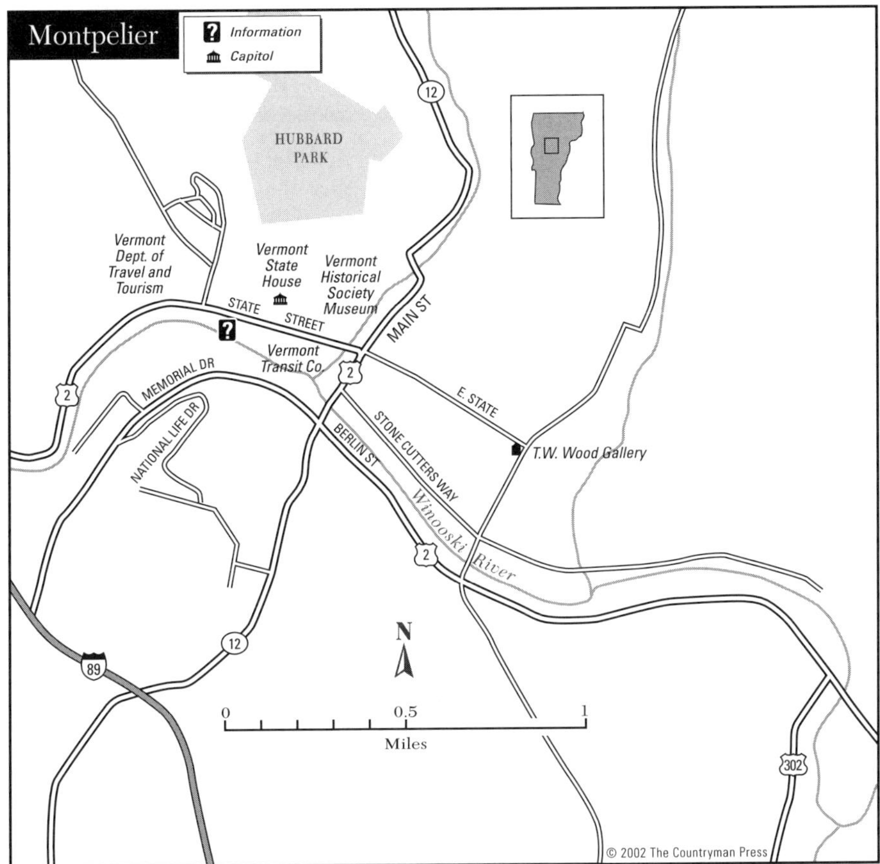

Canada, not to mention England, Scandinavia, Spain, Germany, and the Middle East. This volatile mix of largely underpaid workers who elected a socialist mayor were not afraid to strike for their rights or to shelter victims of strikes elsewhere. In the World War I era, many famous anarchists and socialists spoke here. The **Old Labor Hall** (vintage 1900) on Granite Street (off North Main), the focal point of this struggle, has been restored and can be rented or toured (phone: 802-476-0567). The quarries continue to employ some 2,000 people to produce one-third of the country's memorial stones—for which **Hope Cemetery** and **Elmwood Cemetery** serve as museums (see *Also See*). A formal **Vermont Granite Museum** is taking shape in a former granite shed on the Barre-Montpelier Road; its School of Stone Arts is set to open in fall 2002.

The quarries themselves are southeast of town, primarily in Graniteville, where Millstone Hill has been chipped and chiseled since 1812, when the bedrock was turned into millstones, door stoops, and posts. In the 1830s, huge slabs were hauled by oxen to build the statehouse, but it was only after the Civil War that the railway and a series of inventions enabled Barre to make its mark. The memorial stone business escalated after 1888, when the branch railroad finally linked the quarries to finishing sheds in the valley and to outlets beyond. All but one of the major quarries are owned by Rock of Ages. This company has long made its operations a showcase for visitors, who can view the unforgettable, surrealistic landscape of the quarries themselves, hear the roar of the drills, and watch ant-sized men chip away at the giant pits.

Northfield. This town's mid-19th-century commercial blocks suggest the prosperity that it enjoyed while native son Charles Paine served as governor. Paine actually railroaded the Vermont Central through his hometown instead of the more logical Barre. The old depot, now a bank, stands at one end of the handsome common. Today, the town's pride is Norwich University, a private, coed college of 1,000 cadets, which bills itself as "the oldest private military college in the United States." In the Norwich University Museum in White Memorial Chapel, you learn that this institution sent more than 300 officers into the Civil War. It wasn't until 1867, however, that the college moved to Northfield from its original site in Norwich. More Northfield memorabilia as well as changing exhibits can be seen in the **Northfield Historical Society Museum** housed in the Old Red Brick Schoolhouse, Stagecoach Road (open March through December, Sunday through Wednesday 1–3).

✷ To See

In Montpelier

✐ **The Vermont Historical Society Museum** (802-828-2291), 109 State Street, Montpelier. Open weekdays except Monday, year-round 9–4:30; weekends also during July, August, and foliage season, 10–5. Token admission. This outstanding state museum, maintained by the Vermont Historical Society on the ground floor of the replica of the Pavilion Hotel (which occupied this site between 1870 and 1966), is undergoing renovation at this writing, due to reopen late in 2002. The gallery exhibits and gift store will be expanded and the library, with changing exhibits, is set to moved to the Vermont History Center in the former Spaulding High School in Barre.

NORTHFIELD FALLS

Christina Tree

T. W. Wood Art Gallery at the Vermont College Art Center (802-828-8743) at Vermont College (now a part of Norwich University), College Street (corner of East State Street), Montpelier, open Tuesday through Sunday noon–4. The gallery displays Civil War–era art by local artist Thomas Waterman Wood and mounts excellent shows on contemporary Vermont artists and craftspeople. Token admission.

In Barre

Rock of Ages Quarry Complex (802-476-3119; www.rockofages.com), 773 Main Street, Graniteville. The easiest way to get there, even from Montpelier, is via I-89 exit 6 to Route 63. At the light go straight and follow signs. From the observation deck of the Manufacturing Division (open year-round, Monday through Friday 8–3:30), you'll see stone polished and sculpted into memorials. The Visitors Reception Center, a mile up the road, is open May through October, Monday through Saturday 8:30–5 and Sunday noon–5. Displays explain the geology of granite, and a path leads the short way out back to the state's oldest, 27-acre-wide quarry. From June through mid-October there's also a narrated shuttle tour to a working, 50-acre, 600-foot-deep quarry farther up the hill.

Hope Cemetery, Route 14 just north of downtown Barre. If coming in off I-89 on Route 62, continue straight ahead up Maple Street (Route 14); if on North Main Street (Route 302), turn up Maple. The impressive main gates are a way up on your left; you can drive in. The 6,000 memorials here range from classic tableaux to a half-scale racing car, all sculpted by stonecutters for themselves and their families and among the most elaborate to be found anywhere in the world. **Elmwood Cemetery,** at the opposite end of downtown (Route 302 turns into Washington Street as it heads east; take Hill Street at the first Y and it's right there), also has many striking memorials. Tours of Barre cemeteries can be arranged through the Old Labor Hall (802-476-0567).

COVERED BRIDGES

In Northfield

Off Route 12 in Northfield Falls (turn at the general store) stand three covered bridges: the **Station Bridge,** spanning 100 feet, and the **Newell Bridge** are within sight of each other; farther along Cox Brook Road is the **Upper Bridge,** with a span of 42 feet. Another bridge is just south off Route 12 on Slaughter House Road.

SCENIC DRIVE **Roxbury to Warren.** The road through Roxbury Gap, while not recommended in winter, is spectacular in summer and fall, commanding a breathtaking view of the Green Mountains from the crest of the Roxbury Range. Do not resist the urge to stop, get out, and enjoy this panorama. Ask locally about the hiking trail that follows the ridgeline from the road's highest point.

✳ To Do

BOATING AND FISHING **Wrightsville Dam,** just north of Montpelier; **North Montpelier Pond,** with a fishing access off Route 14; and **Curtis Pond** and **Mirror Lake** in Calais (pronounced *Callus*). **Nelson Pond** and **Sabin Pond** in

Woodbury are both accessible from Route 14, as are **Valley Lake** and **Greenwood Lake** (good for bass and pike). The **Stevens Branch** south of Barre offers brook trout.

East Roxbury Fish Hatchery, 2 miles south of Roxbury on Route 12A. This is a state hatchery in which salmon species are raised; children are allowed to feed the fish.

Reel Vermont (802-223-1869; www.reelvt.com) at the waterfall on Curtis Pond in Calais offers canoe and kayak rentals and guided fishing trips.

Green Mountain Outdoor Adventures (802-229-4246), based in Montpelier, supplies hunting and fishing guides.

GOLF **Montpelier Elks Country Club** (802-223-7457), Country Club Road, Montpelier, nine holes. **Barre Country Club** (802-476-7658), Plainfield Road, Barre, 18 holes. **Northfield Country Club** (485-4515), Roxbury Road, Northfield, nine holes.

HIKING *Guidance:* **The Green Mountain Club** (802-244-7037), RR 1, Box 650, Route 100, Waterbury Center 05677. Encourages general inquiries and trail description updates (see *Hiking* in "What's Where").

Spruce Mountain, Plainfield. An unusually undeveloped state holding of 500 acres, rich in bird life. The trail begins in Jones State Forest, 4.2 miles south of the village; the 3-hour hike is described in *50 Hikes in Vermont* (Backcountry Guides) and in *Day Hiker's Guide to Vermont* (Green Mountain Club).

Worcester Range, north of Montpelier. There are several popular hikes described in the above books, notably **Elmore Mountain** in Elmore State Park (a 3-mile trek yielding a panorama of lakes, farms, and rolling hills; see "Stowe and Waterbury"), **Mount Worcester** (approached from the village of Worcester), and **Mount Hunger.**

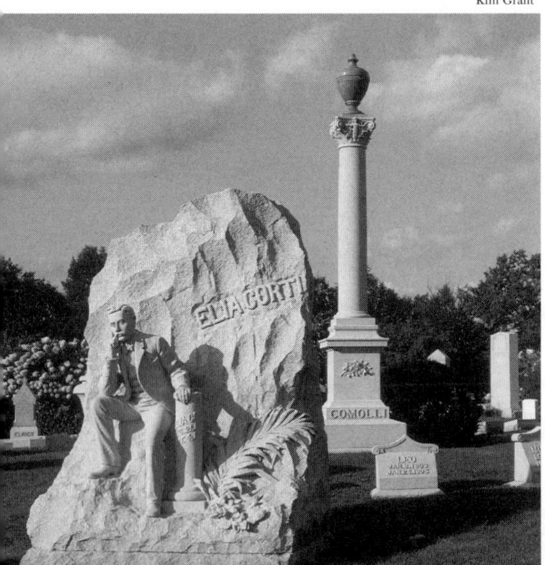

STONECUTTERS' MEMORIALS AT HOPE CEMETERY IN BARRE

Kim Grant

HORSEBACK RIDING **Autumn Harvest Inn** (802-433-1355), Williamstown (2 miles off I-89, exit 5). Trail rides. (See *Lodging.*)

SWIMMING **Wrightsville Dam Recreation Area,** Route 12 north; also numerous swimming holes in the Kents Corner area.

✷ Lodging

In Montpelier

Capitol Plaza (802-223-5252; 1-800-274-5252; www.capitolplaza.com), 100

Vermont State House (802-828-2228), State Street, Montpelier. Open Monday through Friday 8:45–4:15, closed holidays. Friends of the Vermont State House offers tours Monday through Friday 10–3:30, Saturday 11–2:30, July through mid-October, otherwise open for self-guided tours. Visitors are welcome to watch the legislature in action, January through mid-April.

In 1805, when Montpelier was chosen as the "permanent seat of the legislature for holding all their sessions," it was on the condition that the town give land for the capitol and get it built by 1808. The resulting three-story building was nine-sided, with a cupola, and warmed by a two-story stove. Legislators sat on plank seats at pine desks that were said to have been "whittled out of use" by the representatives' jackknives. The whole building had to be demolished in 1836 and was replaced by a granite Grecian temple designed by the Federal-era architect Ammi Young. After it was virtually destroyed by fire, it was rebuilt along the same but larger lines and completed in 1857.

While several chambers are quite opulent, there is noticeable informality in the way the 150 state representatives and senators talk with their constituents while standing in the Hall of Flags or seated on the black walnut sofas (which cost $60 apiece in 1859) at either end. The statue of Ethan Allen on the steps is Danby marble, and the handsome black-and-white floor of the lobby was quarried on Isle La Motte. The lobby is lined with portraits of Vermont-born heroes including Adm. George Dewey, Adm. Charles Clark (like Dewey, a hero of the Spanish-American War), and Calvin Coolidge, 30th president of the United States. Note especially the enormous oil painting by Julian Scott, *The Battle of Cedar Creek, 1864.* The cannon on the front steps was captured from the Hessians at the battle of Bennington in 1777. The Roman lady atop the gold-leafed dome is Ceres, goddess of agriculture.

THE VERMONT STATE HOUSE RISES ABOVE MONTPELIER

Christina Tree

State Street, Montpelier 05602. The former landmark tavern, a downtown hotel with room service, a two-tiered café, and J. Morgans, a steakhouse featuring Sunday brunch, jazz nights, and weekend entertainment as well as conference and reception facilities. Rooms vary from the standard motel models to individually decorated "colonial guest rooms" to an immense apartment-sized, two-bedroom executive suite. From $88 for a standard double to $189 for a suite (higher in foliage season).

✐ **The Inn at Montpelier** (802-223-2727; www.innatmontpelier.com), 147 Main Street, Montpelier 05602. Two stately, adjacent Federal houses have been renovated and luxuriously furnished. Amenities include central air-conditioning, downstairs guest pantries for coffee and tea at any hour, in-room cable TV, bar service, small conference facilities. A marvelous Colonial Revival veranda wraps around the brick Lamb-Langdon house. Of the 19 rooms, the deluxe chambers with fireplaces ($163–177) are the handsomest rooms in town. The smaller king-, queen-, and twin-bedded rooms ($104–145, more in foliage season) are also lovely; all with private bath and continental breakfast. Your hosts are Rita and Rick Rizza. No charge for children 6 and under.

✐ **Betsy's Bed & Breakfast** (802-229-0466), 74 East State Street, Montpelier 05602. Betsy and Jon Anderson are warm, helpful hosts who offer 12 attractive rooms and suites in adjacent Queen Anne and Victorian houses and a carriage house in a quiet hillside neighborhood, a short walk from the middle of town. Rooms have private bath, cable TV, and phone (with voice mail and data ports); five suites have full kitchens. $60–90 ($10 more in foliage season) includes a generous breakfast. Discounts for 3 nights or more.

Comfort Inn at Maplewood (802-229-2222; 1-800-228-5150), RR 4, Box 2110, Montpelier 05602 (take exit 7 off I-89 for 0.2 mile). This handsome and relatively new motor inn has 89 rooms, 18 two-room suites with kitchenette, and a VIP suite with kitchenette and whirlpool. Rates are $59 single, $69 double, $99–210 suites ($10 more during foliage season), with continental breakfast.

Beyond

The Northfield Inn (802-485-8558), 27 Highland Avenue, Northfield 05663. Aglaia Stalb has renovated a grand old 1902 hillside mansion, nicely landscaped with a gazebo overlooking the town. Aglaia is a motherly, hospitable host who worries that her guests are well fed and oriented to her handsome town and its scenic surroundings (which include five covered bridges). There are 12 big, old-fashioned guest rooms, 9 with private bath (several combine into family suites), furnished with antiques, brass or carved-wood beds, and European feather bedding. It's delightfully easy to get lost in this rambling old house with its scattered common spaces, includings a library, parlor, and game room. From $85 to $159 for a suite, including a three-course breakfast and snacks throughout the day.

♘ ♿ **The Autumn Harvest Inn & Restaurant** (802-433-1355), Clark Road, Williamstown 05679, Route 64 east from exit 5 off I-89. This century-old hilltop farm has splendid views and 46 acres now geared to raising and boarding horses (trail rides are available to guests) and in winter trails are used by cross-country skiers and snowmobilliers (they connect to VAST trails). Carolyn White offers 18 plain but bright and cheerful guest rooms with private bath and TV, including one that's handicapped equipped and two semisuites, one with a fireplace. There's a big fireplace in the living room and two dining rooms are open to the public (see *Dining Out*). Guests enjoy the swimming pond, two night-lit tennis courts, and sleigh rides. Rates: $79–159 EP in summer, $59–139 in winter.

Maplecroft Bed & Breakfast (802-476-0760; www.maplecroftvermont.com), 70 Washington Street, Barre 05641. Convenient for anyone resarching Vermont history or geneology next door at the new Vermont History Center (built as a rather grand high school), this stiking Victorian house is on Route 302 just above downtown and the small city park. Built by a granite sculptor in 1887, it is now home to local librarians Paul Heler and Marianne Kotch, who offer three guest rooms, all with private bath and with beds featuring quilts made by Marianne (quilters, librarians, and magicians get a 10 percent discount). Needless to say there are plenty of books around. $70 includes a continental breakfast with homemade jams and scones or popovers.

The Hollow Inn and Motel (802-479-9313; 1-800-998-9444), 278 South Main Street, Barre 05641. With 15 rooms in the inn and and 26 motel units just off I-89, exit 6, this makes a good waystop. Facilities include a landscaped outdoor heated pool and Jacuzzi and an indoor fitness center with whirlpool and sauna. All rooms have VCR and TV, and some have microwave and refrigerator. Double room rates $70–90 in the motel units, $85–105 for a suite in the inn; $10 less for single, depending on the season, including continental breakfast.

✷ Where to Eat

DINING OUT **Chef's Table** (802-229-9202), 118 Main Street, Montpelier. Open Monday through Friday for lunch, Saturday for dinner only. Reservations requested for dinner. This the Montpelier-based New England Culinary Institute's upscale restaurant. Lunch on sweet corn soup and crisp herbed eggplant. The dinner menu might include starters like five-spiced quail and entrées like rosemary-seared swordfish with white beans and truffle oil. Entrées $15–22.

A Single Pebble (802-476-9700), 135 Barre-Montpelier Road, beside Twin City Lanes, Berlin. Open for dinner Tuesday through Saturday. Reservations are a must, even for weeknights; a few days ahead are advisable for weekends. Classic Chinese dinners here are outstanding, the best in the state. The imaginative menu (mock eel made from shiitake mushrooms, for instance, and fried green beans) is designed for group enjoyment, with many dishes hot from the wok. Dishes from $2.95 to $16.95, moderate considering the quality.

Sarducci's (802-223-0229), 3 Main Street, Montpelier. Open Monday through Saturday 11:30 AM–midnight; Sunday 4–midnight. Reserve. Above-average Italian dishes blossom in this very popular, spacious, columned, yellow-walled restaurant with an open wood-fired oven. Request a table overlooking the river. Many daily specials, antipasti, customized pizzas, salads, and 18 pasta choices, including shrimp with angelhair, tomatoes, and garlic. At dinner we can recommend the saltimbocca (sautéed veal with prosciutto and fresh sage in a portobello mushroom sauce, served with risotto). Entrées come with a "mista salad" and are surprisingly reasonable, given both the quality and atmosphere ($10.95–15.95).

The Autumn Harvest Inn & Restaurant (802-433-1355), Route 64, Williamstown. The superb views from the main dining room and wraparound porch complement dinners here Tuesday through Saturday. Begin with baked stuffed mushrooms or crabcakes with honey mustard sauce, and follow with honey Dijon chicken or duck with cranberry Armagnac glaze. $11.75–17.50.

Also see Ariel's Restaurant in Brookfield in "White River Valleys."

EATING OUT

Barre-Montpelier Road

Wayside Restaurant and Bakery (802-223-6611). Open daily 6:30 AM–9:30 PM. Vermont's ultimate family restaurant, featuring "home cooking away from home." Breakfast on corned beef hash and eggs (that comes with homefries and toast for $3.50), sausage gravy on biscuit, or baked oatmeal. Lunch on the soup of the day and maple cream pie, dine on pork liver and bacon ($5.50) or rib-eye steak ($12.95). The children's menu is $2.95. Brian and Karen Zecchinelli offer over 200 menu items to choose from, plus at least four daily specials (all under $6), and they're fully licensed.

In Montpelier

The Main Street Bar and Grill (802-223-3188), 118 Main Street. Open for breakfast, lunch, and dinner daily, Sunday brunch. Montpelier-based New England Culinary Institute's signature eatery, a multi-level restaurant and pub with seasonal outdoor seating and a viewing window into the kitchen. Lunch on poached pear and Stilton salad with ginger bisque and sausage and mussel stew. At dinner begin with a warm beef short rib terrine and then choose between New England leg of venison or pan-seared rainbow trout.

Julio's (802-229-9348), 54 State Street. Open Monday through Saturday for lunch and dinner, opening at 4 on Sunday. A colorful Mexican restaurant that doesn't pretend to be the ultimate in authenticity but fills the bill as a pleasant downtown eatery, good for a grilled eggplant sandwich as well as a taco salad, for a hearty bowl of mussels or goat cheese enchiladas. There's a kids' menu and sidewalk dining, weather permitting. Fully licensed.

La Brioche Bakery & Cafe (802-229-0443), 89 Main Street. Open daily, 6:30 AM–7 PM weekdays, Saturday 8–5:30, Sunday 8–5. The source of pastries and bread for all New England Culinary Institute Montpelier restaurants. Eat in the dining room or on the patio or take out breakfast and sandwiches.

Coffee Corner, corner of Main and State. Open 6–3. A great little diner that's been here forever and specializes in fresh produce, fresh baked bread, booths, and fast, friendly service.

Hunger Mountain Food Co-op (802-223-8004), 623 Stone Cutters Way. Open 8–7:30. Hidden away in a corner of this supermarket-style co-op is an expanded deli with many vegetarian choices and a very attractive glass-sided café area overlooking the river.

Capitol Grounds (802-223-8411), 45 State Street. An inviting coffeehouse filled with the aroma of roasting coffees and comfortable corners in which to sip them. Inquire about jazz, country, and blues nights.

In Barre

Del's (802-476-6684), 248 North Main Street. Open Monday through Saturday for lunch and dinner, Sunday from 4 PM. Sited across from the courthouse, this is a justly popular local gathering spot with a colorful decor and a suspiciously wide selection: pastas, Mexican dishes, pizza, subs. No complaints, however, about a great taco salad and fast, friendly service at lunch. Patrons vouched for the pasta. At dinner chefs Don and Donna Dick offer a choice of "light fare" as well as the regular menu.

All Fired Up (802-476-2036), 9 Depot Square. Just off Main Street. Open daily 11–9. Not much atmosphere but good pizza, baked in an imported Italian wood oven. Also soups like Tuscan sausage and rice; "sandwich tarts" like sausage, caramelized onion, and mozzarella; and fresh ravioli.

Green Mountain Diner (802-476-6292), 240 North Main. Open Monday through Friday 6 AM–9 PM; Saturday 6 AM–7 PM; Sunday 6 AM–2 PM. Friendly booths, a blackboard menu with specials like stew and Spanish pork chops; beer and wine served.

✷ Entertainment

THEATER **Barre Opera House** (802-476-8188), corner of Prospect and Main Streets, Barre. Built in 1899, after fire destroyed its predecessor, this elegant, acoustically outstanding, recently restored 650-seat theater occupies the second and third floors of City Hall. The Barre Players, a community theater, perform spring through fall, and this is also a venue for year-round music, dance, and other theater productions.

Lost Nation Theater Company (802-229-0492; www.lostnationtheater.org), Montpelier City Hall Arts Center, 128 Elm Street, Montpelier. First-rate productions of contemporary plays, classics, and original works year-round by a professional troupe. The Summer Theater Series features five different shows, June through October, 5 nights a week.

FILM **Savoy** (802-229-0509), 26 Main Street, Montpelier, presents art and alternative films with two daily showings, occasional speakers, and special events.

The Capitol (802-229-0343), 93 State Street, Montpelier, and **The Paramount** (802-479-9621), 241 North Main Street, Barre, are both classic old movie houses showing first-run feature films.

✷ Selective Shopping

ARTS STUDIOS AND GALLERIES

The Artisans' Hand (802-229-9492), City Center, 89 Main Street, Montpelier. Open Monday through Saturday 10–5. An exceptional variety of quality Vermont craftwork by a cooperative of some 125 artisans in many media.

SPA (Studio Place Arts), 201 North Main Street, Barre (802-479-7069; www.studioplace.com), an arts center offering classes for both adults and children, maintains the Studio Place Arts Gallery and neighboring Mediums Blend Café.

Thistle Hill Pottery (802-223-8926; www.thistlehillpottery.com), Powder Horn Glen Road, in the hills north of Montpelier. Jennifer Boyd sells her handmade functional stone pottery: dinnerware, vases, lamps, and more; bargains, seconds. Her studio is near Morse Farm.

BOOKSTORES ✐ **Bear Pond Books** (802-229-0774), 77 Main Street, Montpelier. One of the state's most inviting bookstores, heavy on literature, art, and children's books; authors' readings.

Rivendell Books (802-223-3928), 100 Main Street, Montpelier, features a wide stock of new books for adults and children at discount, plus selected remainders and some interesting used titles.

Capitol Stationers (802-223-2393), 54 Main Street, Montpelier, includes new books, with a strong Vermont and New England section.

Barre Books (802-476-3114), 158 North Main Street, Barre. Open until 6, Friday until 7, a good array of general books.

FARMS **Morse Farm** (802-223-2740), County Road (the western extension of Main Street), Montpelier. Open daily, year-round except holidays. The farm itself has been in the same family for three generations. This is a place to come watch sugaring off in March; a large farm stand sells Vermont crafts and cheese as well as produce in summer and fall; Christmas greens in December. Sugar on snow.

Bragg Farm (802-223-5757), Route 14, East Montpelier. Open daily, March 15 through December 24, for maple products, Vermont crafts.

Danforth's Sugarhouse (802-229-9536), Route 2, East Montpelier. A fourth-generation sugaring operation and maple product gift shop open daily year-round.

Grandview Winery (802-456-7012), East Calais. Open late May through November. Off Route 14 south of the village, the tasting room at the farm is set in gardens, hung with Vermont artists.

Knight's Spider Web Farm (802-433-5568; www.spiderwebfarm.com), off Route 14 on Spider Web Road, Williamstown Village. Open daily 9–6; January through March by appointment. The weirdest farm you ever will see: Artists Will and Terry Knight began by preserving, painting, and mounting spiderwebs from their own barn, and now grow spiders that you can watch as they weave their webs and then buy the results, mounted on wood; gifts and pine accessories.

SPECIAL SHOPS **Woodbury Mountain Toys** (802-223-4272), 24 Main Street, Montpelier. This independent specialty toy store carries major lines and some locally made items.

✷ Special Events

Memorial Day weekend: **Open Studios weekend** throughout Vermont (www.vermontcrafts.com).

Early June: **Vermont Dairy Celebration,** statehouse lawn in Montpelier.

June through August: **Montpelier City Band Concerts,** statehouse lawn Wednesday at 4 PM.

July: **Montpelier's Independence**

ANTIQUES

East Barre Antique Mall (802-479-5190), 133 Mill Street, East Barre. Open daily 10–5. Closed Monday. In the middle of this one-street village sandwiched between Routes 302 and 110, an unlikely wooden store houses central Vermont's largest group shop: 350 dealers represented on three floors with plenty of furniture as well as dishes and glassware, one whole room of kitchenware.

Day Celebration, sponsored by the **Onion River Arts Council** (802-229-9408) on the statehouse lawn, features performances and a giant fireworks display. **Barre Homecoming Days** (last weekend): music, fireworks, street dance, art exhibit. **Vermont Quilt Festival,** a 3-day event on July's third full weekend, at Norwich University in Northfield (www.vqf.org), New England's largest annual quilt event.

Labor Day weekend: In Northfield, a pageant, parade of floats, and Norwich cadets.

September: **Old Time Fiddlers' Contest,** Barre Auditorium, one of new England's oldest contests. On the weekend after Labor Day the **Barre Granite Festival** at the evolving Granite Museum (see *Guidance*) is the scene of rock splitting and cutting, a chicken barbecue, and more.

Early October: **Vermont Apple Celebration,** statehouse lawn, Montpelier.

Late October: **Festival of Vermont Crafts,** Montpelier High School (call Central Vermont Chamber of Commerce, 802-229-5711).

December 31: **First Night** celebrations, Montpelier.

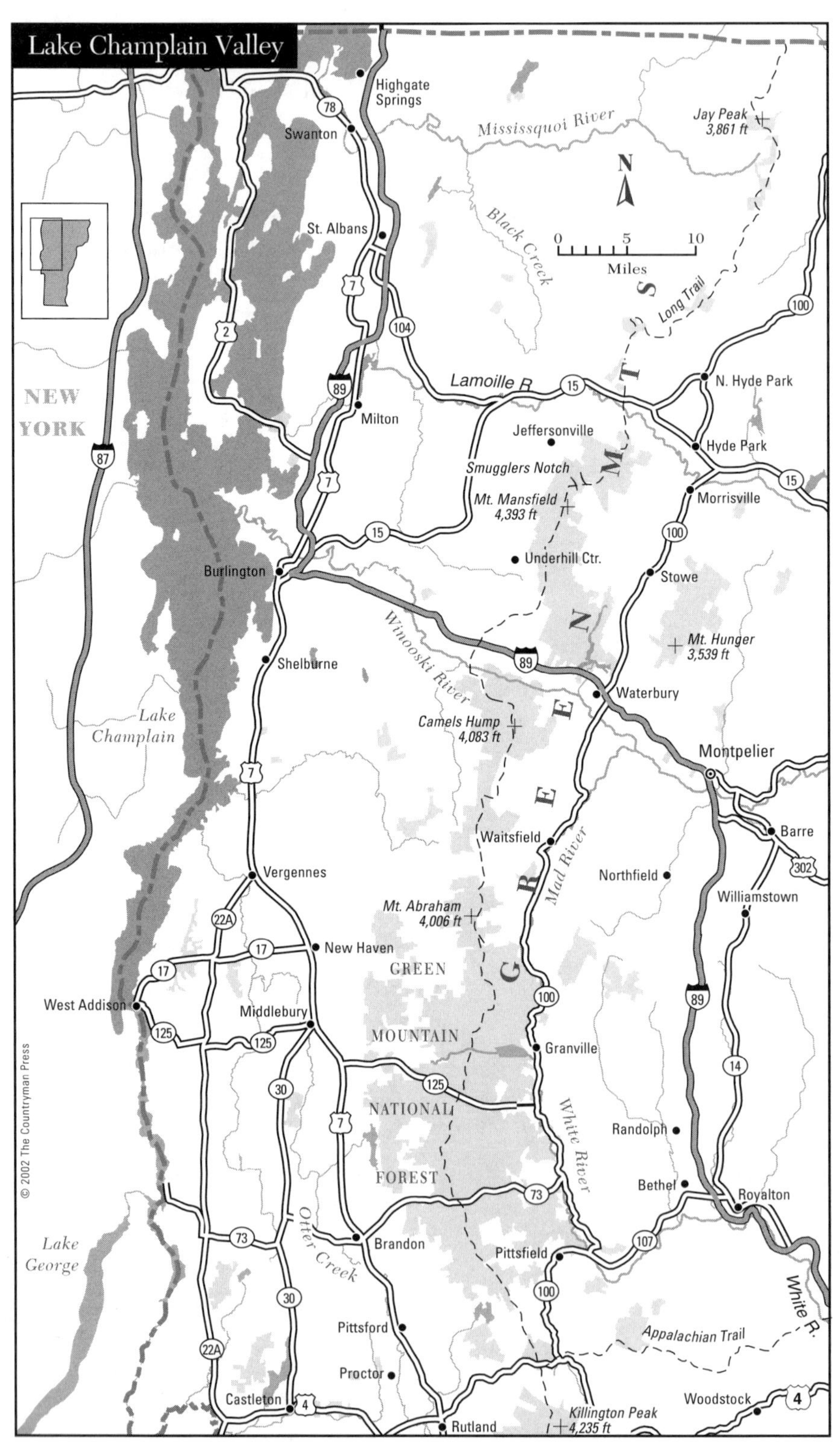
Lake Champlain Valley
Highgate Springs
78
Swanton
Mississquoi River
Jay Peak 3,861 ft
N
St. Albans
Black Creek
0 5 10
Miles
7
2
104
Long Trail
100
NEW YORK
89
Lamoille R.
15
N. Hyde Park
Milton
Jeffersonville
Hyde Park
87
Smugglers Notch
Morrisville
Mt. Mansfield 4,393 ft
Underhill Ctr.
Burlington
Stowe
Winooski River
Mt. Hunger 3,539 ft
Shelburne
Waterbury
Lake Champlain
Camels Hump 4,083 ft
Montpelier
Waitsfield
Barre
302
Mad River
Vergennes
Northfield
Williamstown
Mt. Abraham 4,006 ft
22A
17
New Haven
GREEN
West Addison
Middlebury
125
MOUNTAIN
Granville
30
NATIONAL
FOREST
14
White River
Randolph
Bethel
Royalton
73
Lake George
Brandon
Otter Creek
Pittsfield
107
White R.
Pittsford
Appalachian Trail
Proctor
Castleton
4
Woodstock
Rutland
Killington Peak 4,235 ft
GREEN MTS

Lake Champlain Valley

4

RUTLAND AND THE LOWER CHAMPLAIN VALLEY

ADDISON COUNTY AND ENVIRONS

BURLINGTON REGION

THE NORTHWEST CORNER

Kim Grant

RUTLAND AND THE LOWER CHAMPLAIN VALLEY

Rutland, formerly Vermont's second largest city, has been bypassed in recent years by the population growth in Chittenden County. However, the city remains more than just a convenient commercial adjunct to the Killington-Pico ski resorts. Stolid, early-Victorian mansions and streets crisscrossed with railroad tracks testify to its 19th-century prosperity—when Rutland was known as "the marble city"—and it has retained its industrial base.

Today, city fathers are trying hard to reconstitute the downtown core, buoyed by the return of railroad passenger service. The daily *Rutland Herald,* the oldest newspaper in the state, continues to win frequent journalism awards, including a Pulitzer Prize in 2001.

The long-established shops along Merchants Row and Center Street have held their own in recent years and number upward of 100 within just a few square blocks; they include some genuinely interesting newcomers. This is, moreover, a good restaurant town.

Rutland is the business and shopping center for the Lower Champlain Valley, a broad, gently rolling corridor between New York State and the Green Mountains. In contrast to the rest of Vermont, this valley is actually broad enough to require two major north–south routes. Route 7 is the busier highway. It hugs the Green Mountains and, with the exception of the heavily trafficked strip around Rutland, is a scenic ride. Route 30 on the west is a far quieter way through farm country and by two major lakes, Lake Bomoseen and Lake St. Catherine, both popular summer meccas.

Route 4 is the major east–west road, a four-lane highway from Fair Haven, at the New York line, to Rutland, where it angles north through the middle of town before turning east again, heading uphill to Killington. Route 140 from Wallingford to Poultney is the other old east–west road here, a quiet enough byway through Middletown Springs, where the old mineral waters form the core of a pleasant park.

GUIDANCE The Rutland Region Chamber of Commerce (802-773-2747; 1-800-756-8880; www.rutlandvermont.com), 256 North Main Street, Rutland 05701; visitors center (802-775-0831) at the junction of Routes 7 and 4, open late May through mid-October. The chamber supplies an illustrated *Visitor's Guide.*

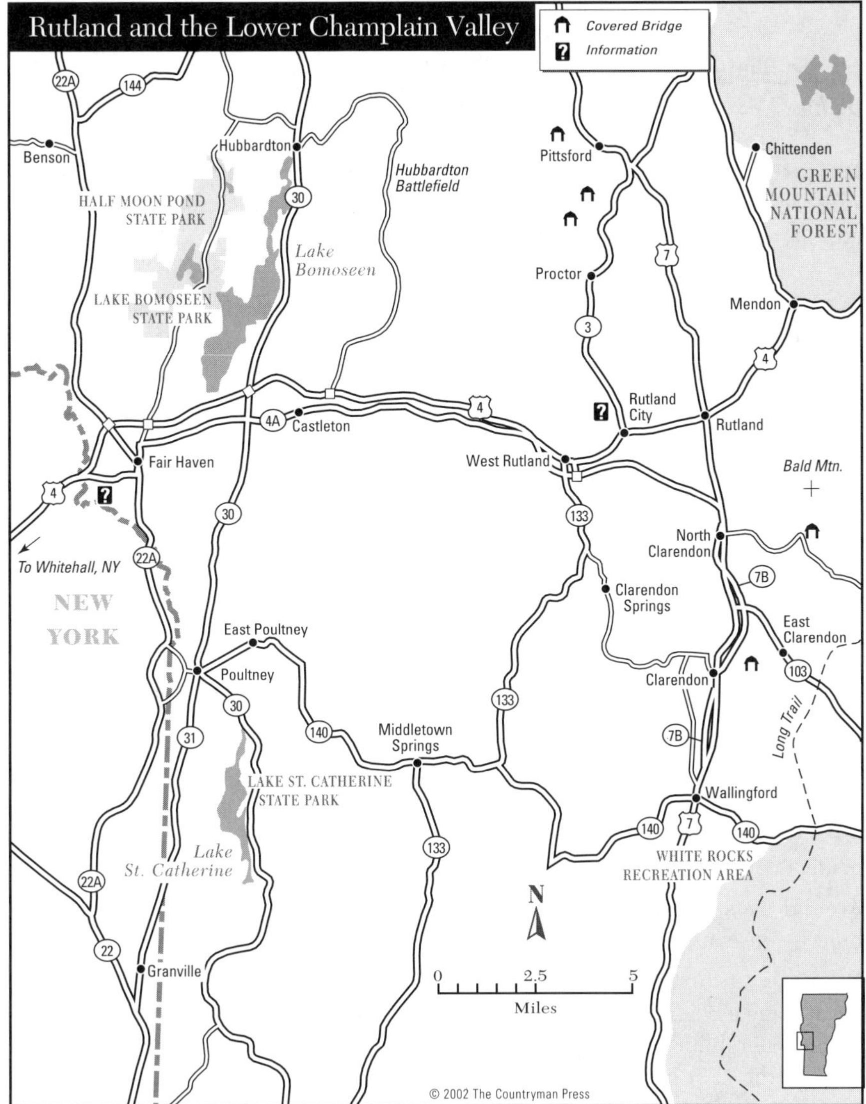

The Vermont Office of Vacation Travel (802-265-4763) maintains a Welcome Center in Fair Haven (open 7 AM–9 PM) on Route 4 near the New York line.

Crossroads of Vermont (1-800-756-8880; www.vermontcrossroads.com) is the regional marketing organization.

Area Chambers of Commerce: Poultney (802-287-2010); Brandon (802-247-6401); Killington (802-773-4181).

GETTING THERE *By train:* **Amtrak** (1-800-USA-RAIL). Daily service to and from New York City on the *Ethan Allen Express.*

By air: **USAirways Express** (1-800-428-4322). USAirways small planes offer daily connecting service to Boston's Logan International Airport and New York's La Guardia Airport.

By car: Routes 7 and 4; Route 103 from Bellows Falls.

By bus: **Vermont Transit,** from Albany, Boston, and other points.

GETTING AROUND *By bus:* **Marble Valley Regional Transit District** (802-773-3244), operator of "The Bus," connecting Killington, Castleton, the Rutland airport, and other points in the area.

MEDICAL EMERGENCY **Rutland Regional Ambulance Service** (911); **Rutland Fire Department Rescue Paramedics** (911); **Rutland Regional Medical Center Fast Track Emergency Service** (802-747-3601), 160 Allen Street.

Rescue squads: Fair Haven/Castleton (911); Poultney (911); Pittsford (911); Wallingford (911).

✷ Villages

Fair Haven, located where Routes 4, 4A, and 22A intersect, is at the core of Vermont's slate industry. One of its earliest developers in the 1780s was the controversial Matthew Lyon, who started an ironworks and published a newspaper called *The Scourge of Aristocracy,* in which he lambasted the Federalists. Elected to Congress in 1796, Lyon had scuffles on the floor of the House and criticized President Adams so violently that he was arrested and jailed under the Alien and Sedition Act. Lyon's case caused such a national uproar that this patently unconstitutional censorship law was soon rescinded. Lyon was reelected to Congress while still in jail and took his seat in time to cast the tie-breaking vote that made Thomas Jefferson president instead of Aaron Burr.

Around the spacious green are three Victorian mansions (two faced with marble) built by descendants of Ira Allen, founder of the University of Vermont.

Poultney, on Route 30, the home of Green Mountain College, also has significant journalistic associations: Horace Greeley, founder of the *New York Tribune,* lived at the venerable Eagle Tavern in East Poultney while he was learning the printing trade at the East Poultney *National Spectator* in the 1820s (and organizing a local temperance society). Working with him was George Jones, who helped to found the *New York Times* in 1851.

It's **East Poultney** that's the picturesque village worth detouring to see. The fine white Baptist church, built in 1805, is the centerpiece, standing on a small green surrounded by late-18th- and early-19th-century houses. The general store is also a classic and a source of good deli sandwiches. Its picnic benches are within earshot of the Poultney River, here a fast-flowing stream.

Castleton, at Routes 4A and 30, has triple historical significance: Ethan Allen and Seth Warner planned the capture of Ticonderoga here; on a nearby hill in Hubbardton, Colonel Warner's scrubby militiamen made a valiant rear-guard stand while halting the British invasion force on July 7, 1777, the only Revolutionary War battle actually fought on Vermont soil; and the town itself is a showcase of Greek Revival houses. One offshoot of the conspiratorial meeting in Remington's Tavern in 1775 was the exploit of the blacksmith Samuel Beach—Vermont's own Paul

Revere—who reputedly ran some 60 miles in 24 hours to recruit more men from the countryside for the raid on Ticonderoga.

After the Revolution, Castleton grew rapidly. Thomas Royal Dake, who arrived in about 1807, left his hallmark of design and workmanship on the pillared houses that line Main Street, including the Ransom-Rehlen mansion, with its 17 Ionic columns; and Dake's masterpiece, the Congregational Meeting House, now the Federated Church, with the lovely pulpit that Dake completed with his own funds. These heirloom houses are open for tours during Castleton's Colonial Days, usually held in late July. Between 1850 and 1870, the West Castleton Railroad and Slate Company was the largest marble plant in the country. During these years, a large Welsh community grew up in the area. The town is also the site of Castleton College, part of the Vermont State College system, which has an active arts center.

Benson, west of Route 22A, 8 miles north of Fair Haven, is one of those tiny proverbial villages "that time forgot" except as a scenic photo op, but which in recent years has developed a creative personality with its artisans and special shops.

✷ To See

MUSEUMS **Chaffee Center for the Visual Arts** (802-775-0356), 16 South Main Street, Rutland. Closed Tuesday, otherwise open 10–5, noon–4 Sunday. One of the state's outstanding art galleries, representing 250 Vermont artists, in a former private house listed on the National Register of Historic Places. It has permanent and periodic exhibits and a youth gallery for school displays. Traditional and contemporary paintings, sculpture, crafts, graphics, and photography are included. (See also *Special Events.*) Donation expected.

Vermont Marble Exhibit (802-459-2300; 1-800-427-1396; www.vermontmarble.com), Route 3 from West Rutland, Proctor. Open daily 9–5:30, mid-May through mid-October. Admission charge. The first commercial marble deposit was discovered and quarried in Vermont in 1784. The Vermont Marble Company, formed in 1870 when Redfield Proctor merged several quarries, has mined one of the state's principal resources. Marble from Proctor and Danby was used for the U.S. Supreme Court building, the Lincoln Memorial, and the Beinecke Library at Yale, among many other notable edifices. Proctor himself served as governor, U.S. senator, and secretary of war. Several other members of the Proctor family and chief executives of the company also filled the governor's chair, forming a political dynasty that lasted nearly a century. The company, run by the Swiss-based Pleuss-Staufer Industries since 1976, was closed down in 1991, but nearly 100,000 people still visit the marble exhibit every year, making it one of the biggest tourist attractions in New England. Featured are a special geological display, a film dramatizing the origins and uses of marble, a gallery of bas-reliefs of American presidents, a gift shop, **Dorothea's Cafe,** replicas of the *Pietà* and the *Last Supper,* a sculptor in residence, and a factory viewing site from which to watch the various stages of transformation from rough-cut blocks to polished slabs.

Slate Valley Museum (518-642-1417). Just across the Vermont border on Water Street in Granville, New York, in the heart of the slate industry's historic base, on a site where immigrant quarry workers once lived in tenements, this 19th-century

Dutch barn reflects the many colors and shapes of slate. It includes a quarry shanty, tools, a mural, paintings, photographs, family artifacts, and a gift shop. Call ahead for hours.

The New England Maple Museum (802-483-9414), Route 7 north of Pittsford. Open daily 8:30–5:30 in November and December; March through May, 10–4; closed January and February. The museum has an attractive display of the history, production, and consumption of maple syrup, once called "sweet water," and its by-products. You can view the Danforth Collection of antique equipment, murals, and a 10-minute slide show, and there is a tasting area and gift shop. Mail-order service. $1.50 admission; group rates.

Norman Rockwell Museum (802-773-6095; www.normanrockwellvt.com), Route 4 east, Rutland. Open daily 9–6. The chronological display of his magazine covers, many ads, posters, portraits, and other published illustrations make this an interesting documentary of changing American graphic styles. Gift shop. Admission charge.

Rutland Historical Society (802-775-2006), 96 Center Street, Rutland. The distinctive, 1860 Nickwackett Fire Station serves as the society's home, open for public use Monday 6–9 PM, Saturday 1–4 PM, and by appointment.

HISTORIC SITES **The Hubbardton Battlefield** (802-273-2282) is in East Hubbardton, 8 miles north of the posted Route 4 exit. A small, hilltop visitors center is open mid-May through mid-October, Wednesday through Sunday 9:30–5:30. Battle buffs won't want to miss the diorama and audiovisual display of this 1777 skirmish, detailing how a small force of Green Mountain Boys led by Col. Seth Warner, together with a Massachusetts militia and a New Hampshire regiment, managed to defeat a far larger British contingent led by General Burgoyne.

Paul P. Harris Memorial, Route 7 south of Rutland, Wallingford. Paul Harris (1868–1947), who founded Rotary International while he was working in Chicago, went to school here in the small brick building on Main Street, where the local club meets Monday at 6:30 PM.

Wilson Castle (802-773-3284), Route 3 from West Rutland toward Proctor. This 32-room, 19th-century stone "château" on a 115-acre estate is furnished with elaborate European and Oriental pieces, stained glass, and a variety of wood paneling. Guided tours given daily, late May through mid-October. Admission charge.

COVERED BRIDGES There are six in the area: the 1836 **Kingsley** or **Mill River Bridge,** East Street, off Airport Road, East Clarendon; the 1880 **Brown Bridge,** off Cold River Road, Shrewsbury; the 1840 **Depot Bridge,** off Route 7 north, Pittsford; the 1849 **Cooley Bridge,** Elm Street, Pittsford; the 1843 **Gorham** or **Goodnough Bridge,** Gorham Bridge Road, off Route 3, Pittsford; and the 1830 **Twin Bridge,** East Pittsford Road, off Route 7 north, Rutland.

FISH HATCHERY **Pittsford National Fish Hatchery** (802-483-6618), Furnace Road, Pittsford. Open 8–4 daily. The Fish and Wildlife Service raises landlocked salmon and lake trout here.

✱ To Do

BIKING There is a lot of great bike riding in this area. The roads west and south of Rutland are little traveled and very scenic. Also, there are snack bars sprinkled throughout the area, which always helps. For information on local routes, contact the **True Wheels Bike Shop** in Killington (802-422-3234).

BOATING Boats can be rented from **Lake Bomoseen Marina** (802-265-4611; www.lakebomoseenmarina.com), run by Vito and Mary Guarino.

GOLF **The Rutland Country Club** (802-773-9153), a mile north of the business section on North Grove Street, Rutland. An 18-hole golf course on rolling terrain; restaurant.

Proctor Pittsford Country Club (802-483-9379), Corn Hill Road, Pittsford. 18 holes, lounge, and restaurant.

Lake St. Catherine Country Club (802-287-9341), Route 30, south of Poultney. 18 holes, lounge, and restaurant.

The Bomoseen Country Club (802-468-5581) in Castleton offers nine holes.

Stonehedge Golf (802-773-2666), Route 103 west, North Clarendon, is a nine-hole, par-3 public course.

HIKING **White Rocks Recreation Area,** Route 140 off Route 7 in Wallingford. Follow signs from the White Rocks Picnic Area. The big feature here is a 2,600-foot, conical white peak surrounded by quartzite boulders that retain ice and snow into summer. We advise picking up a hiking guidebook (see *Hiking and Walking* in "What's Where") before starting out.

HORSEBACK RIDING ✐ **Pond Hill Ranch** (802-468-2449), Pond Hill Road, Castleton, offers trail rides and hayrides.

✐ **Mountain Top Equestrian Center** (802-483-6089), Chittenden. Guided trail rides and pony rides; instruction from Memorial Day through Columbus Day. Also see Mountain Top Inn under *Lodging* in "Killington/Pico Area."

HUNTING **Tinmouth Hunting Preserve** (802-446-2337), East Road, Wallingford, has 800 acres of varied cover where individual and group pheasant, partridge, and quail shoots can be arranged from September through March (except on Sunday). Five sporting clay-shooting areas have been added.

RODEOS **Pond Hill Ranch** (802-468-2449), Castleton. Saturday-night rodeos all summer long and into the fall. Go into Castleton and follow the signs to Pond Hill.

SWIMMING **Elfin Lake Beach,** off Route 140 west, 2 miles southeast of Wallingford. (See also *Green Space.*)

SKIING See *To Do—Skiing* in "Killington/Plymouth Area."

SLEIGH RIDES **Cortina Inn** (802-773-3333), Route 4 East, Mendon. Wednesday, Saturday, and some holidays.

Pond Hill Ranch (802-468-2449), Castleton. One- to 3-hour rides.

FITNESS CENTERS **The Gymnasium** (802-773-5333), 30 Merchants Row, Rutland. A complete wellness and cardiovascular center, open Monday through Friday 6 AM–9 PM, 7–7 Saturday and Sunday.

Vermont Sport & Fitness Center (802-775-9916), 40 Curtis Avenue, Rutland. Outdoor pool, indoor/outdoor tennis, racquetball, cardio equipment.

* Green Space

Lake Bomoseen, just north of Castleton, is a popular local summer colony. The lake gained notoriety in the 1930s because of Alexander Woollcott's summer retreat on Neshobe Island. The portly "Town Crier" entertained such cronies as Harpo Marx, who was known to repel curious interlopers by capering along the shore naked and painted blue.

Bomoseen State Park (802-265-4242; 802-483-2314), Route 4 west of Rutland, exit 3, 5 miles north on Town Road. Its 60 campsites and five lean-tos are set in a lovely wildlife refuge; beach, picnic area, nature program, trails, boat ramp, and rentals.

Half Moon Pond State Park (802-273-3848; 802-483-2314), Fair Haven, off Route 4 west of Rutland, exit 4, 7.5 miles north on Route 30, 2 miles west on Town Road, 1.5 miles south on Town Road. Wooded campsites around a secluded pond; rental canoes; hikes to **High Pond,** a remote body of water in the hills.

Lake St. Catherine State Park (802-287-9185; 802-483-2314), 9.5 miles south of Poultney on Route 30. Fifty-two campsites, sandy beaches, fishing, boat rentals, nature trails.

* Lodging

INN **The Victorian Inn at Wallingford** (802-446-2099; www.thevictorianinn.com), 55 North Main Street, Route 7, Wallingford 05773. This fine, restored, historic village mansion has just four very comfortable guest rooms with private bath, and the atmosphere is family friendly, thanks to the upbeat proprietors, Constantine and Soo Schonbachler. There's a cozy, publike bar and three dining rooms that are both formal and casual, fine settings for superior food (see *Dining Out*). Room rates $120–140 ($20 foliage supplement) with full breakfast.

BED & BREAKFASTS **The Inn at Rutland** (802-773-0575; 1-800-808-0575; www.innatrutland.com), 70 North Main Street, Rutland 05071. This is a large, 1890s town house on Route 7 just north of the center of town, now owned by Leslie and Steven Brenner. All 11 distinctive guest rooms have phone, private bath, and antiques, plus color TV. The differences are in size and position. We suggest a room in the back, away from Route 7. The woodwork in the dining room is exceptional, and the fireplaced living room is attractive. Rates of $90–200 include a full breakfast.

The Phelps House (802-775-4480; 1-800-775-4620; www.thephelpshouse.com), 19 North Street, Rutland 05071. Eight bedrooms, plus a private apartment that sleeps eight; playroom and tennis court. Betty Phelps's wonderfully primitive murals are worth the visit to what has been called "the first Frank Lloyd Wright house built in Vermont." $65–80.

Baker's Bed & Breakfast (802-775-4835; 1-888-778-4835), 80 Campbell Road, Rutland 05071 (off Dorr Drive, south of the business district), is a spacious 1826 redbrick house with an inviting veranda and a swimming pool. Steve and Leslie Baker offer three large bedrooms with private bath. There's a living room, library, and dining room for brunchlike breakfasts, included in the $125 rate.

I. B. Munson House (802-446-2860; 1-888-519-3771; www.ibmunsoninn.com), P.O. Box 427, Route 7, Wallingford 05773, has been refurbished by owners Tom and Jo Ann Bren. It is furnished with classic Victorian antiques and period decor, including claw-foot bathtubs. There are seven guest rooms, all with private bath, two with working fireplace. Rates range from $95 single to $180 double, including full gourmet breakfast.

Maplewood Inn (802-265-8039; 1-800-253-7729; www.maplewoodinn.net), Route 22A south, Fair Haven 05743. Lisa and Don Osborne's historic 1843 Greek Revival farmhouse (on the National Register of Historic Places), set in fields, is decorated in period style with common rooms that ramble on and on. There is a breakfast room with hot-beverage bar, and a parlor with complimentary liqueurs. The Blue Room, Rose Room, and Oak Suite are especially attractive. Four of the five rooms have a fireplace, and all have private bath, cable TV, and air-conditioning. Rates are $80–170, including a continental-plus breakfast buffet.

Memory Lane (802-468-5394), 503 Main Street, Castleton 05735. Antique furniture, toys, dolls, and china fill this Federal-style house, originally the home of the cofounder of the medical school at Castleton College. Now Barbara and Thomas Ettori offer three guest rooms, one with a private bath, at $55–90.

Fair Haven Inn Bed & Breakfast (1-800-325-7074; in Vermont: 1-800-649-1212; www.fairhaveninn.com), 18 Main Street, Fair Haven 05743. Owned by the Lemnotis family, proprietors of the popular restaurant (see *Dining Out*) but in a separate town house with a wraparound veranda, the inn has three bedrooms with private bath starting at $99, cable TV in the den, fax and copier service, wet bar (BYOB), and a sitting room with fireplace.

Priscilla's Victorian Inn (802-235-2299), 52 South Street, Middletown Springs 05757, has vintage gingerbread charm, six large Victorian rooms with private bath, a game room, and English gardens. $95 per room.

White Rocks Inn (802-446-2077), 1774 Route 7, Wallingford, 05773. June and Alfred Matthews's elegantly furnished farmhouse and its spectacular, landmark barn are on the National Register of Historic Places. The five guest rooms, each with private bath, have either king, queen, or double canopy beds (one has twin beds) and can be had for $75–120 double occupancy, including full breakfast. The Milk House Cottage (with a whirlpool bath, living room, and full kitchen) is EP. Children over 8 are welcome.

See also Maple Crest Farm and Buckmaster Inn under *Bed & Breakfasts* in "Okemo Valley Region."

MOTELS

In Rutland 05071

Mendon Mountain Orchards (802-775-5477; www.mendonorchards.com), 16 Route 4, Mendon, is not really a motel but rather a series of pleasant, old-fashioned cabins, surrounded by orchards, with a pool and a shop for homemade goodies, apples in-season, cider, and flowers. $45–60 double in winter, less in summer.

Holiday Inn (802-775-1911; 1-800-HOLIDAY), Routes 7 and 4 south, includes **Paynter's Restaurant,** an indoor pool, sauna and exercise room, **Centre Stage** lounge. $99–299 double.

CAMPGROUNDS See *Green Space* for information on campgrounds in Bomoseen State Park, Half Moon Pond State Park, and Lake St. Catherine State Park.

✷ Where to Eat

DINING OUT See also "Killington/Plymouth Area."

Royal's 121 Hearthside (802-775-0856), 37 North Main Street (junction of Routes 4 and 7), Rutland. Open 11–11. The legendary Ernie Royal is no longer alive, but his spirit lives on, maintained by the owner of what was 121 West. Mesquite and hearthside grill specialties: prime rib, chops, seafood, and lobsters. Moderate.

Little Harry's (802-775-4848), 121 West Street, Rutland. Open 5–10 Wednesday through Sunday. This offspring of the popular Harry's Cafe in Mount Holly occupies the old space of 121 West. Owner Harrison Pearce calls his venture the "general store of ethnic eating." Besides pad Thai, a "signature" noodle dish, Little Harry's offers such fare as lamb chops, trout, Greek salads, and lively Spanish dishes plus burritos and steak sandwiches from what Pearce calls a "user-friendly" menu. Inexpensive to moderate.

ↀ **The Victorian Inn at Wallingford** (802-446-2099), 9 North Main Street, Route 7, Wallingford, serves dinner Tuesday through Saturday and a bountiful Sunday brunch buffet laid out in the kitchen. Closed in November until Thanksgiving. Swiss-born chef-owner Constantine Schonbachler's really exceptional Continental specialties have won a strong local following. There is a banquet room that allows catering for up to 180 people. Moderate.

The Fair Haven Inn (802-265-4907), 5 Adams Street, Fair Haven. In a spacious, neo-Colonial setting, the Lemnotis family serves hearty, tasty Greek and Italian dishes at lunch and dinner. Specials include spanakopita, an appetizer of pastry filled with spinach, feta cheese, and egg; moussaka; and seafood souvlakia. Inexpensive to moderate.

EATING OUT The Palms (802-773-2367), 36 Strongs Avenue, Rutland. Italian cooking is a specialty in Rutland because of all the Italians who came to work in the marble quarries. The Palms offers cooking by the fourth generation of the Sabataso family.

South Station (802-775-1736), at the Trolley Barn, 170 South Main Street, Rutland. Open daily for lunch and dinner, specializing in prime ribs of beef and such munchies as fried potato skins, zucchini sticks, stuffed mushrooms, chicken wings, hearty soups, salads, burgers, and teriyaki beef or chicken, all at moderate prices.

Sweet Tomatoes (802-747-7747), 88 Merchants Row, Rutland, has the same northern Italian flair as its siblings in Burlington and in Lebanon, New Hampshire—wood-fired pizzas and all. Open for lunch Monday through Friday 11:30–2, for dinner nightly from 5 PM. Shrimp sautéed with tomato, Greek olives, basil, garlic, crushed red chiles, and white wine, tossed with linguine, is but one sample dish.

Sawdi's Steak House (802-773-8124), Route 7 north, Pittsford. Open for dinner daily. This roadside landmark specializes in charbroiled steaks, lamb, and seafood; an extensive children's menu.

The Sirloin Saloon (802-773-7900), Route 7 south, Rutland. One in a Vermont minichain (there are three), this colorful restaurant (lots of glasswork, art, and gleaming brass) is a good bet for family dinners. The menu runs from ground sirloin to prime rib.

Panda Pavilion (802-775-6682; 802-775-6794), Route 4 east. Open 11:30–11 Monday through Saturday, 1–10 Sunday. Highly praised Szechuan-Hunan-Mandarin cuisine, like Double Happiness Chicken. Takeout service.

Birdseye Diner (802-468-5817), Main Street, Castleton. This restored 1940s Silk City diner, open all day, is a justifiably popular spot for college students and local residents alike.

LakeShore Pub & Grill (802-273-3000), Route 30, on Lake Bomoseen. This locally popular place features live music on summer weekend evenings.

Wheel Inn (802-537-2755), Lake Street at Stage Road, Benson. Open daily 6 AM–9 PM, this family-friendly place has a loyal following.

Magnolia's (802-773-9500), 217 Woodstock Avenue, Rutland. Open Monday through Friday 10–5, Saturday 10–3. Paul Morini offers New York–style deli sandwiches—oven-roasted meat piled high between slices of hand-cut bread. Want roast beef? Try the Chelsea. Like turkey? Order the Upper West Side. The Bronx is a toasted pressed sandwich with roast pork, boiled ham, and Swiss cheese topped with pickles, butter, and mayonnaise.

Tokyo House, 106 West Street, Rutland. Open for lunch and dinner. Owner George Li also owns restaurants in Saratoga Springs and Lake George, New York. Sushi and sashimi are the calling cards here, but you'll also find filet mignon and noodle soups. Eat in or take out; beer and wine.

Clem & Co. (802-747-3340), Wales Street, Rutland. Great soups, salads, and sandwiches for lunch. Breakfast served until closing at 2 PM. A fast, friendly local eatery.

Also see Costantino's Italian Imports in *Selective Shopping*

COFFEEHOUSE/WINE BAR **Coffee Exchange** (802-775-3337), 101–103 Merchants Row, Rutland. Open Monday through Thursday from 6 AM, from 8 AM Friday through Sunday. "Jazz, java, and jabber" is the theme of this upbeat coffee bar and sophisticated wine room orchestrated by Kevin Lefter at a key downtown intersection. Patrons sip and nosh on exotic beverages and pastries at outdoor tables in summer—perhaps macadamia cream coffee and orange-poppyseed scones. Salads, soups, and sandwiches at lunch.

✷ Entertainment

Crossroads Art Council (802-775-5413), 39 East Center Street, Rutland, sponsors a series of concerts, theater and ballet performances, and an arts education program.

See also LakeShore Pub & Grill under *Eating Out.*

Movieplex 9 (802-775-5500), downtown Rutland Plaza, and **Westway 1-2-3-4** (438-2888), Route 4 in West Rutland, show first-run flicks.

✷ Selective Shopping

BOOKSTORES **Charles E. Tuttle Company** (802-773-8930), Main Street, Rutland, facing the park, has one of the largest stocks of used and rare books in New England. Charles Tuttle began his publishing company in Tokyo right after World War II and built it into a major supplier of beautifully produced books on Oriental art and other Asian subjects.

The Book King (802-773-9232), Merchants Row, Rutland, is a bright, well-stocked store for new adult and children's books, paperbacks, and cards.

✐ **Annie's Book Stop** (802-775-6993), Trolley Square, 120 South Main Street, Rutland. Annie's has a large selection of new books and preread paperbacks; specializes in children's books and books on

CENTER STREET IN DOWNTOWN RUTLAND

Kim Grant

tape, plus educational puzzles and games.

SPECIAL SHOPS **Great Outdoors Trading Company** (802-775-6531), Woodstock Avenue, Rutland, is a vast, complete sporting goods store, with a bike shop, gun shop, archery center, and fly-rod department, among others.

The Seward Vermont Dairy Deli Shop (802-773-2738), 224 North Main Street (Route 7), Rutland. One corner of this vast restaurant (see *Eating Out*) showcases the cheddar cheeses produced by Cabot and Crowley (the Seward family no longer makes its own cheese). One specialty is sharp cheddar, aged more than 9 months. Maple syrup and creamed honey are also available. The ice cream is the showstopper, however.

Costantino's Italian Imports, 802-747-0777, 10 Terrill Street, Rutland. Former antiques dealer Dan Costantino has renovated the former Bartlett's Studio building to create a shop that features shelves of imported Italian meats, cheeses, pasta, and olive oil. In the back a deli offers Italian sandwiches and pasta salads.

Vermont Canvas Products (802-773-7311), 179 Woodstock Avenue, Route 4 east, Rutland, makes customized luggage and handbags. Open daily except Sunday.

Truly Unique (802-773-7742), Route 4 east, Rutland, has an uncommon collection of country antiques, Vermont products, and gifts.

Rocking Horse Country Store (802-773-7882), Route 4 east, Rutland, combines Vermont food products (including its own homemade wine jelly), gifts, antiques, and collectibles.

Fred's Dollhouse and Miniature Center (802-483-6362), 3224 Route 7 north, Pittsford. Open Monday through Saturday 9:30–5, Sunday 11–5, and by appointment. This is where you can get dollhouses and miniature furnishings, accessories, scaled lumber, hardware, electrical systems, and wallpaper, plus dollhouse and furniture kits.

Farrow Gallery & Studio (802-468-5683), Old Yellow Church, Main Street, Castleton, shows Patrick Farrow's limited-edition, award-winning bronze sculptures, along with the work of other Vermont artists.

✷ Special Events

Late February: **Great Benson Fishing Derby,** sponsored by the Fair Haven Rotary Club—many prizes in several categories, including best ice shanty. Tickets for the derby: P.O. Box 131, Bomoseen 05732.

Late July: **Colonial Days,** Castleton (see *Villages*).

Early August: **Art in the Park Summer Arts Festival,** sponsored by the Chaffee Center (802-775-0356), in Main Street Park, junction of Routes 7 and 4 east.

Early September: **Vermont State Fair** (802-775-5200). Midway, exhibits, races, demolition derby, and tractor pulls animate the old fairgrounds on Route 7 south, Rutland.

Mid-October: **Art in the Park Fall Foliage Festival,** sponsored by the Chaffee Center (802-775-0356).

December 31: Rutland's **First Night** celebration.

ADDISON COUNTY AND ENVIRONS

INCLUDING MIDDLEBURY, VERGENNES, BRANDON, AND BRISTOL

Addison County packs as much contrasting scenery within its borders as any county in the country. On the east it includes the high wall of the Green Mountains, laced with hiking trails and pierced by four of the state's highest, most dramatic "gaps" (passes). The mountains drop abruptly through widely scattered hill towns—Lincoln, Ripton, and Goshen—into a 30-mile-wide, farm-filled valley, Vermont's largest concentration of dairy farms and orchards. Lake Champlain is far narrower here than up around Burlington, and the Adirondacks in New York seem higher and nearer, forming an improbable but spectacular backdrop to cows, water, red barns, and apple trees.

This stretch of the Champlain Valley is particularly popular with bicyclists, not only because it's the flattest piece of Vermont, but also because its quiet old farm roads wind through orchards to discoveries like the "Fort Ti Ferry" ("serving people and their vehicles since Mozart was three months old") and "the world's smallest bank" in Orwell.

Middlebury, the hub of Addison County, is among New England's most sophisticated towns, the home of one of its most prestigious private colleges and many interesting shops.

We hope that this book will lure visitors to explore the entire valley: the easily accessible scenery along Route 7 as well as the Lake Champlain shoreline, notched at regular intervals with quiet and accessible bays, and the Green Mountain forest roads, with their occasional but spectacular lake and valley views.

GUIDANCE **Addison County Chamber of Commerce** (802-388-7951; 1-800-SEE-VERMONT; www.midvermont.com), 2 Court Street, Middlebury 05753, in the Painter House (see *Villages—Middlebury*), offers information about every corner of its domain, from Vergennes and Bristol in the north to Orwell in the south. Open Monday through Friday 9–5. This unusually large walk-in information center publishes a map/guide, stocks brochures, and refers visitors to a wide variety of lodgings, from inns and bed & breakfasts to seasonal cottages on Lake

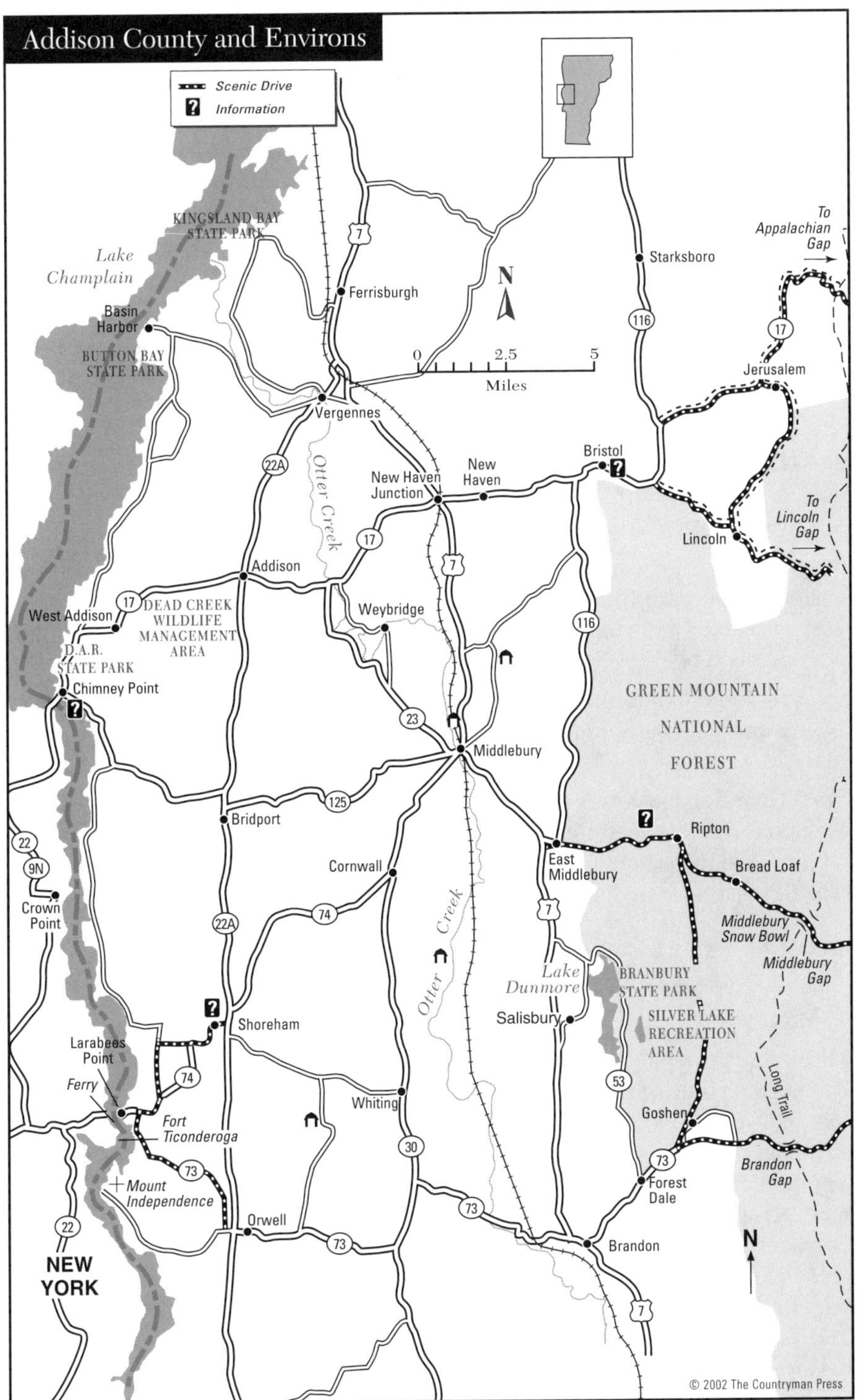
Addison County and Environs
Scenic Drive
Information
KINGSLAND BAY STATE PARK
Lake Champlain
Basin Harbor
BUTTON BAY STATE PARK
Ferrisburgh
Vergennes
Otter Creek
New Haven Junction
New Haven
Bristol
Starksboro
To Appalachian Gap
Jerusalem
Lincoln
To Lincoln Gap
N
0
2.5
5
Miles
Addison
West Addison
DEAD CREEK WILDLIFE MANAGEMENT AREA
D.A.R. STATE PARK
Chimney Point
Weybridge
Middlebury
GREEN MOUNTAIN NATIONAL FOREST
Bridport
Crown Point
Cornwall
East Middlebury
Ripton
Bread Loaf
Middlebury Snow Bowl
Middlebury Gap
Lake Dunmore
BRANBURY STATE PARK
SILVER LAKE RECREATION AREA
Salisbury
Shoreham
Larabees Point
Ferry
Fort Ticonderoga
Whiting
Goshen
Long Trail
Brandon Gap
Forest Dale
Mount Independence
Orwell
Brandon
NEW YORK
© 2002 The Countryman Press

Dunmore. During foliage season, it is unusually resourceful in finding lodging for all comers.

Vergennes Chamber of Commerce (802-877-0080), P.O. Box 335, Vergennes 05491, has an information booth on the common.

Brandon Area Chamber of Commerce (802-247-6401), P.O. Box 267, Brandon 05735; visitors booth on Park Street with brochures and information in front of the library across from the Brandon Inn. There's an informative self-guided walking tour guide to the town's rich architectural heritage.

Moosalamoo, from the Abenaki word possibly meaning "the moose departs," is a dandy map and guide, with site signage, to the trails and other natural features of some 20,000 acres of Green Mountain National Forest, published and distributed by the Moosalamoo Partnership, available at chambers of commerce, the Catamount Trail Association, other outdoor recreation organizations, and several inns. Or call 802-247-6735; 1-800-448-0707.

GETTING THERE *By bus:* **Vermont Transit** (802-864-6811; 1-800-451-3292) stops in Brandon and Vergennes as well as Middlebury. This is the Burlington-to-Albany run, so New Yorkers and Bostonians must change in Rutland.

By car: The major north–south highway is Route 7, but we advise anyone from Boston to approach through the Middlebury Gap (see *Scenic Drives*). From the west you can take the toll bridge at Chimney Point year-round or the seasonal ferries described below.

By ferry: **Lake Champlain Ferry** (802-864-9804) from Essex, New York, to Charlotte operates spring through fall, takes 20 minutes, and puts you just above Vergennes.

Fort Ticonderoga Ferry (802-897-7999), Larrabees Point to Fort Ticonderoga. Memorial Day weekend through June, 8–6 daily; July through Labor Day 8 AM–9 PM, then 8–6 through the last Sunday in October. Cars $6 one-way, $10 round-trip. (See the chapter introduction.)

MEDICAL EMERGENCY Emergency service is available by calling **911.**

✷ Villages

Middlebury (population: 8,000) is the county seat and hub of Addison County. It's also the home of prestigious Middlebury College and one of Vermont's handsomest, liveliest, most welcoming communities. Inns and restaurants serve visitors as well as potential students and their parents, and in recent years it has become a great place to shop. Middlebury College (founded in 1800 and now one of the most sought-after private colleges) owes much to the energy and vision of Gamaliel Painter, a surveyor who settled here before the Revolution. Painter accompanied Ethan Allen on the Fort Ticonderoga raid and returned to Middlebury to become the town's principal landowner, sheriff, judge, and assemblyman. The fine mansion on Court Street, presently housing the information center, belonged to Painter. Another benefactor was Joseph Battell, who owned thousands of acres of forest and mountain land that he left to the college and the state when he died in 1915. He was the proprietor of the famous old summit house, the Bread Loaf Inn, now the nucleus of the summer Bread Loaf School of English and the Bread Loaf Writers Conference. Battell also owned a weekly newspaper in which he fulminated against the invasion of motorcars. Emma Hart Willard, who pioneered in the education of women, was another Middlebury luminary.

The town's proudest buildings—the courthouse, Middlebury Inn, the Battell House, and the fine Congregational church—are grouped, along with compact business blocks, around the common. It's a short walk down Main Street to the churning Otter Creek falls, a centerpiece for dozens of shops that have proliferated in the old mills and marbleworks on both banks of the river, connected by a footbridge. With the Vermont State Craft Center (see *Selective Shopping—Crafts Shops*) as its anchor store, this is now one of Vermont's most interesting places to shop.

Brandon. A peaceful town of some 4,000 inhabitants and a heretofore underrated appeal, Brandon has an unusual array of 19th-century houses in an eclectic and intriguing mix of Federal and Victorian styles. Sited in Rutland County (it's just over the southern border of Addison County) between Otter Creek and the Neshobe River, it was the home of Thomas Davenport, who invented and patented an electric motor in 1838, and the birthplace of Stephen A. Douglas (1813–1861), the "Little Giant" of the famous debates with Abraham Lincoln in 1858, when Douglas was a senator from Illinois. Brandon's hospitality to travelers is growing with the addition of some interesting new places to stay.

MIDDLEBURY CAMPUS

Sally Johnson

Bristol. Billing itself as the "Gateway to the Green Mountains," Bristol is nestled at the foot of Lincoln Gap, at the junctions of north–south Route 116 (less heavily trafficked than Route 7) and east–west Route 17. Its broad Main Street is lined with a delightful mix of stores and restaurants, housed in a 19th-century building that leads to a square green, complete with fountain, park benches, and old cannon. The local site to see is the **Lord's Prayer Rock** (on the south side of Route 17 entering Bristol from the east), a flat rock inscribed with the Lord's Prayer. A physician named Joseph C. Greene commissioned the inscription in 1891, presumably because he was still thankful for having reached that point safely when, as a youth, he was hauling logs over steep roads.

Vergennes, midway between Middlebury and Burlington, has long claimed to be the smallest city (2,300 residents) in the United States. Although 5 miles inland, its history and its present activities are linked closely to Lake Champlain. Otter Creek winds from the city to the lake, and the road leads to Basin Harbor, site of the area's premier resort (see *Lodging—Resort*) and the Lake Champlain Maritime Museum (see *To See—Museums*). We recommend the lake road south from Basin Harbor, by Button Bay State Park and the D.A.R. State Park to Chimney Point. The ruins of the 18th-century fort at Crown Point in New York are just across the Lake Champlain Bridge.

Vergennes's site on an impressive falls and its handsome, early-19th-century commercial buildings suggest an unusual history. This is, in fact, one of the oldest, as well as the smallest, cities in the country. It was founded by Donald McIntosh in 1764 and later named by Ethan Allen for Charles Gravier, Comte de Vergennes, the French minister of foreign affairs who was a strong supporter of the American Revolutionary cause.

In 1811–12, Thomas Macdonough used the Otter Creek Basin just below the falls to build—in record time—three ships, including the 734-ton, 26-gun *Saratoga.* He also equipped nine gunboats, using them all to defeat the British fleet in Lake Champlain off Plattsburgh in 1814.

Shoreham is known for its many orchards. Shoreham Village is a beauty, with a classic Congregational church (1846), a Masonic temple (built in 1852 as the Universalist church), and the graceful St. Genevieve Catholic Church (1873), as well as the old inn and general store (see *Lodging—Inns*). Follow Route 74 southwest

VERGENNES OPERA HOUSE

Sally Johnson

from the village through the orchards; or continue straight on Witherell Road where 74 jogs south, then turn south (left) onto Smith Street along the lake. Either way, you get to Larrabees Point, the site of Teachout's Store, built in 1836 from stones taken from Fort Ticonderoga just across the lake. The excursion boat M/V *Carillon* now departs from this spot; next door, the small, car-carrying "Fort Ti" cable ferry makes the crossing to the fort itself in 6 minutes flat. It has held the franchise from the Vermont and New York legislatures since 1799, but records indicate the service was initiated by Lord Jeffery Amherst in 1757 for use by his soldiers in the campaigns against the French. Continue south on Route 73 to the turnoff for Mount Independence.

Orwell. Best known for Mount Independence (see *Historic Sites*), the small village at the center of this orchard and dairying community circles a long, sloping green with a brick Congregational church (1843) on a rise by the white-clapboard town hall (built in 1810 as the Baptist church). It all overlooks a brief line of shops with the First National Bank of Orwell, billed as "the world's smallest bank," in the middle. Chartered in 1863 (but known as the Farmers Bank for many years, before Lincoln granted it the country's 212th official charter), the bank remains a real center of town, with notices of upcoming events tacked to the authentic old teller's cages. The other village nerve center is **Buxton's Store,** the genuine article.

✷ To See

MUSEUMS **Middlebury College Center for the Arts** (802-443-6433), Route 30, Middlebury. Open Tuesday through Friday 10–5, weekends noon–5. The college's small but distinguished permanent collection of paintings and small sculptures plus changing exhibits are displayed in galleries within the multitiered arts center, which also includes a café and several performance areas.

The Henry Sheldon Museum (802-388-2117), Park Street, Middlebury. Open year-round, Monday through Friday 10–5, also Saturday late May through October. Guided and self-guided tours. This 1829 marble merchant's house has no fewer than six black marble mantels and holds an intimate collection of furnishings, tools, household articles, clothes, books, games, and other artifacts portraying Vermont folkways, all displayed in period rooms. A modern research ell has been added, with a gallery for changing exhibits. There are also frequent special events. $4 per adult, $3.50 for seniors, and $2 for children 6–18.

The Vermont Folklife Center (802-388-4964), 3 Court Street, Middlebury (in Masonic Hall). This growing organization (founded in 1984) collects and presents the traditional arts and folkways of Vermont, primarily through taped interviews. It mounts changing exhibits and sells its publications.

Lake Champlain Maritime Museum (802-475-2022), Basin Harbor, Panton, at the entrance to the Basin Harbor Club off Panton Road west of Vergennes. Open daily 10–5 May 1 through mid-October; $8 adults, $7 seniors, $4 for children ages 6 and up. This museum has been evolving steadily over the last decades. It began with the gift of a local schoolhouse constructed from native limestone in 1808, moved stone by stone (2,000 of them) and reconstructed to house exhibits. The museum's 10 buildings, spread over 3 acres, now house dozens of small craft built

JOSEPH BATTELL BRIDGE

The bridge that Joseph Battell built in downtown Middlebury is but one element of an enormous and enduring legacy of mountaintops and mortar that this eccentric bachelor left to the state of Vermont as a whole and to Middlebury College in particular.

Battell was born in 1839 to a wealthy and influential Vermont family. He attended Middlebury College, but ill health kept him from finishing his degree. Instead, he went off to travel the world; upon his return he bought land in the mountain town of Ripton, where he ran an inn, mainly for his friends. Today that land and those buildings house two of the college's most highly regarded summer programs: the Bread Loaf School of English and the Bread Loaf Writers Conference. In addition to being publisher of the *Middlebury Register,* a local newspaper, Battell was also an author. One of his oddest efforts was a book entitled *Ellen, or, The Whisperings of an Old Pine,* a dense tome that is seldom read but much wondered about.

Battell was a man who loved mountains and woods and hated cars, so much so that he refused to allow cars on the road that ran up to his Ripton inn. Yet it was because of Battell that the stone bridge spanning Otter Creek in downtown Middlebury is still, a century later, a key to the transportation infrastructure in Addison County. The original wooden bridge that carried traffic across the creek burned down a century ago. Middlebury's town fathers, in a fit of economy, decided to build an iron bridge on the site, but Battell was opposed, arguing that a stone bridge would last significantly longer than an iron one. So determined was he that he is said to have paid the difference out of his own pocket.

A pioneering conservationist, Battell used to send his hired man into the woods, armed with blank deeds and instructions to buy as much acreage as he could from any farmer or logger he came across. Over time, he acquired about 35,000 acres, including Camels Hump, which he donated to the state of Vermont for use as a state park. His landholdings also reached over Bread Loaf Mountain from East Middlebury to Hancock, Granville, and Rochester, along Route 100, and followed the spine of the Green Mountains from Mount Ellen south to Brandon Gap. When he died in 1915, most of this land was bequeathed to Middlebury College, which has sold off much of it over the years, keeping only a few hundred acres.

Battell is also the father of the University of Vermont's Morgan Horse Farm (see *To See*). Battell began breeding Morgans on his farm in the latter

1800s, an interest that would prove to be instrumental in saving America's first breed of horse from extinction. He hired architect Clinton Smith to build the beautiful white farm buildings that still stand in Weybridge. With typical Battell intensity, he spent years tracing out pedigrees that resulted in the publication of the first volume of the *Morgan Horse Register* in 1894. Then in 1906 he gave his farm and his Morgan horses to the U.S. government. It remains a working horse farm to this day and supplies stock to Morgan breeders across the country.

Sally Johnson

THE BATTELL BRIDGE IN DOWNTOWN MIDDLEBURY

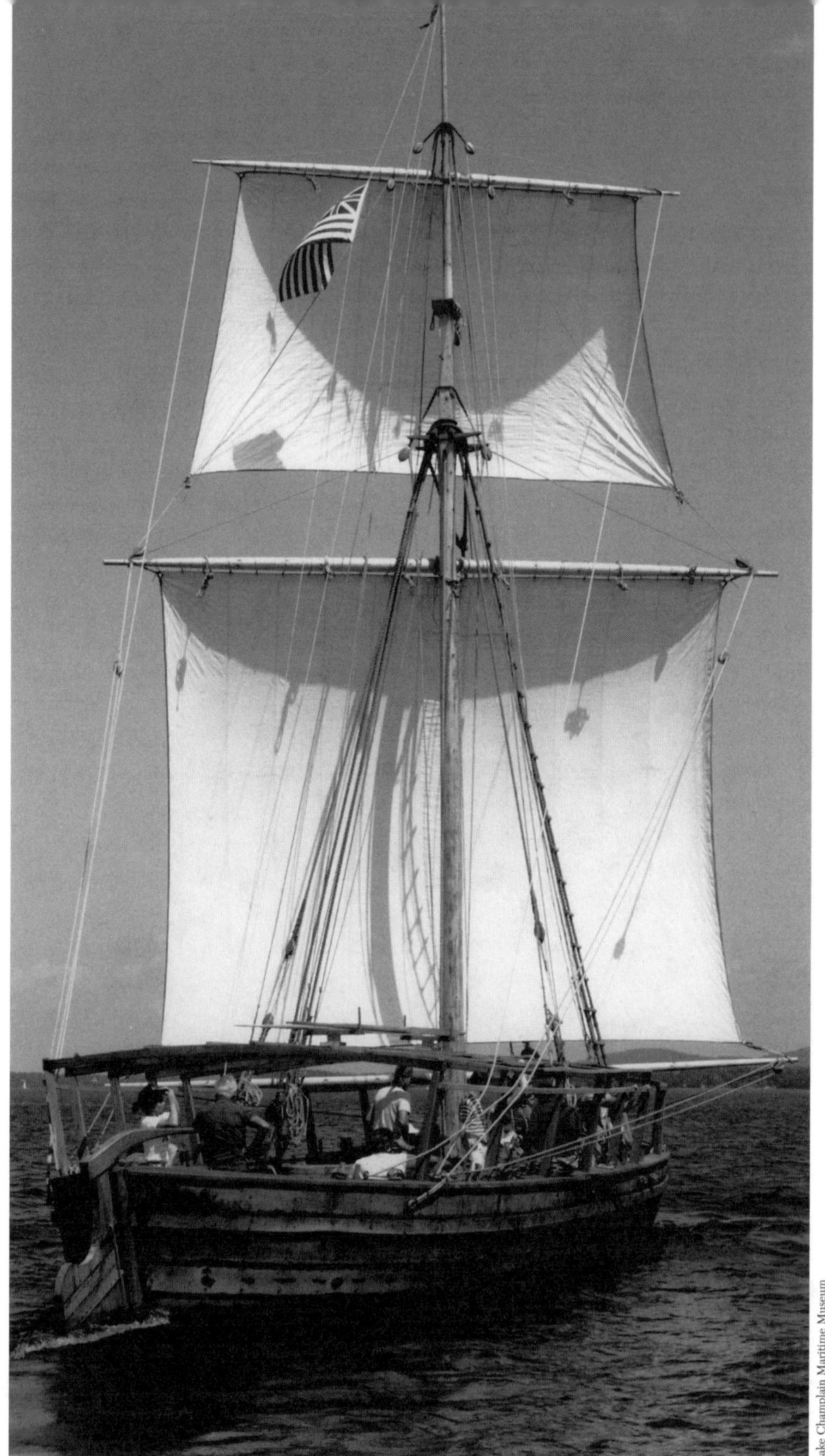
Lake Champlain Maritime Museum

THE GUNBOAT REPLICA *PHILADELPHIA* UNDER SAIL ON LAKE CHAMPLAIN

around the lake over a period of 150 years, and exhibits on a number of chapters in the lake's story, including the saga of the hundreds of wrecks still beneath the surface. Attempts to raise them, you learn, began in the 1930s but have been abandoned because divers and historians have accepted the obvious: Wood that's been submerged in fresh water quickly disintegrates when exposed to air. Instead, the state of Vermont has created five underwater parks; inquire about guided scuba tours, lectures, and field trips, and demonstrations and courses in boatbuilding. A working replica of Benedict Arnold's 54-foot gunboat, *Philadelphia,* built on the spot, is also on view. The bookstore carries a good selection of maritime-related books, prints, clothing, and gifts.

HISTORIC HOMES **Rokeby Museum** (802-877-3406), 3 miles north of Vergennes on Route 7 in Ferrisburgh. Open for guided tours at 11, 12:30, and 2, Thursday through Sunday, May through October, and by appointment year-round. $4 adults, $3 students and seniors. Exhibits evoke the lives of four generations of a Quaker family whose members included pioneers, farmers, and Rowland E. Robinson, the 19th-century author, illustrator, and naturalist. Rokeby was an important stop on the Underground Railway for freedom-seeking slaves before the Civil War.

The John Strong D.A.R. Mansion (802-759-2309), Route 17, west of 22A, West Addison, open mid-May through mid-October, Friday through Sunday 9–5. $2 per adult, $1 seniors and students. This is one of several substantial houses and buildings made of stone taken from the ruins of Fort Crown Point and skidded across frozen Lake Champlain by oxen. General Strong, an early settler and Green Mountain Boy, built his (third) residence here in 1796 with brick from his own clay pits on the "Salt Lick" where he first hunted deer. Furnishings reflect five generations of the family.

HISTORIC SITES **Mount Independence State Historic Site** (802-948-2000), 8 miles west of Orwell on the shore of Lake Champlain, marked from the junction of Route 73 off Route 22A. Grounds open year-round; museum open Memorial Day through Columbus Day, Wednesday through Sunday 9:30–5:30. Opened in 1996, a boat-shaped visitors center exhibits archaeological artifacts and tells the story of the thousands of men who weathered a brutal winter on this fortified peninsula in 1776–77, facing Fort Ticonderoga across a narrow strip of lake. Eventually they defeated the British at Saratoga, one of the most decisive victories of the Revolution. Four marked trails begin at the information center and wander down to the lake through 400 wooded acres.

Fort Ticonderoga (518-585-2821), Ticonderoga, New York. Open mid-May through mid-October daily. $12 per adult, $6 children ages 7–12. The 18th-century stone fort has been restored and includes a museum displaying weapons and uniforms. It was built by the French (who named it Fort Carillon), captured by English Gen. Jeffery Amherst, and held by the British until 1775, when Ethan Allen and his Green Mountain Boys took the fort by surprise, capturing the guns that eventually helped free Boston. The fort is easily accessible from Larrabees Point on the Vermont shore (see *Getting There* and *To Do—Boating*).

Kim Grant

THE UVM MORGAN HORSE FARM IN MIDDLEBURY

Crown Point State Historic Site (518-597-3666), Crown Point, New York. Open mid-May through October, Wednesday through Saturday 10–5, Sunday 1–5. Free. Just across the Lake Champlain Bridge from Chimney Point, West Addison, Vermont. Fifteen miles north of Fort Ticonderoga, Crown Point was once a far larger, more important fortification, and in 1775 it was the source of 29 pieces of cannon captured by the colonists and hauled off to Boston. The complex includes 18th-century ruins and a visitors center.

Chimney Point State Historic Site (802-759-2412), at the Vermont end of the Lake Champlain Bridge, Route 125. Open Memorial Day through Columbus Day, Wednesday through Sunday 9:30–5:30. An 18th-century tavern houses a well-mounted display on Native American and French colonial heritage.

GARDENS **Pinewood Gardens** (802-247-3388), Route 7 south, Brandon. Excellent perennials and annuals for sale, plus display gardens. Open Easter through Christmas.

Rocky Dale Gardens (802-453-2782), 62 Rocky Dale Road, Bristol. Open daily 9–6 except Tuesday. Extensive displays on 3 acres with dramatic rock outcroppings, plus retail nursery.

FARMS AND ORCHARDS **The UVM Morgan Horse Farm** (802-388-2011), open May through October, 9–4 daily. Go through downtown Middlebury, heading west on Route 125, then turn right onto Route 23 (Weybridge Street) and follow signs. Admission. The first "Morgan" was born in the late 1790s and is recognized as the sire of an entire breed of Vermont horse. Col. Joseph Battell began breeding Morgans on this farm in the 1870s and is credited with saving the breed (America's first developed breed of horse) from extinction. The farm is now a breeding and training center operated by the University of Vermont. Guided tours of the stables and paddocks are available, along with an audiovisual presentation about the Morgan horse and farm.

✐ **Yankee Kingdom Orchard** (802-759-2387), Lake Street, West Addison. Overlooking Lake Champlain, pick-your-own apples, strawberries, and pumpkins; also a petting zoo, children's play area, wagon rides, cider pressing. The Yankee Kingdom Festival in early September is a great event for kids.

See also *To Do—Apple Picking.*

BRIDGES OF ADDISON COUNTY The **Pulp Mill Covered Bridge,** between Middlebury and Weybridge, spanning the Otter Creek near the Morgan Horse Farm (see *Farms and Orchards*), is the oldest in the state (1808–20) and the last two-lane span still in use.

Halpin Bridge (1824), Middlebury, 2 miles east of Route 7, off Halpin Road, is Vermont's highest bridge above the streambed.

Station Bridge, across Otter Creek in Cornwall (2 miles east of Route 30 on Swamp Road), is a 136-foot Town lattice bridge built in 1836.

Shoreham Covered Railroad Bridge, East Shoreham off the Whiting-Shoreham Road (turn south onto Shoreham Depot Road); the bridge is marked on area maps. A Howe bridge built in 1897 by the Rutland Railroad, spanning the Lemon Fair River. A designated state historic site.

SCENIC DRIVES **Middlebury Gap.** This is our favorite approach to Addison County from the southeast, and this stretch of Route 125 is more dramatic driving east to west. Begin in Hancock and stop at Texas Falls (see *Green Space*). The road quickly crests at its junction with the Long Trail, near the Middlebury Snow Bowl. Then it's all downhill through the woods until the huge, wooden Bread Loaf Inn (now part of Middlebury College) improbably appears. The Robert Frost Wayside Picnic Area and the Interpretive Trail are a short way beyond. We also like to stop in the small, 19th-century cemetery a bit farther down, where a wind chime strikes softly in a row of maples. The picturesque hill town of Ripton is just below, and as the road continues to plunge into the valley, you glimpse the Adirondacks in the distance.

Brandon Gap. Route 73 is a high road over Goshen Mountain and through Brandon Gap. At the height-of-land, several wooded hiking trails are posted, and a rest area has been sited to catch the full majesty of Mount Horrid's Great Cliff. The road then rushes downhill with Brandon Brook, joining Route 100 and the White River below Rochester.

Note: A well-surfaced woods road (Goshen Road) runs south from Ripton through the national forest, past the turnoffs for Silver Lake (see *Green Space*) and past Blueberry Hill (see *Lodging* and *To Do—Bicycling* and *Cross-Country Skiing*) to Route 73 in the Brandon Gap.

Appalachian Gap. East from Bristol, Route 17 climbs steadily for 4 miles (past the Jerusalem General Store), eases off for a couple of miles, and then zigzags steeply to crest at more than 3,000 feet, yielding some spectacular views before dropping into the Mad River Valley. It's even more spectacular heading west.

Lincoln/Appalachian Gap Loop. From Bristol, follow Route 17/116 to the turnoff for Lincoln 2 miles east of Bristol, past Bartlett Falls (be sure to stop) to Lincoln and out the Dowlingsville Road to Jerusalem, back down on Route 116 to Route 17.

Lincoln Gap. Follow Routes 17/116 east from Bristol, as above, but from Lincoln continue on the narrow Gap Road, unpaved in sections. Again there are beautiful views, and you are quickly down in Warren (see "Sugarbush/Mad River Valley"). *Note:* Unsuitable for trailers and RVs. Closed in winter.

Along Lake Champlain. See *Villages* for Shoreham and Orwell.

✱ To Do

APPLE PICKING September and early October is apple time in Addison County, where you are welcome to pick your own (PYO). The orchards are particularly thick in and around Shoreham: **Atwood Orchards** (802-897-5592) on Barnum Hill, a half mile from its stand on Route 22A (3 miles south of Shoreham Village), offers PYO, also a picnic area and views of Lake Champlain. **Douglas Orchards,** 1 mile west of the village on Route 74, does the same and has a cider press; as does **RidgeView Orchards** (802-897-5991), another mile west on Route 74, with PYO plus honey, blueberries, and raspberries. **Champlain Orchards** (802-897-2777), farther west on Route 74, offers PYO. See also *Farms and Orchards.*

BICYCLING It's no coincidence that the country's first bicycle touring company was founded in this area. According to Bruce Burgess, a pioneer tour leader and current owner of Bicycle Holidays (see below), there just isn't a more rewarding place to bike anywhere than this swath of the Champlain Valley, with its relatively flat terrain and mountain views, its wealth of back roads leading through covered bridges, connecting historic sites and comfortable inns with ample swimming holes, ice cream, and antiquing stops en route. Burgess shares a word of warning: Beware deceptively quiet but narrow, truck-trafficked roads like Route 22A and Route 30.

Bicycle Holidays (802-388-BIKE), Munger Street, Middlebury 05753, offers custom-designed, self-guided tours—both inn-to-inn and camping—for solos, couples, and groups. Rental equipment, airport pickup, and luggage shuttle can be arranged.

Bike Vermont (1-800-257-2226), based in Woodstock, gets good reviews for guided, small-group inn-to-inn tours in this area.

Vermont Bicycle Touring (VBT) (802-453-4811), Box 711, Bristol, the state's oldest bike tour company, offers guided group inn-to-inn tours.

The Bike Center (802-388-6666), 74 Main Street, Middlebury, is a source for a variety of rental bikes.

Country Inns along the Trail (802-247-3300; 1-800-838-3301), Van Cortland Road, Brandon 05733. Bike tours usually begin and end at Churchill House Inn (see *Hiking*), which has a fleet of bikes for rent at $15 per day, including helmet. Other inns are on the itinerary. Brochure from Churchill House (see *Lodging—Inns*).

Mountain Biking at Blueberry Hill (802-247-6735), Goshen. An extensive network of ski trails and woods roads that are well suited to mountain biking; rentals, lessons.

BIRDING **Otter Creek** (see *Boating*), near Lake Champlain in Vergennes, and the **Dead Creek Wildlife Management Area** in Addison (off Route 17) are particularly rich in bird life, especially during migration seasons. See also *Watchable Wildlife* under "What's Where."

BOATING **The M/V *Carillon*,** a 60-foot, 49-passenger replica of a 1920s Thousand Islands luxury motor yacht, operates daily Father's Day through Labor Day. Geared to groups in spring and fall but walk-ons accepted (call ahead), from Teachout's Lakehouse Store and Wharf (802-897-5331) at Larrabees Point. The 1½-hour cruise goes up to Hand's Cove, then across to Fort Ticonderoga (you can debark and catch a later boat), and on to Mount Independence and Mount Defiance, while the captain tells you what was happening along the route in the 1770s. $8.50 per adult, $4.50 per child; group rates.

Boat rentals are available from **Vermont Houseboat Vacations** (802-948-2375), Route 73A, Orwell; **Buoy 39 Marina** (802-948-2411), Route 73A, Orwell; **Waterhouses** (802-252-4433), West Shore Road, Lake Dunmore (rents rowboats, canoes, motorboats, sailboats); **Champlain Bridge Marina** (802-759-2049), West Addison (boat access, pump-out station for boats less than 35 feet); **Chipman Point Marina & Campground** (802-948-2288), Route 73A (dockage for 60 boats, grocery store, pump-out station, game room, swimming, boat rentals); and **Lake Dunmore Kampersville** (802-352-4501), in Salisbury, which also rents rowboats, canoes, sailboats, and motor bugs.

FACTORY TOURS **Otter Creek Brewing** (1-800-473-0727), 85 Exchange Street, Middlebury. Open daily for free guided tours. Free samples, retail sales of its Copper Ale, Stovepipe Porter, and lagers.

FISHING **Otter Creek** is a warm-water stream good for smallmouth bass and northern pike. The cooler **Neshobe River,** especially in Forest Dale, is better for trout, and rainbows can be found in the **Middlebury River** just below Ripton. The **New Haven River** between Lincoln and Bristol and south of New Haven Mills is also good trout fishing.

FITNESS CENTERS **Vermont Sun** (802-388-6888), 88 Exchange Street, Middlebury, is a spacious indoor sports and fitness center with training equipment, an Olympic-sized pool, and racquetball courts. Open daily for members; guests by the day or week.

Middlebury Fitness (802-388-3744), Wilson Road off Route 7 south, Middlebury, features state-of-the-art equipment. Guests by the day or by the week.

GOLF **Ralph Myhre Golf Course** (802-388-3771), Route 30 just south of the Middlebury campus, is owned and operated by the college; 18 holes.

The Basin Harbor Club (802-475-2311), Vergennes, 18 holes (see *Lodging—Resort*).

Neshobe Golf Club (802-247-3611), Town Farm Road (just off Route 73), Brandon. Open April through October. A full-service club; 18 holes.

HIKING **The Green Mountain National Forest District Office** (802-388-4362), Route 7, Middlebury, offers a pamphlet guide to 28 day hikes.

Country Inns along the Trail. Eight other inns collaborate with Churchill House (802-247-3300) to provide lodging along an 80-mile stretch of the Long Trail and some of its side trails, including the section over Mount Mansfield.

Middlebury Area Land Trust (802-388-1007) publishes *Trails Around Middlebury,* a map and guide to 14 miles of trails.

HORSEBACK RIDING **Mazza Horse Service** (802-758-9240), Hemenway Road, Bridport. Trail-ride lessons.

Firefly Ranch (802-453-2223), Bristol. Open May through October for riding. Really a miniranch set off a back road high in the mountains, an expanded chalet with just three guest rooms (private baths), eight horses. Guests must be experienced riders (children 10 and older are accepted); guided trail rides over dirt roads and woods trails, all meals included.

Krawczyk Horse Farm (802-758-2655), East Street, Bridport. Trail rides, leasing, boarding, lessons, tack shop.

SWIMMING **Middlebury Gorge,** East Middlebury, off Route 125 just above the Waybury Inn (see *Lodging—Inns*), where the road suddenly steepens beyond the bridge. Paths lead down to the river.

Bartlett Falls, Bristol. Near the beginning of the Lincoln Gap Road (off Route 116 in Rocky Dale) there's a pulloff for this popular swimming hole. A bronze plaque explains that the land is a gift from Irving Wesley Sr., in memory of his son who died at 19 fighting a 1943 forest fire in British Columbia. It's a beautiful spot by a stream with shallow falls dropping into pools. Swimming shoes are a good idea.

See also Branbury, Button Bay, D.A.R., and Kingsland Bay State Parks and Silver Lake under *Green Space.*

✷ Winter Sports

CROSS-COUNTRY SKIING **Carroll and Jane Rikert Ski Touring Center** at the Bread Loaf Campus of Middlebury College (802-388-2759), Route 125, Ripton, 12 miles from the main campus, is owned and operated by Middlebury College. It has more than 42 km of groomed trails in the area of the Robert Frost Farm and the college ski bowl. Elevations range from 975 to 1,500 feet. Rentals, accessories, repairs.

Blueberry Hill Inn (802-247-6735), Goshen, has 50 km of tracked and groomed trails plus another 20 km of outlying trails on elevations of 1,400–3,100 feet. This is a surefire cross-country mecca during even marginal seasons. The ski center has retail and rental equipment, waxing, and repairs.

DOWNHILL SKIING **Middlebury College Snow Bowl** (802-388-4356), 13 miles east of Middlebury on Route 125, at Bread Loaf. A throwback to a less commercial era of skiing: well-maintained, winding trails with a library in the base lodge! Two double chairs, one triple, a total of 15 trails; 40 percent covered by snowmaking. It also offers a ski school, rentals, cafeteria. Closed December 25. $30 adults weekends; $25 adults weekday.

✷ Green Space

Note: Public preserves are clustered on the eastern and western fringes of the valley.

On or near Lake Champlain

Button Bay State Park (802-475-2377; 802-483-2314), on Panton Road just below Basin Harbor. Named for the unusual, buttonlike clay bank formations, with a splendid view across the lake to the Adirondacks; 72 campsites, picnic areas, swimming, fishing, nature museum, and trails. Rocky Point juts into Lake Champlain like the prow of a ship.

ꝏ **Kingsland Bay State Park** (802-877-3445), Ferrisburgh. Marked from Route 7. Facilities include a picnic area on Lake Champlain, also tennis courts and hiking trails. This is a particularly lovely overlook of Kingsland Bay with lawns that roll down to the lakeside shaded by old maples. Weddings and summer get-togethers are very popular here.

Dead Creek Wildlife Management Area (802-759-2397), 7 miles east of the D.A.R. State Park on Route 17, is a 2,800-acre, semiwilderness tract. Except for certain refuges, it is open to the public. The information booth is not always staffed, because the supervisor is generally in the field, but a self-guided tour folder is available.

D.A.R. State Park (802-759-2354; 802-483-2314), 8 miles west of Addison on Route 17, has a campground with 71 sites and a picnic area. Steps lead down to a smooth shale beach for swimming.

In or near the Green Mountain National Forest

Lake Dunmore, in Salisbury between Brandon and Middlebury on Route 53 off Route 7, is a tranquil, 1,000-acre lake that has licked its once infamous mosquito problem. It is lined with summer cottages at the foot of Mount Moosalamoo and along its hiking trails. On the east shore road is **Branbury State Park** (802-247-5925), with a sandy beach, boating, snack bar, picnic grove, museum nature trail, and hiking to the Falls of Lana. The trail begins just south of the Branbury Park entrance, and it's just a half mile to the picnic area and falls. From Route 53, it's 1.6 miles past these falls up to **Silver Lake,** a mountain lake that was the site of religious camp meetings in the 1880s; a large hotel (actually constructed as a seminary) occupied the site of the present picnic area and stood until around 1940, when it was destroyed by fire. About 1 mile long, it is now part of the Green Mountain

THE ROBERT FROST CABIN

Kim Grant

National Forest, accessible only by foot and mountain bike (0.6 mile via the Goshen Trail from the second parking lot on Forest Road 27, off Goshen Road). There are 31 primitive campsites and a nature trail around the lake; swimming is permitted.

"Robert Frost Country" in the Green Mountain National Forest is a title officially bestowed in 1983 on a wooded piece of the town of Ripton because it is here, in a log cabin, that the poet summered for 39 years. This section of Route 125, between the old Bread Loaf Inn (part of the Middlebury College campus) and the village, has been designated the Robert Frost Memorial Highway; there is also a Robert Frost Interpretive Trail and a Robert Frost Wayside picnic area near the road leading to the farm and cabin. The picnic area has grills and drinking water, and it's shaded by red pines that were pruned by Frost himself. Just east of the wayside, a dirt road leads to the Homer Noble Farm, which Frost bought in 1939. Park in the lot provided and walk past the farm to Frost's cabin (it's not open to the public). The Robert Frost Interpretive Trail, a bit west on the opposite side of Route 125, is an easy walk, just three-quarters of a mile. It begins with a bridge across Beaver Pond (we actually saw a beaver here one time) and winds through woods and meadow, by seven Frost poems mounted along the way. This trail is also popular with cross-country skiers and snowshoers, and with July and August blueberry pickers.

Texas Falls, in Hancock, is easily accessible from the marked road, 3 miles east of the Middlebury Gap. It's a short drive to the parking area, and the succession of falls are just across the road, visible from a series of paths and bridges. There's also a picnic area.

* Lodging

Mid VT for All Seasons Area Guide, Mid VT Map (1-800-733-8376; www.midvermont.com). This comprehensive guide to area lodging is available by calling the 800 number or visiting the web site.

INNS ♿ **Swift House Inn** (802-388-9925; fax: 802-388-9927), 25 Stewart Lane, Middlebury 05753. Formerly the family estate of the legendary philanthropist Jessica Stewart Swift, who lived to be over 100. Antiques, elaborately carved marble fireplaces, formal gardens with more than 20 rosebushes, and other gracious amenities add to the charm of this 1814 mansion. Common space in the inn itself includes a cozy pub as well as two attractive living rooms. A continental breakfast is served in the cherry-paneled main dining room, the library, or the sun porch. There are 10 guest rooms in the main house, 5 in the gatehouse, and 6 in the renovated 1886 carriage house. One room is wheelchair-accessible, as is the dining room. Rates per room with continental breakfast $100–235 for suites with fireplace, sitting area, whirlpool tub, and cable TV.

RESORT

🐾 ♿ **Basin Harbor Club** (802-475-2311; 1-800-622-4000, www.basinharbor.com), Box 7, Vergennes 05491, located on Lake Champlain 5 miles west of town, off Panton Road. Open mid-May through mid-October. This is Vermont's premier family-run resort. The 700-acre retreat offers 136 rooms, most in cottages scattered along the shore. Since 1886, when they began taking in summer boarders, the Beach family have assiduously kept up with the times. Over the years, a large swimming pool, an 18-hole golf course, and even an airstrip have been added. Still, the handsome old farmhouse has been preserved. In summer, Dutchman's-pipe climbs as it always has around the porch pillars, and three grand old maples shade the lawn, which slopes to the extensive flower gardens and the round harbor beyond. There are 18 rooms in the inn, 13 more in the attractive stone Harbor Homestead. The 77 cottages, geared to families (and well-behaved pets), vary in rate depending on size and location. All have phone, fridge, and wet bar; many have fireplace. Eight cottages are handicapped-accessible, with ramps and bathrooms, as are all public areas. The lakeside units are worth the little extra, with views of the lake and the Adirondacks so extraordinary that it's difficult to tear yourself away from the window or deck, especially at sunset.

Basin Harbor manages to please both children and elderly couples. Youngsters can take advantage of the beach, elaborate playground, and lively, supervised (complimentary) children's program available 9 AM–1 PM for ages 3–15, and younger children can also dine together and play until 9 PM. For those ages 10–15, there are golf and tennis clinics, movies, mixers, and video games in the Red Mill, the resort's informal restaurant off by the airstrip. Those who like to dress for dinner have ample opportunity; at the main restaurant, men and boys over 12 must wear jackets and ties. The food is fine (see *Dining Out*). Daily rates per couple $125–330 B&B; with a full American plan, $230–460 per couple; add 15 percent gratuity. Less for children. There are also golf, tennis, and fall foliage packages; inquire about kayaking, horticultural workshops, and birding and nature treks.

Historic Brookside Farms Country Inn & Antique Shop (802-948-2727; www.brooksideinnvt.com), P.O. Box 36, Route 22A, Orwell 05760. White Ionic columns distinguish the front of this stately Greek Revival mansion, enlarged in 1843 and now on the National Register of Historic Places. It's still a 300-acre working farm, owned and operated by Joan Korda. In the

Kim Grant

SWIFT HOUSE INN

main house, guests can browse in the 10,000-volume library, relax in the TV den, and enjoy afternoon tea and a five-course dinner. Here, too, is a two-room suite with a private bath ($175). In the restored tenant farmhouse that doubles as antiques shop are five more guest rooms, two with private bath and three shared ($95–135, including breakfast). Dinner is available by reservation. The grounds are great for nature hikes in summer and fall, cross-country skiing in winter. Cash and traveler's and personal checks accepted; no credit cards.

ꝏ ♿ **Lilac Inn** (802-247-5463; 1-800-221-0720; www.lilacinn.com), 53 Park Street, Brandon 05733. One of New England's most romantic inns, this grand old mansion has been totally restored. Built with an imposing five-arched facade in 1909 by a Brandon-born financier, the mansion, owned by Shelly and Doug Sawyer, has some splendid common spaces (a glassed-in ballroom is the scene of chamber concerts and wedding receptions) and a wide entrance hallway with a grand staircase. There is also a formal garden with a gazebo and cobbled patio, a small living room with a fireplace and floor-to-ceiling bookcases, and a bar with comfortable seating. The nine ample guest rooms all have luxurious bathrooms with deep, claw-foot tubs; each is furnished in antiques and has a hidden TV. The bridal suite has a pewter canopy bed, whirlpool bath, fireplace, and dressing area. There is one handicapped-accessible room. Weddings are a specialty. Rates include a full breakfast, served in the oak-paneled dining room, where dinner is also served Wednesday through Saturday. Rates $185–265 in October, otherwise $120–185. Inquire about MAP, winter weekends featuring music or dramatic readings, and the cottage for four.

Blueberry Hill Inn (802-247-6735; 802-247-6535; 1-800-448-0707; www.blueberryhillinn.com), Goshen 05733, on Forest Road 32 in Ripton. Over the past 27 years, Tony Clark has turned this blue 1820 farmhouse on a high, remote back road into one of New England's most famous country inns. The big lures are fine food, hiking and mountain biking, and, in winter, cross-country skiing. But there is more to it: a sure touch. The rooms—some with lofts, all with full bath—have their share of antiques. The common rooms are sunny and inviting with geraniums blooming in the greenhouse off the kitchen and a stone fireplace in the dining room. Guests are encouraged to mingle, from morning coffee to evening hors d'oeuvres and dinner. This inn has long been known for its food, and current chefs more than deserve the reputation, producing elaborate, creative dinners featuring fresh, local ingredients. The cross-country-ski center, with 75 km of groomed trails, tends to be snowy, thanks to its elevation, if there is any snow in Vermont. MAP rates per person: $125–200, depending on the season, plus 15 percent gratuity; half price for children 12 and under in same room with parent. BYOB. No smoking.

The Middlebury Inn (802-388-4961; 1-800-842-4666; www.middleburyinn.com), 14 Courthouse Square, Middlebury 05753, has been the town's imposing chief hostelry since 1827. The Emanuel family has completely renovated the 75 guest and public rooms. Rooms in the main house are on two floors (there's a 1926 Otis elevator) and are furnished in reproduction antiques. They have private bath, cable TV, air conditioner/heater, and direct-dial phone. There are also 20 motel units with inn-style furnishings, and the adjacent Porter Mansion, full of handsome architectural details, has 10 Victorian rooms. The common rooms include a vast, comfortable lobby with a formal check-in desk and portraits of the Battell family and Robert Frost. Elegant afternoon tea and light dinners are available in the pubby Morgan Tavern; dinner and buffet breakfast are served in the pillared, Wedgwood blue, formal dining room (see *Dining Out*). Lunch is served in the Rose Room and on the front porch in summer and early fall. Thoughtful touches include readable books on shelves near guest rooms and umbrellas for guests to use next to the door. Continental breakfast is included in rates that run $90–375 double, including afternoon tea (plus $38 per person MAP). Inquire about packages. Pets are welcome in the motel units for a small daily fee, and arrangements for baby-sitting can be made.

The Shoreham Inn & Country Store (802-897-5081; out-of-state: 1-800-255-5081), Route 74 west, Shoreham 05770. This friendly, comfortable place is a great antidote if you've overdosed on Laura Ashley wallpaper and mints on the lacy coverlets of antique beds. Rooms are whimsically decorated, some with daybeds for families, and plenty of singles for the many bicyclists and hikers who frequent the inn. There are 10 guest rooms, 9 with private bath. The many-windowed inn, which dates from 1790, sits in the middle of a small village, surrounded by apple country and not far from Larrabees Point, Mount Independence, Fort Ticonderoga, New York, and the college town of Middlebury. The common rooms are filled with pictures, plants, and, frequently, the aroma of coffee, soup, or other things cooking and baking in the kitchen. $65 single with full breakfast, $85–95 double. The Country Store is next door, a source of great deli sandwiches.

MIDDLEBURY INN

Sally Johnson

Churchill House Inn (802-247-3078; 802-877-248-7444; www.churchillhouseinn.com), 3128 Forest Dale Road (Route 73), Brandon 05733. Located west of the Brandon Gap on Route 73, this old farmhouse, run by Richard Daybell, has nine guest rooms furnished in 19th-century style. There are zesty dinners and breakfasts, and canoeing, hiking, bicycling, snowshoeing and cross-country-ski expeditions (see *To Do—Bicycling* and *Hiking*). MAP rates are $180–220 per room plus 15 percent gratuity; inquire about 3- and 5-day packages.

Waybury Inn (802-388-4015; 1-800-348-1810), Route 125, East Middlebury 05740. A historic, 14-room village inn, open all year. Bob Newhart never did sleep here, though guests sometimes ask for "the Loudons" because the exterior served as the "Stratford Inn" on a veteran CBS series. There's no pool, but a swimmin' hole under the nearby bridge serves the purpose. Dinner and Sunday brunch are served year-round. The rates are $80–115 double, including a continental breakfast. Two-night minimum stay on busy weekends and holidays.

Chipman House (802-388-2390; 1-800-890-2390; www.chipmaninn.com), Route 125 on the way to or from Bread Loaf and the Middlebury College Snow Bowl ski area, in the center of the tiny village of Ripton 05766 (population: 400), which consists of a schoolhouse, community meetinghouse, church, and general store. It's also within striking distance of Robert Frost's house and cabin and the Robert Frost Trail. This is an exceptionally attractive 1828 house with nine guest rooms of varying sizes (we suggest requesting one at the back of the house), all with private bath. Guests gather in the lounge/bar and around a very large old hearth or settle into the sunny sitting room near the woodstove. The dining room is lit by candles and decorated with stenciled wallpaper. Innkeepers Joyce Henderson and Bill Pierce offer a five-course dinner on request (prix fixe $25), and both dinner and breakfast guests are encouraged to sit together at long tables. There is also a table for two. Rates are $115–145 per couple ($85–105 single), with breakfast. Closed April and November.

Mary's at Baldwin Creek (802-453-2432; www.marysatbc.com), 1868 North Route 116, Bristol 05443. Open year-round. A classic Vermont farmhouse inn set on 25 acres including a perennial garden with paths down to Baldwin Creek. Mary's is best known for its restaurant (see *Dining Out*). Four guest rooms with private bath includes one two-room suite, which works well for families. Weddings and catered events for up to 200 people. Heated outdoor swimming pool. Chef/innkeeper owned. $75–185, including full breakfast and afternoon tea.

The Brandon Inn (802-247-5766), 20 Park Street, Brandon 05733. A large brick landmark overlooking the village green, this inn dates from 1892 and is on the National Register of Historic Places. Innkeepers Sarah and Louis Pattis have scaled down the number of guest rooms from 46 to 37, refurbishing them nicely. Number 217, a two-room suite, is especially attractive ($155 MAP). Other MAP rates: $65–80 per person for a double; September 18 through October 18 rates are $83.75–100 per person double, MAP, and a 2-day minimum stay is required on weekends. The B&B rate is

$45–77.50 per person. Children under 12 are free in their parent's room (except for meals), and are welcome. There are TV rooms upstairs as well as large living rooms downstairs, and some of the 19th-century furniture and a good deal of the atmosphere survive. The inn's 5 landscaped acres include a swimming pool (with Jacuzzi) and a stretch of the Neshobe River, good for trout fishing. An 18-hole golf course is just up the way. Buses from New York, Boston, and Montreal still stop, as stages once did, at the front door.

BED & BREAKFASTS

In and around Middlebury 05753

♿ **The Inn on the Green** (802-388-7512; 1-888-244-7512), 71 South Pleasant Street. A recent addition to the downtown hospitality scene, this very attractive 1803 Federal town house has two impressive, colorfully decorated suites in the main house, plus eight other spacious rooms, each with private bath, phone, cable TV. There's also a more contemporary carriage house, same amenities. Rates $98–210.

Linens & Lace (802-388-0832; 1-800-808-3897), 29 Seminary Street. This crisply decorated, yellow and white village house has four guest rooms, two with private bath; also spacious sitting and dining rooms, and an inviting kitchen. Rates $99–129.

Fairhill (802-388-3044), 724 East Munger Street, 4 miles east of Middlebury, on 75 acres of woodland, marsh, and meadows. Russell and Fleur Laslocky's 1825 center-chimney Cape has three guest rooms, one with a four-poster double and private bath. The breakfast area is in an 18th-century granary. Rates $75–95.

In and around East Middlebury 05740

Elizabeth's October Pumpkin B&B (802-388-9525; 1-800-237-2007), P.O. Box 226, East Middlebury. A charming 1850 Greek Revival (you can't miss the color) with stenciling; four rooms, $70–90.

By the Way B&B (802-388-6291), P.O. Box 264, East Middlebury. Nancy Simoes provides two spacious guest rooms with private bath, air-conditioning, $65–85; the wraparound veranda is appealing, and an in-ground swimming pool is set in the orchard.

In and around Vergennes 05491

The Strong House Inn (802-877-3337), Route 22A, Vergennes. This is a real beauty, built in the 1830s by Samuel Paddock Strong, a local worthy, in the graceful Federal style, with fine workmanship such as curly maple railings on the freestanding main staircase. Mary and Hugh Bargiel offer six bedrooms, all exceptional, as well as Samuel's Suite—a library with queen-sized sofa bed and fireplace and an adjoining bedroom with queen-sized poster bed, plus an enclosed sun porch with Adirondack views ($185). The Empire Room has mahogany furnishings (queen-sized bed), a working fireplace, and a private half bath ($120); and the sunny English Garden Room with its brass bed (shared bath) is a find at $75. We also wouldn't mind settling for the English Hunt Room, with its sleigh bed ($85). The Victorian Suite has a double four-poster plus a sitting room with a double tapestry sofa bed, cable TV, and air-conditioning ($125). Rates include afternoon tea and a full breakfast and increase by $15 per room in foliage season. Inquire about quilting weekends.

Emersons' Guest House (802-877-3293), 82 Main Street, Vergennes. Six bright and airy guest rooms in this Victorian town house are named for New England writers and poets. $55–90 with full breakfast.

♿ **Whitford House** (802-758-2704; 1-800-746-2704; www.whitfordhouseinn.com), 912 Grandey Road, Addison. On Grandey Road between Nortontown and Townline Roads off Route 22A (ask directions!). Sited 2 miles east of the lake in the middle of rich farmland, it's set among flower gardens on 2 acres of mowed lawns with spectacular views of the Adirondacks from the outdoor deck. Tranquillity and warm hospitality are the hallmarks of Bruce and Barbara Carson's 18th-century farmhouse, with two upstairs bedrooms (king or twin beds) and private baths. A spacious first-floor bedroom has a four-poster double bed and private bath. The Great Room, with its fireplace made from local Panton stone, is a perfect place for relaxing. There is also a cottage with a large bedroom (king-sized bed), sitting room with sofa bed, and full bath. Rates: $110–135 double; $125–150 king or twins; $200–225 cottage (plus $25 for each additional guest). Price includes afternoon tea, full breakfast, and loan of the Carsons' canoe and bicycles. Breakfasts are events in themselves, and visting chefs prepare memorable five-course, prix fixe dinners when reservations are made in advance.

South and west of Middlebury

Quiet Valley Bed & Breakfast (802-897-7887), RD 1, Box 175, Shoreham 05770. A new house built along traditional lines with wide-pine floors to maximize the light and views across the Lemon Fair River to the hills. Bruce Lustgarten burns only applewood in the large, shallow, Rumford-style fireplace in the living room, and Jane enjoys preparing "healthy" breakfasts for guests, who never number more than seven. Four guest rooms, one with a wood-burning stove, two with handmade four-posters and a private bath, the other two with twin beds and shared bath. $85–105 double.

🐾 **Buckswood Bed & Breakfast** (802-948-2054), 633 Route 73E, Orwell 05760. Open year-round. Linda and Bob Martin offer two guest rooms (private baths) and ample common space in their 1814 home, located in a pleasant country setting just east of Orwell Village. Dinner by reservation. Rates of $60–70 per couple include breakfast. Polite pets accepted.

In and around Brandon 05733

The Old Mill Inn (802-247-8002; 1-800-599-0341), Route 73, Stone Mill Dam Road, East Brandon. Owned by Ed and Cindy Thomas, this is an attractive farmhouse set above the Neshobe River, adjoining the Neshobe Golf Club (18 holes; see *To Do—Golf*). Guests enter through a sunny breakfast room and find two large living rooms with wing chairs, a piano, TV, and Cindy's artwork. There's a sense of space here, both inside and out—a porch with wicker chairs is new. The four guest rooms have private bath, stenciling, and carefully chosen antiques. Daisy the golden retriever, two barn cats, miniature horses, chickens, and a rooster are also in residence, and guests can take advantage of the swimming hole in the neighboring rushing stream. $75–95 per couple includes a full country breakfast.

Rosebelle's Victorian Inn (802-247-0098; www.rosebelles.com), 31 Franklin Street, Route 7, Brandon. This nicely restored, mansard-roofed house has a high-ceilinged living room with fireplace and TV and a large dining room—the setting for afternoon tea and full breakfasts that feature gourmet coffees and fresh-baked breads and muffins. Guests with small musical instruments are especially welcome. Hostess Ginette Milot speaks French. The five guest rooms all have private bath. $65–110 double, with a 2-night minimum stay required on holiday weekends and during foliage season.

The Gazebo (802-247-3235; 1-888-858-3235), 25 Grove Street (Route 7), Brandon. This is another attractive in-town, circa-1865 classic house, with a wood-burning stove in the sitting room. It's decorated with folk art and antiques and has four comfortable guest rooms, private baths. Antiques shop on premises; families welcome. Rates include a full breakfast at $65–95 per couple.

🐾 **Hivue Bed & Breakfast Tree Farm** (802-247-3042; 1-800-880-3042), 730 High Pond Road, Brandon. A contemporary lodging that offers on-site trout fishing and walking trails in a 76-acre wildlife habitat. Picture windows in the living room and the deck overlook Pico Peak and the Killington Mountains. One of two guest quarters has a king-sized bed and sleep sofa with a Jacuzzi in the private bath; the other, a king bed and studio couch with bath. $60 per room with continental breakfast. Polite pets accepted.

Judith's Garden (802-247-4707), Goshen-Ripton Road, Goshen. Locally noted for its lovely perennial gardens in a mountainous setting appealing to hikers, walkers, and cross-country skiers who want to take advantage of the Moosalamoo region. Proprietors Judith Irven and Dick Conrad serve smoked salmon and dill quiche among other breakfast dishes. This restored 1830s farmhouse has three attractive bedrooms with private bath; $85–95 includes breakfast.

🐾 **Salisbury Village Bed & Breakfast** (802-352-6006), P.O. Box 214, Salisbury 05769. Not far from Lake Dunmore, this restored farmhouse has four guest rooms with shared bath ($65–75), and welcomes polite pets at $10 per night and even provides day care for them.

In Bristol 05443

🐾 **Crystal Palace Victorian B&B** (802-453-4131; 1-888-674-4131), 48 North Street. This impressive 1897 mansion with a turret provides six guest rooms, $85–130 with full breakfast. Dogs are welcome.

See also Firefly Ranch under *To Do—Horseback Riding*.

COTTAGES **Lake Dunmore.** Some cottagers hope that the lake will remain off the beaten track; however, it's being "discovered." Here are some good bets:

Dunmore Acres (802-247-3126; off-season: 207-499-7491), Brandon 05733, a former summer camp in a lovely setting, has nine two- and three-bedroom housekeeping cabins, a swimming pool, basketball, rec hall, boat dock with canoe and rowboat. $65 per night for a two-bedroom cabin, $70 for a three-bedroom (2-night minimum), and $425 and $450 per week, respectively.

North Cove Cottages (802-352-4236 summer; winter: 617-354-0124), P.O. Box 76, Salisbury 05769. Nine housekeeping cottages, sanded beach, free rowboats; $45–75 per day, $240–430 per week.

Note: The Addison County Chamber of Commerce (802-388-7951; see

Guidance) has a list of rental cottages on both Lake Dunmore and Lake Champlain.

MOTEL 🏵 **The Adams Motor Inn and Restaurant** (802-247-6644; 1-800-759-6537), Route 7 south, Brandon 05733. Open late spring to November. Located on Route 7, 1 mile south of Brandon, this isn't really a motel but rather a shady campus of 20 cozy, one- and two-room cottages of the kind so familiar in premotel motoring days. Most of the cottages have fireplace and cable TV, and there's a stocked trout pond, swimming pool, and miniature golf across the highway. Rates for two: $55–70, without meals (extra $25 a day per person with breakfast and dinner).

FARM VACATION **Cream Hill Farm** (802-897-2101), P.O. Box 205, Shoreham 05770. Rene and Paul Saenger welcome families to their 1,100-acre diversified farm, with beef cattle. This is very much a working farm (meaning it smells like a farm, and its owners may be preoccupied with farm chores). The 1830s renovated farmhouse has two large guest rooms, one with private bath. $40 double, $10 per additional person.

CAMPGROUNDS See *Green Space* for information on campgrounds in Button Bay State Park, D.A.R. State Park, and Lake Dunmore.

✳ Where to Eat

DINING OUT **The Storm Café** (802-388-1063), 3 Mill Street, Middlebury. This intimate, casual spot by the river is considered by many to serve the most imaginative food in town, if not in the state. Dinner is now available 5–9. Moderate.

Fire & Ice Restaurant (802-388-7166; 1-800-367-7166), 26 Seymour Street, Middlebury. Open 11:30–9:30 daily except Monday. "Good Food & Legal Vice," it says of itself; excellent lunch and dinner plus Sunday brunch in an informal stained-glass and mahogany setting that has recently been enlarged. A local favorite since 1974, specializing in steaks ($14.95–20.95), prime rib ($14.95–19.95), and chicken dishes like a fresh boneless breast sautéed in a champagne and mushroom cream sauce ($14.95). The name was inspired by a Robert Frost poem.

Roland's Place (802-453-6309), Route 7, New Haven. A grand old tower-topped mansion, this 1796 house is the setting for dinner and Sunday brunch year-round, lunch May through October. Lunch on seafood crêpes with Newburg sauce ($7.75). Dine on a Vermont game sampler with mushroom risotto ($17.95), vegetable seacake with marinara sauce ($11.50), or one of the other moderately priced entrées. Owner-chef Roland Gaujac has a Provençal background. (Guest rooms available at $65.)

Basin Harbor Club (802-475-2311), Basin Harbor, off Panton Road, 5 miles west of Vergennes. If you don't stay at Basin Harbor, there's all the more reason to drive out for lunch or dinner, to see the lakeside setting and savor the atmosphere. The food is fine, too. The menu and dining room are both large. At dinner (reserve) you might begin with Green Mountain smoked trout, then enjoy seared breast of ginger-soy-marinated duck. The prix fixe is $28 plus 15 percent service charge. The wine list is extensive and excellent. Jacket and tie required.

Tully and Marie's (802-388-4182), 5 Bakery Lane, Middlebury, open daily 11:30 AM–midnight; Sunday brunch. Closed Tuesday in winter. You have the sense of being wined and dined on a small, three-decker art deco ship beached on the bank of Otter Creek. Favorites include the pad Thai, the spring rolls, great soups, and excellent daily specials. The menu changes nightly, and both the wine list and the selection of beers are extensive. The à la carte menu begins at $6, inclusive dinner at $11.

Mr. Up's (802-388-6724), on the Bakery Lane plaza, Middlebury, open daily, lunch–midnight; Sunday brunch buffet 11–2. Dine outdoors on the riverside deck or in the brick-walled, stained-glass, oak-and-greenery setting inside. The menu is equally colorful, ranging from the Ultimate Salad Bar and Bread Board ($6.50) to prime rib ($14.75).

The Middlebury Inn (802-388-4961; 802-388-4666), 14 Courthouse Square, Middlebury, serves breakfast and dinner in the Wedgwood blue Founders Room. Lunch is served in the Rose Room and on the front porch in summer and early fall, and light dinner is served in the **Morgan Tavern.** A popular appetizer here is fried Cabot cheese (deep-fried Vermont cheddar served with apple maple sauce for dipping). The moderately priced menu includes fresh seafood, Angus steaks, and a rotating market special each evening. Dinner includes hot popovers.

Christophe's on the Green (802-877-3413), 5 Green Street, Vergennes. Open for dinner Tuesday through Saturday from early May through October. Reservations suggested. Housed in the old hotel in the middle of town, a first-class French restaurant. You might begin with Cornish hen baked in phyllo, then dine on braised rabbit with mushrooms and tomatoes, served with a garlic flan and *pommes gaufrettes,* and finish with espresso crème caramel served with cardamom cream. All appetizers are $6, entrées $17.50, desserts $5.50. The prix fixe for three courses is $25.

Mary's at Baldwin Creek (802-453-2432), at the junction of Routes 116 and 17, Bristol. Open year-round except Monday for dinner, and Sunday brunch (10:30–2); lunch served in summer. Highly and widely regarded, Mary's moved a few years ago from a village storefront, expanding to fill three rooms of a classic Vermont farmhouse on the banks of Baldwin Creek. Entrées run $10–22, and the menu changes seasonally. Local rabbit, venison, produce, and brews are featured. Local meat and produce from area farms is a mainstay of the menu, especially during warm-weather months.

The Dog Team Tavern (802-388-7651), a jog off Route 7, 4 miles north of Middlebury. Moderately priced, traditional New England fare (sticky buns, relish trays, et al.). Open for dinner daily except Monday; for lunch late spring through foliage season. Gift shop. Opened in the 1930s by Sir Wilfred Grenfell (1865–1940), the British medical missionary who established hospitals, orphanages, schools, and cooperative stores in Labrador and near the Arctic Circle.

The Brandon Inn (802-247-5766), 20 Park Street, Brandon. Open for dinner daily except Tuesday and Wednesday. Austrian-trained owner-chef Louis Pattis and David Bofhinger make moderately priced dinner something of an event, with appetizers like crabcakes with a mango-habanero fruit sauce and entrées like roast duck served with wild blueberry-ginger sauce.

Bobcat Café (802-453-3311), Main Street, Bristol. A beautiful eatery just opened by Chef Robert Fuller. The food is excellent and the prices moderate.

EATING OUT **Rosie's Restaurant** (802-388-7052), 1 mile south of Middlebury on Route 7, is open daily (6 AM–9 PM in winter, until 10 May through November) and serves a lot of good, inexpensive food. This family mecca expands every eight months or so to accommodate its fans. There's a friendly counter and three large, cheerful dining rooms. We lunched on a superb beef and barley soup and a turkey salad on wheat. Dinner choices run from fish-and-chips to Smitty's top sirloin, and there are always stir fries.

Noonie's Deli (802-388-0014), 2 Maple Street (in the Marble Works), Middlebury. Open Monday through Saturday 9–9, Sunday 11–9. Good soups, the best sandwiches in Addison County (a half sandwich is plenty)—on homemade bread, you design it. Eat in or take out.

Squirrel's Nest Restaurant (802-453-6309), Route 116, Bristol. Open daily for breakfast, lunch, and dinner; Sunday brunch. Good family dining. Creemees and take-out year-round.

Amigo's (802-388-3624), on the green, Middlebury, serves Mexican specials from light snacks to full dinners, weekdays from 11:30, Sunday from 4.

Patricia's Restaurant (802-247-3223), Center Street, Brandon, open daily from 11 for lunch and dinner; 1–8 Sunday, when there's a senior citizen discount on complete dinners. Traditional fare like grilled pork chops, fried haddock, and Italian dishes ranging from cheese ravioli to spaghetti with hot sausage.

Bristol Bakery & Café (802-453-3280), 16 Main Street, Bristol. Open daily from 5 AM, except Sunday when it opens at 6. An inviting storefront filled with the aroma of coffee and breads. Stop at least for a muffin and espresso and take home a loaf of sourdough bread; there are also blackboard luncheon specials.

Eat Good Food (802-877-2772), 221 Main Street, Vergennes. A welcome addition to the culinary scene in Vergennes, this is primarily a gourmet take-out, but there are also tables for eating in. A good choice for lunch, dinner, or picnics, it's open Monday through Friday 9 AM–7 PM, Saturday and Sunday 9 AM–6 PM.

Main Street Bistro (802-877-3288), 253 Main Street, Vergennes. Open summer and early fall Monday through Saturday, 5–9:30 PM, this intimate place has earned favorable reviews. Limited seating; no credit cards.

Cubbers (802-453-2400), Main Street, Bristol. A local favorite for red and white-sauce pizza. Eat in or take out.

MICROBREWERY **Otter Creek Brewing** (802-388-0727; 1-800-473-0727), 85 Exchange Street, across the railroad tracks from the Marble Works, Middlebury. Open Monday through Saturday 10–6, Sunday 11–4. Guided tours Saturday 2–4 and Sunday at 2. Ales and other beers can be sampled in the Tasting Room.

✷ Entertainment

Middlebury College Center for the Arts (802-388-3711, ext. SHOW). The theater and concert hall in this dramatic new building on the college campus (Route 30) offer a full series of concerts, recitals, plays, dance companies, and film and video programs.

✷ Selective Shopping

ART GALLERIES **Woody Jackson's Holy Cow** (802-388-6737), Main Street, Middlebury. Woody himself, a Middlebury graduate whose Holstein products have become almost more of a symbol of Vermont than the maple tree, is usually on the premises. His black-and-white Holstein cows, immortalized on Ben & Jerry's ice cream cartons, decorate T-shirts, aprons, coffee mugs, boxer shorts, and more.

✐ **Norton's Gallery** (802-948-2552), Route 73 in Shoreham. The small red gallery overlooking Lake Champlain houses an amazing menagerie of dogs, rabbits, birds, and fish, along with flowers and vegetables—all sculpted from wood in unexpected sizes, unquestionably works of art and a visual delight for children and adults alike.

ANTIQUES SHOP **Middlebury Antique Center** (802-388-6229; in Vermont: 1-800-339-6229), Route 7 at the junction of Route 116 in East Middlebury. A fascinating variety of furniture and furnishings representing 50 dealers.

BOOKSTORES **Vermont Book Shop** (802-388-2061), 38 Main Street, Middlebury, was opened in 1947 by Robert Dike Blair, who retired several years ago as one of New England's best-known booksellers and the publisher of Vermont Books, an imprint for the poems of Walter Hard. John and Laura Scott are now the proprietors. Robert Frost was a frequent customer for more than two decades, and the store now specializes in autographed Frost poetry collections as well as current and out-of-print books about Vermont.

Deerleap Books (802-453-4062), Main Street, Bristol. Open daily except Monday. A small, friendly, and carefully stocked bookstore that entices you to browse and to buy. Author readings are held.

Otter Creek Old and Rare Books (802-388-3241), Main Street, Middlebury, is a book browser's delight: 25,000 very general titles.

✐ **Monroe Street Books** (802-388-1622), 7 Monroe Street, Middlebury. Open 10–6 Memorial Day through October, but it's a good idea to call. Dick and Flanzy Chodkowski have some 20,000 titles; specialties include children's books and cartoon, comic, and graphic art.

Bulwagga Books and Gallery (802-623-6800), corner of Route 30 and Shoreham Road at the Whiting post office. More than 10,000 titles plus an art gallery, handcrafted furniture, and a reading room with mountain views and coffee.

CRAFTS SHOPS **The Vermont State Craft Center at Frog Hollow** (802-388-3177), Middlebury. Open Monday through Saturday 9:30–5, Sunday afternoon, spring through fall. This nonprofit shop combines the natural beauty of Otter Creek falls, just outside its windows, with a dazzling array of the best art and crafts work in Vermont. More than 200 Vermont artisans are represented, and you can come away with anything from a 50¢ postcard to a magnificent, handcrafted $14,000 harpsichord. A feast for the eyes, it's also a serious shopping source with an outstanding selection of pottery, woven clothing, wall hangings, jewelry, and woodwork, among other things.

Sweet Cecily (802-388-3353), Main Street, Middlebury. Nancy Dunn, former Frog Hollow gallery director, has assembled her own selection of ceramics, folk art, hooked rugs, and other items from 100 craftspeople, including Mexican and Amish artisans.

Danforth Pewterers (802-388-0098), 52 Seymour Street, Middlebury, is best known for its distinctive pewter buttons, found in stores throughout New England. Fred and Judi Danforth actually continue a family tradition begun by Revolutionary War hero Thomas Danforth II. They also make pewter jewelry, oil lamps, and tableware.

Robert Compton Potter (802-453-3778), Route 116, Bristol. Open May through October 10–6. Visitors are welcome to watch Robert Compton fashioning his stoneware pottery (plates, vases, lamps, aquasculpture) and Christine Homer at work at her loom, weaving place mats and napkins to complement her husband's dinnerware.

SPECIAL SHOPS **Wood Ware** (802-388-6297), Route 7 south of Middlebury, is the home of good values in furniture, beds, lamps, solid butternut door harps, and dozens of other items. Interesting gift items as well. Open daily except Sunday in the winter.

Kennedy Brothers Marketplace (802-877-2975), Vergennes, just off Route 7, no longer produces its own oak and pine woodenware, but a Factory Marketplace serves as cooperative space for many woodworkers and craftspeople.

FROG HOLLOW SHOPS IN MIDDLEBURY

Kim Grant

✷ Special Events

Late February: **Middlebury College Winter Carnival** (802-388-4356). Ice show, concerts, snow sculpture.

Mid-March: **The Pig Race** winds up with a fine pork barbecue. Information from Blueberry Hill, Goshen (see *Cross-Country Skiing*).

Memorial Day weekend: Middlebury's **Memorial Day parade** is a popular annual event featuring lots of school marching bands, Scouts, Little Leaguers, politicians, floats, and fire trucks. It starts at 9 AM (not sharp), but you can catch the same parade two hours later in **Vergennes** if you prefer to sleep in.

July 4: Bristol hosts one of the most colorful **Independence Day parades** around. Brandon's parade is the day before.

Early July: A 6-day **Festival on the Green,** Middlebury, featuring individual performers and groups such as the Bread & Puppet Theater as well as a potpourri of music from folk to jazz to exotic international talent. No charge for admission.

Early August: **Addison County Field Days** (802-545-2257), New Haven. Livestock and produce fair, horse pull, tractor pull, lumberjacks, demolition derby, and other events. There's also a **Taste of Vermont** dinner one night that requires reservations, but the food is worth the small effort.

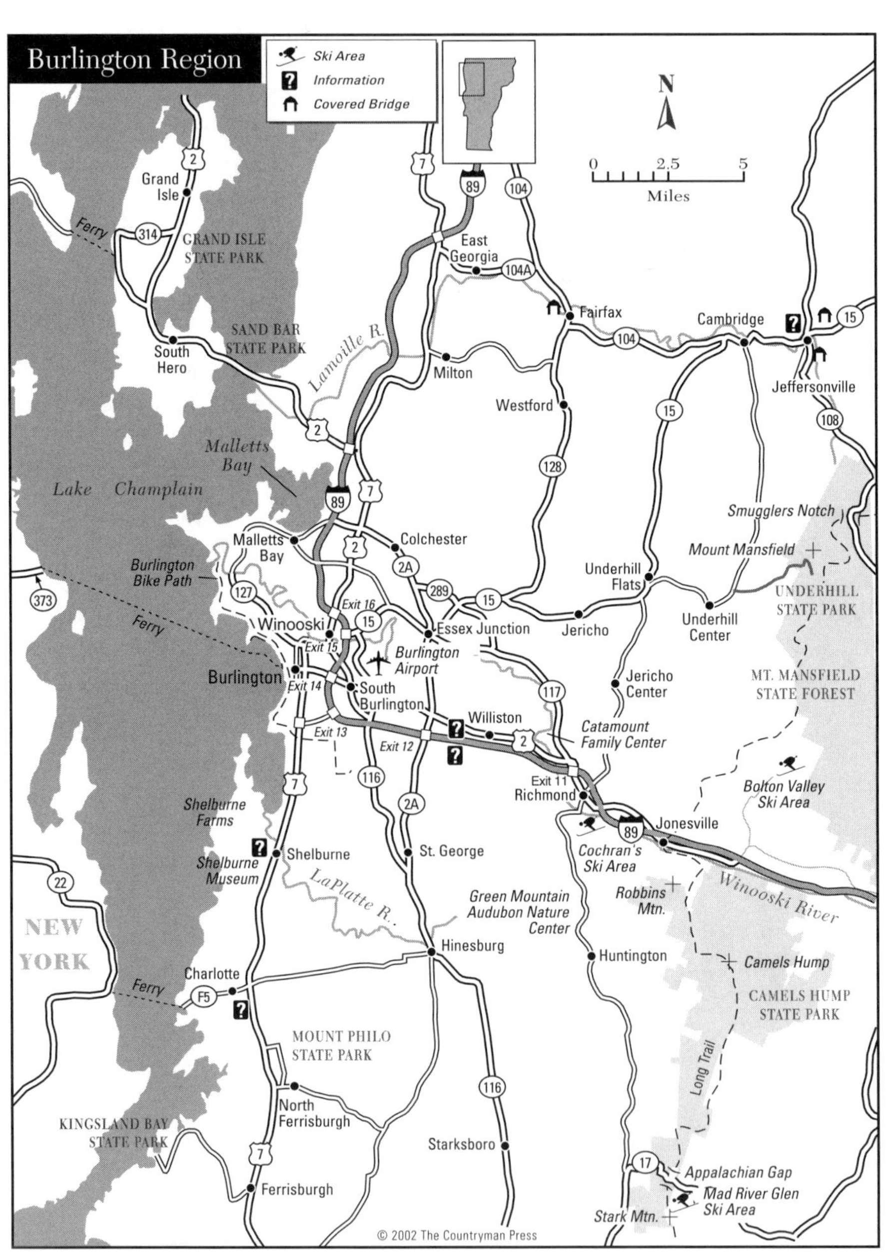
Burlington Region
Ski Area
Information
Covered Bridge
N
0
2.5
5
Miles
Grand Isle
Ferry
GRAND ISLE STATE PARK
SAND BAR STATE PARK
South Hero
Lamoille R.
East Georgia
Fairfax
Cambridge
Jeffersonville
Milton
Westford
Malletts Bay
Lake Champlain
Smugglers Notch
Mount Mansfield
Malletts Bay
Colchester
Burlington Bike Path
Underhill Flats
UNDERHILL STATE PARK
Underhill Center
Exit 16
Winooski
Essex Junction
Jericho
Exit 15
Burlington Airport
Burlington
Exit 14
South Burlington
Jericho Center
MT. MANSFIELD STATE FOREST
Williston
Exit 13
Exit 12
Catamount Family Center
Exit 11
Richmond
Bolton Valley Ski Area
Jonesville
Shelburne Farms
Cochran's Ski Area
Shelburne
St. George
Shelburne Museum
LaPlatte R.
Winooski River
Green Mountain Audubon Nature Center
Robbins Mtn.
NEW YORK
Hinesburg
Huntington
Camels Hump
Charlotte
CAMELS HUMP STATE PARK
MOUNT PHILO STATE PARK
Long Trail
North Ferrisburgh
KINGSLAND BAY STATE PARK
Starksboro
Appalachian Gap
Ferrisburgh
Mad River Glen Ski Area
Stark Mtn.
© 2002 The Countryman Press

BURLINGTON REGION

Superbly sited on a slope overlooking Lake Champlain and the Adirondack Mountains, Burlington is Vermont's financial, educational, medical, and cultural center. While its fringes continue to spread over recent farmland (the core population hovers around 40,000, but the metro count is now more than 150,000), its heart beats ever faster. Few American cities this size offer as lively a downtown, as many interesting shops and affordable, varied restaurants, or as easy an access to boats, bike paths, and ski trails.

"Downtown Vermont" may sound like a contradiction, but that's just what Burlington is. Vermont is known for mountains, white-steepled churches, and cows, for rural beauty and right-spirited residents. Its only real city is backed by and overlooks mountains, has more steeples than high-rises, and offers plenty of green space (more about the cows later). Burlington actually pushes the possibilities of the sophisticated, urban good life—the ecological, healthy, responsible good life, that is.

The community was chartered in 1763, four years after the French were evicted from the Champlain Valley. Ethan Allen, his three brothers, and a cousin were awarded large grants of choice lots along the Onion (now Winooski) River. In 1791 Ira Allen secured the legislative charter for the University of Vermont (UVM), from which the first class, of four, was graduated in 1804. UVM now enrolls more than 9,000; it is now just the largest of the city's four colleges.

Ethan and Ira would have little trouble finding their way around the city today. Main streets run much as they did in the 1780s—from the waterfront uphill past shops to the school Ira founded and on to Winooski Falls, site of Ira's own grist- and sawmills.

Along the waterfront, Federal-style commercial buildings house shops, businesses, and restaurants. The ferry terminal and neighboring Union Station, built during the city's late-19th-century boom period as a lumbering port—when the lakeside trains connected with myriad steamers and barges—are now the summer venue for excursion trains, ferries, and cruise boats. The neo-Victorian Burlington Boathouse is everyone's window on Lake Champlain, a place to rent a row- or sailboat, to sit sipping a morning coffee or sunset apéritif, or to lunch or dine on the water. The adjacent Waterfront Park and promenade are linked by bike paths to a series of other lakeside parks (bike and in-line skate rentals abound), which include swimmable beaches.

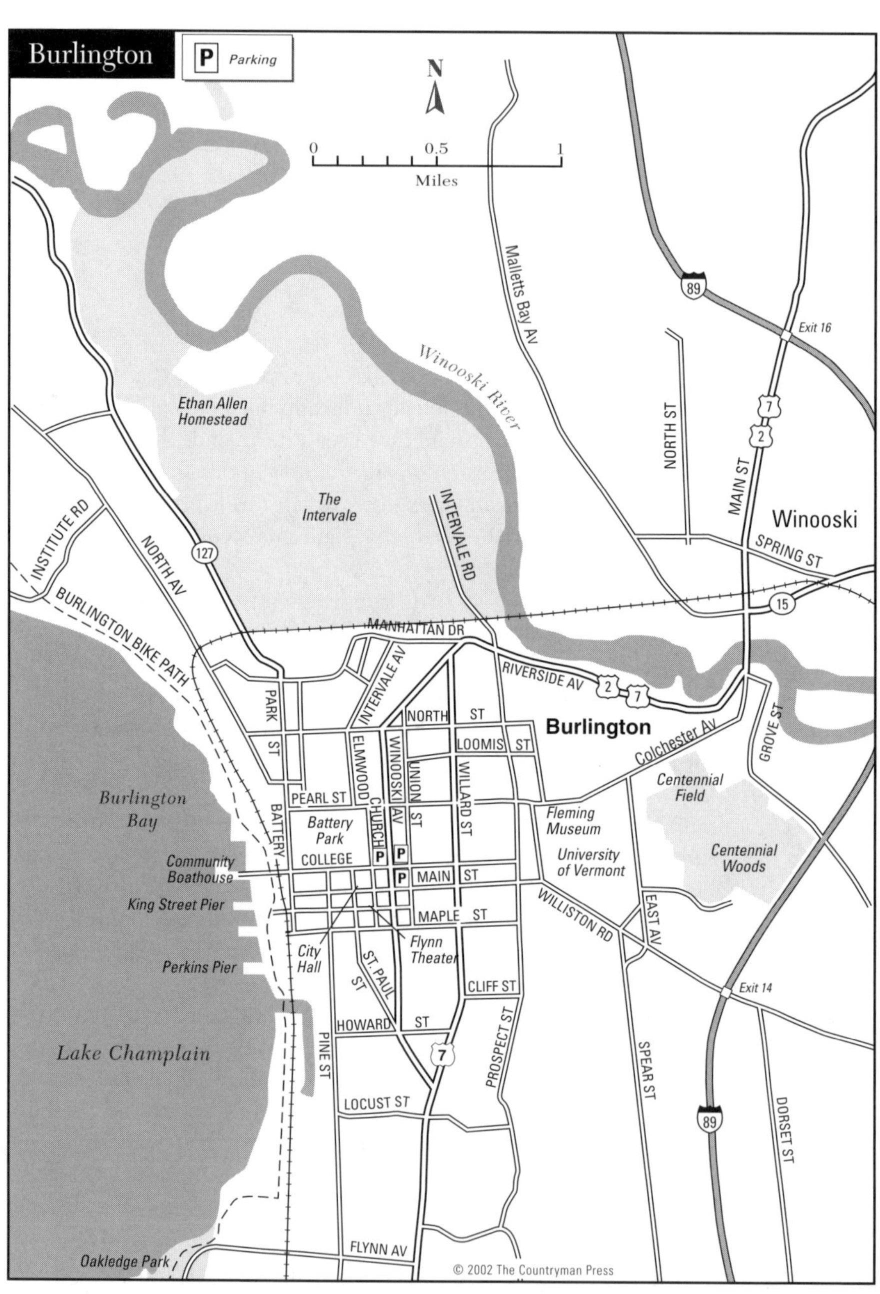
Burlington
Parking
N
0
0.5
1
Miles
Winooski River
Ethan Allen Homestead
The Intervale
Malletts Bay Av
NORTH ST
MAIN ST
Winooski
SPRING ST
Exit 16
INTERVALE RD
INSTITUTE RD
NORTH AV
BURLINGTON BIKE PATH
MANHATTAN DR
RIVERSIDE AV
INTERVALE AV
PARK
ST
NORTH ST
LOOMIS ST
Burlington
Colchester Av
GROVE ST
ELMWOOD
WINOOSKI AV
UNION ST
WILLARD ST
PEARL ST
CHURCH
Centennial Field
Centennial Woods
Burlington Bay
BATTERY
Battery Park
Fleming Museum
University of Vermont
COLLEGE
Community Boathouse
MAIN ST
King Street Pier
MAPLE ST
WILLISTON RD
EAST AV
City Hall
Flynn Theater
Perkins Pier
ST. PAUL ST
CLIFF ST
Exit 14
HOWARD ST
PROSPECT ST
SPEAR ST
Lake Champlain
PINE ST
LOCUST ST
DORSET ST
FLYNN AV
Oakledge Park

Halfway up the hill, the graceful Unitarian Church, designed in 1815 by Peter Banner, stands at the head of Church Street—now a bricked, traffic-free marketplace for four long blocks, a promenade that's become a 21st-century-style common, the place everyone comes to graze.

Theater and music are constants, but Burlington is best when winter winds soften to cool breezes. The city celebrates summer with an exuberance literally trumpeted from the rooftops in its opening salvo to summer: the Discover Jazz Festival. The weeklong celebration includes some 200 performances. Stars perform at the Flynn Center for the Performing Arts but jazz venues include buses, trolleys and ferries, street corners, parks, rooftops, and restaurants. This festival is followed by the Mozart Festival (also in varied venues) and a variety of music, both indoor and out, all summer.

Burlington in the 1950s and '60s was a different place. Docks and waterside rail yards had become privately owned wastelands, littered with rusting debris. The few public beaches were closed due to pollution, and the solution was seen as "urban renewal." In the '70s some 300 homes and 40 small businesses were demolished, and large luxury condo/retail development was planned. Then in 1981, Burlington elected as mayor Bernard Sanders, who had campaigned on the slogan, "The Waterfront Is Not for Sale."

The present waterfront includes several new parks, such as Oakledge (formerly a General Electric property), just south of downtown, and Leddy (site of a former rendering plant) in the North End, and the waterside green space is linked by an 8-mile recreational path that now extends across the Winooski River into Colchester and someday soon will extend across Lake Champlain to the Champlain islands on the bed of the old Rutland Railroad.

Downtown lodging options are mysteriously limited. Still, it is possible to walk from one high-rise hotel and several pleasant B&Bs to sights and water excursions, dining and shopping. Of course it's also appealing to bed down in the real countryside that's still within minutes of the city, so we have included B&Bs in nearby Jericho, Williston, Richmond, and Shelburne.

A couple of decades ago the Shelburne Museum, 6 miles south of the city, was the big sight-to-see in the area, although in recent years this "collection of collections" has been upstaged by Burlington itself. The museum's treasures range from a vintage Champlain Lake steamer to outstanding art and folk art, and at neighboring Shelburne Farms, New England's most fabulous estate, there are plenty of prizewinning cows (and cheese), miles of lakeside walks, and a mansion in which you should dine, sleep, or at least breakfast.

GUIDANCE **The Lake Champlain Regional Chamber of Commerce** (802-863-3489; 877-686-5253; www.vermont.org), 60 Main Street, Burlington 05401. Request brochure guides. Open Monday through Friday 8:30–5 year-round, also weekends 10–2 Memorial Day through Labor Day. Not the most obvious place for an information center (it's housed in the former motor vehicles building, halfway between Church Street and the waterfront), this one is augmented by a staffed information booth at the airport. This is also the regional marketing organization.

Newspapers: The daily ***Burlington Free Press.*** For current entertainment happenings, pick up ***Seven Days,*** a fat, free weekly published Wednesday and available in most shops and cafés.

GETTING THERE *Note:* Burlington is Vermont's single most car-free destination, accessible by bus from Boston and Montreal and by train from New York City and Montreal, blessed with good local public transport and little need to use it.

By air: **Burlington International Airport** (802-863-2874) is just 3 miles from downtown, served by American, Continental Express, United Airlines, USAirways, and Delta Connection. **JetBlue and Northwest** are the two new airlines serving Burlington, and JetBlue has led the way in discounting ticket prices, so there are good deals to be had (www.jetblue.com). A half dozen auto rental firms are at the airport.

By bus: **Vermont Transit Company** (1-800-451-3292 in New York and New England; within Vermont: 1-800-642-3133; from Canada: 1-800-552-8737), headquartered in Burlington, offers service to Albany, Boston, New York City, Montreal, Portland, and many points between. Buses depart from 345 Pine Street, south of the downtown area; plenty of parking.

By car: I-89, Routes 7 and 2.

By ferry: **The Lake Champlain Transportation Company** (802-864-9804; www.ferries.com), King Street Dock, Burlington. Descended from the world's oldest steamboat company, LCTC offers three local car-ferry services. Between mid-May and mid-October, the car ferries make the 75-minute crossing between Burlington and Port Kent, New York. April through early January they also ply between Charlotte, just south of Burlington, and Essex, New York. Year-round service is offered on the 15-minute run between Grand Isle (see "The Northwest Corner") and Plattsburgh, New York.

By train: **Amtrak** (1-800-USA-RAIL; in Canada: 1-800-4-AMTRAK). The *Vermonter* (Washington to St. Albans via New York and Springfield, Massachusetts) stops at Essex Junction, 5 miles north of Burlington. (The station is served by two cab companies and by Burlington CCTA buses; see *Getting Around.*) Faster, more scenic service from New York City is available via the *Adirondack* to Port Kent, New York, connecting with the ferry to Burlington, connecting with the free trolley up Main Street.

GETTING AROUND *By bus:* **Chittenden County Transportation Authority** (802-864-0211). CCTA bus routes radiate from the corner of Cherry and Church Streets (hub of the Church Street Marketplace), serving the Shelburne Museum, the airport, the ferry, and the Champlain Mill in Winooski as well as all the colleges and shopping areas. The fare is $1 and transfers are free. The CCTA also operates the College Street Shuttle, a free trolley on wheels circling the waterfront, Church Street, and UVM.

By trolley: A free, year-round trolley runs up and down the length of College Street, from the medical complex and UVM at the top of the hill to Union Station and the ferry dock on the lake. Stops are marked, and it is timed to meet the Champlain Valley Flyer (See *Getting There—By Train*).

MEDICAL EMERGENCY Until recently, each town has its own emergency number, but now **911** works everywhere in Vermont (hence all the new street addresses). In Burlington, the 24-hour emergency room is at **Fletcher Allen Health Care** (802-847-2434) on the UVM campus, Colchester Avenue.

* Nearby Villages

Jericho. Northeast of Burlington, Jericho is best known for the **Old Red Mill** (Jericho Historical Society: 802-899-3225), on Route 15 at Jericho Corners (open Monday through Saturday 10–5, Sunday 1–5, except January through March when it's open only Wednesday, Saturday, and Sunday). This tower-topped, 1800s red mill set above a gorge is one of the most photographed buildings in Vermont and appropriately houses prints and mementos relating to one of the state's most famous photographers, Wilson A. "Snowflake" Bentley. A Jericho farmer who was the first person in the world to photograph individual snowflakes, Bentley collected more than 5,000 microphotos. A basement museum also tells the story of the many mills that once lined six sets of falls. Sales from the crafts store benefit the preservation of the building, which is owned by the Jericho Historical Society. A 20-acre park behind the mill, along the river, offers picnic tables and hiking trails. Ask directions to nearby Jericho Center, with its oval village common and **Desso's General Store** (802-899-3313), which occupies a gray, wooden building that's architecturally difficult to describe. It's just a genuine, old-fashioned general store. Lil and Gerry Desso carry the usual fresh, frozen, and canned produce, plus socks, mittens, gloves, boots, and so on. The syrup and beans (which, we can attest, bake up nicely) are local.

Richmond. East of Burlington on Route 2 (I-89, exit 11) and the Winooski River, Richmond was badly damaged in the flood of 1927 but still has a brief, architecturally interesting downtown. Turn down Bridge Street and drive by the old Blue Seal grain store (now a restaurant; see *Dining Out*) and the library (a former church) to the **Old Round Church.** This 16-sided building, one of the most unusual in the state, was constructed in 1812–13 as a community meetinghouse to serve five denominations (open daily July 4 through Labor Day 10–4, also weekends in spring and fall).

Shelburne. Beyond the commercial strip that's Shelburne Road (Route 7 south from Burlington) lie two of Vermont's greatest treasures, both the legacy of 19th-century railroad heirs William Seward and Lila Vanderbilt Webb. In the 1880s the couple hired Frederick Law Olmsted to landscape their 4,000-acre lakeside model farm, and in 1946 their daughter-in-law founded a major museum of Americana. Today 1,400 acres of the estate—Shelburne Farms—survive as a combination inn and demonstration farm, complementing the exhibits in no fewer than 37 buildings in the nearby Shelburne Museum. Inevitably shops and attractions continue to multiply along Route 7; the latest, the Vermont Teddy Bear Company Factory and Museum, threatens to draw more visitors than either Shelburne Farms or the Shelburne Museum. (See *To See* for details about all three.)

Winooski is just across the 32-foot Winooski Falls from Burlington. Ira Allen was the first to harness the water that subsequently powered several mammoth, brick, 19th-century mills, attracting the workers from Ireland, Canada, and

Shelburne Museum

AFTER THE WEDDING (1942) BY GRANDMA MOSES

Eastern Europe who settled in the cottages that line its streets. The falls, with its art deco bridge, and the common, framed by the vintage-1867 Winooski Block and the handsome **Champlain Mill** (now a shopping/dining complex), still form the center of town. **St. Michael's College** with its Playhouse (presenting a variety of stage performances) and art gallery (802-654-2535) is just up Allen Street (Route 15).

✷ To See

MUSEUMS AND ATTRACTIONS ✐ ♿ **Shelburne Museum** (802-985-3344; www.shelburnemuseum.org), Route 7, Shelburne (6 miles south of Burlington), is open daily 10–5 late May through late October, with daily tours of selected buildings 1–4 PM through early December. $17.50 adults, $7 youths (6–14). Family cap: $45. Tickets are good for two consecutive days. This fascinating "collection of collections" features American folk art but also includes paintings by Rembrandt, Degas, Monet, and Manet. More than three dozen buildings, many of them historic transplants from around New England, each house a different collection. They are set in 45 landscaped acres that include flower and herb gardens, an apple orchard, and more than 90 varieties of lilacs (the annual Lilac Festival is usually Memorial Day weekend; see *Special Events*).

An adequate description of the collections (more than 80,000 objects) would fill a separate chapter. Highlights include a 1915 steam locomotive and a vintage-1890 private Palace Car; the sidewheeler *Ticonderoga,* in her basin near the Colchester Reef Lighthouse; the amazing folk art in the Stagecoach Inn (weather vanes, cigar-store figures, trade signs, and figureheads); the American paintings (Fitz Hugh Lane, Winslow Homer, and many other lesser-known but superb 19th-century New England painters); the Webb Memorial Building, with its elegant rooms (originally in a New York penthouse) hung with impressionist paintings (including a portrait of the museum's founder, Electra Havemeyer Webb, by Mary Cassatt); and the heirloom quilts (the collection includes some 900 American quilts). There are also the Horseshoe Barn's marvelous carriages; the Castleton Slate Jail; Shaker Shed; Dorset House and its decoys, Audubon game-bird prints, and fowling pieces; a general store; an up-and-down sawmill; an old-fashioned carousel; and much more. The ticket is good for 2 days because you may well want to allow time to absorb it all.

Acquisitions continue but this is still substantially the collection of one woman, gathered at a time when few people were interested in Americana. Electra Havemeyer was 18 in 1910 when she bought her first cigar-store figure. Three years later she married James Watson Webb, of Shelburne (son of the wealthy couple who had built Shelburne Farms; see below). Over the next 30 years she raised five children, traveled widely, and managed homes on Long Island and in Manhattan and a 50,000-acre "camp" in the Adirondacks, as well as the Shelburne estate. Gradually she filled all her holdings (even her indoor tennis court) with her collections, founding the museum in 1947 when her husband retired to Shelburne. Both died in 1960 but their vision for the museum was fulfilled by their son, the late J. Watson Webb Jr.

The **Owl Cottage Family Activity Center** gives kids some hands-on time; a number of displays, such as a model circus parade, are also geared to children. There's a museum shop and cafeteria, picnic areas, and electric trams for the disabled or just footsore. The visitors center is a rare round barn. Inquire about gallery talks, classes in traditional crafts, and frequent special events.

✐ **Shelburne Farms** (802-985-8686; www.shelburnefarms.org), marked from Route 7, Shelburne. The Farm Store and Visitors Center (802-985-8442), with an exceptional introductory film, are open daily year-round, 9–5 (10–5 in the off-season). Mid-May through mid-October, a day pass to the walking trails and children's farmyard and cheese making operation on the 1,400-acre lakeside property costs $10 adults, $9 seniors, $9 children 3–14; full 1½-hour wagon tours are offered five times daily mid-May through mid-October. November through April, no charge for the walking trails. Inquire about inn and garden tours, Breeding Barn tours, and special events.

Much of this grand 1880s lakeside estate is now a nonprofit experimental farm and educational and cultural center. Comprised of 3,800 acres at its zenith, this "duchy" was landscaped by Frederick Law Olmsted (who also designed Central Park) and pioneer forester Gifford Pinchot. It was designed for William Seward Webb and Lila Vanderbilt Webb (it was their daughter-in-law Electra Havemeyer Webb who founded Shelburne Museum). It included, and still does, a model farm with magnificent Norman-style barn buildings and a 110-room brick summer "cottage" on a bluff overlooking Lake

THE CAROUSEL AT THE SHELBURNE MUSEUM

Kim Grant

Kim Grant

THE NORMAN-STYLE BARN AT SHELBURNE FARMS

Champlain.

The mansion is now the Inn at Shelburne Farms (open late May through mid-October; see *Lodging* and *Dining Out*). The immense, five-story, 416-foot Farm Barn (housing pigs, chickens, and other farm animals) is now a place for children to collect eggs, learn to milk a cow, or enjoy a hayride. It also houses the cheese making facility; the Coach Barn, once occupied by locally bred Hackneys, now houses changing art exhibits and frequent workshops. The most recent addition to the holdings is the massive Breeding Barn, where the Hackneys were bred. The farm's prizewinning cheddar cheese, made from its own herd of Brown Swiss cows, is sold, along with other Vermont products, in the Farm Store. A walking trail winds from the visitors center about 1 mile to the top of Lone Tree Hill for sweeping views of Lake Champlain and the Adirondacks. Inquire about naturalist-led bird walks and special events.

Tip: The Inn at Shelburne Farms is open to the public by reservation for breakfast as well as dinner. (No admission fee.) Enjoy the most elegant breakfast in the area, and then stroll the lakeside perennial, herb, and rose gardens.

Burlington waterfront. As noted in the chapter introduction, Burlington's waterfront revival is relatively recent and dramatic. The handsome (vintage-1915) **Union Station** at the base of Main Street is now public space (changing art exhibits) and the King Street Dock remains home to the Lake Champlain Transportation Company (LCTC), established in 1826 (see *Getting There* and *Boating*). At the base of College Street at the College Street Pier, the (1991) Community Boathouse (see *Boating* and *Eating Out*) echoes the design of the Lake Champlain Yacht Club built on this site in 1889; it's flanked by a waterfront park and by the **Lake Champlain Basin Science Center** (802-864-1848, open mid-June through Labor Day 11–5, otherwise weekends and school vacations 12:30–4:30), an "ecomuseum" devoted to the ecology, history, and culture of the Champlain Basin. The Burlington Bike Path (see *Bicycling*) links these sites with the nearby Waterfront Park to the north (it includes a promenade and picnic shelter) and with Perkins Pier (parking, boat launch, and picnic area) just to the south and to several more beaches and parks in both directions. Not surprisingly, shops and restaurants have proliferated along neighboring Battery Street; Battery Park is the setting for free summer concerts Thursday and Sunday and for frequent special events.

Church Street Marketplace. The city's shopping and dining hub, the Church Street Marketplace extends four traffic-free blocks, from the graceful Unitarian Church, designed in 1815 by Peter Banner, to City Hall at the corner of Main Street. A fanciful fountain plays at its head, and the bricked promenade is spotted with benches and boulders from different parts of the state. The marketplace buildings themselves, a mix of 19th-century and art deco styles, house more than 100 shops and an ever-increasing number of restaurants. Walk through one storefront and you are in the Burlington Town Center, a multilevel (stepped into the hillside), multishop complex resembling many in Montreal but few in New England. Unlike Boston's Quincy Market, Church Street is a public thoroughfare, geared as much to residents as to tourists.

Robert Hull Fleming Museum (802-656-0750), Colchester Avenue, on the University of Vermont campus. Open September through April, weekdays 9–4; Saturday and Sunday 1–5; closed Monday May through August and holiday weekends year-round. Limited parking. $3 per adult; over 54 and under 18, $2. Varied collections of art, natural history, archaeology, and geology. Holdings include ancient primitive art from several cultures and continents, a collection of American portraits and landscapes (from the 18th century to contemporary works), and frequent special exhibits, plus a gift shop. The building was designed by the renowned firm of McKim, Mead and White, which also designed UVM's Ira Allen Chapel (1927) and Burlington's City Hall.

Fire House Center for the Arts (802-865-7165), 135 Church Street, Burlington, next to City Hall. Open Wednesday through Sunday noon–6, but noon–8 on Friday. A nonprofit community space, newly renovated and expanded, showcasing work by top Vermont artists. Inquire about First Friday Art Trolley Tours, a free tour of local art galleries the first Friday of every month, April through November (5–7 PM).

The Ethan Allen Homestead (802-865-4556), off Route 127 just north of the downtown Burlington waterfront (take the North Avenue Beaches exit off Route 127, the Northern Connector). Open for tours mid-May to mid-October: in spring, daily 1–5; summer, Monday through Saturday 10–5, Sunday 1–5; mid-October to mid-May, open noon–4 on the weekends. Vermont's godfather is memorialized here in the timber farmhouse in which he lived out the last years of his turbulent life; he died in 1789. The visitors center offers interesting descriptive and multimedia exhibits, and the setting is a working garden and an extensive park with some 4 miles of walking trails along the Winooski River (see also *Green Space*). $5 per adult, $4 seniors, $2.50 ages 5–17; under 5 is free; family rate $14.

ETHAN ALLEN HOMESTEAD Kim Grant

FOR FAMILIES **Vermont Teddy Bear Company Factory and Museum** (802-985-3001; 1-800-829-BEAR), 6655 Shelburne Road, Route 7 at the south end of Shelburne Village. Open daily 9–6, Sunday 10–5. A phenomenon in its own right, the huge, fanciful new birthplace of well over 100,000 teddy bears a year now includes a museum depicting teddy bear history; visitors are also invited to make their own teddy bear ($19–24) and to take the highly entertaining tour ($2 adults, free for children under 12.). There is, of course, a huge teddy bear store (see *Selective Shopping—More Special Stores*).

University of Vermont Dairy Farm (802-862-2151), 500 Spear Street, Burlington. Open daily 9–4; milking 2:30–4. The university's working farm, with its large herd of Holsteins and Jersey cows, along with some horses, is student run, visitor friendly, and the site of frequent horse shows and dog shows.

Justin Morgan Memorial Museum (802-985-8665), Route 7 at Bostwick Road, Shelburne. Open Monday through Friday 8–5, Saturday 10–2. A small museum depicts the Morgan horse story in illustrations and video. Token admission.

✷ To Do

BICYCLING The **Burlington Bike Path** runs for 8 miles along the waterfront, connecting eight different parks, beginning with Oakledge Park in the south (see *Green Space*). A ferry will shuttle you across the Winooski River to the continuation of the path in Colchester and on up to the Champlain Islands. Fun side trips include Ethan Allen Park, the Ethan Allen Homestead, Intervale Community Farms, and the Salmon Hole Fishing Area off Riverside Avenue (see *Fishing*). **Rental bikes** (including tandems, trailers, and trail-a-bikes) and in-line skate rentals are available from the **SkiRack** (802-658-3313), 85 Main Street. This path is used for walking, running, and in-line skating as well as biking. Note that CCTA buses and trolleys have bicycle racks. For serious bicyclists, we recommend the *Burlington Vermont Hiking and Biking Map*, published by Map Adventures (802-253-7489) in Stowe, which

FOR BIRDERS

The Birds of Vermont Museum (802-434-2167), adjacent to the Green Mountain Audubon Center (see *Green Space*) on Sherman Hollow Road, Richmond. Open May through October daily, except Tuesday, 10–4; by appointment in winter. Carvings of more than 200 species of birds by Robert Spear Jr.; also nature trails, recorded birdsongs. $3.50 adults, $1.50 children.

details several Burlington area loops and longer tours on both sides of Lake Champlain, using ferries. Mountain bikers should check out the **Catamount Family Center** (802-879-6001), Governor Chittenden Road, Williston: a 40 km trail system, also rentals and food in the 1796 house built by Vermont's first governor. There is also the **Essex Transportation Trail,** a 3-mile rail-trail from the Essex Police Station to Route 15 (Lang Farm); the **Shelburne Recreation Trail,** from Bay Road through Shelburne Bay Park to Harbor Road; the unpaved **Intervale Bikepath,** from Gardener's Supply on Intervale Avenue to the Ethan Allen Homestead; and **Causeway Park** in Colchester (a packed gravel trail that follows an old railroad bed out into Lake Champlain). **Bolton Valley** (see *Winter Sports*) also offers mountain biking on its cross-country and alpine trails.

BOATING *Note:* The regular LCTC 75-minute ferry crossing from Burlington to Port Kent, New York, is a great ride and a bargain.

Burlington Community Boathouse (802-865-3377), foot of College Street, Burlington. Rowboats, Rhodes and Laser sailboat rentals, captained day sails, sailing lessons, fishing charters, June through October. **Winds of Ireland** (802-863-5090), based here, offers day and sunset sails, bareboat charters, and instruction.

Spirit of Ethan Allen II (802-862-8300). Seasonal, daily scenic cruises aboard a triple-deck, 500-passenger excursion boat, departing from the Burlington Community Boathouse (see above) mid-May through mid-October. Narrated sightseeing, plus sunset cruises, dinner, murder mystery, and variety show cruises. Sight-seeing cruise fare: $7.95 adult, $3.95 ages 3–11.

Lake Champlain Cruise & Charter (802-864-9804), King Street Dock, Burlington. Two regular ferries offer sunset, dinner, brunch, music, and other specialty cruises.

Also note: Day sails and local marinas are listed with the Lake Champlain Chamber of Commerce (see *Guidance*).

A SUNSET CRUISE ON THE *SPIRIT OF ETHAN ALLEN II*

Kim Grant

Kim Grant

THE LAKE CHAMPLAIN COMMUNITY BOATHOUSE

DIVING Lake Champlain Historic Underwater Preserves (802-457-2022). The Vermont Division for Historic Preservation maintains five shipwrecks, identified by Coast Guard–approved buoys, at various points on Lake Champlain; all are open to scuba divers. The *Horse Ferry,* the *Coal Barge,* and the *General Butler* are off Burlington. The *Phoenix* and the *Diamond Island Stone Boat* are in Colchester and Vergennes, respectively. **Waterfront Diving** (802-865-2771), 214 Battery Street, Burlington, provides equipment rentals, instruction in snorkeling, underwater archaeology, video, and scuba, and charters to historic preserved shipwrecks. See also *Boating.*

FISHING Champ Charters (802-864-3792), Burlington, offers charter boats. Check out **Schirmer's Fly Shop** (802-863-6105), 34 Mills Avenue, South Burlington, specializing in Ed Schirmer's own flies, instruction, tackle, and accessories. The **Salmon Hole fishing area** off Riverside Avenue, just beyond Tortilla Flats Mexican Restaurant, is a popular local spot.

GOLF Vermont National Country Club (802-864-7770), Dorset Street, South Burlington, 18 holes; **Marble Island Resort** (802-864-6800), Marble Island Road, Malletts Bay, Colchester, 9 holes; **Rocky Ridge Golf Club** (802-482-2191), St. George (5 miles south on Route 2A from exit 12 off I-89), 18 holes; **Kwiniaska** (802-985-3672), Spear Street, Shelburne, 18 holes; **Williston Golf Course** (802-878-3747), Williston, 18 holes; **Essex Country Club** (802-879-3232), Old Stage Road, Essex Junction, 18 holes;. **Cedar Knoll Country Club** (802-482-3186), Hinesburg, 27 holes.

HIKING See Camels Hump State Park under *Green Space.*

HORSEBACK RIDING **Georgia Stables** (802-524-3395; 802-893-7268), Beebe Hill Road, Georgia. Trail riding for all abilities.

KAYAKING **True North Kayak Tours** (802-860-1910). Jane and David Yagoda are an experienced Burlington-based mother-and-son team who offer instruction and guided tours from a variety of locations on Lake Champlain. Inquire about multiday paddles through the Champlain islands with B&B lodging.

PaddleWays (802-660-8606). Burlington-based Michele Rose offers 3-hour tours, instructional classes, full-day and multiday tours on Lake Champlain.

Umiak Outfitters (802-253-2317), based in Stowe, also offers guided kayaking on Lake Champlain in the Burlington area.

SPECTATOR SPORTS 🖍 **The Vermont Expos** (802-655-4200), Burlington's minor league baseball team, play at Centennial Field (off Colchester Avenue) all summer. You can park at UVM and take a shuttle bus to the game. The season is mid-June through September 1, tickets are cheap, the park is lovely, the concession food is pretty good, and there's a giant Day-Glo dancing Champ mascot for the kids. All in all, a great time—and the baseball isn't bad. The Expos operate a souvenir store in the Champlain Mill (802-655-9477), Winooski (see *Selective Shopping—More Special Stores*).

SWIMMING **North Beach Park** (802-862-0942), off North Avenue at Institute Road, Burlington (turn at the high school), provides tent and trailer sites plus swimming from a long, sandy beach, mid-May through October; vehicle charge. (Just before the park is the entrance to Rock Point, where the Episcopal Diocese of Vermont maintains Bishop Hopkins' Hall School, the bishop's residence, a conference center, and an outdoor chapel.)

Other beaches: **Leddy Park,** also off North Avenue; **Oakledge Park,** off Route 7 south of the city, at the end of Flynn Avenue; **Red Rocks Park,** South Burlington's public beach on Queen City Park Road.

✱ Winter Sports

CROSS-COUNTRY SKIING *Northern Vermont Adventure Skiing,* a weatherproof map ($6.95) detailing cross-country trails throughout the region, is available at local outlets and from Map Adventures (802-253-7489), 846 Cottage Club Road, Stowe 05672.

Bolton Valley (802-434-3444), Bolton. Ownership changed but this 105 km network of trails didn't. Ranging in elevation from 1,600 to 3,200 feet, this is Vermont's highest cross-country system, with snow that usually lasts well into April. A total of 45 km are machine groomed, meaning tracked for the most part, rolled elsewhere. There is a wide and gently sloping 3.6-mile Broadway and a few short trails for beginners, but most of the terrain is backwoods, much of it splendidly high wilderness country. You can take an alpine lift to the peak of Ricker Mountain and ski Old Turnpike, then keep going on cross-country trails for a total of 7 miles. There are rentals in the cross-country center, and experienced skiers are welcome to stay in the area's high huts by reservation. Telemarking is a specialty here, along with guided tours.

The legendary 12-mile **Bolton-to-Trapp trail** originates here (this is by far the preferred direction to ski it), but requires spotting a car at the other end or on Moscow Road. Inquire about the exciting new telemark/backcountry trail beginning at the top of Bolton's Wilderness Chair and meandering down into Little River State Park in Waterbury/Stowe. Again, a car needs to be spotted at the other end.

Catamount Family Center (802-879-6001), 421 Governor Chittenden Road, Williston. The 40 km of trails—30 of them machine tracked, 2 km lit—are on rolling terrain, geared to all abilities. Guided tours, rentals, instruction, warming hut. $12.

Note: See *Green Space* for more about local parks with trails that lend themselves to cross-country skiing.

DOWNHILL SKIING **Bolton Valley** (802-434-3444; 1-877-926-5866), Bolton. This substantial ski mountain has the highest base elevation in the East. It has changed hands frequently in recent years but now seems firmly financed by a consortium of local businesspeople. Its base facilities were renovated in '99. The 50 ski trails and slopes (seven lifts, including one quad and four double chairs) here are on 3,680-foot Bolton Mountain, which towers above its neighbors in a lonely stretch of country 20 miles east of Burlington, 20 miles west of Montpelier. Set atop a 4-mile access road that is, in turn, a long way up Route 2 from anything else, it offers a genuinely self-contained resort atmosphere guaranteed to make you want to stay put for a week (see *Lodging—Beyond Burlington*). Half-day and night-skiing prices also available.

✐ **Cochran Ski Area** (802-434-2479), Cochran Road, Richmond. A small, family-owned and -oriented ski area run by a family of former Olympic skiers.

Note: See also Smugglers Notch in "North of the Notch and the Lamoille River Valley," "Stowe and Waterbury," and "Sugarbush/Mad River Valley." Five major alpine areas are within easy striking distance of Burlington.

ICE SKATING **Leddy Arena** (802-864-0123), Leddy Park, Burlington. Rentals.

Skating from **Waterfront Park** on Lake Champlain is also a special rite of winter; flags indicate ice safety.

SLEIGH RIDES **Shelburne Farms** (802-985-8442) offers rides in 12- to 15-passenger sleighs. For a description of the setting, see *To See—Museums and Attractions*.

✷ Green Space

Burlington Parks and Recreation (802-865-7247). Request a copy of the Burlington *Bike Paths & Parks* map or pick it up at the chamber of commerce (see *Guidance*). Burlington's lakeside parks are superb (see chapter introduction).

Oakledge Park (take Flynn Avenue off Pine Street or Route 7) offers swimming and picnicking (parking fee, but you can bike or walk in). **Red Rocks Park** just south, occupying the peninsula that divides Burlington from South Burlington (take Queen City Parkway off Route 7), offers walking trails (no bikes allowed) as well as a beach. See also *Bicycling* and *Swimming*. **Ethan Allen Park** (North Avenue) is a 67-acre preserve, once part of Ethan's farm (it's near the Homestead; see *To See—Museums and Attractions*) and webbed with trails that climb to the Pinnacle and to a stone tower built on Indian Rock in 1905 (open Memorial Day through Labor Day, Wednesday through Sunday noon–8); both high points offer panoramic views of Lake Champlain.

Winooski Valley Park District (802-863-5744) consists of more than two dozen well-run parks, including beaches (see *Swimming*), boat launches, tennis courts, and an extensive riverside bike path (see *Bicycling*). **The Intervale** (entrance on Riverside Avenue) along the Winooski River offers walking as well as bike trails and includes Intervale Community Farms (802-660-3508), Gardener's Supply (retail and catalog outlet; see *Selective Shopping—More Special Stores*), and a seasonal organic farm stand. Also along the Winooski: a children's discovery garden and walking trails in the 67-acre park around the Ethan Allen Homestead (park headquarters), at **Macrea Farm Park,** and **Half Moon Cove Park. Delta Park** at the mouth of the Winooski River is a magical place with a sandy trail traversing woods to a wetland observation platform. **Centennial Woods** offers nature trails; access is from East Avenue.

Bayside Park (802-655-0811), Colchester. The site of a 1920s resort, the park now offers sports facilities, a beach, and walking trails. In winter this is also a popular spot for ice fishing, ice Windsurfing, and skating.

For Sand Bar State Park and other green space to the north, see "The Islands."

To the east

Underhill State Park (802-899-3022), within the Mount Mansfield State Forest, offers camping (mid-May through mid-October), a Civilian Conservation Corps log picnic pavilion, and four trails to the summit ridge of Mount Mansfield. It's accessed from the Pleasant Valley Road west of Underhill Center.

The Green Mountain Audubon Nature Center (802-434-3068), Huntington. (Turn right at Round Church in Richmond; go 5 miles south to Sherman Hollow Road.) Trails wind through 230 acres of representative habitats (beaver ponds, orchards, and woodlands). Interpretive classes are given. Groups are welcome to watch (and help in) the wood-fired sugaring conducted each year. Open all year, but call ahead to confirm.

Camels Hump State Park. Ver-

TEACHOUT'S GENERAL STORE ON THE SHORES OF LAKE CHAMPLAIN

Kim Grant

mont's most distinctive and third highest mountain (4,083 feet) is best accessed from Huntington via East Street, then East Street to Camels Hump Road. Request a free map and permission for primitive camping (at lower elevations) from the Vermont State Parks in Waterbury (802-241-3655; 1-800-VERMONT; www.vtstateparks.com). The **Green Mountain Club** (802-244-7037) on Route 100 in Waterbury Center also has maps and maintains shelters, lodging, and the Hump Brook Tenting Area. Camping facilities are also available in nearby Little River State Park. The name "Camel's Rump" was used on Ira Allen's map in 1798 but by 1830 it was known as "Camel's Hump." *Note:* All trails and roads within the park are closed during mud season.

To the south

LaPlatte River Marsh Natural Area, Shelburne; parking on Bay Road. Managed by The Nature Conservancy of Vermont, this 211-acre preserve at the mouth of the LaPlatte River is rich in bird life. It is traversed by an easy trail (45 minutes round-trip).

Shelburne Bay Park, Shelburne. (Park on Bay Road, across from the entrance to the Shelburne Farms visitors center; see *To See—Museums and Atttractions.*) The Shelburne Recreation Department maintains a blue-blazed trail along the bay through mixed woods.

Shelburne Farms. See *To See—Museums and Atttractions.* Five miles of easy trails on 1,400 acres landscaped by Frederick Law Olmsted.

H. Lawrence Achilles Natural Area, Shelburne, access off Pond Road. A short hiking trail leads to Shelburne Pond.

Mount Philo State Park (802-425-2390; 802-372-5060), Charlotte. A small mountaintop picnic area and campground, with spectacular views of the valley, lake, and Adirondacks. A short but steep ascent off Route 7 (not recommended for trailers or large RVs); 15 campsites; $1 per adult admission.

Kingsland Bay State Park (802-877-3445), Ferrisburgh. West from Route 7 on Little Chicago Lane, about 1.5 miles north onto Slang Road, 3 miles to Lake Champlain. Picnic areas, tennis courts, on 130 acres.

✱ Lodging

In Burlington 05401

HOTELS ♿ **The Radisson Hotel** (802-658-6500; 1-800-333-3333), 60 Battery Street. The view and location can't be beat. It's worth paying a slight premium for a room overlooking the lake and its backdrop of the Adirondacks. Families may prefer the cabana rooms, however, handy to the indoor swimming pool, Jacuzzi, and fitness room. Complimentary parking is offered in the adjacent garage, and the shops and restaurants of downtown Burlington are steps away. Request a corner room, facing south as well as west. In the hotel itself, the Oak Street Café serves three daily meals, and Seasons on the Lake, the hotel's upscale dining room, has a spectacular view. Rates range from $149–219 all year long; inquire about B&B packages, free shuttle service to the airport.

🐾 **The Sheraton-Burlington** (802-865-6600; 1-800-325-3525), 870 Williston Road. With 309 rooms, this is Vermont's largest hotel and the city's convention and trade center. It's set on campus like grounds in South Burlington at the top of the hill behind the UVM campus and the medical center, near the I-89 (exit 14W), Route 2 interchange with easy bus access to downtown. $99–220 per room. Small pets permitted.

BED & BREAKFASTS **Willard Street Inn** (802-651-8710; 1-800-577-8712; www.willardstreetinn.com), 349 South Willard Street. The classiest place to stay in Burlington, a brick mansion built grandly in the 1880s up on the Hill (adjoining the UVM and Champlain College campuses). It offers 14 guest rooms, all with private bath. Guests enter a cherry-paneled foyer and are drawn to the many-windowed, flower-filled solarium with a woodstove, where guests breakfast. There is also a spacious living room with a grand piano and hearth, and a dining room. Guest rooms are decorated individually and range in size and detailing from the master bedroom to former maids' rooms but all are tastefully done and equipped with phone, TV, and air-conditioning. Top dollar is for a canopy bed, lake view, and private bath (but lake views can also be enjoyed for far less). $130–225 includes a full breakfast.

Lang House (802-652-2500; 1-802-877-919-9799; www.langhouse.com), 360 Main Street. Well-known innkeepers Bev Watson and Bobbe Maynes teamed up to open the newest B&B. They offer nine rooms with private bath in a restored 1881 Eastlake Victorian, done in period furnishings and antiques. Everything is close by, and a chef prepares breakfast. $125–200, breakfast included.

Howard Street Guest House (802-864-4668; www.together.net/~agray), 153 Howard Street. Available by the night year-round. A beautiful space in a detached carriage barn: a sunny, open living room, dining area and minimal kitchen with skylights, all furnished with flair, including a queen bed and a pullout sofa. Andrea Gray's house is in a quiet residential area, within easy walking distance of the waterfront and Church Street Marketplace (see *To See—Museums and Attractions*). $120 for the room. Good for a romantic getaway or a businessperson requiring space to spread out. Ten percent discount for stays of more than 3 days.

Burlington Redstone (802-862-0508; www.burlingtonredstone.com), 497 South Willard Street. A long but possible walk from downtown, nearer to UVM, this handsome mansion was built in 1906 of local redstone. Helen Sellstedt offers two guest rooms with shared bath and one with private, along with gracious common spaces, including an invitingly landscaped garden. No children under 13, please. $99–135 includes a full breakfast.

Beyond Burlington

RESORT ✐ **Bolton Valley Resort** (phone/fax: 802-434-3444), Bolton Valley 05477. A mountaintop cluster of condominiums, lodge, restaurants, shops, and a sports center set on 5,000 wooded acres. In winter, Bolton Valley is a ski resort (see *To Do—Downhill Skiing* and *Cross-Country Skiing*); in summer the focus is on tennis, mountain biking, and golf, with formal programs for children. An outdoor pool, an extensive network of hiking trails, and a nearby 18-hole golf course are also part of the summer picture. Facilities include the renovated (in 1999) 150-room slope-side hotel (some rooms have a fireplace and kitchenette) and more than 120 one- to four-bedroom condominium units. The sports center houses an exercise room, pool, tennis courts, and game room. Rates for the hotel rooms range $89–319; for a condominium unit, $149–649.

INNS **Inn at Shelburne Farms** (802-985-8498; www.shelburnefarms.org), Shelburne 05482. Open mid-May through mid-October. Guests are treated to a peerless taste of Edwardian grandeur. The 45-room, Queen Anne–style mansion was built by William Seward and Lila Vanderbilt Webb on a bluff overlooking Lake Champlain. Completed in 1899, the house is the centerpiece of a 1,400-acre estate (see Shelburne Farms under *To See—Museums and Attractions*).

Perhaps because its transition from mansion to inn in 1987 entailed a $1.6 million restoration but no sale (the Webb family have turned the estate into a nonprofit environmental education organization), there is a rare sense of a time as well as place here. Turn-of-the-20th-century furnishings predominate (most are original), and you feel like an invited rather than a paying guest. You can play billiards in the richly paneled game room, leaf through one of the 6,000 leather-bound books, or play the piano in the library. Common space includes the Main Hall, a magnificent room divided into sitting areas with fireplaces and dominated by a very grand staircase. There's also an elegant tearoom (tea is served daily) and the Marble Room, a formal dining room with silk damask wall coverings, a marble floor, and long windows overlooking the formal gardens and lake. Don't miss the third-floor playroom, with its dollhouses.

Guest rooms vary in size and elegance, from the second-floor master bedroom to servants' quarters, which means room prices also vary. The Green Room, in which we slept, was painstakingly but far from fussily decorated (its wallpaper was specially made) to echo the mauve-and-green fabric in a splashy '20s screen. With its alcove desk, freestanding old mirror, fresh flowers, luxurious turn-of-the-century bath, and water view, there was a sense of comfort and space. Guests have access to tennis, boating, a swimming beach, and walking trails. Rates for the 24 luxurious, individualized bedrooms (17 with private bath): $200–365 double with private bath, $95–180 with shared bath (rates include a 15 percent service charge). There is a 2-night minimum stay on weekends. Breakfast and dinner are extra, and memorable. No smoking.

♿ **The Inn at Essex** (802-878-1100; 1-800-727-4295), 70 Essex Way (Route 15 east), Essex Junction 05452. There are innlike common spaces, and the 120 rooms and suites are decorated with country-chic wallpapers and fabrics; 30 have working fireplace and 2 have Jacuzzi. The large, neo-Colonial complex is set in landscaped gardens in a commercial, suburban area handy to IBM, 10 miles northeast of downtown Burlington. Facilities include a conference center and an outdoor heated swimming pool. A free shuttle to the airport is also offered. $179–499 includes continental breakfast. Inquire about special packages. Butler's, the inn's formal restaurant (see *Dining Out*), and the more casual café are both staffed by students from the New England Culinary Institute.

BED & BREAKFASTS **Willow Pond Farm** (802-985-8505), 20 Cheese-factory Lane, Shelburne 05482. Open early spring to late fall. If we had special sections for birders and gardeners, Sawyer and Zita Lee's elegant home would top both lists. Zita inherited the 200-acre farm and in 1990 the couple designed and built this exceptional retirement house, a blending of old lines and modern spaces. Many windows let in the view of rose and perennial gardens, with their many bird feeders, and the small pond. The property also borders Shelburne Pond, a haven for ospreys, pileated woodpeckers, mergansers, bluebirds, and wild turkeys, among others. The living room/dining room overlooks the gardens and ponds and conveys an unusual sense of light and space. A woodstove, wing chairs, and sofas invite you to sit, surrounded by books, art, and treasures well chosen by several discerning generations. A full breakfast and the Lees' special cappuccino blend are served at the formal, oval table in the dining area or out on the terrace. The upstairs master bedroom overlooks the Adirondacks, and there is a sleeping loft for kids. The two smaller rooms are also furnished in fine antiques, Oriental carpets, and handmade quilts on the king- and queen-sized beds. All have private bath. Just minutes from downtown Burlington and from Shelburne Farms (see *To See—Museums and Attractions*), with a way-out-in-the-country feel. $85–120 with breakfast. There is a 2-night minimum.

♿ **Heart of the Village Inn** (802-985-2800; 1-877-808-8134; www.heartofthevillage.com), 5347 Shelburne Road, P.O. Box 953, Shelburne 05482-0953. A handsome 1880s home next to the town green and library (1816) and across from town hall. Bobbe Maynes, one of the three original owner-innkeepers, coveted this house for years and, when it came on the market, bought it. Some $500,000 in renovations later, this is a comfortable showplace of a B&B with hosts Bobbe and Stephanie Spaulding, who never seem to run out of energy, perhaps because they take turns. The two living rooms, dining room, and five guest rooms are all carefully, comfortably decorated. All have air-conditioning and in-room connections for phones and cable TVs, as well as private bath; the carriage barn houses the four most deluxe rooms, a honeymoon suite with a whirlpool bath, and one room with wheelchair access. Rates are $95–205, with breakfast and afternoon refreshments included.

🐾 **Homeplace** (802-899-4694), P.O. Box 96, Old Pump Road (off Route 15), Jericho 05465. The sprawling house is set in a 100-acre wood with hiking paths. Guests can meet horses, sheep, ducks, chickens, cats, dogs, and a donkey. The guest area is separated from the family quarters and includes a large library and living room. Four rooms, two with private bath and two with shared (twin or double beds). Mariot Huessy asks $65 single, $75 double, $85 with private bath, full breakfast included. $10 per extra person in the room; pets possible for a small fee.

ꝏ ♿ **Sinclair Inn Bed & Breakfast** (802-899-2234; 1-800-433-4658), 389 Route 15, Jericho 05465. This fully restored 1890 Queen Anne "painted lady" is located in a village setting within easy driving distance of Burlington. All six rooms have private bath and air-conditioning, but you may prefer to relax in the extensive perennial gardens or sit by the waterfall overlooking the Green Mountains. Nancy Ames is your hostess. $70–150 per couple includes a full breakfast. Children over 12 welcome.

🐾 **A Mansfield View B&B** (802-899-

4793), 58 Sand Hill Road, Underhill Center 05490. A handsome Garrison Colonial home set on 5 acres with views east to Mount Mansfield. There are two guest rooms with a shared bath, one with a double, the second with twin beds, both with individual heat control. The house is furnished in antiques, and there's a player piano, a sun room, and an open porch overlooking busy bird feeders as well as the mountains. Rates are $45–75, with breakfast included. Pets negotiable.

The Richmond Victorian Inn (802-434-4410; 1-888-242-3362), 191 East Main Street, P.O. Box 652, Richmond 05477. On Route 2 in the village of Richmond (2 miles off I-89), this exceptionally clean and classy house was formerly owned by the Harringtons of ham and other specialty food fame (the home store is still across the street). There are six comfortable guest rooms, all with private bath, all individually decorated with antiques and equipped with good reading lights. Children over 12, please. Gail Clark will pick up Long Trail hikers. Rates: $85–125 for a double including full breakfast.

Maple Grove Farm B&B (802-878-4875), 3715 Oak Hill Road, Williston 05495. Open year-round. Ginger and David Isham are the fourth generation of the Isham family to operate this 120-acre farm, one of the last four in this historic town just east of Burlington. While they have sold their dairy herd, the Ishams still raise cattle, and the vintage-1852 Gothic Revival farmhouse retains its surrounding fields and sugarhouse. Guests are comfortably bedded in three rooms vacated by the family's six grown children. One room has a double bed, and the other two have queen beds. Baths are shared, breakfast is full, and children are welcome. Common space includes a big living room and a den with piano. $50–75, discounts for more than 3 nights.

Black Bear Inn (802-434-2126; 1-800-395-6335; www.blkbearinn.com), 4010 Bolton Access Road, Bolton 05477. Built in the '60s as a ski lodge, now very much a hilltop country inn known for its fine food. Chef-owner Ken Richardson is a Culinary Institute of America grad (see *Dining Out*). The 25 rooms all have private bath and country decor and range from standard to luxurious (hot tubs and gas fireplaces). Richardson has weathered the changing fortunes at Bolton Valley Resort, with which he shares this hilltop, and continues to offer access to the resort's many facilities. This is also a favorite place for groups (one family group has been coming for 30 years), at which time the dining room is closed. $49–205. Pets are invited to stay at the Bone & Biscuit Inn.

Elliot House (802-985-1412; 1-800-860-4405; elliothouse.com), 5779 Dorset Street, Shelburne 05482. This 1865 Greek Revival farmhouse adjoins conservation land with a view west to the Adirondacks. Anne and George Voland offer three bedrooms, all with private bath; there's also a sitting room with piano. Guests are welcome to walk the meadows; sheep, chickens, and ducks are in residence. Rates: $80 per room with full breakfast.

The Millhouse Bed & Breakfast (802-453-2008; 1-800-859-5758), 394 State Prison Hollow Road, Starksboro 05487 (just off Route 116, south of Hinesburg). Open mid-May through mid-October. While it's 25 miles from Burlington, this gem of a bed & breakfast run by Pat and Ron Messer isn't really in any other region (as defined by our chapters) either. The friends who tipped us off to it found it convenient enough to use while visiting their daughter at UVM. The house retains its graceful 1831 lines and sits just above a rushing brook, near enough so that the sound of the water is constant. The sleeping arrangements include the upstairs master bedroom (shared bath) and two suites, one with three bedrooms (a large twin bedroom and two small single rooms) and another composed of two double bedrooms plus private baths. The house (on the National Register of Historic Places) is tastefully, comfortably decorated with plenty of common space, including a great back porch. The downstairs suite is handicapped-accessible. Rates, including a breakfast and afternoon snack, are $80–100. Inquire about the studio cottage on the falls (where pets are allowed).

By the Old Mill Stream (802-482-3613; www.bythestream.com), 84 Richmond Road, Hinesburg 05461. This is a pleasant place: an 1860s rambling farmhouse with wide, wooden floorboards and tin ceilings. There are three upstairs guest rooms, two with private bath, and a double living room and dining room; grounds include gardens that border a waterfall (it powered the mill for Isaiah Dow, who built the house). $70–105 includes a full breakfast.

MOTOR INNS 🐾 ✐ ♿ **Hawthorn Suites** (802-860-1212; 1-800-527-1133; www.harthotels.com), 401 Dorset Street (just off Route 2), South Burlington 05403. Opened in 1998 by Chuck and Ralph DesLauriers, with an open timbered lobby, featuring suites with separate living rooms (containing fold-out couches) and bedrooms: 73 one-bedroom suites and 6 two-bedroom. Facilities include an indoor pool, a spa/Jacuzzi, and fitness machines. While it's located in the heart of South Burlington's strip malls, it's just minutes from downtown Burlington. Ralph DesLauriers developed Bolton Valley Resort and ran it for 30 years and Chuck's background is in hotel management; both men grew up in South Burlington on the family farm on which their parents ran one of the area's first motor inns. $99–280 (depending on length of stay) includes a breakfast buffet.

🐾 ✐ ♿ **The Wilson Inn** (802-879-1515; 1-800-521-2334; www.wilsoninn.com), 10 Kellogg Road, Essex Junction 05452. The 42 units all include a bedroom, living room, and full kitchen. Handy to IBM rather than Burlington (10 miles away), it can work for families as well as businesspeople. Amenities include a free breakfast buffet, a grocery shopping service, and access to the neighboring fitness center. Some handicapped-accessible units available. One-bedroom units are $94–124; two-bedroom, $114–144. Luxury suites available; discounts for longer stays.

🐾 ✐ ♿ **Marriott Residence Inn** (802-878-2001; 1-800-331-3131), 35 Hurricane Lane, Williston 05495. At exit 12 off I-89, this glossy, all-suite motor hotel has an indoor pool, spa, and Sport Court; free breakfast buffet. The one-bedroom-plus living room and kitchen suite is as low as $99 on weekends; the duplex, two-bedroom suite is $160 in high season. There's a pet charge.

🐾 ✐ **Hampton Inn** (802-655-6177; 1-800-HAMPTON), 42 Lower Mountain View Drive, Route 7 north, Colchester 05446, exit 16 off I-89. North of Burlington, one of the chain's latest: 188 well-furnished one- and two-room suites, indoor pool, Jacuzzi, fitness facilities, free airport shuttle, and continental breakfast.

✳ Where to Eat

Note: Burlington offers the best choice of restaurants and cafés between

Boston and Montreal, but the best are not all downtown.

DINING OUT **Inn at Shelburne Farms** (802-985-8498; www.shelburnefarms.org), Shelburne. Open for dinner by reservation from mid-May to late October. This turn-of-the-21st-century manor offers imaginative cuisine in a magnificent setting: walls covered in fin de siècle silk damask from Spain, a black-and-white marble floor, and a stunning sunset view of Lake Champlain and the Adirondacks. You might begin with chilled Amish peach and sparkling wine soup and dine on naturally raised beef tenderloin with sweet corn and Swiss chard polenta ($29) or pan-roasted chicken with a ragout of beets, fingerling potato, fava beans, *haricots verts,* and roasted pepper tapenade ($21). Dessert might be a chocolate truffle cake with peppermint ice cream, mixed berry Napoleon with sweet mascarpone cream, or Vermont-made cheeses with poached figs and crostini. Smokers can have coffee served on the terrace. Breakfast, open to the public by reservation, is also an event: granola pancakes, brioche French toast, eggplant and cheddar frittata, or poached eggs with herbed hollandaise and homefries.

Café Shelburne (802-985-3939), Route 7, Shelburne. Open for dinner daily except Monday. Located across the road from the Shelburne Museum, this chef-owned and -operated authentically French bistro serves consistently fabulous fare. Lobster over homemade fettuccine and a hunter's plate that includes quail, rabbit, and venison are stars in an overall excellent menu. The desserts are to die for. It's one of the best restaurants in the state. Entrées: $19–24.

Pauline's Café & Restaurant (802-862-1081), 1834 Shelburne Road (Route 7 south). Open daily for lunch, brunch, and dinner, also Sunday brunch. It is worth braving the strip development traffic. In the elegant simplicity of the downstairs café or the more formal upstairs dining rooms, subtle cuisine featuring wild and local ingredients (mushrooms, cattail shoots, sea beans, fresh black and white truffles, for example) is artfully presented in sensible portions. Entrées might be pork loin scaloppine with apricot, sherry, and herb sauce; loin of Vermont rabbit with artichoke hearts and mushrooms; or veal tenderloin with wild mushrooms. Café: moderate. Upstairs: expensive.

Butler's (802-878-1100), the Inn at Essex, Route 15, Essex Junction. Open for dinner nightly. In the deft hands of the New England Culinary Institute, the cuisine in this elegantly formal, green-walled room with high-backed, upholstered chairs is a visual as well as gustatory treat. Dinner might start with asparagus leek soup ($3.75) and Chef Jacques's rich country pâté ($5.75); proceed to grilled breast of duck with fig chutney ($16), crisp-skin salmon with fennel risotto ($17), or grilled rack of lamb with polenta and broccoli rabe ($21). Elaborate desserts might include a caramelized phyllo Napoleon with cranberry compote.

Smokejacks (802-658-1119), 156 Church Street, Burlington. Open daily for lunch and dinner. The decor is understated, almost stark in contrast to what even the menu describes as "bold food." Culinary Institute of America–trained Leslie Myers and Don Kelp obviously strive to be creative. Chances are we will never again have the opportunity to lunch on black bean turkey chili soup with sour cream, corn, and pumpkin seeds. We're glad we did! Dinner entrées like balsamic-grilled Cavendish quail and "paella" (including a crispy duck leg as well as the usual seafood and sausage). Request a cheese plate and a glass of wine (the wine selection is long and interesting); also great martinis. Moderate to expensive.

Blue Seal Restaurant (802-434-5949), Bridge Street, Richmond. Open Tuesday through Saturday 5:30–9:30. Reservations suggested. Housed in a vintage-1854 feed store, chef-owner Debra Weinstein's casual restaurant may not look—or charge—the part, but it's right up there with the Burlington area's finest. The menu changes frequently, but you might begin with a savory tart (sweet potatoes, apples, and grilled red onions) and dine on pan-roasted salmon with roasted garlic mashed potatoes, herb oil, and salsa, or marinated portobello mushrooms with grilled new potatoes, sautéed spinach, and goat cheese. A favorite dessert is double-layered devil's food cake with coffee swirl ice cream. Entrées: $10.50–16.

Black Bear Inn (802-434-2920), at the Bolton Valley Resort, off Route 2 in Bolton. Reservations requested. Chef-owner Ken Richardson is a Culinary Institute of America graduate who has turned his hilltop lodge into a dining destination for Burlington residents. The menu, which changes nightly, is limited to five entrées so you might want to call to check, and to reserve. You might begin with escargots sautéed with roasted garlic and red wine (or a cream of carrot and red pepper soup), then dine on a center-cut rib pork chop with wild rice and cranberry relish or a confit of duck with broccoli rabe, sausage, and sage. Entrées run $12.95–17.95.

Opaline (802-660-8875), 1 Lawson Lane, Burlington. This French restaurant has only a few tables, so reservations are a must. The food is expensive but very good. Heed the warning in the parking lot and get a sticker from the maître d' or you will get towed, an unpleasant finish to an otherwise excellent dining experience.

Iron Wolf (802-865-4462), 86 St. Paul Street, Burlington. Dinner is served Tuesday through Saturday from 5:30 PM. Reservations recommended. Diners have been known to wax poetic about the juicy filet of beef. They cannot say enough about chef Claus Bockwoldt's filet of pork with its port wine and veal stock reduction, or his butter-soft lamb and white beans. Entrées $13–21.50. Wine store open from 11 AM to closing.

Waiting Room (802-862-3455), 156 St. Paul Street, Burlington. Open 5:30 PM until 2 AM Tuesday through Sunday. Reservations accepted. The Waiting Room brought metropolitan flavor to the Burlington after-hours scene when it opened in August 2001. Nightly jazz performances complement a sophisticated dinner menu served until midnight along with an extensive wine selection and well-stocked bar. Live music starts at 10:30 every night except Sunday, when it starts at 7. Appetizers $7–12; entrées $14–25; desserts $7.

EATING OUT *Note*: Thanks to their largely student patronage, many of the following restaurants offer "dining-out" quality at "eating-out" prices.

In Burlington

Sweetwater's (802-864-9800), 120 Church Street (corner of College

Street). Open Monday through Saturday 11:30 AM–1:30 AM, Sunday 10:30–1 AM. Housed in a former and splendidly restored 1920s bank building, this is a deservedly popular spot. Note the fresco depicting a number of recognizable Burlingtonians cavorting down Church Street with Bacchus. You might lunch on a burger, a salmon sandwich, or a choice of daily specials; dine on wood-grilled chicken served with sun-dried tomatoes and shiitake mushrooms. Dinner entrées are well prepared; sandwiches, flatbread pizza, and salads are always available. The square bar is one of Burlington's prime rendezvous spots. Moderate

Trattoria Delia (802-864-5253), 152 St. Paul Street. Open daily 5–10. A dimly lit, nicely decorated space with a helpful, knowledgeable waitstaff, tempting antipasti and pastas, a wide choice of entrées (ranging from chicken to wild boar), nightly specials, and regional Italian wines. Moderate. Reservations.

Daily Planet (802-862-9647), 15 Center Street. Open Monday through Saturday 11:30–3 for lunch, 3–5 for the bar menu, 5–10:30 for dinner; also a weekend brunch. The atmosphere is light and casual with a solarium and airy dining room, both filled with small tables covered in bright oilcloths at lunchtime, linen for dinner. Unusual soups of the day are a specialty, along with tapas, nachos, burritos, and entrées ranging from grilled lamb loin to Vietnamese seafood and a variety of pastas. Planet burgers and fajitas are also usually on the menu. Dinner entrées from $11.95 for tempeh vegetable stir fry to $19.95 for rack of lamb.

NECI Commons (802-862-6324), 25 Church Street. Open daily for light breakfast, lunch, dinner, and take-out. This three-story former clothing store is now filled with New England Culinary Institute students both learning and putting what they've learned into practice. The space includes several dining rooms, varying in tone, all hip and inviting. Generally excellent and innovative cuisine.

Sakura (802-863-1988), 2 Church Street. Lunch Monday through Saturday, dinner daily. Vermont's first (but no longer its only) Japanese restaurant is a resounding success. At lunch its soothing ambience is an oasis of calm and an appropriate setting for savoring sushi and sashimi dishes or simply deep-fried salmon served with a tangy sauce. Vegetarians will appreciate dishes like avocado, bean curd, boiled spinach, vegetable tempura, and hijiki (cooked seaweed). Lone diners appreciate the seats lining the long sushi bar.

Sweet Tomatoes (802-660-9533), 83 Church Street, in the cellar of the old Howard Opera House at the marketplace. A fine, busy place with an excellent northern Italian menu, plus top-drawer, wood-fired pizzas. You might lunch on the pasta of the day and dine on fusilli sautéed with wood-smoked chicken, sweet peas, mushrooms, plum tomatoes, black pepper, rosemary, and light cream. Outdoor tables in summer. Italian mineral water and wines featured. Moderate.

Five Spice Café (802-864-4045), 175 Church Street. Open Monday through Saturday for lunch and dinner, Sunday 11–3 for dim sum brunch. The dishes are from a variety of Asian countries—Thailand, Vietnam, Indonesia, and India, as well as China—and the spices are as hot as you care to take them. The atmosphere is appealing. Try the ginger-tangerine cheesecake.

Parima Restaurant (802-864-7917),

185 Pearl Street. Open for lunch and dinner. Polished wood and brass and ornate glass lamps are the unlikely but pleasing decor for a wide selection of classic Thai dishes.

Halvorson's Upstreet Cafe (802-658-0278), 16 Church Street. Open for lunch, dinner, and brunch. An old landmark that's expanded its basic all-American menu and added beer and wine to meet the changing nature of the street. In summer, check out its hidden courtyard; inquire about Thursday-night jazz.

Red Square Bar and Grill (802-859-8909), 136 Church Street. Open afternoons for people-watching and for dinner. Jack O'Brien's attractive space features a copper bar, local art, music 6 nights a week, and is best known for its Sunday gospel brunch: $13.95 includes the music.

Stone Soup (802-862-7616), 211 College Street. Open Monday through Friday 7–7, Saturday 8–5, closed Sunday. A hugely popular storefront café specializing in vegetarian dishes, great soups, salads, and breads. Inexpensive.

Cobblestone Deli & Market (802-865-3354), 152 Battery Street. Open daily, 7–7 weekdays, Saturday 8–6, Sunday 8–5. No view (wrong side of Battery Street) but a pleasant café with a good deli: soups, sandwiches, coffees, wines, and microbrews. Pick up a sandwich to take on the bike path or to picnic by the lake.

Leunig's Bistro (802-863-3759), Church and College Streets. Open daily for breakfast, lunch, and dinner. In classic bistro style, Leunig's has dark wood, gleaming coffee machines, streetside tables, and status as the hub of Church Street. Frequent live entertainment.

Henry's Diner (802-862-9010), 155 Bank Street, is a long-established, authentic diner around the corner from the Church Street Marketplace. Here you can get the meat loaf and thick gravy you've been hankering for. Closed Monday.

Nectar's (802-658-4771), 188 Main Street. A basic eatery for breakfast and lunch but famed for its french fries with gravy and its owner's association with the musical group Phish. Because it has a cabaret license (nightly music), it's the only restaurant in town that allows smoking.

Bove's Cafe (802-864-6651), 68 Pearl Street. Open Tuesday through Sunday for lunch and dinner. An old favorite with booths and a row of tables between; traditional Italian menu, full bar. Inexpensive.

The Vermont Pub and Brewery (802-865-0500), 144 College Street. Open daily 11:30 AM–1 AM. Housed in a modern building but with an old beer-hall atmosphere (tile floor, huge bar, brass), specializing in ales and lagers brewed on the premises. The menu includes Cornish pasties, cock-a-leekie pie, bratwurst, and fish-and-chips.

India House (802-862-7800), 207 Colchester Avenue. Lunch and dinner Tuesday through Saturday; Sunday brunch. This warm and hospitable restaurant serves traditional curries, tandoori chicken, and the like, plus puffy poori bread.

Sai-Gon Cafe (802-863-5637), 133–135 Bank Street. Lunch and dinner in this attractive eatery, serving authentic Thai cuisine.

Penny Cluse Cafe (802-651-8834), 169 Cherry Street, in the old Ben & Jerry's building. Innovative, healthy, hearty breakfasts and lunches. Famous for black beans, polenta, great biscuits.

On the waterfront

Mona's (802-658-6662), 3 Main Street. Open daily for lunch and dinner and Sunday for brunch. An open kitchen sets the tone in this casual place with a great view of the lake and the Adirondacks, good for southern flatbread pizza, cheddar and ale soup, or herb-roasted chicken with cornbread stuffing, sun-dried tomatoes, and artichoke hearts. Save room for the chocolate Grand Marnier mousse served in an almond cookie tulip with white chocolate and coconut macaroons.

Dockside Cafe (802-864-5206), 209 Battery Street. Open for lunch and dinner; Sunday brunch. Housed in the depths of one of the city's oldest waterfront buildings, with outdoor dining in good weather. A variety of tapas are featured, along with high-priced entrées.

The Ice House (802-864-1800), 171 Battery Street. Open for lunch and dinner daily, Sunday brunch, with seasonal open-air decks overlooking the ferry slip and marina. This was a pioneer of the city's upscale restaurant scene, a 19th-century icehouse with massive walls and timbers. American regional dishes feature seafood and Vermont lamb. We recommend the shrimp pico (shrimp and crabmeat stuffing in puff pastry with lobster cream sauce; $18.50). You might lunch on sautéed chicken with garlic, herbs, and white wine in a tomato cream sauce on tortellini ($6.95). Save room for hot cheesecake.

✐ **Shanty on the Shore** (802-864-0238), 181 Battery Street. Open daily 11–11. Handy to the ferry with great lake views from inside as well as out; good for burgers and sandwiches as well as seafood platters, even escargots. A children's menu and choice of exotic drinks also offered.

Breakwater Cafe & Grill (802-864-9804), King Street Dock. Part of the LCTC ferry complex, an informal dockside space serving sandwiches, fried baskets, soups, and salads all day and evening in summer; inquire about frequent live music.

THE *CARILLON* FERRY ON LAKE CHAMPLAIN

Kim Grant

Whitecaps (802-862-1240), at the Boathouse. Open Memorial Day through Labor Day, 7:30 AM–sunset. A relaxing, casual spot; small menu; bar; moderate prices.

In Winooski

Papa Frank's (802-655-2433), 13 West Center Street. Open Monday through Friday 11–10, Saturday 4–10. A red-sauce Italian neighborhood restaurant that caters to families as well as students. Good for pizza, calzones, but also classic dishes. The vegetables are fresh, and garlic bread comes with your order. A bit tricky to find if you're driving because of one-way streets, but it's just a couple of blocks from the Champlain Mill.

Sneakers (802-655-9081), 36 Main Street, serves a great breakfast and lunch Monday through Friday, dinner Monday through Saturday, weekend brunch. Locals consider this the best breakfast in the area; options include eggs Benedict and freshly squeezed orange juice. The dinner special may be seafood or lamb. Inquire about live music on weekends.

Waterworks (802-655-2044), the Champlain Mill. Open for lunch, dinner, and Sunday brunch. Occupying the prime space in the turn-of-the-20th-century mill, overlooking the dam spillway and rapids of the Winooski River. You can dine outside in a greenhouse area or savor the view through the mill's long windows. The large menu ranges from sandwiches to Wiener schnitzel, steak, stir fries, and nightly specials.

In Colchester

Colchester Reef Lighthouse (802-655-0200), 8 Mountain View Drive, adjacent to the Hampton Inn just off I-89, exit 16. Lunch, dinner, and Sunday brunch. Nowhere near the water, but a bustling, cheerful, steak-and-seafood place, with the biggest salad bar around; good for families (kids' menu). Full bar.

Libby's Blue Line Diner (802-655-0343), 1 Roosevelt Avenue, Route 7, Colchester, with its tile floor and marble counters, attracts itinerant diner buffs and area fans for breakfast, lunch, and dinner daily. Try the banana bread French toast.

Williston Road to Richmond

Daily Bread Bakery Café (802-434-3148), Richmond Center. Open daily 8–4. People leave I-89 south (turn right at the Cumberland Farms and look for the aqua sign at the end of a parking lot on your left) just to drop by for breakfast, lunch, or Saturday and Sunday brunch, or even for a slice or two of maple bread.

Al's French Frys (802-862-9203), 1251 Williston Road, South Burlington. Really, that's how it's spelled. Open daily 10:30 AM–midnight. Burlington's own (amazingly fast) fast-food joint, spanking clean and small-town friendly with first-class fries, burgers, dogs, and shakes. Handy enough to I-89, exit 14E, to work well as roadfood.

On Shelburne Road (Route 7 south)

Perry's Fish House (802-862-1300), 1080 Shelburne Road. Open Monday through Saturday 5–10, Sunday 4–10. A big, bustling, landlocked pier with an extensive menu of moderately priced, first-rate seafood that attracts large numbers of locals. Specialties include batter-fried clams. Children's menu.

Harrington's (802-985-2000), Shelburne. Across from the Shelburne Museum, a good bet if you can snag one of the few tables and don't mind

Kim Grant

A SIDEWALK CAFÉ ON CHURCH STREET

the Styrofoam at the excellent deli here. Specialties include the "World's Best Ham Sandwich" (Harrington's is known for its corn-smoked ham), also smoked turkey, quiche, homemade soups, sausage chili made with Harrington's own pork sausages, and chocolate mousse.

ALFRESCO

In Burlington

Beansie's Bus, Battery Park. Early April through autumn, this old yellow school bus parks daily by the lake and dispenses its famous french fries; the hamburgers, dogs, and grilled cheese on a bun are incidental.

The Hot Dog Lady. Lois Bodoky has her imitators, but she was the first and she's still the most reasonably priced and all-around best. Look for her cart at noon every day at the Church Street Marketplace: $1 hot dog with kraut.

CAFFEINE/SNACKS

In Burlington

Mirabelle's (802-658-3074), 198 Main Street. A delightful bakery-eatery featuring special teas, espresso, pastries, sandwiches, and light fare. Look for the waterfront offshoot.

Muddy Waters (802-658-0466), 184 Main Street, just up from Church Street. Excellent coffee, homemade desserts, vegan specials, smoothies, beer and wine by the glass, brick walls, sofas, lots of reading material and earnest conversation.

Uncommon Grounds (802-865-6227), 42 Church Street. They roast their own here, and also sell tea and pastries. A good people-watching spot.

Speeder and Earl's. A small counter and café tables at 104 Church Street, a zany shop at 412 Pine Street, same complex as the Fresh Market (see *Selective Shopping—Food and Drink*), featuring their own blends and assorted pastries.

Ben & Jerry's (802-862-9620), 36 Church Street. This isn't the original location, but the world's legendary ice cream makers did get their start in the neighborhood.

✷ Entertainment

Note: For current arts and entertainment in Burlington, call the **Burlington City Arts line** at 802-865-7166, or check *Seven Days,* a free weekly publication that's available everywhere around town.

MUSIC **Vermont Mozart Festival performances** (802-862-7352), 110 Main Street, Burlington 05401. Summer concerts in various settings—on ferries, at the Shelburne Museum and/or Shelburne Farms (see *To See—Museums and Attractions*), at the Basin Harbor Club (see "Addison County and Environs"), in churches. Winter chamber series.

Vermont Symphony Orchestra (802-864-5741), 77 College Street, Burlington. One of the country's first statewide philharmonics presents a five-concert Chittenden County series at the Flynn Center; outdoor summer pops at Shelburne Farms (see *To See—Museums and Attractions*) and elsewhere.

St. Michael's College concerts (802-655-2000), in Winooski, feature jazz, pop, and classical productions.

Burlington Oratorio Society (802-864-0471). A volunteer, 50-voice choir presents several concerts a year.

The Discover Jazz Festival (Flynn box office: 802-86-FLYNN; www.discoverjazz.com), Burlington, 10 days in early June, a jazz extravaganza that fills city parks, clubs, restaurants, ferries.

Battery Park Summer Concert Series, Burlington, Thursday and Sunday nights.

THEATER **Flynn Center for the Performing Arts** (802-86-FLYNN), 153 Main Street, Burlington. The city's prime stage for music and live performance is a refurbished art deco movie house, now home to plays, musical comedies, jazz concerts, and lectures, in addition to movies. It now has a gallery and several smaller performances spaces as well.

Royall Tyler Theater (802-656-2095), at the University of Vermont, Burlington, stages an eclectic, top-notch seasonal repertory of classic and contemporary plays.

St. Michael's College Theater Department (802-654-2000), Winooski, presents two major productions, fall and spring; also an excellent summer playhouse series (802-654-2281).

Lane Series (802-656-4455) sponsors major musical and theatrical performances around Burlington fall through spring.

DRIVE-IN **Sunset Drive-In** (802-862-1800), Route 127 off North Avenue, Colchester. It's for real: three screens, a snack bar, and a kiddie playground.

MUSICAL VENUES For jazz, blues, rock, and dance clubs, check out these nightspots, all in Burlington: **Nectar's** (802-658-4771; see *Eating Out*), 188 Main Street, and above it, **Club Metronome** (802-865-4563). **135 Pearl Street** (802-863-2343) is the area's gay and lesbian rallying point; dance floor and cabaret theater downstairs, bar and dining room up. **Red Square Bar and Grill** (see *Eating Out*) offers frequent nightly music and a Sunday gospel brunch. **Leunig's Bistro, Halvorson's Upstreet Café,** and **Sweetwater's** on Church Street (see *Eating Out*) also frequently offer live entertainment. **Higher Ground** (802-654-8888), 1 Main Street, Winooski (next to the Champlain Spectrum Mall) offers live music.

✷ Selective Shopping

In downtown Burlington

The Church Street Marketplace. Nearly a hundred stores, restaurants, and services line several blocks of Church Street, nicely paved, landscaped, closed to traffic, and enlivened by seasonal arts and crafts shows, weekend festivals, and wandering entertainers (and street people).

Pine Street area. A small yet delectable cluster of businesses on Pine Street between Marble Avenue and Howard Street, just south of the Vermont Transit terminal. Parking is never a problem. Highlights include the Fresh Market, the Burlington

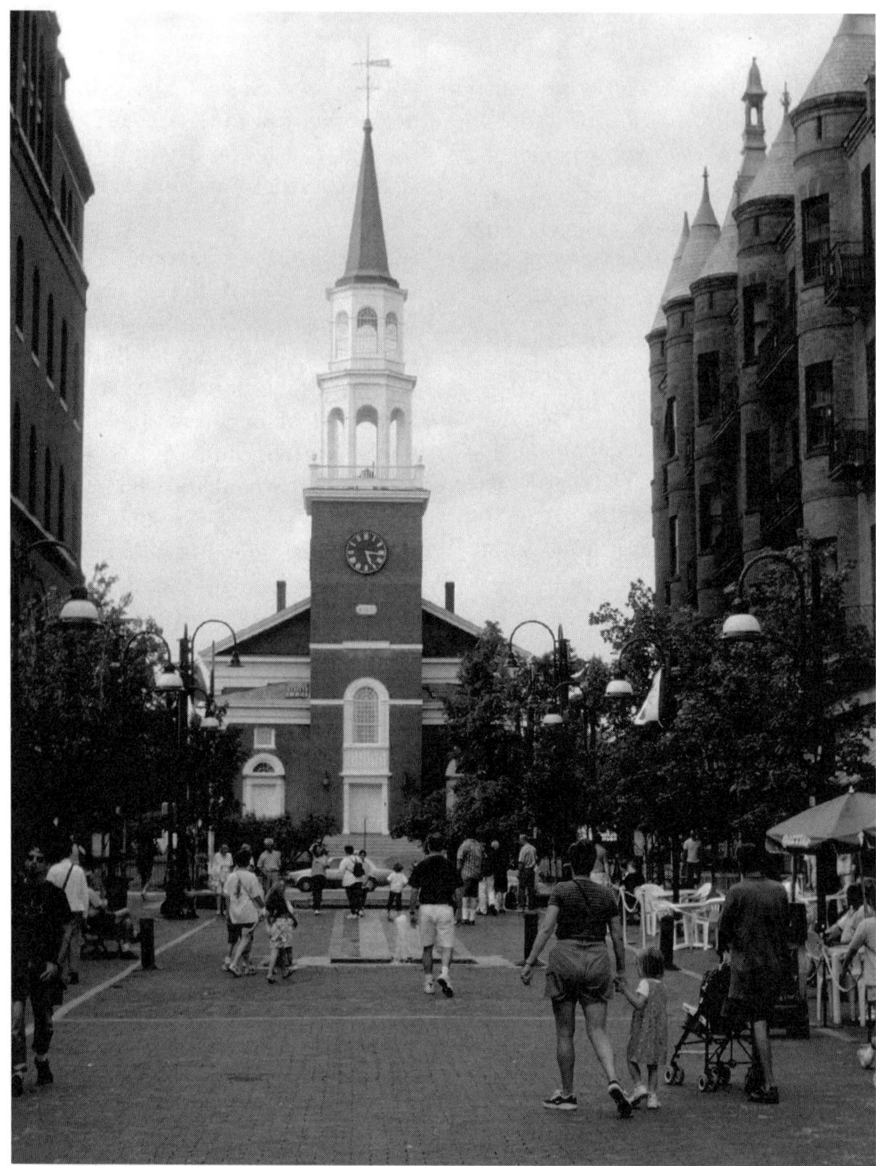

THE CHURCH STREET PEDESTRIAN MALL IN DOWNTOWN BURLINGTON Kim Grant

Futon Co., Speeder and Earl's Coffee, and Beverly's Cafe; a number of smaller craft businesses are behind Speeder and Earl's.

Burlington Town Center. This vast indoor agora, mostly underground, has 80 stores stocking just about everything, linked to a parking garage and Filene's. Several food stalls for grazers.

ART GALLERIES **Fire House Art Gallery,** 135 Church Street, Burlington. Pick up a copy of the *First Friday Art Trolley Tours* pamphlet guide (see *To Do—Museums and Attractions*). The trolley only runs first Fridays, but the map is a good gallery locator any day. On our own tour we were most impressed with the **Doll-Anstadt Gallery** (802-864-3661), 91 College Street. Ruby

Anstadt offers a mix of striking paintings (changing shows) and decorative art.

Furchgott & Sourdiffe Gallery (802-985-3848), 86 Falls Road, Shelburne. A tasteful gallery in an old farmhouse, offering local art.

Also check out the **Exquisite Corpse Artiste,** 47 Maple Street (802-864-8040), just off Battery Street.

ANTIQUES SHOPS **Ethan Allen Antique Shop** (802-863-3764), Williston Road, Route 2 east of Burlington, has a large stock of early American and country furniture and accessories. Open daily; Sunday by appointment.

Architectural Salvage Warehouse (802-658-5011), 53 Main Street, offers artifacts from old houses and buildings.

Burlington Centre for Antiques (802-985-4911), 3093 Shelburne Road, south of Burlington. Open daily year-round. Two large floors offer quality antiques in every size and shape from more than 70 dealers.

Route 7 Antiques (802-859-0917), 388 Shelburne Road in the south end of town. Open Tuesday through Sunday. An intimate collection of elderly and antique items, reasonably priced.

Champlain Valley Antique Center (802-985-8116), 4067 Shelburne Road, Shelburne, offers the wares of 25 dealers. Also try **Upstairs Antiques** (802-859-8966), on Flynn Avenue in Burlington.

BOOKSTORES The small **Everyday Book Shop** (802-862-5191) on College Street is the lone surviving independent bookstore in the downtown area. **Waldenbooks'** branch (802-658-6019) is in the Burlington Town Center on the lower level. **Barnes & Noble** (802-864-8001), 102 Dorset Street, is a two-story book department store in South Burlington, and **Borders Books** (802-865-2711) is at 29 Church Street.

Antiquarian books can be found at **Bygone Books** (802-862-4397; 31 Main Street), Burlington's oldest and most appealing antiquarian bookstore; also at **North Country Books** and **Crow Bookshop,** both on upper Church Street. In Williston, **Beliveau Books** (802-482-2540), at Goose Creek Farms, specializing in Vermont, military history, and nature, is open by appointment.

CRAFTS SHOPS **Frog Hollow on the Marketplace** (802-863-6458), 86 Church Street, is a branch of the Vermont State Craft Center of Middlebury, a showcase for fine things crafted in the state, from furniture and art glass to handwoven scarves.

Designers Circle (802-864-4238), 52 Church Street, features beautifully crafted jewelry. **Bennington Potters North** (1-800-205-8033), 127 College Street, sells kitchenware, home furnishings, glass, and woodenware, and Bennington pottery at "factory prices." **Church and Maple Glass Studio** (802-863-3880), 225 Church Street. Closed Sunday. Bud Shriner, a former emergency room physician, bought the old Yellow Cab garage several years ago and has transformed it into a glassblowing studio with a reasonably priced array of crafted glass.

FARM **Vermont Wildflower Farm** (802-425-3500), Route 7, Charlotte (5 miles south of the Shelburne Museum). Open May to October, 10–5 daily. A multimedia show; 6 acres of wildflowers in test fields and woodland settings; flowers and trees labeled along paths; a large gift shop; and "the largest wildflower seed center in the East." Nominal admission.

FOOD AND DRINK **Lake Champlain Chocolates** (802-864-1807), 750 Pine Street, Burlington. Open 7 days. The home of the American Truffle, and other expensive candy, discounts some of its premium chocolates. Tours possible with advance reservations.

Snowflake Chocolates, Route 15, Jericho Corners. Bob and Martha Pollak's handcrafted chocolates are so good. Try the dark, liqueur-laced truffles.

Fresh Market (802-863-3968; 1-800-447-1205), 400 Pine Street, Burlington. Formerly the Cheese Outlet, this market still specializes in cheeses from Vermont as well as from around the world. Also most other Vermont products, and a source of sandwiches, baked goods, wines, deli meats, fresh produce, and exotic deli items.

Magic Hat Brewing Company (802-658-BREW), 5 Bartlett Bay Road, South Burlington (turn off Route 7 at the Jiffy Lube). A microbrewery offering free tours and samples, Wednesday through Saturday; also a retail store.

Note: The **Saturday Farmer's Market** in City Hall Park (8:30–2:30 summer through fall) is good for baked goods, clothes, and art as well as fruits and veggies.

SPORTS STORES **Burton Snowboards** (802-862-4500), 80 Industrial Parkway (near Oakledge Park), Burlington. Open Monday through Friday 8–6, Saturday noon–5. The factory's retail and factory outlet for Vermont's name-brand snow- and skateboards and gear. Also check out the downtown Burlington store (802-863-0539) at 145 Cherry Streeet.

The Outdoor Gear Exchange (802-860-0190), 191 Bank Street, Burlington. Used and new outdoor sporting equipment: cross-country skiing, snowshoeing, rock climbing, hiking, and backpacking gear. It's rock climbing central.

The Downhill Edge and Ski Rack (802-862-2282), 65–85 Main Street, Burlington. This combined store features high-performance sailboards, gives lessons, and offers rentals at Leddy Beach and the Marble Island Resort. It's also a major source of cycling, running, in-line skate, and ski gear and wear, as well as rentals.

Climb High (802-985-5055), 2438 Shelburne Road, Shelburne. Hiking, biking, rock climbing, cross-country skiing—you name it, this store has got the gear for it, plus quick and reasonable repairs. The best part is that you don't have to drive into downtown Burlington.

VINTAGE CLOTHING AND FURNISHINGS **Old Gold** (802-864-7786), 180 Main Street, is a fun and funky store. **Battery Street Jeans** (802-865-6223), 182 Battery Street, offers more grungy but cool clothing. **Recycle North** (appliances, furniture, books) and **Garment Gallery** (clothing and jewelry) are similar shops at 266 Pine Street. All are in Burlington.

MORE SPECIAL STORES

In Burlington

Peace and Justice Store (802-863-8326), 21 Church Street, run by the city's active Peace and Justice Coalition, a source of alternative publications and Third World–crafted items—jewelry, cards, clothing—all purchased from wholesalers committed to nonexploitation and social justice. The bulletin board is also worth checking.

Gardener's Supply (802-660-3505), 128 Intervale Road. One of the largest catalog seed and garden suppliers in New England, with a retail store and nursery adjacent to demonstration gardens along the Winooski River.

Apple Mountain (802-658-0500), 30 Church Street, is a Vermont products gift and food shop; on the touristy side, but fun.

In the Charlotte-Shelburne area

Dakin Farm (802-425-3971), Route 7, Ferrisburg (and the Champlain Mill, Winooski), is one of the principal purveyors of cob-smoked hams and bacon. This roadside store also stocks a variety of other Vermont food products and gifts.

Shelburne Farm Store and Visitors Center (802-985-8442), open daily year-round 9–5 (10–5 in the off-season; see a full description of what this place is about under *To See—Museums and Atractions*). The store features the prizewinning cheddar cheeses made from the milk of the estate's own Brown Swiss herd. A variety of Vermont products are also stocked.

Harrington's, Route 7, across from the Shelburne Museum, Shelburne, has been known for years for its delectable (and expensive) corncob-smoked hams, bacon, turkey, pork chops, and other goodies. The shop also displays an array of cheeses, maple products, griddlecake mixes, jams, fruit butters, relishes, baked goods, wines, and coffees. Harrington's headquarters (Route 2, Richmond) include a smaller store.

The Shelburne Country Store, Route 7, Shelburne, encloses several gift galleries under the same roof—a sweets shop, foods, lamp shades.

The Vermont Teddy Bear Factory Store (802-985-3001; 1-800-829-BEAR), 6655 Shelburne Road (Route 7), Shelburne (see *To See—For Families*) is immense.

In Winooski

The Champlain Mill (802-655-9477), 1 Main Street, a creatively converted woolen mill, holds 30 smart shops, including the **Book Rack and Children's Pages** (802-655-0231), a well-stocked bookshop, plus two good restaurants, a bakery, and a deli; also several interesting clothing stores.

Blackthorne Forge (802-655-7676), 94 West Canal Street. Assorted traditional fixtures, plus unusual sculptured clocks.

Also in greater Burlington

University Mall (802-863-1066), Dorset and Williston Streets (I-89, exit 14E), South Burlington. Your basic shopping mall with 70 stores; Ames, Sears, and J. C. Penneys are the anchors. The **Essex Outlet Fair** (802-657-2777), Routes 15 and 289 in Essex, includes Polo Ralph Lauren, Jones New York, Levis, Jockey, and Bali, plus a new cinema complex.

Special Events

February: **Burlington Winter Festival,** at Waterfront Park—dogsled rides, snow and ice sculptures (802-864-0123).

Saturday before Lent: **Magic Hat Mardi Gras**—a parade and block party at the Church Street Market place.

March: **Vermont Flower Show** at the

Sheraton in South Burlington: 3 days of color and fragrance mark the end of winter.

May: **Lilac Sunday** at Shelburne Museum (802-985-3346). A festival of 19th-century food and games when the museum's many lilac bushes are in peak bloom.

Early June: **Arts Alive,** a showcase of Vermont artists. **Vintage auto rally** at the Shelburne Museum (802-985-3346). **Discover Jazz Festival**—for 9 days, the entire city of Burlington becomes a stage for more than 200 musicians (see *Entertainment*). **Lake Champlain International Fishing Derby**—for details about registration and prizes, check with the chamber of commerce (see *Guidance*).

Late June: **Green Mountain Chew Chew,** Burlington, a 3-day food festival featuring more than 50 restaurants; continuous family entertainment. **Showcase of Agriculture** at the American Morgan Horse Association (802-985-4944), adjacent to the Shelburne Museum.

Early July: Gala **Independence Day celebrations** on the Burlington waterfront; fireworks over the lake with live bands in Battery Park, children's entertainment, a parade of boats, and blessing of the fleet.

Mid-July through mid-August: **Vermont Mozart Festival** performances in various locations, including Lake Champlain ferries (see *Entertainment*).

Mid-August: **The Shelburne Craft Fair** at Shelburne Farms features dozens of exhibitors.

Late August: **Champlain Valley Exposition,** Essex Junction Fair grounds. A big, busy, traditional county fair with livestock and produce exhibits, trotting races, midway, rides, spun-sugar candy—the works.

Mid-September: **Annual Harvest Festival,** Shelburne Farms (802-985-8686). **Fools-A-Float**—a parade of land and sea craft, downtown Burlington. **Art Hop**—Open-studio weekend in Burlington.

Early October: **Marketfest**—celebrates Burlington's cultural diversity.

Early December: **Christmas Weekend** at the Shelburne Museum—a 19th-century festival; call 802-985-3344 for dates and details.

December 31: **First Night** (802-863-6005); the end-of-the-year gala—parades, fireworks, music, mimes, and other performances that transform downtown Burlington into a happy "happening."

THE NORTHWEST CORNER

Interstate 89 is the quickest but not the most rewarding route from Burlington to the Canadian border. At the very least, motorists should detour for a meal in St. Albans and a sense of the farm country around Swanton. We strongly recommend allowing a few extra hours—or days—for the route up through the Champlain islands, Vermont's Martha's Vineyard but as yet unspoiled.

THE ISLANDS

The cows and silos, hay fields and mountain views couldn't be more Vermont. But what about those beaches and sailboats? They're part of the picture, too, in this land chain composed of the Alburg peninsula and three islands—Isle La Motte, North Hero, and South Hero.

The Champlain islands straggle 30 miles south from the Canadian border. Thin and flat, they offer some of the most spectacular views in New England: east to the highest of the Green Mountains and west to the Adirondacks. They also divide the northern reach of the largest lake in the East into two long, skinny arms, freckled with smaller outer islands. It's a waterscape well known to fishermen and sailors.

This is Grand Isle County, Vermont's smallest (with a year-round population of 4,000). It was homesteaded by Ebenezer Allen in 1783 and has been a quiet summer retreat since the 1870s.

In the 19th century, visitors arrived by lake steamer to stay at farms. Around the turn of the century, a railway spawned several hotels, and with the advent of automobiles and Prohibition, Route 2—the high road down the spine of the islands—became one of the most popular roads to Montreal, a status it maintained until I-89 opened in the 1960s.

Happily, the 1960s, as well as the '70s, '80s, and '90s, like the interstate, seem to have passed these islands by. The selection of North Hero as summer home of the Royal Lipizzan Stallions (see *Entertainment*) in the 1990s is the biggest thing that's happened here since Theodore Roosevelt's visit in 1901. (It was here at Lt. Gov. Nelson Fisk's estate that Vice Pres. Theodore Roosevelt, who was attending a Vermont Fish and Game League banquet learned that Pres. William McKinley, also a visitor here in 1897, had been shot in Buffalo, New York.)

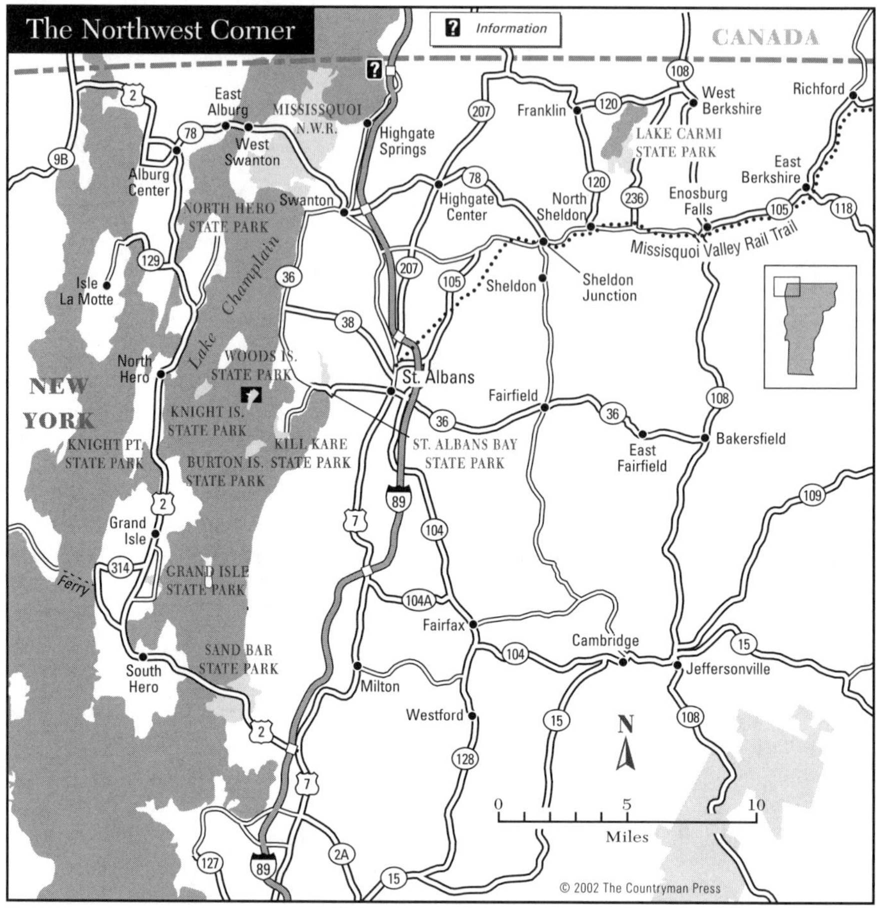

Isle La Motte is the smallest and quietest of the islands, and it's crossed and circled by narrow roads beloved by bicyclists. St. Anne's Shrine near the northern tip marks the site of a 17th-century French fort, and a rocky, tree-topped hump in the middle of a cow pasture at the southern end of the island is said to be the oldest coral reef in the world. Other evidence of the island's geological distinction can be seen in its stone houses, as well as in the marble facades of New York's Radio City Music Hall and the U.S. Capitol building. A quarry for the unique black Isle La Motte limestone marble is once again being worked after years of closure.

The rural, laid-back beauty of these islands is fragile. Their waterside farms and orchards are threatened, not by tourism, but by quiet, steady suburbanization. Burlington is just south of Grand Isle, and Montreal is just 60 miles north.

Viewed primarily as a summer destination, this is a great place to visit in September and October when its many orchards are being harvested and bicycling is at its best. Roads are little trafficked, mysteriously overlooked by mainstream leaf-peepers.

GUIDANCE **Champlain Islands Chamber of Commerce** (802-372-5683; info@champlainislands.com; www.champlainislands.com), P.O. Box 213, North Hero 05474, next door to the Hero's Welcome General Store (see *Selective Shopping—Special Stores*), maintains a year-round office and publishes a list of accommodations, restaurants, marinas, campgrounds, and trailer parks.

Also see **www.islandsandfarms.com.**

GETTING THERE From New York State and Montreal, Route 2 from Rouses Point, and from Vermont, Route 78 from Swanton (an exit on I-89). From Vermont on the south, I-89 exit 17 to Route 2, which runs the length of the islands.

Lake Champlain Transportation (802-864-9804) offers year-round, 15-minute ferry crossings between Gordon's Landing, Grand Isle, and Cumberland Head, New York.

MEDICAL EMERGENCY North and South Hero **(911)**. Marine emergencies (802-372-5590).

✷ Must See

St. Anne's Shrine (802-928-3362), Isle La Motte, Route 129. An open-sided Victorian chapel on the shore marks the site of Vermont's first French settlement in 1666. There are daily outdoor Masses in summer and Sunday services as long as weather permits. The shrine is a pleasant and peaceful place with a public beach, a cafeteria, and a picnic area in a large pine grove, presumably descended from what Samuel de Champlain described as "the most beautiful pines as I have ever seen" near this spot. Champlain himself is honored here with a massive granite statue, which was carved in Vermont's Pavilion at Montreal's 1967 Expo. The complex is maintained by the Edmundites, the order that runs St. Michael's College in Winooski.

FISK FARM RUIN ON ISLE LA MOTTE

Christina Tree

ST. ANNE'S SHRINE ON ISLE LA MOTTE

VDT

✷ Also See

Hyde Log Cabin, Route 2, Grand Isle. Open July through Labor Day, 11–5 Wednesday through Sunday. Built by Jedediah Hyde in 1783, the cabin was restored by the Vermont Board of Historic Sites in 1956 and leased to the Grand Isle Historical Society, which has furnished it with appealing 18th-century artifacts—furniture, kitchenware, toys, tools, and fabrics. $1.

Isle La Motte Historical Society. Open July through August, Saturday 2–4. This old stone school building and blacksmith shop is on Route 129, 4 miles south of the bridge. Displays include a sculpture of local stone that's been partially polished, graphically illustrating that the stone used in many local buildings is marble. The nearby Chazian Reef, said to be the oldest coral reef in the world, is 450 million years old. Coral rock can harden into limestone that, over millennia, can turn to marble.

The Fisk Quarry Preserve, Isle La Motte. The reef is actually comprised of 1,000 acres underlying the entire southern third of Isle la Motte. The one reef site that currently can be visited by the public is at the Fisk Quarry Preserve, which adjoins Fisk Farm (see *Lodging*). Owned by the Isle La Motte Reef Preservation Trust, the preserve offers a pedestrian footpath with public viewing area where ancient reef-building organisms can be seen in the quarry walls. Parking is 600 feet to the south of the path. The Preservation Trust asks the public to park only in the designated area, and not alongside the road.

Fish Culture Station (802-372-3171), Bell Hill Road, Grand Isle. Just beyond the Plattsburgh, New York, ferry on Route 314, look for the large hatchery (it's precisely 2 miles up Route 314 from Route 2), open 8–4 daily. Fish are brought to the facility as freshly spawned eggs (up to 2.2 million eggs at any one time), incubated, then transferred to a series of tanks; well worth checking out.

✷ To Do

BICYCLING With its flat roads (little trafficked once you are off Route 2) and splendid views, the islands are popular biking country. Isle La Motte is especially well suited to bicycling. There are five interpretive theme loops that roam through the gently rolling terrain, easily followed with the help of a map available at the chamber of commerce. New in 2002 will be a completed rail-trail that links South Hero with Colchester by following the railbed of the old Rutland Railroad. The trip takes you on a magnificent journey across Lake Champlain. Lake views don't get any better than this, and it's flat to boot. The chambers of commerce have maps to guide you. The trial run in August 2001 was a smashing success.

For **rental bikes** check with **Hero's Welcome General Store** (802-372-4161; see *Selective Shopping—Special Stores*), North Hero Village, and **Bike Shed Rentals** (802-928-3440), Isle La Motte, West Shore Road, 1 mile south of St. Anne's Shrine. Open daily July through August, weekends in June, September, and October. Both Ruthcliffe Lodge and Terry Lodge (see *Lodging*) offer bikes to their guests. **Mountain Lake Expeditions** (802-777-7646) has instituted a very helpful delivery service that deposits bicycles, kayaks, or canoes right at your front door.

BIRDING Located on one of the major flyways, the islands are particularly rich in bird life: Herons, eagles, ospreys, cormorants, among others, migrate through the area. Prime birding sites include the South Hero Swamp and Mud Creek in Alburg and the Sand Bar Wildlife Refuge across from Sand Bar State Park. See also Knight's Island under *Green Space.*

BOATING Rental boats are available in North Hero from **Anchor Island Marina** (802-372-5131), **Charlie's Northland Lodge** (802-372-8822), and **Hero's Welcome** (802-372-4161; kayaks and canoes only). In South Hero, **Apple Tree Bay** (802-372-3922) offers canoes, sailboats, and pontoon boats. **Tudhope Sailing Center and Marina** (802-372-5320), at the bridge in Grand Isle, also offers sailboats, powerboats, boat slips, sailing instruction, and charters**. Mountain Lake Expeditions** (see *Bicycling*) will bring kayaks and canoes right to your door.

BOAT EXCURSIONS **Driftwood Tours** (802-373-0022), North Hero, offers several daytime, sunset, and moonlight cruises in a boat that seats a maximum of six passengers. Capt. Holly Poulin offers nature and fishing tours and also does dinner cruises in conjunction with the North Hero House. The trips take 2 hours and leave from the North Hero House Pier.

Ferry Cruise (802-864-9804), Route 314, Grand Isle. If you don't get out on the water any other way, be sure to take the 15-minute ferry to Plattsburgh, New York, and back.

FISHING Lake Champlain is considered one of the finest freshwater fisheries in America. With the right bait and a little luck, you can catch trout, salmon, smelt, walleye, bass, pike, muskellunge, and perch. Don't expect area fishermen to give away their favorite spots, but you can find hints, maps, equipment, bait, and advice from local fishing pundit Charlie North at **Charlie's Northland** in North Hero (see *Selective Shopping—Special Stores*).

GOLF **Alburg Country Club** (802-796-3586), Route 129, 3 miles west of South Alburg; 18 holes, gentle, shady terrain, snack bar.

Barcomb Hill Country Club at Apple Tree Bay (802-372-5398), Route 2, South Hero. Open May until late October. A par-3 executive golf course. Rental carts and clubs.

Wilcox Golf Course (802-372-8343), Grand Isle, offers nine lakeside holes, golf carts, pro shop, rentals.

Beaver Creek Mini Golf (802-372-5811), Route 2, North Hero. Open Memorial Day through Labor Day. An 18-hole miniature golf course.

✷ Green Space

Alburg Dunes State Park (802-796-4170), Alburg. Recently opened, features a shallow sandy beach, excellent for swimming with young ones, rare flora and fauna; limited day use only. Call for directions or ask locally.

North Hero State Park (802-372-8727) has 99 wooded tent or trailer sites and 18 lean-to sites arranged in three loops, each with a rest room and hot showers (no hookups); mostly in lowland forests with access to open fields, a beach, boat launch, boat rentals, and picnic and children's play areas.

Grand Isle State Park (802-372-4300) has 155 campsites, including 33 lean-tos (no hook-ups) on 226 acres, with a beach, nature trail, and recreation building.

Knight's Island State Park by way of Burton Island State Park (802-524-6353). Taxi service used to be available to Knight's Island, but now you must get there by private boat or by making private arrangements through the folks at Burton Island. The camping at Knight's Island is primitive (there are no facilities) and even clothing is optional! To maximize privacy, campsites are hidden from public view. Not to be missed is the brochure-guided "Walk of Change" that explores island ecology.

Knight Point State Park (802-372-8389), located on the southern tip of North Hero, is the best place to swim, especially if you have small children. A former farm facing The Gut, a quiet, almost landlocked bay, its grounds include a fine brick house and a nature trail that loops around the point, through maple and oak groves. From the sandy beach you can watch sailboats and yachts pass through the drawbridge between the islands. Canoes and rowboats are available for rental in the park.

Sand Bar State Park (802-372-8240) fills to capacity on sunny weekends in summer, but this oasis with its sandy beach and adjacent waterfowl area is a fine place to relax on weekdays.

See also *Green Space* in "St. Albans and Swanton" for the Missisquoi National Wildlife Refuge.

✷ Lodging

Note: See *Green Space* for information on campgrounds in North Hero and Grand Isle State Parks. Families who don't camp tend to rent cottages for a week or more. The chamber of commerce (see *Guidance*) can furnish details about numerous old-fashioned lakeside cottage clusters.

INNS AND BED & BREAKFASTS

Thomas Mott B&B (802-796-4402; 1-800-348-0843), 63 Blue Rock Road, Alburg 05440. This 1838 English country cottage with a splendid view of the Green Mountains is a real find. Hosts Lee and Linda Mickey keep a fridge is full of complimentary Ben & Jerry's ice cream. There are three bedrooms, each with private bath, and a suite with two bedrooms and shared bath. Guests are welcome to use the canoes and the swimming/fishing dock. Cross-country skiers and snowmobilers are at home here in winter (local rentals available), with 40 miles of dedicated trails adjacent. More daring guests can try skydiving or paragliding from the Franklin County Airport in Swanton. $85–165.

♿ **North Hero House** (802-372-4732; 1-888-525-3644; www.northhero-house.com), Route 2, North Hero 05474. Open year-round. This century-old summer hotel has a new lease on life thanks to New York investment manager Walt Blasberg, who put almost $1 million into renovations in 1997. Now it's a prim gray with black shutters and masses of red geraniums. All the rooms—the 9 upstairs and 15 more across Route 2—have been totally refurbished, and many baths now have Jacuzzi. The inn offers a comfortable sitting area, also an inviting pub and small library, and a large public dining room and table-filled solarium beyond (see *Dining Out*). Facilities include a long, grassy dock at which Champlain steamers once moored; canoes, kayaks, power- and pedal boats are available. Our favorite (alas, the most expensive) rooms are in the buildings that face, even extend out over the lake, so that you fall asleep to lapping water. In summer: $95–205 per couple B&B weekdays, $125–255 weekends; $10 per child. In winter (October 24 through May 15): $75–155 weekdays, $95–195 weekends.

OVERLOOKING LAKE CHAMPLAIN IN NORTH HERO

Kim Grant

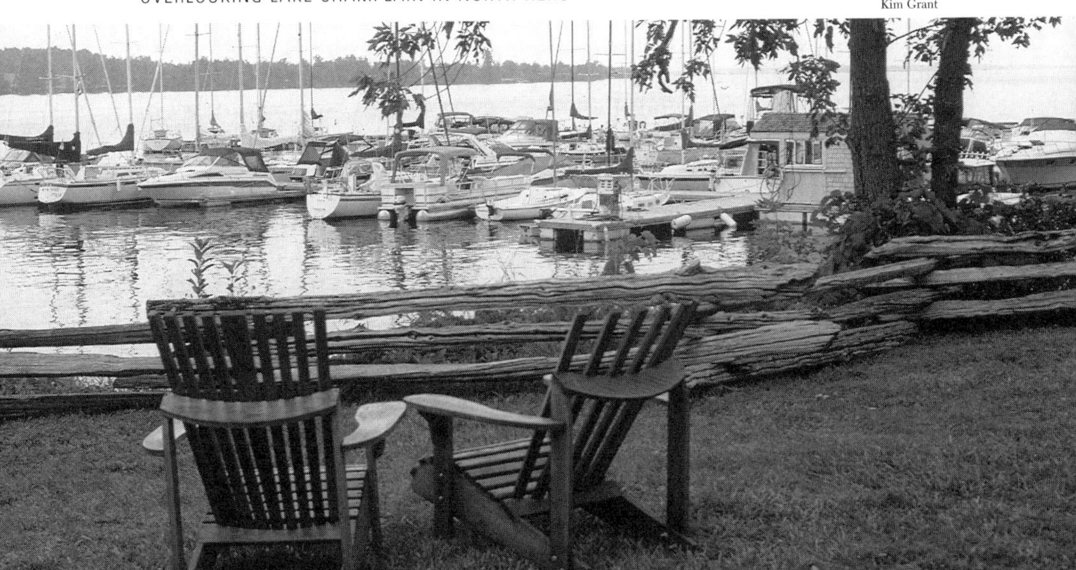

Fisk Farm (802-928-3364), 44 West Shore Road, Isle La Motte 05463. The clapboard home that once served as a store and post office now has two guest rooms, both facing the lake. Common space includes a pleasant living room and old-fashioned front porch. There are also two guest cottages. The former Ice House, built of wood and stone next to the main house, is a beauty, a place we would like to reserve for a special occasion, but only in warm weather (it has a fireplace but no other heating). There is a rustic Shore Cottage, said to have been built as a playhouse in North Hero and brought across the ice. The ruins of a gray stone mansion have been preserved in the front garden, the scene of Sunday teas, and the horse and carriage barn has been preserved as an art gallery. The mansion burned in 1924, but thanks to Linda Fitch, who has dedicated the last few years to restoring the property, it's an exceptionally tranquil place that offers a window into not only the history of Vermont but also the world (see Fisk Quarry Preserve under *To See*). Rates begin at $75 in the main house with a continental breakfast. Rates begin at $85 for the Shore Cottage and $110 for the Ice House (both of which have their own kitchen) but vary according to the length of time reserved and the season. Guests may help themselves to the herb garden.

Ruthcliffe Lodge & Restaurant (802-928-3200; 1-800-769-8162), 1002 Quarry Road, Isle La Motte 05463, open Mother's Day through Columbus Day. Way out at the end of Old Quarry Road, this lakeside compound includes a small motel and lodge with a total of nine rooms and a suite, seven of which feature lakeside panoramas and private bath. Mark and Kathy Infante are warm hosts, and the food is well known and highly rated (see *Dining Out*); three meals a day are served. There's a 40-foot water's-edge patio for dining, as well as the cozy dining room in the lodge. Swimming and fishing are out the front door; rental boats and bikes are available. Rates range from $87 for a double room with a half bath to $129 for a two-room adjoining unit with a bath and a half, including a full country breakfast.

The Ransom Bay Inn (1-800-729-3393), 4 Center Bay Road, Alburg 05440. A stone house built beautifully in the 1790s, originally a stagecoach stop, set back from Route 2 within walking distance of a small beach. Plenty of common space: an open-beamed living room area opening on a patio and a more formal parlor, two large airy and two smaller guest rooms, all nicely furnished and with private bath. $60 single, $75–85 double, includes full breakfast. Dinner served to guests with advance notice ($18).

Paradise Bay Bed & Breakfast (802-372-5393), 50 Light House Road, South Hero 05486. This is a very gracious new house in a secluded setting with plenty of deck space overlooking the lake. The two large, nicely furnished guest rooms share a bath in a separate wing. $75–100 per couple.

Charlie's Northland Lodge (802-372-8822; 802-372-3829), 3829 Route 2, North Hero 05474, open all year, built by Charlie's grandparents early in the 19th century. Two guest rooms, furnished in country antiques, share a bath, a private entrance, and guest parlor. $55–65 double includes continental breakfast. It's part of a nifty little complex that includes a sporting and gift shop, boat and motor rentals, fishing licenses, bait, and tackle. Housekeeping cottages available.

Terry Lodge (802-928-3264), Isle La Motte 05463. Open May 15 through October 15. A friendly, family kind of place in a superb location: on a quiet road not far from St. Anne's Shrine, across a narrow road from the lake with a fine lakeside deck and swim raft. Most of the seven rooms in the lodge itself have lake views. Breakfast and dinner (family-style) are served. There's also a four-unit motel, a housekeeping cottage ($475 per week), and a housekeeping apartment ($425 per week) in the rear. Bikes and rowboats are available. Lodge rooms are $85–90 with breakfast, $105–110 per couple MAP. Request one of the front rooms with a lake view.

The Allenholm Orchards Bed & Breakfast (802-372-5566; 1-888-721-5666), 150 South Street, South Hero 05486. Pam and Ray Allen offer a guest suite—a bedroom furnished in family antiques, including a queen-sized canopy bed, and a large living room with a TV, VCR, board games, and full-sized pool table, plus a full private bath, patio, and rose garden. A country breakfast is served upstairs in the dining room or, if preferred, on your patio. The suite is on the lower level of the Allens' modern home; it opens onto more than 100 acres of apples, billed as Vermont's oldest commercial orchard. Established in 1870s, it's now owned and operated by the sixth generation of Allens. $90 per couple for the bedroom, $150 for the entire suite.

Ferry Watch Inn (802-372-3935), 121 West Shore Road, Grand Isle, 05458. This wonderfully restored lakefront home, originally built in 1800, overlooks the broad lake with spectacular views of the Adirondacks and the most wonderful sunsets. Janet and Troy Wert offer three guest rooms (two with shared bath; one with private bath) with antique double beds renowned for their comfort. The property is within walking distance of a nine-hole golf course. $85–95 per room includes full county breakfast.

OTHER LODGING 🐾 ✐ **Shore Acres Inn and Restaurant** (802-372-8722; www.shoreacres.com), 237 Shore Acres Drive, North Hero 05474. Motel rooms open May through early October. This pleasant motel commands one of the most spectacular views of any lodging place in Vermont. Set in sweeping, peaceful, beautifully groomed grounds, 19 comfortable rooms face the lake and the Green Mountains. There's a bar/lounge; breakfast and dinner are served (see *Dining Out*). There are also four guest rooms in the garden house, away from the lake. Susan and Mike Tranby have worked hard to make this an exceptionally friendly as well as comfortable place. Amenities include lawn chairs, two clay tennis courts, a driving range, lawn games, and a half mile of private shore for swimming. All rooms have been upgraded and have either a queen, king, two twins, or two doubles, TV, and ceiling fan or air conditioner when lake breezes fail. $85–155 per room.

Wilcox Cove Cottages & Golf Course (802-372-8343 in summer; 802-879-7807 in winter), Route 314, mailing address: 3 Camp Court, Grand Isle 05458. Open June through mid-September. This homey, lakeside cottage colony and nine-hole public golf course, less than a mile from the ferry, is a real find (adults preferred). Each of the 11 cottages has a living room, dining area, fully equipped kitchen, one bedroom with twin beds, bathroom with shower, and one or two screen porches. They are completely furnished except for sheets, pillowcases, and bath and kitchen towels, and can be rented for about $400 a week including green fees. Occupancy is limited to two people unless arrangements are made in advance.

✱ Where to Eat

DINING OUT **Sand Bar Inn at Apple Island Resort** (802-372-6911), Route 2, South Hero. Chef Jim Kowalski has turned this popular eatery into a fine-dining restaurant with a casual atmosphere right on the lake. He does a blackberry duck breast appetizer with arugula salad and a walnut and Stilton crostini ($9). Entrées include a stuffed, bacon-wrapped filet mignon ($22) and a poached halibut and lobster claw dish with steamed vegetables and grapefruit beurre blanc ($19). Reservations are suggested. In season, the restaurant is open daily from 5 to 9. The chef also does private parties.

Shore Acres (802-372-8722), Route 2, North Hero. Reservations for dinner are a must much of the time. Also open for breakfast May through October and for lunch in July and August; dinner also served weekends until New Year's. The dining room's large windows command a sweeping view of the lake, with Mount Mansfield and its flanking peaks in the distance. It's a very attractive room with a large fieldstone hearth. You might begin with coconut-beer-battered shrimp ($5.25) or grilled homemade polenta ($3.95) and dine on Apple Island chicken or roast rack of lamb. Entrées ($12.95–21.95) come with home-baked bread, a salad, and seasonal vegetables. The chocolate pie is famous.

Ruthcliffe Lodge (802-928-3200), Old Quarry Road, Isle La Motte. Open mid-May through Columbus Day for dinner, July and August for lunch. Overnight moorings available for dinner guests. Be sure to reserve for dinner before you drive out to this rustic building, way off the main drag and overlooking the lake. Dine in the pine-paneled dining room or outside on the deck. Owner-chef Mark Infante specializes in Italian dishes like chicken Marsala and veal Sorrentina, but the menu might also include shrimp scampi Ruthcliffe or a full rack of lamb. Entrée prices include soup, salad, and vegetables. Entrées $17–22.

North Hero House (802-372-8237), Route 2, North Hero. Open mid-May through September. This historic old inn is known as a good bet for lunch as well as dinner (reserve). Although the dining room does not overlook the lake, it does feature a flower- and plant-filled greenhouse. The menu changes constantly, with entrées like salmon and steaks prepared in a variety of ways and a choice of pastas. Friday night there's always a lobster feast down on the dock. Entrées $13.95–18.95.

WEDDING RECEPTIONS ⚭ **Grand Isle Lake House,** East Shore Road, Grand Isle. For details and reservations, contact Bev Watson at 802-865-2522. Built on Robinson's Point as the Island Villa Hotel in 1903, this is a classic mansard-roofed 25-room summer hotel with a wraparound porch, set in 55 acres of lawn that sweep to the lake. From 1957 until 1993, it was a summer girls camp run by the Sisters of Mercy. Since 1997 it has been owned by the

Preservation Trust of Vermont, which has restored the upstairs rooms beautifully, as it has the lobby, kitchen, and dining rooms. It is currently available as a site for conferences and wedding receptions (80 can sit down in the dining room and another 125 guests on the porch; tents on the lawn can accommodate 250 guests).

EATING OUT **Hero's Welcome** (802-372-4161), Route 2, North Hero Village. Open daily, year-round, an upscale general store with a good deli, a bakery, and café. Great sandwiches and freshly made soups.

South Wind Market and Café (802-372-3721), Route 2, South Hero. Two local women have turned this spot into a find for salads and sandwiches, not to mention ice cream and a baked good or two. With a little advance notice, they'll pack a picnic for your Thursday-night outing at the Snow Farm Winery (see *Selective Shopping—Winery*).

Margo's (802-372-6112), Route 2, Grand Isle. Behind this simple facade lies a cozy, popular bakery-café serving continental breakfast and light lunches indoors, outdoors, or to go, and featuring the work of local artists.

Grand Isle Ferry Dock Snack Bar, South Hero. Breakfast, 7–11 AM; open until 8 PM on Friday, otherwise until 6. Don't miss the french fries or the homemade bread that Chuck and Ruth Hager make for sandwiches. Check out the orange and peach julep. Tables inside and picnic tables outside.

Northern Café (802-796-3003), Route 2, Alburg. Open daily 7 AM–9 PM. Nothing special from the road, but it can hit the spot when a grilled cheese or homemade soup is what you want. Dinner specials as well as predictable fare.

Links on the Lake (802-796-3586), Route 129, Alburg. Good food and reasonable prices in a pretty setting at the Alburg Country Club.

Note: See also Fisk Farm under *Lodging* and inquire about Tea Garden Art Shows with music on summer Sundays, 1–5.

✷ Entertainment

Royal Lipizzan Stallions (802-372-5683), mid-July through August, performing Thursday through Sunday at the Herrmann Farm, Route 2, North Hero. Tickets through the chamber of commerce (see *Guidance*). Visitors welcome every day. These are elegant and unusually strong white horses bred in the 16th century for battle and show, known for their intricate maneuvers, many executed while in midair. Only a few hundred representatives of the breed survive. Colonel Herrmann's family have been training Lipizzans since 1618, when their ancestors received some as a gift from Hapsburg Austrian Emperor Ferdinand II. The Herrmanns winter in Florida and come to North Hero for 6 weeks each summer.

Music at Snow Farm Vineyard (802-372-9463), West Shore Road, South Hero. If you fancy meeting the locals, a popular event is the Thursday summer music series beginning at 6:30 PM on the vineyard's lawn. The music ranges, over the course of the summer, from classical to rock. It's free, and all you need to bring is a picnic and a chair. You can buy your wine on site.

✷ Selective Shopping

ANTIQUES Pick up a current copy of the pamphlet guide *Antique the Champlain Islands* at **Hero's Welcome**

General Store (see *Selective Shopping—Special Stores*). The usual count is a half dozen shops, but they are all seasonal and tend to close as one thing, open as another. Standbys include the **Alburg Country Store,** Main Street (Route 2), middle of Alburg Village, the **Back Chamber Antiques Store,** North Hero Village, and **Simply Country,** south of the village. Also check with **Alburg Auction House,** Lake Street, Alburg, open Saturday 2–6 and 7–midnight.

CRAFTS **McGuire Family Furnituremakers** (802-928-3118), Route 129, Isle La Motte. Open year-round but call. Two generations of this talented family are involved in the day-to-day production of stunning furniture in spare, heirloom early American designs: beds, tables, grandfather clocks, dressers—anything you want designed, and some surprisingly affordable. The showroom fills the common rooms of a classic old brick house in the village of Isle La Motte.

Black Cat Gallery (802-372-8748), Hyde Road and Route 2, Grand Isle. The gallery showcases woven baskets, clothing, jewelry and high-end crafts from 60 Vermont artisans.

Island Craft Shop, located next to the Hero's Welcome main store and open daily mid-May through mid-October. Works of local and area artisans.

ORCHARDS **Allenholm Farm** (802-372-5566), 111 South Street, South Hero. Open July through December 24, 9–5. A sixth-generation, 100-acre apple orchard with a farmstead selling Vermont cheese, honey and maple syrup, jams and jellies, and Papa Ray's famous homemade pies. There's also a petting paddock with rabbits, goats, horses, and donkeys. See also *Special Events* (the Allens are the power behind the October Apple Fest).

Hall's Orchard (802-928-3418; 802-928-3226), Spaulding Road, Isle La Motte. The 1820s brick house sits across from the orchard that has been in the same family since the house was built. The apples we bought here on a crisp October morning are the best we can remember finding anywhere.

Hackett's Orchard (802-372-4848), 86 South Street, South Hero. Perennials, syrup, and pies in spring; small fruits and fresh-picked vegetables in summer; apples, cider, and pumpkins in fall. The farmstand has a family picnic and play area. Fresh cider doughnuts are a specialty.

SPECIAL STORES **Hero's Welcome General Store** (1-800-372-HERO; fax: 802-372-3205), P.O. Box 202, Route 2, North Hero. Former Pier 1 CEO Bob Camp and his wife, Bev, have transformed this 19th-century landmark into a bright, smart, multilevel emporium: café and bakery, gift shop, art gallery, grocery, Vermont gourmet food products, sports clothes, wine shop, and bookstore, retaining its flavor as a community gathering spot. They offer canoe and bike rentals as well as lake cruises (see *Boating*), and have plans for other magnetic features and services.

Charlie's Northland Sporting and Gift Shop. A serious fishing-gear source, but also assorted sportswear and gifts.

WINERY **Snow Farm Vineyard** (802-372-9463), 190 West Shore Road (follow signs from Route 2 or Route 314), South Hero. Open Memorial Day through October 31, 10–4:30. Vineyard tours are offered daily at 11 and 2. This pioneering Lake Champlain vineyard is the fruition of several years' hard work by lawyers Molly and Harrison Lebowitz. Visitors enter a barnlike building that is the winery/showroom with a tasting counter. There they learn that this is still a relatively new operation (opened in 1997). Initially it is processing and bottling wine from grapes grown in New York's Finger Lakes, gradually mixing these with the harvest from vines on Snow Farm's 10 acres. The farm's blanc de noirs was awarded a bronze medal at the 1998 Eastern International Wine Competition. (See also *Entertainment.*)

✷ Special Events

Note: Check with the chamber of commerce (see *Guidance*) about weekly events. See Fisk Farm under *Lodging;* inquire about Tea Garden Art Shows with music, summer Sundays.

June (second weekend): **Taste of the Islands: Food & Wine,** South Hero. Local food purveyors show off their culinary creations, accompanied by Snow Farm Vineyard wines. *Third weekend:* **Celebrate Champlain! Islands Festival,** Grand Isle. Classes and demos on Windsurfing, kayaking, sailing and canoeing; music and BBQ.

July 4: **Parades** and **barbecue**s in South Hero and Alburg.

Mid-July through August: **Lipizzan Stallions** (see *Entertainment*).

August (first weekend): **Grand Isle County Art Show & Sale.** *Last weekend:* **Northumbrian Pipers Convention Community Dance and Concert,** North Hero Town Hall.

September (first weekend): **Teddy Roosevelt Toast**. Isle La Motte, at the Fisk Farm. Presentation pays tribute to a person or group that has furthered T. R.'s mission with respect to our natural resources and cultural heritage.

October (first weekend): **Apple Fest**—crafts fair, a "press off," plenty of food and fun.

MUSEUMS AND PUBLIC BUILDINGS FLANK THE TOWN GREEN IN ST. ALBANS

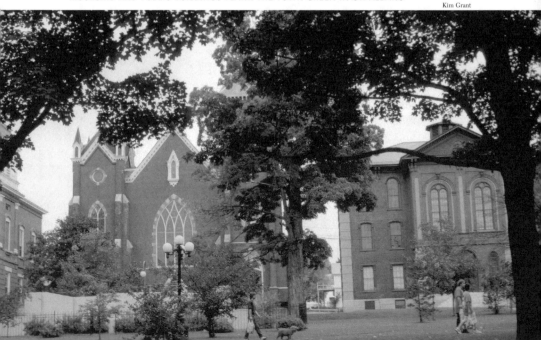

Kim Grant

Once an important railroad center and still the Franklin County seat, St. Albans (population: 8,082), on Route 7, is showing signs of revitalization. Its firm place in the history books was assured on October 19, 1864, when 22 armed Confederate soldiers, who had infiltrated the town in mufti, held up the three banks, stole horses, and escaped back to Canada with $201,000, making this the northernmost engagement of the Civil War. One of the raiders was wounded and eventually died, as did Elinus J. Morrison, a visiting builder who was shot by the bandits. The surviving Confederates were arrested in Montreal, tried, but never extradited; their leader, Lt. Bennett H. Young, rose to the rank of general. When he visited Montreal again in 1911, a group of St. Albans dignitaries paid him a courtesy call at the Ritz-Carlton!

Swanton was settled by the French about 1700 and later named for a British captain in the French and Indian Wars. It is now (population: 4,622) is growing again after a long period of relative stagnation. During World War I, the long-abandoned Robin Hood–Remington Arms plant produced millions of rounds of ammunition for the Allied armies. At one end of the village green dwell a pair of royal swans. This park is the focus for the Swanton Summer Festival (see *Special Events*). The tribal headquarters of the Abenaki are in the old railway depot.

GUIDANCE **The St. Albans Area Chamber of Commerce** (802-524-2444; www.stalbanschamber.com), 2 North Main Street, St. Albans 05478, provides brochures and general information.

The Swanton Chamber of Commerce (802-868-7200), Swanton 05488, has an information booth at the north end of the village green.

MEDICAL EMERGENCY **Northwestern Medical Center** (802-524-5911; 1-800-696-0321), St. Albans.

✷ To See and Do

Franklin County Historical Society (802-527-7933), facing Taylor Park, open June through September, Tuesday through Saturday 1–4. This museum was established by the St. Albans Historical Society in 1971 in a three-story brick schoolhouse erected in 1861. The Beaumont Room has been fitted up as a fascinating, old-time country doctor's office. Another room has period costumes, a third houses Central Vermont Railroad memorabilia. Upstairs are farm tools, a maple sugaring exhibit, and other artifacts of the region. Admission is free; contributions appreciated.

Chester A. Arthur Birthplace, North Fairfield. A replica of the little house where the 21st (and usually underrated) president was born can be found 10 miles east on Route 36 to Fairfield (open June through mid-October, Wednesday through Sunday and holidays, 9:30–5:30). In the visitors center, exhibits examine the controversy over the actual site of Arthur's birth, which had an impact on the question of his eligibility to serve as president. Arthur's conduct as president in light of his reputation as a leading New York State political boss is also examined.

GOLF **Champlain Country Club** (802-524-9895), Route 7, 3 miles north of St. Albans. Nine holes, some terraced. Snack bar.

Enosburg Falls Country Club (802-527-2296), Routes 105 and 108, Enosburg Falls, 18 holes.

Richford Country Club (802-848-3527), 84 Intervale Avenue, Richford, nine holes, established 1930.

Enosburg Falls Country Club (802-527-2296), Routes 105 and 108, Enosburg Falls, 18 holes.

Richford Country Club (802-848-3527), 84 Intervale Avenue, Richford; nine holes, established 1930.

BIKING **Missisquoi Valley Rail Trail** (802-524-5958), 140 South Main Street, St. Albans. The Northwest Regional Planning Commission supervises this 26.5-mile-long trail, converted from the abandoned Central Vermont Railroad bed into a path for cross-country skiing, bike riding, hiking, snowmobiling, dogsledding, snowshoeing, and just plain strolling, but not for ATVs or dirt bikes. It leads from St. Albans to Sheldon Junction, from there to Enosburg Falls, and winds up in Richford. You can stop along the trail at **The Abbey** restaurant for lunch (or breakfast if you're a real early bird). A free map guide shows trailside facilities.

Porter's Bike Shop (802-868-7417), Grand Avenue, Swanton is a find for out-of-luck bicyclists. Mr. Porter—or at least we assumed it was Mr. Porter—houses an impressive array of bike parts in his small shop, and he's a handy man to have around when something on the bike gets broken.

CANOEING AND FISHING **Raven Ridge Canoe Rental and Guide Service** (802-527-4616; 1-888-527-4616), Enosburg. Chas Salmon and Olga Lermontov provide fishing guides for bass, trout, northern pike, and walleye. They rent kayaks and canoes (with life jackets) and shuttle you to and from the river. They also take families and groups on wildlife-viewing and photographic expeditions.

✷ Green Space

St. Albans Bay State Park, 4 miles west on Route 36, is a good place for picnics, but the water is too shallow and weedy for decent swimming.

Kamp Kill Kare State Park (802-524-6021), once a fashionable summer hotel site and then, for years, a famous boys summer camp; on Point Road off Route 36, St. Albans Bay. It can be crowded on weekends, but it's usually blissfully quiet other days; swim beach, playgrounds, boat rentals, access to Burton Island.

Burton Island State Park (802-524-6353), a lovely, 350-acre island reached from Kill Kare by park boat or by your own. Facilities include 42 campsites, including 22 lean-tos, and a 100-slip marina with electrical hook-ups and 20 moorings. Campers' gear is transported to campsites by park vehicle. Fishing off this beautiful haven is usually excellent. Also accessible for day use; swim beach, food concession, hiking trails, boat rentals.

Lake Carmi State Park (802-527-8383), exit 19 off I-89, 2 miles on Route 104; 1.5 miles north on Route 105; 3 miles north of Route 108, in Enosburg Falls. Set in rolling farmlands, the 482-acre park has 178 wooded campsites, including 35 lean-tos and some on the beach of this sizable lake; nature trails; boat ramp and rentals.

Wood's Island State Park (802-879-6565), 2 miles north of Burton Island. Primitive camping on an island of 125 acres. Five widely spaced campsites with no facilities; fires are not allowed. The island is unstaffed, although there are daily ranger patrols; reservations for campsites must be made through Burton Island State Park (see above). There is no public transportation to the island; the best boat access is from Kill Kare.

The Missisquoi National Wildlife Refuge (802-868-4781), on the river's delta, lies 2 miles west of Swanton on Route 78 to East Alburg and the islands. Habitats are about equally divided among brushland, timberland, and marsh, through which wind Black Creek and Maquam Creek Trails, adding up to about 1.5 miles or a 2-hour ramble; both are appropriately marked for the flora and fauna represented. It's open most of the time, but call ahead to confirm.

✷ Lodging

RESORT **The Tyler Place Family Resort** (802-868-4000), Box 901, Route 7, Highgate Springs 05460. Open late May through mid-September. One of the country's oldest and most popular family resorts continues to thrive on 165 acres of woods, meadows, and a mile of undeveloped lakeshore. At the height of the season, it is rather like a jolly, crowded cruise ship with a lively crew; its faithful partisans have been returning year after year for three generations of the Tyler family's management. (Mrs. T, the grande dame, passed away in 1996—she was over 90—but the tradition continues.) They provide just about every conceivable form of recreation for adults and children 2–17 years of age, with separate programs and dining for each group (special arrangements for infants). The children's recreation centers are exceptional.

There are heated indoor and outdoor swimming and wading pools, six tennis courts, and equipment for kayaking, fishing, and Windsurfing. Accommodations vary: the contemporary inn, plus 27 fireplaced cottages, a farm, and a guest house, a total of 58 cottages and family suites. Each unit has two or more bedrooms, air-conditioning, and a pantry or kitchen unit. The inn has a spacious dining room with good food, and a big lounge with bar. Call or write for rates, which range upward from $123 per adult per day from late June to early September; special rates for children; lower prices during the spring, early summer, and fall, plus learning retreats for the whole family.

FARM VACATION **Berkson Farms** (802-527-2522), Route 108 north, Enosburg Falls 05450. A mile north of the village, this 600-acre working dairy farm welcomes families year-round. The renovated, nicely maintained, 130-year-old farmhouse, managed by Dick and Joanne Keesler, can accommodate 8 to 10 people in four bedrooms, one of which has a private bath. There's a spacious living room and a library as well as a comfy family and game room with TV and

VCR. But the main attractions, especially for kids, are the cows, ducks, sheep, and goats, along with sugaring in-season. Cross-country skiing can be enjoyed, along with hayrides and local swimming holes, and there's golf at the nearby 18-hole Enosburg Falls Country Club (see *To Do—Golf*). Rates are $55–65 per couple, including a full breakfast. Dinner is available for $15 per adult, $10 per child. A weeklong vacation including three meals a day costs $330 per adult, $180 per child (ages 2–12). Well-behaved pets accepted.

BED & BREAKFASTS **Country Essence B&B** (802-868-4247; www.countryessence.com), RD 2, Box 95, Swanton 05488, 1.5 miles north of the village on Route 7. Armand and Cheryl Messier provide two pretty rooms with private bath, reached by a private staircase entrance in their 1850s homestead on 12 groomed acres. There's an in-ground swimming pool. $60–65 per room double occupancy with country breakfast. French is spoken.

Bayview B&B (802-524-5609), 860 Hathaway Point Road, St. Albans 05478. Located on Hathaway Point amid the colony of bayside cottages, this simple remodeled farmhouse with a nice screened-in porch has three rooms with shared bath at $50–65 per room. Continental breakfast. Weekly rates.

Wagner Road B&B (802-849-6030; 1-800-842-6030), 92 Fairfield Street, St. Albans 05478 (on Wagner Road, off Route 104, near Silver Lake). Gail and Ned Shulman's 1806 Cape Cod, located on 103 acres in Fairfax, has doubles at $60–70 with full breakfast; swimming pool in summer, cross-country trails in winter.

The Old Mill River Place (802-524-7211), Georgia Shore Road, St. Albans 05478, is a classic five-bay brick Federal built in 1799 as a wedding present for Sarah Allen Evarts, Ethan Allen's niece, occupied by the Neville and Bright families since 1926. There are three antiques-furnished rooms with private bath: Evarts has a lake view; Wheeler has twin cannonball low-post beds; Percival features a queen-sized four-poster and fireplace. $60–65 per double, including afternoon tea and generous country breakfast.

The Inn at Buck Hollow Farm (802-849-2400; www.buckhollow.com), 2150 Buck Hollow Road, Fairfax 05454, on Buck Hollow Road off Route 104, occupies a renovated 1790s carriage house on 400 spectacular acres. Each of the four rooms (with two shared bath) is decorated with antiques, queen-sized four-poster, and TV. Guests are encouraged to use the four-person outdoor hot tub and the heated pool; and children have a play area and can ride the pony. Rates range from $73 per room or $93 per night for one to three people in the suite; $103 for four, including full country breakfast.

Tetreault's Hillside View Farm (802-827-4480), 143 South Road, Fairfield 05455, is warm hospitable home in a quiet village. There's a fireplace in the family room, lots of antique furniture and braided rugs. French spoken. Rates $50–60 per double.

OTHER LODGING **Comfort Inn & Suites** (802-524-3300; 1-800-228-5150; www.vtcomfortinn.com), 167 Fairfax Road, Route 104, at exit 19 off I-89, St. Albans 05478. This new branch of the well-known chain has 63 guest rooms and suites, complimentary continental breakfast, indoor pool, and fitness room, at $60–130 with special rates for families, seniors, and business groups.

The Cadillac Motel (802-524-2191), 213 South Main Street, St. Albans 05478, is a pleasant cluster of 54 units surrounding a swimming pool, with minigolf, badminton, and a coffee shop in summer. $49–79 double.

♿ **Econo Lodge** (802-524-5956; 1-800-55-ECONO; www.econolodge.com), 287 South Main Street, St. Albans 05478, has a AAA rating and the look of a B&B. Rooms range $45–115 per night, and "senior-friendly" rooms are available.

CAMPGROUNDS See Burton Island State Park, Lake Carmi State Park, and Wood's Island State Park under *Green Space*.

Homestead Campground (802-524-2356), exit 18 off I-89 in Georgia, offers 160 shaded campsites with water and electric hook-up, laundry facilities, hot showers, cabin and camper rentals, a playground, and two swimming pools. The season is May 1 through October 15.

✷ Where to Eat

Jeff's Maine Seafood (802-524-6135), 65 North Main Street, St. Albans, obviously began as a fish shop and deli and has expanded into an attractive restaurant with specialties like pecan-crusted salmon ($16) and a New York strip steak with wild mushrooms ($18). Open for lunch and dinner Monday through Saturday. (This is one of the top chowder houses in the state.)

The Old Foundry Restaurant (802-524-9665), 3 Federal Street, St. Albans. Housed in one of the city's few 1840s buildings to have escaped the town's big 1895 fire, this is a great setting for traditional fare, like charbroiled rib steak and fillet mignon (both $14.95), fried seafood, and charbroiled salmon filet ($13.95).

Chow!Bella (802-524-1405), 28 North Main Street, St. Albans. An intimate wine bar with an eclectic menu, especially vegetarian dishes and fish. The atmosphere is welcoming and hospitable. Open for lunch and dinner daily except Sunday.

Simple Pleasures Cafe (802-527-0669), 84 North Main Street, St. Albans. Cappuccino, sandwiches, baked goods.

McGuel's Irish Burro (802-527-1276), 1820 Lake Street, St. Albans. The owners are Irish, and the food is Mexican. Prices are very reasonable: Combo platters run $8–11. Fajitas are a house specialty. The restaurant is open 11:30 AM –8 or 10 PM, depending on the day. The same menu is available in the pub.

Foothills Bakery (802-849-6601), 1123 Main Street, Fairfax. This bakery, housed in the old post office and much beloved by a local clientele, serves freshly baked muffins, scones, Danishes, cinnamon buns, and frittata early on, then sandwiches on fat slices of homemade bread. Open 6–6 except on Friday, when it closes at 4 PM.

Chester's in the Square (802-827-3974), Route 36, Fairfield. Chester's is named after Chester Arthur. Home-baked ham and turkey sandwiches, cream of celery soup, shepherd's pie, chowders, cookies, and all the comfort food you could ever want. Closed Sunday.

Uncle Sam's Restaurant (802-527-7340), 51 South Main Street, St. Albans. A bright, casual place serving breakfast all day, plus lunch and dinner.

My-T-Fine Creamery Restaurant (802-868-4616), 73 First Street, Swanton. Open daily for home-style breakfast, lunch, and dinner.

The Pines Restaurant (802-868-4819), Route 7, Swanton. A good place for family fare.

✷ Selective Shopping

Better Planet (802-524-6835), 44 North Main Street, St. Albans, is a bright place for books, toys, games, puzzles, hobby kits, and art supplies.

Richford Antique and Craft Center (802-848-3836), 66 Main Street, Richford. Open daily 10–5. Twenty rooms filled with antiques, crafts, and collectibles.

✷ Special Events

Early through mid-April: **Maple Sugar Festival,** St. Albans. For 3 days the town turns into a nearly nonstop "sugarin' off" party, courtesy of the local maple producers, augmented by arts and crafts and antiques shows and other events.

Last week of July: **Swanton Summer Festival**—parades, band concerts, square dancing, arts and crafts shows.

Mid-September: **Civil War Days** (802-524-2444), St. Albans. A lively weekend of encampments at Taylor Park, a tour of an Underground Railroad home, echoes of the 1864 Confederate Raid, parade, barbecue, music, and a crafts show.

Stowe Area and North of the Notch

5

STOWE AND WATERBURY

NORTH OF THE NOTCH AND THE LAMOILLE VALLEY

Kim Grant

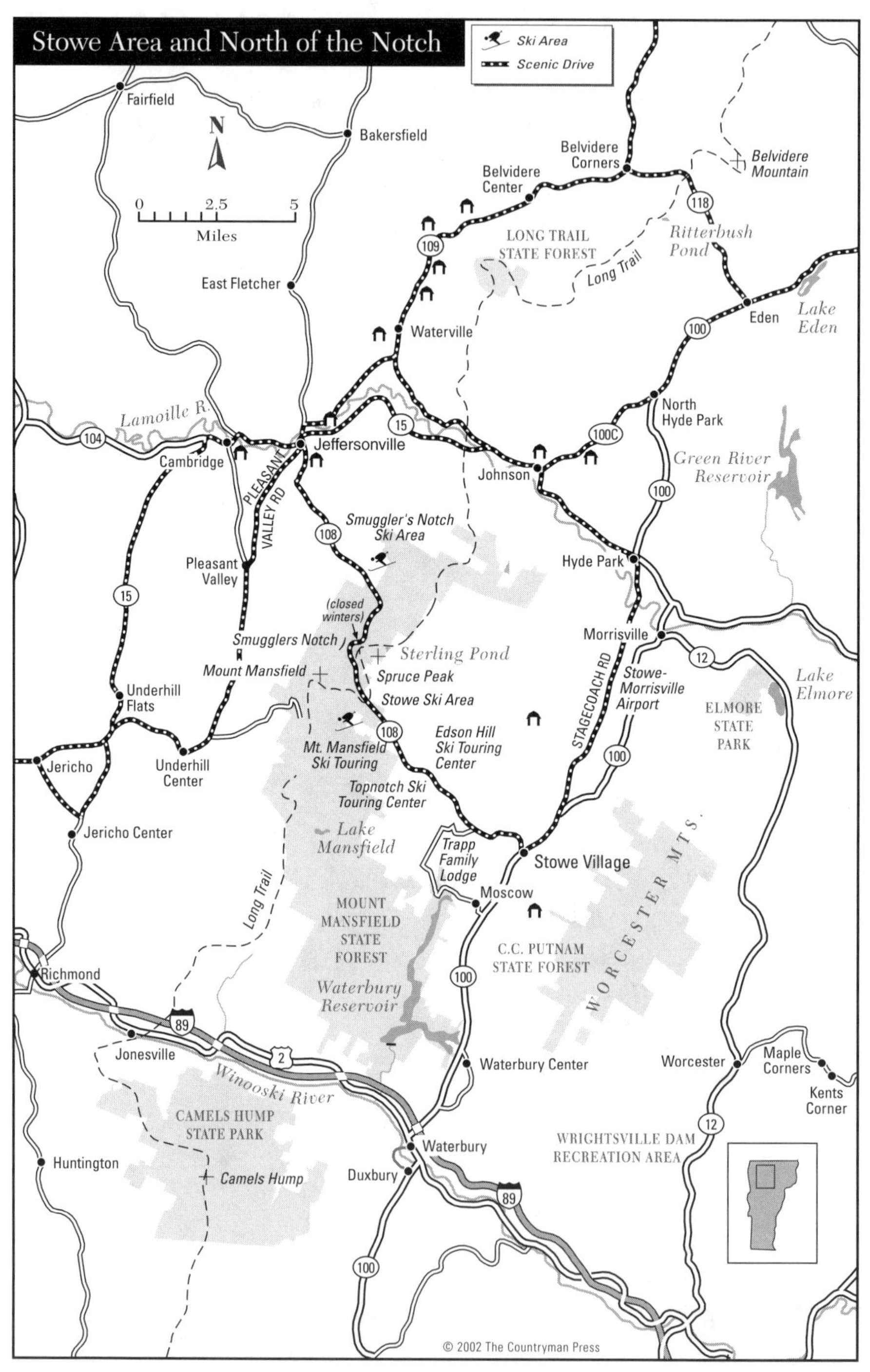
Stowe Area and North of the Notch
Ski Area
Scenic Drive
N
0 2.5 5
Miles
Fairfield
Bakersfield
East Fletcher
Belvidere Corners
Belvidere Center
Belvidere Mountain
LONG TRAIL STATE FOREST
Long Trail
Ritterbush Pond
Waterville
Eden
Lake Eden
Lamoille R.
Cambridge
Jeffersonville
Johnson
North Hyde Park
Green River Reservoir
PLEASANT VALLEY RD
Smuggler's Notch Ski Area
Pleasant Valley
Hyde Park
(closed winters)
Smugglers Notch
Mount Mansfield
Sterling Pond
Spruce Peak
Stowe Ski Area
Morrisville
Stowe-Morrisville Airport
STAGECOACH RD
Lake Elmore
ELMORE STATE PARK
Underhill Flats
Jericho
Underhill Center
Mt. Mansfield Ski Touring
Edson Hill Ski Touring Center
Topnotch Ski Touring Center
Jericho Center
Lake Mansfield
Trapp Family Lodge
Stowe Village
WORCESTER MTS.
Moscow
Long Trail
MOUNT MANSFIELD STATE FOREST
C.C. PUTNAM STATE FOREST
Richmond
Waterbury Reservoir
Jonesville
Winooski River
Waterbury Center
Worcester
Maple Corners
Kents Corner
CAMELS HUMP STATE PARK
Huntington
Camels Hump
Waterbury
Duxbury
WRIGHTSVILLE DAM RECREATION AREA
104
15
108
109
118
100
100C
12
89
2
© 2002 The Countryman Press

STOWE AND WATERBURY

Known as the "ski capital of the East," Stowe is the state's premier summer resort as well. A 200-year-old village that looks like a classic Vermont village should look, it's set against the massive backdrop of Mount Mansfield, which looks just like Vermont's highest mountain should look.

By the mid–19th century, men were already taxing their imaginations and funds to entice visitors up onto the heights of Mount Mansfield—which bears an uncanny resemblance to the upturned profile of a rather jowly man. In 1858 an inn was built under the Nose, a project that entailed constructing a 100-yard log trestle above a chasm and several miles of corduroy road made from hemlock. In Stowe Village at that time, a hotel, the Mansfield House, accommodated 600 guests.

Swedish families moved into Stowe in 1912 and began using their skis to get around. Then, in 1914, the Dartmouth College librarian skied down the Toll Road. Serious skiing, however, didn't begin until 1933, when the Civilian Conservation Corps cut a 4-mile-plus trail for just that purpose. The following year the town formed its own Mount Mansfield Ski Club, setting up basic lodging near the bottom of the ski trail in a former logging camp. By 1937, a rope tow had been rigged from the camp to the top of the trail, powered by a Cadillac engine. Lift tickets cost 50¢ per day, $5 per season.

While its name keeps changing, the Mount Mansfield Company (also known as Stowe Resort Co.) is still the same outfit formed in 1951 from the various small concerns that had evolved in the 1930s and '40s to serve skiers, and it's still owned by the same insurance company. The good news is continuity and an immense sense of pride and history. The bad news is a sometimes slow response to the demands of this quickly changing industry, although the company has become much more aggressive over the past decade.

What the "Mountain Company" does, it always does first-class. Just as it was a Cadillac engine (not the Ford used elsewhere) that first hauled Stowe skiers, the eight-passenger gondola, installed in 1991, is one of the world's fastest, and the Cliff House in the summit Octagon offers lunch complete with a view. On the other hand, a small '50s base lodge, expanded and renovated a couple of times, still serves the mountain's primary trail network—although not for long.

The Mountain Company is finally focusing on its most basic need: water. In the '90s it became painfully clear that natural snow in northern New England is too fickle a base for the huge business that skiing has become. Ski operators and skiers alike are not about to invest big bucks unless they can depend on snow, and to make snow you need water.

Stowe has won approval for its Master Plan that includes a village of 400 housing units at the base of Spruce Peak, along with a new Spruce base lodge, an 18-hole golf course, and a lift that will ferry skiers between Mansfield and Spruce across Route 108 without removing their skis. Also in the works are plans to expand the Mansfield base lodge, add two new lifts, and enlarge the Inn at the Mountain. The plan calls for all this to be accomplished over the next decade.

In the meantime, the quality of alpine skiing and snowboarding at Stowe remains high. The more than 150 km cross-country-ski network is outstanding, not only in its extent but also in its quality, thanks in good part to its elevation: Many trails meander off the high walls of the cul-de-sac in which the resort nestles, and you can usually count on snow on many miles of trail through April.

Stowe actually now attracts more visitors in summer and fall than it does in winter. From June through mid-October, it offers a superb golf course, tennis courts, theater, an alpine slide, and gondola rides to the top of the mountain, as well as hiking, biking, fishing, and special events every week of the summer and fall. Year-round it boasts more than 2,200 rooms, accommodating a total of 7,500 visitors on any given night. There are also more than 50 restaurants and 100 or so shops.

What's most amazing about Stowe is the way it has managed to keep its commercial side low-key and tasteful, a sideshow to the natural beauty of the place. Even in nonskiing months, most visitors are lured from their cars and onto their feet and bicycles, thanks to the 5.5-mile Stowe Recreation Path, which parallels the Mountain Road from the village (albeit at a more forgiving grade) to Mount Mansfield, through cornfields, wildflowers, and raspberry patches.

A CHURCH IN STOWE

Kim Grant

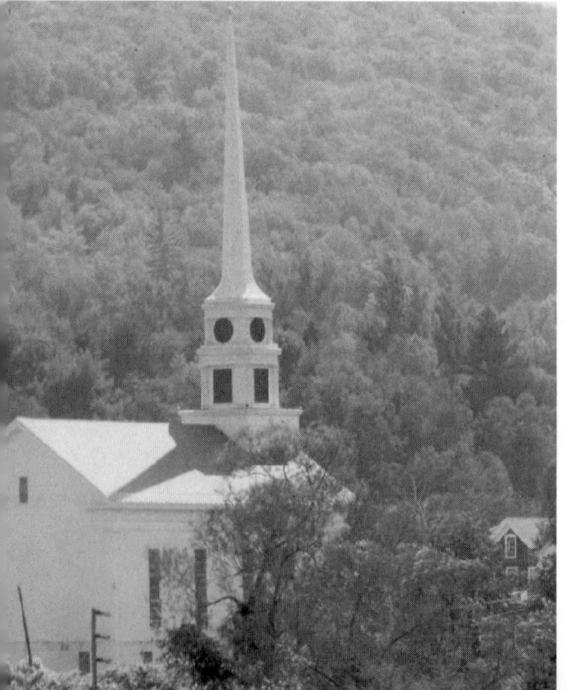

In warm-weather months, Stowe is also an excellent pivot from which to explore northern Vermont: 30 miles from Burlington, just over the Notch from the little-touristed Lamoille Valley, and a short drive from both Montpelier and Barre on the one hand and the Northeast Kingdom on the other. Lodging options range from funky to fabulous, including a number of self-contained resorts as well as inns, lodges, motels, and condominiums. The Stowe Area Association has been in business since 1936, matching visitors with lodgings they can afford and enjoy.

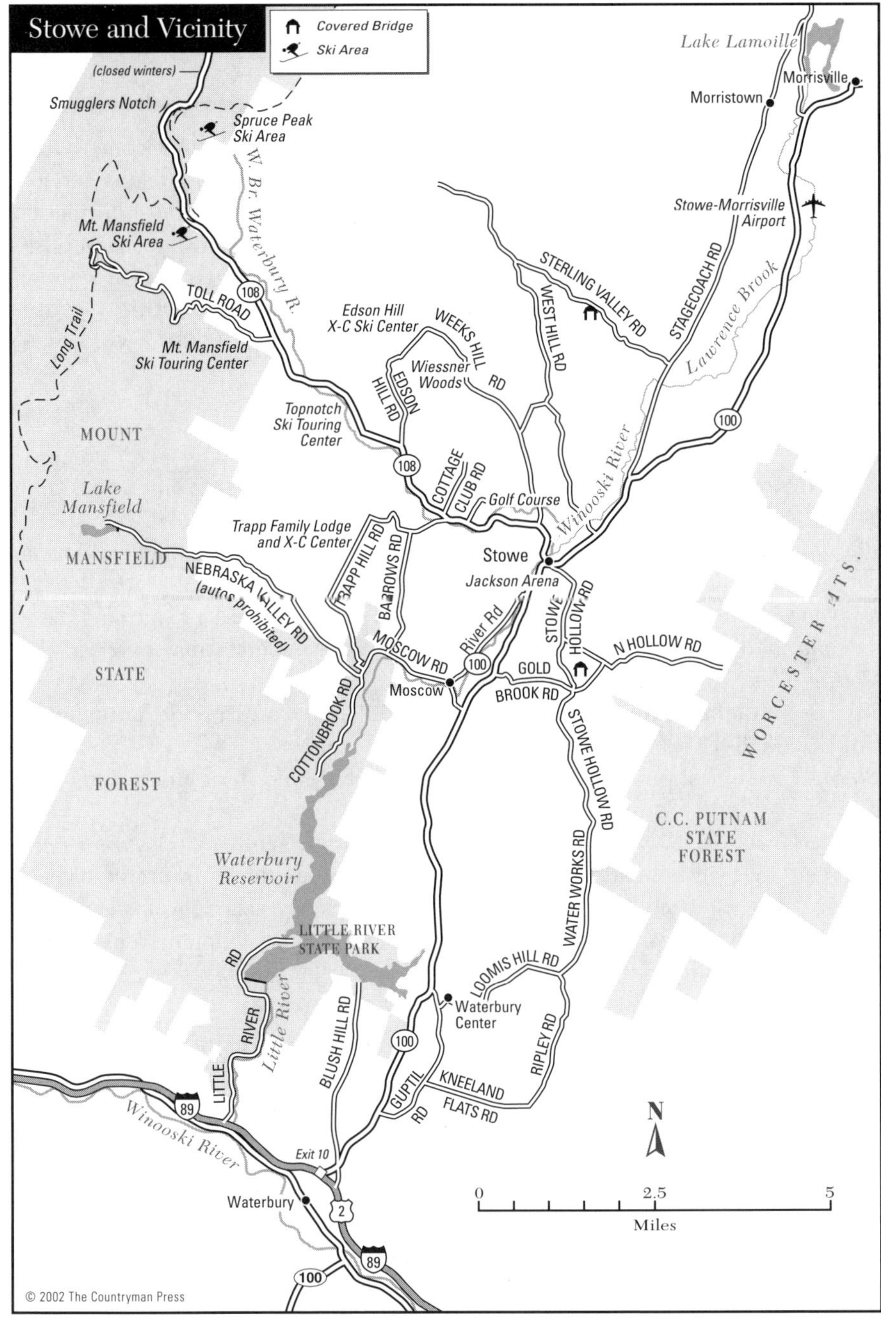

Most Stowe-bound visitors know Waterbury, 10 miles down Route 100, simply as an I-89 exit; they know the strip just to the north as the home of Ben & Jerry's ice cream factory, one of the state's most popular attractions. The old town itself lies along a southward bend in the Winooski River, and several interesting shops and restaurants are housed in the brief downtown between the traffic light and the railroad station. Waterbury Reservoir, accessible from Waterbury Center, is the obvious place in this area to swim and paddle a canoe or kayak.

GUIDANCE **The Stowe Area Association** (802-253-7321; for toll-free reservations: 1-800-247-8693; Box 1320, Stowe 05672; www.gostowe.com). Open daily November through March, 9–8; the rest of the year 9–5. This service, housed in its own building in the middle of Stowe Village, provides information on more than 60 local lodging places and will make reservations; it also publishes seasonal guides listing most things in the area and is a walk-in source of advice about what's going on. The **Stowe-Smuggler's Notch Region Marketing Organization** is another good source of information (1-877-247-8693; www.stowesmugglers.com).

GETTING THERE

By bus: **Vermont Transit/Greyhound** stops in Waterbury with connections from Boston, New York, and points south.
By train: **Amtrak** from Washington, D.C., New York City, and Springfield, Massachusetts, stops in Waterbury.
By plane: The Stowe-Morrisville Airport, 7 miles north, provides private plane services and charters. Burlington Airport, 34 miles away, is served by major carriers (see *Getting There* in "Burlington Region").
Taxi: **Peg's Pickup/Stowe Taxi** (1-800-370-9490), also **Countryside Transportation:** 802-888-5405.
By car: From most points, I-89 exit 10, and 15 minutes north on Route 100.

GETTING AROUND During winter season, the **Town Trolley** circles the 7 miles between the village and the mountain every 30 minutes; from the village, 7:30 AM–4:30 PM; from the mountain, 8 AM–5 PM. Pick up a schedule. Trolley tokens are $1, and 1-week passes cost $10. Tuesday and Thursday shopping runs to Morrisville are also offered; in summer inquire about trolley tours.

MEDICAL EMERGENCY Stowe Rescue Squad, police (**911**); Waterbury (**911**); **Copley Hospital** (802-888-4231), Morrisville.

✷ To See

Mount Mansfield, the highest point in Vermont—4,395 feet (it gained 2 feet when it was remeasured in 1998) at the Chin—yields a truly spectacular view, accessible primarily in summer, unless you can clamber up to the summit from the Cliff House restaurant at the top of the gondola over ice and snow. In summer there are two easy ways up: the Toll Road and an eight-passenger gondola.

The Toll Road (802-253-3000) begins 7 miles up Route 108 from the village of Stowe; look for the sign on the left just before the Inn at the Mountain (see *Lodging—Resorts*). Open late May through mid-October, weather permitting, 10–5. $14 per car and $8 per motorcycle in 2001, but raised annually; bikes and foot traffic, free. First laid in the mid–19th century, this steep, winding road led to a

AT THE BEN & JERRY'S ICE CREAM FACTORY IN WATERBURY

Kim Grant

hotel that served the public until 1957. (It was demolished in the mid-1960s.) The road also serves as a ski trail in winter. It terminates at the Mount Mansfield Summit Station, just below the Nose (4,062 feet). A half-mile Tundra Trail follows the Long Trail (red-and-white blazes on the rocks) north to Drift Rock (the trek should take 20 minutes); another mile along the trail brings you to the summit of Mount Mansfield (round trip: 2 hours).

The gondola (802-253-7311) at Stowe operates mid-June through mid-October, weather permitting, 9–5; $11 per adult; $7 per junior (6–12); $9 for seniors (65 and older); $29 for a family of four round-trip. The eight-passenger gondola runs from Midway Lodge to the Cliff House (see *Dining Out*); a half hour's trek brings you up to the Chin. However you get there, the view from the summit (the Chin) is spectacular on a clear day: west across 20 miles of farmland to Lake Champlain; east to the Worcester Range across the Stowe Valley; north to Jay Peak (35 miles distant) across the Lamoille Valley; and south, back along the Green Mountains, to Camels Hump. Mount Washington is visible to the east, Whiteface to the west.

Stowe Village. A classic, early-19th-century Vermont village with a spired white meetinghouse at one end of Main Street and a brick stagecoach inn at the other, a satisfying variety of stores and restaurants all within an easy stroll. The former wooden high school (one block up School Street from Main) is now the **Helen Day Art Center** (802-253-8358), open in summer daily noon–5 except Monday, closed Sunday too in winter. The changing art exhibits are frequently well worth checking out ($3 per adult, $1 seniors, and 50¢ students). The mid-19th-century Bloody Brook Schoolhouse next door is open on request in summer months.

Smugglers Notch is the high (elevation: 2,162 feet), extremely winding and narrow stretch of Route 108 just north of Mount Mansfield, with 1,000-foot cliffs towering on either side. The first carriage road through this pass wasn't opened until 1894, but the name reflects its heavy use as a route to smuggle cattle down from

Canada during the War of 1812. One of two formally designated State Scenic Roads in Vermont, Smugglers Notch is known for rock formations: Smugglers Head, Elephant Head, the Hunter and His Dog, the Big Spring, Smugglers Cave, and the Natural Refrigerator. The Notch is closed in winter, inviting cross-country skiing and snowshoeing. See also *To See* in the "North of the Notch" chapter.

Ben & Jerry's Ice Cream Factory Tours (802-882-1260), Route 100, take exit 10 off I-89, Waterbury. No American ice cream has a story, let alone a taste, to match that of the totally Vermont-made sweet and creamy stuff concocted by high school buddies Ben Cohen and Jerry Greenfield who have sold the company to Unilever. More than two decades ago, they began churning out Dastardly Mash and Heath Bar Crunch in a Burlington garage; they have now outgrown this seemingly mammoth plant, which has outstripped the Shelburne Museum (see *Museums* in "Burlington Region") as Vermont's number one attraction. A half-hour tour of the plant is offered all year, daily 10–5. The gift store, selling an amazing number of things relating to cows and Vermont, is open 10–6, as is the Scoop Shop. The tour includes a multimedia show, a look (from an observation platform) at the production room, and a free sample of one of the many "euphoric flavors." The grounds include picnic facilities and some sample black-and-white cows. $2 adults, children free.

COVERED BRIDGES The **Gold Brook Bridge** in Stowe Hollow, also known as Emily's Bridge because Emily is said to have taken her life from it (in different ways and for different reasons in the different stories) and reportedly returns to haunt it on occasion. There is another picturesque bridge across the Sterling Brook, off the Stagecoach Road, north of the village.

SCENIC DRIVES Not only is Stowe pleasantly situated for touring in all directions, but it is also organized to offer visitors well-researched printed tours. Pick up a copy of *Roads and Tours* from the **Stowe Area Association** (see *Guidance*). Don't fail to drive Smugglers Notch (see *To See*).

CYCLISTS ON THE STOWE RECREATION PATH

© Dennis Curran

✷ To Do

AIR RIDES For **hot-air ballooning,** inquire at Stoweflake Mountain Resort and Spa (802-253-7355; see *Lodging—Resorts*). Whitcomb Aviation, based at the Stowe-Morrisville State Airport (802-888-7845), offers **glider rides,** instruction, and rentals (see *Getting There*).

ALPINE SLIDE **Stowe's alpine slide**

(802-253-3500) is accessed from the Spruce Peak Base Lodge, Mountain Road, Stowe. Open late June to early September, 9:30–5. $9 per adult, $7 per junior or senior; discounts for five-ride packages.

BIKING The equipage here is a mountain bike, and the rental sources are the **Mountain Sports & Bike Shop** (802-253-7919), **AJ's Mountain Bikes** (802-253-4593; 1-800-226-6257), **Pinnacle Ski & Sports** (802-253-7222; 1-800-458-9996), **Stowe Action Outfitters** (802-253-7975), and **Topnotch Resort** (802-253-8585), all on the Mountain Road (Route 108) in Stowe. Neophytes usually head for the 5.5-mile **Stowe Recreation Path** (see *Hiking and Walking*); next there's a 10-mile loop through part of the Mount Mansfield State Forest (see *Green Space*) and into the Cottonbrook Basin. The **Mountain Sports & Bike Shop** and the **Inn at Turner Mill** (802-253-2062), both along the Mountain Road, offer mountain-biking tours. Pick up a copy of the *Mt. Mansfield/Stowe Area Biking Map/Guide* published by Map Adventures in Stowe (802-253-7489); it maps and describes 32 local mountain-bike trail and road rides.

BOATING Canoes can be rented from **Stowe Action Outfitters** (802-253-7975) and from **Umiak Outfitters** (802-253-2317), Stowe. Umiak also offers kayak rentals, lessons, and guided trips on the Winooksi and Lamoille Rivers, on Lake Champlain, and throughout the state.

CAMPING **Little River Camping Areas** (802-244-7103; 1-800-658-6934 is the off-season reservations number), Waterbury 05676. Six miles north of Waterbury on the Waterbury Reservoir: 64 campsites, including 6 lean-tos, swimming, hiking, rental boats, snowmobile trails in Little River State Park.

See also *Green Space* for information on camping in Smugglers Notch and Elmore State Park.

CARRIAGE RIDES **Edson Hill Manor, Golden Eagle Resort,** and **Stowehof Inn** in Stowe (see *Lodging—Resorts*) all offer carriage rides. **Charlie Horse Sleigh Rides at Topnotch** (802-253-2215) in Stowe offers carriage and wagon rides.

FISHING The Little River in Stowe is a favorite for brook trout, along with Sterling Pond on top of Spruce Peak and Sterling Brook. Contact **Reel Vermont** (802-223-1869), geared to guiding everyone (families included) from neophytes to pros. **Catamount Fishing Adventures** (802-253-8500), run by Willy Dietrich, is located in Stowe. It offers year-round guide service, including ice fishing. **Fly Fish Vermont** (802-253-3964; www.flyfishvt.com) is another Stowe resource.

GOLF **Stowe Country Club** (802-253-4893), an 18-hole course with a 40-acre driving range, putting green, restaurant, bar, pro shop, lessons; inquire about the Stowe Golf School. **Stoweflake Mountain Resort and Spa** (802-253-7355), adjacent to the Stowe Country Club, also offers instruction. The **Farm Resort** (802-888-3525), Route 100, 6 miles north of Stowe in Morrisville, offers nine holes and a driving range.

Blush Hill Country Club (802-244-8974), a nine-hole course in Waterbury, has marvelous views.

Country Club of Vermont (802-244-1800), Waterbury. This 18-hole course gets rave reviews.

HEALTH SPAS **The Stowe Athletic Club** (802-253-2541) at the Green Mountain Inn, the **Spa at Topnotch** (802-253-8585), **Golden Eagle Resort Motor Inn** (802-253-4811), and **Stoweflake Spa & Sports Club** (802-253-7355) all offer spa facilities. **Trapp Family Lodge** (802-253-8511) offers massage services. The **Stowe Gym** (802-253-2176) on the Mountain Road has state-of-the-art machines, aerobics and spinning classes, and more.

HIKING AND WALKING **Green Mountain Club (GMC)** (802-244-7037; www.greenmountainclub.org), a few miles south of Stowe Village on Route 100 in Waterbury Center, maintains a Hiker's Center stocked with hiking maps, guides, and gear. Inquire about workshops and special events.

Stowe Recreation Path is a 5.5-mile paved path that begins in Stowe Village behind the Community Church, winds up through cornfields, wildflowers, and raspberry patches, and parallels Mountain Road (but at a more forgiving pitch). It's open to walkers, joggers, bicyclists, etc. Note the **Quiet Path** along the Mayo River, a mile loop off the main path (it begins across from the Golden Eagle; see *Lodging—Resorts*) reserved for walkers (no mountain bikers or in-line skaters).

Mount Mansfield. See the introduction to this section and *To See* for a general description of Vermont's highest mountain. For walkers (as opposed to hikers), it's best to take the Toll Road or gondola up and follow the Tundra Trail (see *To See*). Serious hikers should at least purchase the weatherproof map of the Mount Mansfield region and can profit from the *Long Trail Guide,* both published by the Green Mountain Club. A naturalist is on hand May through November along the heavily traveled, 2.5-mile section of the Long Trail between the Forehead and the Chin; the Green Mountain Club maintains Butler Lodge, a half mile south of the Forehead, and Taft Lodge, below the Chin, as shelters for hikers.

Smugglers Notch. The Long Trail North, clearly marked, provides an easy, mile-plus hike to Sterling Pond, a beautiful spot at 3,000 feet, and fish-stocked, too. The Elephant's Head can be reached from the state picnic area on Route 108; a 2-mile trail leads to this landmark—from which you can also continue on to Sterling Pond and thence out to Route 108 only a couple of miles above the picnic area. No one should drive through Smugglers Notch without stopping to see the **Smugglers Cave** and to clamber around on the rocks.

Other local hikes are detailed in *Day Hikers Guide to Vermont,* which is published by the Green Mountain Club and available from the Stowe Area Association (see *Guidance*): **Belvidere Mountain** in Eden, a 3½-hour trek yielding good views in all directions; **Ritterbush Pond** and **Devil's Gulch,** also in Eden, about 2½ hours round-trip (see *Hiking* in "North of the Notch"); and **Elmore Mountain** in Elmore State Park (see *Green Space*), a 2- to 3-hour hike with spectacular views.

Camels Hump, from Waterbury. See "Burlington Region" for details. This trail is also detailed in *50 Hikes in Vermont* (Backcountry Publications). One trail starts from Crouching Lion Farm in Duxbury; it's a 6½-hour round-trip hike to the unspoiled summit of Vermont's third highest mountain. Pick up a map at the GMC Hiker's Center (see above).

Little River Trail System, Mount Mansfield State Forest, Waterbury. There are seven beautiful trails through the Ricker Basin and Cotton Brook area, once a settlement for 50 families who left behind cellar holes, stone fences, cemeteries, lilacs, and apple trees. Accessible from both Stowe and Waterbury. Pick up the self-guiding booklet from the Vermont State Department of Forests, Parks and Recreation in Waterbury (802-241-3678).

See also "Barre/Montpelier Area" chapter for hiking in the Worcester Range.

Note: The *Northern Vermont Hiking Trails Map/Guide* published by Map Adventures (802-253-7489) in Stowe is worth picking up.

HORSEBACK RIDING **Topnotch Stables** (802-253-8585), Mountain Road, Stowe, offers trail rides and carriage lessons. **Edson Hill Manor** (802-253-7371), Stowe (see *Lodging—Resorts*), gives private lessons, trail rides. Also **Stowehof Inn** (802-253-9722; see *Lodging—Resorts*), the **Mountain View Equestrian Center** (802-253-9901), and **Peterson Brook Farm** (802-253-9052), all in Stowe. **Wild Branch Trail Horse Adventures** (802-888-9233) does guided rides.

IN-LINE SKATING **Stowe-in-Line Skate Park** (802-253-3000) at the base of Spruce Peak features a speed oval, a half-pipe, freestyle ramps, and a timed downhill slalom course; $8 half day, $15 full day, less for children under 13. Rentals available.

ROCK CLIMBING Check with **Umiak Outfitters** (802-253-2317) in Stowe for instruction and ropes course.

SWIMMING **Waterbury Reservoir** is the obvious local beach. **Forest Pool** on Notchbrook Road, **Sterling Falls,** and the swimming holes in **Ranch Valley** are all worth checking; ask locally for directions. Many lodging places also have their own pools that nonguests may use for a fee.

TENNIS **The Racquet Club at Topnotch** (802-253-9308), Stowe. Four indoor and 11 outdoor courts, pro shop, instruction, videotape, 8 AM–11 PM.

Stowe Mountain Resort Tennis Courts (802-253-7311), six well-maintained clay courts adjacent to the Inn at the Mountain (see *Lodging—Resorts*), 8–6, available by the hour (dress: whites required).

Free public courts can be found at the town recreation area off School Street. A number of inns have courts available to the public; inquire at the Stowe Area Association (802-253-7321; see *Guidance*).

✷ Winter Sports

CROSS-COUNTRY SKIING A 150 km network of trails that connect ski centers in this area adds up to some of the best ski touring in New England. Given the high elevation of much of this terrain, the trails tend to have snow when few other areas do, and on windy, icy days, cross-country can be better in Stowe than downhill. All four touring centers (in Stowe) honor the others' trail tickets (if you ski, not drive, from one to the next).

Trapp Family Lodge Cross-Country Ski Center (802-253-8511). Located on the Trapp Hill Road, off by itself in the upper reaches of the valley, this is one of the oldest and most beautiful commercial trail systems—40 km of set trails and a total of 85 km of trails at elevations of 1,100–3,000 feet. The basic route here is up and up to a cabin in the woods, a source of homemade soups and chili. Start early enough in the day and you can continue along ridge trails or connect with the Mount Mansfield system. Lessons, equipment rental and sales, and outstanding pastries are all available, as well as guided tours.

Stowe Mountain Resort Cross-Country Center (802-253-3688), Mountain Road. Located near the Inn at the Mountain (see *Lodging—Resorts*), this center offers 35 km of set trails, plus 45 km of backcountry trails, at elevations of 1,200–2,800 feet. Trail fees are $12 adults, $6 for seniors. It's possible to take the Toll House lift partway up the Toll Road and ski down (a good place to practice telemarking). You can also take the quad close enough to the summit to enable you to climb to the very top (via the Toll Road) for a spectacular view out across Lake Champlain; the descent via the Toll Road is relatively easy. Another beautiful trail circles Sterling Pond high in the saddle between Spruce and Madonna Mountains (accessible via chairlift). Connecting trails link this system with the Trapp Family Lodge trails (see above) along some of Stowe's oldest ski trails, such as Ranch Camp and Steeple, dating to the 1920s, now backcountry trails winding along the curved inner face of the mountain.

Edson Hill Ski Touring Center (802-253-7371), Edson Hill Road. Relatively uncrowded on the uplands north of the Mountain Road, the area offers 30 miles of set trails, 25 more on outlying trails at elevations between 1,200 and 2,150 feet; instruction, rental, sales, full lunches, and guided tours available.

Topnotch Touring Center (802-253-8585), Mountain Road, Stowe. Novice to expert trails, a total of 25 km; instruction, rental, café, and restaurant available, also changing rooms.

Backcountry tours are offered by the **Stowe Mountain Resort** (802-253-3688) and **Trapp Family Lodge** (802-253-8511). *Remember:* Backcountry skiing is best done with a guide if you don't know the area.

DOWNHILL SKIING ✐ **Stowe Mountain Resort** (1-800-253-4SKI; www.stowe.com for information, snow reports and slopeside lodging). See the chapter introduction for the history and proposed future of the ski resort. The oldest section of the Mount Mansfield Base Lodge looks exactly as it did in the 1950s and continues to serve the mountain's primary trail network: the legendary expert Front Four trails that plunge down the mountain's face, and a half dozen intermediate trails that snake down its more forgiving slopes. A quad (wear a neck warmer and/or face mask) goes up to the 1940s-era Octagon. With the exception of Starr and Goat, which are too steep to cover or groom, most trails here are coated with man-made as well as natural snow, and conditions are usually fine. It's an easy traverse from this side of the mountain to the trails served by the gondola up to the Cliff House, from which long, ego-building runs like Perry Merrill sweep to the valley floor. Stowe regulars ski Mount Mansfield in the morning, switching after lunch to south-facing Spruce Peak across Route 108. Spruce Peak, with its Children's Adventure Center (connected by free shuttles every 20 minutes), serves as home to the ski school and children's programs, and several lifts access extensive novice trails. *Lifts:* Eight-passenger gondola, one high-speed quad chairlift, seven double and triple chairlifts, two surface. *Trails:* 48, also glade skiing; 25 percent expert, 59 percent intermediate, 16 percent beginner. *Vertical drop:* 2,360 feet on Mount Mansfield, 1,550 feet on Spruce Peak. *Snowmaking:* Covers 73 percent of the terrain trails served by 9 of the 11 lifts. *Facilities:* Eight restaurants, including those in the Inn at the Mountain (see *Lodging—Resorts*), three base lodges, plus the Octagon Web Cafe (you can send free e-mail postcards) and the Cliff House at the top of the busiest lifts; cafeterias, rentals, ski shops, shuttle bus. *Ski school:* 200 instructors; a lift especially designed for beginners at Spruce Peak, where novices learn to make the transition from easy to intermediate trails. *Night skiing:* More than 20 acres on Mount Mansfield are lighted Thursday through Saturday nights 5–9. *For children:* Daycare from 6 weeks in Cubs Infant Daycare. The Children's Learning Center offers daycare or a combo of care and lessons at Spruce Peak. *Rates:* $58 per adult midweek and weekend; $38 per child under 13 and seniors 65 and older; 5 and under free. Add $2 to the ticket price for holidays.

(*Note:* For downhill skiing at **Smugglers' Notch,** see "North of the Notch"; it is possible to ski back and forth between the two areas when the Spruce Chair is working.)

ICE CLIMBING See Expedition Stowe under *Special Events.* The **Inn at Turner Mill** (802-253-2062; see *Lodging—Inns*) offers ice climbing expeditions, led by the owner, an avid climber. Smugglers Notch itself is favored by ice climbers.

ICE SKATING Ice skating is available at the Olympic-sized **Jackson Arena** (802-253-4402) in the village. Call for public skating times. Rentals are $4.50 plus tax, and admission is $2.50 per person. There's also skating on the pond at **Commodores Inn** (802-253-7131; see *Lodging—Motels*).

SLEIGH RIDES In Stowe, sleigh rides are found at **Stoweflake Resort** (802-253-7355), **Stowehof Inn** (802-253-9722), **Edson Hill Manor** (802-253-7371, not Tuesday or Thursday), and **Trapp Family Lodge** (802-253-5813) (see *Lodging—Resorts*); **Mountain View Equestrian** (802-253-9901); and **Charlie Horse Sleigh Rides** (802-253-2215).

SNOWBOARD RENTALS **Misty Mountain Snowboards** (802-253-3040), top of the Mountain Road, Stowe. They advertise "the fastest snowboard rentals in town."

SNOWMOBILING **Stowe Snowmobile Tours** (802-253-6221) offers rentals and tours of the Mount Mansfield State Forest, and is also a source of information about local trails. **Smugglers' Notch Snowmobile Tours** (1-800-347-8266), based at Sterling Ridge Inn, on the other side of the Notch in Jeffersonville (see "North of the Notch"), also offers guided trips from the Stowe side.

SNOWSHOEING Tubbs, New England's leading snowshoe manufacturer, is located in Stowe but at this writing it offers no retail store or visitor outreach program. On the other hand, **Umiak Outdoor Outfitters** (802-253-2317) offers guided moonlit snowshoe tours, fondue dinner tours, and even a package tour at the Ben & Jerry's Factory in Waterbury so you can snowshoe before you eat the ice cream. **Trapp Family Lodge Cross-Country Ski Center** (see *Cross-Country Skiing*) has designated more than 15 km of its trails as snowshoe-only. The **Stowe Mountain Resort Cross-Country Center** (see *Cross-Country Skiing*) has cut 5 km of dedicated trails and permits snowshoers on all 80 km of its cross-country trails. **Topnotch at Stowe Resort** has also designated some snowshoe-recommended routes, and permits snowshoes on all 20 km of its trails.

The obvious place to go is, of course, up the unplowed stretch of Route 108 into Smugglers Notch (see *To See*), and the more adventurous can also access more than 40 miles of hiking terrain on and around Mount Mansfield, but it's best to check with the **Green Mountain Club** (see *Hiking and Walking*), which also sponsors a mid-February Snowshoe Festival (see *Special Events*). Local rental sources are plentiful. Pick up a copy of ***Northern Vermont Adventure Skiing,*** a weatherproof map/guide ($6.95 but worth the money) detailing trails throughout the region. It's available at Umiak and other local stores in Stowe.

✵ Green Space

For fees and reservation rules, see *Campgrounds* in "What's Where."

Mount Mansfield State Forest. The largest state forest in Vermont—27,436 acres—much of which lies on the other (western) flank of the mountain. The 10-mile Cottonbrook Trail starts at Cottonbrook Road off Nebraska Valley Road in Stowe. Follow the blazes.

Smugglers Notch State Park (802-253-4014), Stowe 05672; 10 miles up Mountain Road (Route 108) from Stowe Village, open mid-May through mid-October. Thirty-eight campsites, including 14 lean-tos. A few miles beyond the camping area, just beyond the highest point on this high, winding road—open only late May through November, weather permitting—is a turnoff with parking, toilet, and an information center. For details on the trails from this area, see *Hiking and Walking;* for background, see "North of the Notch."

Elmore State Park (802-888-2982), Lake Elmore 05657. Open mid-May through mid-October, 14 miles north of Stowe on Route 100, then east to Morrisville, south 5 miles on Route 12; 709 acres with a beach, bathhouse, rental boats, 64 sites for tents and trailers including 5 lean-tos, picnicking, hiking trail up Elmore Mountain.

Wiessner Woods. An 80-acre preserve with nature trails maintained by the Stowe Land Trust. The entrance is on Edson Hill Road, the next right after the entrance to Stowehof Inn (see *Lodging—Resorts*).

✷ Lodging

Most accommodations are found either in Stowe Village or along—or just off—the 7.2-mile Mountain Road (Route 108), which connects the village with the ski slopes. Unless otherwise noted, all are in Stowe 05672.

RESORTS ✐ ♿ **The Trapp Family Lodge** (802-253-8511; 1-800-826-7000; www.trappfamily.com), 700 Trapp Hill Road, is an alpine-modern version of the fabled Austrian schloss once owned by the family of *Sound of Music* fame. Johannes von Trapp lives nearby and remains involved in the property's day-to-day operations. The 73-room lodge with its 17-room luxury wing offers ample common space: a charming greenhouse sitting room, three common rooms with fireplaces, and a library, cocktail lounge, large dining room, and conference facilities. Twenty more rooms are in the motel-style Lower Lodge, and 100 guest house time-share units (inquire about vacancies) are ranged in tiers on the slope below, commanding sweeping views of the Worcester Range. The inn's 2,700 acres are webbed with cross-country-ski trails, also good for splendid walks. There are tennis courts and a spring-fed pool as well as an indoor pool, sauna, and workout room in the Sports Center. Come in late March (when the sugarhouse is operating and the sun is warm but there is still snow on the high and wooded trails) or in early December (when there is usually snow), and you can pay $98 for the same room that costs $180 (per couple) during foliage season. A 3-day minimum is mandatory in peak periods like foliage and Christmas. Inquire about family packages (children 16 and under stay free), and about nature walks, snowshoeing, sleigh rides, and children's, exercise, and cross-country-ski programs. $98–283 EP; the suites and Maria's own former quarters (the von Trapp Suite) go for $295–645 EP.

Edson Hill Manor (802-253-7371; 1-800-621-0284), 1500 Edson Hill Road. Set on 225 cultivated acres on a high slope, the manor was built in the 1940s with brick from the old Sherwood Hotel of Burlington. Most of the living room beams were hewn for Ira and Ethan Allen's barn, which stood in North Burlington for more than a century. In the inn itself, the nine guest rooms are each very individual, most with wood-burning fireplaces and hand-painted mural in the bath. The honeymoon suite with a view over the gardens is Room 3, and Room 5 has gables, a canopy bed, and the same view. Four carriage houses, each with three or four units, are ranged in tiers behind the main house; these have knotty-pine walls, wing chairs and reproduction antiques, fireplaces, sitting areas, books, and a comfortable, spacious, in-the-woods feel. Under the ownership of William O'Neill and family, the small dining room has acquired an enviable reputation (see *Dining Out*). Living rooms are furnished in genuine antiques, hung with exceptional art. Facilities include a stable and trails for horseback riding, outdoor pool, stocked trout pond, and 40 km of cross-country trails. Rates are $110–210 per couple B&B; MAP and multiday packages available, more expensive during foliage season; add 15 percent for service.

Green Mountain Inn (802-253-7301; 1-800-253-7302), 18 Main Street. The brick-and-clapboard face of this landmark dates back to 1833, when it was built as a private home. In the 1850s it became a hotel, and it last changed ownership in 1982, when it was acquired by a Canadian, Marvin Gameroff, who has since tastefully renovated the rooms in the inn itself, outfitting them with country furniture especially made for the inn, adding niceties like salt-glaze stoneware lamps and appealing art. Public spaces have also been tastefully redecorated, settings for the collection of striking watercolors of local scenes by Walton Blodgett. The Clubhouse rooms, each with queen-sized four-poster, fireplace, VCR, and Jacuzzi, have been added in landscaped grounds beyond the swimming pool, a couple also with fully equipped kitchens. The 15-room Annex Building has been renovated, too. The dining options: a formal Main Street Dining Room, and the downstairs Whip Bar & Grill, which offers a poolside patio in summer and a fire in colder months (see *Eating Out*). Afternoon tea and cookies are served in the living room. $99–289 per room in winter and summer (2-night minimum stay on weekends), less in the off-season. The suites and efficiencies are more. Guests enjoy complimentary use of Athletic Club facilities, located just the other side of the pool.

Inn at the Mountain and Condominiums (802-253-7311; 1-800-253-4754), Mountain Road. The Mount Mansfield Company's luxurious 34-room lodge, also a number of town houses, and truly luxurious one-, two-, and three-bedroom Mountain Club condominiums, are currently the closest lodging to the lifts. Facilities include H. H. Bingham's restaurant, clay tennis courts, swimming pools, and the Toll House Health Spa. From $129–199 EP per room in the inn to $199–529 for a three-bedroom, three-bath condo sleeping up to eight people comfortably (children under 12 stay free). Less through numerous packages.

Stowehof Inn (802-253-9722; 1-800-932-7136), 2 miles off Route 108. A fantasy world from the moment you step through its sod-roofed porte cochère, supported by two maple trees. No two of the 44 guest rooms are alike (some suites, a few fireplaced demisuites with optional kitchenette). The public rooms are quixotically furnished with mementos, like the divining rod that located the water source for the building. Windows everywhere let in the view. Facilities include a taproom, a dining room known for nouvelle French dishes (see *Dining Out*), tennis courts, a putting range, a pool with a view, a sauna, and cross-country-ski trails connecting with the larger network. The Stowehof specializes in weddings. On the adjacent working farm, guests can see cattle and ride horses. Rates are $103–225 per couple B&B.

Topnotch at Stowe Resort (802-253-8585; 1-800-451-8686; www.topnotch-resort.com), P.O. Box 1458, Mountain Road. Uncommonly comfortable rooms, luxurious areas for lounging, the convivial Buttertub Bistro, and the stately, glass-sided, highly rated main dining room at Maxwell's. The health-and-fitness spa (see *To Do—Health Spas*) offers a program as well as superb facilities, including an indoor pool with a waterfall. Contemporary sculpture surrounds the outdoor swimming pool. A red barn down across the Mountain Road serves as a cross-country-ski center in winter (50 km of groomed trails that connect with other trail systems in Stowe); riding stable, indoor and outdoor tennis courts, and a handy skating rink.

Rates begin at $170 for a double room, run $276–576 for a suite, and town houses are $275–555 per unit. Rates include use of the pool and Jacuzzi; the exercise program is $15 extra. A $52 MAP plan is offered; inquire about spa packages. Pets welcome.

♿ **Golden Eagle Resort Motor Inn** (802-253-4811; 1-800-626-1010), 511 Mountain Road. The 12-unit motel that Herb and Ann Hillman bought in 1963 has evolved through two generations into an amazing 60-acre complex with 76 rooms, 11 efficiencies, 4 condos, 1 guest house, and two apartments. Family geared as well as owned, it offers a lot for children. In summer, there's a formal hiking and crafts program on selected days for 3- to 12-year-olds, and on certain nights, year-round, there are movies with popcorn. Amenities include a playground as well as an attractive health spa with indoor pool, large whirlpool, sauna, Universal exercise equipment, massage service, and exercise classes (see *To Do—Health Spas*). There are also outdoor heated pools (swimming lessons are offered); a clay tennis court; fish-stocked ponds; shuffleboard, badminton, lawn games, and game rooms; and a coffee shop and restaurants. Throughout, you have the sense of a well-run resort. A 50-acre wildlife area with walking trails adjoins the property. Breakfast is included in $99–209 per room; fully handicapped-accessible rooms; also shuttle service to the Amtrak station.

Stoweflake Mountain Resort & Spa (802-253-7355; 1-800-253-2232; www.stoweflake.com), Mountain Road. The small ski lodge that the Baraw family opened more than 30 years ago has mushroomed into a full-facility, 94-room resort (including 40 new luxury suites) and 36 town houses. There are bright, comfortable, inn-style rooms in the original lodge and many nicely furnished motel rooms (besides its own motel wing, the resort includes the former Nordic Motor Inn). All rooms have cable TV, phone, and private bath, and common space includes a library and lobby with fireplaces and sitting area, along with a large living room with a sunken fireplace. The Spa & Sports Club includes a Cybex Circuit, racquetball/squash court, indoor pool, Jacuzzi, sauna, and steam and massage rooms. There are also tennis courts, badminton, volleyball, croquet, horseshoes, and a professional putting green and driving ranges. The links at the Stowe Country Club adjoin the property (see *To Do—Golf*). Dining options include Winfield's Bistro and the pubby Charlie B's. $150–280 per room or suite; $320–850 for townhouse units; MAP rates and many packages.

INNS AND BED & BREAKFASTS ♿ **The Gables Inn** (802-253-7730; 1-800-GABLES1; www.gablesinn.com), 1457 Mountain Road. Randy Stern and Annette Monachelli are warm, personable hosts who have created one of Stowe's most relaxing and welcoming inns. Common rooms include a comfortable living room with fireplace, a plant-filled solarium, and a downstairs game room/lounge (BYOB). There's a swimming pool on the landscaped grounds, which angle off from Mountain Road, across from an open stretch of the Stowe Recreation Path (see *To Do—Hiking and Walking*). The hot tub is right outside the door, the better to hop into in winter. Each of the 12 rooms (all with private bath) in the main house is different. Four in the Carriage House (handicapped-accessible) feature whirlpool and fireplace; the two Riverview suites in the neighboring house across the brook have a fridge, microwave, and coffeemaker, as well as a fireplace and double Jacuzzi. After skiing, there is always Brie and crackers or a pot of cheese fondue in the den; dinner at 6:30 (by reservation) is candlelit. The famously good breakfasts are also open to the public and generally considered the best in town (see *Eating Out*). Rates are $110–235 B&B in high season, $78–165 in low season; dinner is optional.

Stone Hill Inn (802-253-6282), 89 Houston Farm Road (off Route 108), Stowe 05672. A luxury bed & breakfast run by Amy and Hap Jordan. Nine guest rooms all have two-person Jacuzzi, comfy king-sized beds, and gas fireplace. Hap cooks breakfast, which is taken in a sunny room overlooking woods and fields. $250–375 per room, depending on the season.

Three Bears at the Fountain (802-253-7671; 1-800-898-9634; www.three-bearsbandb.com), Route 100 north. Suzanne and Stephen Vazzano run this wonderful old farmhouse and converted barn as a bed & breakfast. Notice the fountain out front. Rates $100–200 per room.

Fiddler's Green Inn (802-253-8124; 1-800-882-5346; www.FiddlersGreenInn.com), 4859 Mountain Road, 5 miles from the village toward the mountain. Less than a mile from the lifts, this pleasant, yellow, 1820s farmhouse can sleep no more than 18 guests (making it great for small groups) in seven comfortable guest rooms tucked under the eaves. Guests gather around the fieldstone hearth in the living room and at the long table off the sunny kitchen. BYOB. Hammocking or hiking and skiing, depending on the season, are close by. In summer and winter longtime owners Bud and Carol McKeon cater to bicyclists and cross-country skiers. Room rates are $60–125 B&B; dinner possible on request. Families welcome.

The Inn at Turner Mill (802-253-2062; 1-800-992-0016), 56 Turner Mill Lane. Sequestered in the pines by Notch Brook, off Mountain Road just a mile from the lifts, this complex was splendidly built in the 1930s by a woman doctor. Its 10 wooded acres include a mountain stream and "refreshing" swimming hole; there's also an outdoor pool. The family-geared efficiencies and apartments are nicely decorated, with cable TV, some with hearth, access to sauna, Jacuzzi, and cross-country trails. Greg and Mitzi Speer are friendly hosts who can find a baby-sitter and help with transfers from Burlington or Waterbury. Mitzi is a justice of the peace. Greg's passions are hiking and biking, cross-country skiing, snowshoeing, and ice climbing and he offers guided tours. (He also frequently just accompanies guests.) Snowshoe rentals are available, and guests get a half day free. When it was built, this was as high as a car could drive up the Mountain Road, and the Civilian Conservation Corps ski trails (now cross-country-ski trails) are within easy striking distance. Rates: $60–110 per couple in low, and $115–280 in high season. Breakfast is served in summer only.

Ski Inn (802-253-4050), 5037 Mountain Road. Harriette Heyer has been welcoming guests to Stowe's oldest ski lodge—one of the handiest places to the lifts—since Pearl Harbor Day, and she specializes in solo travelers. Designed as a ski lodge, the inn is set back from the Mountain Road amid hemlocks and evergreens. The 10 guest rooms are bright and meticulously clean, each with both a double and a single bed; shared and private baths. There is a pine-paneled BYOB bar and attractive sitting and dining rooms. Stowe's cross-country network can be accessed from the back door. $55–65 per person MAP (dinners are hearty) in winter; $55–65 per room with continental breakfast in summer.

Brass Lantern Inn (802-253-2229; 1-800-729-2980; www.brasslanterninn.com), 717 Maple Street (Route 100), is a welcoming B&B at the northern edge of the village. Your host is Andy Aldrich, a Vermonter raised on a Richmond dairy farm, a builder of prizewinning homes. His work is evident in this nicely renovated 1800s building, with its planked floors and comfortable common rooms. The nine stenciled or papered guest rooms are furnished with antiques and handstitched quilts; all have private bath, some have whirlpool tub, some a wood-burning fireplace. A small pub and porch are for guests only. Guests enjoy gym privileges at the Stowe Athletic Club (see *To Do—Health Spas*). Breakfast is a serious affair, maybe sourdough French toast, apple crêpes, or broccoli and mushroom quiche. $80–130 in low season, $90–165 in regular, and $100–225 per couple in high season. Small weddings are a specialty.

Auberge de Stowe (802-253-7787; 1-800-387-8789; www.aubergedestowe.com), 692 South Main Street. This 18th-century brick farmhouse and converted carriage house (it was the Bittersweet Inn) is a find. Shawn and Chantal Kerivan offer eight rooms, including one suite, six with private bath. The house is right on Route 100 along the river, but there is a view and a sense of space in the back. Amenities include a comfortable living room, a game room with BYOB bar, a good-sized swimming pool, a large lawn, and a hot tub. Rates, which are less than $100 per room, include a substantial continental breakfast with homemade pastries. The owners speak both German and French.

♿ **Ten Acres Lodge** (802-253-7638; 1-800-327-7357), 14 Barrows Road. This 1840s red-clapboard inn has a luxurious feel and a reputation for fine dining. We recommend the suites with fireplace, sitting area, and a balcony in Hill House Suite, a newish complex up behind the old inn. Many of the rooms have been completely refurbished. The two cottages, one with two and the other with three bedrooms, and with kitchen and fireplace, are also exceptional. The grounds include a pool, tennis court, and hot tub. Doubles are $115–440.

Ye Olde England Inn (802-253-7558; 1-800-477-3771; www.englandinn.com), 433 Mountain Road. Anglophiles can revel in the English accent, decor, and menu. The rooms are unabashedly luxurious, from the 17 Laura Ashley–style rooms in the inn to the two 2-bedroom English "cottages" beside the swimming pool (each with fireplace, Jacuzzi, and kitchen). There are 10 suites on a rise behind the inn, each with a four-poster bed, Jacuzzi, deck, and lounge with a fireplace, wet bar, fridge, and microwave. A full English breakfast and tea are included in $99–395 rates, except in the cottages.

Mr. Pickwick's Pub & Restaurant serves lunch and dinner (see *Eating Out*). The extravagant breakfasts are served in Copperfield's, the inn's other dining room.

Foxfire Inn (802-253-4887), 1606 Pucker Street Route 100 north of Stowe Village. This early-19th-century farmhouse is set on 70 wooded hillside acres. The five guest rooms have wide-board floors (several have exposed beams) and are furnished with antiques, each with private bath. Downstairs there is plenty of space for guests away from the large, public dining room, well respected for its Italian fare (see *Dining Out*). $65–115 per double room includes a full breakfast served in the garden room.

Commodores Inn (802-253-7131; 1-800-44-STOWE; www.commodoresinn.com), P.O. Box 970, Route 100 south. Megan Goss runs this establishment with 72 large rooms, all with private bath (request one in the back, overlooking the lake). There's a living room with a fireplace; also two Jacuzzis and saunas and an outdoor pool. The Stowe Yacht Club Steakhouse and Sport Lounge (a popular watering hole and spot for an evening burger) overlooks a 3-acre lake on which model sailboat races are regularly held. $78–162 per person in winter; less in summer and multidays year-round. Breakfast is included.

In Waterbury 05676

The Inn at Blush Hill (802-244-7529; 1-800-736-7522; www.blushhill.com), 784 Blush Hill Road, off Route 100, hidden away on 5 hilltop acres with spectacular views across the valley and reservoir (good for boating and swimming). All five rooms have private bath, one has a fireplace, another has a 15-foot-wide view of the mountains, and a third, a Jacuzzi bath. The handsome, wine-red, gabled cape dates to 1790, and the living room has that nice snug feel (there's a vintage-1840 hearth and an oak armoire that opens into an entertainment center). Country breakfasts are served on an old farmhand's table in the sunny, many-windowed kitchen. Your hostess is Pam Gosselin. $85–160 per couple includes a full breakfast and evening refreshments.

The Old Stagecoach Inn (802-244-5056; 1-800-262-2206), 18 North Main Street. A classic stagecoach inn built in 1826 with a triple-tiered porch but substantially altered in the 1880s, when a millionaire from Ohio added oak woodwork, ornate fireplaces, and stained glass. Renovated in 1987, the inn is run by John and Jack Barwick. There are eight guest rooms and three efficiency suites, all tastefully furnished but varying widely—from a queen-bedded room with a sitting area, fireplace, and private bath to small rooms with a shared bath. Two efficiency suites are studios; the other has two bedrooms and a sitting area. Many of the rooms are large enough to accommodate families. Coco, the African gray parrot, sits by the fireplace in the living room adjoining the library, with its fully licensed bar. Regular-season rates are $55–120 per room; foliage season and winter holidays $60–180. A full breakfast, including a selection of hot dishes, is included. Pets possible.

Grünberg Haus (802-244-7726; 1-800-800-7760; www.grunberghaus.com), 94 Pine Street, Route 100 south of Waterbury. This secluded, Tyrolean-style chalet has 11 guest rooms, 5 with private bath, and three cabins. (The cabins are open from May through October.) Innkeepers Jeff and Linda

Connor serve a full breakfast of homemade breads and baked goods, a fresh-fruit creation, and a main dish such as ricotta-stuffed French toast. Facilities include a garden deck with a warm-weather Jacuzzi and self-serve pub and game room. Hiking and snowshoe trails behind the inn feed into a 20 km cross-country trail system. The dark-wood-beamed common rooms include a large fieldstone fireplace. In winter, the inn offers discounts at Stowe, Sugarbush, Bolton, and Mad River Glen (all within easy striking distance) and keeps four sets of snowshoes on hand. Rates are $66–115 or from $375 a week in low season, $101–175 in high. Dog in residence.

In Waterbury Center 05677

♿ **The Black Locust Inn** (802-244-7490; 1-800-366-5592; www.blacklocustinn.com), 5088 Waterbury/Stowe Road (Route 100). This is an 1832 three-gabled home with six rooms that have private bath, polished wood floors, and stained-glass transoms. One king-bedded room is handicapped-accessible. Len, Nancy, and Valerie Vignole (assisted by golden retriever Lady) get great reviews for hospitality. $119–235 includes three-course breakfasts and afternoon appetizers.

MOTELS

In Stowe 05672

Buccaneer Country Lodge (802-253-4772; 1-800-543-1293; www.buccaneerlodge.com), 3214 Mountain Road. This is the former home of Olympian Billy Kidd. Karen and Rod Zbikowski offer 12 rooms and suites, all with private bath, recently renovated and furnished in antiques, equipped with TV and a small fridge. Two rooms have fully equipped kitchens; four have a fireplace, and two come with two-person whirlpool tub. Common space includes a game room, pool table, and outdoor pool and Jacuzzi. Amenities include two fieldstone fireplaces, spectacular views of Mount Mansfield, and English gardens in summer. $65–299 per room with full breakfast.

Alpenrose (802-253-7277; 1-800-962-7002), 2619 Mountain Road. A pleasant, small motel with just two rooms, three efficiencies with kitchenettes; direct access to cross-country network and the Stowe Rec Path. $60–68 per room in winter.

In Waterbury 05676

Holiday Inn (802-244-7822; 1-800-HOLIDAY), 45 Blush Hill Road, exit 10 north, I-89. There are 79 rooms with private bath and a restaurant serving three meals. Amenities include an indoor pool, tennis court, and sauna. Positioned just off the interstate, this is a popular waystop with family-geared rates and access to Sugarbush as well as Stowe. The activity center features sauna and hot tub, high-end weight and aerobic equipment. $89–179 per couple; many family-sized rooms; no meals included.

CONDOMINIUMS **Stowe Country Rentals** (802-253-8132; 1-800-639-1990; www.stowecountryrentals.com) handles condos and houses. **Country Village Rentals** (802-253-8777; 1-800-320-8777; www.cvrandr.com) specializes in upscale homes, both old and new. **All Seasons Rentals** (802-253-7353; 1-800-54-STOWE; www.stowe rentals.com), **Blue Heron Rentals** (802-253-7791; 1-800-42-HERON; www.blueheronrentals.com), and **Rentals at Stowe** (802-253-9786; 1-800-848-9120, ext. 624; www.rentalsatstowe.com) also rent homes and condos.

The Village Green at Stowe (802-253-9705; 1-800-451-3297), 1003 Cape Cod Road, Stowe 05672. Seven nicely designed buildings set on 40 acres (surrounded by the Stowe Country Club links; see *To Do—Golf*) contain 73 two- and three-bedroom town houses, all brightly furnished. A recreation building has a heated indoor pool, Jacuzzi, sauna, game and changing rooms; also an outdoor pool and two tennis courts. Winter rates excluding holidays begin at $280–375 per night for a two-bedroom unit with a minimum of 2 nights; less for additional nights. $235–310 per night in summer, more for three-bedroom units; weekly rates.

🐾 **Notch Brook Condominiums** (802-253-4882; 1-800-253-4882), 1229 Notch Brook Road, Stowe, 05672. In the shadow of Spruce Peak with a spectacular view of Mount Mansfield, an unusually well-built (though no one seems to know why Vermont architect Robert Burley designed them with flat roofs) complex of 36 rooms and 35 condominiums ranging from doubles through three-bedroom town houses. Most rooms are available by the day and week. Amenities include saunas, tennis, an outdoor pool that's heated for winter use, and complimentary continental breakfast. $80–325 per unit in winter, less in summer; more in peak holiday periods.

1836 Cabins (802-244-8533), Box 128, Waterbury Center 05677, are tucked into a pine forest whose logging roads become cross-country-ski trails in winter. Completely furnished one- and two-bedroom units with kitchen, TV; telephone on request. Rates $99 for two, standard; $139 for deluxe (gas fireplaces); more over holidays.

DORMS 🏵 **Round Hearth at Stowe** (802-253-7223), 39 Edson Hill Road, Stowe 05672. A dormitory-style operation, complete with chaperones and all sorts of amenities for teen groups, such as DJ dances on Saturday nights, outdoor hot tubs, and large-screen TVs. Merry and Grady Vigneau do everything from winter ski trips to summer sports camps and basket-making workshops. They also own and operate the **Red Fox Alpine Lodge at Smugglers Notch.** Call for group rates.

CAMPGROUNDS See *Green Space* for information on campgrounds in Smugglers Notch.

✷ Where to Eat

DINING OUT **Blue Moon Cafe** (802-253-7006), 35 School Street, Stowe. Open for dinner daily. A very small, candlelit bistro with a huge reputation. Former Ten Acres Lodge chef Jack Pickett prepares "contemporary American" dishes. The menu changes weekly but you might begin with a trio of smoked fish with blini, capers, and crème fraîche ($8) or Tuscan bread soup ($5.50), then dine on braised Glover rabbit with foraged mushrooms and grilled polenta ($22) or miso-poached salmon with wasabi mashed potatoes ($19.25). Dinner for two with wine is about $90.

Ten Acres Lodge (802-253-7638), Luce Hill Road, Stowe. Chef Matt Larson has taken over the dining room, producing a varied, seasonal menu that changes frequently. Recent offerings included a winter minestrone with arugula pesto ($7) or seared sea scallops with a citrus and roasted fennel salad ($11). And those were only the appetizers! Entrées impressed us with their creativity: honey-soy-glazed quail with roasted sweet potato puree ($23) and forest mushroom ravioli with oven-dried tomatoes and braised greens ($18). The wine cellar is extensive and the bar is open all the time.

Cliff House (802-253-3665), in the Octagon at Mount Mansfield's summit. Dinner is a thing of the past, but lunch is served 11–3 each day. It's impossible to beat the view, and where else would you go out to lunch via a gondola? You might begin with a cup of Atlantic lobster bisque ($5.95) or baked Brie in pastry ($8.95). Winter warmers include a lamb stew ($12.95) or shepherd's pie ($11.95).

Edson Hill Manor (802-253-7371), 1500 Edson Hill Road, Stowe. Open for dinner nightly in-season; reservations required. The small, gracious dining room at this low-key resort has soared to the top of local restaurant ratings. The menu changes daily. The appetizer menu ($9–11) might feature smoked duck French toast and Cajun paella. Entrées ($19–24) might be bacon-roasted Chilean sea bass, seared rare tuna loin, or roast rack of New Zealand lamb.

Isle de France (802-253-7751), 1899 Mountain Road, Stowe. Open for dinner nightly except Monday. A classic French restaurant in the grand manner, with a formal dining room worthy of a Ritz. You might begin with escargots ($8.50) and dine on entrecôte béarnaise ($22.50). **Claudine's Bistro** offers less formal and expensive options, with entrées from $12.75.

Foxfire Inn and Italian Restaurant (802-253-4887), Route 100, north of Stowe Village. Dinner nightly. Favored by local residents for a predictably good night out. The setting is a 1850s country farmhouse, and the menu is large. You might begin with rolled eggplant (baked with ricotta and prosciutto, mozzarella and Romano cheese) ($5) and dine on veal saltimbocca ($17.75) or chicken stuffed with Gorgonzola cheese, pancetta, and figs sautéed in a creamy Marsala wine sauce ($15.95).

Emily's at Stowehof Inn (802-253-9722, 2 miles off Route 108). American nouvelle cuisine in a dramatic dining room. In winter you might dine on a mixed grill of antelope and smoked venison sausage ($22.95), tuna à la Niçoise ($21.95), or Muscovy breast of duck ($21.50). Inquire about sleigh-ride and dinner packages in winter. **Coslin's Pub** offers less formal fare, complimentary appetizers during ski season, and live jazz on Friday night.

Trapp Family Dining Room (802-253-8511), Trapp Hill Road, Stowe. The lodge offers noteworthy formal dining with a three-course ($34) and five-course ($40) prix fixe menu; always includes Austrian specialties, like Wiener schnitzel with spaetzle, but also varied fare, like fresh sea scallops sautéed in a Riesling cream sauce and roasted stuffed quails with pear schnapps served with braised red cabbage. Lighter meals are served in the lounge.

Mist Grill (802-244-2233), 95 Stowe Street, Waterbury. A vintage-1807 gristmill houses this "New England bistro," good for continental breakfast on weekdays, lunch beginning at 11:15, bistro fare from 5:30 on most nights, and family-style Sunday-night dinners. There's also a brunch menu on Saturday and Sunday. About the only day you can't eat here is Monday. Chef Steve Schimoler has just published *The Mist Grill Cookbook*, if you want to preview his recipes. Suffice it to say the food is very good.

In Stowe

Gracie's Restaurant (802-253-8741), Main Street, Carlson Building, Stowe Village. Open from 11:30 AM to midnight, this richly paneled pub with booths, a hearth, and heavily dog-themed decor is a great place to eat when you pull into town late. We have enjoyed dining alone on one of Gracie's outstanding burgers at the bar, and on the nightly special (shrimp jambalaya or Gracie's scampi) with friends. At lunch we recommend Gracie's famous chicken sandwich served with bacon, mayo, and guacamole ($7.95) or the vegetable flatbread ($6.95). Gracie, who was owners Paul and Sue Archdeacon's dog (his picture hangs at the bottom the stairs), was a fixture at the Shed all those years Paul worked there as bartender.

McCarthy's Restaurant (802-253-8626), Mountain Road next to the Stowe Cinema. Open 6:30–3 daily. The local gathering place: quick, cheerful service, an open black-and-white-checked tile kitchen, oilcloths on the tables, wood skis on the walls, and deep wooden booths. Daily specials for breakfast and lunch, plus a big breakfast menu and a wide selection of soups and sandwiches on homemade breads. Kids' menu, boxed lunches to go. Great all around.

Restaurant Swisspot (802-253-4622), Stowe Village. An old reliable, open nightly for lunch and dinner. Soups, quiche, and fondue are lovingly prepared. For lunch, there are tempting burgers with Swiss cheeses, and a wide variety of sandwiches. Fondues are a specialty of the house; try the Swiss cheese fondue ($25 for two) or beef fondue bourguignon for two ($33). Other options range from Wiener schnitzel ($16) to pesto shrimp ($15). Children's menu. Try the Matterhorn sundae with hot Tobler sauce ($4).

Trapp Family Austrian Tea Room (802-253-8511), Trapp Hill Road, 10:30–5:30 daily, is fully licensed and specializes in hot *glühwein* and café Viennese, soups, Austrian wursts, sandwiches, and Bavarian desserts, served up by dirndl-clad fräuleins. This attractive building is a part of the Trapp family complex. The view is spectacular, especially from the terrace in summer.

The Gables Inn (802-253-7730; 1-800-GABLES-1), 1457 Mountain Road. Breakfast served 8–10:30 daily, Sunday and holiday brunch until 12:30. Breakfast is an event, served on the enclosed front porch and in the cheerful dining room. The daily blackboard breakfast specials might include French toast stuffed with cream cheese, walnuts, and molasses ($6.50); a Vermont cheddar cheese omelet with mushrooms, peppers, onions, and garden herbs ($5.75); kippers with onions ($7). Dinner at the Gables might begin with escargots ($7), and move on to Chicken Dipeppo (penne with broccoli, chicken, and Asiago cheese; $14) or pan-seared duck breast in a mandarin orange compote ($18). The restaurant offers a selection of beer and wines.

The Shed (802-253-4364), Mountain Road, open daily for lunch and dinner, also Sunday buffet brunch and a late-night menu (10–midnight). Ken Strong's old landmark pub has expanded over the years into a complex that includes a microbrewery as well as a large, greenhouse-style dining room. The varied menu includes salads, tacos, baked onion soup, zucchini boats, barbecued ribs, seafood strudel, and, of course, Shed burgers. Children's menu.

Whip Bar & Grill (802-253-7301), Main Street at the Green Mountain Inn. Open daily 11:30–9:30; Sunday brunch is a specialty. For charm and good food at palatable prices, the

Whip is difficult to beat. The antique buggy whips, brass dumbwaiter, and vintage photos recall the tavern's status. It boasts Stowe's first liquor license, from 1833. In summer there's patio dining and a view of lawns and the pool; in winter the focus is on a roaring hearth. There is a blackboard menu, always a choice of grilled meats or fish, a raw bar, and specials ranging from pan-blackened fish to Montreal smoked meat with hot mustard. Dinner specials include grilled sea scallops with a honey-lemon-thyme glaze and maple-marinated pork chops served with apple-rhubarb chutney.

✐ **Miguel's Stowe-Away Lodge and Restaurant** (802-253-7574), 3148 Mountain Road. This snug old farmhouse, the original Miguel's, is a reliably good bet featuring innovative Mexican fare, like carnitas de cordero (marinated lamb served with rice and beans), as well as the usual Tex-Mex "especiales" and a gringo and full children's menu. This is the place for margaritas.

Mr. Pickwick's Pub & Restaurant at Ye Olde England Inn (802-253-7558), 433 Mountain Road. Open for lunch, dinner, and Sunday brunch. "A Dickens of a place" offers bangers and mash ($13.95) or grilled wild boar chop with ragout of white beans ($24.95). Vermont rabbit loin wrapped in pancetta ($19.95) and caribou scaloppine ($23.95) are among the exotic dinner entrées. There is a vast collection of beers, single-malt whiskeys, wines, and what-have-you on the menu.

Trattoria La Festa (802-253-8480), 4080 Mountain Road. Dinner served daily except Sunday (open on long weekends). On the upper reaches of the Mountain Road with terrace dining in summer, a pleasant dining room that's owned by three experienced chefs, two of them brothers born and raised in Aprilia, a small coastal town not far from Rome. True to the nature of an Italian trattoria, the food is varied. Reliably delicious antipasti, such as carpaccio di carne (thin slices of filet mignon with onions, capers, extra-virgin olive oil; $7.50); specialty pastas like penne Michelangelo (penne sautéed with fresh vegetables and grilled shrimp in a garlic wine sauce; $14.50); and four-course, family-style dinners can be preordered.

Moscow Tea House (802-253-2955), Moscow. Open year-round, Thursday through Saturday, noon–5. Call ahead for reservations. Homemade pastries and savories are served with herbal and regular teas on the veranda and in the combination tearoom/gift shop with dried herbs and flowers hanging from the rafters.

Dutch Pancake Cafe (802-253-5330), 900 Mountain Road at the Grey Fox Inn. Open daily 7:30–11 AM, for Sunday brunch until 12:30 PM, and for dinner 5:30–8:30 PM. There are about as many types of pancakes (more than 80) served here as you could think of, and then some, ranging from peaches and cream to shredded potato leek with cheese ($5.25–9.75). Dinner could be flatbread pizzas, hearty sandwiches, or . . . pancakes.

✐ **Depot Street Malt Shoppe** (802-253-4269), Depot Street, Stowe Village. A consciously '50s decor with a reasonably priced menu to match, a great lunch stop with old-style fountain treats like malted frappes, egg creams, and banana splits.

In Waterbury

Arvad's (802-244-8973), 3 South Main Street. Open daily 11:30–11:30. A great waystop (just off I-89, exit 10), an attractive brick-walls-and-hanging-plants decor, varied lunch and dinner menus, a full bar. Dine on pasta primavera ($12) or chicken, beef, pork, or shrimp stir fry ($13). Nightly specials; try the Cabot fries (made with the local cheddar).

Mist Grill (802-244-2233), 95 Stowe Street. Open daily. Baked goods and coffee from 6:30 AM to 4 PM; breakfast 7–10:30; lunch 11–2:30; Sunday dinner 5–8. Housed in a vintage-1807 mill, this new restaurant offers good atmosphere and food. Lunch features soups, salads, grilled panini, sandwiches, burgers, and cold cuts. Reasonably priced Sunday-night suppers are family-style, a choice of four entrées—maybe roast chicken, beef Burgundy, polenta lasagna, and seafood risotto. See also *Dining Out*.

✷ Entertainment

Stowe Cinema (802-253-4678), at the Stowe Center, Route 108. Standard seats as well as bar viewing area for first-run films.

The Lamoille County Players (802-888-4507) stage plays at the Hyde Park Opera House, Hyde Park.

Stowe Theater Guild (802-253-3961), staged upstairs at the Akeley Memorial Building in Stowe Village, offers a series of summer musicals and Broadway favorites.

Stowe Performing Arts (802-253-7792) presents a series of three summer Sunday-evening concerts followed by three **Vermont Mozart Festival** concerts held in the natural amphitheater of the Trapp Family Meadow. Patrons are invited to bring a preconcert picnic. The setting is spectacular, with the sun sinking over Nebraska Notch.

APRÈS-SKI There are reputedly 50 bars in Stowe. Along the Mountain Road, look for après-ski action at the **Matterhorn** (802-253-2800), with live music every weekend during ski season. **Charlie B's,** at Stoweflake, is also usually lively, as is **Mr. Pickwick's Pub,** source of one of Vermont's largest selections of beers (the better to wash down its steak-and-kidney pie).

✷ Selective Shopping

ARTISANS **Stowe Craft Gallery, Shimmering Glass & Design Center** (802-253-4693), Mountain Road, Stowe. Outstanding crafts from throughout the country including contemporary crafts, jewelry, and wearables. The interior design showroom features lighting, rugs, hardware, and furniture.

Little River Hotglass Studio & Gallery (802-253-0889), 593 Moscow Road, Moscow. We are kicking ourselves for not stocking up on the lovely, reasonably priced glass Christmas balls that Michael Trimpol creates in this small and very attractive studio just off Route 100. The specialty is exquisite colored glass creations: weights, bowls, balls, and perfume bottles. Open to the public from Thursday through Sunday.

Ziemke Glass Blowing Studio (802-244-6126), Route 100, Waterbury Center. Showroom open daily 10–6. Glass is usually blown Thursday through Sunday.

Stowe Gems (802-253-7000), in the village near the Helen Day Art Center. Barry Tricker polishes and sets exquisite stones, including tanzanite, tourmaline, Tahitian pearls, and freshwater pearls.

Samara's Cards & Gifts (802-253-

8318), Red Barn Shops, Mountain Road, Stowe. An exceptional selection of work by Vermont artisans: quilts, soft sculpture, jewelry, wooden toys, batik, stained glass, and more.

Vermont Clay Studio (802-244-1126), Route 100, Waterbury, open daily 10–6. Pottery sold, made, and taught.

Vermont Rug Makers (802-253-6288), Stowe Village. A branch of the Johnson store: distinctive, locally handwoven rugs and hangings, also a stock of imported Turkish and Oriental rugs.

Moriarty Hat & Sweater Shop (802-253-4052), Stowe. Many long years ago, Mrs. Moriarty began knitting caps for Stowe skiers, and her distinctive style caught on. It is now widely imitated, but the originals remain a Stowe tradition.

FOOD AND DRINK **Cabot Annex Store** (802-244-6334), 2653 Waterbury-Stowe Road (Route 100), Waterbury, 1.4 miles north of Ben & Jerry's, in the same complex as Lake Champlain Chocolates (see below). Open daily, year-round. While the prizewinning cheese isn't made here, this is its major showcase, displaying a full line of dairy products (plenty of samples), along with other Vermont specialty foods and crafts.

Lake Champlain Chocolates (802-241-4150), Route 100, Waterbury. This is the chocolate maker that started out in Burlington and has expanded into other parts of the state. Open 9–6 daily.

Green Mountain Coffee Roasters (802-244-5621), 33 Coffee Lane, Waterbury. Sample these famous blends at the factory outlet.

Cold Hollow Cider Mill (802-244-8771; 1-800-3-APPLES), Route 100, Waterbury, is one of New England's largest producers of fresh apple cider; visitors can watch it being pressed and sample the varieties. The retail stores in this big red barn complex stock every conceivable kind of apple jelly, butters, sauces, natural fruit preserves, honey, pancake mixes, pickles, and mustards, plus Vermont books and other gifts. Open daily 8–6, year-round.

OTHER **Bear Pond Books** (802-253-8236), Depot Building, Stowe Village. Open daily. An excellent full-service bookstore; calendars, cassettes, and cards, too.

Brick House Book Shop (802-888-4300), Stagecoach Road, Morristown Corners. Open daily except Monday. Proprietor Alexandra Heller has amassed 70,000 old books, fiction and nonfiction, hardcover and paperback. She also offers a search and mail service.

Shaw's General Store (802-253-4040), 54 Main Street, Stowe Village. Established in 1895 and still a family business, a source of shoelaces and cheap socks as well as expensive ski togs and Vermont souvenirs.

Lackey's Variety Store (802-253-7624), Main Street, Stowe Village, open 8:30–8:30 daily. An 1840s building that has housed many enterprises and is now "just a variety store," according to Frank Lackey, its owner of more than 48 years. An anomaly in this resort village, it still stocks nail clippers, india ink, shoe polish, scissors, not to mention patent medicine and magazines. The walls are hung with posters for '30s ocean liners and long-vanished local movie houses and lined with antique bottles, boxes, and other fascinating ephemera.

Stafford's Country Store and Pharmacy (802-253-7361), Main Street, Stowe Village. The village's full-service pharmacy (parking in the rear), also a selection of European music boxes, toys, books, and Vermont products.

Stowe Street Emporium (802-244-5321), 23 Stowe Street, Waterbury. A large, eclectic selection of clothing and gifts.

Fly Fish Vermont (802-253-3964), 954 South Main Street, Stowe, carries a full line of name-brand fishing gear. Bob Shannon also offer full- and half-day instructional tours.

Straw Corner Mercantile (802-253-3700), Mountain Road, Stowe. Folk art, Americana gifts, and decorative accessories. Shaker boxes, Nantucket baskets, cards, calendars, boxes, and earthenware.

Misty Meadows Herb and Perennial Farm (802-253-8247), 785 Stagecoach Road, Stowe. Open mid-May through fall, 9–5 daily. Display gardens feature herbs and perennials in a farm setting; also potpourri, everlasting wreaths, seasonings, and herbs.

Nebraska Knoll Sugar Farm (802-253-4655), 256 Falls Brook Lane. The sugarhouse is open in-season, and syrup and maple cream are available year-round. We advise calling before, especially in winter when the steep back road (especially if you come via Trapp's) is four-wheel-drive only (we chickened out three-fourths of the way there).

See also the Johnson Woolen Mill in "North of the Notch"; the short and scenic drive there is certainly worth the effort.

✷ Special Events

Mid-January: **Winter Carnival** is one of the oldest and most gala village winter carnivals in the country: a week of snow sculptures, sled-dog races, ski races, public feeds.

February: **Stowe Derby** (last weekend of the month), the country's oldest downhill/cross-country race: a 10-mile race from the summit of Mount Mansfield to Stowe Village, which usually attracts about 300 entrants.

Easter festivities: **Easter parade** at Spruce Peak; **Easter egg hunt.**

May: Lamoille County Players present **musicals** at the Hyde Park Opera House.

Late June: **Stowe Flower Festival.**

July 4: **Parades, fireworks, Stowe Marathon,** the world's shortest marathon; separate festivities in the village of Moscow, too small for its own band, so they parade to the music of radios.

Mid-July: **Stoweflake Hot-Air Balloon Festival,** Stowe Country Club. **International Food and Wine Festival,** Stoweflake Resort Field.

Late July: **Stowe Performing Arts Summer Festival,** a week of concerts ranging from chamber to symphony music, including bands and choral groups, presented in a number of places. **Lamoille County Field Days,** a weekend agricultural fair in Morrisville—tractor pulling, crafts, children's rides.

Early August: Annual **antique and classic car rally,** 3 days.

Late August: Lamoille County Players stage a **musical** in the Hyde Park Opera House.

September (last weekend): **Stowe Foliage Craft Fair,** Topnotch Field.

NORTH OF THE NOTCH AND THE LAMOILLE VALLEY

Vermont's most dramatic road winds up and up from Stowe through narrow, 2,162-foot-high Smugglers Notch, then down and around cliffs and boulders. Just as it straightens and drops through woodland, motorists are startled by the apparition of a condominium town rising out of nowhere (Smugglers' Notch Resort, a self-contained, family-geared village that accommodates some 2,000 people). However, as Route 108 continues to descend and finally levels into Jeffersonville on the valley floor, it's clear that this is a totally different place from the tourist-trod turf south of the Notch. This is the Lamoille Valley.

Smugglers Notch, as well as the village of Jeffersonville, is in Cambridge, one of several towns worth exploring along the Lamoille River. Jeffersonville has been a gathering place for artists since the 1930s, and Johnson, 9 miles west along Route 15, is also now an arts center. It's easy to see why artists like this luminous landscape: open, gently rolling farm country. The Lamoille River itself is beloved by fishermen and canoeists, and bicyclists enthuse about the little-trafficked roads.

While Smugglers Notch is the more dramatic approach, the prime access to the Lamoille Valley region is Route 100, the main road north from Stowe, which joins Route 15 (the major east–west road) at Morrisville, the commercial center for north-central Vermont. Just west on Route 15 is Hyde Park, the picturesque county seat, famed for its year-round theater.

North of the Lamoille Valley is the even less-trafficked Missisquoi River Valley, and between the two lies some beautiful, very Vermont country.

GUIDANCE **Stowe–Smugglers Notch Regional Marketing Organization** (1-877-247-8693; www.stowesmugglers.com), Morrisville, is a source of information for the entire region.

Lamoille Valley Chamber of Commerce (802-888-7607), P.O. Box 445, 43 Portland Street, Morrisville 05661. The office in the Tegu Building in Morrisville is open year-round. A summer information booth is at the junction of Routes 15 and 100 at the Morrisville Mobil station. Open May through October.

GETTING THERE *By air:* See "Burlington Region." Given 48 hours' notice, Smugglers' Notch Resort (see *Lodging—Resort*) arranges transfers for guests.

By train: **Amtrak** stops at Essex Junction (1-800-872-7245).

By car: When the Notch is closed in winter, the route from Stowe via Morrisville is 26 miles, but in summer via Route 108 it is 18 miles from Stowe.

MEDICAL EMERGENCY Jeffersonville, Johnson (**911**).
Cambridge Regional Health Center (**911**).
Cambridge Rescue: Dial **911.**

✷ To See

Smugglers Notch. During the War of 1812, Vermonters hid cattle and other supplies in the Notch prior to smuggling them into Canada to feed the British army—who were fighting the U.S. Army at the time. A path through the high pass has existed since Native American days, but it wasn't until 1910 that the present road was built, which, with its 18 percent grade, is as steep as many ski trails and more winding than most. Realizing that drivers are too engrossed with the challenge of the road to admire the wild and wonderful scenery, the state's Forests and Parks Department has thoughtfully provided a turnoff just beyond the height-of-land. An information booth here is staffed in warm-weather months; this is a restful spot by a mountain brook where you can picnic, even grill hot dogs. The Big Spring is here, and you can ask about hiking distances to the other local landmarks: the Elephant Head, King Rock, the Hunter and His Dog (an outstanding rock formation), Singing Bird, the Smugglers Cave, Smugglers Face, and the natural reservoir. See *To Do—Hiking and Walking* in the "Stowe and Waterbury" chapter for details about the easy trail to Sterling Pond and about the trail to the Elephant Head.

COVERED BRIDGES **In and around Jeffersonville.** Look for the **Scott Bridge** on Canyon Road across the Brewster River near the old mill that's now Kelly's Restaurant; the 84½-foot-long bridge is 0.1 mile down the road. To find the **Poland Bridge** (1887) from the junction of Routes 108 and 15, drive north and turn onto Route 109, angling off on the road along the river; the bridge is in 0.2 mile. Heading west on Route 15 toward Cambridge Village, look for Lower Valley Road; the **Gates Farm Bridge** (1897) is a few hundred feet from where the present road crosses the river.

In Waterville and Belvidere. Back on Route 109, continue north to Waterville and at Waterville Town Hall (on your right), turn left; the **Church Street Bridge** (1877) is in 0.1 mile. Back on Route 109, continue north; the **Montgomery Bridge** (1887) is east of the highway, 1.2 miles north of town hall. Go another 0.5 mile north on Route 109 and turn right; the **Kissin' Bridge** (1877) is in 0.1 mile. Continue north on Route 109, and 1.5 miles from the Waterville Elementary School (just after the bridge over the North Branch), turn left and go 0.5 mile to the **Mill Bridge** (1895). Back on Route 109, continue north 0.9 mile and turn left to find the **Morgan Bridge** (1887). See the "Jay Peak Area" chapter for a description of six more covered bridges another dozen miles north in Montgomery. *Note:* For detailed descriptions of all these sites, see *Covered Bridges of Vermont,* by Ed Barna (The Countryman Press).

In Johnson. Take Route 100C north from its junction with Route 15 for 2.6 miles and turn right; the **Scribner Bridge** (around 1919) is 0.3 mile on your right.

GALLERIES **Mary Bryan Memorial Art Gallery** (802-644-5100), Main Street, Jeffersonville. Open daily 11–5. Built by Alden Bryan in memory of his wife and fellow artist, Mary Bryan, this minimuseum has changing exhibits featuring artists who have worked in Jeffersonville.

Vermont Studio Center (802-635-2727), Johnson. Over the past 16 years, this nonprofit center has absorbed 20 buildings in the village of Johnson. The lecture hall is a former meetinghouse, and the gallery, exhibiting the work of artists in residence, is in a former grain mill one street back from Main, down by the river. Some 50 professional artists and writers from throughout the country are usually here at any given time. They come to take advantage of the studio space and the chance to learn from each other through lectures and critiques. Inquire about gallery openings and evening slide shows and lectures.

Dibden Center for the Arts (802-635-2356), Johnson State College, Johnson. Open during the academic year, Tuesday through Saturday 10–3. Changing solo and group shows.

SCENIC DRIVES Four loop routes are especially appealing from Jeffersonville:

Stowe/Hyde Park (44-mile loop). Take Route 108 through Smugglers Notch to Stowe Village, drive up the old Stagecoach Road to Hyde Park (be sure to see the old Opera House), and head back through Johnson.

A LANDSCAPE PAINTER IN JOHNSON

Kim Grant

Belvidere/Eden (40-mile loop). From Jeffersonville, Route 109 follows the North Branch of the Lamoille River north (see *Covered Bridges*) to Belvidere Corners; here take Route 118, which soon crosses the Long Trail (see *To Do—Hiking*) and continues to the village of Eden. Lake Eden, 1 mile north on Route 100, is good for swimming and boating; return on Routes 100, 100C, and 15 via Johnson.

Jericho/Cambridge (38-mile loop). From Jeffersonville, drive southwest on Pleasant Valley Road, a magnificent drive with the Green Mountains rising abruptly on your left. Go through Underhill Center to the junction with Route 15 but continue south on Jericho Center Road; return via Jericho (see the "Burlington Region" chapter for a description of Jericho and Jericho Center) and Route 15 to Cambridge Village, then drive back along Route 15 (see *Covered Bridges*) to Jeffersonville.

Jeffersonville/Johnson (18-mile loop). From the junction of Routes 15 and 108, head north on Route 108, but turn onto Route 109 (note the Poland Covered Bridge on your right). Take your first right, Hogback Road, which shadows the north bank of the Lamoille River most of the way into Johnson. Return via Route 15.

HISTORIC HOUSE **The Noyes House Museum** (802-888-7617), Route 100, Morrisville. Open mid-June until September, 1–5 or by appointment. Suggested donation: $3 adult, $1 student. The 18 rooms of this brick, Federal-style house are furnished and filled with varied memorabilia, including an 1,800-piece pitcher and Toby jug collection.

✷ To Do

BICYCLING **Rentals:** Mountain-bike rentals are available in Jeffersonville at **Foot of the Notch Bicycles** (802-644-8182) and in Morrisville at **PowerPlay Sports** (802-333-6557), Route 100.

Bicycle touring: Smugglers Notch Inn (802-644-2412; see *Lodging—Inns and Bed & Breakfasts*). The owners can help with local bike routes. **Mannsview Inn** (802-644-8321; see *Lodging—Inns and Bed & Breakfasts*) offers canoeing/cycling packages.

The **Cambridge Greenway** recreation path runs 1.3 miles along the Lamoille River from Jeffersonville east.

Missisquoi Valley Rail Trail, a 26.5-mile-long rec path, traverses the northern tier of this region, following the Missisquoi River from Enosburg Falls to Richford. For a map, call the **Northwest Regional Planning Commission** (802-524-5989).

CANOEING AND KAYAKING The **Lamoille River** from Jeffersonville to Cambridge is considered good for novices in spring and early summer; two small sets of rapids.

Smugglers' Notch Canoe Touring (1-800-937-6266), based at the Mannsview Inn, Jeffersonville, rents canoes and kayaks and offers shuttle service. Paddles are all flat and Class I water.

NAVIGATING SMUGGLERS NOTCH

Kim Grant

Green River Canoe & Kayaks (802-644-8336), based at Smugglers' Notch Resort (see *Lodging—Resorts*). Guided canoe and kayaking trips, also instruction and rentals.

See also Sterling Ridge Inn under *Lodging—Inns and Bed & Breakfasts.*

FISHING The stretch of the Lamoille River between Cambridge and Johnson is reputedly great fly- and spin-fishing for brown trout.

Smugglers' Notch Resort (802-644-8851) offers twice-weekly fly-casting clinics in-season.

The Fishing Hole (802-888-6210), 81 Bridge Street, Morrisville, offers year-round fishing supplies, and guide service May through September. For fly-fishing, see also the Golden Maple on the Lamoille in Wolcott (see *To Do—Fishing* under "St. Johnsbury, Craftsbury, and Burke Mountain Area").

HIKING **Prospect Rock, Johnson.** An easy hike yields an exceptional view of the Lamoille River Valley and the high mountains to the south. Look for a steel bridge to the Ithiel Falls Camp Meeting Ground. Hike north on the white-blazed Long Trail 0.7 mile to the summit.

Belvidere Mountain–Ritterbush Pond and **Devil's Gulch.** These are basically two stretches of the Long Trail; one heads north (3½ hours round-trip) to the summit of Belvidere Mountain, the other heads south (2¾ hours round-trip) to a gulch filled with rocks and ferns. Both are described in the Green Mountain Club's *Long Trail Guide.*

HORSEBACK RIDING **Lajoie Stables at Vermont Horse Park** (802-644-5347), 4306 Route 108, Jeffersonville, across the road from Smugglers' Notch Resort, offers guided trail rides, pony rides for kids, hay- and sleigh rides, year-round.

LLAMA TREKS **Northern Vermont Llama Treks** (802-644-2257), Waterville. Treks depart from the Smugglers' Notch Resort (see *Lodging—Resort*) and head into the backcountry. Geoff and Lindsay Chandler offer half-day treks on Tuesday, Wednesday, and Thursday in the summer, with full-day options in the fall. Day treks are $80 per person (picnic and snack included), and half-day treks are $40 per person (including snacks). Family rates available.

Applecheek Farm (802-888-4482), 567 McFarlane Road, Hyde Park. Trek on "wilderness trails," with or without a picnic. Trekking season is spring and fall with a break in the heat of the summer. Rates: $90 for two, $15 each additional person with a maximum of 10.

PICNICKING There are several outstanding roadside picnic areas: On Route 108, 0.2 mile north of the junction with Route 15 at Jeffersonville, picnic benches on the bank of the Lamoille; on Route 108 south of Jeffersonville Village on the east side of the highway; on Route 108 in Smugglers Notch itself (see *To See*); on Route 15, just 1.5 miles east of the Cambridge/Johnson line.

SWIMMING **Brewster River Gorge,** accessible from Route 108 south of Jeffersonville (turn off at the covered bridge).

Smugglers' Notch Resort (802-644-8851; 1-800-451-8752; see *Lodging*) features an elaborate summer water park with eight pools and three water slides as well as a winter pool.

TENNIS Courts at **Smugglers' Notch Resort** (see *Lodging*), and a summer program of clinics for adults and children and daily instruction at the TenPro Tennis School.

WALKING See the Cambridge Greenway recreation path under *Bicycling*.

Lamoille County Nature Center (802-888-4965), Cole Hill Road, Morrisville. Two nature trails offer easy walking and the chance to see deer, bear, and a variety of birds, also lady's slippers in early summer. Inquire about programs offered in the outdoor amphitheater.

✷ Winter Sports

CROSS-COUNTRY SKIING **Nordic Ski and Snowshoe Adventure Center** (802-644-8851), Smugglers' Notch Resort (see *Lodging*). Narrow trails wind up and down through the trees, then climb meadows away from the resort complex, a total of 14 miles of set trails; rentals; also telemark, skate skiing, and snowshoe rentals; lessons and tours; repairs in the warming hut, where there is cocoa on the woodstove.

Smugglers Notch. The stretch of Route 108 that is closed to traffic for snow season is open to cross-country skiers. Guided tours are offered by the Nordic Adventure Center (see above).

DOWNHILL SKIING **Smugglers' Notch Resort** (802-644-8851; U.S.: 1-800-451-8752; Canada: 1-800-356-8679; www.smuggs.com), Jeffersonville. In 1956, a group of local residents organized Smugglers' Notch Ski Ways on Sterling Mountain, a western shoulder of 3,640-foot-high Madonna. In 1963 a high-powered group headed by IBM board chairman Tom Watson gained a controlling interest and began developing the area as Madonna Mountain, a self-contained, Aspen-style resort. Only two owners later, with 550 condominiums, Smugglers' is a major ski resort sporting a natural snow bowl with a satisfying variety of terrain: beginners trails on Morse Mountain (2,250 feet), some world-class trails and glade skiing on Madonna itself, along with intermediate runs that predominate on Sterling Mountain.

The only way to the summit of Madonna, which commands one of the most spectacular views in New England—from Mount Washington to Mount Mansfield—is a 17-minute ride on the longest (and coldest) chairlift in the East, and the way down can be via some of the region's steepest or longest runs. The ideal time to ski this mountain is early March, when it's relatively warm, and midweek, when it's empty. Obviously, this is a place you come, anytime during ski season, for a 5-day ski week—which automatically includes lessons for all family members. *Lifts:* Six double chairlifts, two surface. *Trails:* 70, including two 3.5-mile trails; 25 percent expert, 53 percent intermediate, 22 percent beginner. *Vertical drop:* 2,610 feet. *Snowmaking:* 60 percent. *Facilities:* Mountain Lodge, base lodge with ski shop, rentals, cafeteria, pub. The reception center/ski shop at Morse Mountain has a Village Center, source of rentals and tickets; the complex also includes a ski shop and deli. Top of the Notch warming hut is at the Sterling chair terminal. Snowboarding. *Ski school:* Group and private lessons at Morse and Madonna, beginners at Morse. Children's ski and snowboarding camp. *For children:* Daycare for infants. Discovery Ski Camp for 3- to 5-year-olds—all day with hot lunch and two lessons, mountain games, and races. Adventure Ski Camp for 6- to 10-year-olds: all day with hot lunch and two lessons; games and races. The Notch Squad is for ages 11–14. Explorer Ski Program for 15- to 17-year-olds begins at 1:15; lesson and evening activities; teen center. *Rates:* $48 for adults; youths 7–17, $34. Kids 6 and under ski free. *Note:* Lodging packages greatly reduce ski-week rates.

ICE SKATING **Smugglers' Notch Resort** rink (flooded tennis courts) is lighted at night as part of its FunZone.

SLEIGH RIDES **Applecheek Farm** (802-888-4482), 567 McFarlane Road, Hyde Park. John and Judy Clark's gentle Belgians, Sparky and Sam, take you through the woods by day or night.

LaJoie Stables at Vermont Horse Park (802-644-5347), Route 108 across from Smugglers' Notch Resort. Sleigh rides offered all winter. See also *Horseback Riding*.

SNOWMOBILING **Smugglers' Notch Snowmobile Tours** (800-347-8266), Junction Hill Road, Jefferson. Evening 1-hour tours through Smugglers Notch. Customized day tours from 2 to 4 hours. Ride on new Polaris machines.

✷ Lodging

RESORT **Smugglers' Notch Resort** (802-644-8851; 1-800-451-8752; UK: 0800-169-8219), 4323 Route 108 South, Smugglers' Notch 05464. More than 550 condominium units in a variety of shapes accommodate a total of 2,400 people. Geared to families and groups (facilities include a conference center), the resort offers a year-round combination of good things: skiing, swimming (the pool is protected by a heated bubble in winter), tennis, and a varied program of summer activities, including a supervised children's schedule of fishing, horseback rides, movies, hikes, and games. Summer tennis and other packages are offered. The resort excels at catering to children, with a variety of very distinct facilities and programs geared to different ages. Alice's Wonderland, the nursery for newborns and tots, is particularly impressive, as is the program for teens. In winter, a Club Smugglers' 5-day ski week includes lodging, skiing, snowboarding, lessons, use of the FunZone, pool, tubing, a dinner out, and other extras from $99 per adult per day, from $85 per youth (7–17), kids 6 and under stay free. In summer, a comparable program, including Familyfest Camp Programs for youngsters, begins at $1,485 per week for a two-child family. Add 12 percent for combined state tax and service charge. *Note:* Condominium units are all individually owned and vary from fairly basic (just what you want with kids) to luxury units with TV as well as Jacuzzi in the bath. Units also vary widely in location, from roadside to slope-side to up in the woods.

INNS AND BED & BREAKFASTS

ꝏ **Smugglers Notch Inn** (802-644-2412; 1-800-845-3101), 55 Church Street, P.O. Box 280, Jeffersonville 05464. Dating in part from the 18th century, this is a comfortable village inn that's been gentrified without losing its old-fashioned appeal. The living room retains its decorative tin ceiling as well as its brick fireplace, and remains a casual, inviting space with plenty of books and games. A fully licensed, half-circular bar with a copper footrail fills a corner on the way to the columned dining room (see *Dining Out*), which is hung with paintings by artists who have stayed here over the years, a good place for weddings and reunions. The 11 guest rooms all have private bath and country quilts; the room we slept comfortably in was warmed by a gas fireplace. Facilities include an outdoor hot tub and swimming pool. Innkeepers Paul, Roberta, and Lori will hand out maps of good local bike routes. $60–125 per room includes a full breakfast.

✐ **Sterling Ridge Inn** (802-644-8265; 1-800-347-8266; www.vermont-cabins.com), 155 Sterling Ridge Drive, Jeffersonville 05464. Built in 1988 expressly as a small inn, with a wall of windows in the spacious living room/dining room commanding a magnificent mountain view. The lodge has three- or four-bedroom suites, making it ideal for larger gatherings. Back beyond the pond, Scott and Susan Peterson have built 8 one- and two-bedroom log cabins, each nicely designed with a fireplace, cathedral ceiling, fully equipped kitchen, and outdoor grill. The inn's 80 acres are webbed with 20 km of trails; facilities include a hot tub and outdoor pool. Mountain bikes and a canoe (with shuttle service) are also available. Rates $75–280.

Mannsview Inn (802-644-8321; 1-888-937-6266), 916 Route 108 South, Jeffersonville 05464. The most popular spot in the house is the solarium, a greens-filled dining area off the open kitchen with a view of the mountains. There's also a library and a billiard room, year-round outdoor Jacuzzi, and common room with big-screen TV. Kelley and Bette Mann offer canoe trips on the Lamoille River (see *Canoeing*). Seven guest rooms include two suites with fireplaces and Jacuzzis, three rooms with private bath and two with shared bath. Rates range $65–185 per room double occupancy, with breakfast included.

Jefferson House (802-644-2030; 1-800-253-9630), 71 Main Street, Jeffersonville 05464. Three bedrooms in a Victorian village house with original woodwork throughout the home, also a wraparound porch with swings and an upstairs deck. $60–85 double with complete breakfast.

Fitch Hill Inn (802-888-3834; 1-800-639-2903; www.fitchhillinn.com), 258 Fitch Hill Road, Hyde Park 05655. Handy to many parts of the North Country, this hilltop house is elegantly maintained. The four double guest rooms, each named for a state (our favorite is Vermont), are all nicely furnished and equipped with ceiling fans;

a studio apartment and a suite can be combined to sleep up to six. There is ample common room, an outdoor hot tub, and a library of videos for the VCR. $85–205, depending on season, includes a full breakfast.

Three Mountain Lodge (802-644-5736), Route 108, Smugglers' Notch Road, Jeffersonville. Originally built in 1966 by the University of Vermont for its outing club, the lodge later housed the UVM and Johnson State College ski teams. Steve and Colleen Blood now offer a guest cottage adjacent to the lodge for travelers looking for comfortable private accommodations. Nightly rates for the cottage range $65–85 with a maximum occupancy of four.

Also see Berkson Farms under *Lodging—Farm Vacation* in "The Northwest Corner."

CAMPGROUND **Brewster River Campground** (802-644-2126), 110 Campground Drive, off Route 108, Jeffersonville. Just 20 "low-tech" tent sites, one tepee, and several lean-tos on 20 secluded acres with a fire pit and picnic tables, a modern bathhouse (hot showers); no pets (but there's a local kennel). Tent sites are $20 per night.

✷ Where to Eat

DINING OUT **Hearth & Candle** (802-644-8090), Smugglers' Notch Resort, Jeffersonville. Housed in a New England–style house, one of the first structures built in the condo village, this is the most formal place to eat in town. The atmosphere is upscale English pub. Moderate.

Hungry Lion Restaurant (802-644-5848), at the Smugglers Notch Inn, Route 108 between Jeffersonville and Smugglers. Open daily 4–closing. This restaurant does a full menu of pasta, beef, seafood, poultry, and vegetarian dishes. Entrées range $8–23. Maple-marinated pork chops are a specialty of the house. The **Lion's Den Pub** features microbrews on tap.

See also Persico's Plum & Main, below.

EATING OUT **Persico's Plum & Main** (802-635-7596), Main Street, Johnson. Open 6 AM–8 PM weekdays, until 9 Friday and Saturday, 8–1 Sunday. Culinary Institute of America graduate Pat Persico could be writing his own ticket in Stowe, but this Johnson native would rather serve local folks along with the stray skier and leaf-peeper. The breakfast specials might include apple cinnamon griddlecakes with homefries and syrup, or a bacon, cheddar, and onion omelet. The lunch menu covers the basics, but the ingredients are fresh and locally grown and the soup homemade. The dinner menu changes nightly but could include baked fresh haddock with a spinach seafood stuffing or prime rib of beef. BYOB. Inquire about specialty nights (Mexican or Italian, for example).

Dinner's Dunn at the Windridge Bakery (802-644-8219), 158 Main Street, Jeffersonville. Open for breakfast and lunch from Sunday through Tuesday, for breakfast, lunch, and dinner from Wednesday through Saturday. This was a dry-goods store until it became one of New England's outstanding bakeries and coffee shops. Great breakfasts; homemade soups and sandwiches for lunch. Breads are still a specialty, along with breakfast omelets. The newest part of the operation is the dining room, which features homemade flatbread pizza, steak, pasta, Italian and French dishes, and nightly specials. $9–17.

Adam's Apple Cafe (802-888-4737), corner of Main and Congress Streets, Morrisville. Healthy fare for all. Open for lunch Monday through Saturday, dinner Thursday through Saturday, and Sunday brunch.

Melben's Restaurant (802-888-3009), 105 Portland Street, Morrisville. Across from the Bijou Theater, Melben's offers moderately prices Italian specialties and fresh seafood.

♿ **Hilary's** (802-888-5352), Route 100, Northgate Plaza, Morrisville. Breakfast, lunch, dinner, and Sunday brunch are all served in this pleasant place that's good for everything from sandwiches to seafood, from vegetarian dishes to steak. Fully licensed.

Café Banditos (802-644-8884), Route 108, Jeffersonville, across from the Village at Smugglers' Notch. A spacious old house offers yet another family- and skier-geared dining option: Ver-Mex. Burgers, ribs, and homemade soups augment tacos, fajitas, and enchiladas. Children's menu. Live music most Fridays.

Three Mountain Lodge (802-644-5736), Route 108, Smugglers' Notch Road, Jeffersonville. The restaurant attached to the Three Mountain Lodge (see *Lodging*) features fresh New England seafood, Black Angus beef, vegetarian entrées, homemade pasta, and homemade ice cream. Daily and seasonal specials. Moderate.

Jana's (802-644-5454) at the junction of Routes 15 and 108, Jeffersonville. Open 5 AM–9 PM weekdays, from 6 AM weekends. A family restaurant that's nicely decorated, Jana's has a coloring menu for children and a collection of antique sleds. Try a pita rabbit for lunch and Vermont chicken cordon bleu for dinner. Fried baskets, pizzas, and most staples are served.

The Cupboard (802-644-2069), junction of Routes 15 and 108, Jeffersonville. Open from 5 AM weekdays, 6 AM–11 PM Saturday, until 10 Sunday. Good for a wide variety of hot and cold subs, deli chili, French bread pizzas, maple baked beans, and other goodies, especially its maple-frosted cinnamon-raisin bread.

French Press Café (802-635-2638), Main Street, Johnson. Open 8–8. A middle-of-the-village place to linger at the counter or around tables over coffees, teas, and pastries. Poetry readings on occasion. Jason, the owner, also has opened **Gelis Restaurant** (802-635-9200) across the street from the café. He serves vegetarian fare and seafood 5–11 PM every day but Tuesday.

✱ Entertainment

Lamoille County Players (802-888-4507); call for summer schedule of productions.

The Cambridge Arts Council stages theater, concerts, and coffeehouses in Jeffersonville. Check local bulletin boards.

Vermont Studio Center Lecture and Reading Series. For a schedule of the frequent presentations by artists and writers, call the center (802-635-2727).

✱ Selective Shopping

ANTIQUES **1829 House Antiques** (802-644-2912), Route 15, Jeffersonville (2.5 miles east of the village). Open year-round daily except Sunday. Carolyn and Richard Hover's great old barn is filled on three floors with a wide assortment of country furniture and furnishings representing 40 dealers.

Pocketful O' Posies (802-644-2989), 60 Main Street, Jeffersonville. Located in the old Noble Pearl Building, this center represents more than 30 dealers and consigners.

Smugglers' Notch Antique Center (802-644-8321), Route 108 south, near the Mannsview Inn. This dairy barn turned antiques center represents 16 dealers, and specializes in custom-made and antique furniture. Open daily May through October 10–5, Friday through Sunday from November through April.

The Buggyman Antiques Shops (802-635-2110; 802-635-7664), Route 15, Johnson. Open daily 10–5. A big old barn and 18th-century farmhouse filled with antiques, including wagons, buggies, and sleighs.

Victorian House Antiques (802-635-9549), Johnson. A multidealer and consignment shop.

By Vermont Hands (802-635-7664), Route 15, Johnson (1 mile west of the village), carries fine antiques and some locally made furniture.

ART AND CRAFTS GALLERIES **Quilts by Elaine** (802-644-6635; www.quiltsbyelaine.com), 127 Main Street, Jeffersonville. Open 9–5 daily except Wednesday. Elaine Van Dusen makes great quilts from crib to king sized as well as wall hangings.

Vermont Rug Makers (802-635-2434), Route 100C east of Johnson, and Main Street in Stowe. Handmade rugs from around the world. Open 10–5 except Sunday.

Milk Room Gallery (802-644-5122), Main Street, Jeffersonville. Alison Earl offers custom framing as well as original artwork by 38 local artists.

Boyden Farm, intersection of Routes 15 and 104, just west of Cambridge Village. The second story of this amazing shop/winery (see below) is filled with exquisite, locally made furniture and furnishings. Local crafts are also displayed downstairs.

FARMS AND A WINERY **Boyden Farm and Winery** (802-644-8151), at the intersection of Routes 15 and 104, just west of Cambridge Village. Open Tuesday through Sunday 10–5 June through December, otherwise Friday through Sunday 10–5. At this fourth-generation working dairy, bordering the Lamoille River, David Boyden has turned an 1878 carriage barn into a microwinery producing both fruit and grape wines. Wine tours and tastings are offered, and the apple wine we brought home ($6.95) was excellent. Maple syrup and Vermont products and crafts (see above) are also sold. Inquire about farm tours.

Applecheek Farm (802-888-4482), 567 McFarlane Road, Hyde Park. Call before coming. A dairy farm with Holsteins and Jerseys, maple-sugaring operation; other farm animals include llamas, emus, draft horses, miniature horses. Picnic with llama treks, barbecue with horse and wagon rides (see also *To Do—Llama Treks* and *Sleigh Rides*).

SPECIALTY STORES **Johnson Woolen Mills** (802-635-7185; 1-877-635-WOOL), Main Street, Johnson. Open year-round 8–5 daily except Sunday; Saturday 9–4. Although wool is no longer manufactured in this picturesque mill, the fine line of clothing for which Johnson Woolen Mills has long been known is made on the premises. This mill's label can still be found in shops throughout the country, and its famous, heavy green wool work pants, a uniform of Vermont farmers, are especially popular in Alaska. Although there are few discounts at the factory store, the selection of wool jackets and pants—for men, women, and children—is exceptional. The mail-order catalog is filled with sweaters, wool ties, hunting jackets, blankets, and other staples available in the shop.

Marvin's Country Store (802-635-2329), Main Street, Johnson, is open Monday through Saturday 9–5:30, Sunday 11–4. This is the retail outlet for the Marvin family's maple products, plus a variety of Vermont gifts.

The Studio Store (802-635-2203; 1-800-887-2203), Johnson, adjacent to the Vermont Studio Center (see *To See—Galleries*). Open Wednesday through Saturday 10–6, Sunday noon–5. A fully stocked artist's supply store, independently owned.

Arthur's Department Store (802-888-3125), Morrisville. Arthur and Theresa Breault and their daughter, Adrienne, do their buying in New York and Boston; they have created an unexpectedly fine and friendly source of clothing and footwear for men, women, juniors, and children. **The Cellar Shop** offers genuine bargains.

Vermont Maple Outlet (802-644-5482), Route 15 between Jefferson and Cambridge. A nice selection of cheese, syrup, handmade jams, and gift boxes.

Forget-Me-Not Shop (802-635-2335), Route 15, 1.5 miles west of Johnson. This eclectic store carries international military surplus clothing and gear, gift items of all sorts, and famous label clothing at discounted prices. Open daily 9–9.

✷ Events

January (last weekend): **Winterfest**—primitive biathlon (muzzle loaders and snowshoes).

March: **Marchfest.** Four weeks of special events at Smugglers' Notch Resort: Nordic, alpine races, broomball tournaments, crafts shows, folk dances, snow sculpture, fireworks, ball.

June (first weekend): **Vermont Dairy Festival**—arts and crafts, horse pulling, stage shows, 2-hour Saturday parade, country-and-western jamboree Sunday.

July 4: **Celebration,** Jeffersonville. Outstanding small-town parade at 10 AM followed by a chicken barbecue, games, crafts, cow-flop bingo, and a frog-jumping contest on the green behind the elementary school. Evening music at Smugglers' Notch Resort (see *Lodging*), food, fireworks.

September: **Labor Day Festivities** in Cambridge—barbecue on the green, flea market; family road run (3.1 miles) from Jeffersonville to Cambridge along back roads.

The Northeast Kingdom 6

ST. JOHNSBURY, CRAFTSBURY, AND BURKE MOUNTAIN AREA

JAY PEAK AREA

NEWPORT AND THE NORTH COUNTRY

Kim Grant

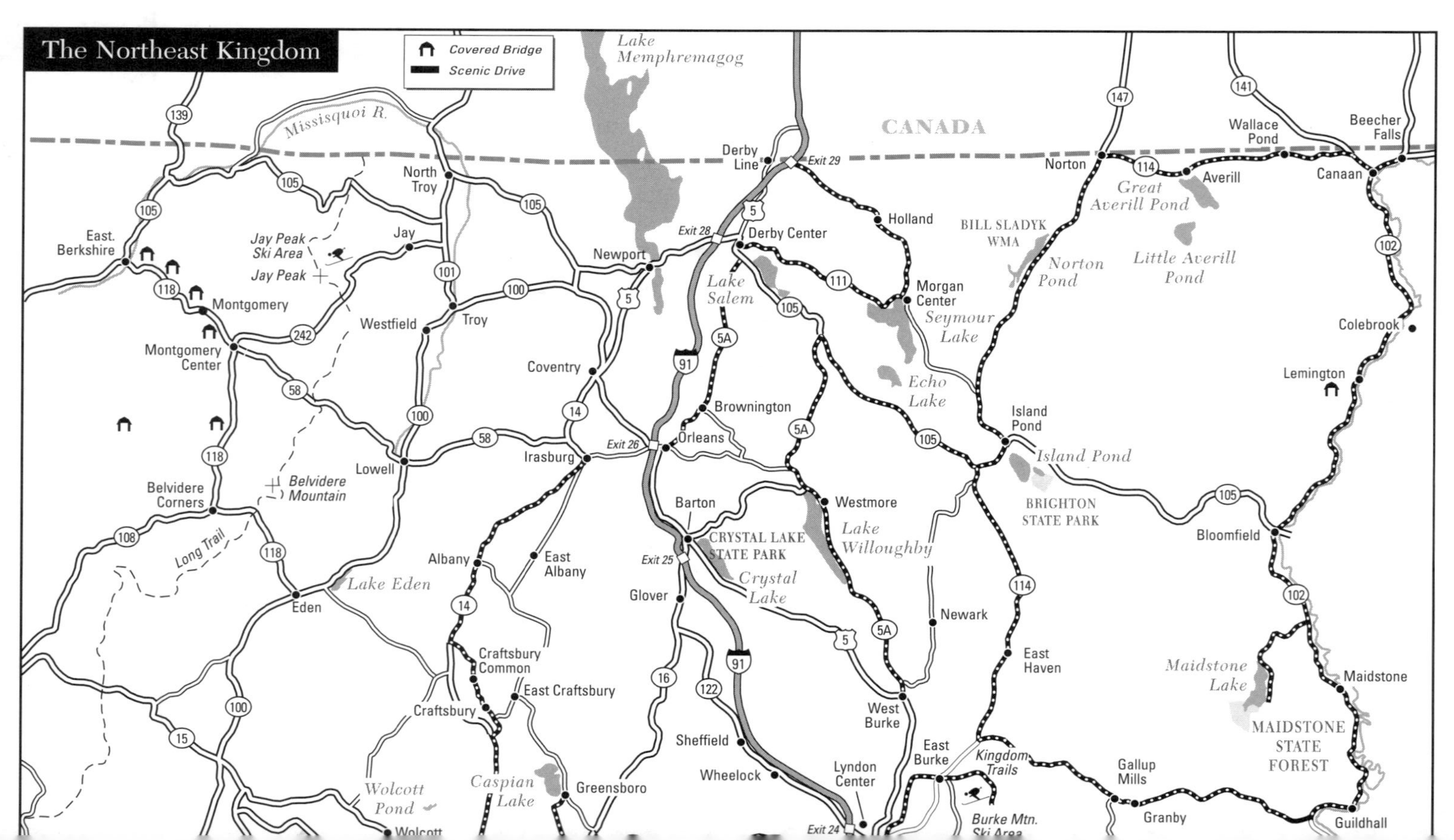
The Northeast Kingdom
Covered Bridge
Scenic Drive
CANADA
Lake Memphremagog
Missisquoi R.
East. Berkshire
Montgomery
Montgomery Center
Jay Peak Ski Area
Jay Peak
Jay
North Troy
Troy
Westfield
Newport
Coventry
Derby Line
Derby Center
Exit 29
Exit 28
Exit 26
Exit 25
Exit 24
Holland
Morgan Center
Seymour Lake
Echo Lake
Lake Salem
Brownington
Orleans
Irasburg
Lowell
Belvidere Mountain
Belvidere Corners
Long Trail
Eden
Lake Eden
Albany
East Albany
Craftsbury Common
East Craftsbury
Craftsbury
Caspian Lake
Greensboro
Wolcott Pond
Wolcott
Barton
CRYSTAL LAKE STATE PARK
Crystal Lake
Glover
Sheffield
Wheelock
Lyndon Center
West Burke
East Burke
Kingdom Trails
Burke Mtn. Ski Area
Westmore
Lake Willoughby
Newark
East Haven
Island Pond
BRIGHTON STATE PARK
BILL SLADYK WMA
Norton
Norton Pond
Great Averill Pond
Little Averill Pond
Averill
Wallace Pond
Beecher Falls
Canaan
Colebrook
Lemington
Bloomfield
Maidstone Lake
Maidstone
MAIDSTONE STATE FOREST
Gallup Mills
Granby
Guildhall

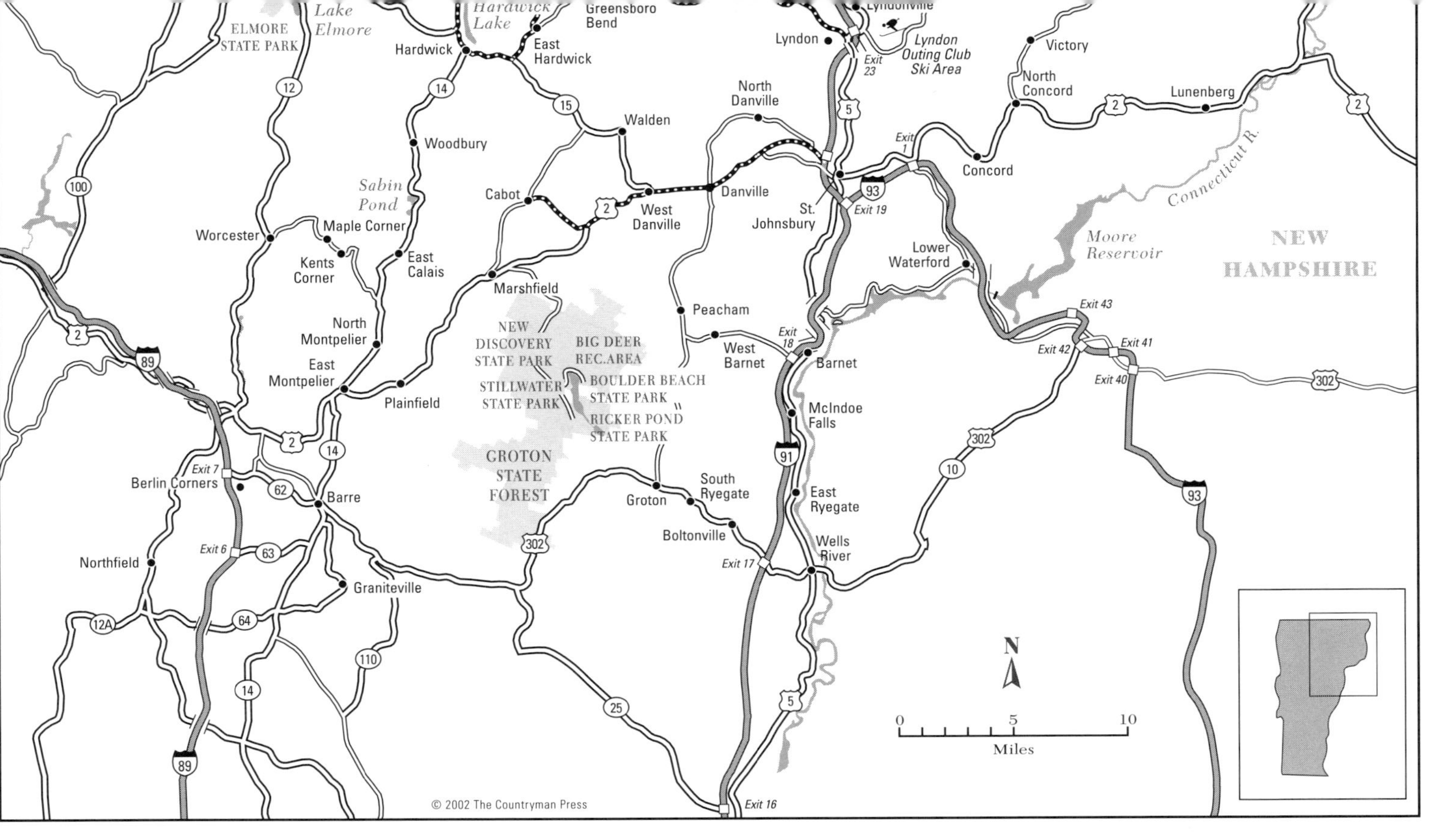
ELMORE STATE PARK
Lake Elmore
Hardwick
East Hardwick
Greensboro Bend
Lyndon
Lyndon Outing Club Ski Area
Exit 23
Victory
North Concord
Lunenberg
Woodbury
Walden
North Danville
Exit 1
Concord
Connecticut R.
Sabin Pond
Cabot
West Danville
Danville
St. Johnsbury
Exit 19
Worcester
Maple Corner
Kents Corner
East Calais
Marshfield
Peacham
Lower Waterford
Moore Reservoir
NEW HAMPSHIRE
North Montpelier
East Montpelier
NEW DISCOVERY STATE PARK
BIG DEER REC.AREA
West Barnet
Exit 18
Barnet
Exit 43
Exit 42
Exit 41
Exit 40
Plainfield
STILLWATER STATE PARK
BOULDER BEACH STATE PARK
RICKER POND STATE PARK
McIndoe Falls
Exit 7
Berlin Corners
Barre
GROTON STATE FOREST
Groton
South Ryegate
East Ryegate
Boltonville
Wells River
Exit 17
Northfield
Exit 6
Graniteville
N
0 5 10
Miles
Exit 16
© 2002 The Countryman Press

ST. JOHNSBURY, CRAFTSBURY, AND BURKE MOUNTAIN

With a population of 7,600, St. Johnsbury is the largest community in the Northeast Kingdom. Thanks to the Fairbanks family, who began manufacturing their world-famous scale here in the 1830s, it is graced with an outstanding museum of natural and local history, a handsome athenaeum, and an outstanding academy. The general late-19th-century affluence that St. J (as it is affectionately known) enjoyed as an active rail junction and industrial center has been commemorated in ornate brick along Railroad Street and sloping Eastern Avenue and in the fine mansions along Main Street, set high above the commercial downtown. In the 1960s, when Fairbanks became a division of a conglomerate—which threatened to move the scaleworks south—townspeople themselves raised the money to subsidize a new plant. The point is that this is a spirited community boasting one of the country's oldest town bands, a busy calendar of concerts, lectures, and plays, and all the shops and services needed by residents of the picturesque villages along the Connecticut River to the south, the rolling hills to the southwest and northwest, and the lonely woodlands to the east. Less than a dozen miles north, the wide, main street of Lyndonville is also lined with useful shops. Burke Mountain, a short way up Route 114, is accessible by car as well as by foot in summer and draws skiers from throughout the Northeast in winter.

As Route 2 climbs steeply west from St. J to Danville, a spectacular panorama of the White Mountains unfolds to the east. The village of Danville itself is a beauty, and the back roads running south to Peacham and north to Walden follow ridges with long views. Continue northwest to Cabot and on to Craftsbury, where fields roll away like waves to the mountains in the distance.

Craftsbury is a composite of scattered villages, most of which you drive through in a trice. It's Craftsbury Common, with its common so vast that it dwarfs the surrounding white homes, academy, and church, that compels you to stop. It's so high that the countryside drops away on all sides.

Get lost in the surrounding web of well-maintained dirt roads. Eventually you hit a paved, numbered road, and in the meantime you find some of Vermont's most breathtaking farmscape, spotted with small lakes and large ponds. Don't miss Greensboro, an early-20th-century summer compound on Caspian Lake.

In Hardwick, a small trading center for the southwestern corner of the Kingdom, Main Street is unexpectedly Victorian, a reminder of the town's heyday as one

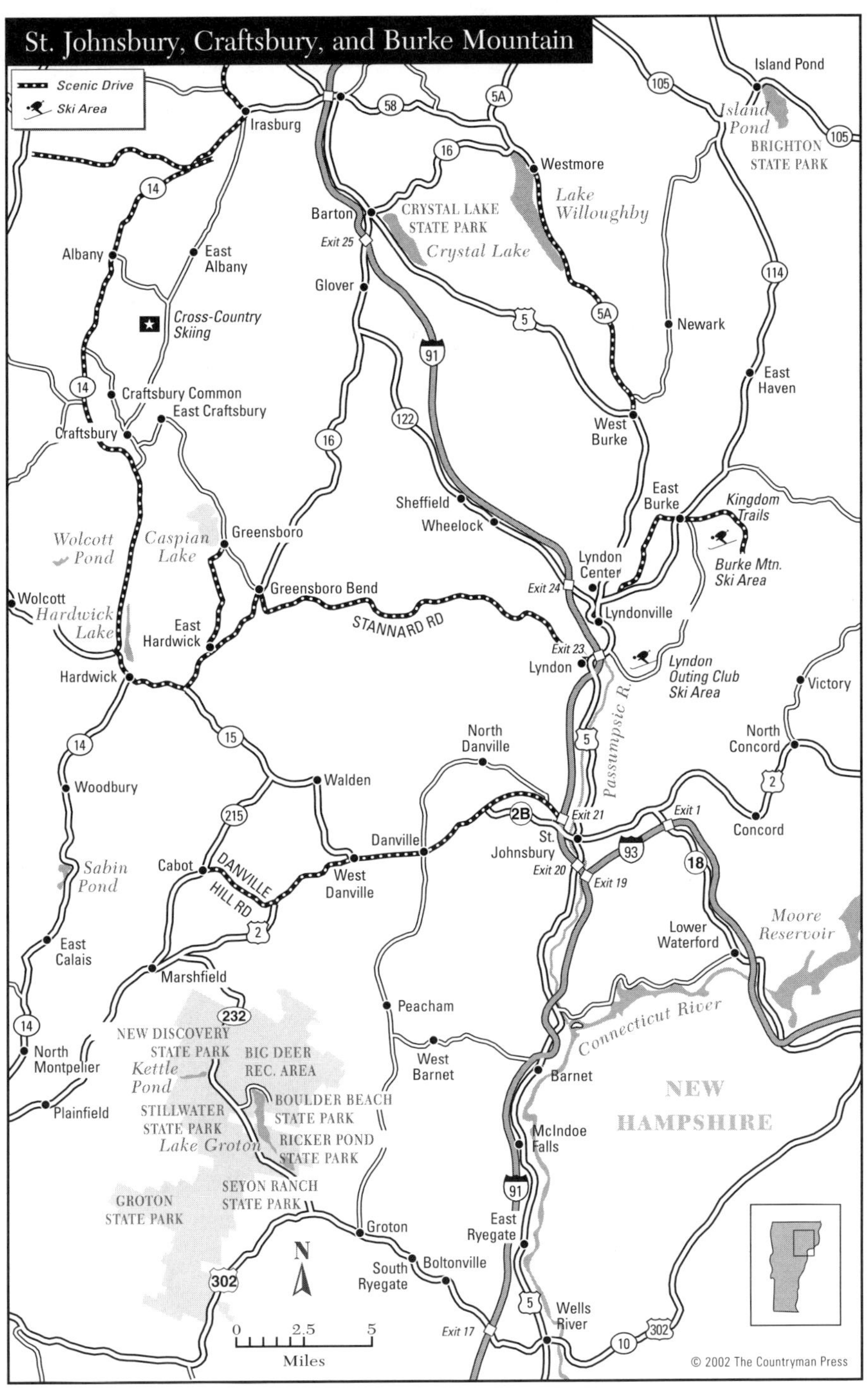
St. Johnsbury, Craftsbury, and Burke Mountain
Scenic Drive
Ski Area
Irasburg
Island Pond
Island Pond
BRIGHTON STATE PARK
Westmore
Lake Willoughby
Barton
CRYSTAL LAKE STATE PARK
Crystal Lake
Exit 25
Glover
Albany
East Albany
Cross-Country Skiing
Newark
East Haven
Craftsbury Common
East Craftsbury
Craftsbury
West Burke
Sheffield
Wheelock
East Burke
Kingdom Trails
Burke Mtn. Ski Area
Wolcott Pond
Caspian Lake
Greensboro
Greensboro Bend
Lyndon Center
Exit 24
Lyndonville
Wolcott
Hardwick Lake
East Hardwick
STANNARD RD
Exit 23
Lyndon
Lyndon Outing Club Ski Area
Hardwick
Victory
Passumpsic R.
North Danville
North Concord
Woodbury
Walden
Exit 21
Exit 1
Concord
Danville
St. Johnsbury
Exit 20
Exit 19
Cabot
DANVILLE HILL RD
West Danville
Sabin Pond
Lower Waterford
Moore Reservoir
East Calais
Marshfield
Peacham
Connecticut River
NEW DISCOVERY STATE PARK
BIG DEER REC. AREA
North Montpelier
Kettle Pond
West Barnet
Barnet
BOULDER BEACH STATE PARK
Plainfield
STILLWATER STATE PARK
RICKER POND STATE PARK
Lake Groton
NEW HAMPSHIRE
McIndoe Falls
SEYON RANCH STATE PARK
GROTON STATE PARK
Groton
East Ryegate
South Ryegate
Boltonville
Wells River
Exit 17
0 2.5 5
Miles
© 2002 The Countryman Press

NORTHEAST KINGDOM FARMSTEAD

Kim Grant

of the world's largest granite processors. The granite was actually in Woodbury, 5 miles south, whence it arrived by rail. Thousands of skilled European craftsmen moved to town beginning in the 1870s and continuing into the 1920s; a number of French Canadians remain.

Barton, this area's northernmost commercial center, also obviously boomed in the late 19th century, when six passenger trains a day stopped in summer, bringing guests to fill the town's big (long gone) hotels or the gingerbread "camps" (still there) on Crystal Lake.

Lake Willoughby, between Barton and East Burke, is one of Vermont's most hauntingly beautiful lakes. Mounts Hor and Pisgah, which rise abruptly from opposite shores, create a fjordlike effect when viewed from the public beach in Westmore at the northern end or from the southern tip of the lake. Mostly undeveloped, Willoughby is surrounded for much of its length by state forest, and the water is stocked with salmon and rainbow trout. A well-known resort area in the days of grand hotels and steamboats, it now has a limited, loyal following of sailors, Windsurfers (there is always a breeze here), and year-round fishermen.

GUIDANCE **Northeast Kingdom Chamber of Commerce** (802-748-3678; 1-800-639-6379; www.vermontnekchamber.org), 357 Western Avenue, St. Johnsbury 05819. The chamber maintains a year-round walk-in office, also a seasonal information booth at the corner of Main Street and Eastern Avenue; a source for lodging, dining, and general information for a 35-mile radius around St. Johnsbury.

The Lyndon Area Chamber of Commerce (802-626-9696; www.lyndonvermont.com), P.O. Box 886, Lyndonville 05851, publishes a leaflet guide and maintains a seasonal information booth on the common.

For cottage listings on Crystal Lake in Barton and Lake Parker in Glover, you can check with the **Barton Chamber of Commerce** (802-525-1137; www.bartonareachamber.com), P.O. Box 403, Barton 05822.

See also Northeast Kingdom Travel and Tourism Association in the box.

WHAT'S IN A NAME?

"You know, this is such beautiful country up here. It ought to be called the Northeast Kingdom of Vermont."

It was in 1949 that Sen. George Aiken made this remark to a group in Lyndonville. Since then, word has gotten around that that's what Vermont's three northeastern counties—Orleans, Caledonia, and Essex—should be calling themselves. This is, after all, a world unto itself: the state's most rural and lake-spotted corner, encompassing nearly 2,000 square miles. Aside from a few dramatic elevations, such as Jay Peak on its northwestern fringe and Burke Mountain at its heart, this is a predominantly high, open, glacially carved plateau of humped hills and rolling farmland, with some lonely timber country along the northern reaches of the Connecticut River. Neither of the ski areas draws patrons enough to change the look of the surrounding landscape. In the era of trains and steamboats, there were many more summer hotels than there are now; yet you can still stay in an unexpected range of places—from elegant country inns and full resorts to ski lodges and condominiums, from summer cottages to working farms. And all the amenities are here: golf, tennis, and horseback riding as well as plenty of hiking, fishing, canoeing, and winter sports that include ice fishing, tracking and snowshoeing, some of the state's best snowmobiling, and cross-country as well as downhill skiing. But they may take some searching out, and in the process you may stumble across some people and places of memorable beauty.

The Northeast Kingdom has a voice. Listen at a lunch counter, in a general store, at a church supper, at a county fair, or during the peerless Northeast Kingdom Foliage Festival. Admittedly it's fading, but you can sharpen your ear with Howard Frank Mosher's beautifully written books—*Northern Borders, Where the Rivers Flow North, A Stranger in the Kingdom,* and *Disappearances.* Kingdom-based filmmaker and arts activist Jay Craven has turned the last three into films.

Unfortunately, while this is the single most distinctive corner of the entire state, 2,000 square miles is too large an area to describe without dividing it into three smaller sections. If you have a particular passion such as canoeing, cross-country skiing, fishing, hiking, or mountain biking, check *To Do* under all three.

The Northeast Kingdom Travel and Tourism Association (802-723-5300; 1-888-884-8001; fax: 802-723-5300; e-mail: info@travelthekingdom.com), a nonprofit umbrella organization representing 10 local chambers of commerce, publishes a useful *Four Season Guide* and a *Heritage Tour Map,* and also maintains an excellent web site, www.travelthekingdom.com.

GETTING THERE *By bus:* Check with **Vermont Transit** (1-800-642-3133) about schedules to St. Johnsbury from Boston, New York, and Connecticut via White River Junction. At this writing, buses stop in Barnet, St. Johnsbury, Lyndonville, Barton, Orleans, and Newport.

By car: I-93, completed in the 1980s, makes the Northeast Kingdom far more accessible from the southeast than is still generally realized. Bostonians, for instance, can be in St. Johnsbury in 3 hours. It also enables you to bypass St. J entirely en route to the Craftsbury area.

Note that I-91 works like a fireman's pole, a quick way to move north–south through the Kingdom. In snow, beware the high, open, 16-mile stretch of highway between Lyndon Center and Barton.

MEDICAL EMERGENCY Dial **911.**

Emergency services are available at **Northeastern Vermont Regional Hospital** (802-748-8141), St. Johnsbury; **Lyndon State College Rescue Squad** (802-626-5053), Lyndonville; Craftsbury (802-472-6666); Glover (802-525-3505); Barton (802-525-3505); Orleans (802-754-6366).

* Towns and Villages

Peacham. High on a ridge overlooking the White Mountains, this is a tiny but aristocratic village settled just after the Revolution, with a library at the four corners, a fine historical house, and a general store specializing in fresh-baked croissants and gourmet fare. Peacham has an unusual number of retired professors, literati, artistic luminaries, and ambassadors per capita. All three Peachams (South, East, and Center) are worth exploring, as are the roads between.

Barnet. An old Scots settlement, the village of Barnet itself is on a curve of the Connecticut River, almost lost today in a curious intertwining of I-91 and Route 5. **Pearson's General Store** marks the middle of town, and **Goodwillie House** (802-633-2542), built in 1790 by a Scottish pastor, served as a stop on the Underground Railroad and now houses the collections of the Barnet Historical Society. Drive east to Barnet Center to find Harvey's Lake (good for both fishing and swimming) and the long-established **Karme-Choling Buddhist Meditation Center** (802-633-2384). From the road it appears to be a traditional white farmhouse, but inside the house has been dramatically altered to let in the sun and a sense of the surroundings, creating a Tibetan-style temple. It provides housing for guests, who are welcome to stay overnight, and for retreats. Drop-in visitors are also welcome. Child care is offered.

Danville. Until 1855, Danville was the shire town of Caledonia County. It is an exceptionally beautiful town set high on a plateau, around a large green complete with bandstand, Civil War monument, and general store. The imposing town hall was built as the county courthouse, and the small, square Passumpsic Savings Bank is one of the safest strongholds around, thanks to devices installed after it was last held up, in 1935. Danville is known primarily as the headquarters for the American Society of Dowsers. In **Dowsers' Hall** (802-684-3417; open weekdays

9–5 and occasionally on weekends), you learn that dowsing is the knack of finding water through the use of a forked stick, a pair of angle rods, or a pendulum. Staff are always willing to demonstrate the art or to turn on the introductory video. Dowsing equipment and books are sold. Occasional weekend workshops are also offered. The American Society of Dowsers boasts 5,600 members throughout the world. The owner of the **Danville Morgan Horse Farm** (see *To See—Farms*) provides tours and enjoys talking about the breed.

West Danville is a crossroads (Routes 15 and 2) village. **Hastings Store** is a great, old-fashioned general store–cum–post office, and one of the world's smallest libraries sits across the road at Joe's Pond. There is a public beach with picnic and sanitary facilities at the pond. The water from Joe's Pond (an old summer resort) is said to empty, eventually, into Long Island Sound, while that from Molly's Pond (a mile south, named for Joe's squaw) presumably winds up in the Gulf of St. Lawrence.

Cabot. Known during the War of 1812 for its distilleries (the whiskey was sold to Canadians), this distinctly upcountry village is now famed for its cheese. The **Cabot Farmers Co-op Creamery** is Vermont's major producer, and its visitors center is a popular attraction (see *To See*).

Lyndonville. An up-and-down roll of land encompassing the villages of Lyndonville, Lyndon Center, Lyndon Corner, Red Village, and East Lyndon, and the neighborhoods of Vail Hill, Pudding Hill, Darling Hill, and Squabble Hollow.

CRAFTSBURY COMMON

Kim Grant

Lyndon isn't a tourist town but it offers real, down-home hospitality and five covered bridges (see *To See*). The village of Lyndonville was developed by the Passumpsic River Railroad Co. in the 1860s. Besides a handsome (long gone) station and a number of brick rail shops, the company laid out broad streets, planted elm trees, and landscaped Bandstand Park. The former home of Dr. Vanila L. Shores is filled with Victoriana, town memorabilia, and special exhibits (see *To See—Museums*). **Lyndon State College** is on Vail Hill (T. N. Vail was the first president of AT&T; he came here to buy a horse and bought a farm, which eventually turned into 20 farms, much of which is now occupied by campus). Lyndonville's famous product is Bag Balm (see *Selective Shopping—Special Shops*).

East Burke. A small village with a beautiful library and historical society building (the **Old Museum,** 802-626-9823, open June through October, Wednesday and Saturday afternoons; also by appointment), some attractive lodging, shops, and restaurants geared to alpine skiers at Burke Mountain, known because of its excellent terrain and reasonable prices as the Vermonter's Mountain. Burke Mountain Cross-Country center also offers some 80 km of high, wooded trails (see *To Do—Winter Sports*).

Greensboro. Shaped like an hourglass, Caspian Lake has a century-old following. The unusual purity of its water is checked three times weekly in-season by its association of cottage owners—who include noted authors, educators, and socialites—all of whom mingle in **Willey's Store** in the center of Greensboro (see *Selective Shopping—General Stores*). There is a public beach and resort facilities maintained by Highland Lodge, also open in winter for cross-country skiing. Greensboro also claims Vermont's oldest (nine-hole) golf course.

Craftsbury Common. Few places convey such a sense of tranquillity and order. In summer, petunias bloom in the post office window boxes, and the green of the grass contrasts crisply with the white fence. In winter, the general whitewash of this scene contrasts with the blue of the sky. Throughout the year there are nearby places to stay and books to check out at the desk beneath the imposing portraits of Ebenezer and Samuel Crafts in the village library.

Unlike most North Country pioneers, Ebenezer was university educated (Yale, class of 1740). Forced to sell his tavern in Sturbridge, Massachusetts (the still-popular Publick House), due to war debts, he made his way here over the Bayley-Hazen Military Road, eventually bringing his family and 150 of his Sturbridge neighbors this way on sleds. Ebenezer saw to it that a church and school were established soon after the saw- and gristmills. His son Samuel, a Harvard graduate who served two terms as Vermont's governor, founded the Academy, which still serves as the public high school for the town. The **Sterling College** campus adds to the variety.

Many farmers welcome visitors to their sugarhouses during "sugaring" season in late March and early April and sell syrup from their farmhouses year-round. Inns and B&Bs offer year-round lodging, and **Craftsbury Outdoor Center** offers basic accommodations and one of the most extensive and dependable cross-country-ski networks in New England; its summer sculling program is also nationally recognized. Mountain biking, walking, Elderhostel, and a variety of other programs are offered. The extensive web of well-surfaced dirt roads meandering in all directions is beloved by bicyclists and horseback riders.

Barton. The hotels are now gone, but Crystal Lake remains beautiful, with a clifflike promontory on one side and public beaches at its northern rim. There is golf here, and the town of Barton itself packs an astounding number of services into its small downtown. The Crystal Lake Falls Historical Association maintains the **Pierce House Museum** (802-525-6251) on Water Street, next to the old-fashioned office of the *Barton Chronicle,* an excellent little weekly covering much of Orleans and Essex Counties.

Brownington Village is a crossroads full of outstanding, early-19th-century buildings, the core of a once proud hill town long since eclipsed by such valley centers as Barton, Orleans, and Newport. There are 19th-century gardens behind the **Eaton House** and a spectacular panorama from the wooden observatory set up in a meadow behind the church. A descriptive walking tour booklet is available at the Old Stone House Museum (see *To See—Museums*), the big attraction in the village.

Wolcott, a small village that fronts on Route 15 and backs on the Lamoille River, and has long been known for its big store. In the early decades of the century the store was Charles E. Haskell's, famed as the "most general store in the entire Northeast" (teakettles, church pews, whatever). Now O. C. Buck's, probably the largest furniture (and then some) store in Vermont, dominates the town in a startling way: Most village buildings are painted chocolate brown to show that they belong to Buck's. To the east of the village the Fisher Covered Bridge, built in 1908, is said to be the nation's only surviving covered railroad bridge. The Golden Maple Bed & Breakfast on the western edge of town specializes in fly-fishing.

✷ To See

MUSEUMS ✐ **The Fairbanks Museum and Planetarium** (802-748-2372; www.fairbanksmuseum.com), Main and Prospect Streets, St. Johnsbury. Open daily, year-round, Monday through Saturday 9–5, Sunday 1–5; $5 adults, $4 seniors, $3 ages 5–17; $12 families; $3 for planetarium shows, which are Saturday and Sunday, 1:30 year-round. This is still a wonderfully old-fashioned "Cabinet of Curiosities." Its main hall, which is capped by a 30-foot-high, barrel-vaulted ceiling, is filled with thousands of stuffed animals: from mice to moose, from bats to bears (including a superb polar bear), birds galore (from hummingbirds to passenger pigeons), reptiles and fish, insects' nests; also fossils, rocks, and minerals. Historical exhibits are drawn from the collection of 95,000 objects and "ethnological" exhibits from a 5,000-piece collection representing most of the world's far corners. "I wish the museum to be the people's school . . . to teach the village the meaning of nature and religion," explained Franklin Fairbanks at the museum's 1880 dedication. In the planetarium, which seats just 50 people, you learn about the night sky as it appears in the Northeast Kingdom. The museum is a U.S. weather observation station, and daily forecasts are a popular feature on Vermont Public Radio. There is also a fine little gift shop. The Kitchel Center, a resource

FAIRBANKS MUSEUM

library for studies and information about the Northeast Kingdom, is open Tuesday and Thursday 2–4.

St. Johnsbury Athenaeum (802-748-8291), Main Street, St. Johnsbury. Open Monday and Wednesday 9–8, closed Sunday, otherwise 10–5:30. Donation. The big attraction is the art gallery in the rear of this fascinating public library. Said to be the oldest unaltered gallery in the country, it has a distinctly 19th-century feel. Smaller canvases and sculptures are grouped around the outsized painting *Domes of Yosemite,* by Albert Bierstadt. Natural light through an arched skylight enhances the effect of looking into the Yosemite Valley.

Bread and Puppet Theater Museum (802-525-3031), Route 122, Glover. Open June through October, 10–5. The internationally known Bread and Puppet Theater tours in winter, but in summer its farmhouse on this back road displays the huge and haunting puppet dwarfs, giants, devils, and other fantastic figures of good and evil, the artistic expressions of Polish-born Peter Schumann. Inquire about Sunday-afternoon performances, staged in the meadow across the road.

The Old Stone House Museum (802-754-2022), off Route 58 east of Orleans in Brownington. Open May 15 through October 15 (call for hours); modest admission charge. This is the Orleans County Historical Society Museum, housed in a four-story granite building dating back to 1836, built as a dormitory for a rural academy. The structure resembles the earliest dorms at Middlebury College, from which Alexander Twilight, the school's principal and building's architect, graduated in 1823. There is some question about whether Twilight was—as Middlebury College claims—the first African American graduate of an American college. There is no question about the beauty of the building and the historical collections: Rooms represent 10 of the 18 towns in Orleans County and also hold 18th- and 19th-century weapons, tools, paintings, furniture, and decorative arts. Pick up a walking tour (see Brownington under *Villages*).

Shores Memorial Museum (802-626-8547), 202 Center Street, Lyndon Center. Open June through August, Saturday and Sunday 2–4 and by appointment. What you notice first is the portrait of Vanila Shores as a young woman. Both the girl's parents followed the poor scholar when she went to Bates College, again when she moved on to Smith College and then to Johns Hopkins. Shores's house is now filled with Victorian items—hair wreaths and horsehair couches, vintage clothing and old toys, and—most notably—tops once made in town and sold around the world. Changing exhibits.

OTHER **Cabot Creamery Visitors Center** (802-563-2231; 1-800-837-4261; www.cabotcheese.com), Cabot. Open year-round except January, daily June through October 9–5, Monday through Saturday the rest of the year, 9–4. Cabot was judged "best cheddar in the world" at the 1998 World Championship Cheese Contest (the industry's Olympics). Now owned by Agri-Mark (a cooperative of 1,650 farms), the center showcases its 80-year history as a true Vermont cooperative. There's a video and half-hour tour of the plant ($1 includes samples). The store features every conceivable variety of cheese product, plus spreads and yogurt as well as other Vermont goods.

Maple Grove Farms of Vermont (802-748-5141), Route 2 east, St. Johnsbury. Open May 30 through late October. Guided tours are offered daily 8–4:30 of "the world's largest maple candy factory." In business since 1904, this is an old-fashioned factory in which maple candy is made from molds. A film in the adjacent museum depicts maple production and displays tools of the trade.

John Woodruff Memorial Library (802-586-9692), in East Craftsbury, was a general store built in the 1840s by the grandfather of the late Miss Jean Simpson. She converted it into one of New England's most pleasant libraries; most titles are in the room once used for bolts of cloth and groceries (old shelves and counters remain), and there is a special back room for youngsters, with a Ping-Pong table amid the books. Open Wednesday and Saturday 9–noon, 2–5, and 7–9:30; Sunday noon–1:30.

COVERED BRIDGES All five within northern Caledonia County are in Lyndonville—one 120-foot, 1865 bridge across the Passumpsic, 3 miles north of town off Route 114; one as you enter town, a genuine 1869 bridge moved from its orig-

WORK IN PROGRESS AT THE ST. JOHNSBURY ATHENEUM

Robert C. Jenks

inal site; two in Lyndon Corner (one dating from 1879, the other from 1881, both west off Route 5); the fifth in Lyndon Center on Route 122.

FARMS In Danville, the owner of the **Danville Morgan Horse Farm** (802-684-2251) provides tours and enjoys talking about the breed (call ahead), and just north of Danville Village at **Emergo Farm** (802-684-2215), the Websters "just love to show off" their fifth-generation, prizewinning dairy operation (see also *Lodging*). Susan Houston at **Maple Leaf Llamas** (802-586-2674) in Craftsbury Common welcomes visitors who call ahead, as does **Oooh Ahhh Baby Llamas** (802-563-2929; 1-800-674-8023) on Cobb Road in Hardwick. At **Cedar Grove Farm** (802-593-3650) in Peacham visitors are welcome to see how Jubilee beef cattle (a new breed) are raised; **Coburn Hill Blueberry Farm** (802-586-2202) in Craftsbury invites pick-your-own customers August through frost. We have not had a chance to check the **Perry Farm** (802-754-2396) in Brownington (a small dairy farm with Morgan horses and maple syrup) or **Garvin Hill Farm** (802-533-7436) in Greensboro, raising beefalo and free-range chicken, both offering B&B. Ditto for the **MacBain Homestead** (802-563-2025), a working dairy farm offering a reasonably priced three-room apartment on Mack Mountain Road between East Cabot and Peacham (handy to Harvey's Lake). See also *Selective Shopping—Gardens* and *Sugarhouses.*

SCENIC DRIVES **Route 2 West from St. Johnsbury to Danville.** As the road climbs steadily, the White Mountains rise like a white wall in the distance. This actually works better if you are driving east from Danville. Either way, be sure to pull off to appreciate the panorama.

THE OLD STONE HOUSE MUSEUM

Kim Grant

Danville Hill Road. Continue west on Route 2 from West Danville, past Joe's Pond, and after the Craft Shop at Molly's Pond (see *Selective Shopping—Crafts Shops*) take the right-hand turn marked for Cabot. This is a high road with long mountain views; note the Birdman (see *Crafts Shops*) along the way and the Cabot Creamery Visitors' Center in Cabot.

Up Burke Mountain. A 2.5-mile auto road to the summit of Burke Mountain (3,267 feet) commands a sweeping view of the North Country; picnic areas are provided halfway and at the summit. This preserve was formerly the 10,000-acre Darling State Forest, donated to the state in 1933. The road was constructed by the Civilian Conservation Corps. The toll road and campsites in the Sugar House Campground are open May 25 through October 15.

Darling Hill Road from Route 114 in East Burke, 5 miles south to Route 114 in Lyndonville, follows a ridge past a magnificent former estate that once encompassed many old homesteads and still offers great views. The bright yellow main house, on a private drive, has been beautifully restored.

Greensboro Village to East Hardwick. The road passes through Hardwick Street (that's the name of the hamlet) and a fine collection of Federal and Greek Revival houses; from Greensboro Village to Hardwick it makes a beeline through high and open farm country; and from Craftsbury Common north to Route 14 through Albany and Irasburg, it follows the rich farmland of the Black River Valley.

West Burke to Westmore. The stretch of Route 5A along Lake Willoughby is one of the most breathtaking anywhere.

Greensboro Bend to Lyndon. An old ridge road with splendid views, 17-mile **Stannard Road** is unpaved but usually well graveled most of the way. Check locally, though, because there are occasional washouts.

✷ To Do

BIKING **Vermont Adventure Company** (802-525-3154; 1-866-542-7204; www.vtadventureco.com), 425 Goodwin Mountain Lane, Westmore. Biking and hiking vacation packages as well as guided day tours and recreational rental equipment.

Craftsbury Outdoor Center (1-800-729-7751; www.craftsbury.com), Craftsbury Common, rents 21-speed fat-tire bikes and offers instruction and guide service on 200 miles of dirt roads and more than 100 miles of cross-country-ski trails (see also *Lodging*).

East Burke Sports (802-626-3215), Route 114, East Burke Village. A full-service cycle shop whose owners have developed an extensive off-road trail system and offer maps, guided tours, and rentals. Owner John Worth has been instrumental in developing the extensive Kingdom Trails network (see *Biking and Walking Trails*); call the shop for details. A map of the Kingdom Trail Association network can be had here for $5.

BIKING AND WALKING TRAILS **Bayley-Hazen Military Road.** Begun at Wells River on the Connecticut River in 1776 by Gen. Jacob Bayley, continued in

1778–79 by Gen. Moses Hazen, this 48-mile road was a flop as the invasion route it was intended to be, but it served settlers well after the Revolution when it came time to establish towns in this area. A historical but not very practical map is available from the Northeastern Vermont Development Association (802-748-5181), 44 Main Street, St. Johnsbury. The beautiful dirt stretch from Hazen's Notch to Lowell is noted in the "Jay Peak Area" chapter; the next stretch to Albany is now a walking/riding trail. It continues unmarked through Craftsbury and is marked on its way through Greensboro, where a monument commemorates its story; the first couple of miles of the road is a pleasant walk, from the granite marker at the northern end of Main Street in Wells River to Ticklenaked Pond in Boltonville (a good place for a swim and a picnic).

Kingdom Trail Association (John Worth: 802-626-3215). The East Burke area is webbed with more than 75 miles of trails: alpine ski trails on Burke Mountain, cross-country-ski trails at the Burke touring center, several loops in East Burke Village, snowmobile trails maintained by VAST, cross-country trails up on Darling Hill, and several more miles of trails specifically maintained by this nonprofit organization. Hikers have the right-of-way but this is clearly mountain-biker heaven. For a map, send $6 ($5 for the map, $1 for handling) to Kingdom Trails, P.O. Box 204, East Burke 05832.

See also Craftsbury Outdoor Center trails under *Biking*, the Vermont Leadership Center trails in "Newport and the North Country," and Hazen's Notch Association trails in "Jay Peak Area."

BOAT RENTALS **Injun Joe Court** (802-684-3430), Route 2, West Danville; **Harvey's Lake Campground** (802-633-2213), West Barnet; **Village Sport Shop** (802-626-8448), Lyndonville. (See also *Camping*.) Also **Anglin' Canoe & Boat Rental** on Crystal Lake in Barton (802-525-3904; 802-723-6693). See also *Canoeing* and *Sculling*. This area is pocked with lakes, and launches are shown on the state map.

CAMPING **Groton State Forest,** Marshfield 05658. A 25,623-acre preserve with four separate campgrounds, a beach area, yet another area for fly-fishing, and one for group camping, all listed below (access is from the Marshfield-Groton Highway, Route 232). **New Discovery Campground** (802-584-3820) has a total of 47 campsites, 14 of them lean-tos; beach privileges and hiking trails; primitive camping. **Stillwater Campground** (802-584-3822), on the west side of Lake Groton, has a total of 63 tent sites, 16 lean-tos; campers' beach and boat launch; rental boats, dump station. **Ricker Pond Campground** (802-584-3821) has a total of 33 campsites, 22 lean-tos, on the south side of Ricker Pond; campers' beach, rental boats, nature trail, dump station. **Seyon Fly-Fishing Area** (802-584-3829), on Noyes Pond, features an old lodge, frequently booked by groups. (See *Fishing*.) **Kettle Pond** (802-584-3820), on the south side of the pond; walk-in fishing, group camping, hiking, and snowmobiling. There are also a number of **private campgrounds,** and the list is included in the Northeast Kingdom travel guide, available by calling 1-800-884-8001.

CANOEING East of St. Johnsbury, the **Moore** and **Comerford Reservoirs,** created by dams, are good for canoeing (there are two boat launches in Lower Waterford) as we found out one evening, listening to birdcalls and watching a baby beaver swim steadily toward a beaver lodge beneath the pines. Below the Comerford Dam, the stretch of the Connecticut River south to McIndoe Falls (now the McIndoe Dam) is excellent, and the portage around the dam is not difficult. For a canoe/camping guide to the Connecticut from Wells River south, contact the **Upper Valley Land Trust** (603-643-6626). Other rivers that invite canoeing are the **Passumpsic** and **Moose,** which join the Sleeper at St. Johnsbury. A boat launch on the Moose River can be accessed from Concord Avenue in St. J, and look for a boat launch on the Passumpsic in Passumpsic Village, 5 miles south of St. Johnsbury. For rentals, check with the outlets listed under *Boating.* (See also East Burke Sports under *Biking.*) For details about canoeing the uppermost stretch of the Connecticut River and the Clyde River, see "Newport and the North Country."

Highland Lodge (see *Lodging*) also has canoes for its guests, and **Craftsbury Outdoor Center** (see *Biking*) rents canoes for use on Great and Little Hosmer Ponds and on the Black River.

FISHING Fishing is huge here. See the pamphlet *Vermont Guide to Fishing* available from the Vermont Fish and Wildlife Department in Waterbury (802-241-3711) or check the Northeast Kingdom Chamber of Commerce web site (see *Guidance*) for details about which fish are available where. Check the state highway map for local access points. Willoughby is known as the prime fishing lake, but Caspian and other lakes are also good for salmon, lake and rainbow trout, and perch. There are trout in the streams, too. (See also *To Do—Camping.*)

Willoughby Falls Wildlife Management Area. From Orleans drive east on Route 58 for 0.2 mile. At the BROWNINGTON sign bear left and drive 0.1 mile to the Vermont Fish and Wildlife parking area. Between the last week in April and the second week in May, wild rainbow trout climb the falls here, jumping high to clear the whitewater to reach their spawning ground.

♿ A handicapped-accessible fishing platform has been constructed in Passumpsic Village on the Passumpsic River.

Lodging geared to fishermen includes **Crystal Lake B&B** (802-525-4670) on Crystal Lake in Barton, which is open 6 months of the year and offers fishing from its dock as well as rental boats and canoes; **Golden Maple Inn** (802-888-6614; 1-800-639-5234), on the Lamoille River in Wolcott Village, which offers a fly-fishing school, canoe rentals, and guide services; **Seyon Ranch,** a lodge on Noyes Pond within the Seyon Recreation Area (May to October: 802-584-3829; otherwise: 802-479-3241), offers nominally priced group and individual reservations; trout fishing, with flies only, from boats rented at the site. See also Quimby Country and Seymour Lake Lodge in the "Newport and the North Country" section.

GOLF **Mountain View Country Club** (802-533-9294), Greensboro, nine holes. Established 1898; open to nonmembers midweek only. Use of carts permitted only for health reasons.

St. Johnsbury Country Club (802-748-9894; 1-800-718-8899), off Route 5 north, open daily mid-May through October, PGA rated, 18 holes. (Original nine holes designed in 1923; added nine holes designed by Geoffrey Cornish.) Cart rentals, great little restaurant, lounge.

Orleans Country Club (802-754-9392), Route 58, near Lake Willoughby. April through November; 18 holes, rentals, instruction.

Barton Golf Course (802-525-1126), Telfer Hill. April through September. Nine holes, cart rentals, low fees.

HAY- AND SLEIGH RIDES In the Craftsbury area, **Coachworks Farm** (802-586-2818), Page Pond Road, Albany, offers hayrides. On Darling Hill, both the **Wildflower Inn** and the **Inn at Mountain View Creamery** offer sleigh rides (see Burke Mountain–area *Lodging*).

Perry Farm (802-754-2396) in Brownington offers hay- and sleigh rides for groups of up to 10 people for $50, extra for every person above that number.

HEALTH SPAS **St. Johnsbury Academy Field House** (802-748-8683), Main Street, St. Johnsbury, has a pool, track, weight room with Nautilus and free weights, and three racquetball courts. These are open to the public at certain hours; call ahead for times and rates.

Old Mill Racquet & Fitness Center (802-748-5313), Perkins Street, St. Johnsbury. Indoor tennis, racquetball, aerobics, Nautilus, free weights, sauna, Jacuzzi. Day passes are $10 for adults, $5 for students and seniors.

CoachWorks Farm (802-755-6342), Page Pond Road, Albany near Craftsbury Common, is an amazingly sophisticated facility; there's an indoor lap pool, sauna, steam bath, massage, and weight machines. Day passes are available.

HIKING AND WALKING **Mount Pisgah** and **Mount Hor,** Lake Willoughby. Named respectively for the place where the Lord sent Moses to view the Promised Land and for the place Moses' brother Aaron died after the Lord commanded him to go there, these twin mountains, separated by a narrow stretch of lake, form Willoughby Gap. Both are within the 7,000-acre Willoughby State Forest and offer well-maintained hiking trails. Mount Pisgah (2,751 feet) on the east side of the lake (access marked from Route 5A) has fairly short climbs yielding spectacular views of the White Mountains; trails up Mount Hor (2,648 feet) begin on the Civilian Conservation Corps road, 1.8 miles west of its junction with Route 5A, and also offer panoramic views of the Green Mountains to the west. For details, consult *50 Hikes in Vermont* (Backcountry Guides) and *Day Hiker's Guide to Vermont* (Green Mountain Club).

Wheeler Mountain. The trail begins on Wheeler Mountain Road, which leaves the north side of Route 5, 8.3 miles north of West Burke and 5 miles south of Barton Village. From the highway, the unpaved road climbs to the trailhead, 1.9 miles.

Bald Mountain. There are excellent views from the abandoned fire tower at the summit of this, the tallest peak in the Willoughby Lake area. Trails ascend to the summit from both the north (Lookout's Trail, 2.8 miles) and the south (Long Pond Trail, 2.1 miles). From the north side of Bald Mountain, you can hike on trails and wilderness roads all the way to the summit of Mount Hor, and Haystack Mountain (a side trip) has excellent views and two trails. Details can be found in *Day Hiker's Guide to Vermont* (see *Hiking and Walking* in "What's Where").

Willoughby Gap Expeditions (802-626-5936; 802-626-8047). Naturalists Craig Erickson and Fife Hubbard lead expeditions Saturday and Sunday from East Burke Village to study the geology, flora, and fauna of Willoughby Gap. Private tours by appointment.

HORSEBACK RIDING **Rohan Farm** (802-467-3701), East Burke. Brian Kelly offers trail rides and cross-country treks geared to intermediate and better riders over the web of bridle paths on Darling Ridge and the adjacent mountains.

Greenhope Horse Farm B&B (802-533-7772), Walden. A long-established riding center with a summer camp and instruction, along with trail riding for experienced riders, on 140 acres connecting with local trails and dirt roads. Inquire about year-round B&B.

Perry Farm (802-754-2396) in Brownington offers hour-long trail rides at $25 per person, as does the **DND Farm** (802-626-8237) in East Burke.

RUNNING **Craftsbury Outdoor Center** (802-586-7767; 1-800-729-7751; www.craftsbury.com), Craftsbury Common, offers six 1-week camp sessions between June 30 and August 10; training for triathlons, marathons, the Stowe road race, and other excursions at around $500 per week.

SCULLING **Craftsbury Outdoor Center** (802-586-7767; 1-800-729-7751; www.craftsbury.com), Craftsbury Common, offers a nationally acclaimed summer sculling program; novices welcome.

SWIMMING **Harvey's Lake** in West Barnet; **Miles Pond** in Concord; public beaches in **Groton State Forest;** a small beach at **Ticklenaked Pond** in Boltonville; **Joe's Pond** in West Danville; **Molly's Pond** in Marshfield; public pools in St. Johnsbury and **Powers Park** in Lyndonville. In Glover, **Shadow Lake Beach,** marked from Route 16, is a delightful spot. There is also a public beach on **Caspian Lake,** near Greensboro Village. In Barton, **Crystal Lake State Beach** just east of the village on Route 15 is open daily in-season 10–8, with lifeguard, bathhouse, and picnic facilities; and **Pageant Park,** a mile farther east on Route 16, is a town-owned park open daily until 10 PM, also with a bathhouse and camping (primarily tenting). **May Pond,** also along Route 16 in Barton, is a great spot for swimming, canoeing, and kayaking.

Lake Willoughby has small public beaches at both its northern and southern tips. **Boulder Beach Day Use Area** (802-584-3820) in Groton State Forest has a public beach, picnic area, snack bar, bathhouse.

✷ Winter Sports

CROSS-COUNTRY SKIING Inquire about the **Ski the Kingdom Cross-country Trail Pass** (1-800-729-7751), good on all 220 miles of commercially maintained cross-country trails in this area. *Note:* There are two exceptionally high, dependably snowy, and spectacularly beautiful trail systems in this area, one in Craftsbury and the second in and around East Burke.

Craftsbury Outdoor Center Nordic Ski Center (802-586-7767; 1-800-729-7751; www.craftsbury.com), Craftsbury Common, grooms 105 km of its 130 km marked and maintained trail system; it offers rentals, instruction, lodging packages (trail fee). The system connects with **Highland Lodge** (802-533-2647; see *Lodging*) in Greensboro, which offers a total of 60 km of trails, 15 of them well groomed. The only major New England cross-country system that's nowhere near an alpine ski hill, the Craftsbury Outdoor Center/Highland Lodge trails web the kind of red-barn–spotted farmscape that's equated with, but increasingly rare in, Vermont. They traverse rolling fields, woods, and maple and evergreen groves, with stunning views of the distant Green Mountains. Thanks to their elevation and Craftsbury's exceptional grooming, they also represent some of the most dependable cross-country skiing in the Northeast and usually remain skiable well into March and sugaring season.

Burke Mountain Cross-Country (802-626-8338; 1-800-786-8338), East Burke. Well-groomed trails begin at 1,300 feet and wind through woods that yield to panoramic views. Rentals, lessons, guided tours; 62 km of tracked trails, an 80 km

CROSS-COUNTRY SKIING AT CRAFTSBURY CENTER

© Dennis Curran

system that connects with the evolving Kingdom Trails (see *To Do—Biking and Walking Trails*). Trails climb to 2,400 feet.

The Wildflower Inn and the **Inn at Mountain View Farm** (see *Lodging* for both) on Darling Hill between East Burke and Lyndonville offer adjoining trail systems with fabulous views; nominal donation.

Groton State Forest. Snowed-over roads, good for 20 km of cross-country skiing.

Sugarmill Farm (1-800-688-7978), Route 16, Barton. Eleven km of marked trails meander through the farm; 800- to 1,400-foot elevations. $5 trail fee.

See also Hazen's Notch in "Jay Peak Area."

DOWNHILL SKIING AND SNOWBOARDING **Burke Mountain** (802-626-3322), East Burke. This little ski area has had a rough go of it over the last few years, but it's still in operation. The adult weekend rate is $39 ($19 on weekdays in the spring!), which is hard to beat. The Burke Ski Academy bought and subsidized the mountain during the 2001–02 season, but its future remains uncertain. This is a small, friendly mountain with kids' programs, and the Northeast Kingdom gets more than its share of snow. The mountain doesn't offer lodging, but there's plenty in the area. The message is: call ahead.

Lyndon Outing Club (802-626-8465), Hill Street, Lyndonville. An old-fashioned, nonprofit town ski hill with a lodge, maintained by the Lyndon Outing Club since 1937. Open Tuesday, Wednesday, and Friday for night skiing 6:30–9:30, weekends 10–4; a T-bar is the workhorse lift and a rope tow serves the beginners' trail; snowboarding is permitted, and several cross-country trails are also maintained. Weekends $12 per adult, $8 weeknights.

SNOWMOBILING **The Northeast Kingdom Chamber of Commerce** (see *Guidance*) publishes a local snowmobiling map and directs inquiries to the local club from which it's necessary to purchase a VAST membership in order to use the trails. Rentals are available from **All Around Power Equipment** (802-748-1413), Route 5 north, St. Johnsbury.

Kingdom Cat Corp. (802-723-9702; www.kingdomcat.com) on Cross Street in Island Pond is by far the largest snowmobile rental operation in the area, and Island Pond is at the center of the state's snowmobile culture.

✷ Green Space

Barr Hill Nature Preserve, Greensboro. Turn right at the town hall and go about a half mile to Barr Hill Road (another left). The trails at Barr Hill, managed by The Vermont Nature Conservancy, overlook Caspian Lake. Don't miss the view from the top.

Victory Basin, alias Victory Bog. This 4,970-acre preserve administered by the Vermont Fish and Wildlife Department includes a 25-acre boreal bog with rare plant life, 1,800 acres of wetlands, 1,084 acres of hardwoods, and 71 acres of clearings and old fields. The dirt road access is via Victory; there are three parking areas: Mitchell's Landing, Lee Hill, and Damons Crossing.

Kim Grant

ROLLING FARMLAND NEAR EAST BURKE

Hurricane Brook Wildlife Management Area, off Route 114, south of Norton Pond: 9,500 forested acres, also accessible via a gravel road past Holland Pond from Holland Village. A detailed map is available from the Fish and Wildlife Department in Waterbury.

Waterford Dam at Moore Reservoir. New England Power offers guided tours of the huge complex of turbines. There are also picnic sites and a boat launch here. The approach is from the New Hampshire side of the Connecticut River, just below Lower Waterford, Vermont, off Route 135.

In St. Johnsbury

Fred Mold Park, near the confluence of the Passumpsic and Moose Rivers, is a great picnic spot by a waterfall and old mill. **The Arlington Preserve,** accessible from Waterman Circle, is a 33-acre nature preserve with woods, meadows, and rock outcroppings.

See also *Biking, Biking and Walking Trails,* and *Camping.*

✷ Lodging

In the St. Johnsbury area

Rabbit Hill Inn (802-748-5168; 1-800-76-BUNNY), Route 18, Lower Waterford 05848. Brian and Leslie Mulcahy welcome you to this pillared landmark, an inn since 1795. All 15 rooms and five suites are romantic confections, with canopy bed, antiques, and "indulging" bathroom. Many have working fireplace, Jacuzzi for two, and private porch. All have been painstakingly furnished, complete with a "room diary." Summer swimming and fishing in a freshwater pond, canoeing, and golf privileges; winter cross-country skiing, and snowshoeing. Rooms $265–295, suites $300–410 per couple, breakfast, afternoon tea, and five-course, candlelit dinner included. Add 15 percent service charge.

Broadview Farm (802-748-9902), 2627 McDowell Road, North Danville 05828. Open Memorial Day through October. This shingle-style country mansion has been in Molly Newell's family since 1901. It's set on 300 acres with a panoramic view of mountains, on a farm road in North Danville that, Molly assures us, was once the Boston-Montreal Road. In the late 19th century, before its shingles and gables, this old farmhouse took in summer boarders, advertising its 2,000-foot elevation as a sure escape from malaria and hay fever. Today the elevation suggests dependable cross-country skiing. Molly has thoroughly renovated the old place, removing 4,000 pounds of radiators, replacing windows, and gutting and redesigning the kitchen, while preserving the fine woodwork, detailing, and maple floors throughout the house. The four guest rooms are furnished with family antiques (check out the great oak set in the Yellow Room). Baths are private or shared; $55–120 double includes a full breakfast.

The Albro Nichols House (802-751-8434), 7 Boynton Avenue, St. Johnsbury 05819. This 1840s Federal-style house sits up behind Arnold Park at the head of Main Street, a flowery, quiet setting that's still within strolling distance of St. Johnsbury's museums, galleries, theaters, shops, and restaurants. Margaret Ryan is a former prep school dean and a high school theater director who clues in guests to the Kingdom's cultural scene. The pleasant, square Rose Room with private bath ($80) is on the ground floor; the upstairs rooms (both $60), one with twin beds, the other with a double (this would be a delightful room for a single person, too), share a book-lined sitting room and a bath. Common rooms feature plenty of books and interesting art; a full breakfast is included.

Branch Brook Bed & Breakfast (802-626-8316; 1-800-572-7712; bbbb@together.net), P.O. Box 217, Lyndon 05849. This is an exceptional house with long, graceful parlor windows, built in the 1850s, beautifully converted to a B&B by Ted and Ann Tolman. The room with a pencil-post, canopy bed, locally crafted from cherrywood, is worthy of brides; two rooms are tucked under exposed beams, furnished with antiques. All but two of the five have private bath. Prices are $65–85 per couple with a hearty breakfast; Ann Tolman has a food-service background and prides herself on breakfasts prepared on her English Aga cooker. Two of Lyndon's five covered bridges are within walking distance.

Emergo Farm B&B (802-684-2215; 1-888-383-1185; emergo@together.net), 261 Webster Hill, Danville 05828. Just north of the village, this strikingly handsome farm is a prizewinning, fifth-generation working dairy farm. The upstairs apartment has two bedrooms, full kitchen, sitting room, and bath, ideal for a family or two couples (a pullout in the sitting room sleeps extra kids). Rooms are also available individually with shared bath. The farm's 200 acres include a hilltop with panoramic views of much of the Kingdom. Historical and present-day farm tours are offered, and livestock includes a pet goat and turkeys as well as 130 head of cattle (80 milking cows). $70–140 per room includes breakfast, served downstairs in the dining room.

Country Cottage B&B (802-426-3655), 3314 Route 232, Marshfield 05658. Dan and Judy Lloyd, who used to run the Creamery Inn in Cabot, now own and operate this new establishment in Marshfield. They have two guest rooms with private bath and are convenient to walks in the nearby state park. Children welcome, but no pets please. Rates range from $75–85, including full breakfast.

The Inn at Maplemont Farm (802-633-4880; 1-800-230-1617), Route 5, Barnet 05821. Tom and Sherry Tolle's trim, well-kept, large yellow farmhouse sits in a bucolic setting on 43 acres across the road from the Connecticut River. The three guest rooms are pleasant, all with private bath; South Peacham, the ground-floor twin, is particularly attractive. Pet and livestock accommodations are available if you arrange in advance. $80–110 per night, with hearty breakfast and afternoon refreshments.

Sherryland (802-684-3354), Danville 05828. Caroline Sherry's large, 19th-century farmhouse is on a pleasant country road about a mile south of the village green. Five guest rooms are genuinely homelike. No meals; still only $32 double, $28 single, $5 per cot.

Echo Ledge Farm Inn (802-748-4750), Route 2, P.O. Box 46, East St. Johnsbury 05838. Open year-round. The Lamotte family runs this bed & breakfast on a farm established in 1793. Six comfortable bedrooms, five with private bath. Afternoon tea, plenty of books. $47–67; $5 less single, $10 extra for use of one or two daybeds.

Ha'Penny Gourmet (802-592-3317; 1-800-471-7655), Peacham 05862 (see also *Selective Shopping—General Stores*). Mark Moore and Karen Stawiecki, proprietors of the unusual Peacham Store, have three cozy bedrooms over the shop. $75–85 double, with a sumptuous breakfast of freshly made croissants and homemade jams. Dinner by reservation.

Long Meadow Inn (802-757-2538; 1-800-394-2538), Route 5, Wells River 05081. This stately brick Federal by the river, once a stagecoach stop, is now nicely restored (and extensively fireproofed) by Roy and Ellen Canlon. There are five pretty guest rooms, two with private bath. $25–30 per person, less for 3 or more days.

The Old Homestead (802-633-4016; 1-877-OLD-HOME), 1573 Route 5 south, Barnet 05821. Gail Arnaar is a musician who welcomes other musicians in particular, everyone in general, to this handsome old house. Guest rooms range from small ($48 single) to a $95 family room; inquire about $65 per weekend per couple.

In the Burke Mountain area

ꝏ ✐ **The Wildflower Inn** (802-626-8310; 1-800-627-8310; www.wildflowerinn.com), 2059 Darling Hill Road, Lyndonville 05851. This is a fine old farmhouse set high on a ridge with a spectacular view, surrounded by its own 500 acres including gardens and trails maintained for hiking, mountain biking, and cross-country skiing. Jim and Mary O'Reilly have eight children (five boys, three girls), and other children are particularly welcome. There is a big playroom in the main house; a daily (except Sunday) supervised morning arts, crafts, and summer nature program for children ages 4 and up in the big barn; a variety of animals to relate to in the petting barn; a sports complex with basketball, a batting cage, and tennis court and playing field beyond. Adult spaces include an indoor sauna and hot tub, an attractive parlor and library—stocked with games and the kind of books you really want to read—and a fine little art gallery. The landscaped pool commands a spectacular view of rolling hills. Dinner is a multi-course event (see *Dining Out*), but for children, there's the option of parent-free dining at Daisy's Diner, open only in the summer. Breakfast is a three-course production, and tea is also served. Upstairs in the main house, two family suites have great views. There are nine more suites, including a romantic one off by itself in the old schoolhouse, complete with whirlpool bath. There are also 10 rooms in the former carriage house across the road. $95–280 per couple B&B plus $25 per teen, $20 per child ages 4–11, and free for ages 3 and under. Christmastime is especially festive here.

ꝏ **The Inn at Mountain View Farm** (802-626-9924), Darling Hill Road, East Burke 05832. Like the Wildflower Inn, this is part of a onetime 9,000-acre hilltop estate owned by Elmer Darling, a Burke native, who built this creamery in 1890 to supply dairy products to his Fifth Avenue hotel (it used to churn out 600 pounds of butter a month and 70 pounds of cheese per day). The inn is still set among restored barns and backed by 440 acres that spread across a high ridge and are laced with trails maintained for walking, mountain biking, and cross-country skiing. Marilyn Pastore has tastefully decorated the 12 guest rooms (private baths) with antiques, wicker, and bright fabrics. The downstairs sitting rooms are also nicely furnished, and a patio with tables, chairs, and striped market umbrellas is set in perennial gardens. A weekend bistro serves lunch and dinner (see *Dining Out*). This is a favorite for weddings and with bike groups. $115–180 per room includes a full breakfast that might include a vegetable frittata as well as fruit, yogurt, muffins, and cereals. Inquire about the neighboring Victorian farmhouse, sleeping six: two bedrooms, two baths, a Jacuzzi, full kitchen, and parlor, $1,800 per week.

ꝏ **The Old Cutter Inn** (802-626-5152; 1-800-295-1943), 143 Pinkham Road, East Burke 05832. Closed April and November. This 1845 farmhouse just minutes from Burke Mountain has been owned and operated by Swiss-born chef Fritz Walther since 1977. It's a spotless, cozy inn with a suite plus nine rooms, five with private bath, and a two-bedroom apartment next to the barn. Its excellent dining room is open to the public every night except Wednesday (when it still serves guests); you can choose between the formal dining room (see *Dining Out*) and a friendly, less expensive pub. The grounds include a heated, landscaped swimming pool and views of Willoughby Gap. The inn can accommodate wedding receptions and rehearsal dinners of up to 44 people. $60–62 with shared bath; $72 with private bath; $10 per extra person in room; MAP available; multiday packages; cheaper in the off-season. No pets.

THE BARN AT THE INN AT MOUNTAIN VIEW FARM

Kim Grant

The Village Inn of East Burke (802-626-3161; 802-793-4517), Box 186, East Burke 05832. This friendly bed & breakfast owned by Lorraine and George Willy offers five rooms, all large enough to accommodate families and all with private bath; in the common space are a woodstove, books, and games. Guests can use a separate kitchen with stove and refrigerator. $45 single, $60 per couple includes a light breakfast.

Burke Mountain Condominiums (802-626-8903; 1-800-541-5480), Burke Hollow Road, East Burke 05832. About 90 slope-side units in the rental pool are salted around the ski area's access roads. They range from studios to four-bedroom apartments accommodating 11. All have woodstove or fireplace, TV, and trail access; 2-night weekend packages from $199 per person; 5-night midweek, from $281 per person.

In the Craftsbury area

The Inn on the Common (802-586-9619; 1-800-521-2233), Craftsbury Common 05827. The most regal lodging in the Kingdom has been offered since 1978 by Michael and Penny Schmidt. Guest rooms and suites are impeccably tasteful, with matching paper and curtains, well-chosen antiques, brass and four-poster beds, and original art. The 16 rooms, 5 with woodstove or fireplace, some with canopy beds, are divided among three Federal-style buildings close to the common. Guests congregate in the library for cocktails and dine formally at candlelit tables (see *Dining Out*). In summer, you can take advantage of the solar-heated pool, the perennial gardens, lawn croquet, and the tennis court. Inquire about packages featuring mountain biking, running, sculling, and cross-country-skiing programs at nearby Craftsbury Outdoor Center (see *Winter Sports*), and the inn also offers access to superbly equipped Coachworks (see *Health Spas*). $150–265 single occupancy, $230–290 per couple, MAP, plus tax and 15 percent service. Children (special rates), smokers, and pets ($15 per stay) are all welcome.

Highland Lodge (802-533-2647; www.highlandlodge.com), Greensboro 05841. Open May 30 through October 16 and December 20 through March 15. A fine, Victorian-era inn on the shore of Caspian Lake that manages to be both airy in warm weather and cozy in winter, now managed by the second generation of Smiths (David, Wilhelmina, and Alex)—hosts whose warmth is reflected in the atmosphere of their public rooms. Common rooms include a comfortable library with desks and armchairs, a game room, a living room with fireplace, and a sitting room with baby grand piano. Upstairs are 11 rooms, all with private bath. There are also 11 cottages (4 remain open in winter). In summer, facilities include tennis courts and a pleasant beach with bathhouse and boats, along with the nature trails on the property and in the adjacent Barr Hill Nature Preserve (see *Green Space*); in winter the draw is cross-country skiing on the extensive network radiating from the inn's touring center, rising to unusual elevations with superb views. Inside, there is plenty of space to read and get away from other guests, along with nice corners in which to socialize. For children, there's an organized summer program (ages 4–9). In the lodge, $112–157 per person, $20–65 per child depending on age, MAP; in a cottage, $120–140 per person; inquire about family rates; 15 percent gratuity, as well as breakfast and dinner, is included. Less in May and weekdays in June, September, October, January, and March.

Craftsbury Bed & Breakfast (802-586-2206; www.scenesofvermont.com/craftsburybb), Craftsbury Common 05827. Margaret Ramsdell welcomes guests to her farmhouse on Wylie Hill, with views that (even by local standards) are hard to beat. Generally known as Margie's Place, this friendly, informal B&B caters to skiers, bicyclists, and hikers. The two upstairs rooms (sharing a bath) have the longest views, but the four additional ground-floor guest rooms (sharing two baths) are perfectly pleasant. There's an inviting living room, and the door to the big country kitchen—with its glowing soapstone stove, backed by gleaming copper—is always open. In winter (December through early April), guests can ski out the door and onto 105 km of groomed trails maintained by the Craftsbury Outdoor Center (see below). $60–85 includes a full breakfast (maybe cinnamon-apple pancakes or eggs with cheddar cheese). Dinner possible.

Craftsbury Outdoor Center (802-586-7767; 1-800-729-7751; www.craftsbury.com), P.O. Box 31, Lost Nation Road, Craftsbury Common 05827. Recreational facilities are the big attractions here, with accommodations for 90 guests divided between two rustic lodges: 9 large doubles and 31 smaller rooms sharing lavatory-style hall bathrooms, 3 larger rooms with private bath, 2 efficiency apartments, and 3 housekeeping cottages sleeping four. Three meals are served, buffet-style, in the dining hall. Guests come for the programs offered: running, sculling, walking, mountain biking, and cross-country skiing; or they stay and enjoy the outdoors at their own pace. Facilities include swimming at Lake Hosmer, exercise rooms, sauna, tennis courts, and 140 acres. From $136–230 per person including three plentiful meals with vegetarian options; family and multiday rates available. (See also *To Do—Biking, Sculling, Running,* and *Cross-Country Skiing.*)

Lakeview Inn (802-533-2291; www.hcr.net/lakeview), P.O. Box 95, Main Street, Greensboro 05841. Open year-round. Built in 1872 as a summer boardinghouse, this handsome clapboard inn served that purpose right up until the 1980s (it housed the musicians who performed in Summer Music from Greensboro), but it had stood abandoned for eight years when Kathy Unser and John Hunt took it on, painstakingly restoring it. It has since been added to the National Register of Historic Places and was an Editor's Pick by Yankee Magazine in 2001. Much of the ground floor is now an informal restaurant (see *Eating Out*), and there is a small first-floor guest sitting room with a big-screen TV. Upstairs is another common room. There are nine guest rooms with private bath, one of which is handicapped-accessible, and a top-floor three-bedroom suite sleeps six. $125–250 (for the suite) includes breakfast.

Craftsbury Inn (802-586-2848; 1-800-336-2848), Route 14, Craftsbury 05826, a village with a delightful general store just downhill from Craftsbury Common. The handsome 1850 Greek Revival–style inn was built as a private residence in the 1850s with a second-story, wraparound porch. There are unusually attractive living and game rooms dressed with interesting artwork. Upstairs, the 10 guest rooms are also nicely decorated, some with canopy beds, all with quilts made to match the wallpaper. Dinner is taken seriously (see *Dining Out*). Rates $140–160 per couple, MAP; $90–110 B&B plus 15 percent for service. Midweek packages, single rates.

Whetstone Brook Bed & Breakfast (802-586-6916), 1037 South Craftsbury Road, Craftsbury 05826-4220. An 1826 Vermont classic Cape that, with additions, has been home to six generations of the Wilson family is now Audrey and Bryce Wilson's retirement project, a pleasant B&B. There's a piano in the living room, an Aga stove in the kitchen, and the small round tables in the dining room are positioned to view the meadow through the French doors. Two upstairs rooms share a bath (a third is rented if everyone belongs to the same group), and the ground-floor Apple Blossom Room has a queen bed and private bath. $80–90 includes a full breakfast.

Somerset House (802-472-5484; 1-800-838-8074), 130 Highland Avenue, Hardwick 05843. A vernacular 1890s Victorian home with perennial flower gardens and four guest rooms, one with private bath, three sharing two baths. English hostess Ruth Gaillard serves a full breakfast with an egg entrée or crêpes, fresh fruit. Ask for a tower room. $69–80 double, $50–60 single.

Golden Maple Inn (802-888-6614; 1-800-639-5234), Route 15, Wolcott Village 05680, offers four spacious guest rooms and a fireplace suite, all with private bath, in an 1865 riverside home. Fy-fishing is the real specialty (a fly-fishing school and guide service can be arranged; see *To Do—Fishing*). The ground-floor Geneve Suite with gas woodstove goes for $94 and up, and the second-floor Captain's Cabin and Alpine Glow, with private bath, are $84 and up. The River Suite can sleep four and goes for $99. Full breakfasts.

Village House Inn (802-755-6722), P.O. Box 228, Route 14, Albany 05820. This fine Victorian village house with a wraparound porch is a full-service inn with eight bedrooms (private baths) just minutes from Craftsbury Common and adjacent to the Catamount cross-country-ski trail. From $65 per couple, including breakfast. See also *Dining Out*.

Maple Manor B&B (802-525-9591), 77 Maple Lane, West Glover 05875. A charming Victorian inn on 250 acres. Rates are $99–175 with breakfast and afternoon tea.

On Lake Willoughby

ꝏ **Fox Hall** (802-525-6930), mailing address: 145 Fox Hall Lane, Barton 05822. Ken and Sherry Pyden have transformed the main house of a turn-of-the-20th-century mansion, which served for many decades as a girls camp, into a comfortable bed & breakfast. Common space is ample and the eight guest rooms, some round, four with private bath, are furnished with antiques. All offer views of Lake Willoughby. The 76 acres include lake frontage and a dock. Guests have access to canoes, paddleboats, and Windsurfers, and can swim off the dock. But they may never want to leave the wide old porch, which commands one of the most dramatic views in Vermont, right down Willoughby Gap. Sherry has a thing about moose—which she collects in many forms. Inquire about summer music and theater in the pavilion behind the inn. $79–109 in summer and fall, less mid-October through June, an exceptional breakfast included.

♿ **WilloughVale Inn on Lake Willoughby** (802-525-4123; 1-800-594-9102; www.willoughvale.com), RR 2, Box 403, Westmore 05860. This nifty place has an efficiency suite and seven unique upstairs rooms, one handicapped-accessible room downstairs, and 4 two-bedroom housekeeping cottages with fireplaces across the road, on the lake. There's a taproom and light dinner; breakfast is

LAKE WILLOUGHBY

Kim Grant

also available for guests. The original farmhouse here dated back to the mid-1800s, and by the early 1900s it was a restaurant. After several years of vacancy, the old house was replaced by a new inn, tastefully built along traditional lines with windows that maximize the spectacular lake view. It is now owned and operated by the Gameroff family, who also own the Green Mountain Inn (see *Lodging* in "Stowe and Waterbury"). Elegant public areas give guests some private space beyond their quarters, some of which are quite spacious; all have private bath, furnishings specifically made for them, and water views. In the main inn, standard rooms with queen beds are $89 in low season and $109–139 in high; the Lupine Room, with four-poster and Jacuzzi, is $99–119 in low, $134–154 in high; and the Harter Suite, with living-dining room and kitchen, is $79–99 in low, $125–145 in high (plus $2 per room per night as housekeeping gratuity). The cottages are $109–119 in low season, $179–275 nightly, $1,170 weekly in high. Canoe, bicycle, snowshoe, and snowmobile rentals are available on the premises. Inquire about packages that combine WilloughVale and Green Mountain Inn stays.

In the Barton/Orleans area

Heermansmith Farm Inn (802-754-8866), 550 Heermanville Road, Coventry 05825. Up a hill and out a back road beyond a small village you will find this farm, which has been in the same family since 1807. Jack Smith offers six rooms upstairs in the snug, 1860s farmhouse that sits amid fields of hay and pastureland skirted by the Black River. It is well known as one of the region's leading restaurants (see *Dining Out*). Three of the rooms, with private bath, are in a new wing, and three others, also with private bath, are in the original part of the house, one about as Vermont as a guest room can be, complete with antique bed, handmade quilt, and a crazy window. Books line the walls throughout the inn, including in the dining rooms. Guests can enjoy the lounge by day. $60 single, $75 double, B&B.

Brick House (802-754-2108), P.O. Box 33, Irasburg 05845. Roger and Jo Sweatt welcome you to their 1875 brick house just off the common in this small, very Vermont village. There are three guest rooms, one twin bedded with private bath and two (one with a lace-topped canopy bed and the other with a brass bed) sharing a bath. A breakfast, which might include Jo's crustless mushroom quiche, is included in $45 double, $30 single, $50 for the family room with a pullout bed. Add $5 for 1-night stays on weekends.

Crystal Lake B&B (802-525-4670), Route 5, Barton 05822. This trim white house, open from Memorial Day through Halloween, sits right on Crystal Lake, and the view is across its width. The three rooms with private bath are bright, nicely furnished, with lake views. There are lots of books and reading alcoves. Guests can fish and swim from the dock, and boats and canoes can be rented. $85 per couple, $75 single includes breakfast. A waterfront apartment goes for $650 per week.

MOTELS **Fairbanks Inn** (802-748-5666), 401 Western Avenue (Route 2 east), St. Johnsbury 05819. This three-story, 46-unit, quite luxurious motel has central air-conditioning, heated pool, and fitness center privileges. $65–125 per room. Pets accepted in some rooms.

Aime's Motel (802-748-3194; 1-800-504-6663), junction of Routes 2 and 18, Box 332, St. Johnsbury 05819. This small, family-geared motel is located right next to a rushing stream. There are 16 rooms, which a reader tells us are sparkling clean. $37–70 double includes morning coffee. Pets accepted.

CAMPGROUNDS For a complete listing, see *To Do—Camping.*

* Where to Eat

DINING OUT **Inn on the Common** (802-586-9619; 1-800-521-2233), Craftsbury Common. The menu at this elegant inn changes daily; outside guests with reservations are welcome. Meals are in the formal dining room at either common or small tables (patrons tend to meet over cocktails in the library before dinner), or (weather permitting) on the adjoining patio. The menu changes nightly. On a late-October evening you might begin with a shrimp, roasted pepper, and spinach appetizer, then a cream of celery soup followed by a salad. Then choose from pan-seared rib-eye buffalo, chicken breast sautéed with a sesame-honey-ginger glaze, or sautéed medallions of tuna with lemon caper buerre blanc. Dessert can be cheesecake with kiwi puree. $35 prix fixe includes after-dinner coffee and chocolates in the library. The wine list is a passion of innkeeper Michael Schmidt.

Heermansmith Farm Inn (802-754-8866), Heermanville Road, Coventry. Closed Monday and Tuesday in the off-season, otherwise open for dinner nightly, year-round. Reservations appreciated. The farm itself is locally known for the quality of its produce, especially strawberries. The restaurant is the candlelit interior of the old farmhouse, walls lined with books, white-linen-covered tables well spaced. You might begin with mushrooms en cassoulet (sautéed in a sherried cream sauce and nestled in a warm pastry puff shell, $5.95) and dine on Duck

Heermansmith, roasted crisp with a strawberry and Chambord fruit sauce ($16.95). A lighter menu is offered in the Library Lounge.

The Inn at Mountain View Farm (802-626-9924), Darling Hill Road, East Burke. Open Friday, Saturday, and Sunday for lunch and dinner. This brick-walled room, once the heart of a working creamery, is an attractive dining room with a varied menu that includes entrées ranging from a layered polenta terrine with roasted vegetables and French feta ($10.95) to roasted New Zealand lamb ($19.95). Specials vary each night, as do the featured wines.

The Wildflower Inn (802-626-8310), between Lyndonville and East Burke on Darling Hill Road. Open for dinner June through mid-October, Monday through Saturday; in winter Thursday, Friday, and Saturday. Positioned as it is at the rear of the inn, overlooking flower gardens and a spread of valley with mountains rolling into the distance, this is a delightful place to dine. Entrées might include salmon and sole lattice with pesto, Irish beef stew, and marinated rib-eye steak. $12–20.

Rabbit Hill Inn (802-748-5168; 1-800-76-BUNNY), Route 18 in Lower Waterford. Open to outside guests by reservation, space permitting. The elegant dining room holds just 15 tables, and both food and atmosphere are carefully orchestrated. There's candlelight and crystal, harp or flute music many nights, and a choice of five-course dinners. Entrées might range from broccoli-cheddar crêpes filled with mushrooms, leeks, and sun-dried tomatoes to poached red snapper in red peppercorn broth with olive pancetta to smoked tenderloin of beef. Appetizer or soup, and bread, sorbet, salad, dessert, and beverage are included in the $37 prix fixe.

The Old Cutter Inn (802-626-5152), Burke Hollow Road, East Burke. Open for dinner daily except Wednesday, also for Sunday brunch; closed November and April. Owner Fritz Walther prepares a few of his native specialties, like Rahmschnitzel (pork medallions sautéed in butter with shallots, deglazed with white wine, and finished with fresh mushrooms in a light cream sauce). He is also known for his beef Wellington and veal dishes. Less formal fare, like smoked trout, Swiss bratwurst, and forster-schnitten, is served in the tavern, a favorite local gathering place. Entrées $13.25–18.95, less in the tavern.

Creamery Restaurant (802-684-3616), Danville. Open Tuesday through Friday for lunch and dinner; Saturday for dinner only. A former creamery nicely converted into a gracious little restaurant that many feel is the best in the St. J area. A blackboard menu features homemade soups and salads, pies, and a choice of meat and seafood dishes. Moderate; less expensive pub menu downstairs.

The Village House Inn (802-755-6722), Route 14, Albany. Open for dinner Friday and Saturday, year-round. Right in the middle of this small village, the inn—a Victorian home—rides a reputations for quality that chef-owner Jon Ryan established during the years he was chef at Heermansmith Farm, where wife Kate managed the dining room, as she does this one, a long, narrow, many-windowed space with tables on the porch, too, in warm weather. Entrées range from grilled Cajun chicken on a bed of spinach ($10.95), to fresh tomato fettuccine primavera pesto ($11.95), to veal

Oscar ($17.95), to salmon en croute (which we can personally recommend, $16.95). Desserts are superior and wines are reasonably priced.

Craftsbury Inn (802-586-2848), Craftsbury. Dinner is open to the public by reservation May through October, Wednesday through Sunday 6:30–8:30. The small dining room has just eight tables and a choice of four entrées. Chef-owner Blake Gleason offers a limited menu that changes seasonally but might include sautéed mushrooms and goat cheese in puff pastry for starters ($4.75) and sautéed pork medallions served with apricot brandy sauce ($15.95).

Highland Lodge (802-533-2647), Greensboro. The inn is open late May through mid-October and Christmas week through mid-March. Breakfast, lunch (except Monday), and dinner (by reservation) are served in the inn's attractive dining room and, weather permitting, on the porch. Dinner entrées could include Vermont leg of lamb with roasted garlic sauce, farmed salmon fillet with mustard and tarragon, or triple orange chicken breast. Begin with wild mushroom soup and French walnut rolls and end with bittersweet chocolate cake. Lunch features interesting croissants, salads, and soups as well as the usual sandwiches. Specials, too, can be interesting. Dinner entrées $14.75–16.75, with a lighter menu available.

EATING OUT **River Garden Café** (802-626-3514), Route 114, East Burke Village. Open daily for lunch and dinner. A hugely and justly popular place with an attractive decor and varied menu, from salads, burgers, pizza, eggplant Parmesan, and pastas to filet mignon ($21.95); homemade breads and desserts. A café atmosphere, casual and pleasant, with a year-round back porch and summer patio dining within earshot of the river. Readers have recommended it highly.

Lakeview Inn (802-533-2291), Main Street, Greensboro. Open daily for breakfast, lunch, and light fare until 4, later in summer. This is a meeting spot for miles around, an expansive, comfortable dining room with a bakery and deli serving soups, chili, salads, and such. Definitely worth checking.

Candlepin Restaurant (802-525-6513), Route 5 north of Barton. Open 7 days a week featuring family-style breakfast, lunch, and dinner.

Village Restaurant (802-472-5701), junction of Routes 14 and 15, Hardwick, offers three squares in a basic, clean, comfortable, no-frills, dinerlike place in the center of town.

Miss Lyndonville Diner (802-626-9890), Route 5 south, Lyndonville. Open from 6 AM until supper, famed for strawberry pancakes with whipped cream for breakfast, pie, homemade French toast, and jumbo eggs. This is one of the famous railroad diners, along with Miss Newport and Miss Bellows Falls, that made their way to Vermont years ago. When they came, they brought with them the best of classic diner fare.

Danville Restaurant (802-684-3484), Danville Village. Housed in a village house, open 6 AM–9 PM, this family restaurant is good for all three meals at reasonable prices in a friendly atmosphere. Both counter and table service, from hamburgers to full-course meals, daily specials.

In St. Johnsbury

Cucina de Gerardo (802-748-6772), 1216 Railroad Street (in the old creamery building). Everyone's favorite place for gourmet pizzas, chicken pesto, and mussels marinara. Far closer to Italy than you might suspect you could come in St. J. Most entrées are in the $8.95–13.95 range.

Northern Lights Bookshop Cafe (802-748-4463), 79 Railroad Street. Open daily from 9:30 for bagels, croissants, currant scones, sour cream coffee cake, and assorted omelets; at lunch for soups, salads, and sandwiches; until 4 PM for pastries; and until 8:30 Thursday, Friday, and Saturday nights for dinner. Espresso, cappuccino, and teas all day. Begun as a bookstore café, this bright, imaginative space now fills a second storefront. The dinner menu features regional American dishes; beer and wine are served. Inquire about Thursday-evening jazz (see also *Selective Shopping—Bookstores*).

♣ ✐ ♿ **Cindy's Pasta** (802-748-4848), Route 5 south of the Green Mountain Mall. Open 6:30 AM through lunch Monday and Tuesday, 6:30 AM through dinner Wednesday through Saturday, closed Sunday. Cindy gets up at 5:30 to start baking the day's breads, and the pasta is all made on premises. The seafood scampi goes for $17.25, while a hearty portion of meat or vegetable lasagna is $9.50. Lunch is salads and sandwiches.

St. Jay Diner (802-748-9751), Memorial Drive (Route 5 north). Open Sunday through Thursday 7:30 AM–8 PM, Friday and Saturday 7:30 AM–9 PM. Formerly the Miss Vermont Diner, now owned by the owners of Warners Gallery (see below). Known for reliable roadfood.

In Wells River

✐ **Warners Gallery Restaurant** (802-429-2120), Route 302. Open for dinner nightly and for Sunday brunch. Often crowded for dinner; reserve. Good range of moderately priced entrées like stuffed shrimp and prime ribs. Children's menu. Boasts "best Sunday brunch in the Northeast." All entrées come with the large salad bar (includes peel-and-eat shrimp and sticky buns); on Wednesday, the second dinner is half price. Children under 12 are free on Friday. Fully licensed.

Happy Hours Restaurant (802-757-3466), Route 5. Open daily 11:30–8. This solid, pine-paneled family restaurant in the middle of town serves lunch and dinner, fully licensed.

✐ **P&H Truck Stop** (802-429-2141), Route 302 just off I-91. Open 24 hours, a genuine trucker's haven with showers and hearty grub. Popular with families as well.

TEA **The Brick House** (802-472-5512), East Hardwick, features 3 acres of perennial gardens, the backdrop for English cream teas, served by English-born Judith Kane. Aside from a variety of teas and lemonades, the teas include cucumber sandwiches, scones, ham, fresh cream, and pastries. Reservations.

✷ Entertainment

Catamount Film and Arts Company (802-748-2600), 60 Eastern Avenue, St. Johnsbury. Established in 1975 as a nonprofit cultural organization serving northern Vermont and New Hampshire, Catamount stages a variety of "showcase events" at sites throughout the region, weekend film screenings at the Catamount Arts Center (the former St. Johnsbury post office), and changing shows in its gallery. Summer productions include performances of

Circus Smirkus, a summerlong circus workshop for area youths ages 10–18.

Star Theater (802-748-4900; 802-748-9511), 18 Eastern Avenue, St. Johnsbury. Cinemas 1-2-3; first-run movies.

Lyndon Corner Grange (802-748-8829) sponsors dances every Saturday night at the Grange Hall. A three-piece band plays for the over-50 crowd. BYOB; dancing begins at 9 PM. $3 admission; call for reservations.

Summer Music from Greensboro, based at the Congregational church in Greensboro, is a series of chamber and choral music concerts in July and August.

Craftsbury Chamber Players have brought chamber music to northern Vermont for 25 years. The 6-week summer series runs mid-July through August, Thursday evenings, at the Hardwick Town House. There are also shorter, Thursday-afternoon free concerts at the Town House. Most performers are faculty members at the Juilliard School of Music in New York City.

The Vermont Symphony Orchestra plays regularly at Burke Mountain in summer; check local calendars for other musical performances at Burke.

Vermont Children's Theater (802-626-8838), Darling Hill Road, Lyndonville. Local youngsters perform amazingly well. Performances the last two weekends in July are by thespians ages 8–12 and, in August, ages 13–18.

Circus Smirkus (802-533-7443; 1-800-532-7443) in Greensboro. A children's circus camp stages frequent performances in July and August.

BAND CONCERTS **St. Johnsbury Town Band concerts,** weekly all summer at the bandstand in Town Hall Park. Monday 8 PM. **Lyndonville Town Band concerts,** every Wednesday in summer at 8 PM in the park. **Craftsbury band concerts** at the band shell on the common, Sundays at 7 in July and August.

In **Greensboro.** Concerts on the dock at Caspian Lake, sponsored by the Greensboro Association, summer Sundays at 7:30.

* Selective Shopping

ANTIQUES SHOPS **Farr's Antiques** (802-684-3333), Peacham Road, Danville. Oak tables, chairs, dressers, and other assorted furniture and furnishings fill three floors of a former granary.

Route 5 Collectibles (802-626-5430), Route 5, Lyndonville. A multidealer and consignment shop.

Norman Dion's (802-754-8770), Irasburg. Ask directions from the general store. It's just a short way out of the village, up a farm road; there's no sign, but you'll see the warehouse-like complex on your right before you get to the Castle (you'll know when you do). This is a local institution, a vast collection of trash and treasure, well known to antiques dealers from near and far.

BOOKSTORES **The American Society of Dowsers Bookstore** (802-748-8565; 1-800-711-9497), 430 Railroad Street, St. Johnsbury. This is an amazing store. Everything you ever wanted to know about dowsing and dowsing equipment is here, but also a host of New Age books and tapes on healing, chakras, earth mysteries, the esoteric and metaphysical, reiki, runes, and well-being, not to mention labyrinth T-shirts, crystals, and more.

✐ **Northern Lights Bookshop** (802-748-4463), 79 Railroad Street, St. Johnsbury. A bright, lively, full-service bookstore that's a real part of St. Johnsbury's cultural life. The stock is unusually extensive, with many Vermont-based writers, a large children's section, also cards, magazines, and children's toys. The popular café (see *Eating Out*) displays work by local artists (see *Galleries*). Inquire about author's readings and music.

The Galaxy Bookshop (802-472-5533), 7 Mill Street, Hardwick. Since Linda Ramsdell moved her shop into a vintage-1910 bank building, she offers not only ample space for her stock but also probably the only drive-through book and rental audiotape (call ahead) service in the country. Audiotapes? Local farmers listen while driving tractors and doing chores. This is a full-service bookstore specializing in Vermont writers and unusual titles; armchairs invite lingering.

Green Mountain Books & Prints (802-626-5051), 100 Broad Street, Lyndonville (Route 5 on the corner of the common). Open Monday through Thursday 10–4, Friday 10–6, Saturday 10–1. Ellen Doyle is the second generation of her family to preside over this book lover's heaven: an unusual mix of new and used books; many new, discounted titles; new and old prints; and rare books. Doyle seems to know something about every book in this 4,000-plus square-foot space. Vermontiana, Native American, and children's books are specialties, but the range is wide and patrons are welcome to sit in a corner for as long as they wish. Bigger than it looks at first: There are separate children's and fiction rooms.

That Book Store (802-748-1722), 71 Eastern Avenue, St. Johnsbury. Monday through Saturday 10–8, Sunday 11–8 . . . "usually." A big old hardware

HASTINGS GENERAL STORE IN WEST DANVILLE

Kim Grant

space is filled with used and antiquarian books, postcards, and "paper ephemera."

Country Bear Books (802-626-3469), Main Street, Lyndonville. Open daily, Friday till 8 PM, Sunday to 4. An extraordinarily large and eclectic stock of new—and remaindered—books, most at discount prices.

Marketplace Vintage Books (802-525-4291), Post Office Square, Barton. Buys and sells used, new, and collectible books.

CHEESE **Cabot Creamery Visitors Center** (802-563-2231; www.cabotcheese.com), Cabot. Open year-round except January, June through October 9–5 daily, in the off-season Monday through Saturday 9–4. For details, see *To See*.

Kingsey Cheese of Vermont (802-472-5763), Hardwick Industrial Park, Wolcott Street, Hardwick. Founded in Quebec, this is an rBGH-free milk cheese; check out the retail shop.

Northeast Kingdom Sheep Milk Cheese (802-533-2360), Skunk Hollow Farm, Greensboro. Visitors are discouraged at the farm itself, but this exceptional cheese is available at the Lake View Inn (see *Lodging*) and other locations in Greensboro.

CRAFTS SHOPS **Northeast Kingdom Artisans Guild** (802-748-0158), 101 Railroad Street, St. Johnsbury. Open Monday through Saturday. This cooperative showcases some magnifcent work in many media.

The Peacham Corner Guild (802-592-3332), Route 2. Open June through October, daily 10–5, Sunday 11–5. Handcrafted gifts, small antiques.

Birdman (802-563-2877), Danville Hill Road between Route 2 and Cabot. Open July through October, Monday through Saturday 8–5; November through June by chance or appointment. Edmund Menard produces small, impressively fantailed birds: Christmas ornaments, a bird necklace, earrings, lapel pins, and more.

The Craft Shop at Molly's Pond, on Route 2, west of West Danville. Open June through November, closed Sunday. One of the state's first outstanding crafts shops, here for more than 30 years, specializing in original metal jewelry, fine pottery, weavings, blown glass, and Sabra Field prints. Shopkeeper Martha Price knows all the craftspeople personally.

The Miller's Thumb (802-533-2960), Greensboro Village. A former gristmill with a spectacular view of the stream churning down falls below, through a window in the floor. Open June through mid-September, a gallery with crafts. A trove of art, crafts, and gift items, many made locally; check out the furniture and clothing upstairs.

Steffi's Studio (802-754-6012), Irasburg green. Steffi Huess crafts gold and silver jewelry, and sells it along with other local arts and crafts right from the front room in her home.

GALLERIES *Note:* St. Johnsbury's most famous art gallery is the St. Johnsbury Athenaeum (see *To See—Museums*), but an unusual quantity and quality of original art is displayed within a short walk along Eastern Avenue and Railroad Street:

Catamount Art Gallery (802-748-2600), 60 Eastern Avenue, mounts shows representing regional artists.

Inquire about special August and December crafts sales.

Windhorse Visual Art Center (802-751-8303), 56 Eastern Avenue. This trio of octagonal buildings, set back above Eastern Avenue, has recently been developed as Windhorse Commons. The most striking of the buildings dates from 1854 and features a (recent) mural painted on the curved central stairwell, depicting Caledonia County history and landscapes. The gallery at the top of the stairs features changing exhibits.

Wool Away (802-748-5767), 13 Eastern Avenue. Open Tuesday through Saturday. This is an outstanding knitting supply shop featuring fiber arts and the paintings, multimedia works, and sketches by Nicholas Piliero.

The St. Johnsbury Art League (802-748-6233), 71 Railroad Avenue. The restored Merchants National Bank block and its atrium constitute a gallery of architectural history and a fine showcase for changing exhibits, plus a room for the permanent display of paintings by Frank Mason.

The Art Cache (802-626-5711), East Burke. Marty Martin's long-established gallery in an 1856 schoolhouse exhibits a wide range of art from throughout the country.

Stephen Huneck Gallery (802-748-5593), St. Johnsbury. Huneck's stylish, carved wooden animals and bold, fanciful furniture, panels, jewelry, and even Christmas-tree ornaments are being widely exhibited and shown in the permanent collections of the Smithsonian and other museums. Ask directions.

See also Northern Lights Bookshop under *Bookstores* (shows change monthly and include crafts as well as traditional media) and Northeast Kingdom Artisans Guild under *Crafts Shops* (paintings and prints are displayed).

GARDENS **Vermont Daylilies** (802-533-7155), Barr Hill Road, Greensboro. David and Andrea Perham offer some 400 varieties of daylilies; also B&B.

Labour of Love Gardens (802-525-6695), Route 16, Glover. An acre of public gardens on the Barton River, mid-May until frost, plus antiques and crafts.

Stone's Throw Gardens (802-586-2805), East Craftsbury, features displays of perennials and roses around a restored 1795 farmhouse; nursery open May 1 through late August, Wednesday through Sunday.

Perennial Pleasures Nursery (802-472-5512), East Hardwick. Sited at the Brick House (see *Lodging*) and run by Rachel Kane, this unusual nursery specializes in authentic 17th-, 18th-, and 19th-century restoration gardens. There are 3 acres of flowering perennial and herb gardens, grassy walks, and arbors; more than 375 varieties of plants are available. See also *Where to Eat—Tea*.

Stillmeadow Farm (802-755-671), South Albany. In their greenhouses at this handsome dairy farm that's been in the same family since the 1830s, Bruce and Elizabeth Urie now sell a variety of annuals; syrup too.

GENERAL STORES **Danville General Store** (802-684-3691), on the green, includes a collection of local crafts and foods, such as Clover Hill Farm fudge, Julie Kempton's children's clothes, Partridge Lane Woodworks, and Marylyn Magnus's wool rugs. Mail-order catalog.

Hastings Store (802-684-3398), West Danville. See West Danville under *Towns and Villages*.

Bailey's & Burke General Store (802-626-9250), Route 114, East Burke. Open 6:30 AM–9 PM weekdays, 8–9 Sunday, closes at 8 in winter. This classic old general store has been nicely fancied up by longtime local residents Jody Fried and Bill Turner. The second-floor gallery has been restored and displays work by local craftsmen. Downstairs are breads, pies, cookies, and coffee cakes baked daily right here; also a gourmet deli featuring specialty pizzas, cheeses, cold cuts, fresh fruits and vegetables, and basic staples. A selection of wines, coffees, and teas, and a back room full of wicker complete the scene.

Currier's Quality Market (802-525-8822), Glover. The number of stuffed (formerly live) animals festooned from the rafters and counters is impressive in this old-style emporium.

Craftsbury General Store (802-586-2811), Craftsbury Village. A genuine, old-style village store under the same ownership for many years; a source of information about the area and a full stock of everything.

Pierce's Marketplace (802-525-3400), Barton: state liquor store, downstairs a separate fishing and hunting supply store. Vermont gifts and books, sports equipment and clothes, groceries, beer and wine, deli, hunting and fishing licenses.

Ha'Penny Gourmet, the Peacham Store (802-592-3310), Peacham Village. Crafts, collectibles, and specialty foods. Gourmet food to take out. It's the kind of place that grows as it comes into focus, especially if you check out the back rooms and the upstairs gallery.

Bayley-Hazen Country Store (802-592-3630), South Peacham. An upscale country store with a gallery featuring local artists.

Willey's Store (802-533-2621), Greensboro Village. One of the biggest and best general stores in the state; an extensive grocery, produce and meat section, hardware, toys, and just about everything else you should have brought for a vacation but forgot.

Lake Parker Country Store (802-525-6985; 1-800-893-6985), Main Street, West Glover. By Lake Parker. Good for basics plus sandwiches and baked goods. They also do catering.

Northern Exposure Country Store (802-525-3789), Route 5A at Lake Willoughby. Deli, grinders, fishing and hunting licenses, crafts, Green Mountain coffee.

SPECIAL SHOPS **Through the Woods** (802-748-5369), 107 Eastern Avenue, St. Johnsbury. Specializes in crafts and collectibles for the home. An interesting shop with lots of unusual items.

Kingdom Toys (802-751-8690), 438 Railroad Street, St. Johnsbury. It bills itself as the *only* real toy store in the Northeast Kingdom—and it may well be.

Moose River Lake and Lodge Store (802-748-2423), 69 Railroad Street, St. Johnsbury, features an eye-popping collection of antiques, rustic furniture, and accessories for the home, camp, or cabin: taxidermy specialties, antlers and skulls, prints, pack baskets, fishing creels and snowshoes, folk art, and more.

The Old Forge (802-533-2241) at the Lake View Inn, Greensboro. Open daily, year-round, 10–5; 1–5 on Sunday. Karen Clobber Atwood's long-established outlet for Scottish designer sweaters and other woolens has moved from East Craftsbury to this old village inn (separate entrance; see *Lodging*).

Peter Glenn Ski & Sports (802-748-3433), 115 Railroad Street, St. Johnsbury. A full four-season sports shops, top quality at good prices.

Caplan's Army Store Work & Sportswear (802-748-3236), 112 Railroad Street, St. Johnsbury. Established in 1927 as a serious source of quilted jackets, skiwear, Woolrich sweaters, hunting boots, and such; good value and friendly service.

Bag Balm, Route 5, Lyndonville. Developed in 1899 as an antiseptic ointment for cattle, Bag Balm proved particularly effective for chapped udders and is still used by Vermont farmers. In recent years, its campy, old-fashioned green tins began to appear in Madison Avenue pharmacies and ski resort boutiques, at three or four times the price they fetch locally. The factory is an old, red, double-porched building at the southern end of town. Factory tours and sales are discouraged because the company, which turns out some 6,000 tins a day, has only four employees, so visit the Lyndonville Pharmacy, which stocks Bag Balm at realistic prices. The company is owned by John Norris, who inherited the business from his father in 1933.

Evansville Trading Post (802-754-6305), Route 58 between Orleans and Lake Willoughby. A crafts cooperative for local Abenaki Indian products and special events May through October. A big powwow is usually scheduled for the first weekend in August.

Trout River Brewing Company (802-626-3984; 1-888-BYO-BREW), Route 5, Lyndonville. Open for tours daily 11–6, until 7 Friday and 4 on Sunday. The three signature beers here are a Rainbow Red (medium-bodied), a Caramel Porter (dark), and a Scottish Ale.

Castle Shoppe (802-754-2057), 4887 Burton Hill Road, Irasburg. An unusual home furnishings store in a very out-of-the-way place. To get there, leave the Irasburg common with the white church on your right, take a left at the next church and then bear left at the Y in the road. The shop is open officially on weekends and most days but Monday during the week, although from Tuesday through Thursday, it's best to call ahead.

SUGARHOUSES **Sugarmill Farm Maple Museum** (802-525-3701), Route 16 south of Barton Village. The Auger family has turned its former dairy farm into a combination maple museum, working maple operation, dairy parlor, and gift shop selling its own syrup and locally crafted items. Attractions include a tractor-drawn wagon trip through the orchards, a covered bridge, a film on sugaring, a sugarhouse, vintage farm and sugaring tools, and picnic tables. Ben & Jerry's is served year-round; sugar-on-snow in-season.

Rowell Sugarhouse (802-563-2756), Route 15, Walden. Visitors are welcome year-round. Maple cream and candy as well as sugar; also Vermont honey and sheepskins.

LaPlant's Sugarhouse (802-467-3900), 3 miles north of West Burke on Route 5, offers horse-drawn sleigh- and hayrides as well as sugarhouse tours.

David and Myra Houston (802-223-7307), West Hill in Cabot. Here 250–500 taps and buckets are gathered with oxen; up to 10 visitors at a time are welcome during boiling off.

Tamarlane Farm (802-626-3265), Pudding Hill, Lyndonville. This family farm prides itself on the quality of its syrup.

Goodrich's Sugarhouse (802-563-9917), just off Route 2 by Molly's Pond in East Cabot. A family tradition for seven generations, open to visitors March through December with a full line of award-winning maple products.

Martin Calderwood (802-586-2297), South Albany Road, Craftsbury. Here sap from 1,900 taps is gathered with a tractor and sled. Sugar parties arranged on request.

Harry F. Sweat (802-586-2838), Craftsbury, on the road from the common to Craftsbury Center. There are 3,000 taps; sugar parties arranged.

Bruce and Elizabeth Urie (802-755-6713), at **Stillmeadow Farm,** South Albany, have a sugar shack right on this picturesque back road, across from the old red dairy barn. The farm has been in the Urie family since the 1820s, and the syrup is outstanding and reasonably priced.

Peter and Sandra Gebbie at **Maplehurst Farm** (802-533-2984), Greensboro, put out 7,000 taps and will arrange sugaring parties; syrup is sold year-round in their friendly kitchen.

Beverly and George Young (802-533-2964), Greensboro Bend, put out 1,100 taps and will arrange sugar parties.

See also *To See—Other.* Request the *Maple in Caledonia County* pamphlet, available from the Northeast Kindgom Chamber of Commerce (see *Guidance*).

✳ Special Events

February: **Snowflake Festival Winter Carnival,** Lyndonville-Burke. Events include a crafts show, snow sculpture, ski races for all ages and abilities, sleigh rides, music, and art.

March: **Open sugarhouses.**

May: In East Burke, the **Annual White-Water Canoe Race** on the Passumpsic River, May 1.

June: **Lumberman's Day** at Burke Mountain. In Lyndonville, the **Caledonia Classic Auto Show,** first Sunday in June.

July: **Antiques and Uniques Fair** in Craftsbury Common. Burklyn **Summer Festival of Vermont Arts and Crafts,** Bandstand Park, Lyndonville. **Stars and Stripes Pageant,** Lyndonville, last weekend—big auction, parade featuring Bread and Puppet Uncle Sam, barbecue. **Hardwick Annual Fiddlers' Contest,** also the last weekend.

July and August: **Circus Smirkus** (802-533-7443), Greensboro. A children's circus camp stages frequent performances.

July through October: **Farmer's Market,** Saturday and Wednesday until noon at the Middle School on Western Avenue, St. Johnsbuy.

August: **Old Home Day,** Craftsbury Common (parade, games, crafts). **Danville Fair**, **Orleans County Fair** in Barton, old-fashioned event at the extensive fairground. **Old Stone House Day**—open house, picnic lunch, crafts demonstrations at the museum in Brownington Village. **Caledonia County Fair,** Lyndonville; fourth weekend, Thursday through Sunday. **Dowsers National Convention** (802-684-3410), held at Lyndon State College. Annual **Star Party** at Fairbanks Museum and Planetarium (see *To See—Museums*): a week of special events, St. Johnsbury.

September through October: **Northeast Kingdom Fall Foliage Festival,** the last week in September or first one in October. Eight towns take turns hosting visitors, feeding them breakfast, lunch, and dinner, and guiding them to beauty spots and points of interest within their borders. In Walden, the specialty is Christmas wreath making; in Cabot, there is a tour of the cheese factory; in Plainfield, farm tours; in Peacham, sugar-on-snow parties in the hillside sugarhouse; in Barnet, there's usually a ham dinner at the Barnet Center Church; and in St. Johnsbury, the windup. For details, contact Mrs. Lee Hatch (802-563-2472).

December: **Burklyn Christmas Crafts Fair,** the first weekend—a major gathering of North Country craftspeople and artists in St. J.

December 31: **First Night celebrations** (802-748-4561).

JAY PEAK AREA

Jay Peak towers like a sentinel above a wide valley in which the state of Vermont and the province of Quebec meet at three border crossings and mingle in the waters of Lake Memphremagog—and in general ambience. The sentinel itself has fallen to the French. The face of Vermont's northernmost peak is owned by Mont-Saint-Saveur International, and more than half of the patrons at Jay Peak ski area hail from across the border. Montreal is less than 2 hours away.

In summer and fall as well as in winter, a new 60-passenger aerial tram hoists visitors to the 3,861-foot summit of Jay Peak. The view sweeps from Mount Washington to Montreal, back across the lake, down the spine of the Green Mountains and southwest across Lake Champlain to the Adirondacks.

In winter, storms sweep down from Canada or roll in from Lake Champlain, showering the clutch of mountains around Jay with dependable quantities of snow. Admittedly, given its exposed position, Jay can be windy and frigid in January and February (we try to visit in March), the reason—along with spectacular snowfall—that regulars are drawn by "off-piste" skiing through glades and into the back-country beyond. In nearby Hazen's Notch cross-country skiers also find some of the most dependably snowy and beautiful trails in New England.

Walk the length of the border between New England and Canada and you will not find a more distinctive stretch than this western fringe of the Northeast Kingdom. This is big-sky farm and logging country with isolated mountains and unexpectedly high passes. It has a haunting quality. Lodging is limited to a total of some 1,200 "pillows" in the hotel and condominiums at Jay Peak itself and to a smaller number in widely scattered lodges and B&Bs. Some are along Route 242, which climbs 4 miles from Jay Village, a crossroads inn, gas station, and general store, to the Jay Peak access road, then dips steeply 9 miles down to Montgomery Center, a lively village with a choice of places to stay and eat. Montgomery, known for its six covered bridges, is 2 more miles to the west, and the Hazen's Notch angles back east over a high woods pass and down through fields into Lowell. An inviting drive in summer, it's open only for the first 4 miles in winter, just far enough to access magnificent snowshoeing and cross-country ski trails.

In contrast to most ski resort areas, this one attracts relatively few transients. Innkeepers, restaurateurs, and shopkeepers are a mix of self-sufficient natives and

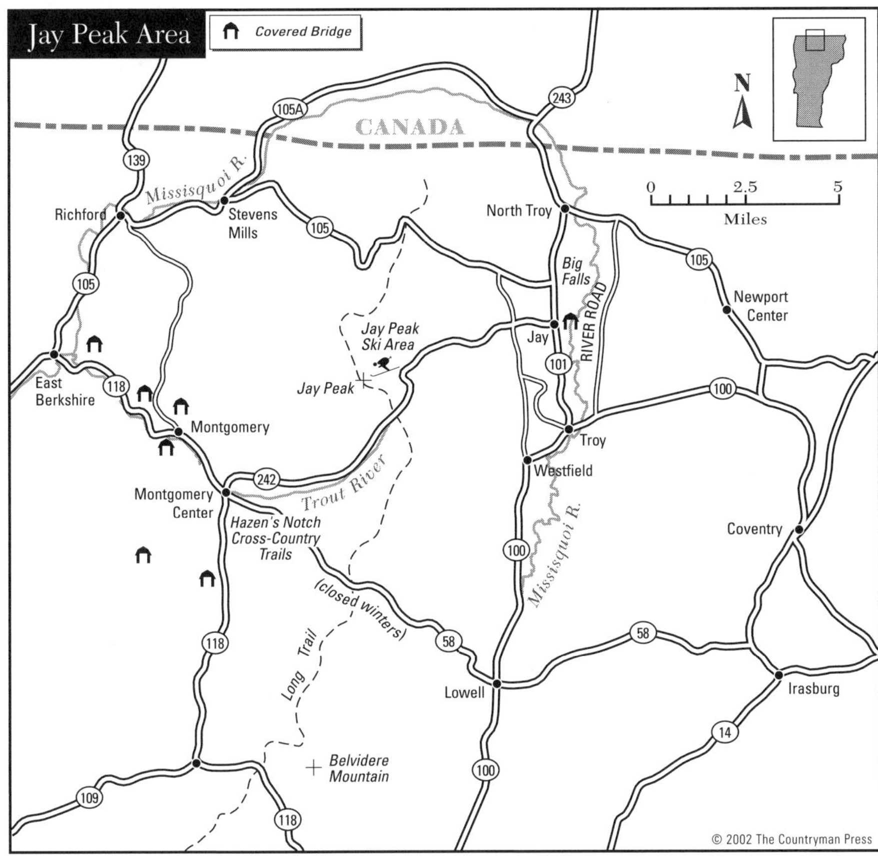

the interesting kind of people who tend to gather in the world's beautiful back-and-behind places.

GUIDANCE **Jay Peak Travel Service** (802-988-2611; outside Vermont: 1-800-451-4449; www.jaypeakresort.com), Jay 05859, is based at Jay Peak Resort. The Jay Peak Area Association (802-988-2259; 1-800-882-7460; www.jaypeakvermontorg) is manned by area members.

GETTING THERE *By air:* **Burlington International Airport,** a 1½-hour drive.

By train: **Amtrak** service to St. Albans.

By bus: **Greyhound** and **Vermont Transit** service to Newport; host lodges will generally pick up.

By car: From points south take I-91 exit 26 at Orleans and follow Route 5 north 4 miles to Coventry, then north on Route 14 and then south on Route 100, 11 miles to Troy. Travel 3 miles north on Route 101 to the turnoff for Jay on Route 242. Believe it or not, this is shorter and less confusing than exiting in Newport.

WHEN TO GO Foliage and winter seasons both begin early here: By the last week in September color is substantial but the inns are empty. The area only fills on winter weekends, when buses from Montreal augment the crowds on the slopes. Midweek is relatively empty all season except during Canadian school vacations (check) but during Presidents' Week (public school vacation in New England) it's the one major mountain that isn't crowded. Given the windchill factor, we like to ski here in March, which can be glorious. For cross-country it's great all winter. July through October is very quiet.

MEDICAL EMERGENCY **Montgomery** (802-933-4000); **North Country Hospital & Medical Center** (802-334-7331), Prouty Drive, Newport. **911** now covers the area.

✷ To See

Jay Peak summit. The spectacular view from the top is accessible via the new 60-person tram at Jay Peak Resort (802-966-2611), Route 242, Jay. It operates daily during ski season and from the last weekend in June through Labor Day, then in foliage season, mid-September through Columbus Day, 10–5. $10 adults, $6 children, $30 family pass.

Hazen's Notch. From Montgomery Center, an unpromising narrow road, Route 58, climbs steeply east, quickly changing to dirt. In winter, it is open only for the first 4 miles and is the site of a popular ski-touring spot (see *Winter Sports—Cross-Country Skiing*). In summer, it's a beautiful road, dappled with sunlight through the thick foliage. Look for a picnic spot near the height-of-land, close to a clear roadside spring. A historic site plaque says the road through the high pass was built by Gen. Moses Hazen in 1778–79, commissioned by George Washington himself. The road was begun in 1776, 48 miles to the southeast at the town of Wells River on the Connecticut River, and was intended to reach St. John, Quebec. It was abandoned on this spot in April 1779 when the news that British patrols might use it as an invasion route (it was meant to work the other way) reached the camp at Hazen's Notch.

Montgomery and its covered bridges. Montgomery boasts a grand total of six Town lattice covered bridges: one right in Montgomery Village over Black Falls Creek; one south on Route 118; another nearby but 3 miles off Route 118 on West Hill on an abandoned side road over a waterfall; another northwest on Route 118 over the Trout River; and two in Montgomery Center, both a mile west of Route 118 over the Trout River (see area map). Montgomery Village itself is

BIG FALLS OF THE MISSISQUOI

River Road hugs the river, paralleling Route 101 between Troy and North Troy. You can access the falls from either town or from Vielleux Road off Route 101 at its junction with Route 105. This last is the prettiest route, through farmland and through the **covered bridge** south of the falls. Look for the unmarked pull-off in a grove of pine trees. The falls, thundering though a deep gorge, are awe-inspiringly magnificent .

picturesque. It began as a lumbering center and was for a long time one of the world's major producers of timothy grass seed culture. The Montgomery Historical Society's collection is housed in an 1835 wooden church, open June through September at stated hours; the society also sponsors Saturday-evening concerts on the common in July and August (see *Special Events*).

St. Benoit du Lac (819-843-4080), Austin, Quebec. Open daily. This non-cloistered French Benedictine monastery, founded in 1912, is sited on the west shore of Lake Memphremagog in a fjordlike section. It's an impressive building, and the resident monks welcome visitors for daily Mass and vespers (usually at 5 PM), at which Gregorian chant is sung. The monastery shop sells Gregorian music records, also hard cider, cheese, vestments, and religious articles. The easiest route from Newport is via the North Troy border crossing, then through Mansonville, South Bolton, and Austin.

✷ To Do

BICYCLE TOURING A time-honored and -tested 22.6- or 33.7-mile ride begins at the Black Lantern (see *Lodging—Inns*) in Montgomery Village, passes two covered bridges along Route 118 north, and takes you to East Berkshire; you can simply continue to Enosburg Falls, where Lake Carmi offers camping and swimming, turn onto the Richford Road, and loop back to Montgomery or loop up into Canada.

The **Missisquoi Valley Rail Trail** begins in Richford and runs 26.4 miles west to St. Albans (for a booklet guide to the trail, phone 802-524-5989). Also see *Mountain Biking* below.

CANOEING The 86-mile-long **Missisquoi River** makes a complete loop around Jay, passes briefly through Quebec, and continues across Vermont to empty into Lake Champlain. The upper half of the river near Jay offers spring fast water, and the lower reaches are gentle and broad, good spring and summer ground for beginners and those who enjoy traversing outstanding rural landscape. For canoes and boat rentals, contact the **Missisquoi Riverbend B&B** (802-744-9991), Route 100, Troy.

FISHING The **Trout River** deserves its name. Brook trout can also be found in the **Missisquoi,** and **Lake Memphremagog** harbors smallmouth bass and salmon, among other species. See "Newport and the North Country" for boat rentals in Newport. See *To Do—Canoeing* for boat rentals.

HIKING The **Long Trail** terminates its 262-mile route at the Canadian border, 10 miles north of Jay Peak, but the trek up Jay itself is what most hikers look for here. The most popular ascent is from Route 242, 1.2 miles west of the entrance to the ski area; the round-trip hike takes 3 hours. For details on this and the section of the trail between Hazen's Notch and Route 242, also for the final, fairly flat leg to the border, see the *Long Trail Guide,* published by the Green Mountain Club, which maintains the trail and four shelters in this area.

MOUNTAIN BIKING The **Jay Peak Ski and Summer Resort** (802-988-2611; 1-800-451-4449) maintains a network of trails for experienced mountain bikers via its aerial tramway, which will transport them and their bikes to the 3,861-foot summit from which several routes descend: 20 miles of alpine and 15 miles of cross-country.

SWIMMING A number of inns have their own pools. The most popular local swimming hole is at Jay Four Corners, downstream from the Route 101 bridge.

TENNIS ✐ **Jay Peak Resort** (802-988-2611) maintains tennis courts in warm-weather months.

WALKING ✐ **Hazen's Notch Association and Outdoor Education Center** (802-326-4789), Route 58, Montgomery Center. Sharon and Rolf Anderson, who directed Vermont Voyageur Expeditions for 10 years, have reorganized their programs, offering nature and ecology day camps for children 6–9, Adventure Day and Overnight Camps for ages 10–12, and Voyageur Camp/Wilderness trips for ages 13–16. They also supervise the self-guided use of 10 miles of trails over 500 acres of privately owned conservation lands for hiking and nature study in spring, summer, and fall; for snowshoeing and cross-country skiing in winter. Park and walk 15 minutes to Bear Paw Pond. Inquire about frequent nature walks, fly-fishing workshops, and other special events.

* Winter Sports

CROSS-COUNTRY SKIING **Hazen's Notch Cross-Country Ski Center** (802-326-4708), Route 58, Montgomery Center. This outstanding touring center offers 30 km of meticulously tracked trails, some with fine views of Jay and the Cold Hollow Mountains. A total of 45 km of marked trails connect the network with the Catamount Trail. In business since 1978, when Val Schadinger and Rolf Anderson first laid out the trails, Hazen's Notch's rustic, noncommercial atmosphere has attracted a loyal following. Early and late in the season, this tends to be one of a half dozen cross-country networks in New England that have snow (elevation: 1,000–1,670 feet). *Note:* B&B rooms are also offered.

Jay Peak Resort (802-988-2611) maintains 20 km of trails near the base of the mountain.

DOWNHILL SKIING ✐ **Jay Peak** (information and reservations: 802-988-2611; 1-800-451-4449 including Canada; snow conditions: 802-988-9601; www.jaypeakresort.com). While there's an easy-intermediate trail (Northway) off the summit, Jay Peak regulars duck into glades right off the top. Jay's 20 glades and extreme chutes are what draw many of its regulars, who like to strike out into 150 acres of backcountry terrain. Unlike regular runs, wooded trails ("glades") cannot be covered by man-made snow and so require a lot of the natural stuff, which is what Jay Peak has in spades: an average of 330 inches annually. That's twice the snow many New England areas receive.

The original trails here are stateside, on a shoulder of Jay Peak. Still considered some of the toughest runs in Vermont, they were carved 30 years ago by local residents. An enterprising Kiwanis group (it included the parish priest) convinced the Vermont Legislature to reroute existing roads up over the high ridge from which Jay's access road arises, thus linking it to northwestern Vermont as well as to the Northeast Kingdom. They also imported an Austrian skimeister to create a true trail system and ski school. Then in the early '60s the lumber company Weyerhaeuser Corporation acquired the ski area and installed a Swiss-built tramway to Jay's Peak, which it topped with a Sky Haus tram station, a building that emphasizes the crest of the summit and gives it a distinctly Matterhorn-like cap. Weyerhaeuser also built the large, sturdy, Tyrolean-style base complex that still stands and includes a 48-room hotel.

Christian Tremblay

JAY PEAK

Since 1978 the resort has been owned by the Montreal-based owners of Saint-Saveur, a lucrative Laurentian ski area. The original trams have been replaced with sleek cars, lifts have been improved, and condominiums have been proliferating. A 27-hole golf course and greatly expanded base facilities are planned. Weekends can be mobbed by Montrealers, but midweek is frequently wide open, and spring skiing is superb. *Lifts:* 60-passenger tram; one quad chair, one triple, two doubles; two T-bars. *Trails and slopes:* 64 trails, glades, and chutes totaling more than 50 miles of skiing, spread over two peaks, connected by a ridgeline. *Off-piste skiing:* 150 acres. *Vertical drop:* 2,153 feet. *Snowboarding:* Permanent half-pipe course; Jay is now Burton Board demo center; rentals, instruction for beginners. *Snowmaking:* 75 percent of the total 385 acres. *Snowshoeing:* Weekly snowshoeing walks led by a naturalist. *Facilities:* Austria Haus and Tram Haus base lodges with cafeteria, pub, and ski and rental shop. Sky Haus cafeteria at summit, nursery and daycare facilities. Rentals. A lighted skating rink and skate rentals. Van service is offered from Burlington Airport (80 miles away) and from the Amtrak station in St. Albans (a 45-minute drive). *Ski school:* U.S. and Canadian certified instructors, adult and junior racing clinics, American Teaching Method (ATM). Telemarking instruction and rentals offered. *For children:* Mountain Explorers for both skiing and snowboarding 5- to 12-year-old group, kinderschool for ages 2–5. Daycare for ages 2–7. *Rates:* \$52 adult, \$38 junior (14 and under)

SLEIGH RIDES **Rose Apple Acres Farm** (802-988-4300). See *Bed & Breakfasts.*

SNOWMOBILING The area is webbed with **Vermont Association of Snow Travelers** (VAST) trails; check with the local inns.

TRACKING Offered at the **Hazen's Notch Association** center (802-326-4789), Route 58, Montgomery Center (see *Walking*).

✷ Lodging

On-mountain

Hotel Jay (1-800-451-4449), Route 242, Jay 05859. Located right at the lifts, an attractive lodge with 48 big rooms, each with two double beds, color TV, phones, and private bath; a pleasant public dining room, a game room, family room, sauna, Jacuzzi, outdoor pool (summer only). Rates are reasonable, especially in the off-season. In winter, a 2-day package including lift, lodging, two breakfasts, and one dinner can be had for $227 per person (except over the holidays).

Jay Peak Condominiums (from Vermont: 802-988-2611; from out of state: 1-800-451-4449). A total of 120 condos and town houses, constructed in clusters: studios and two- and three-bedroom units accommodate from 4 to 10 people; all have fireplace, living room, and fully equipped kitchen. The Village Townhouses accommodate up to six people and are luxurious. From $50 per person in the off-season and from $199 including lifts for 2 nights during ski season.

INNS **Black Lantern Inn** (802-326-4507; 1-800-255-8661; www.blacklantern.com), Montgomery 05470. A white-pillared, brick inn built in 1803 as the Montgomery Village stage stop. Deb and Bob Winders, the new owners, have upgraded several guest rooms of which there are now 16, including 2 "minisuites" upstairs with sitting area, gas fireplace, steam shower, and Jacuzzi. All rooms are nicely decorated, with private bath. Four suites with fireplace and whirlpool bath in the neighboring Burdett House are truly comfortable (our fireplace drew beautifully, and the rooms were thoughtfully furnished; hooked rugs, a few antiques, a TV—everything but a phone). The inn itself also offers a small reading/talking area, warmed by a soapstone stove; a cozy taproom; and a small, charming dining room (see *Dining Out*). This is not a place for children. Beyond the porch is the village with its six covered bridges, and from the back there is a view of Hazen's Notch (see *To See*). $75–95 per room, $105–145 per suite B&B.

Inglenook Lodge (802-988-2880; 1-800-331-4346; www.inglenookvermont.com), Route 202, Jay 05859. This classic family-run lodge near the Jay Peak access road offers a great view. It has 10 large and 8 smaller rooms, a sunken lounge with circular fireplace, an indoor swimming pool, Jacuzzi, and sauna. $69–89 per couple B&B, $138 MAP. Owner Janice Kruse also manages **Trillium Woods at Jay,** on Route 242 between the village and the mountain. These are town houses holding eight, with Jacuzzi, fireplace, and sauna; $350 per night in ski season, available by the week and month in summer. More in foliage season.

The Inn on Trout River (802-326-4391; 1-800-338-7049; www.troutinn.com), P.O. Box 76, Montgomery Center 05471. Built grandly by a lumber baron, this attractive village house offers 10 guest rooms with private bath, and one suite with a brass bed and woodstove. There are also hearths in the dining room, library, and foyer. The innkeepers are Michael and Lee Forman. The convivial Hobo Cafe and more formal Lemoine's Restaurant are open to the public (see *Where to Eat*). $86–132 per person B&B. Inquire about the service charge.

BED & BREAKFASTS **Rose Apple Acres Farm** (802-988-4300; 1-877-879-9135; fax: 802-988-2309), 721 East Hill Road, North Troy 05859. Jay and Camilla Meads's comfortable house sits on 52 acres, good for cross-country skiing. It's a real farm with goats, sheep, and horses. Located 10 miles from Jay Peak, near a covered bridge on the Missisquoi River; good for fishing. Sleigh rides by reservation. There are two guest rooms, one with private bath. Camilla makes porcelain dolls in her studio (see *Selective Shopping*) and the couple also breed and sell Morgan horses. The Meads cater to hikers with a special rate of $35 per person; they will shuttle hikers to and from the trailhead. Otherwise, rates range $50–60, including breakfast.

Woodshed Lodge (802-988-4444; 1-800-495-4445), Route 242, Jay 05459. Just 3 miles from Jay Peak, this landmark old lodge is maintained by John and Chris Engler, who cater to families. Three of the seven rooms have private bath, four share two baths. There's a sitting room upstairs and a library/TV lounge downstairs. $35–40 per person includes breakfast; there are 5-day and weekend specials; 20 percent discount for children 10 and under. Dinner by arrangement.

Hazen's Notch B&B at the Cross-Country Ski and Hiking Center (802-326-4708), Route 58, Montgomery Center 05471. Val Schadinger has restored an old farmhouse and offers three bedrooms and baths, a living room with a woodstove, and breakfast with mountain views. Cross-country trails radiate from the neighboring touring center. $60–70 per room, continental breakfast included.

Phineas Swann B&B (802-326-4306; www.phineasswann.com), Main Street, Montgomery Center 05471. Michael Bindler and Glen Bartolomeo are the hosts in this bright gingerbread Victorian with its delightful sun room and wood-burning fireplaces. In the main house four guest rooms are decorated with period antiques and Laura Ashley patterns. $99–109 per room includes full breakfast (like raspberry French toast) and afternoon tea with fresh pastries. There are also two suites with sitting room, fireplace, and Jacuzzi in the Carriage House: $175 for two bedrooms, $135 for one bedroom. Add 10 percent gratuity in the rooms, 13 percent gratuity in suites.

Missisquoi Riverbend B&B (802-744-9999; www.riverbendvt.com), 6198 Route 100, Troy 05868. A Victorian farmhouse on the edge of the village offers 15 acres on the Missisquoi River. Innkeeper Paul Becker enjoys introducing guests to the delights of paddling (canoes available). The house offers two guest rooms with shared bath and a suite with private bath. This is a comfortable, casual place with fireplaces in the living room and library. Inquire about horseback riding. $85–115 includes a full breakfast.

Idyllwild East Bed & Breakfast (802-988-9830; www.idyllwildeast.com), 1287 Route 101. Proncell and Dortha Johnson's contemporary house is remarkably roomy. The three attractive guest rooms (two with shared bath) are off a big entry-level family room with a wood-burning stove and TV. On the second floor is a larger, brighter "great room" with a dining area and eat-in kitchen. Common space also includes a back deck and more than three landscaped acres. $75 single, $95 double with breakfast, family and meal plan rates.

English Rose Inn (802-326-3232; www.theenglishroseinn.com), 195 Mountain Road (Route 242), Montgomery Center 05471. The former Eagle Lodge has a new identity. Gary and Mary Jane Bouchard-Pike (he from Britain, she from Highgate Springs) spent 2 years renovating the rambling 1850 farmhouse before opening with 14 redecroated rooms, 2 of them suites (all with private bath). Lacy curtains, Victorian antiques, and knickknacks have been added, and the dining room is now open to the public as Paddington's (see *Dining Out*), but there is still ample common space, including a reading room and upstairs sitting room. $40–135 includes a full breakfast and afternoon tea. The high end is for a suite with fireplace and Jacuzzi.

✱ Where to Eat

DINING OUT **Black Lantern Inn** (802-326-4507), Montgomery Village. Dinner is served nightly in-season, less often in spring and summer. Phone to reserve. The low-beamed dining room of this delightful old inn is the setting for candlelight dinners that might begin with shrimp bisque or spinach-stuffed mushrooms and feature roast half duck with raspberry reduction or mustard-crusted rack of lamb. Entrées $12–20.

North Troy Village Restaurant (802-988-4063), Main Street, North Troy. Open at 5 PM daily except Tuesday. Irene McDermott has earned an enthusiastic following. The attractive dining room in this 1890s village hotel is the scene of memorable meals. The menu is extensive and features seafood and prime rib specials. There's a kids' menu and "mini-meals," like a 5-ounce tournedo (why don't others do this?). *Warning:* the "Little Bear Cut" is enormous. Entrées $9.95–15.95.

Paddington's (802-326-3232), Route 242 between the Jay Peak access road and Montgomery Center. Open Thursday through Sunday 5–9:30. We can't claim to have dined here yet, but chef-owners Gary and Mary Jane Bouchard-Pike both hold culinary school degrees and spent their lives in the restaurant business before opening the dining room of this old inn (formerly the Eagle Lodge) as a restaurant featuring Gary's native cuisine. Specialties include prime rib with Yorkshire pudding and Cornish pasty (golden flaky crust filled with Vermont cheddar, a blend of fresh herbs, and veggies). Entrées start at $12.95, including house salad, vegetables, starch, and fresh baked bread.

Lemoine's at the Inn on Trout River (802-326-4391), Main Street, Montgomery Center. Serving nightly in winter, check off-season. The lacy dining room in this handsome old house is the setting for heart-healthy meals featuring entrées like turkey tenderloin with celery sauce ($11.95) and grilled leg of lamb with pesto and sun-dried tomatoes ($15.95). Full dinners run $20.50–24.25.

Hotel Jay (802-988-2611) at Jay Peak. Dinner is served 6–9, and reservations are a must in winter. In summer, dinner is served only Friday through Sunday. The big, functional dining room is cheery, and the menu features dishes like veal Gruyère and fillet of salmon.

EATING OUT ✿ **The Belfry** (802-326-4400), Route 242, between Montgomery Center and the Jay Peak access road. Open nightly 4 PM until late. No reservations, and during ski season you'd better get here early if you want a booth. Built in 1902 as schoolhouse, this is the area's most popular pub, and the food's good, thanks to longtime manager Chaneile Politier who now owns it, along with Marty Lumbra, who drives the local school bus. If you've been here a day or two, chances are you will recognize someone in the crowd around the mirrored oak and marble back bar. The soup is homemade, and the blackboard lists daily specials, like pan-blackened fish and grilled lamb chops. The set menu features "belfry steak" ("price depends on the chef's mood"), salads, burgers, and deep-fried mushrooms. Inquire about music.

✿ ✐ **J. R.'s Café** (802-326-4682), Main Street, Montgomery Center. Open 6:30 AM–10 PM, later on weekends. The best place around for lunch, not bad for dinner either. Bigger than it looks from its greenhouse-style front, this is a genuine gathering spot for the area. Breakfast options include bagels, smoked salmon, and eggs any style, and the breads (including wheat onion, six-grain, and herb) are baked daily, for sale separately as well as used in sandwiches. Soups are a luncheon specialty, and at dinner the menu ranges from sautéed scampi through pastas, to J. R.'s Texas rib platter. Fully licensed with a pub in back. J. R., who frequently presides behind the counter, also crafts the stained glass set in the walls and windows.

Hobo Cafe at the Inn on Trout River (802-326-4391), Main Street, Montgomery Center. A pub atmosphere and menu, with reasonably priced dinners like BBQ ribs and chicken.

Kilgore's General Store, Main Street, Montgomery Center. Open daily except Tuesday, 7 AM–5 PM. Steve and Karen Houghtaling, transplants from New Jersey, operate this picturesque old store. Sample the chili and cheese, place your order, and poke through antiques and crafts on the store's balustraded mezzanine, then lunch at the genuine old marble soda fountain or at a table by the woodstove.

The Old Bobbin Mill Retaurant & Pub (802-744-6341), Route 100, Westfield. Open daily except Monday 6 AM–9 PM. Local fiddlers gather for Wednesday breakfast. This a genuine old lumber turned bobbin mill, turned crafts shop, turned pub and restaurant. Menus and servings are large and prices low. A cheeseburger deluxe with the works is $3.50 even at dinnertime. Other choices include Vermont roast turkey with sage dressing and homemade gravy and hot roast beef, sliced thin and stacked on bread, topped with brown gravy.

Jay Country Store (802-988-4040), Jay Village. Open daily. The sandwiches at the counter and in the sunny solarium are the best in the village, reflecting the quality of the store's deli.

✷ Selective Shopping

Jay Country Store (802-988-4040), Jay Village. Open daily. Art and Peggy

Moran's store forms the center of Jay Village, selling papers, gas, food, and wine basics, also a deli (see *Eating Out*), plus an interesting assortment of gift items (we bought a stunning Vermont-designed wool ski cap made in Nepal here), cards, books, and an art gallery that has been growing over the years, featuring limited-edition prints by Will Moses (great-grandson of Grandma Moses), varied landscapes.

Kilgore's General Store (802-326-4681), Main Street, Montgomery Center. A fine old store with an interior balcony, nicely restored with a classic soda fountain and cases stocked with munchies (ideal for hikers and bikers). The store also sells crafts, antiques, and Vermont specialty items.

Couture's Maple Shop (802-744-733; 1-800-845-2733), Route 100, Westfield. A long-established maple producer: maple candy, cream, granulated sugar, pancake mix, and salad dressing, as well as syrup; will ship anywhere.

The Tickle Trunk (802-988-4731), Crossroads, Jay, is full of clocks, books, Victorian and country antiques, vintage clothing, and work by local artists and artisans.

KILGORE'S GENERAL STORE

Chris Tree

Rose Apple Acres Dolls (802-988-4300), East Hill Road, North Troy. Modern porcelain figures (the idea is to make dolls resembling a particular child), plus sculpture and doll-making classes and supplies.

The Pink Lady (802-848-3836), 66 Main Street, Richford. Open daily, 10–5. Subtitled "the Richford Antique and Gift Center," this elaborate Victorian mill owner's mansion now offers 21 rooms filled with antiques, art, vintage and new clothing, jewelry, mirrors, lamps, crafts, and more.

Red Barn Studio (802-326-4672), 32 Fuller Bridge Road, Montgomery (behind the Methodist Church), is open May through November by chance or appointment, showcasing local artists.

✷ Special Events

January: **Hazen's Notch Ski Race,** last Sunday.

Mid-February: **Winter Festival**—varied events including a race from the summit of Jay Peak to Jay Village.

July and August: **Concerts on the common,** presented by the Montgomery Historical Society on Saturday evening (802-326-4404), and during September in the Montgomery Village church.

Mid-August: **Jay Day.**

October (first weekend): **Octoberfest,** Jay Peak—big annual arts and crafts fair.

NEWPORT AND THE NORTH COUNTRY

The Northeast Kingdom is blessed with some of the most beautiful lakes in Vermont. The largest of these is Memphremagog, stretching more than 30 miles from Newport, Vermont, to Magog, Quebec. Only 5 miles lie within the United States.

At the height of railroad passenger service, large wooden hotels rose on the shores of these lakes. In Newport, the 400-room Memphremagog House stood next to the railroad station, Newport House was across the street, and the New City Hotel was nearby. Guests came by train from Boston and Philadelphia. Lindbergh came with his *Spirit of Saint Louis*, and there was a racetrack and a paddle-wheeler. Until recently the city's past splendor was recalled only in photos. The past few year's infusion of public funding seems, however, to be working. The new Waterfront Gateway (off Main Street) works as a downtown window on the water, a place to sit or eat, to board an excursion boat, or to stroll along the new lakeside walkway. On the second floor of the new State Office Building the Memphremagog Historical Society of Newport has mounted blown-up archival photos and a permanent display on northern Vermont Abenaki people, from Paleolithic through current times. The building is also decorated with murals. Several new clothing shops and a real restaurant or two have opened in neighboring blocks.

From Prospect Hill, site of St. Mary, Star of the Sea, a towering cathedral, Newport slopes to the lake, which actually seems to surround it. Downtown Newport separates the lake proper from South Bay, and the shoreline offers access points for sailing, canoeing, fishing, and swimming.

Memphremagog (stress on the third syllable) has a split personality. The two-thirds of the lake north of the Canadian border is not only French speaking (although there are English pockets like Georgeville) but also more of a resort area. Montreal is just an hour's drive from the resort town of Magog. In stark contrast is the American end of the lake, which is the end of the road (I-91) from New York and Boston. It remains a delightful refuge for frugal flatlanders, especially those who like to fish, hike, observe wildlife, or generally steep themselves in the beauty of this high, rolling—still pastoral—countryside.

Less than a dozen miles northeast of Newport is the split-nationality community of Derby Line, Vermont, and Rock Island, Quebec. This is a major border crossing (I-91 continues north as Highway 55), linking with the major east–west

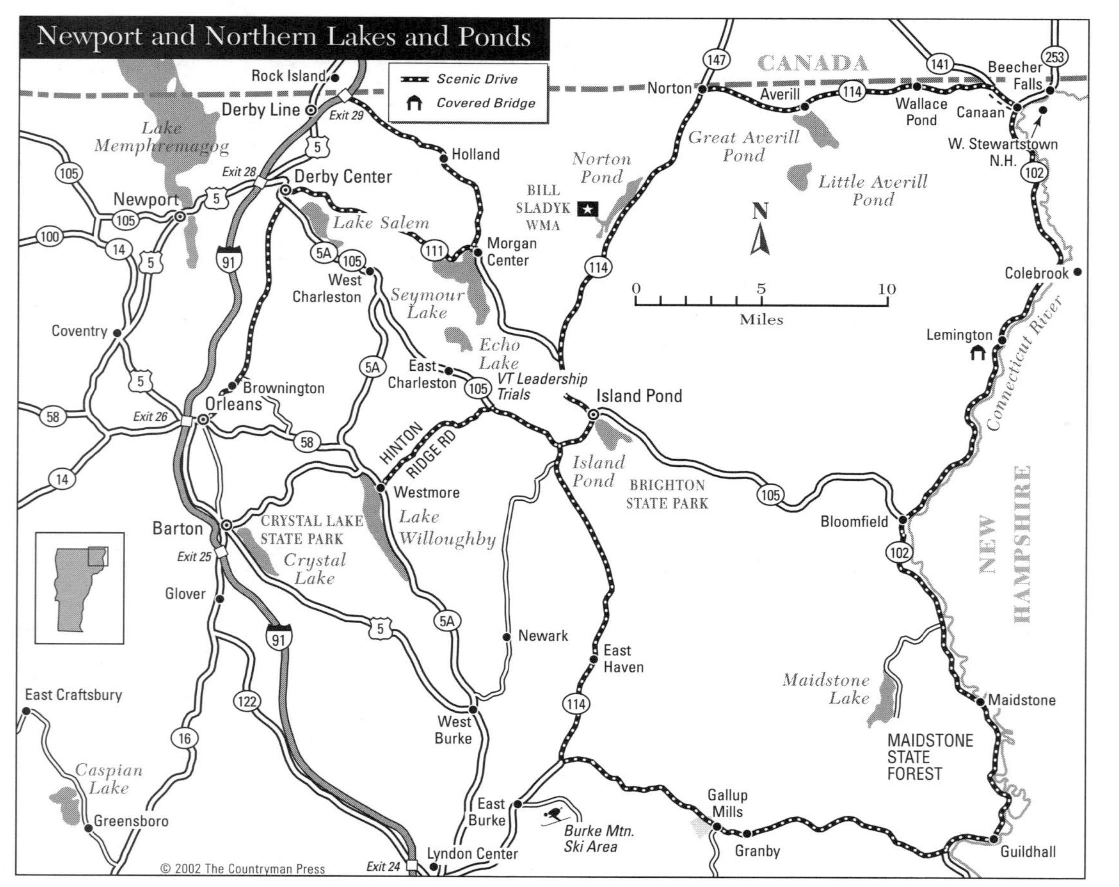

Newport and Northern Lakes and Ponds
Scenic Drive
Covered Bridge
CANADA
NEW HAMPSHIRE
Rock Island
Derby Line
Exit 29
Exit 28
Derby Center
Holland
Lake Memphremagog
Newport
Lake Salem
Morgan Center
BILL SLADYK WMA
Norton Pond
Norton
Averill
Great Averill Pond
Little Averill Pond
Wallace Pond
Canaan
Beecher Falls
W. Stewartstown N.H.
Colebrook
Lemington
Connecticut River
West Charleston
Seymour Lake
Echo Lake
East Charleston
VT Leadership Trials
Island Pond
Coventry
Brownington
Orleans
Exit 26
HINTON RIDGE RD
Westmore
Lake Willoughby
BRIGHTON STATE PARK
Bloomfield
Barton
CRYSTAL LAKE STATE PARK
Crystal Lake
Exit 25
Glover
Newark
East Haven
Maidstone Lake
Maidstone
MAIDSTONE STATE FOREST
East Craftsbury
Caspian Lake
Greensboro
West Burke
East Burke
Burke Mtn. Ski Area
Gallup Mills
Granby
Guildhall
Lyndon Center
Exit 24
0 5 10
Miles
N

highway between Montreal and Quebec City. The international line runs right through the Haskell Opera House in Derby Line—the audience in America attends concerts in Canada.

West of Derby Center you are quickly in little-trafficked lake country: Lakes Derby and Salem, Seymour and Echo all have good fishing, and dozens of smaller ponds have boat launches. Island Pond is a town as well as a lake. A sign in front of the city-sized depot reads, "Pioneer railroad planner John A. Poor's dream of an international railroad connecting Montreal, Canada, with the ice-free harbor of Portland, Maine, became a reality on July 18, 1854, when the first through trains met at this great halfway point on the Grand Trunk Railway." During the late 19th century and into the 20th, Island Pond hummed with the business of servicing frequent passenger trains and freight trains transporting logs and wood pulp. No longer. Today it's a funky village on a pond with an island in its center. The Twelve Tribes, a religious community, has rooted here, buying and restoring many of the Victorian houses and operating the town's one big specialty store. Winter is now the season here. Island Pond is the region's snowmobiling capital.

For travelers, Island Pond still looms large on the map because you have to pass through it to get to the empty (of people, but teeming with moose, black bear, and other wildlife), lake-pocked land surrounding in every direction. There's good fishing around Averill and in this lonely stretch of the Connecticut River as it dwindles into a stream. Better fishing still is to be found in the Connecticut Lakes just over the New Hampshire line.

GUIDANCE **Vermont North Country Chamber of Commerce** (802-334-7782; www.vtnorthcountry.com) maintains a walk-in visitors center on the Causeway in Newport, open daily year-round, in summer and fall 9–5, in winter 9:30–4:30.

ALICE WARD MEMORIAL LIBRARY IN CANAAN

Christina Tree

The **Derby Line Welcome Center** (802-873-3311) on I-91 south, with rest rooms, at the border serves arriving Canadians.

The **Northeast Kingdom Travel and Tourism Association** (1-888-884-8001) publishes *A Day in the Kingdom,* a cultural heritage tour map and audio tour, a pamphlet guide, and a magazine.

GETTING AROUND Two pieces of advice: 1. Avoid driving lonely stretches after dark and if you must, do so slowly, watching for moose, which are difficult to spot at night and deadly if you collide at high speed. 2. Gas up. Pumps are few and far between and tempting woods roads abound.

WHEN TO COME Snowmobilers and ice fishermen come in winter, and fishermen in spring. Otherwise this is summer country.

✷ To See

LAKES **Lake Memphremagog,** Vermont's second largest lake, 33 miles long, only 5 miles of which are within the United States. Memphremagog stretches north from Newport. See St. Benoit du Lac (see *To See* in "Jay Peak Area") and listings under *To Do* for *Boating, Fishing,* and *Swimming.*

Seymour Lake. There is a public beach in the tiny village of Morgan Center, also the spot to rent boats for fishing for landlocked salmon. In winter, this lake is peppered with fishing shanties, and there is a system of cross-country trails (ungroomed).

Echo Lake. Much smaller than Seymour Lake and adjoining it on the south, this lake is circled by a dirt road and gently rolling hills. There is also public boat access. Good fishing for trout and landlocked salmon.

Island Pond is actually a small lake with a 20-acre island off the sandy beach and a wooded campground in Brighton State Park (see *Green Space*). Boating and fishing are both easily accessible.

See also *To Do—Boat Excursion.*

SCENIC DRIVE

Island Pond/Lake Willoughby shortcut. An easy route to navigate from Westmore on Lake Willoughby: Turn north in the middle of the village on Hinton Ridge Road and follow it through high, rolling farmland and forest (never mind name changes) until it reaches a T-intersection. Turn right and right again onto Route 105 into Island Pond. The reverse direction is even more beautiful but tricky at the beginning (left onto Hudson Road off Route 105 and then your second left onto Westmore Road).

✷ To Do

BOATING Aluminum boats (14 feet) with small motors, also pontoons and sailboats, may be rented at **Newport Marine** (802-334-5911) at Eastside Restaurant

VDT

NEWPORT LAKEFRONT

Docks, Farrants Point, on Lake Memphremagog in Newport. Boats are also available at both **Brighton State Park** in Island Pond and at **Maidstone State Park** (see *Green Space*).

BOAT EXCURSION ***Newport's Princess*** (802-334-6617), 225 Sias Avenue at Newport City Dock, Newport. This excursion group offers frequent cruises from mid-May through September.

CANOEING **Vermont Leadership Center** (802-723-6551; www.vtlc.org), 10 Mile Square Road, East Charleston (5 miles west of Island Pond), offers rental canoes on the Clyde River. On the Connecticut River, Canaan is a good place to put in, but there are several rapids at the start. Canoeing is also good below Colebrook, New Hampshire, for 3 miles but then rather fast for an equal distance. (See also *Fishing*.)

FISHING **Quimby Country** (see *Lodging*), a self-contained resort that includes 70-acre Forest Lake, is a half mile from 1,200-acre Big Averill, both lonely and remote but good for trout and salmon; rowboats can be rented here by the day.

Guides can be found through the **Vermont Leadership Center** (see *Green Space*); for the upper Connecticut, contact **Osprey Fishing Adventures** (603-922-3800). Ken Hastings of Columbia, New Hampshire, is the fishing guru for this stretch of the river. Check the state highway map for local access points to ponds. The **Connecticut Lakes** in adjacent northern New Hampshire (see *Scenic Drives*) offer world-class trout fishing. There are also landlocked salmon and brown, brook, lake, and rainbow trout in dozens of ponds with boat access, as well as in the lakes we describe here. There is a **state fish hatchery in Newark; Newark Pond** has an access and is good for yellow perch along with trout. Rental boats, bait, and tackle are available at the sites listed under *Boating*. **Lake Memphremagog** is good for smelt, smallmouth bass, and walleyes, in addition to

ISLAND POND LOOP

This 66-mile loop circles the northeastern corner of Vermont, beginning in Island Pond and heading north on Route 114. The Canadian National Railway's Grand Trunk line from Montreal to Portland, Maine, hugs the highway the full 16 miles to Norton. This railway was once Montreal's winter lifeline to Europe, as goods could not be shipped in or out of the frozen port of Montreal during the coldest months. About halfway to **Norton,** near the south end of long and slender **Norton Pond** (there's a boat launch on Route 114), a gravel road to the left leads into the **Bill Sladyk Wildlife Management Area** (see *Green Space*), frequented by hunters, fishermen, and loggers. Just before reaching the tiny village of Norton (opposite slightly larger Stanhope, Quebec), the forest thins out and farmland reappears. Norton is the site of the notorious Earth People's Park, a 1960s-style, loosely governed hippie commune that has survived but has dwindled from hundreds to perhaps two dozen residents. The road passes several farms, a school, and the **Norton Country Store** (open daily 7 AM–9 PM), then swings abruptly eastward to avoid the imposing Canadian port-of-entry.

Continuing eastward along the border, Route 114 reenters the forest, passing a series of lakes, most of which are dotted with hunting and fishing camps. The largest of the lakes is **Big Averill.** For directions to the boat launch, stop by the **Lakeview Store** (open daily 8–7), where owner Priscilla Roy sells the wool that she spins, also weaving supplies and locally handcrafted items. East of the store a road leads to **Quimby Country,** one of Vermont's oldest and most interesting resorts (see *Lodging*). Shortly after passing Big Averill, you leave the St. Lawrence watershed and begin a rapid descent into the Connecticut River Valley. Halfway from Averill to Canaan, the road skirts the south shore of sizable **Wallace Pond,** almost entirely within the province of Quebec.

Canaan, 14 miles east of Norton, is a pleasant pocket of civilization with a handsome green, Fletcher Park, with a lovely Greek Revival building in its far corner. Built as a tavern in 1846 and said to have served for a while as the northernmost U.S. stop on the Underground Railroad, this is now the **Alice M. Ward Memorial Library** (802-266-7135), worth a stop to see the the Cannan Historical Society's changing exhibits upstairs.

In **Bessie's Diner** (see *Eating Out*), across from the green on Route 114, a framed tintype depicts Canaan as the village was when a covered bridge spanned the Connecticut River here, connecting it with West Stewartstown, New Hampshire. Today you barely notice the river, here just a fledgling stream, spanned by a brief bridge. Turn north along this stream if you want to see the village of Beecher Falls, 2 miles north. The small, sagging village is dominated by the huge Ethan Allen Furniture plant (closed at this writing) and is a Canadian border crossing. Across another brief bridge is Stewartstown, New Hampshire.

In reality these far corners of Vermont and New Hampshire form a region of their own, a fishing, snowmobiling, and moose-watching mecca known by various names but most accurately as the Connecticut Lakes. You might want to detour north on Route 3 in New Hampshire (Vermont ends at Beecher Falls). A state-operated information center (with rest rooms) south of Pittsburg orients visitors to the series of four lakes strung along the 22 semiwilderness miles north of town. This stretch of Route 3 is known as "Moose Alley" for reasons easy to grasp if you drive it on a summer evening. Fishing lodges and rental camps, salted away around these lakes, way outnumber lodging options contained in the entire vast area of Vermont covered by this chapter, but you see few from the road. Diehard Connecticut river buffs may want to hike into its source, a small pond accessible via a path beside the Route 3 border station (rest rooms).

From Canaan, the loop turns south on Route 102, through river-bottom farmland, through Lemington, past the impressively long Columbia covered bridge, which demands a photo stop. This stretch of the river valley alternately narrows and widens, and the road tunnels through forest, broken occasionally by farms, fields, and glimpses of impressive mountains. In Bloomfield (the store may or may not be open), the Grand Trunk railroad line angles east across the road, heading for Portland. Here our route turns west on Route 105 (it's 16 miles back to Island Pond).

For another great detour, however, continue at least the mile down Route 102 to **Brunswick Springs,** once the site of a mineral springs resort. Said to be a sacred Abenaki site, the resort's buildings repeatedly burned and are all gone, but the springs still run pure. Another 4 miles south on Route 102 (and 5 miles in on a dirt road) bring you to **Maidstone State Park,** offering camping and swimming as well as fishing (see *Green Space*). The Connecticut River widens noticeably the farther south you drive on Route 102, and views of the White Mountains are increasingly dramatic. If you continue another 7 miles south to Guildhall, you are informed by a billboard-sized sign that the town was "discovered" in 1754, chartered in 1761, and settled in 1764, making it the oldest town in northeastern Vermont (by contrast, Norton was not settled until 1860).

An attractive, square green is flanked by historically interesting buildings: a tiny courthouse, church, town hall (the Guild Hall, 1798), and an ornate 1909 Classical Revival library with stained-glass windows. An unassuming white-clapboard house serves as a county lockup.

Two miles downriver from Guildhall, a town road marked GRANBY runs west off Route 102, beginning as a paved road but becoming gravel well before reaching the tiny hamlets of Granby and Gallup Mills, about 8 miles from Route 102. This is wild, wooded, and boggy country, good for spotting moose and bear. Lumber camps and sawmills once peppered this area, and there was even a steam railway. The road finally descends about 8 miles west of Granby to reach Route 114, joining it a couple of miles north of East Burke (see "St. Johnsbury, Craftsbury, and Burke Mountain"). Take Route 114 some 12 miles north through rolling, mixed farm- and forestland to its junction with Route 105, 2 miles west of Island Pond.

salmon and trout. Ice fishing is particularly popular on Memphremagog and Seymour Lake. The pamphlet *Vermont Guide to Fishing*, prepared by the Vermont Fish and Wildlife Department, available locally, tells where to find what.

FOR FAMILIES ✐ **Cow Town Elk Ranch** (802-766-5068), Derby Center, intersection of Routes 5 and 105. Visitors welcome anytime. Derby once had so many dairies that it was known as Cow Town, but Doug Nelson's is now the only big dairy operation left (1,000 head), and he also raises elk (the herd numbered 130 with 40 calves due when we last checked). There's parking and a sign answering the 10 most frequently asked questions. Nelson harvests the velvet for the Asian trade in June, so you might want to come before, when the antlers are at their most majestic. Spring is also calving time. Please don't feed the elk, and be cautious: They're friendly, but they're still wild animals.

GOLF **Newport Country Club** (802-334-7751), off Mount Vernon Street, overlooking the lake. Eighteen holes, rentals, instruction, restaurant; April through November.

Dufferin Heights Golf Club (819-876-5528), Stanstead, Quebec. May through November. Nine holes, cart rentals, restaurant.

Grandad's Invitational, Newark. This nine-hole course is a local legend. Ask around for directions and leave your fee in the mailbox.

HIKING **Bluff Mountain** (elevation: 2,380 feet) looms over Island Pond to the north. It is a popular climb, with spectacular views. The trail starts from Route 114, north of the village. Inquire locally for directions.

Monadnock Mountain (elevation: 3,140 feet), in Lemington, towers over the Connecticut River and Colebrook, New Hampshire. A trail runs west, beginning as a driveway off Route 102 near the bridge to Colebrook. An abandoned fire tower crowns the summit.

SWIMMING In Newport, try **Prouty Beach,** a public facility on Lake Memphremagog. On Seymour Lake there is a public beach in Morgan Center. There are state facilities at Island Pond, a large beach that is sandy and shallow for quite a way out, great for children.

✷ Winter Sports

CROSS-COUNTRY SKIING There are no commercial cross-country centers in northern Essex County. With all the wild, open land, you might find paying to ski somewhat appalling. There is a vast network of wilderness snowmobile trails that are marked by snowmobile clubs and open to skiers. See also Vermont Leadership Center under *Green Space*.

DOWNHILL SKIING On Lake Memphremagog, **Owl's Head** (450-292-5592), Mansonville, Quebec, offers 25 trails, including a steep expert run down the face of the mountain. Snowmaking covers 80 percent of the terrain, and there are six double chairlifts, one quad. Facilities include condominiums and a new apartment hotel, moderately priced. Burke Mountain and Jay Peak are nearby (see "St. Johnsbury, Craftsbury, and Burke Mountain" and "Jay Peak Area").

SNOWMOBILING A *Northeast Kingdom Snowmobile Map* is free from the Northeast Kingdom Chamber of Commerce (1-800-639-6379). Island Pond is the snowmobiling capital of the Kingdom, from which groomed VAST (Vermont Association of Snow Travelers: 802-229-0005) trails radiate in all directions. Check with Kingdom Cat Corp. (802-723-9702) for rentals and information about local sledding.

✷ Green Space

Brighton State Park (802-723-4360), Island Pond, southeast of the village of Island Pond on the south shore of Island Pond and the west shore of Spectacle Pond. Facilities include 84 campsites, of which 21 have lean-tos; also a swimming beach, dump station, snack bar, picnic area, bathhouse, boat rentals, nature trail, and naturalist in residence.

Maidstone State Park (802-676-3930) in the town of Brunswick. Open daily Memorial Day through Labor Day. Five miles south of Bloomfield on Route 102, then 5 miles on dirt road, this is a forest of maple, beech, and hemlock around a large lake, with a beach, picnic area, rental boats, picnic shelter, hiking trails, and 83 campsites, including 37 lean-tos.

Vermont Leadership Center (802-723-6551), 10 Mile Square Road, East Charleston (5 miles west of Island Pond), is a 600-acre preserve with 40 miles of walking/skiing and snowshoeing trails traversing neighboring private property. Aside from its formal nature hikes, guided canoeing, and frequent outreach programs, the center also serves as an informal clearinghouse for local canoe, fishing, tracking, and nature guides.

Bill Sladyk Wildlife Management Area, off Route 114, south of Norton Pond: 9,500 forested acres, also accessible via a gravel road past Holland Pond from Holland Village. A detailed map is available from the Fish and Wildlife Department in Waterbury (802-241-3700).

* Lodging

Water's Edge B&B (802-334-7726), 324 Wishing Well Avenue, Newport 0585. Several miles north of downtown Newport, Pat Bryan's contemporary house sits right on the edge of Lake Memphremagog. Common space is tasteful and includes a deck. The three guest rooms include a queen room with a lake view ($75), a splendid corner queen with two windows on the lake ($90), and a suite with a sitting area and gas stove. All rooms have private bath and TV. In summer guests have use of the canoe, rowboat, and dock; in winter there's snowmobile and ice-fishing access right out the front door. Bird-watching year-round. Rates include a continental-plus breakfast. Residents include Lily, a big, gentle dog, and Shadow, a small black cat.

Seymour Lake Lodge (802-895-2752; www.seymourlakelodge.com), Route 111, Morgan 05853. Brian and Joan Du Moulin both grew up right around here (on opposite sides of the border) and maintain a casual, homey lodge, the kind that's increasingly hard to find. They accommodate 16 guests in six rooms (there are five baths). Guests also have access to the kitchen (freezer, stove, microwave). Breakfast is served 7–9. The Du Moulins also operate an antiques shop on the premises. The inn is open for winter ice fishing and snowmobiling or cross-country skiing on the lake; in summer and fall it caters to fishermen, bicylists, and families. Boat rentals and fishing licenses are available locally, and there's a swim beach across the road. $45 single, $49 double without breakfast. In winter $50 per person. Children 12 and under, $10.

Lakefront Inn & Motel (802-723-6507; www.thelakefrontinn.com), Cross Street, Island Pond 05846. A tidy, two-story motel, also a building housing the lobby and suites with one, two or three bedrooms (some with fireplace) in the center of the village overlooking the pond. Four of the 20 units have built-in kitchenette. A small dock is reserved for motel guests, and a heated multibay garage is available for guests to work on servicing their snowmobiles in winter. Just across a vacant lot are public tennis courts, a beach, picnic area, boat launch, a lighted ice hockey rink, and children's playground. Robert and Sharon Dexter charge $79 per room, $295 per efficiency for two people in winter (high season), $10 per extra person. Summer rates are lower.

The Birchwood B&B (802-873-9104; birchwood@together.net), 48 Main Street, Derby Line 05830. Betty and Dick Fletcher's handsome 1920s village house has three spacious, antiques-furnished (the couple owns an antiques store), immaculate bedrooms with private bath. Rooms include the Double Bed Chamber

🐾 ✐ **Quimby Country** (802-822-5533; www.quimbycountry.com), P.O. Box 20, Averill 05901, is about as north (less than 3 miles from Canada) and as east (10 miles from New Hampshire) as you can get in the Kingdom. This unique 650-acre resort is a 19th-century lodge and grouping of 20 cabins overlooking 70-acre Forest Lake. It is also a quarter mile from 1,200-acre Big Averill, 4 miles from 400-acre Little Averill, and surrounded by its own woodland, which, in turn, is surrounded by forest owned by paper companies. Begun as a fishing lodge, Quimby Country evolved into a family-oriented resort under the proprietorship of Hortense Quimby, attracting a large following in the process. Fearful that the place might change when it came up for sale upon Miss Quimby's death, a number of regular guests formed a corporation and bought it. When the place is in full operation, late June through late August, the rates are $132 per adult, $58–69 per child depending on age, with all three meals and a supervised children's program geared to ages 6–15 that includes swimming, hiking, overnight camping, and rainy-day activities. Reasonable rates during spring fishing season (May 10 through June 27), and again August 30 through foliage season when cottages are available on a housekeeping basis. This is a great place for family reunions.

QUIMBY COUNTRY

Chris Tree

(antique pineapple bed), the blue-and-white Queen Canopy Chamber, and the green-and-pink Twin Bed Room, $90 with a full breakfast in the stately dining room. The fireplace in the formally furnished living room is frequently lit, and guests gather around the long formal dining table for candlelit breakfasts.

CAMPGROUNDS See Brighton State Park and Maidstone State Forest in *Green Space.*

✷ Where to Eat

DINING OUT **Abbie Lane** (802-334-3090) at Bay View Lodge & Motel, Route 5, Newport. Open for dinner Tuesday through Sunday, 5–9 PM. Recently moved, Alisa and Ed Levy are known for offering the best dining around. You might begin with a bowl of mussels steamed in rice wine, tossed with fresh ginger, shallots, basil, mint, and cilantro, and feast on porcini and morel-mushroom-crusted seared pork loin stuffed with fresh mushrooms and herbs in a sauce of pan juices and red Dubonnet, potatoes au gratin, and sautéed vegetables. Entrées $11.95–19.95; early-bird specials.

Lago Trattoria (802-334-8222), 95 Main Street, Newport. Open Monday through Saturday, 4:30–10. Chef-owner Frank Richardi claims not to fry anything except calamari, a departure for downtown Newport, as is the sophisticated modern Italian decor. The menu incudes pastas and staples like chicken Marsala and cacciatore. Try the flattened breast of chicken stuffed with crumbled sausage stuffing, four cheeses, roasted pepper, and fresh basil. Entrées: $11.50–$18.

The East Side (802-334-2340), 47 Landing Street, Newport. Open for lunch and dinner weekdays, breakfast on weekends. Closed Monday. Formerly The Landing, this is a large old landmark with a seasonal outside deck and dock. The reasonably priced lunch menu might include lamb stew and biscuits or grilled chicken salad; the dinner menu is also moderately priced. The night's special might be marinated center-cut pork chop, deep-fried oysters, or Yankee pot roast (all under $12). Many locals come just for dessert (try the pecan ribbon). Live entertainment Friday and Saturday.

Quimby Country (802-822-5533), Route 114, Averill (see *Lodging*). Open to the public for dinner by reservation only, offering a rotating menu of two entrées, plus a children's entrée; Sunday-night buffet. Moderate.

Sutton Place Restaurant (603-237-8842), 152 Main Street, Colebrook, New Hampshire. Lunch Tuesday through Saturday and dinner every night. Don and Carmela Kelsea have created an intimate dining place in the front parlors of a Queen Anne–style house in the center of town. Dinner entrées include steak, chicken, and seafood. Moderate.

EATING OUT **Bessie's Diner** (802-266-3310), 166 Gale Street, Canaan. Open weekdays from 6, Saturday from 7, and Sunday from 8; closes at 8 every night. Admittedly we're suckers for cheap and friendly, but Vernon and Bonnie Crawford's place is so pleasant and wholesome—ditto for the food—that we can't rave enough. On our last visit we went for the special: cabbage soup and a tuna fish casserole (real tuna with rice, beans, and onions). The menu includes burgers, 30 different kinds of sandwiches, open-faced bagel-wiches (try the Grump-Fish), subs, and wraps. Poutines (Quebec-style french fries with gravy and cheese curds) are a specialty, and a wide choice of dinner choices average $6.75. Service is fast and friendly. Wine and beer. Cow Licks, an ice cream window, operates summers.

Jennifer's Restaurant (802-723-6135), Cross Street, Island Pond. Open daily for breakfast, lunch, and dinner, with a children's menu. The town's gathering spot, a cheery restaurant known for good food, especially seafood—which even coastal residents find inexplicably outstanding. Hearty breakfast sandwiches, and roast turkey, surf and turf for dinner. Beer and wine served.

Derby Cow Palace (802-766-4724), Main Street (Route 5), Derby. This is the newest venture for Doug Nelson, owner of the largest local dairy operation and of Cow Town Elk Ranch. Needless to say, the pleasant log restaurant specializes in beef, from burgers to prime rib. Fully licensed, with a bar menu.

La Vielle Douane (819-876-2776), 33 Rue Pricipale, Rock Island, Quebec. Literally "the old customs" house, steps across the border from Derby Line, this is your standard Greek feautring souvlaki and pizza but it's a full family restaurant menu and it's fun to order *"truite arc-en-ciel"* instead of rainbow trout. Fully licensed.

The Brown Cow (802-334-7887), 900 East Main Street, Newport, open daily 6 AM–7 PM except Sunday, when it's 7–1. This is a nice spot to linger over breakfast (served all day); sandwich and salad lunches, reasonably priced dinners. Homemade ice cream on homemade pie.

Miss Newport Diner (802-334-7742), East Main Street, Newport. Open 5 AM–11 PM daily except Saturday, when it closes at 10:30 PM. Blueberry pancakes and fresh muffins are the specialty, along with homemade soup and friendly natives; choice of stools and booths.

Friendly Pizza (802-723-4616), Derby Street (Route 105), Island Pond. John Koxarakis offers a wide variety of pizzas, also steaks, spaghetti, sandwiches, grinders, and Greek salad in his small eatery on the southern fringe of the village.

Northland Restaurant and Lounge (802-266-9947), Canaan. A large, clean, comfortable place offering three squares. The spacious adjoining bar/lounge/dance floor hosts rock and country-rock bands Saturday evening.

✷ Entertainment

North Country Concert Association (802-723-6027), Box 601 in Newport, sponsors a dance, theater, and concert series in various locations throughout the area.

♿ **Haskell Opera House** (819-876-2020; tickets also on sale at the Woodknot Bookshop in Newport: 802-334-6720), in Derby. This splendid vintage-1904 theater has perfect acoustics, three antique sets, a rare roll-up curtain depicting scenes of Venice, and a rococo interior. Its season runs late April through mid-October and includes performances by a resident theater company, opera, dance, and a variety of outstanding concerts.

Piggery Theater (819-842-2431), North Hatley, Quebec. June through August, summer theater.

✷ Selective Shopping

Sel-Bar Weaving (802-334-6565), in the old South School, Weaver Street, Newport. Open Monday through Thursday 8–5, Friday until 4. East on Main Street across the Long Bridge (don't turn onto the Causeway), take your first right on Glen Road, then your second left (Weaver Street). A small factory outlet, housed in the big white school building in which place mats, napkins, and homespun linens are made, offers a large choice of styles, seconds, and discontinued patterns. We use these place mats day in and day out (they machine-wash) and send them as wedding gifts to far places because they mail so well. Mats and tablecloths come in a variety of colors. The big annual sale is the weekend before Thanksgiving.

Bogner Factory Outlet (802-334-0135), 150 Main Street, Newport. Looking more like a boutique than the outlet it is—for the nationally known ski- and sportswear made in town.

Woodknot Books (802-334-6720), Main Street, Newport. Open 9–5 except Sunday, Friday until 7. A good selection of books and magazines.

Great Outdoors (802-334-2851), 177 Main Street, Newport. In summer, the store features an extensive array of fishing gear and sells fishing licenses; four-season sporting goods.

Simon the Tanner (802-723-4452), Cross and Main Streets, Island Pond. Open daily except Saturday, closing at 3 on Friday, otherwise 9–5, until 8 on Thursday. This is an unlikely spot for such a huge shoe store, but here it is selling a wide variety of name-brand shoes—Birkenstock and Clarks sandals, Dansko and Stegmann clogs, Doc Martens, work boots, winter boots, Tubbs snowshoes, and a big selection of athletic shoes, all at below-usual prices. There's also a bargain basement. Candles, specialty food, wrought iron, natural soaps, and body-care products made by the Twelve Tribes, an international sect that rooted in Island Pond several decades ago, restoring a number of houses and winning the respect of the community.

Lakeview Store (802-822-5570), Route 114, Averill. Open daily 8–7. A no-nonsense general store except for the fabulous wools and some handcrafted items: bowls, sweaters, baskets, also weaving supplies. Pick a fleece at a nearby Swanson Oldfarm and the store's owner, Priscilla Roy, will spin it.

✷ Special Events

February: **Newport Winter Carnival, Island Pond Snowmobile Races.**

March: **Sugaring** throughout the region.

July: **Memphremagog International Aquafest**—a swim race from Newport to Magog in Canada (32 miles), also a water-ski tournament, parade, public suppers, and more.

August (last week): **North Country Moose Festival.** Based in Colebrook, New Hampshire, a series of colorful events on both sides of the Connecticut River.

November: Annual **Hunters Supper.**

INDEX

4 Corners Farm, 221
40 Putney Road, 78
135 Pearl Street, 403
1811 House, 138–39
1824 House Inn, 308
1829 House Antiques, 467
1830 Shire Town Inn, The, 239
1836 Cabins, 450
1836 Country Store Village, 113

A

A. R. Nowes, 51
Abbie Lane, 534
Abenaki Indians, 38
Abenaki Museum, 38
Act 250, 11
Adam's Apple Cafe, 467
Adams Farm, 104
Adams Motor Inn and Restaurant, 368
Adavasi Imports, 93–94
Addison County, 344–73; entertainment, 371; events, 373; getting there/around, 346; green space, 359–60; guidance, 344, 346; lodging, 360–68; map, 345; restaurants, 368–70; shopping, 371–72; sights/activities, 349–59; villages of, 346–49
Addison County Field Days, 17
Adventure Guides of Vermont, 37, 46
aerial rides, 257
agricultural facts, 16–17
agricultural fairs, 17.
Aiken, George, 67–68
Aime's Motel, 500
air service, 17, 378
airplane rides, 100
airports, 17
AJ's Mountain Bikes, 437
Albany, 498, 501–2
Albany Airport, 17
Albro Nichols House, 493
Alburg, 415
Alburg Auction House, 420
Alburg Country Club, 414
Alburg Country Store, 420
Alburg Dune State Park, 414
Alexandra B&B, 118
Alice M. Ward Memorial Library, 528
Alice's Patisserie & Cafe, 36, 217
All Fired Up, 327
All Seasons Inn Motel, 186
All Things Bright and Beautiful, 314
Alldays & Onions, 121
Allen Brothers Farms & Orchards, 172
Allenholm Farm, 31, 420
Allenholm Orchards Bed & Breakfast, 417
Allis State Park, 284, 286, 290
Alonzo's Pasta and Grille, 111
Alpenrose, 449
Alpine lifts, 26
alpine slides, 26, 133, 258, 436–37
Alpine Traders, 102
Al's French Frys, 401
American Classics, 247
American Country Designs, 93
American Flatbread Kitchen, 312
American Maple Products, 44
American Museum of Fly Fishing, 128
American Precision Museum, 39, 47, 202, 203
American Revolution, 39
American Society of Dowsers Bookstore, The, 504
Amigo's, 370
Amos Brown House, 109
Amtrak, 17–18
Amy's Bakery Arts Café, 86
Anatolia, 170
Anchor, 111
Anchor Island Marina, 413
Andover, 183, 185
Andrie Rose Inn and Luxury Suites, The, 180–81, 188
Anglin' Canoe & Boat Rental, 486
Annie's Book Stop, 342–43
Annual Balloon Adventure, 19
Anthony's Restaurant, 28
antiquarian booksellers, 18
antiques, 18; Addison County, 371; Barre/Montpelier area, 328; Bellows Falls/Grafton, 171; Burlington region, 405; Champlain Islands, 419–20; Lamoille Valley, 467–68; Lower Connecticut and West River Valleys, 89–91; Manchester area, 155; Mount Snow/Wilmington area, 111–12; Northeast Kingdom, 504; Okemo Valley Region, 190; Sugarbush/Mad River Valley, 313; Woodstock/Quechee area, 246–47
Antiques Collaborative, 246–47
Appalachian Gap, 33, 303, 355
Appalachian Trail Conference, 37
Apple Barn & Country Bake Shop, 122
Apple Island Resort, 418

Apple Mountain, 407
Applebutter Inn, 240
Applecheek Farm, 462, 464, 468
apples/apple picking, 18, 75, 356
Applewoods, 112
Architectural Salvage Warehouse, 405
Ardmore Inn, 239
area code, 16
Ariel's Restaurant & Pond Village Pub, 290
Arjuna, 250
Arlington, 126, 128, 140–42, 150, 152, 159
Arlington Inn, The, 140–41, 150
Arlington Preserve, 492
Art Building, The, 91
Art Cache, The, 507
art galleries, 18–19; Addison County, 371; Barre/Montpelier area, 327; Bellows Falls/Grafton, 171–72; Bennington, 122; Burlington region, 404–5; Lamoille Valley, 459, 468; Lower Connecticut and West River Valleys, 91; Manchester area, 155–56; Northeast Kingdom, 506–7; Okemo Valley Region, 190; Sugarbush/Mad River Valley, 313–14; Woodstock/Quechee area, 247
art/artisans: Bellows Falls/Grafton, 171; Mount Snow/Wilmington area, 112–13; Stowe area, 454; Upper Valley, 219; Woodstock/Quechee area, 247, 250
Arthur's Department Store, 469
Artisans Gallery, 314
Artisans' Hand, 327
Artist's Loft B&B and Gallery, The, 79, 91
Arts Center at Middlebury College, 19
arts centers, 88
Arts Council of Windham County, 19
arts councils, 19
Arvad's, 36, 453–54
Ascent of Nature, 80
Ascutney Mountain Resort, 205, 207, 208
Ascutney State Park, 207–8
Atwood Orchards, 356
Auberge de Stowe, 447
auctions, 19, 91
Auntie M's Attic, 90
Austin's Antiquarian Books, 113
Autumn Harvest Inn & Restaurant, 322, 326
Averill, 533
Averill's Restaurant & Bob's Tavern, 169

B

Baba-A-Louis Bakery, 188
Back Behind Saloon, 273
Back Chamber Antiques Store, 420
Back Side Cafe, 87
Bag Balm, 509
Bailey's & Burke General Store, 508
Bailey's Mills Bed & Breakfast, 241
Baker Memorial Library, 199
Baker's Bed & Breakfast, 339
Baker's Pond, 284
Bald Mountain, 263, 488–89
Ball Mountain Lake, 43, 74
ballooning, 19, 204, 231, 252, 436
Balloons Over New England, 19, 231
Baltimore Covered Bridge, 204
band concerts, 504
Barcomb Hill Country Club, 414
Barn Restaurant and Tavern, 152
Barnard, 236–37, 240–41, 243
Barnard Inn, the, 243
Barnes & Noble, 405
Barnet, 478, 493, 494
Barn-It All Antiques and Collectibles, 313
barns, 19–20
Barnstead Inn, The, 146–47
Barr Hill Nature Preserve, 491
Barr House, 239
Barre Books, 328
Barre Country Club, 322
Barre Opera House, 48, 327
Barre/Montpelier area, 316–29; about, 316, 318–20; entertainment, 327; events, 328–29; getting there/around, 318; guidance, 316, 318; map, 317; restaurants, 325–27; shopping, 327–29; sights/activities, 321–23
Barrows House, The, 142–43, 148
Bartleby's Books and Music, 113
Bartlett Falls, 358
Barton, 476, 481, 498, 499–500, 506
Barton Golf Course, 488
baseball, 387
Basin Harbor Club, 26, 34, 42, 48–49, 358, 361, 368–69
Basketville, 94
Bass Restaurant, 311
Basta, Peter, 131
Battell, Joseph, 350–51
Battenkill, 131
Battenkill Anglers, 131
Battenkill Canoe, 24, 117, 131
Battenkill Inn, The, 140
Battenkill River, 32
Battenkill Sports Cycle Shop, 130
Battery Park Summer Concert Series, 403
Battery Street Jeans, 406
Battleground, The, 309
Bayley-Hazen Country Store, 508
Bayley-Hazen Military Road, 485–86
Bayside Park, 389
Bayview B&B, 425
beaches, 54–55, 102–3, 337, 387, 489, 531; *See also* swimming
Beadnicks, 94
Bean Heads, 111
Beansie's Bus, 402
Bear Creek Mountain Club, 264
Bear Pond Books, 327–28, 455
Beattie's Trailside Lodge, 269–70
Beaver Creek Mini Golf, 414
Beaver Meadow, 211
Beckwood Pond, 80
bed & breakfasts, 20; *See also* lodging
Beecher Falls, 529
Belfry, The, 521
Beliveau Books, 405
Belle of Brattleboro, 21
Bellows Falls: about, 161, 162–63; entertainment, 170–71; events, 172; getting there/around, 162; guidance, 161; lodging, 168–69; map, 162; restaurants, 169–70; shopping, 171–72; sights/activities, 166, 167
Bellows Falls Country Club, 167
Belmont General Store, 191
Belvidere, 458, 460
Belvidere Mountain, 438–39, 462
Ben & Jerry's, 41, 402, 436
Bennington, 114–22; entertainment, 121; events, 122; get-

ting there/around, 115; guidance, 115; history, 38, 39; lodging, 118–20; map, 114; restaurants, 120–21; shopping, 121–22; sights/activities, 116–18
Bennington Battle Monument, 39, 116
Bennington Bookshop, 121
Bennington Center for the Arts, 117
Bennington Historic Bike Route, 20
Bennington Museum, 18, 39, 47, 116
Bennington Potters, 30, 122, 405
Bennington Station, 120
Benson, 335
Bentley's Restaurant, 245
Berkson Farms, 31, 424–25
Beside Myself Gallery, 155–56
Bessie's Diner, 528, 534–35
Best Diner, 151
Best Western, 186
Bethel, 280, 288, 291
Better Planet, 427
Bicycle Holidays, 20, 204, 356
bicycling, 20–21; Addison County, 356–57; Burlington region, 384–85; Champlain Islands, 413; Grafton, 166; Jay Peak area, 515; Killington/Plymouth area, 257–58; Lamoille Valley, 460; Lower Connecticut and West River Valleys, 70; Manchester area, 130; Northeast Kingdom, 485; Okemo Valley Region, 177; Rutland/Lower Champlain Valley, 337; St. Albans/Swanton, 423; Stowe area, 437; Sugarbush/Mad River Valley, 299; Upper Valley, 204–5; White River Valleys, 283; Woodstock/Quechee area, 231
Big Averill, 528
Big Black Bear Shop at Mary Meyer, 93
Big Falls of the Missisquoi, 514
Bike Center, The, 356
bike paths, 20
Bike Shed Rentals, 413
Bike Vermont, 20, 177, 204, 231, 299, 356
Bill Sladyk Wildlife Management Area, 528, 532
Billings Farm & Museum, 26, 40, 47, 49, 229
Billings, Frederick, 227
Bill's Country Store, 274
Bingo Brook, 285
Birch Meadow Farm, 289
Birchwood B&B, The, 532, 534
birding, 21, 357, 384, 413
Birdman, 506
Birds of Vermont Museum, 21, 384
Birdseye Diner, 341
Bistro Henry, 149
Bittersweet Farm, 31
Black Bear Inn, 394, 397
Black Cat Gallery, 420
Black Lantern Inn, 518, 520
Black Locust Inn, 449
Black Mountain Natural Area, 72
Black Newt Ironworks Sculpture Studio, 313–14
Black River Academy Historical Museum, 175
Black River Brewing Company, 22, 189
Black River Produce, 191
Black Swan, The, 148
Blackthorne Forge, 407
Blue Benn Diner, 28, 121
Blue Moon Cafe, 450
Blue Ridge Outfitters, 258
Blue Seal Restaurant, 397
Blue Tooth, The, 313
Blueberry Hill, 34, 51
Blueberry Hill Inn, 46, 358–59, 362–63
Blueberry Lake, 302
Blueberry Lake Cross-Country Ski Center, 303
Bluff Mountain, 530
Blush Hill Country Club, 438
Blythedale Farm, 26
Boardman House, 80
boating, 21–22; Addison County, 357; Barre/Montpelier area, 321–22; Burlington region, 385; Champlain Islands, 413; Connecticut River, 166–67; Lower Connecticut and West River Valleys, 70–71; Mount Snow/Wilmington area, 100–1; Newport/North Country, 526–27; Northeast Kingdom, 486; Okemo Valley Region, 177; Rutland/Lower Champlain Valley, 337; Stowe area, 437; Upper Valley, 205; White River Valleys, 283; Woodstock/Quechee area, 231
Bobbin Mill, 302
Bobcat Café, 370
Bogner Factory Outlet, 536
Bolton, 394, 397
Bolton Valley, 46
Bolton Valley Resort, 51, 52, 385, 387–88, 391–92
Bolton-to-Trapp trail, 388
Bomoseen Country Club, 337
Bomoseen State Park, 338
Bondville, 153
Bondville Fair, 17
Bonnie's Bundles, 190
Book Cellar, The, 91
Book King, The, 342
Book Rack and Children's Pages, 407
bookstores, 22; Addison County, 371; antiquarian, 18; Barre/Montpelier area, 327–28; Bennington, 121; Burlington region, 405; Lower Connecticut and West River Valleys, 91–92; Manchester area, 156; Mount Snow/Wilmington area, 113; Northeast Kingdom, 504–6; Okemo Valley Region, 190; Rutland, 342–43; Stowe area, 455; Upper Valley, 219; Woodstock/Quechee area, 250
Borders Books, 405
Borter's Jewelry Studio, 94
Boulder Beach Day Use Area, 489
Bove's Cafe, 399
bowling, 101
Boyd Family Farm, 104–5
Boyden Farm and Winery, 18, 57, 468
Bradford, 201, 215–16, 219, 220–21
Bradford Country Club, 206
Bradford Village Store, 36, 217
Bradley House, 314
Bragg Farm, 328
Braintree Hill, 285
Branbury State Park, 359
Branch Brook Bed & Breakfast, 493
Brandon, 347, 354, 358, 362, 364, 366–67, 370
Brandon Gap, 33, 355
Brandon Inn, The, 364–65, 369–70
Brandywine Glassworks, 92
Brass Lantern Inn, 447
Brattleboro: about, 63–65;

entertainment, 88–89; events, 94–95; guidance, 61–62; lodging, 78–79, 81; map, 64; restaurants, 81, 84, 85–87, 88; shopping, 89–94; sights/activities, 68–76
Brattleboro Area Chamber of Commerce, 61
Brattleboro Bicycle Shop, 70
Brattleboro Books, 92
Brattleboro Country Club, 72
Brattleboro Farmer's Market, 75, 86
Brattleboro Food Co-op, 93
Brattleboro Historical Society, 65
Brattleboro Museum and Art Center, 68
Brattleboro Music Center, 88–89
Brattleboro Outing Club Ski Hut, 73
Brattleboro Retreat Petting Farm, 69
Brattleboro Winter Carnival, 94
Bread and Puppet Theater Museum, 482
Breakwater Cafe & Grill, 400
breweries, 22–23, 88, 111, 189, 218, 274, 357, 370, 509
Brewster River Campground, 466
Brewster River Gorge, 34, 463
Brick House Book Shop, 455
Brick House, The, 500, 503
Bridge Street Bakery, 314
Bridge Street Studio & Gallery, 314
bridges, covered. *See* covered bridges
Bridges Family Resort and Tennis Club, 300, 302, 305
Bridgewater, 248–49
Bridgewater Corners, 267, 271
Bridgewater Country Store, 248
Bridgewater Mill, The, 248–49
Briggs Ltd., 220
Brighton State Park, 527, 531
Bristol, 347–48, 354, 364, 367, 369, 370, 372
Bristol Bakery & Café, 370
British School of Falconry, 133
Broadview Farm, 492
Brockway Mills Gorge, 34
Bromley, 47, 135
Bromley Alpine Slide, 133
Bromley Mountain, 133
Bromley Thrill Sleds, 133
Bromley Village, 147
Brookfield, 43, 279–80, 286–87, 289, 290
Brookfield Guest House, 288
Brookfield Gulf, 34, 285
Brookline, 66, 72
Brooks Memorial Library, 63
Brooksies Family Restaurant, 291
Brown Cow, The, 535
Brown River, 34
Brownington Village, 481
Brownsville, 210, 216
Brownsville General Store, 216
Brunswick Springs, 529
Bryant House, The, 153
Buccaneer Country Lodge, 449
Buckmaster Inn, The, 185
Buckswood Bed & Breakfast, 366
Buddhist Meditation Center Karme Choling, 53
Buggyman Antiques Shops, The, 468
Bulwagga Books and Gallery, 371
Bundy Fine Arts Center, The, 313
Buoy 39 Marina, 357
Burke Mountain, 47, 474, 485, 491, 494–96
Burke Mountain Condominiums, 496
Burke Mountain Cross-Country, 490–91
Burlington Bike Path, 20, 384
Burlington Center for Antiques, 405
Burlington City Arts Line, 402
Burlington Community Boathouse, 385
Burlington Gem and Mineral Club, 50
Burlington International Airport, 17
Burlington Oratorio Society, 403
Burlington Parks and Recreation, 388
Burlington Redstone, 391
Burlington region, 374–408; about, 375, 377; events, 407–8; getting there/around, 378; green space, 388–90; guidance, 377–79; lodging, 390–95; map, 374, 376; restaurants, 395–402; shopping, 403–7; sights/activities, 380–88; villages of, 379–80
Burlington Town Center, 404
Burton Farm Lodge, 210
Burton Island State Park, 423
Burton Isle, 43
Burton Snowboards, 406
bus service, 23
Butler's, 396
Butterfly Heaven, 69
Buttermilk Falls, 178
Butternut on the Mountain, 270
Buttery, The, 151
Button Bay State Park, 359
By the Old Mill Stream, 395
By the Way B&B, 365
By Vermont Hands, 468
Bygone Books, 405

C

C&B Guided Rides, 178
Cabin Fever Quilts, 314
Caboose Corner, 172
Cabot, 479
Cabot Annex Store, 455
Cabot Creamery Visitors Center, 25, 483, 506
Cabot Farmers Co–op Creamery, 479
Cadillac Motel, The, 426
Café Banditos, 467
Cafe Beyond, 86
Café Shelburne, 396
Cafe, The, 170
Calvin Coolidge Historic Site, 177, 261–62
Calvin Coolidge State Forest, 265
Cambridge, 460
Cambridge Arts Council, 467
Cambridge Greenway, 460
Camelot Village, 121
Camels Hump State Park, 389–90, 439
Camp Plymouth State Park, 177, 178
campgrounds, 23–24; Lake Champlain Valley, 426; Lamoille Valley, 466; Lower Connecticut and West River Valleys, 81; Manchester area, 130–31; Northeast Kingdom, 486; Stowe area, 437; White River Valleys, 289–90
camps: children's, 23; day, 101; summer day, 302
Canaan, 528
Candeleros, 151
Candle in the Night, A, 94
Candle Mill Village, 159
Candlelight Bed & Breakfast, The, 108
Candlepin Restaurant, 502

canoeing, 24–25, 117, 131, 205, 258, 299, 423, 460, 486, 487, 515, 527
Canterbury House, 238–39
Capitol Grounds, 326
Capitol Plaza, 322, 324
Capitol Stationers, 328
Capitol, The, 327
Caplan's Army Store Work & Sportswear, 509
Cappuccino's Cafe, 189
Carlson's Antiques, 155
Carriage House of Woodstock, 240
carriage rides, 437
Carriage Trade Antiques Center, 155
Carroll and Jane Rikert Ski Touring Center, 358
Cascades Lodge, 269
Cascades Lodge Restaurant, 273
Casey's Caboose, 272–73
Castle at Proctorsville, The, 11
Castle Inn, The, 40
Castle Shoppe, 509
Castle, The, 181, 188
Castleton, 334–35, 337, 339, 341, 343
Catamount Art Gallery, 506–7
Catamount Family Center, 46, 385, 388
Catamount Film and Arts Center, 19, 503–4
Catamount Fishing Adventures, 437
Catamount Trail, 51
Cavendish, 186
Cavendish Gorge, 34
Cavendish Pointe Hotel, 186
Cavendish Trail Horse Rides, 178
CCC Road, 177
Cedar Circle Farm, 221
Cedar Grove Farm, 484
Cedar Knoll Country Club, 386
Centennial Woods, 389
Central Vermont Music Festival, 47
Chaffee Center for the Visual Arts, 19, 335
chairlifts, 101, 133
Champ Charters, 386
Champlain Bridge Marina, 357
Champlain Islands, 409–21; about, 409–10; entertainment, 419; getting there/around, 411; green space, 414; guidance, 411; lodging, 415–18; restaurants, 418–19; shopping, 419–21; sights/activities, 411–14
Champlain Mill, The, 380, 407
Champlain Orchards, 356
Champlain Valley Antique Center, 405
Champlain Valley Exposition, 17
Chandler Gallery, 19
Chandler Music Hall, 48, 293
Chantecleer, 147–48
Chapman's, 220
Charity's Tavern, 273
Charles E. Tuttle Company, 342
Charles Orvis Inn, 137
Charleston House, The, 238
Charlestown, NH, 202–3
Charlie B's, 454
Charlie Horse Sleigh Rides, 437
Charlie's Northland Lodge, 413, 414, 416–17
Charlie's Northland Sporting and Gift Shop, 420
Charlotte, 407
Charles Shackleton Furniture, 247
cheese, 25–26, 75, 190–91, 506
Chef's Table, 325
Chelsea, 279, 286, 291, 292
Chelsea Royal Diner, 28, 36, 87
Chelsea Station, 291
Chester, 173, 175–76, 181, 182–83, 185, 186, 188, 190, 191
Chester A. Arthur Birthplace, 422
Chester Art Guild, 19, 175–76, 190
Chester Depot, 176
Chester Historical Society, 176
Chester House, The, 183
Chesterfield Inn, 78
Chesterfield, NH, 78
Chester's in the Square, 426
Chez Henri, 310
children, 23, 26
Chimney Point State Historic Site, 38, 354
China Wok, 170
Chipman House, 51, 364
Chipman Point Marina & Campground, 357
Chipman Stables, 132
Chittenden, 267, 267–68, 272, 337
Chittenden Brook Campground, 289–90
Chittenden Reservoir, 258
Chocolate Barn, The, 122
Choices Restaurant, 272
Chow!Bella, 426
Christmas trees, 26–27, 292
Christophe's on the Green, 369
Christo's, 152
Church and Maple Glass Studio, 405
Church Street Antiques, 247
Church Street Bridge, 458
Church Street Marketplace, 383, 403
churches, 198
Churchill House Inn, 51, 364
Cider Hill Farm, 219, 221
cideries, 18
Cilley Bridge, 281
Cilly General Store, 269
Cindy's Diner, 28
Cindy's Pasta, 503
Circus Smirkus, 504
civil unions, 27
Civil War, 39
Clarendon Gorge, 34
Classic Snow Tours, 136
Claudine's Bistro, 451
Clear Lake Furniture, 191
Clearwater Sports, 24, 299, 302, 303
Clem & Co., 341
Cliff House, 451
Climb High, 406
Club Car, The, 219
Club Metronome, 403
Coachworks Farm, 488
Cobblestone Deli & Market, 399
Coburn Hill Blueberry Farm, 484
Cochran Ski Area, 388
Coffee Corner, 326
Coffee Country, 87
Coffee Exchange, 341–42
Colatina Exit, 215
Colchester, 389, 395, 401
Colchester Reef Lighthouse, 401
Cold Hollow Cider Mill, 455
Cold Hollow Llamas, 43
Coleman, Abner W., 12
Collected Works Books & The Cafe Beyond, 91
colleges, 27
Colonial House Inn & Motel, 144
Columns Motor Lodge, The, 289
Combes Family Inn, The, 185–86
Comerford Reservoir, 487
Comfort Inn & Suites, 425–26

Common Man Restaurant, The, 311
Commodores Inn, 441, 448
Common Ground, 85, 89
condominiums, 49, 108, 147, 186–87, 270, 309–10, 449–50
Connecticut Lakes, 527
Connecticut River, 27, 71, 163, 195, 196
Connecticut River Fish Ladder, 69
Connecticut River Joint Commissions, 205
Connecticut River Tours, 71
Cooley Bridge, 336
Coolidge, Calvin, 260–62
Cooper Hill Inn, 107
Cooper-Webber House, 287
Copeland Furniture, 30, 220
Corners Inn Restaurant, The, 271
Cornish, NH, 203
Cornucopia of Dorset, 143–44
Cortina Health Club, 259
Cortina Inn and Resort, 264, 266, 338
Coslin's Pub, 451
Costantino's Italian Imports, 343
cottages, 49, 367
Country Bear Books, 506
Country Casuals, 50
Country Club of Vermont, 438
Country Cottage B&B, 493
Country Creemee Restaurant, 216
Country Essence B&B, 425
Country Girl Diner, 28, 188
Country Inns along the Trail, 356, 358
Country Pursuits Centre, 131
Country Willows B&B, 141
Countryman's Pleasure, The, 271
Couture's Maple Shop, 522
Coventry, 499–500
Cover to Cover Books, 293
covered bridges, 27, 68–69, 117, 165, 203–4, 230–31, 281, 321, 336, 355, 436, 458–59, 483–84, 514–15
Cow Town Elk Ranch, 530
Crackerbarrel Fiddle Festival, 31
Craft Haus, 112
Craft Shop at Fletcher Farm, 190
Craft Shop at Molly's Pond, The, 506
crafts, 28; Addison County, 371–72; Bennington, 121–22; Burlington region, 405; Champlain Islands, 420; Lamoille Valley, 468; Lower Connecticut and West River Valleys, 92; Manchester area, 156; Mount Snow/Wilmington area, 112–13; Northeast Kingdom, 506; Okemo Valley Region, 190; Sugarbush/Mad River Valley, 314; Upper Valley, 219
Craftsbury, 474, 496–98, 500, 502, 508
Craftsbury Bed & Breakfast, 497
Craftsbury Center Resort, 51
Craftsbury Center, The, 46, 51, 54
Craftsbury Chamber Players, 48, 504
Craftsbury Common, 480
Craftsbury General Store, 508
Craftsbury Inn, 497, 502
Craftsbury Outdoor Center, 480–81, 485, 487, 489, 490, 497
Crazy Mountain, 273
Cream Hill Farm, 368
Creamery Bridge, 68
Creamery Restaurant, 501
credit cards, 45
Crisanver House, 183, 185
Crosby House, 78–79
Cross-Country Center, 302
cross-country skiing, 51–52; Addison County, 358–59; Bennington, 117–18; Burlington region, 387–88; Grafton, 167; Killington/Plymouth area, 263; Lamoille Valley, 463; Lower Connecticut and West River Valleys, 73; Manchester area, 134–35; Mount Snow/Wilmington area, 103; Newport/North Country, 531; Northeast Kingdom, 490, 516; Okemo Valley Region, 179; Stowe area, 440; Sugarbush/Mad River Valley, 302–3; Upper Valley, 206; White River Valleys, 285–86; Woodstock/Quechee area, 233–34
Crossroad Farm, 221
Crossroads Arts Council, 19, 342
Crow Bookshop, 405
Crow Hill Gallery, 190
Crowley Cheese Factory and Shop, 25, 176, 190–91
Crown Point Country Club, 206
Crown Point State Historic Site, 354
Crow's Bakery, 191
Crystal Lake B&B, 487, 500
Crystal Lake State Park, 489
Crystal Palace Victorian B&B, 367
Cubbers, 370
Cucina de Gerardo, 502–3
Cupboard, The, 467
Currier's Quality Market, 508
Curtis' Barbecue, 36, 87
Curtis Pond, 321
Cuttingsville, 184, 191
Cycle-Inn-Vermont, 20
Cyclery Plus, 231

D

D. Lasser Ceramics, 156
D&H Recreation Trail, 20–21
D&K's Little Petting Farm, 69
Daily Bread Bakery Café, 401
Daily Planet, 398
dairy farms, 16
Dakin Farm, 407
Dan and Whit's General Store, 220
Dana Hill Stable, 301
Dana House, 40, 47, 230
Dana L. Thompson Recreation Area, 133, 134
Danby, 127, 130, 142, 148–49, 152, 155
Danby Antiques Center, 155
Danby Marble Company, 156
Danforth Pewterers, 372
Danforth's Sugarhouse, 328
Dan's Windsor Diner, 216
Danville, 474, 478–79, 484–85, 493, 501–2, 504, 506–8
Danville General Store, 507–8
Danville Morgan Horse Farm, 479, 484
Danville Restaurant, 502
D.A.R. State Park, 359
Darling Family Inn, 144
Darling Kelly's Motel, 119–20
Dartmouth Bookstore, The, 219
Dartmouth College, 195, 199
Dartmouth Film Society, 218
David Crandall's, 249
Day Art Center, 435
day camps, 101
Dead Creek Wildlife Management Area, 21, 357, 359
Debbie's Corner Café, 291

Deer Brook Inn, 239–40
Deer Leap Trail, 259, 263
Deer Meadow Inn, 308
Deerfield River, 101
Deerhill Inn, 106–7, 109
Deerleap Books, 371
Delectable Mountain, 93
Del's, 326–27
Delta Park, 389
Den, The, 311–12
Department of Forests, Parks and Recreation, 53–54
Depot Bridge, 336
Depot Street Malt Shoppe, 453
Derby Cow Palace, 535
Derby Line, 523, 525
Designer Outlets Center, 157
Designers Circle, 405
Desso's General Store, 379
DévalKarts, 133
Devil's Gulch, 439, 462
Dewey Pond Wildlife Sanctuary, 235–36
Dibden Center for the Arts, 48, 459
diners, 28
Dinners' Dunn at the Windridge Bakery, 466–67
Discover Jazz Festival, 47, 403
diving, 386
Dixie's Country Kitchen, 291
Dixie's II, 291
DJ's Restaurant, 189
DND Farm, 489
Dockside Cafe, 400
Dog Team Tavern, The, 369
dogsledding, 104
Doll-Anstadt Gallery, 404–5
Don's Diner, 28
Dormy Grill, 132
Dorothea's Cafe, 335
Dorset, 126–27, 142–44, 147–48, 149, 156, 157–58
Dorset Craft Center, 156
Dorset Inn, The, 142, 149
Dorset Playhouse, 55, 153–54
Dorset Quarry, 133
Dorset Tennis Club, 134
Dot's Restaurant, 110
Douglas Orchards, 356
Doveberry Inn, 107, 110
Dover, 97
Dover Hill Road, 99–100
Dovetail Inn, 144
Down in the Valley, 113
Downhill Edge and Ski Rack, The, 406
Downstairs at the Playhouse, 150
Dowser's Hall, 478
Dr. George A. Russell Collection of Vermontiana, 128
Driftwood Tours, 413
drive-ins, 219, 403
driving schools, 131
Dufferin Heights Golf Club, 530
Dummerston, 76
Dunmore Acres, 367
Dunne's Grill, 189
Dutch Pancake Cafe, 453
Dutton Berry Farm and Stand, 76
Dutton Pines State Park, 74
Dwight Miller & Son, 75

E

East Barre Antique Mall, 328
East Burke, 480, 485, 494–95, 496, 501
East Burke Sports, 46, 485
East Dummerston, 70, 75
East Good Food, 370
East Hardwick, 485
East Poultney, 334
East Roxbury Fish Hatchery, 322
East Side, The, 534
Eastern Vermont Rivers & Byways, 277
Eastman Long & Sons, 315
Eaton House, 481
Eaton's Sugar House, 36, 291, 292
Eben House, 240
Echo Lake, 526
Echo Lake Inn, 177, 181, 187–88
Echo Ledge Farm Inn, 31, 494
Econo Lodge, 426
Eden, 460
Edson Hill Manor, 51, 437, 439, 443–444, 451
Edson Hill Ski Touring Center, 440
Egan's Big World Pub and Grill, 312
Elaine Beckwith Gallery, 91
Elderhostel, 54
Elfin Lake Beach, 337
Elizabeth's October Pumpkin B&B, 365
Elliot House, 394
Elmore Mountain, 322, 439
Elmore State Park, 442–43
Elmwood Cemetery, 319, 321
Elysian Hills, 76
Emerald Lake State Park, 131, 134
emergencies, 29
Emergo Farm Bed and Breakfast, 31, 484, 493
Emerson's Guest House, 366
Emily's at Stowehof Inn, 451
English Rose Inn, 520
equestrian sports, 29
Equinox Hotel, 53, 123, 134, 136, 137, 149
Equinox House, The, 12
Equinox Mountain Antiques Center, 155
Equinox Nursery, 158–59
Equinox Preservation Trust, 136
Equinox Ski Touring Center, 135
Equinox Square, 157
Equinox Village Shops, 158
Eshqua Bog, 235
Essex Country Club, 386
Essex Ferry, 31
Essex Junction, 392, 395, 396
Essex Outlet Fair, 407
Essex Transportation Trail, 385
Ethan Allen Antique Shop, 405
Ethan Allen Homestead, 38, 383
Ethan Allen Park, 389
Etna, NH, 212–13
Evansville Trading Post, 509
Everyday Book Shop, 405
Everyone's Books, 91
Exquisite Corpse Artiste, 405

F

F. H. Gillingham & Sons, 250
factory tours, 357, 436
Fair Haven, 334, 339
Fair Haven Inn Bed & Breakfast, 339
Fair Haven Inn, The, 340
Fair Winds Farm, 73, 76
Fairbanks Inn, 500
Fairbanks Museum and Planetarium, 26, 47, 50, 481–82
Fairhill, 365
Fairlee, 204, 206, 208, 211, 217, 219, 220
Fairlee Diner, 29, 36, 217
Fairlee Drive-In, 219
Fairlee Marine, 205
Fairlee Village, 201
Fall Wave Soaring Encampment, 53
family sights/activities, 69, 258–59, 384, 530

Farina Family Diner and Restaurant, 28, 246
Farm Barn, 20
Farm Resort, 438
farm stands, 314
farm vacations, 30–31, 368
Farmbrook Motel, 270
farmers' markets, 30, 75, 86, 221, 246, 406
farming, 16–17
farms, 30; Addison County, 354–55; Barre/Montpelier area, 328; Bellows Falls/Grafton, 172; Burlington region, 384, 405–6; herb, 35; Lamoille Valley, 468; Lower Connecticut and West River Valleys, 75; Mount Snow/Wilmington area, 104–5; Northeast Kingdom, 484; pick-your-own, 49; sheep, 50; Sugarbush/Mad River Valley, 299; Upper Valley, 221; White River Valleys, 285
Farm-Way, Inc., 220–21
Farrar Mansur House, 40, 129
Farrow Gallery & Studio, 343
Farr's Antiques, 504
Fat Hat Factory, 251
Faulkner Park, 235
Fayston, 298, 301, 309
Featherbed Inn, The, 308
Fernwood Llama Farm, 43
ferries, 31
Ferrisburgh, 353, 359
Ferry Cruise, 413
Ferry Watch Inn, 417
Fiddler's Green Inn, 446
fiddling, 31
film. *See* cinemas
Fine Arts Center, 48
Fire & Ice Restaurant, 368
Fire House Art Gallery, 404
Fire House Center for the Arts, 383
Firefly Ranch, 358
FireStones, 245–46
Fish Culture Station, 412
fish hatchery, 336, 527
Fish Ladder and Visitors Center, 166
fishing, 32–33; Addison County, 357; Barre/Montpelier area, 321–22; Burlington region, 386; Champlain Islands, 413–14; Killington/Plymouth area, 258; Lamoille Valley, 462; Lower Connecticut and West River Valleys, 71–72; Manchester area, 131; Mount Snow/Wilmington area, 101; Newport/North Country, 527, 530; Northeast Kingdom, 487, 515; Okemo Valley Region, 177; St. Albans/Swanton, 423; Stowe area, 437; Sugarbush/Mad River Valley, 300; Upper Valley, 206; White River Valleys, 283–84; Woodstock/Quechee area, 231
Fishing Hole, The, 462
Fisk Farm, 416
Fisk Quarry Preserve, The, 412
Fitch Hill Inn, 465–66
fitness centers, 259, 300, 338, 357
Five Spice Café, 398
Flag Hill Farm, 18, 57
Flames Stables, 102, 104
Flat Road Diner, 151
flea markets, 90, 111–12
Fletcher Farm Craft School, 54, 178
Fletcher Library, 175
Flint Bridge, 281
Floating Bridge at Sunset Lake, 280
Fly Fish Vermont, 437, 456
fly-fishing, 131; *See also* fishing
Flynn Center for the Performing Arts, 403
foliage, 33
Foot of the Notch Bicycles, 460
Foothills Bakery, 426
Forest Care Nature Walks, 102
Forest Pool, 439
Forget-Me-Not Shop, 469
Forlie-Ballou, 191–92
Fort at Number Four, 38, 202–3
Fort Drummer State Park, 74
Fort Ticonderoga, 353
Fort Ticonderoga Ferry, 31
Fortune Cookie Chinese Restaurant, 121
FossilGlass, 250
Four Chimneys Inn, The, 118, 120
Four Columns Inn, 76–77, 84
Four Seasons Touring, 37
Fox and Pheasant Inn, 270
Fox Creek Inn, 263, 267–68, 272
Fox Hall, 498
Fox Stand Inn, 291
Foxfire Inn and Italian Restaurant, 448, 451
Framery of Vermont, The, 172
Franklin County Historical Society, 422
Franklin Farm, 76
Frank's Franks, 170
Fraser's Antiques, 247
Fred Mold Park, 492
Fred's Dollhouse and Miniature Center, 343
French Press Café, 467
Fresh Market, 406
Friendly Pizza, 535
Friends of Music at Guilford, 89
Frog Hollow at the Equinox, 156
Frog Hollow on the Marketplace, 405
Frog's Leap Inn, 146
Front Porch Theater Company, 170
Frost, Robert, 360
Fullerton Inn, The, 181, 188
Furchgott & Sourdiffe Gallery, 405

G

Gables Inn, The, 445–46, 452
Galaxy Bookshop, The, 505
Gallery in the Woods, 112
Gallery North Star, 155, 172
Gallery on the Green, 247
Gallery Walk, 89
Gandy Dancer Café', 216–17
gaps, 33–34
Garden Café, 150
Gardener's Supply, 407
gardens, 34, 507
Garment Gallery, 406
Garvin Hill Farm, 484
Gates Farm Bridge, 458
Gazebo, The, 367
Gelis Restaurant, 467
General Butler, 51
general stores, 34, 157–58, 191, 220, 455, 507–8
Georgia Stables, 387
Gibson House, 213
Gifford Woods State Park, 265
Gillies Seafood Restaurant and Raw Bar, 87
Gleneagles Golf Course, 132
Glenwood, 211–12
glider rides, 53, 301, 436
Gold Brook Bridge, 436
Golden Eagle Resort, 53, 437, 438
Golden Eagle Resort Motor Inn, 445
Golden Maple Inn, 487, 498

Golden Stage Inn, The, 182
golf, 34–35; Addison County, 357–58; Barre/Montpelier area, 322; Bellows Falls, 167; Bennington, 117; Burlington region, 386; Champlain Islands, 414; Killington/Plymouth area, 259; Lower Connecticut and West River Valleys, 72; Manchester area, 132; Mount Snow/Wilmington area, 101–2; Newport/North Country, 530; Northeast Kingdom, 487–88; Okemo Valley Region, 177–78; Rutland/Lower Champlain Valley, 337; St. Albans/Swanton, 423; Stowe area, 437–38; Sugarbush/Mad River Valley, 300; Upper Valley, 206; White River Valleys, 284; Woodstock/Quechee area, 231–32
gondolas, 435
Goodnough Bridge, 336
Goodrich's Sugarhouse, 510
Goodwillie House, 478
gorges, 34
Gorham Bridge, 336
Goshen, 358–59, 362–63, 367
Gourmet Café and Deli, 151
Governor's Inn, The, 181, 187
Gracie's Restaurant, 452
Grafton, 163–65; about, 161; entertainment, 170–71; guidance, 162; lodging, 167–68; map, 162; restaurants, 169; shopping, 171–72; sights/activities, 165–66, 167
Grafton Gathering Places Antiques, 171
Grafton Historical Society Museum, 165
Grafton Museum of Natural History, 165
Grafton Ponds, 51, 166, 167
Grafton Swimming Pond, 167
Grafton Village Cheese Company, 25, 165
Grand Isle, 43
Grand Isle Ferry Dock Snack Bar, 419
Grand Isle Lake House, 56, 418–19
Grand Isle State Park, 414
Grand Summit Hotel and Crown Club, The, 105
Grand View Winery, 18, 57, 117
Grandad's Invitational, 530
Grandview Winery, 328
Graniteville, 319
Gran'ma Frisby's, 152
Granville, 292–93, 314, 315
Granville Gulf, 34
Great Benson Fishing Derby, 33
Great Outdoors Trading Company, 343
Great Outdoors, 536
Great Rivers Arts Institute, 171
Green Mountain Audubon Nature Center, 21, 389
Green Mountain Bikes, 283
Green Mountain Blue Cheese, 25
Green Mountain Books & Prints, 505
Green Mountain Boys, 38–39, 115, 195
Green Mountain Club, 37, 300, 322, 390, 438, 442
Green Mountain Coffee Roasters, 455
Green Mountain Cultural Center, 313
Green Mountain Diner, 28, 327
Green Mountain Expeditions, 102
Green Mountain Flagship Co., 100
Green Mountain Flyer (train), 73, 167, 178
Green Mountain Guild, 55
Green Mountain Horse Association, 29, 233
Green Mountain Inn, 444
Green Mountain National Forest, 24, 35, 130, 284, 286, 289–90, 292, 358, 359–60
Green Mountain National Forest Ranger Office and Visitors Center, 277, 280, 297
Green Mountain National Golf Course, 259
Green Mountain Orchards, 75
Green Mountain Outdoor Adventures, 322
Green Mountain Polo Club, 29
Green Mountain Railroad, 49
Green Mountains, 35
Green Mountain Ski Touring Club, 285
Green Mountain Spinnery, 92
Green Mountain Sugar House, 191
Green River Bridge House, 81
Green River Canoe & Kayak, 24, 462
Green River Inn, 142
Green Trails Inn, 286–87
Green Trails Ski Touring Center, 286
Greendale Campground, 131
Greenhope Horse Farm B&B, 489
Greenhurst Inn, 288
Greensboro, 480, 485, 496, 497, 502, 504, 506, 509
Greenwood Lake, 322
Greenwood Lodge & Campsites, 120
Greenwood School, 67
Gregory's, 110
Greystone Bed & Breakfast, 241
Grist Mill, 272
Grist Mill Gallery of Fine Art, 190
Groton State Forest, 486, 491
Grout Pond Recreation Area, 104, 136
Grünberg Haus, 448–49
Guildhall, 529
Guilford, 68, 74, 76, 81, 89
Guilford Historical Society, 68
gulfs, 34
Guy Bridge, 281
Gymnasium, The, 338

H

H & M Orchard, 76
H. Lawrence Achilles Natural Area, 390
Hackett's Orchard, 420
Half Moon Cove Park, 389
Half Moon Pond State Park, 338
Halfway House, 28
Hall's Orchard, 420
Halpin Bridge, 355
Halvorson's Upstreet Cafe, 399
Hamilton Falls, 73
Hampton Inn, 395
Hancock, 292, 306–7
Hancock Hotel, 313
handicapped access, 35
Handle Road, 100
hang gliding, 206
Hanover Country Club, 206
Hanover, NH, 199, 202, 205, 218, 219
Ha'Penny Gourmet, 494, 508
Hapgood Pond Recreation Area, 131, 133
Happy Hours Restaurant, 503
Hardwick, 474, 476, 498, 505
Harlow's Sugar House, 76
Harmonyville, 91, 93
Harpoon Brewery, 22, 218

Harriman Reservoir, 97, 101, 102–3
Harriman's Restaurant, 105
Harrington's, 401–2, 407
Harry F. Sweat, 510
Harry's Cafe, 188–89
Hartness House, 11, 208–9, 214
Hartshorn's Farm Stand, 314
Harvey's Lake, 489
Harvey's Lake Campground, 486
Harvey's Mountain View Inn, 30–31, 288–89
Harwood Hill Motel, 120
Haskell Opera House, 535
Hastings barn, 19
Hastings Store, 479, 508
Haverhill, NH, 201, 213
Hawk Center, 263
Hawk Inn and Mountain Resort, 178, 266
Hawk North, Vermont's Mountain Hideaway, 289
Hawkins House, 121
Hawthorn Suites, 395
hay rides, 488
Haystack, 97, 101, 113
Hazen's Notch, 514
Hazen's Notch Association and Outdoor Education Center, 516
Hazen's Notch Association Trails, 37–38, 51
Hazen's Notch B&B, 519
Hazen's Notch Cross-Country Ski Center, 516
health spas, 232, 259, 438, 488
Heart of the Village Inn, 393
Heart of Vermont Llama Hikes, 285
Hearth & Candle, 466
Hearthstone Books, 92
Heermansmith Farm Inn, 499–500, 500–1
Helen Day Art Center, 19
Hemenway Bowl Mill, 293
Hemenway Bowl Mill Store, 315
Hemingway's, 271
Hemmings Motor News, 117
Henry Farm Inn, 182
Henry House, The, 118–19
Henry Sheldon Museum, 349
Henry's Diner, 28, 399
herbs, 35
Herdsmen Leathers, 158
Hermitage Inn, The, 109
Hermitage Ski Touring Center, 103
Hermitage Sporting Clays and Hunting Preserve, 102
Hermitage, The, 106
Hero's Welcome General Store, 413, 419, 420
Herrin House Inn, 240
Hickins Mountain Mowings, 76
Hickory Ridge House, 79
Hidden Orchard Farms, 172
High Brook Horse and Harness, 251
High Country Marine, 101
High Country Snowmobile Tours, 74, 104
High Pastures, 185
High Pond, 338
Higher Ground, 403
Highland Lodge, 42, 51, 487, 490, 496, 502
highway travel, 36
Hiker's Center, 37
hiking/walking, 36–38; Addison County, 358; Barre/Montpelier area, 322; Killington/Plymouth area, 259, 263; Lamoille Valley, 462, 463; Lower Connecticut and West River Valleys, 72; Manchester area, 132; Mount Snow/Wilmington area, 102; Newport/North Country, 530–31; Northeast Kingdom, 485–86, 488–89, 515; Rutland/Lower Champlain Valley, 337; Stowe area, 438; Sugarbush/Mad River Valley, 300, 302; White River Valleys, 284
Hilary's, 467
Hildene, 40, 123, 128–29
Hildene Ski Touring Center, 134–35
Hill Farm Inn, 141
Hillbilly Flea Market, 249
Hinesburg, 395
Historic Bennington Walking Tours, 116
Historic Brookside Farms Country Inn & Antique Shop, 361–62
Historic Hildene, 34
historic homes/sites, 128–29, 198, 202–3, 230, 282, 336, 353–54, 460
historical societies, 40
Historical Society of Windham County, 66
history, 11–13, 12–13, 38–40, 115, 198
Hivue Bed & Breakfast Tree Farm, 367
Hobo Cafe, 521
Holiday Inn, 340, 449
Hollister Hill Farm, 31
Hollow Inn and Motel, The, 325
Homeplace, 393
Homestead Campground, 426
HoneyBee B&B, 119
Hood Museum of Art, 202
Hooker-Dunham Arts Center, 88
Hope Cemetery, 319, 321
Hopkins Center for the Arts, 218
horseback riding: Addison County, 358; Barre/Montpelier area, 322; Bennington, 117; Burlington region, 387; Killington/Plymouth area, 263; Lamoille Valley, 462; Lower Connecticut and West River Valleys, 72–73; Manchester area, 132–33; Mount Snow/Wilmington area, 102; Northeast Kingdom, 489; Okemo Valley Region, 178; Rutland/Lower Champlain Valley, 337; Stowe area, 439; Sugarbush/Mad River Valley, 300–1; White River Valleys, 284; Woodstock/Quechee area, 232–33
Horses for Hire, 132
hostels, 212
Hot Dog Lady, The, 402
hot-air ballooning, 19, 204, 231, 252, 436
Hotel Coolidge, The, 212
Hotel Jay, 518, 521
hotels. *See* lodging
Houston, David and Myra, 510
Howard Street Guest House, 391
Howe Bridge, 281
Hubbard Park, 318
Hubbardton Battlefield, 39, 336
Hugging Bear Inn & Shoppe, 183
Hundredth Monkey Bookstore, The, 219
Hunger Mountain Food Co-op, 326
Hungry Bear, The, 36, 217
Hungry Lion Restaurant, 466
hunting, 40–41, 102, 133, 337
Huntington, 389
Hurricane Brook Wildlife Management Area, 492
Hurricane Forest, 236
Hyde Log Cabin, 412

Hyde Park, 457, 459, 465–66, 468
Hyde Park Opera House, 48
Hyde-Away Inn, 312, 313

I

I. B. Munson House, 339
I Wonda Book Shoppe, 219
ice climbing, 441
ice cream, 41, 88, 153
Ice House, The, 400
ice skating, 136, 234–35, 305, 388, 441, 464
Idyllwild East Bed & Breakfast, 520
Images from the Past, 122
India House, 399
information, 41–42
Inglenook Lodge, 518
Injun Joe Court, 486
Inn at Blush Hill, 448
Inn at Buck Hollow Farm, 425
Inn at Chelsea Farm, 241
Inn at Cranberry Farm, The, 185
Inn at Essex, The, 392
Inn at High View, The, 183
Inn at Idlewood, The, 290
Inn at Johnnycake Flats, 288
Inn at Long Trail, The, 269, 272
Inn at Mad River Barn, 306
Inn at Manchester, The, 138
Inn at Maplemont Farm, The, 493
Inn at Mountain View Farm, 488, 491, 494–95, 501
Inn at Ormsby Hill, 137–38
Inn at Quail Run, The, 108
Inn at Round Barn Farm, 19, 307
Inn at Rutland, The, 338–39
Inn at Sawmill Farm, The, 106, 109
Inn at Saxtons River, 168, 169
Inn at Shelburne Farms, 11, 31, 34, 40, 392, 396
Inn at South Newfane, 78
Inn at the Mountain and Condominiums, 444
Inn at Turner Mill, 437, 441, 446
Inn at Valley Farms, The, 168
Inn at West View Farm, 143, 148
Inn at Willow Pond, 140
Inn at Windsor, The, 210
Inn at Woodchuck Farm, The, 168
Inn of the Six Mountains, The, 269
Inn on the Common, 48, 496, 500
Inn on the Covered Bridge Green, The, 141
Inn on the Green, 365
Inn on Trout River, The, 519
Inn Victoria, 182–83
Inn Victoria Teapot Shop, 191
inns, 42; *See also* lodging
International Herbs, 122
Intervale, The, 389
Inverness Ski Shop, 299, 305
Ira Allen House, 141–42
Irasburg, 500, 504, 506, 509
Irene Collins, 293
Iron Wolf, 397
Island Craft Shop, 420
Island Pond, 525, 526
Island Pond Loop, 528–30
Isle de France, 451
Isle La Motte, 38, 409, 410, 416, 417, 418, 420
Isle La Motte Historical Society, 412

J

J. J. Hapgood Store, 157
J. K. Adams Co., Factory and Factory Store, 157
J. R.'s Café, 521
Jack Winner Antiques, 90
Jackson Arena, 441
Jackson House Inn, The, 34, 237
Jackson House Restaurant, The, 244
Jacksonville, 97, 99, 108
Jake's Marketplace Café, 152
Jamaica, 61; about, 67; lodging, 77, 80; restaurants, 84; shopping, 91, 93, 94; sights/activities, 69
Jamaica Country Store, 94
Jamaica State Park, 72, 73, 74
Jana's, 467
Japanese Cuisine by Michiko, 189
Jasper Murdock's Alehouse, 22–23, 217, 218
Jay Branch Gorge, 34
Jay Country Store, 521–22
Jay Peak, 46, 514, 516–17
Jay Peak area, 512–22; about, 512–13; events, 522; getting there/around, 513; guidance, 513–14; lodging, 518–20; map, 513; restaurants, 520–21; shopping, 521–22; sights/activities, 514–18
Jay Peak Condominiums, 518
Jay Peak Resort, 45–46
Jay Peak Ski and Summer Resort, 516
Jay's, 312
Jefferson House, 465
Jeffersonville, 458, 460, 465, 466, 467, 468
Jeff's Maine Seafood, 426
Jelly Bean Tree, 172
Jelly Mill, The, 158
Jennifer's Restaurant, 535
Jericho, 379, 393, 460
John James Audubon Art Gallery, 190
John McLeod, Ltd., 112
John Strong D.A.R. Mansion, The, 353
John Woodruff Memorial Library, 483
Johnny Seesaw's, 144–45, 150
Johnson, 459, 460, 466, 468, 469
Johnson Woolen Mills, 30, 468–69
Jolly Butcher, 87
Jonathon's Table, 152
Joseph Battell Bridge, 350–51
Joseph Smith Memorial and Birthplace, 280–81
Joshua Gold Pottery, 92
Joslin round barn, 19
Joy Wah, 170
Judith's Garden B&B, 34, 367
Judy Jensen Clay Studio, 293
Julio's, 326
Junior Soaring Camp, 302
Juniper Hill Inn, 204, 209, 214
Justin Morgan Memorial Museum, 384
Justin Morrill Homestead, 40, 282

K

Kamp Kill Kare State Park, 423
Kaos Fine Art Gallery, 112
Karibu Tulé's A Taste of Africa, 214
Karl Pfister, 132, 136
Karme-Choling Buddhist Meditation Center, 478
Kayak King, 258
kayaking, 24–25, 71, 258, 387, 460
Kedron Valley Inn, The, 237, 244–45
Kedron Valley Stables, 232–33
Kendall Homestead, 242

Kennedy Brothers Marketplace, 372
Kenyon's Variety Store, 300
Kettle Brook, 187
Kettle Pond, 486
Kevin's at Mikes Place III, 121
Kilgore's General Store, 521, 522
Killdeer Farm, 221
Killington, 34, 45
Killington Balloon Adventures, 19, 231
Killington Grand Resort Hotel & Conference Center, 265–66
Killington Hiking Center, 263
Killington K1 Express, 257
Killington Mountain Bike Center, 257–58
Killington Music Festival, 47, 274
Killington Peak, 46, 255, 257
Killington Resort, 259, 263–64
Killington Resort Villages, 270
Killington School for Tennis at the Cortina Inn, 263
Killington Skyeship Express, 257
Killington Snowmobile Tours, 265
Killington Snowshoe Tours, 265
Killington/Pico, 52
Killington/Pico Adventure Center, 258
Killington/Plymouth area, 255–74; activities, 257–65; entertainment, 274; events, 274; getting there/around, 257; green space, 265; guidance, 255, 257; lodging, 265–70; map, 256; restaurants, 271–74; shopping, 274
Kimberly Farms Riding Stables, 117
King Arthur Flour Baker's Store, 219–20
Kingdom Cat Corp., 491
Kingdom Toys, 508
Kingdom Trail Association, 486
Kingdom Trails, 37, 46
Kingsey Cheese of Vermont, 506
Kingsland Bay State Park, 359, 390
Kingsley Bridge, 336
Kinhaven Music School, 48, 153
Kipling Cinemas, 89
Kipling, Rudyard, 82–83
Kissin' Bridge, 458
Klara Simpla, 113
Knight Point State Park, 414
Knight's Island State Park, 414
Knight's Spider Web Farm, 328
Knotty Pine Motel, 119
Krawczyk Horse Farm, 358
Kristal Gallery, 313
Kristina's Café, 292
Kwiniaska, 386

L

L. A. Burdick Café, 170
La Brioche Bakery & Cafe, 326
La Poule à Dents, 215
La Vielle Douane, 535
Labour of Love Gardens, 507
Lackey's Variety Store, 455
Lago Trattoria, 534
Lajoie Stables at Vermont Horse Park, 462, 464
Lake Bomoseen, 338
Lake Bomoseen Marina, 337
Lake Carmi State Park, 424
Lake Champagne, 285
Lake Champagne Campground, 289
Lake Champlain, 39, 43, 359
Lake Champlain Basin Science Center, 382–83
Lake Champlain Chocolates, 406, 455
Lake Champlain Cruise & Charter, 385
Lake Champlain Ferries, 31
Lake Champlain Fishing Derby, 33
Lake Champlain Historic Underwater Preserves, 386
Lake Champlain Maritime Museum, 39, 51, 349, 353
Lake Dunmore, 359, 367
Lake Dunmore Kampersville, 357
Lake Fairlee, 201
Lake Memphremagog, 515, 526, 527, 530
Lake Morey, 201
Lake Morey Inn Resort, 35, 42, 206, 208
Lake Ninevah, 177
Lake Parker Country Store, 508
Lake Runnemede, 198
Lake Shaftsbury State Park, 118
Lake St. Catherine Country Club, 337
Lake St. Catherine State Park, 338
Lake Willoughby, 476, 489, 498–99, 509, 526
Lakefront Inn & Motel, 532
lakes, 42–43
Lakes End Cheese, 25
LakeShore Pub & Grill, 341
Lakeview Inn, 497, 502
Lakeview Store, 528, 536
Lamb and Lamb Company, 50
Lamoille County Nature Center, 463
Lamoille County Players, 454, 467
Lamoille River, 460
Lamoille Valley, 457–69; entertainment, 467; events, 469; getting there/around, 457–58; guidance, 457–58; lodging, 464–66; restaurants, 466–67; shopping, 467–69; sights/activities, 458–64
land trusts, 48
Landgrove, 145, 150
Landgrove Inn, The, 145, 150
Landmark College, 67
landscape, 33–34
Lane Series, 403
Laney's Restaurant, 151
Lang House, 391
LaPlant's Sugarhouse, 509
LaPlatte River Marsh Natural Area, 390
Lareau Farm, 302
Lareau Farm Country Inn, 307
Larkin Bridge, 281
Latchis Hotel, 81, 88
Latchis Theater, 89
Lawrence's Smoke House, 94
Le Petit Chef, 109–10
Le Tagge Sale, 90
Lebanon Opera House, 218
Leddy Arena, 388
Leddy Park, 387
Ledgewood Condominiums, 187
Ledyard Canoe Club, 205
Left Bank Antiques, 112
Lemoine's at the Inn on Trout River, 520
Leslie's, 169
lessons, 54
Letamaya Restaurant, 85
Leunig's Bistro, 399, 403
Libby's Blue Line Diner, 28, 36, 401
Liberty Hill Farm, 30, 288
libraries, 43
Liftline Lodge, 147
Lilac Inn, 362
Lilac Mountain Farm, 31, 75–76
Lily Pond, 71
Lincoln Bridge, 230

Lincoln Gap, 33, 303, 356
Lincoln Inn, The, 238, 245
Lincoln, Robert Todd, 128
Linda's Place, 86
Linens & Lace, 365
Links on the Lake, 419
Lippitts at the Three Stallion Inn, 290–91
Little Harry's, 340
Little River Camping Areas, 437
Little River Hotglass Studio & Gallery, 454
Little River Trail System, 439
Little Rooster Cafe, 150–51
Little Village Coffee Shop, 292
Living Memorial Park, 73, 74
llama trekking, 43, 102, 233, 285, 462
Loch Lyme Lodge and Cottages, 213
lodging: Addison County, 360–68; Barre/Montpelier area, 322, 324–25; Bellows Falls, 168–69; Bennington, 118–20; Burlington region, 390–95; Champlain Islands, 415–18; Grafton, 167–68; Jay Peak area, 518–20; Killington/Plymouth area, 265–70; Lamoille Valley, 464–66; Lower Connecticut and West River Valleys, 76–85; Manchester area, 137–47; Mount Snow/Wilmington area, 105–9; Newport/North Country, 532–34; Northeast Kingdom, 492–500; Okemo Valley Region, 180–87; prices, 5; Rutland/Lower Champlain Valley, 338–40; Saxtons River, 168; St. Albans/Swanton, 424–26; St. Johnsbury area, 494–94; Stowe area, 443–50; Sugarbush/Mad River Valley, 305–10; Upper Valley, 208–13; White River Valleys, 286–90; Woodstock/Quechee area, 236–42
Londonderry, 134, 146, 148, 149, 156
Londonderry Inn, The, 146
Long Meadow Inn, 494
Long Trail, 37, 102, 132, 300, 515
Long Trail Brewing, 22
Long Trail Brewing Company, 274
Long Trail House, 147
Lord's Prayer Rock, 347
Lost Nation Theater Company, 327
Lots-O-Balls, 301
Lower Champlain Valley, 332–43; entertainment, 342; events, 343; green space, 338; lodging, 338–40; map, 333; restaurants, 340–42; shopping, 342; sights/activities, 335–38; villages of, 334–35
Lower Connecticut and West River Valleys: entertainment, 88–89; events, 94–95; getting there/around, 62; green space, 74; guidance, 61–62; lodging, 76–85; map, 60; medical emergency, 63; restaurants, 81–88; seasons, 62; shopping, 89–94; sights/activities, 68–76; towns of, 61, 63–68
Lucca, 85
Lucy S. Gratwick Fine Handweaving, 92
Ludlow, 173; about, 175; activities, 177, 177–78, 179; lodging, 180–82, 185–86, 186; restaurants, 187, 188–89; shopping, 191
Ludlow Cooking Co., 189
Luminosity Stained Glass Studio, 314
Lye Brook Wilderness, 132
Lyme Angler, 206
Lyme, NH, 213
Lyndon, 485, 493
Lyndon Corner Grange, 504
Lyndon Outing Club, 491
Lyndon State College, 54, 480
Lyndonville, 479–80, 494, 502, 504, 505, 506, 509, 510

M

MacBain Homestead, 484
Mach's General Store, 158
Macrea Farm Park, 389
Mad River Carriage Co., 305
Mad River Chorale, 313
Mad River Flick, 313
Mad River Glen, 51, 295, 300, 302, 303, 304–5
Mad River Greenway, 299, 302
Mad River Inn, The, 308–9
Mad River Path Association, 302
Mad River Valley. *See* Sugarbush/Mad River Valley
magazines, 43–44
Magic Hat Brewing Co., 22, 406
Magic Mountain Ski Area, 136
Magnolia's, 341
Magnus Wools, 50
Mohican Moccasin Factory, 122
Maidstone State Park, 527, 529, 531
Main Street Arts, 171
Main Street Bar and Grill, The, 326
Main Street Bistro, 370
Major Farm, 75
Manchester area, 123–60; about, 123, 125; entertainment, 153–54; events, 159–60; getting there/around, 125–26; green space, 136; guidance, 125; lodging, 137–47; map, 124; medical emergency, 126; restaurants, 147–53; shopping, 155–59; sights/activities, 127–36; villages of, 126–27
Manchester Commons, 157
Manchester Highlands Inn, 138
Manchester Music Festival, 47, 153
Manchester Pizza House, 152
Manchester Square, 157
Manchester View, The, 146
Mannsview Inn, 460, 465
Mansfield View B&B, A, 393–94
Manyu's Boutique, 113
Map Adventures, 45, 46
Maple Crest Farm, 30, 176–77, 184
Maple Forest Monastery and Green Mountain Dharma Center, 53
Maple Grove Farm B&B, 394
Maple Grove Farms of Vermont, 44, 483
Maple Leaf Inn, 240–41
Maple Leaf Llamas, 484
Maple Leaf Malt & Brewing, 111
Maple Manor B&B, 498
Maple Museum, 44
Maple Ridge Sheep Farm, 50, 285
maple sugaring, 44–45, 75–76, 191, 292, 315, 328, 509–10
Maplecroft Bed & Breakfast, 325
Maplehurst Farm, 510
Maplewood Inn, 339
Marble Island Resort, 386
Marble West Inn, 143
Margo's, 419
Marilyn Bruno's, 152
Marina Restaurant, The, 86
Marketplace Vintage Books, 506

Marlboro, 97, 108, 110–11, 112
Marlboro Historical Society, 99
Marlboro Music Festival, 47, 97, 112
Marriott Residence Inn, 395
Marsh, George Perkins, 226
Marsh-Billings-Rockefeller National Historic Park, 40, 227, 228, 229–30, 235
Marshfield, 493
Martha Canfield Public Library, 128
Martin Calderwood, 510
Marvin Newton House, 280
Marvin's Country Store, 469
Mary Bryan Art Gallery, 459
Mary's at Baldwin Creek, 364, 369
Matterhorn, 454
May Pond, 489
Mazza Horse Service, 358
McCarthy's Restaurant, 452
McGrath's Irish Pub at the Inn at Long Trail, 272, 274
McGuel's Irish Burro, 426
McGuire Family Furnituremakers, 420
McKinley's, 216
McMorland's Steak and Seafood, 120
McNeil's Brewery, 22, 88
Meadowbrook Inn, the, 145
MeadowLark Inn, 79
Meadows at Quechee Inn at Marshland Farm, 245
Meadowsweet Herb Farm, 35, 177, 191
Melben's Restaurant, 467
Memorial Hall Center for the Arts, 111
Memory Lane, 339
Memphremagog, 523
Memphremagog Historical Society, 38
Mendon, 268, 271, 272, 273, 340
Mendon Mountain Orchards, 340
Merck Forest and Farmland Center, 136
Merriam House, 293
Metcalf barn, 19
Mettowee Valley Farm, 50
Michael Egan Blown Glass, 292–93, 314
Michael's Restaurant at the Powderhound, 311
Middle Bridge, 231
Middlebury: about, 344, 346–47; entertainment, 371; lodging, 360, 363, 364, 364–65; restaurants, 368–70; sights/activities, 349, 354–59
Middlebury Antique Center, 371
Middlebury Area Land Trust, 358
Middlebury College, 54
Middlebury College Center for the Arts, 48, 349, 371
Middlebury College Snow Bowl, 359
Middlebury Fitness, 357
Middlebury Gap, 33, 283, 355
Middlebury Gorge, 358
Middlebury Inn, The, 363, 369
Middlebury River, 357
Middletown, 339
Middy Waters, 402
Miguel's Stowe-Away Lodge and Restaurant, 312, 453
Mika's, 151
Mildred's Fine Foods Deli, 111
Milk Room Gallery, 468
Mill Bridge, 281, 458
Mill Brook Antiques, 247
Mill Brook Bed & Breakfast, 210
Mill Pond, 206
Mill River Bridge, 336
Millbrook Inn & Restaurant, 306, 310
Millbrook Path, 302
Miller Farm, 76
Miller's Thumb, The, 506
Millhouse Bed & Breakfast, The, 394–95
mini golf, 232, 301
Mirabelle's, 402
Miranda Thomas Pottery, 247
Mirror Lake, 321
Miss Bellows Falls Diner, 28, 169
Miss Lyndonville Diner, 28, 36, 502
Miss Newport Diner, 28, 36, 535
Miss Vermont, 28
Missisquoi National Wildlife Refuge, 21, 424
Missisquoi River, 515
Missisquoi Riverbend B&B, 515, 519
Missisquoi River Valley, 457
Missisquoi Valley Rail Trail, 20, 423, 460, 515
Mist Grill, 451, 454
Mistral's at Toll Gate, 148
Misty Meadows Herb and Perennial Farm, 456
Misty Mountain Lodge, 105–6
Misty Mountain Snowboards, 442
Misty Valley Books, 190
Mocha Joe's, 87
Mole's Eye Café, 89
Molly Stark Inn, 118
Molly Stark State Park, 104
Molly Stark Trail, 69–70, 98
Monadnock Mountain, 531
Mona's, 400
money, 45
Monroe Street Books, 371
Montague Golf Club, 284
Montgomery, 514–15, 518, 519, 520, 521, 522
Montgomery Bridge, 458
Montgomery Center, 516
Montpelier. *See* Barre/Montpelier area
Montpelier Elks Country Club, 322
Montshire Museum of Science, 26, 201–2, 205
Montshire Museum of Science Trails, 208
Moondance Grille, The, 272
Moore barn, 19
Moore Reservoir, 487
Moose Mountain Lodge, 212–13
Moose River Lake and Lodge Store, 508
Moretown, 298
Morgan, 532
Morgan Bridge, 458
Morgan Tavern, 369
Morgan's Pub at the Three Stallion Inn, 291
Moriarty Hat & Sweater Shop, 455
Morning Star Café, 216
Morningside Flight Park, 206
Morrill, Justin, 282
Morrisville, 457, 467, 469
Morrisville/Stowe State Airport, 53
Morse Farm, 328
Moscow Tea House, 453
motels. *See* lodging
Mother Myrick's Ice Cream Parlor & Fudge Factory, 153
Mother Shapiro's, 273
Mount Anthony Country Club, 117, 120
Mount Ascutney, 47, 198, 206
Mount Equinox, 47, 123, 129–30, 132
Mount Hor, 488
Mount Hunger, 322

Mount Independence State Historic Site, 39, 353
Mount Mansfield, 46, 434, 438
Mount Mansfield Company, 431–32
Mount Mansfield State Forest, 442
Mount Mills Beach, 102
Mount Peg Trails, 235
Mount Philo State Park, 390
Mount Pisgah, 488
Mount Snow, 34, 47, 52, 73
Mount Snow Condominiums, 108
Mount Snow Country Club, 101
Mount Snow Day Camps, 101
Mount Snow/Haystack, 103
Mount Snow Resort Mountain Bike Center, 45
Mount Snow/Wilmington area, 96–113; entertainment, 111; events, 113; getting there/around, 98; guidance, 97; lodging, 105–9; map, 96; restaurants, 109–11; seasons, 98; shopping, 111–13; sights/activities, 98–105
Mount Tom, 233, 235
Mount Worcester, 322
Mountain Bike School and Touring Center, 102
mountain biking, 45–46, 102, 299, 516
Mountain Biking at Blueberry Hill, 357
Mountain Creamery, 245
Mountain Cycology, 177
Mountain Golf School, 259
Mountain Green Health Club, 259
Mountain Lake Expeditions, 413
Mountain Meadows, 51
Mountain Meadows Lodge, 266–67, 273
Mountain Meadows Munchkins, 258–59
Mountain Meadows Ski Touring Center, 263
Mountain Park Cinema, 111
Mountain Riders, 130
mountain rides, 133
Mountain Sports & Bike Shop, 437
Mountain Top Equestrian Center, 337
Mountain Top Inn, 51, 267
Mountain Top Ski Touring Center, 263
Mountain Top Stables, 263
Mountain Valley Farm, 299, 305
Mountain View Country Club, 487
Mountain View Equestrian Center, 439
Mountain View Inn, 308
Mountain View Stables, 102
mountaintops, 46–47
movies. *See* cinemas
Moxley Bridge, 281
Mr. Pickwick's Pub & Restaurant, 453, 454
Mr. Up's, 369
Mrs. Brady's, 273
Mt. Riders, 70
mud season, 47
Mulligans, 152–53
museums, 47; Addison County, 349, 353; art, 18–19; Bennington, 116–17; Burlington region, 380–81, 384; Grafton, 165; Lower Connecticut and West River Valleys, 68; Manchester area, 127–28; Mount Snow/Wilmington area, 98; Northeast Kingdom, 481–82; Rutland/Lower Champlain Valley, 335–36; Upper Valley, 201–2
music: Bellows Falls/Grafton, 171; Burlington region, 402–3; festivals, 47–48, 88, 95, 112, 153, 274, 402, 403; fiddling, 31; Killington/Plymouth area, 274; Manchester area, 153; Northeast Kingdom, 504; opera, 48; Upper Valley, 218; venues, 89, 219, 274, 403
Music at Snow Farm Vineyard, 419
M/V *Carillon*, 21, 357
M/V *Mountain Mills*, 22
My-T-Fine Creamery Restaurant, 427

N

National Championship Fiddle Contest, 31
National Survey, The, 190
Native American petroglyphs, 166
Native Americans, 38
Nature Conservancy, The, 48
nature preserves, 48
nature walks, 133
Naulakha, 82–83
Nebraska Knoll Sugar Farm, 456
NECI Commons, 398
Nectar's, 399, 403
Neighborly Farms of Vermont, 26, 285
Nelson Pond, 321–22
Neshobe Golf Club, 358
Neshobe River, 357
New Discovery Campground, 486
New England Culinary Institute (NECI), 318
New England Maple Museum, 45, 336
New England Specialties Shoppe, 251
New Falls Cinema, 170
New Haven, 368
New Homestead, The, 288
New Life Fitness Vacations, 53
New Life Hiking Spa, 259
Newbury, 201, 211–12
Newell Bridge, 321
Newfane, 61, 72–73, 76; about, 65–66; lodging, 76–77, 78, 80, 80–81; restaurants, 84, 85; shopping, 90, 91–92, 94
Newfane Country Store, 94
Newfane Flea Market, 90
Newport, 532
Newport Country Club, 530
Newport Marine, 526–27
Newport/North Country, 523–36; about, 523, 525; entertainment, 535–36; events, 536; green space, 531–32; guidance, 525–26; lodging, 532–34; map, 524; restaurants, 534–35; shopping, 536; sights/activities, 526–31
Newport's Princess, 21–22, 527
Next Chapter, 156
Night with a Native Bed & Breakfast, 183
Nightspot, The, 274
Nikki's, 187
Noonie's Deli, 370
Nordic Adventures, 286
Nordic Inn, 51
Nordic Ski and Snowshoe Adventure Center, 463
Norman Dion's, 504
Norman Rockwell Exhibition, 128
Norman Rockwell Museum, 336
Norman Williams Public Library, The, 230
North Air, 100
North Beach Park, 387

North Country. *See* Newport/North Country
North Country Books, 405
North Country Concert Association, 48, 535
North Cove Cottages, 367–68
North Hartland Lake Recreation Area, 235
North Hero, 409, 415, 416–17, 418, 419, 420
North Hero House, 415, 418
North Hero State Park, 414
North Hollow Farm, 292
North Montpelier Pond, 321
North River Winery, 18, 57, 99
North Springfield Lake, 206
North Star Bowl and Mini Golf, 101
North Star Canoes, 24, 205
North Troy Village Restaurant, 520
North Wind Inn Touring, 37
Northeast Fiddling Association, 31
Northeast Kingdom: about, 477; entertainment, 503–4; events, 510–11; guidance, 476, 478; Jay Peak area, 512–22; map, 472–73; Newport/North Country, 523–36; restaurants, 500–3; shopping, 504–10; St. Johnsbury, Craftsbury, and Burke Mountain, 474–511
Northeast Kingdom Artisans Guild, 506
Northeast Kingdom Sheep Milk, 506
Northeast Kingdom Travel and Tourism Association, 477
Northern Café, 419
Northern Excursions, 177
Northern Exposure Country Store, 508
Northern Lights Bookshop, 505
Northern Lights Bookshop Cafe, 503
Northern Stage, 218
Northern Vermont Llama Treks, 43, 462
Northfield, 316, 320, 321, 322
Northfield Country Club, 322
Northfield Historical Society Museum, 320
Northland Restaurant and Lounge, 535
Northshire Bookstore, The, 156
Northwest Corner: Champlain Islands, 409–21; map, 410; St. Albans/Swanton, 422–27
Norton, 528
Norton's Gallery, 371
Norwich, 199, 201–2, 209–10, 211, 215, 217, 218, 219–20, 221
Norwich Bookstore, The, 219
Norwich Farmer's Market, 221
Norwich Inn, 209–10, 215
Notch Brook Condominiums, 450
Noyes House Museum, 460
Nugget, The, 218
Nu-tique, 90
Nutmeg Inn, 106

O

Oak Bluffs Cottage Pottery, 121
Oak Meadow School, 67
Oakledge Park, 387, 389
Oasis, 28
October Country Inn, The, 267
Offerings, 94
Okemo, 34, 52, 179–80
Okemo Inn, The, 181–82
Okemo Lantern Lodge, 182
Okemo Mountain Lodge, 186–87
Okemo Mountain Resort, 175, 180, 186–87
Okemo Valley Golf Club, 177–78
Okemo Valley Nordic Center, 179
Okemo Valley Region, 173–92; activities, 177–80; events, 192; getting there/around, 173, 175; guidance, 173; lodging, 180–87; map, 174; medical emergency, 173; restaurants, 187–90; scenic drives, 176–77; shopping, 190–92; villages of, 175–76
Old & New England Books, 91–92
Old Bobbin Mill Restaurant, 521
Old Constitution House, The, 203
Old Cork's Antiques, 91
Old Cutter Inn, The, 494–95, 501
Old Forge, The, 509
Old Foundry Restaurant, 426
Old Gold, 406
Old Hancock Hotel, 292
Old Homestead, The, 494
Old Inn Marketplace, 248–49
Old Labor Hall, 319
Old Mill Inn, The, 366
Old Mill Racquet & Fitness Center, 488
Old Mill River Place, 425
Old Museum, 480
Old Newfane Inn, 78, 85
Old Red Mill, 379
Old Round Church, 379
Old Schoolhouse Books, 293
Old South Congregational Church, 198
Old Stagecoach Inn, The, 448
Old Stone House Museum, 47, 482, 484
Old Tavern, The, 167, 169
Old Town Farm Inn, 185, 189
Oldcastle Theatre Company, 121
Onion Flats, 291
Onion River Arts Council, 19
Only Village Store, 293
Oona's, 169
Oooh Ahhh Baby Llamas, 484
Opaline, 397
Open Studio Weekend, 28
Opera House, 48
opera houses, 48, 218, 327, 535
Opera North, 218
Orb Weaver Farm, 25
orchards, 420
Orleans, 499–500
Orleans Country Club, 488
Orleans County Fair, 17
Orvis Company, 32, 133
Orvis Fishing Schools, 131
Orvis Retail Store, 158
Orwell, 349, 361–62
Osprey Fishing Adventures, 527
Ott Dog Snack Bar, 246
Ottauquechee River Valley. *See* Woodstock/Quechee area
Ottauquechee Valley Winery, 57, 251
Otter Creek, 357
Otter Creek Brewing, 22, 357, 370
Otter Creek Old and Rare Books, 371
Outback Food & Spirits, 153
Outback Pizza, 274
Outdoor Gear Exchange, The, 406
Outlet Center, The, 93
Ovations Restaurant, 272
Over Andover, 190
Owl Cottage Family Activity Center, 381
Owl's Head, 531

P

P&H Truck Stop, 28, 36, 218, 503
Paddington's, 520
PaddleWays, 387
Page's Ice Cream, 88
Palmer House Resort, 146
Palmer's Maple Products, 315
Palms, The, 340
Panda Pavilion, 341
Pane e Salute Italian Bakery, 245
Panton, 349
Papa Frank's, 401
Paperback Palace, 92
Parade Gallery, 313
Paradise Bay Bed & Breakfast, 416
Paradise Motor Inn, 119
Paradise Restaurant, 121
Paramount, The, 327
Parent Farmhouse, The, 31
Parima Restaurant, 398–99
Parish Players, The, 218
Parker barn, 19
Parker House Inn, 238, 244
Park-McCullough House, 40, 116–17
Parkway Diner, 28
Patricia's Restaurant, 370
Paul P. Harris Memorial, 336
Pauline's Café & Restaurant, 396
Pawlet, 127, 152
Peace and Justice Store, 406–7
Peacemaker Cruises, 166
Peach Brook Inn, 211
Peacham, 478, 494, 508
Peacham Corner Guild, The, 506
Pearson's General Store, 478
Peel Gallery, 155
Peltier's General Merchandise, 151, 157–58
Penelope's on the Square, 213–14
Penny Cluse Cafe, 399–400
Pentangle Council on the Arts, 19, 246
Peppino's Ristorante Italiano, 273
Perennial Pleasures Nursery, 507
Perfect Pear Café, 36, 215–16
Perfect Wife, The, 149
Performing Arts Festival, 48
Perkins Geology Hall, 50
Perry Farm, 484, 488, 489
Perry's Fish House, 401
Persico's Plum & Main, 466
Peru, 130, 131, 133, 134, 135, 144–45, 150, 157
Peter Bramhall, 250
Peter Glenn Ski & Sports, 509
Peter Haven's, 84
Peterson Brook Farm, 439
pets, 48–49
Petticoat Junction, 133
Peyton Place, 215
Phantom Theater, 313
Phelps House, The, 339
Philadelphia, 352
Phineas Swann B&B, 519
Phoenix, 51
Pickle Barrel, 274
picnics, 246, 285, 462
Pico Resort Hotel, 270
Pico Sports Center, 259
Pie in the Sky, 31
Pierce House Museum, 481
Pierce's Marketplace, 508
Piermont Inn, 213
Piero's Trattoria at the Orchard Inn, 111
Piggery Theater, 536
Pikes Falls, 73
Pines Restaurant, The, 427
Pines, The, 291
Pinewoods Gardens, 354
Pink Lady, The, 522
Pinnacle Ski & Sports, 437
Pippin Inn, The, 240
Pitcher Inn, 305–6, 310
Pittsfield, 289
Pittsfield Inn, The, 268
Pittsford, 341, 343
Pittsford Fish Hatchery, 336
Pizza Jerks, 274
Pizza Paul and Mary, 170
Placidia Farm Bed & Breakfast, 289
Plattsburgh Ferry, 31
Playhouse Movie Theatre, The, 292
Pleasant Street Books, 247
Plymouth. *See* Killington/Plymouth area
Plymouth Cheese Company, 25
Plymouth Notch, 177, 260–62
Pocketful O' Posies, 468
Poland Bridge, 458
Polka Dot, The, 29, 217
polo clubs, 29, 233, 301
Polonaise Art Gallery, 247
POMG Bike Tours of Vermont, 20, 205
Pompanoosuc Mills, 30, 220
Poncho's Wreck, 110
Pond Hill Ranch, 337, 338
Pond House at Shattuck Hill Farm, The, 210
Pond Ridge, 242
Popple Fields, 186
Porter House of Fine Crafts, The, 156
Porter's Bike Shop, 423
Post Mills Airport, 19, 204
Post Mills Aviation, 53
Pot Belly Restaurant and Pub, 189
Poultney, 334
Powderhound Lodge, 309–10
PowerPlay Sports, 460
Powers barn, 19
Ppeppers Bar & Grill, 273
Practice Tee, The, 132
prices, 42
Prince and the Pauper, The, 243
Priscilla's Victorian Inn, 339
Proctor Pittsford Country Club, 337
Proctorsville, 181, 182, 186, 188, 191
Prospect Rock, 462
Prouty Beach, 531
public radio, 55
Pulp Mill Covered Bridge, 355
Putney, 61; about, 67–68; entertainment, 88, 89; lodging, 79–80, 81; restaurants, 84, 87; shopping, 92, 94; sights/activities, 69, 70, 75, 76
Putney Artisans Craft Tour, 67
Putney Bicycle Club, 70
Putney Clayschool, 92
Putney Diner, 36, 87
Putney Inn, The, 36, 81, 84
Putney Mountain, 72
Putney Mountain Road, 69
Putney Mountain Winery, 18, 57, 88
Putney School, 67

Q

Quaigh Design Centre, 112
Quail's Nest, The, 142
quarries, 319–20
Quechee. *See* Woodstock/Quechee area
Quechee Balloon Festival, 231
Quechee Club Ski Area, 234
Quechee Gorge, 34, 229
Quechee Gorge Mini Golf, 232
Quechee Gorge State Park, 235
Quechee Gorge Village, 251
Quechee Gorge Village Antique Mall, 246

Quechee Inn at Marshland Farm, 237
Quechee Lakes Resort, 242
Quechee Polo Club, 29, 233
Quiet Valley Bed & Breakfast, 366
quilts, 49
Quilts by Elaine, 468
Quimby Country, 32, 42, 527, 528, 533, 534

R

Rabbit Hill Inn, 492, 501
Racquet Club at Topnotch, 439
radio stations, 55
Radisson Hotel, The, 390
railroad excursions, 49, 73, 167, 178
Ralph Myhre Golf Course, 357
Ranch Valley, 439
Randall Drive-In Movie Theatre, 292
Randolph, 280, 284, 285, 287, 289, 290–91, 291, 292, 293; guidance, 275, 277; lodging, 338–40
Randolph Historical Society Museum, 280
Ranney Brook Farm, 80
Ranney-Crawford House, 79–80
Ransom Bay Inn, The, 416
Raptor Store, The, 293
Raspberries and Tyme, 188
Raven Ridge Canoe Rental and Guide Service, 423
Reading, 214, 241
Readmore Bed & Breakfast & Books, 168–69
Recycle North, 406
Red Barn Gallery, 190
Red Barn Studio, 522
Red Clover Inn, 268, 272
Red Cupboard Gift Shop, 251
Red Rocks Park, 387, 389
Red Shutter Inn, The, 106, 110
Red Square Bar and Grill, 399, 403
Redrock Farm, 292
Reel Vermont, 322, 437
Reluctant Panther Inn & Restaurant, 139, 149
rentals, 49. *See* lodging
Restaurant at Willow Pond, 149
Restaurant Swisspot, 452
restaurants, 50; Addison County, 368–70; Barre/Montpelier area, 325–27; Bellows Falls, 169–70; Bennington, 120–21; Burlington region, 395–402; Champlain Islands, 418–19; Grafton, 169; Jay Peak area, 520–21; Killington/Plymouth area, 271–74; Lamoille Valley, 466–67; Lower Connecticut and West River Valleys, 81–88; Manchester area, 147–53; Mount Snow/Wilmington area, 109–11; Newport/North Country, 534–35; Northeast Kingdom, 500–3; Okemo Valley Region, 187–90; Rutland/Lower Champlain Valley, 340–42; Saxtons River, 169–70; St. Albans/Swanton, 426–27; Stowe area, 450–54; Sugarbush/Mad River Valley, 310–13; Upper Valley, 213–18; White River Valleys, 290–92; Woodstock/Quechee area, 243–46
retreats, 53
Revolutionary War, 38–39
Richard Bissell Fine Woodworking, 92
Richford, 522
Richford Antique and Craft Center, 427
Richmond, 379, 397, 401
Richmond Victorian Inn, The, 394
Ricker Pond Campground, 486
RidgeView Orchards, 356
Riley Rink at Hunter Park, 136
Ritterbush Pond, 439, 462
Rivendell Books, 328
River Bend Lodge, 74
River City Cafe, 217
River Excitement, 206
River Gallery School, 91
River Garden Café, 502
River Meadow Farm, 140
River Mist B&B, 168
River Tavern, The, 271
Riverdale Antiques, 91
Riverside Farm Stables, 263, 284
Riverview Cafe, 85–86
Roadhouse Restaurant, The, 111
roadside restaurants, 35–36
Robb Family Farm, 73–74, 75
Robert Compton Potter, 372
Robert Frost Cabin, 283, 360
Robert Hull Fleming Museum, 18–19, 383
Robert O. Caulfield Art Gallery, 247
Rochester, 277, 280, 284, 286, 288–89, 291–92, 293
Rochester Café & Country Store, 291–92
Rochester Historical Society, 280
Rochester Mountain, 281
Rock Art Brewery, 23
rock climbing, 233, 439
Rock Island, Quebec, 523, 525
Rock of Ages Quarry and Exhibit, 50
Rock of Ages Quarry Complex, 321
Rock River, 73
Rock River Bed & Breakfast, 80–81
Rock Swap and Mineral Show, 50
Rockefeller, Laurance, 227
Rockefeller Mansion, 228
rockhounding, 50
Rocking Horse Country Store, 343
Rockingham, 169, 172
Rockingham Meeting House, 166
Rocky Dale Gardens, 354
Rocky Ridge Golf Club, 386
rodeos, 337
Rohan Farm, 489
Rokeby Museum, 353
Roland's Place, 368
Rood Pond, 284
Rooster Ridge Farm, 31
Rootswork, 299
Rose Apple Acres Dolls, 522
Rose Apple Acres Farm, 31, 518, 519
Rose Arbour Tea Room, 188
Rosebelle's Victorian Inn, 366–67
Rosie's Restaurant, 370
Round Barn Farm, 19–20
Round Barn Merinos, 50
Round Hearth at Stowe, 450
Round Robin Farm, 31, 289
Route 5 Collectibles, 504
Route 7 Antiques, 405
Rowell Sugarhouse, 509
Rowell's Inn, 185
Roxbury, 288, 321
Roxbury State Fish Hatchery, 284
Royal Lipizzan Stallions, 419
Royall Tyler Theatre, 403
Royal's 121 Hearthside, 340
Royalton, 291
running, 489
Russian School, 54

Ruthcliffe Lodge & Restaurant, 416, 418
Rutland, 332–43; about, 332; entertainment, 342; events, 343; getting there/around, 333–34; green space, 338; guidance, 332–34; map, 333; restaurants, 340–42; shopping, 342; sights/activities, 335–38
Rutland Country Club, 337
Rutland Historical Society, 336
Rutland State Airport, 17

S

Sabin Pond, 321–22
Sackett's Brook Gallery, 91
Sai-Gon Cafe, 399
Saint-Gaudens National Historic Site, The, 203
Sakura, 398
Salisbury Village Bed & Breakfast, 367
Salmon Bridge, 204
Salmon Hole, 386
Salt Ash Inn, 268
Salt Ash Inn and Brew Pub, 23
Samara's Cards & Gifts, 454–55
Sam's Army and Navy Dept. Store, 93
Sam's Outdoor Outfitters, 172
Sam's Steak House, 189
Samuel Safford Inne, 119
Sand Bar Inn, 418
Sand Bar State Park, 414
Sandglass Theater, 89
Santa's Land, 69
Sarducci's, 325
Savoy, 327
Sawdi's Steak House, 341
Saxtons River, 161, 162, 165, 168, 169, 170, 171, 172
Saxtons River Historical Museum, 165
Saxtons River Playhouse, 170
scenic drives: Addison County, 355–56; Barre/Montpelier area, 321; Lamoille Valley, 459–60; Lower Connecticut and West River Valleys, 69–70; Manchester area, 129–30; Mount Snow/Wilmington area, 98–100; Newport/North Country, 526; Northeast Kingdom, 484–85; Okemo Valley Region, 176–77; Stowe area, 436; Sugarbush/Mad River Valley, 301, 303; White River Valleys, 281, 283; Woodstock/Quechee area, 231
Schirmer's Fly Shop, 386
schools: summer self-improvement, 54
Scotland by the Yard, 251
Scott Bridge, 68–69, 458
Scribner Bridge, 459
sculling, 489
Seed House Café, 214, 216
Sel-Bar Weaving, 536
self-improvement vacations, 178
Seth Warner Inn, 140
Seward Vermont Dairy Deli Shop, 343
Seymour Lake, 526
Seymour Lake Lodge, 532
Seyon Fly-Fishing Area, 486
Seyon Ranch, 487
Shackleton Furniture, 30
Shaftsbury, 119
Shaftsbury Historical Society, 117
Shanty on the Shore, 400
Sharon, 289, 290, 291
Sharon Historical Society, 278
Sharon Village, 277–78
Shaw's General Store, 455
Shearer Hill Farm, 108
Shed, The, 23, 452
sheep, 50
Shelburne, 379, 380–81, 384, 390, 392–93, 394, 396, 401–2, 407
Shelburne Bay Park, 390
Shelburne Country Store, 407
Shelburne Farms, 20, 25, 381–82, 388, 390
Shelburne Farm Store and Visitors Center, 407
Shelburne Museum, 19, 26, 40, 47, 49, 380–81
Shelburne Recreation Trail, 385
Shelburne Vineyard, 57
Sheldon Museum, 40, 47
Shepherd's Pie Restaurant and Deli, 216
Sheraton-Burlington, The, 390–91
Sherryland, 493
Shimmering Glass & Design Center, 454
Shin La Restaurant, 85
shipwrecks, 51
Shire Inn, The, 286
Shiretown Books, 250
Shops at the Shack, 274
Shore Acres Inn and Restaurant, 417, 418
Shoreham, 348–49, 363, 366, 371
Shoreham Covered Railroad Bridge, 355
Shoreham Inn & Country Store, The, 363
Shores Memorial Museum, 482
Shrewsbury, 176–77, 183, 185, 191
Sign of the Raven, 171
Silas Griffith Inn, 142, 148–49
Silloway Farms, 292
Silver Lake State Park, 231, 233, 234, 235, 359–60
Silver Maple Lodge & Cottages, 204, 211
Simon Pearce Glass, 219, 249
Simon Pearce Restaurant, 243–44
Simon the Tanner, 536
Simple Pleasures Cafe, 426
Simply Country, 420
Sinclair Inn Bed & Breakfast, 393
Singing Spindle Spinnery, 50
Single Pebble, A, 325
Singleton's Store, 191
Sirloin Saloon, 151, 341
Sitzmark, 104
Sitzmark Golf & Tennis Club, 102
Sitzmark Lodge, 103
Skatium, The, 305
Ski Inn, 447
ski resorts, 13
Ski Shack, The, 274
Ski the Kingdom Cross-country Trail Pass, 490
Ski Touring Center, 233
skiing: cross-country. *See* cross-country skiing
skiing, downhill, 52; Addison County, 359; Ascutney Mountain Resort, 207; Bennington, 117–18; Burlington region, 388; Jay Peak, 516–17; Killington Resort, 263–64; Lower Connecticut and West River Valleys, 73; Manchester area, 135–36; Mount Snow/Haystack, 97, 103; Newport/North Country, 531; Northeast Kingdom, 491; Okemo, 179–80; Smugglers Notch, 463–64; Stowe Mountain Resort, 440–41; Stratton Mountain, 147; Sugarbush/Mad River Valley,

303–5; Woodstock/Quechee area, 234
skijoring, 305
Skunk Hollow Tavern, 214
Skyline Restaurant, 110–11
Slate Valley Museum, 335–36
sleigh rides, 52, 73–74, 104, 136, 264, 305, 338, 388, 441, 464, 488, 518
Smokejacks, 396–97
smoking, 5
Smugglers' Notch, 33–34, 52, 435–36, 438, 457, 458, 463
Smugglers' Notch Antique Center, 468
Smugglers Notch Canoe Touring, 24, 460
Smugglers Notch Inn, 460, 465
Smugglers' Notch Resort, 462, 463–65
Smuggler's Notch Snowmobile Tours, 442
Smugglers' Notch Snowmobile Tours, 464
Smugglers' Notch State Park, 442
Sneakers, 401
Snow Farm Vineyard and Winery, 57, 420–21
snowboarding, 52, 442, 491
Snowdoggin' Inc., 104
Snowflake Chocolates, 406
snowmobiling, 52, 74, 104, 118, 136, 178, 265, 442, 464, 491, 518, 531
Snowresort Rentals, 108
snowshoeing, 52–53, 265, 302–3, 442
soaring, 53, 301
Solitude Village, 187
Somerset House, 498
Somerset Reservoir, 97, 101
South Hero, 409, 416, 417, 418, 419, 420, 420–21
South Road Pottery, 219
South Royalton House, 291
South Royalton Village, 278
South Shire Inn, 118
South Station, 341
South Wind Market & Café, 419
Southern Vermont Arts Center, 19, 48, 127–28, 155
Southern Vermont Fly Fisherman, 131
Southern Vermont Natural History Museum, 98
Spa at the Woods, The, 259
Spa at Topnotch, 438
SPA (Studio Place Arts), 327
spas, 53, 232, 259, 438
spectator sports, 387
Speeder and Earl's, 402
Spirit of Ethan Allen II, 21, 385
spiritual centers/retreats, 53
Spooner's, 245
Spotted Crow, The, 310–11
Spring Hill Farm, 50
Springfield, 197, 206, 207, 208–9, 213–14, 216
Springfield Art & Historical Society, 197
Spruce Mountain, 322
Squirrel's Nest Restaurant, 370
St. Albans, 422–27; events, 427; lodging, 424–26; restaurants, 426–27; shopping, 427; sights/activities, 422–24
St. Albans State Park, 423
St. Anne's Shrine, 38, 411, 412
St. Benoit du Lac, 515
St. Jay Diner, 503
St. Johnsbury: about, 474; entertainment, 503–4; green space, 492; lodging, 494–94, 500; restaurants, 502–3; shopping, 504–8; sights, 481–85
St. Johnsbury Academy Field House, 488
St. Johnsbury Art League, The, 507
St. Johnsbury Athenaeum, 482
St, Johnsbury Country Club, 488
St. Michael's College, 380, 403
Stafford's Country Store and Pharmacy, 456
Stanley Bill Sales, 74
Star Lake, 178
Star Theater, 504
Stark Mountain Bike Works, 299
Starksboro, 394–95
State House, 318, 323
State of Bean, A, 189–90
Station Bridge, 321, 355
Station Restaurant and Ice Cream Parlor, 152
Stave Puzzles, 220
Steak Place, The, 311
Steffi's Studio, 506
Stephen Huneck Gallery, 507
Stephen Huneck Studio, 247
Sterling College, 480
Sterling Falls, 439
Sterling Ridge Inn, 465
Stevens Branch, 322
Stillmeadow Farm, 507, 510
Stillwater Campground, 486
Stone Cottage Collectibles, 182
Stone Hearth Inn, 186
Stone Hill Inn, 446
Stone House Antiques, 190
Stone Soldier Pottery, 99
Stone Soup, 399
Stone Soup Restaurant, 290
Stone Village, 176
Stonecrest Farm, 211
Stonehedge Golf, 337
Stone's Throw Gardens, 507
Store, The, 314–15
Storm Café, The, 368
Storrs Pond Recreation Area, 206
Stoughton Pond, 206
Stowe Action Outfitters, 437
Stowe and Waterbury, 431–56; about, 431–34; entertainment, 454; events, 456; green space, 442–43; guidance, 434; lodging, 443–50; map, 433; shopping, 454–56; sights/activities, 434–42
Stowe area, 34, 52; Lamoille Valley, 457–69; map, 430; Stowe and Waterbury, 431–56
Stowe Athletic Club, 438
Stowe Cinema, 454
Stowe Country Club, 437
Stowe Craft Gallery, 454
Stowe Derby, 456
Stowe Gems, 454
Stowe Gym, 438
Stowe Mountain Resort, 440–41
Stowe Mountain Resort Cross-Country Center, 440, 442
Stowe Mountain Resort Tennis Courts, 439
Stowe Performing Arts, 454
Stowe Recreation Path, 437, 438
Stowe Snowmobile Tours, 442
Stowe Street Emporium, 456
Stowe Theatre Guild, 454
Stowe Village, 435
Stoweflake Mountain Resort and Spa, 19, 53, 437–38, 445
Stowehof Inn, 437, 439, 444
Stowe-in-Line Skate Park, 439
Strafford, 279, 289, 290
Stratton Condominiums, 147
Stratton Golf School, 132
Stratton Mountain, 34, 46–47, 52, 73, 125, 133, 134, 135–36
Stratton Mountain Inn, 147
Stratton Mountain Resort, 45
Stratton Ski Touring Center, 134
Stratton Sports, 130
Stratton Village Lodge, 147

Strattonfest, 153
Straw Corner Mercantile, 456
Stream & Brook Fly-fishing, 258
Strong House Inn, The, 365
Studio Store, The, 469
Sugar & Spice, 273
Sugarbush Airport, 53
Sugarbush Farm, 26, 251
Sugarbush Golf Course, 300
Sugarbush Health & Racquet Club, 300
Sugarbush Inn, 305
Sugarbush Polo Club, 29, 301
Sugarbush Resort, 34, 45, 52, 295, 302, 303–4
Sugarbush Resort Condos, 309
Sugarbush Soaring, 53
Sugarbush Sports Center, 302
Sugarbush Village Condominiums, 309
Sugarbush/Mad River Valley, 295–315; about, 295–97; activities, 298–305; entertainment, 313; events, 315; getting there/around, 297; guidance, 297; lodging, 305–10; map, 296; restaurants, 310–13; shopping, 313–15; villages of, 298
Sugarbush-Warren Airport, 301
sugarhouses. *See* maple sugaring
Sugarmill Farm, 45, 491
Sugarmill Farm Maple Museum, 509
Sugartree Inn, The, 309
Suicide Six Downhill Ski Area, 234
Silver Forest of Vermont, 94
summer camps, 302
Summer Music from Greensboro, 504
Summer Music School, 47–48
Summit Lodge, 263, 268–69
Sumner Mansion, The, 210–11
Sun of the Heart Bookstore, 249
Sunbowl Ranch, 132
Sunderland, 155
Sunrise Montessori School, 302
Sunrise Mountain Village, 270
Sunset Drive-In, 403
Sunset Lake, 284
Susan Sargent Designs, 156
Sutton Place Restaurant, 534
Swanton, 38, 422–27; events, 427; lodging, 424–26; restaurants, 426–27; shopping, 427; sights/activities, 422–24
Swe Den Nor Ltd., 113
Sweet Cecily, 372
Sweet Onion Inn, 306–7
Sweet Pond State Park, 68, 73
Sweet Tomatoes, 341, 398
Sweet Tree Farm, 76
Sweetwater's, 397–98
Swift House Inn, 360, 362
swimming, 54–55; Addison County, 358; Barre/Montpelier area, 322; Burlington region, 387; Grafton, 167; Lamoille Valley, 463; Lower Connecticut and West River Valleys, 73; Manchester area, 133–34; Mount Snow/Wilmington area, 102–3; Newport/North Country, 531; Northeast Kingdom, 489, 516; Okemo Valley Region, 178; Rutland, 337; Stowe area, 439; Sugarbush/Mad River Valley, 302; Upper Valley, 206; White River Valleys, 285; Woodstock/Quechee area, 233
Swiss Inn, 146, 149
symbols, key to, 5

T

T. J. Buckley's, 28, 81, 84
T. W. Wood Art Gallery, 318, 321
Taddingers, 113
Taddingers/Orvis Fly Fishing School, 101
Taft Hill, 93
Taftsville, 240, 251
Taftsville Bridge, 231
Taftsville Country Store, 251
Talbot's Herb and Perennial Farm, 35, 251
Tamarlane Farm, 510
Taylor Farm, 25–26
telemarking, 302–3
Tempest Book Shop, 315
Ten Acres Lodge, 447, 450–51
tennis, 55, 103, 117, 134, 231–32, 263, 302, 439, 463
Terry Lodge, 417
Tetreault's Hillside View Farm, 425
Texas Falls, 284
That Book Store, 505–6
theater, 55; Barre/Montpelier area, 327; Bellows Falls/Grafton, 170; Bennington, 121; Burlington region, 403; Lower Connecticut and West River Valleys, 89; Manchester area, 153–54; Newport/North Country, 536; Upper Valley, 218
Theodore's Tavern, 273
Thetford, 199, 201, 220
Thetford Hill State Park, 208
Thetford Historical Society, 201
Third Rail, The, 36, 217
Thistle Hill Pottery, 327
Thomas Mott B&B, 415
Thomas Waterman Wood Art Gallery, 19
Three Bears at the Fountain, 446
Three Church Street, 238
Three Clock Inn, The, 148
Three Mountain Cafe, 313
Three Mountain Inn, 77, 84
Three Mountain Lodge, 466, 467
Three Rivers Gallery, 171
Three Stallion Inn, 46, 283, 287
Through the Woods, 508
Tickle Trunk, 522
Ticonderoga, NY, 353
Tilting at Windmills Gallery, 155
Timber Creek Cross Country Touring Center, 103
Tinmouth Hunting Preserve, 337
Tip-Top Café, 214–15
Titcomb Bridge, 204
Todd Gallery, 155
Tokyo House, 341
Toll Road, The, 434–35
Tom & Sally's Handmade Chocolates, 94
Toonerville Trail, 207
Top of the Hill Grill, 86–87
Topnotch, 48, 53
Topnotch at Stowe Resort, 442, 444–45
Topnotch Stables, 439
Topnotch Touring Center, 440
tourism: high season, 35; history, 12–13
Townshend, 61; about, 66–67; lodging, 77, 80; restaurants, 85, 87; shopping, 93
Townshend Auction Gallery, 91
Townshend Country Inn, 87
Townshend Dam Diner, 87
Townshend Furniture, 30, 93
Townshend Lake Recreation Area, 73
Townshend Outdoors, 71, 73
Townshend State Park, 74
Tracks of Vermont, 132
Tracy's Midway, 284

Trail's End, A Country Inn, 107–8
train rides, 134
train service, 17–18
Trapp Family Austin Tea Room, 452
Trapp Family Dining Room, 451
Trapp Family Lodge, 51, 438, 440, 442, 443
Trattoria Delia, 398
Trattoria La Festa, 453
Treasure Island, 206
Trout River, 515
Trout River Brewing Co., 23, 509
Troy, 519
True North Kayak Tours, 387
True Wheels, 258
True Wheels Bike Shop, 337
Truly Unique, 343
tubing, 285
Tucker Hill Lodge, 306
Tudhope Sailing Center and Marina, 413
Tulip Tree Crafts, 314
Tully and Marie's, 369
Tunbridge, 278, 285
Tunbridge World's Fair, 17, 278
Tupper Farm Lodge, 287
Turnpike Road Pottery, 112
Tuttle, Fred, 32
Twice Upon a Time, 89–90
Twilight Tea Lounge, 88
Twin Bridge, 336
Twin Farms, 236–37
Twinbrooks Tours, 118
Two Tannery Road, 110
Tyler Gallery, 91
Tyler Place Family Resort, The, 26, 42, 424
Tyson, 177, 181, 187–88

U

Umiak Outdoor Outfitters, 24, 37, 387, 437, 439, 442
Umpleby's, 246, 249
Uncle Sam's Restaurant, 426–27
Uncommon Grounds, 402
Underground Railroad, 39
Underhill Center, 393–94
Underhill State Park, 389
Underwater Historical Preserves, 51
Unicorn, 250
Union Station, 382
University Mall, 407
University of Vermont Dairy Farm, 384
Up for Breakfast, 151
Upper Bridge, 321
Upper Connecticut River Valley, 195–21; about, 195; entertainment, 218–19; events, 221; getting there/around, 196; green space, 207–8; guidance, 196–97; lodging, 208–13; map, 194, 200; restaurants, 213–18; river towns of, 195–21; shopping, 219–21; sights/activities, 201–7; villages of, 197–201
Upper Falls Bridge, 204
Upper Valley Land Trust, 205
Upstairs Antiques, 405
UVM Morgan Horse Farm, The, 354–55

V

Vail Field, 232, 234–35
Valley Lake, 322
Valley Pizzeria, 312
Valley Players, 313
Vergennes, 348, 358, 361, 365–66, 369, 370, 372
Vergennes Opera House, 48
Vermont: history of, 11–13, 38–40, 198; landscape of, 10–11, 33–34; map of, 6–8
Vermont Adventure Company, 485
Vermont Antiquarian Booksellers Association, 18
Vermont Artisan Designs, 92
Vermont Arts Council, 19
Vermont Association of Snow Travelers (VAST), 52
Vermont Bach Festival, 48
Vermont Bicycle Touring, 20, 356
Vermont Book Shop, 371
Vermont Butter & Cheese Company, 26
Vermont Camping Association, 23
Vermont Canoe Touring Center, 24, 70–71
Vermont Canvas Products, 343
Vermont Chamber of Commerce, 41–42
Vermont Children's Theater, 504
Vermont Clay Studio, 455
Vermont Country Bird Houses, 159
Vermont Country Store, 34, 157, 172
Vermont Country Walkers, 37
Vermont Craft Gallery, 219
Vermont Daylilies, 507
Vermont Department of Tourism and Marketing, 41
Vermont Expos, 387
Vermont Fish and Wildlife Department, 32
Vermont Fly Fishing School, 231
Vermont Folklife Center, The, 349
Vermont Granite Museum, 319
Vermont Higher Education Council, 27
Vermont Historical Society Library, 43
Vermont Historical Society Museum, 40, 318, 320
Vermont History Expo, 40
Vermont Houseboat Vacations, 357
Vermont Icelandic Horse Farm, 300–1, 305
Vermont Industries Factory Store, 191
Vermont Inn, The, 268, 271
Vermont Institute of Natural Science, 21, 26, 133, 230
Vermont Jazz Center, 89
Vermont Land Trust, 11, 48
Vermont Leadership Center, 37, 527, 531–32
Vermont Maple Festival, 44
Vermont Maple Outlet, 469
Vermont Marble, 30
Vermont Marble Company Exhibit, 50, 335
Vermont Mozart Festival, 47, 402, 454
Vermont Museum & Gallery Alliance, 47
Vermont National Country Club, 386
Vermont Outdoor Guide Association, 33, 37
Vermont Pack & Paddle Outfitters, 299, 300
Vermont Pub and Brewery, The, 399
Vermont Public Radio, 56
Vermont Quarter Horse Association, 29
Vermont Quilt Festival, 49
Vermont Raptor Center, 21, 230
Vermont Rug Makers, 455, 468
Vermont Salvage Exchange, 220
Vermont Sheep and Wool Festival, 50
Vermont Shepherd Cheese, 25
Vermont Ski & Sports, 249
Vermont Ski Areas Association, 51

Vermont Skiing Today Snow-Line, 52
Vermont Sport & Fitness Center, 338
Vermont State Craft Center, 28, 371–72
Vermont State Fair, 17
Vermont State House, 323
Vermont Studio Center, 54, 459, 467
Vermont Summer Horse Festival, 29
Vermont Sun, 357
Vermont Symphony Orchestra, 48, 153, 402–3, 504
Vermont Technical College, 285
Vermont Technical College Farm, 292
Vermont Teddy Bear Company Factory and Museum, 384, 407
Vermont Transit, 23
Vermont Valley Flyer (train), 134
Vermont Wildflower Farm, 405–6
Vermont Workshop, 250
Vermonter Motor Lodge, 119
Vernon, 69, 71, 76
Victorian House Antiques, 468
Victorian Inn at Wallingford, The, 338, 340
Victory Basin, 21, 491
Viking Nordic Centre, 134
Village Butcher, The, 246
Village Country Inn, The, 139
Village Green at Stowe, The, 450
Village House Inn, 498, 501–2
Village Inn, 51
Village Inn of East Burke, The, 496
Village Inn of Woodstock, The, 239
Village Path, 302
Village Restaurant, 502
Village Sport Shop, 486
Village Square Booksellers, 172
Vitriesse Glass Gallery, 156

W

W. E. Pierce General Store, 177
Wagner Road B&B, 425
Wait Farm Motor Inn, 309
Waiting Room, 397
Waitsfield, 298, 300–1, 306, 307, 308, 309, 310–11, 312, 313–14, 315
Waitsfield Pottery, 314
Walden, 509
Waldenbooks, 405
Walker Farm, 76
Walker's Restaurant, 86, 89
walking. *See* hiking/walking
Wall, The, 233
Wallace Pond, 528
Wallingford, 337, 338, 339, 339–40
Walpole Inn, The, 168, 169
Walpole, NH, 165, 168, 169, 171
Wantastiquet Mountain, 72
Ward Fishing Access, 302
Ward's Cove Beach, 102–3
Wardsboro, 97
Wares Grove, 73
Warner Gallery Restaurant, 218, 503
Warren Antiques, 313
Warren Falls, 302
Warren House Restaurant & Rupert's Bar, 311
Warren Path, 302
Warren Store and More, 312–13, 314
Warren Village, 298, 300, 302–3, 305–10, 311, 312, 321
Wasp Diner, The, 246
Waterbury. *See* Stowe and Waterbury
Waterbury Reservoir, 439
waterfalls, 55–56
Waterford, 501
Waterford Dam at Moore Reservoir, 492
Waterfront Diving, 386
Waterfront Park, 388
Water's Edge B&B, 532
Waterville, 458
Waterworks, 401
Waybury Inn, 364
Wayside Restaurant and Bakery, 28, 36, 326
weather reports, 56
Weatherhead Hollow Pond, 72
Weathersfield Center, 197
Weathersfield Historical Society, 197
Weathertop Lodge, 309
Weathervane, The, 147
web sites, 56
weddings, 56, 418–19
Wells River, 212, 494, 503
West Burke, 485
West Danville, 479
West Dover, 70, 97, 103, 106–7, 109, 110, 113
West Dover Inn, 107
West Dummerston, 70
West Hill House, 307–8
West Hill Recreation Area, 178
West Hill Shop, 46, 70, 73
West Mountain Inn, 141, 150
West River, 71, 73
West River Lodge, 80
West River Stables at Meadowbrook Farm, 72
West River Valley. *See* Lower Connecticut and West River Valleys
West Wind Fine Art, 155
Westfield, 521, 522
Westminster, 75
Westmore, 485, 498–99
Weston, 127, 129, 130, 144, 150, 153, 155, 157, 158
Weston Antiques Barn, 155
Weston Antiques Fair, 18
Weston Bowl Mill, 30
Weston House Quilt Collection, 156
Weston Mill Museum, 129
Weston Playhouse, 55, 154
Weston Priory, 53
Weston Village Store, The, 158
Wheel Inn, 341
Wheeler Farm, 104
Wheeler Mountain, 488
Whetstone Brook Bed & Breakfast, 497–98
Whetstone Inn, 108
Whip Bar & Grill, 452–53
Whipple Tree Bed & Breakfast, The, 212
Whipple Tree, The, 250
White Dog Tavern, 152
White House of Wilmington, The, 105, 110
White House Winter Activity Center, 103
White River, 285
White River Golf Club, 284
White River Junction, 198, 212, 214–15, 216–17, 218, 219, 220
White River National Fish Hatchery, 284
White River Valleys, 275–94; entertainment, 292; events, 293–94; getting there/around, 277; green space, 286; guidance, 275, 277; lodging, 286–90; map, 276; restaurants, 290–92; shopping, 292–93; sights/activities, 280–86; villages of, 277–80
White Rocks Inn, 339–40

White Rocks Recreation Area, 337
Whitecaps, 401
white-water rafting, 56–57, 71
Whitford House, 366
Whitingham, 97, 99, 109
Whitingham Farm, 102, 104
Whitingham Lake. *See* Harriman Reservoir
Whitney Brook, 186
Whittemore Theater, 89
Who Is Sylvia?, 247
Wiessner Woods, 443
Wigren & Barlow, 247
Wilburton Inn, 40, 139–40, 148
Wilcox Brothers Dairy, 153
Wilcox Cove Cottages & Golf Course, 417–18
Wilcox Golf Course, 414
Wild Branch Trail Horse Adventures, 439
Wild Grass, 245
Wild Wings Ski Touring Center, 134
Wilder, 211
Wilder Homestead Inn, 144
Wilderness Trails, 24, 205, 231, 234, 235
Wildflower Inn, The, 488, 491, 494, 501
wildlife, 55
Wiley Inn, The, 145
Wilgus State Park, 205, 207
Willard Street Inn, 391
Willey's Store, 480, 508
Williamstown, 322, 328
Williamstown Gulf, 34
Williston, 388, 394, 395
Williston Golf Course, 386
Willoughby Falls Wildlife Management Area, 487
Willoughby Gap Expeditions, 489
WilloughVale Inn on Lake Willoughby, 498–99
Willow Hill Farm, 25
Willow Pond Farm, 392–93
Wilmington, 101, 102
Wilmington Antique & Flea Market, 111–12
Wilmington area. *See* Mount Snow/Wilmington area
Wilson Castle, 40, 336
Wilson, Frank, 68
Wilson Inn, The, 395
Wilson, John, 66
Winchester Stables, 72–73
Windham, 132, 178
Windham Art Gallery, 91
Windham Brewery, 88
Windham Country Club, 167
Windham Foundation, 165
Windham Golf Club, 72, 132, 178
Windham Hill Inn, 77, 85
Windhorse Visual Art Center, 507
Winds of Ireland, 385
Windsor, 198, 202, 203, 210, 214, 216, 219, 221
Windsor-Cornish Covered Bridge, 203–4
Windsor Country Club, 206
Windsor Diner, 28–29
Windsor House, 198
Windsor Station Restaurant, 214
wineries, 18, 57, 88, 99, 117, 251, 328, 420–21, 468
Winhall Brook, 24
Winooski, 379–80, 401, 407
Winooski Valley Park District, 389
Winslow House, 239
Winterplace, 187
Wobbly Barn, The, 274
Wolcott, 481, 498
Wood Ware, 372
Woodbury Mountain Toys, 328
Woodford State Park, 118
Woodknot Books, 536
Wood's Island State Park, 424
Woodshed Lodge, 519
Woodstock Clayworks, 250
Woodstock Country Club, 231–32
Woodstock Farmers' Market, 246
Woodstock Folk Art, 247
Woodstock Health & Fitness Center, 232
Woodstock House, 239
Woodstock Inn and Resort, 34–35. 49, 234, 236, 244
Woodstock Llama Trekking, 43, 233
Woodstock Pharmacy, 250
Woodstock Potters, 250
Woodstock Recreation Center, 233
Woodstock Sports, 231, 235
Woodstock Walking Tour, 228–29
Woodstocker, 239
Woodstock/Quechee area, 222–52; about, 222, 229; entertainment, 246; events, 251–52; green space, 235–36; guidance, 222–23; lodging, 236–42; maps, 224, 225; restaurants, 243–46; shopping, 246–51; sights/activities, 229–35; villages of, 223–29
Woody Jackson's Holy Cow, 371
wool, 50
Wool Away, 507
Wooly Hill Farm, 50
Worcester Range, 322
World Learning, 63, 65
Wrightsville Dam, 321
Wrightsville Dam Recreation Area, 322

Y

Yankee Bookshop, The, 250
Yankee Kingdom Orchard, 355
Ye Olde New England Inn, 447–48
Ye Olde Tavern, 150
Yellow Barn, 47
Yellow Barn Music School and Festival, 67, 88
Yoga Vermont, 53
Young, Beverly and George, 510

Z

Ziemke Glass Blowing Studio, 454
Ziter's Putney Inn Market & Deli, 87
Zoar Outdoor, 101
Zoey's Deli & Bakery, 152
Zola's Grille, 271